'Derivatives and Risk Management in Shipping'

First Edition

by

Professor Dr. Manolis G. Kavussanos

Athens University of Economics and Business, Greece

and

Assistant Professor Dr. Ilias D. Visvikis

ALBA Graduate Business School, Greece

© 2006
Professor Dr. Manolis G. Kavussanos
Professor Dr. Ilias D. Visvikis
ISBN 13: 978 1 85609 310 1
ISBN 10: 1 85609 310 7

OTHER BOOKS IN THE SERIES

Business Finance for Risk Management
Business Organisation and Finance
Corporate Risk Management
Information Systems Risk
Insurance, Non Marine – An Introduction
Liability Exposures
Liability Risk and the Law
Local Government a Text for Risk Managers
Risk Analysis
Risk Control
Risk and the Business Environment
Risk Financing
Risk Management in Healthcare
Risk Management Organisation and Context
Treasury Risk Management

British Library Cataloguing in Publication Data

Kavussanos, Manolis G.
  Derivatives and risk management in shipping
  1. Shipping – Finance 2. Derivative securities. 3. Risk management
  I. Title II. Visvikis, Ilias D.
  332.6'457

ISBN-13: 9781856093101
ISBN-10: 1856093107

Notice of Terms of Use

While the advice given in this document ("document") has been developed using the best information currently available, it is intended purely as guidance to be used at the user's own risk. No responsibility is accepted by any person, firm, corporation or organisation [who or which has been in any way concerned with the furnishing of information or data, the compilation or any translation, publishing, supply or sale of the document] for the accuracy of any information or advice given in the document or any omission from the document or for any consequence whatsoever resulting directly or indirectly from compliance with or adoption of guidance contained in the document even if caused by a failure to exercise reasonable care.

Published by
Witherby Seamanship International
4 Dunlop Square
Deans Estate
Livingston EH54 8SB
United Kingdom
Tel No: +44(0)1506 463 227
Fax No: +44(0)1506 468 999
Email: info@emailws.com
www.witherbyseamanship.com

[5880]

ABOUT THE AUTHORS

Professor Manolis G. Kavussanos (mkavus@aueb.gr) holds a B.Sc. and M.Sc. (Economics) from University of London – Queen Mary College and Birkbeck College, respectively, and Ph.D. (Applied Economics) from City University Cass Business School, London. He has held various academic posts at Cass Business School, including Reader of Shipping Economics and Finance. There, he launched the M.Sc. program in Trade, Transport and Finance and remained its Director until he joined Athens University of Economics and Business, as Professor of Finance, where he is the Director of the Research Centre for Finance. He has also lectured as a visiting professor at Erasmus University, Rotterdam, University of Piraeus, Hellenic Open University and LUISS University, Rome. He has written extensively in the areas of finance, shipping and applied economics and has been the author of numerous pieces of award winning academic work presented in conferences around the globe and published in top international refereed journals and in invited chapters in collective book volumes. He has published books, edited journal guest volumes, organised international conferences and serves on the editorial board of academic journals. He has provided expertise in finance, transportation and educational matters to organisations such as the Commission of the European Communities, Governmental bodies and other public and private sector companies. He has been included in the Marquis publication "*Who is Who in the World*" and "*Who is Who in Science and Technology*". He has developed the area of risk analysis and management in shipping, which remains among his current research interests in addition to futures, forwards and option derivatives, asset valuation, the market microstructure of financial markets, seasonality and forecasting.

Assistant Professor Ilias D. Visvikis (ivisviki@alba.edu.gr) holds a B.Sc. in Business Administration from University of Aegean, Greece, an M.Sc. in International Financial Markets from University of Southampton, an M.Sc. in International Shipping from University of Plymouth, and a Ph.D. in Finance from City University Cass Business School, London. His doctoral thesis was supported financially by the North Atlantic Treaty Organization (NATO) and the Ministry of Economy and Finance of Greece under the Euro-Atlantic Partnership Council Research Fellowship. He is elected as an Assistant Professor of Finance and is the Academic Director of the MBA in Shipping Program at ALBA Graduate Business School, Greece. He has lectured at Hellenic Open University, Erasmus University, Rotterdam and University of Piraeus and tutored in City University's Cass Business School in London. His research work has been published in international journals and practitioner magazines, in the areas of finance and shipping, and presented at international academic conferences. He held posts in the Central Securities Depository of Greece, in shipping companies in various departments, and in the Derivatives Market of the Athens Exchange. At the same time, he has provided consultancy services to private companies in the areas of finance and risk management. His current research interests include financial and shipping derivatives, financial risk management, portfolio management, and initial public offerings.

PREFACE

Shipping carrying bulk cargo is a fiercely competitive international industry characterised by large, mostly unpredictable, volatilities in its rates and prices. This is because tramp freight rates are determined under conditions of perfect competition, at the balance of demand with supply for freight services. The level of this inflexible derived demand depends on a number of factors, which by nature are highly uncertain, and include: world economic activity and global politics; the economics of the commodities being traded and as a consequence, the distances traveled; the discovery of new natural resources or the depletion of old ones and their world trade patterns and to some extent competition with other modes of transport. The supply for freight services, on the other hand, is rather rigid under tight market conditions which becomes flat in weak markets and can only be changed in the short term by changing vessel speeds and lay-up rates. In the longer term, more permanent changes in supply can take place by building new ships and / or scrapping older ones. Moreover, depending on market conditions, it takes one to three years to build and deliver new ships and influence the longer term supply for freight services. These conditions produce highly cyclical, seasonal and volatile freight rates, which translate into highly cyclical, seasonal and volatile income and costs for the cargo carriers and shippers respectively. Some elements of transportation costs, such as fuel prices, are also rather unpredictable, contributing to the uncertainty of the business environment in the sector.

However, shipping is a highly capital intensive industry, a situation which enhances further the risks for those involved in the sector. The investment cost of purchasing a vessel, new or second-hand, amounts to several million US$, which, just like freight rates, is highly volatile and unpredictable. This is expected, as ship prices should reflect the income and its volatility that these vessels are anticipated to produce for its owner. As a consequence of rapid price changes, the timing of vessel acquisitions and sales is an extremely important decision for investors in the sector. The high initial investment cost by itself creates a large fixed cost element for the shipping business, which has to be recovered during the lifetime of the vessel from its operation. Given the high fluctuations in income and costs, the situation involves high business risks for the investor operating in this environment, as it increases the uncertainty of recovering the initial cost of the investment. Furthermore, as vessel acquisitions mostly involve large loans, a further obligation for payments to serve the borrowed capital is created. This enhances further the business risk for the shipping entrepreneur. Moreover, as companies commonly borrow at variable rates of interest, further uncertainty and risk is involved as a consequence of interest rate change.

It should be borne in mind that in this international industry, payments may involve several currencies. For instance, income is usually in US$, but operating and other costs may be in local currencies, such as in the Euro or Japanese yen. Shipbuilding contracts are structured for payment in the shipbuilder's local currency and Shipowners and other market agents involved in the industry are also exposed to exchange rate movements. No doubt other risks can be thought of, including fluctuations in scrap vessel prices, piracy, accidents, etc.

Despite the extremely risky environment that a synthesis of the above risks seems to indicate as the framework into which market participants in the sector operate, it is ironic that there is no single textbook at the moment of writing devoted to systematically analysing, measuring and proposing strategies for managing all aspects of risks in the shipping industry. Risk management is a constantly developing area, with more and more enterprises entering into its practice for their business, as they realise that often their survival amongst competitors hangs on the effective management of the risks that they face. This is particularly important for shipping, for the reasons explained briefly above, and analysed extensively in this book. Volatile and cyclical rates and prices, makes risk management a vital issue and takes a central role in the effective strategic management of business. These risks, if managed effectively, can stabilise cash-flows, with positive repercussions for business in a number of directions.

Market participants in the industry are broadly aware of the business risks that they face, as they need to deal with them on a daily basis. They are managed by most in what may be called 'traditional' methods. These are examined systematically in the first chapter of this book, with new evidence uncovered, which can help market participants identify and control risks more precisely than before. However, there is another set of instruments outside the traditional shipping industry, which have developed in order to manage risks even more effectively, in a cheaper and more flexible way and is the main focus of this book. These are financial derivative products, which have made their way into shipping enterprises. They were available first for interest rate and foreign exchange risk management, and since 1985 for freight rate risk management. Since then, other shipping derivative products have been introduced for the management of risks emanating from fluctuations in ship prices, scrap prices and bunker prices amongst others. All these are thoroughly analysed in this book and many practical applications substantiate their use in various circumstances, both for risk management and investment purposes.

Despite the inroads of financial derivatives into the shipping industry, they are not used to the same extent as in other sectors of the economy. Only a relatively small number of market practitioners use them, with volumes of trading constituting only a proportion of the volume of trading in the underlying physical market. This compares poorly with other mature derivative markets, where the volume of trading is several times that of the underlying spot market. Surveys conducted and personal contacts of the authors with practitioners in the industry indicate that part of the reason for this is the lack of understanding of their use and of the potential that they offer.

Since January 2004 a series of educational seminars have been introduced by the authors aiming to cover this gap in the market. The positive response of participants and others in the market and of colleagues, undergraduate and postgraduate students at universities, where the material has been taught, has made it increasingly evident that a book is also needed to collect all the relevant issues together. These calls, for the development and publication of such a book, have been a great motivation in going ahead with this project. Such a book will be of great value to the shipping business, as to how derivatives can be used in the day-to-day practice of risk management through both traditional and derivatives strategies. Analysis of the economic factors underlying the relevant relationships is also an important aspect of the book. Moreover, the book can provide the educational material for undergraduate and postgraduate courses in shipping risk management and for more general courses in ship finance, shipping economics and ship management.

A number of studies relating to shipping derivatives and risk management have been presented in conferences and business meetings around the world and published in long established, well known, academic and practitioner journals. This book, following the maxim that *"the whole is more than the sum of the parts"*, draws together their most important conclusions in a single place, discusses them critically and evaluates their contribution to our knowledge in the subject matter. Thus, the book deals with the issue of risk management in the shipping industry at different levels. First, it provides the theory underlying the use of derivatives. Second, it deals with the practice of the use of derivatives for risk management and investment purposes. We think it is important to consider the relevant theoretical relationships in order to be able to understand and explain what we observe in the real world. At the same time we try to link theory with practical applications. For every theoretical concept discussed, a number of examples and practical uses of it are presented. No doubt more could be developed under different circumstances, provided the reader has become familiar with how these tools work in practice. Third, the book analyses the sources of risk in the shipping business and proposes *"traditional"* strategies for risk management at both the investment and operational level of the business. Fourth, traditional methods of risk management are compared and contrasted with those involving financial derivatives. Fifth, the different solutions offered by the various types of derivative products are compared and contrasted between them. Sixth, practical applications of derivatives are examined. Seventh, a number of concepts presented in this book appear for the first time in the literature here. Eighth, for researchers in the area it can become a stepping stone for work which can further enhance our knowledge of risk management and derivatives in the shipping industry. Finally, it can provide solutions and become a point of reference for other industries with similar characteristics, wishing to deal with the issue of risk management through the use of derivatives. For instance, the non-storability of the freight service is one such special feature and requires modification of the derivatives pricing formula in order to deal with it. These special characteristics of the industry and its common ground with other industries are analysed extensively in the main body of the book.

One of the important decisions that must be made by an author who is writing in the area of derivatives is the use of mathematics and statistics. If the level of mathematics and statistics is too high, the material may not be readily understood by many practitioners and students. On the other hand, if it is too simple, some important issues and concepts may not be described sufficiently. We have tried to eliminate nonessential mathematics and statistics as much as possible, providing instead appropriate referencing to the relevant literature.

Chapter one provides an introduction to the book in order to: identify the market segmentation in the shipping industry and the market conditions prevailing in each segment of the sector; to examine the fundamental relationships governing rates and prices in shipping and through that understanding the structure of returns and risks present and the implications for 'traditional' risk management strategies; to identify all possible sources of business risks that exist in the shipping industry; to present the recent evidence on the classification of these risks by sector and type of market; and to outline some traditional strategies which shipowners use to manage these risks. The deficiencies of the strategies are discussed, followed by an introduction of how financial derivatives can provide solutions to these deficiencies and be used for the more efficient management of risks.

Chapter two considers the theory and practice of financial derivatives. Its aim is to introduce to the non specialist in derivatives these types of contracts, and can be a good revision for those with prior knowledge of financial derivatives. The chapter: identifies the reasons for using financial derivatives; describes the basic derivatives instruments, including futures, forwards, swaps and options, discussing their specifications, characteristics, trading issues, pricing and their use for hedging and speculation purposes; presents the accounting treatment of derivatives transactions and tax issues; analyses the issue of credit risk in derivatives transactions and the use of credit derivatives; and presents the Value-at-Risk (VaR) model for measuring market risk.

Chapter three is a major chapter in the book, as it discusses how derivative instruments may be used to manage the risk which is considered as the most important of all in the shipping industry, namely freight rate risk. The chapter: provides a historical overview of freight rate derivatives; presents the underlying *"commodities"* of freight derivatives, upon which these derivatives are written; these are freight indices, constructed by the Baltic Exchange and by Platts; presents the freight futures contracts, offered by the International Maritime Exchange (IMAREX) and the New York Mercantile Exchange (NYMEX); discusses Freight Forward Agreements (FFAs) and FFAs cleared by the London Clearing House Clearnet (LCH.Clearnet) and examines their use, their advantages, disadvantages and other relevant issues that their users must be aware of; freight options are also discussed with hedging, arbitrage and investment strategies examined in the process; applications of freight derivatives are examined throughout demonstrating the relevant calculations assumed by freight derivatives positions under various circumstances, including trading in the dry-bulk and tanker sectors, non-cleared and cleared transactions, and voyage and time-charter applications, amongst others; compares and contrasts the traditional strategies which have been used for risk management in shipping to the flexible solutions provided by freight derivatives; shows how Value-at-Risk (VaR) may be used to monitor freight market risks and become a decision tool on whether to use derivatives for freight risk management purposes; discusses the important role of brokers in freight derivatives trading; reviews the economics and presents the empirical evidence and published research on freight derivatives markets.

Chapter four presents the use of bunker derivatives products for the risk management of fluctuations in bunker prices. Specifically, the chapter presents a historical overview of the bunker market; considers the economic variables affecting bunker prices; describes the alternative bunker derivatives products, including forward bunker agreements, petroleum futures contracts, bunker swaps, and bunker options; and presents the empirical evidence and many applications utilising these products.

Chapter five considers the issue of management of risks emanating from fluctuations in vessel values and scrap prices. Highly volatile vessel values, combined with a lengthy Sales and Purchase (S&P) process and relatively low liquidity in the physical market, can make market timing difficult and have adverse effects on the Return on Equity (ROE) of investors. During September 2003, the Baltic Exchange launched the vessel value derivatives contracts, namely the Sale and Purchase Forward Agreements (SPFAs), which are based on the second-hand value of selected types of vessels. Their uses, characteristics and practical applications are presented in this chapter, deriving formulas for their fair valuation. Moreover, risks emanating from fluctuations in vessel demolition prices are also considered and the use of scrapping derivatives for bulk carriers and tankers is examined.

Chapter six takes up the issue of foreign exchange risk which is present in the international shipping environment. It demonstrates how the use of foreign exchange rate derivatives products can be used to manage this risk. This is achieved through instruments like: (i) money market hedges, through borrowing and lending; (ii) currency forwards, available Over-the-Counter (OTC) and tailor-made to the needs of the customer; (iii) currency swaps, being a combination of forward and money market instruments; (iv) currency futures, traded on exchanges; and (v) currency options, both OTC and exchange traded, which allow companies to hedge against movements in one direction while retaining exposure in the other.

Chapter seven introduces interest rate derivatives for uses in the shipping industry. Market agents in the sector may use these tools to: (i) protect the value of their financial assets; and to (ii) lock in favourable interest rates for the finance of their investments through bank loans and bonds. The chapter describes the underlying "*commodities*" of interest rate derivatives, such as T-Bonds, T-Notes, T-Bills, Eurodollar and LIBOR; presents interest rate derivatives contracts, such as forwards, futures, swaps and options, providing a number of examples of their uses in the shipping environment.

A few words are in order on how to approach reading the book. The book is self-contained, as Chapters 1 and 2 provide respectively the background knowledge on shipping markets and on financial derivatives, required to follow the rest of the book, for readers with no prior knowledge in shipping or in derivatives, respectively. However, even if the reader is familiar with shipping matters it is still important to read Chapter 1, as it provides the framework upon which the rest of the book is based. Readers familiar with the use of derivatives may skip Chapter 2, while those with no prior knowledge of financial derivatives may wish to spend more time on this chapter. Readers that wish to concentrate on risk management emanating from the operation of vessels, can read Chapters 1, 3 and 4, as they deal respectively with 'traditional' risk management strategies and analysis, with freight rate derivatives and with bunker price derivatives. If asset price fluctuations are important, as they are for shipowners, then Chapter 5 must be added, as it deals with derivatives on asset (vessel) prices, including demolition prices. Finally, Chapters 6 and 7, which treat the issues of exchange rate and interest rate risk management, can be added to complete the picture of risk management for businesses involved in shipping.

It would be impossible to name everybody that has assisted at various stages of developing the material in this book. However, we would like to thank for their comments participants at various shipping and finance conferences and professional events around the globe, where parts of the material in the book have been presented. We thankfully acknowledge journal editors and anonymous referees for their comments and suggestions and for their time they have taken to read the work as well as for publishing different versions of the material. For the same reason we wish to thank seminar participants in the two-day executive program on "*Shipping*

Derivatives and Risk Management", pioneered and run by the authors since January 2004, and to undergraduate and postgraduate students at Athens Univeristy of Economics and Business for reading the material carefully and providing comments. We are also grateful, for their beneficial comments and suggestions on our work, to: Captain Costas Kanellopoulos and Captain Tassos Tzanis from Nereus Shipping S.A., Mr. Michael McClure from Navios Corporation, Mr. Panayotis Bachtis from O.W. Bunker Malta Ltd., Mr. Pierre Aury from Clarksons, Mr. Knut Møystad and Mr. Morten Erik Pettersen from IMAREX, Professor Nickolaos Travlos from ALBA Graduate Business School, Dr. Dimitris Georgoutsos, Dr. Raphael Markellos, Mr. Dimitris Dimitrakopoulos, Mr. Psychogios and Mr. Dotsis from Athens University of Economics and Business. Finally, our greatest thanks go to our families for their continuous support and encouragement over the years. Of course any remaining errors or omissions are our own responsibility.

Athens, January 2006

Manolis G. Kavussanos   **Ilias D. Visvikis**

INTRODUCTION

It is now over 20 years since the first real effort was made to launch a shipping derivatives market. When, in 1985, the Baltic Exchange opened its market trading freight contracts against a settlement index they could hardly have set themselves a more difficult task. Shipping was at the trough of the 1980s depression and the freight derivative product, existing only on paper, was a tough sell to a generation of shipowners brought up to trade physical ships and cargoes.

Perhaps because of this difficult start, the growth of the shipping derivatives market was painfully slow and the BIFFEX contract trading system, which started to run down in the mid-1990s, never really gained enough depth to make it a serious hedging instrument, far less a speculative vehicle. But since 1997 the FFA market has gradually gained credibility and during the last five years has become a serious business. Serious markets need serious players and this must surely be the ideal time to launch the first authoritative book on "Derivatives and Risk Management in Shipping" for more than fifteen years.

This new volume by Professors Kavussanos and Visvikis is well timed, providing an ideal blend of theory and practice from two acknowledged experts in the field. The structure is thoroughly practical. In the first chapter the shipping business risks are examined; the second chapter explains what products are on offer; and the third deals with the use of freight derivatives for risk management. The remaining chapters cover bunkers, vessel values, residual values, foreign exchange and interest rates. A neat and well-rounded book that will help to spread the gospel of professionalism amongst existing traders and newcomers to the shipping derivatives markets.

Martin Stopford
April 2006

BRIEF TABLE OF CONTENTS

EXTENDED TABLE OF CONTENTS

13

LIST OF TABLES

CHAPTER 4

CHAPTER 5

CHAPTER 6

CHAPTER 7

LIST OF FIGURES

LIST OF ABBREVIATIONS

ADP	Alternative Delivery Procedure
API	All Publications Index
ARA	Amsterdam – Rotterdam – Antwerp
ARIMA	Autoregressive Integrated Moving Average
ASBA	Association of Shipbrokers and Agents
AWB	Australian Wheat Board
BAF	Bunker Adjustment Factor
BaSVA	Baltic Ship Valuation Assessment
BCI	Baltic Capesize Index
BCTI	Baltic Clean Tanker Index
BCV	Barge Carrying Vessels
BDA	Baltic Demolition Assessment
BDCI	Baltic Dirty Tanker Index
BDI	Baltic Dry Index
BFI	Baltic Freight Index
BHI	Baltic Handysize Index
BHMI	Baltic HandyMax Index
BIFFEX	Baltic International Freight Futures Exchange
BIS	Bank of International Settlements
BITR	Baltic International Tanker Routes Index
BM&F	Bolsa Mercadorias & de Futuros
BPI	Baltic Panamax Index
BSI	Baltic Supramax Index
BSPA	Baltic Sale & Purchase Assessments
CAD	Capital Adequacy Directive
CBM	Cubic Meter
CBOT	Chicago Board of Trade
CFaR	Cash-Flow-at-Risk
CFD	Contract For Difference
CFT	Cinnober Financial Technology
CFTC	Commodity Futures Trading Commission
CIF	Cost, Insurance and Freight
CME	Chicago Mercantile Exchange
COA	Contracts of Affreightment
CODELCO	Chile Copper Corporation
COMEX	Commodity Mercantile Exchange
CST	Centistokes
DNB	Den Norske Bank
DOE	US Department of Energy
DWT	Deadweight Tonnes
EaR	Earnings-at-Risk
EBIT	Earnings Before Interest and Tax
ECM	Exempted Commercial Market
EDSP	Exchange Delivery Settlement Price
EFP	Exchange for Physicals
EHTS	Expectations Hypothesis of the Term Structure
EMH	Efficient Market Hypothesis
EUREX	European Derivatives Exchange
FASB	Financial Accounting Standards Board
FFA	Forward Freight Agreement
FFABA	Forward Freight Agreement Brokers Association
FIFC	Freight Indices and Futures Committee
FMIUG	Freight Market & Indices Users Group
FOB	Free on Board
FONASBA	Federation of National Associations of Ship Brokers and Agents

FoSVA	Forward Ship Valuation Agreement
FRA	Forward Rate Agreements
FSAct	Financial Services Act
FSMA	Financial Services and Markets Act
FT	Financial Times
GARCH	Generalised Autoregressive Conditional Heteroskedasticity
GBM	Geometric Brownian Motion
HSFO	High Sulphur Fuel Oil
HSS	Heavy Grain, Soya and Sorghum
IAS	International Accounting Standard
ICE	Intercontinental Exchange
IFO	Intermediate Fuel Oil
IFOs	IMAREX Freight Option Contracts
IMAREX	International Maritime Exchange
IMM	International Monetary Market
INTEX	International Futures Exchange
IPE	International Petroleum Exchange
IRR	Internal Rate of Return
ISDA	International Swap & Derivatives Association
ITFI	International Tanker Freight Index
LCE	London Commodity Exchange
LCH	London Clearing House
LDT	Light Displacement Ton
LED	LIBOR-Eurodollar Spread
LIBOR	London InterBank Offer Rates
LIFFE	London International Financial Futures and Options Exchange
LMIS	Lloyds Maritime Information Services
LOA	Length Over All
LPG	Liquefied Petroleum Gas
LR	Long Range Product Carriers
LRS	Lloyds Register of Shipping
LSE	Lloyd's Shipping Economist
LTBP	London Tanker Brokers' Panel
LTLD	Long Ton Light Displacement
MECO	Middle East Crude Oil
MOB	Municipals-Over-Bonds spread
MPS	Market Place Service
MR	Middle Range Product Carriers
MRSS	Markov Regime Switching Seasonal regression
MT	Metric Tonnes
MVHR	Minimum Variance Hedge Ratio
N.Y.	New York
NCSC	National Coal Supply Corp
NOB	Notes-Over-Bonds Spread
NOS	Norwegian Options and Futures Clearing-house
NPV	Net Present Value
NYMEX	New York Mercantile Exchange
NYSE	New York Stock Exchange
NWE	Nortwestern Europe
OCC	Options Clearing Corporation
OLS	Ordinary Least Squares
OPEC	Organization of Petroleum Exporting Countries
OTC	Over-The-Counter
PaR	Profits-at-Risk
PBOT	Philadelphia Board of Trade
PSD	Parcel Size Distribution
PSD	Parcel Size Distribution
RBS	Royal Bank of Scotland
ROE	Return on Equity

S&P	Sales & Purchase
S/P	Standard & Poors
SES	Stock Exchange of Singapore
SRW	Segmented Random Walk Model
SGX	Singapore Exchange
SIMEX	Singapore International Monetary Exchange
SPAN	Standard Portfolio Analysis of Risk
SPFA	Sale & Purchase Forward Agreement
SSY	Simpson Spence and Young
T/C	Time-charter
TCE	Time-Charter Equivalent
TED	T-Bill-Eurodollar Spread
TIFFE	Tokyo International Financial Futures Exchange
TIFFEX	Tanker International Freight Futures Exchange
TKR	Tanker
TSE	Tokyo Stock Exchange
UK	United Kingdom
ULCC	Ultra Large Crude Carrier
US	United States
VaR	Value at Risk
VECM	Vector Error-Correction Model
VLCC	Very Large Crude Carriers
WS	Worldscale
WTI	West Texas Intermediate

CHAPTER 1. Business Risks in Shipping: Empirical Regularities and Traditional Investment and Risk Management Strategies

1.1. Introduction

Any business decision whose outcome is uncertain is thought to contain risks for the parties involved. Uncertainty of outcomes in decisions is a fact of life, particularly so in business. "*Variables*" are used to describe uncertain outcomes, whose values are often outside the influence of the business itself. Examples of such variables with uncertain outcomes in the shipping industry include freight rates, bunker prices, port and canal charges and so on, with uncertainty in freight rates taking a prominent place amongst them. All produce fluctuations in the final profits of shipowners, by affecting either the revenue side or the cost side of their balance-sheet. Such fluctuations may be undesirable for the parties involved, and a number of actions can be taken to mitigate their impact. Such uncertainty then can be said to bring "*discomfort*" or "*disutility*", in technical terms, to parties facing these risks, and they require compensation for this discomfort. This compensation usually comes in the form of increased benefit, a monetary benefit when we are referring to financial decisions.

Practitioners and academics have developed techniques which can cushion the discomfort, and can compensate for risks involved in decisions involving sums of money. Specifically, financial derivatives products have been developed and introduced into business, thereby allowing for better management of business risks. Moreover, the increased investment choices offered by these products have made them very popular with investors in most sectors of the economy. Financial derivatives have also found their way into the shipping industry since 1985, but have still some way to catch up to reach similar levels of popularity as those available in other sectors of the economy.

The aim of this first chapter of the book is to analyse the sources of business risks that exist in the shipping industry in order to describe the background environment into which participants in the sector operate. It is the first step in the practice of risk management to identify the sources of risk in the sector, to measure them and subsequently to seek ways to manage them. It is argued in this book, by comparing the traditional risk management strategies employed in the sector, that the use of financial derivatives can provide better solutions. Chapter 1 then sets the scene of presenting the recent evidence on the classification of these risks by shipping sub-sector and type of market in the shipping industry. It outlines some traditional strategies, which emanate from these observations and which shipowners and charterers alike use to manage these risks. The deficiencies of the strategies are discussed, followed by an introduction of how financial derivatives can provide solutions to these deficiencies and be used for the more efficient management of risks. The rest of the book then is devoted to analysing and proposing techniques of using this extra market – often referred to as the "*paper*" market – made available to participants in the industry, to provide more flexible and cheaper solutions to risk management. Each separate chapter tackles the issue of how derivatives can be used for the better management of the risks identified in this chapter.

The rest of the chapter is organised as follows: Section 1.2 identifies the possible sources of risk in the shipping industry. Section 1.3 outlines the sequence of commercial decisions that investors in the shipping industry have to make. Section 1.4

considers the cash-flow position of the shipowner and thus provides the basis for the discussion to follow in the rest of the book. Section 1.5 describes the market segmentation of the shipping industry. Section 1.6 considers the market conditions prevailing in the different cargo carrying segments of the industry. Section 1.7 continues the discussion of the previous section, identifying the relationships that determine freight rates for different duration contracts and the factors affecting them. Section 1.8 takes up the issue of volatility and risks in the spot (voyage) and time-charter (period) markets, while section 1.9 extends the discussion to risk levels emanating from fluctuations in vessel values. Section 1.10 summarizes the traditional risk management strategies. Section 1.11 introduces the role that derivatives can play in the management of risk in the shipping industry. Section 1.12 concludes the chapter.

1.2. The Sources of Risk in the Shipping Industry

Risk management in an industry which is riddled with cyclicalities in its rates and prices and which has made and destroyed millionaires over the years is extremely important. Market agents (shipowners and charterers) operating in the international markets of the shipping industry face substantial risks. For our purposes, the structure of the balance-sheet, the cash-flow and the profit and loss statements of a business can be used to identify the sources of risks that it faces. These risks may be broadly classified into the following informal categories:

1) **Business risk**, which is caused by fluctuations in Earnings Before Interest and Taxes (EBIT). In turn, this depends on the variability of the quantity demanded, on the price variability of the "*product*" (the freight service) sold and on the variability of input prices. Thus, the variabilities of the factors affecting EBIT constitute the sources of business risks and include: Freight rates, voyage costs[1], operating costs[2] and foreign exchange rates – as income in this international business is in US$, while costs are in domestic currency.

   To illustrate this issue, consider the Baltic Dry Index (BDI) presented in Figure 1.1, which shows how freight rates in the dry-bulk sector of the shipping industry have fluctuated between August 2002 and December 2005, a period selected just to make the point. In August 2002 the index stood at 1000, rising to 2500 by September 2003. A month later it jumped to 4200, while by February 2004 it reached the unprecedented level of 5450, more than double its value only a few months earlier. Then by June of the same year its value fell to 2900, only to pick up again and return to the even higher level of 5520 by December 2004. By the summer of 2005 the index was again down at 2200. Such great fluctuations in freight rates, within short periods of time, are typical in the tramp sector of the shipping industry, which, as discussed later in this chapter, operates under conditions of perfect competition. That is, freight rates are determined on a day to day basis at the balance of supply and demand for freight services. These fluctuations or volatility or uncertainty in freight rates represent uncertainty of the income received by the shipowner and affects the EBIT of the business. The same is also true for the charterers

---

[1] **Voyage costs** include broking commission, fuel costs, port charges, tugs, canal dues, etc. Fuel costs form the largest part of these, and are subject to the highest fluctuations. The rest of the costs can be safely assumed to rise with inflation and are not therefore subject to high volatility.

[2] **Operating costs** include manning, repairs and maintenance, stores and lubes, insurance, and administration. They are fairly constant or "*predictable*" (rising in line with inflation), in comparison to other types of costs, and have low volatility.

wishing to hire the vessels, as their cost side is affected by such volatility in their transportation costs.

Rational investors are assumed to (seek high returns but) dislike such uncertainty, as it makes their cash-flow position unpredictable, can lead to great gains, but also to disastrous losses. If such volatility in revenue for the shipping business is compiled with other risks and sometimes with wrong decisions regarding other sides of the business, it can lead to the business failures observed in the sector in the past. This argument can also provide the rationale for participants in the sector to enter into risk management strategies, either "*traditional*" or through financial derivatives.

Figure 1.1. Baltic Dry Index (08/2002 – 12/2005)

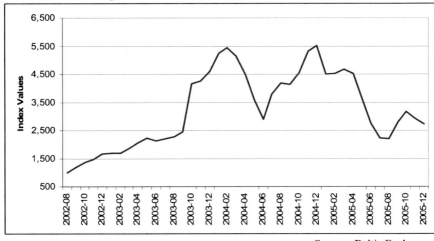

Source: Baltic Exchange

While Figure 1.1 was used to illustrate the point of the risks involved when participating in the dry-bulk sector of the freight market, over the short period August 2002 to December 2005, a similar story of high freight rate volatilities is observed when examining longer periods and other sub-markets of the bulk shipping sector. These are discussed in detail throughout the book, but a cursory view of freight rate changes illustrated in Figures 1.6, 1.7, 1.9, 1.10, 3.1 and 3.2 helps make the point further.

The same is also true when considering bunker prices, on the cost side of the shipping business. Being a product of crude oil, a substantial part of their volatility emanates from the fluctuations observed in crude oil prices in Figure 1.2; the rest of the volatility in bunker prices depends on local market conditions and random effects. As can be observed in the figure, Brent Crude oil prices have changed substantially over the period, from values of approximately US$18.5/bbl in December 2001, to the high values of US$64/bbl in September 2005. Figures 4.2 and 4.3 in Chapter 4 of this book illustrate how bunker prices have fluctuated in the main refueling ports of Houston, Rotterdam and Singapore over the period 1992 to 2005, while Figure 4.1 shows the fluctuations in Brent crude oil price from 1990 to 2005.

The degree of influence of the existence of fixed operating costs on earnings (EBIT) is known as operating leverage[3]. Since the fixed cost for offering the freight service involves investment in the value of the asset – the vessel – offering the service, vessel price fluctuations also contribute to business risks. Figure 1.3 presents newbuilding and 5-year old second-hand prices in US $/dwt as well as scrapping prices in US $/ldt of dry-bulk vessels, for the period January 2003 to December 2005[4]. In line with freight rates, vessel values (effectively, for different ages) have changed substantially within a short period of time. It is observed for instance, that 5-year old vessels had an average price of approximately US $300/dwt in January 2003, which increased to US $573/dwt by March 2004, fell back to US $448/dwt in June, reached a high of US $703/dwt in May 2005, falling back again to US $591/dwt in December 2005. These translate into significant sums as can be observed in such Figures as 1.19, 1.20, 5.1, 5.2, 5.3 and 5.4, which present historical prices of newbuilding, 5-year old second-hand and scrap vessel values for various categories of vessels in sectors of the shipping industry. For instance, a Capesize vessel in May 2005 cost approximately US $72 million, while a 300,000 dwt VLCC vessel cost around US $130 million during the same period. The sums invested are large, making the sector one with high operating leverage. Typically, industries, apart from shipping, with high fixed costs include the automobile industry, the steel industry, airlines, etc.

Figure 1.2. Brent Crude Oil (01/2000 – 10/2005)

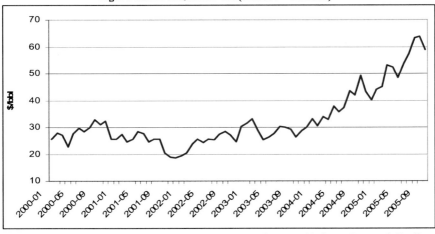

Source: Clarksons Research Studies

The ability to adjust freight rates for changes in input costs can be considered part of the business risk of the company. Different sectors of the shipping industry are affected differently by this factor; thus, in tramp shipping, which operates under conditions of perfect competition, higher costs cannot be passed on to higher freight rates to the same extend they can in the liner sector,

---

[3] The **degree of operating leverage** at a given level of sales is defined as:
[(% Change in EBIT) / (% Change in Sales)]

[4] dwt stands for deadweight and measures the carrying capacity of the vessel. ldt stands for light displacement ton and measures the metal content of the vessel. The former is used as the unit of measurement in the sale and purchase market for vessels, while the latter measurement is important in the scrapping market.

as the latter operates under oligopolistic conditions and as a consequence prices are controlled. The less the ability of the company to influence freight rates, the higher is the business risk it faces. This is the case in the perfectly competitive tramp shipping markets. In some fast changing sectors, the ability to develop new products and respond in a timely cost effective manner is important, as outdated products do not serve the market and will not sell.

Figure 1.3. Bulk Carrier Average Newbuilding (in US $/dwt), Second-Hand (in US$/dwt) and Scrapping Prices (in US $/ldt) (01/2003 – 12/2005)

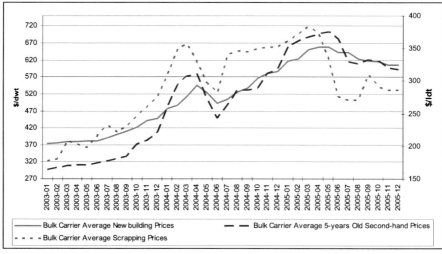

Source: Clarksons Research Studies

2) **Liquidity risk** refers to the inability to sell company assets on short notice at market prices. Tangible assets are more difficult to sell, if the need arises, in comparison to paper/financial assets. However, each class of tangible or of financial assets themselves, have different degrees of liquidity, as we discuss in later chapters of the book.

3) **Default risk** represents the possibility that a company that has borrowed funds (e.g. through a bond issue) is unable to make interest or principal payments on its debt.

4) **Financial risk** depends on the way the company's investments are financed. Too much borrowing, for instance, increases the financial leverage of the company and its debt obligations. These fixed financial obligations, arising from the need to serve its debts, is a source of risk for a company[5]. This is particularly important in industries, such as shipping, where a large part of the funds used by businesses to finance the acquisition of the assets are in the form of debt. Often a distinction is made between operational leverage and financial leverage of the company; multiplying the two provides the degree of total leverage of the business. The shipping industry is highly cyclical (high degree of operating leverage), which when coupled with high degree of borrowed funds (high degree of financial leverage), can result in a very high degree of total leverage for the company. It can explain the high profits and the excessive defaults observed in the sector over its long history.

---

[5] Formally, the **degree of financial leverage**, at a given level of sales, is defined as:
[(%Change in Earnings Per Share, EPS) / (%Change in EBIT)]

5) **Credit risk** can be present in several types of decisions for the business. For instance, the fixing of a 12-month time-charter contract for a vessel may entail credit risk, as it may turn out that the counterparty will not fulfil its agreement to pay the rates due. A loan agreement comprises credit risk, as well as a position in a derivatives contract does.

6) **Market risk**, for a company listed in the stock exchange, is the risk that the stock's price will change due to changes in the stock market. This is a result of company stock prices being correlated with the rest of the market and as a result of being affected by changes in the stock market. Market risk is important, as it affects the cost of capital for the company, and increases the probability that the company with low market value will be taken over, amongst other things. However, market risk may also refer to risks that come about from fluctuations in prices, such as freight rates, interest rates, exchange rates, etc.

7) **Political risk** refers to factors which affect the business and are caused by political decisions. For instance, a war or political unrest in a region that the business operates in, a canal closure, etc, may affect the business balance-sheet and cash-flow positions. Sometimes, political risk and exchange rate risk are classified under the joint heading of *"foreign risk exposure"*, and is important for businesses operating across country borders at the international level. The shipping industry is a prime example of this. A number of political events have had a great influence on the industry in the past. They include the Korean War of 1950, the Suez Canal closures of 1956, 1967 and 1973, the Gulf Wars of 1991 and 2003, all of which have had an important influence on freight rates in the shipping industry.

8) **Technical and physical risk**. Companies operating in the shipping industry are susceptible to the risk of breaking down of the vessel. A consequence of this is loss of income and loss of reputation for the company, amongst others. Loss or damage to the vessel is also included here. Insurance is commonly taken against these risks.

Notice that the above list of risks that businesses in the sector face is only indicative and certainly not exhaustive. Moreover, boundaries between the categories are often blurred and at times overlapping. For instance, market risk and credit risk overlap, while liquidity risk compounds other risks, such as market risk and credit risk. However, classifying risks serves the purpose of identifying them and then targeting their management with specific *"instruments"* that are available to the management of the company.

1.3. Business Decisions Facing the International Investor

A good way to start in analysing risks is to highlight the commercial decisions that an international investor, who considers becoming a shipowner, is facing in her investment decision-making:

1) The investor has a choice of investments to employ her funds. They include stocks, shares, property, the construction industry, shipping, etc. Risks and returns of alternative investments must be compared in constructing her portfolio of assets. Thus, she may decide to enter shipping, either because she sees the possibility of enough rewards in comparison to other sectors, or because of tradition or even, as a sector which can provide further diversification in her portfolio of activities.

2) The next question is whether to enter the shipping industry by buying or leasing vessels. In the first instance, she becomes a shipowner and commits

capital in buying the vessels. In case she decides to lease the vessel though, she does not have to reserve the large capital amounts required to purchase the vessel; she abstains from financial leverage, while certain tax advantages are involved in the decision.

3) Once owning the vessels, shipowners must decide on what routes to operate them and what kind of contract to seek for them?[6] As shown later on in this chapter, the choice of freight contract is important, in terms of the rewards and the risks that it carries. Moreover, some of the traditional strategies followed in the market to achieve risk reduction in relation to freight rates are based on the choice of freight contract. We analyse this further later on.

4) A decision must also be taken on what kind of vessels to purchase – these are described further down this book. The choice of vessel requires the identification of opportunities to service a particular market, but also the expertise/comparative advantage in operating certain types of vessels in particular routes around the globe. The reasons for choosing to invest in particular sectors may well be historical or serve a role in the decision to form a portfolio of different assets, which will be operated in different trades/routes. As we see further down this chapter the opportunities and the rewards differ, according to the vessel type/size. This has been formally shown in Kavussanos (1996a,b, 1997, 1998, 2003), where it is also recognised that both the dry-bulk and the tanker sectors of the shipping industry have distinct submarkets, served by specific vessel sizes. This issue is pursued further later in this chapter of the book.

5) A very important decision is when to buy the vessels and when to sell them. Correct timing can bring great rewards in terms of capital gains, as vessel prices fluctuate considerably in short periods of time – see Figures 1.3, 1.19 and 1.20. They may also lead to disasters if vessels are bought when they are expensive and never manage to ride the business cycle. The return on capital then is greatly affected by the purchase value of the asset. One cannot escape from mentioning the practice of a number of shipowners (particularly Greeks), to exploit the possibility of asset play with the assets-vessels. Often, more money is made from this asset play than from the operation of the vessels themselves. The sums involved are very large and can make or break fortunes. Moreover, buying and selling the vessels quickly is relatively easy.

6) If it is decided to buy vessels, a decision needs to be made on how to finance their purchase. Should the shipowner use debt or equity? What kind of debt to use – would a bank loan serve the purpose of financing or is a bond issue preferred? What kind of equity capital should be used to finance the vessels? Should retained earnings be used, private placement, shareholding, other? What is the optimal mix of debt and equity (capital structure) of the company? These are all important questions, and decisions on these affect the value of the business as well as its cost of capital.

---

[6] The available contracts to the owner/charterer include: (i) **Voyage Charters**, paid as freight per ton to move goods from port A to port B, all costs paid by the shipowner; (ii) **Contracts of Affreightment (COA)**, under which the shipowner carries goods in specified routes for a period of time using ships of his choice. The two major differences between this form of charter and consecutive voyage charters are that under a COA the actual vessel is not precisely designated and the voyages are not undertaken on a round-trip basis; (iii) **Time-Charters** - trip/time, under which the shipowner earns hire every 15 days or every month. He operates the vessel under instructions from the charterer who pays voyage costs; and (iv) **Bareboat Charters**, under which the vessel is rented to another party for operation, usually for a long period of time.

7) Finally, taking into consideration the set of financial tools that are now available to the industry, there is a question of whether to use financial derivative instruments to manage the risk in such markets as the freight, bunker, vessel value, scrap value, foreign exchange and interest rate markets. These are derivative markets, which exist outside the shipping industry and can serve the role of risk management. They provide cheap, flexible tools for risk reduction. The main aim of this book is to describe how these tools can be used to provide effective risk management for the shipping industry. Moreover, the book outlines the traditional strategies used by owners for risk management, and compares and contrasts solutions offered by financial derivatives with them.

1.4. The Cash-flow Position of the Shipowner

All the above commercial decisions, and the rewards and the risks that they carry, are analysed best by viewing vessels as investments – as assets in portfolios. Vessels generate a stream of income through their provision of freight services, and a possible capital gain (loss) by selling the assets at a price higher (lower) than what they are bought at. These are then compared with alternative investments in the world economy and a decision is taken on whether to participate or not in the shipping industry and in what form. This book concentrates in examining the position of investors who decide to participate in the shipping industry, for all the reasons mentioned above. More specifically, the book considers the risks that emanate from all the above decisions and how to moderate them. These are examined according to the type of market the company is exposed to, which includes the freight market, the vessel fuel market, the market for vessels (new, second-hand and scrapping) and the interest and exchange rate markets. It is assumed here that the volatility of operating costs is very low and as a consequence, these costs are very predictable during the course of the year. The above issues become more evident by examining the shipowner's cash-flow, where:

Overall Cash-flow= Operating Revenue – Operating Costs (Fixed) – Voyage Costs (Variable)
    – Capital Costs (Fixed or Variable)
    + Capital Gain

Table 1.1. Shipowner's Cash-flow in Spot (Voyage) and Time-charter (T/C) Markets

Spot (Voyage) Market	Time-Charter Market
Voyage Hire (Revenue, in US$)	T/C Hire (Revenue, in US$)
less: Operating Costs (in Domestic currency, e.g. Euro)	less: Operating Costs (in Domestic currency, e.g. Euro)
less: Voyage Costs	-
= Operating Earnings	**= Operating Earnings**
Less: Capital Costs (from loans)	**Less: Capital Costs (from loans)**
Plus: Capital Gain/Loss from buying and selling the vessel	**Plus: Capital Gain/Loss** from buying and selling the vessel
= Overall Cash-flow	**= Overall Cash-flow**

Notes: Source: Kavussanos, 2002
- For definitions of Operating Costs and Voyage Costs refer to Footnotes 1 and 2 of this chapter.
- Capital Costs refer to debt servicing through capital repayment.

This relationship is also presented in Table 1.1, distinguishing in its two columns between operation of the vessel in the spot (voyage) and in the time-charter market. Thus, the cash-flow is affected by demand and freight rates in the freight market (and by the type of fixture secured), by fuel costs determined in the bunker market, by capital costs determined in the capital and money markets, by vessel prices determined in the market for vessels and by exchange rates, which affect all the above categories. More specifically, businesses are concerned not only about the level but also about the volatility of their cash-flow, which is a coordinate of the volatilities of each constituent part of the cash-flow. As mentioned earlier, it is assumed that rational entrepreneurs dislike the uncertainty that comes along with highly volatile cash-flows. However, they may be prepared to exchange such higher risks with higher returns and visa-versa.

Therefore, it is important to recognize that, in making commercial decisions the owner has in mind that greater rewards usually come by undertaking higher risks. Usually, such risks are measured by the volatility of the variable a decision has to be made for. For example, because freight rates fluctuate widely, say from month to month, substantial gains or losses may occur, depending on what happens in the market in subsequent months. Fluctuations in freight rates around their average values over a period of time may be used typically as measures of freight risk; technically, by their variance or by their standard deviation[7]. High (low) standard deviations reflect high (low) volatility in rates and of the risks involved in operating the vessels. Before embarking into the task of analyzing risks in the sector and considering ways of managing it, it is instructive to examine the segmentation of the shipping industry.

1.5. Market Segmentation of the Shipping Industry

The shipping industry comprises a number of broad sectors, according to the characteristics of the vessels involved in carrying the cargos or passengers in these sectors. They include the cruise shipping sector, the dry-bulk shipping sector, the liner sector, etc. The characteristics of the vessels involved in each sector, have developed to serve the purpose for which they are built. For instance, certain dry-bulk cargo carrying vessels have fitted cranes on board, in order to enable them to load and unload cargo in ports where the infrastructure is not sufficient. Moreover, the economics of the industries, which generate the demand for the service the vessels offer, have been very important in determining the vessel characteristics. Thus, coal and iron ore are typically cheap commodities, which unless they are carried in large quantities their freight cost per ton may not make it worth transporting from more distant producing regions of the world. Technical developments in vessel design have been instrumental to that effect. Larger vessel sizes, more efficient engines, smoother hulls have been made possible through developments in naval engineering.

---

[7] The variance of a variable X, calculated from a sample of n observations, with mean value $\overline{X} = \sum_{i=1}^{n} X_i / n$, is defined as $S^2 = \sum_{i=1}^{n}(X_i - \overline{X})^2 / (n-1)$. The standard deviation of X is simply the square root of the variance – denoted S. Notice that $\sum_{i=1}^{n} X_i = X_1 + X_2 + ... + X_n$, while $\sum_{i=1}^{n}(X_i - \overline{X})^2 = (X_1 - \overline{X})^2 + (X_2 - \overline{X})^2 + ... + (X_n - \overline{X})^2$. The summation operator $\sum_{i=1}^{n}$ is used as a short hand notation to the long sums displayed above.

This book concentrates in the ocean cargo carrying sector of the shipping industry, although the conclusions drawn and the risk management techniques developed are also applicable to other sectors of the industry – or even to other industries/businesses with similar characteristics. The reason for concentrating in the bulk sector is that conditions of perfect competition prevail and this makes freight rates and prices rather volatile. This is not the case with other sub-sectors of shipping, at least to the same extent as in the tramp markets.

1.5.1. General Cargo and Bulk Cargo Movements

The growth in international trade over time has been the driving force behind seaborne transportation. It is argued that 95% of world trade, in volume terms, is carried by vessels. The development in international seaborne trade, by major commodities carried by sea from 1986 to 2005, is shown in Figure 1.4. As can be observed, total seaborne trade has almost doubled over these years, and the point should be made that this has been a continuation of the growth in world trade observed over previous decades also.

The liberalization of international trade, the trend towards the transnationalisation of business, with the associated expansion of industrial processes over countries and continents of the world and the discovery of new sources of raw materials has seen world trade flourish. The economies of scale associated with seaborne transportation have played its role in facilitating these changes. This in itself has called for the construction of specialized types of vessels of various sizes, which can carry these commodities between regions of the world. Therefore, specialized markets have developed for each of these vessels, with common driving forces, but also distinct features in terms of factors affecting demand, supply, and as a consequence risk and return profiles. These features are established in studies such as those of Glen (1997) and Kavussanos (1996a,b, 1997, 1998).

Figure 1.4. World Seaborne Trade by Commodities

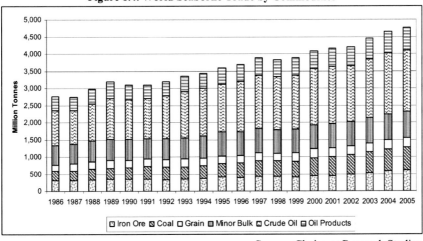

Source: Clarksons Research Studies

To understand the distinction of vessel sizes into categories, the Parcel Size Distribution (PSD) of each commodity, which determines the shipping consignment of the cargo carried by vessels, is useful – see Stopford (1997). It rests on the observation that some commodities are typically moved in larger sizes than others.

For example, iron ore and grain consignments are much larger than phosphate rock or bauxite and alumna. Furthermore, the consignment size or PSD of each commodity changes over time and may be different on different routes. The PSD depends on:

- Commodity demand and shipping supply economics. For instance, low value goods move in large consignments as economies of scale in transportation develop and make the freight cost per unit very low. Such examples include crude oil, coal, iron ore, etc. The economics of the industrial processes generating the demand for raw materials and finished products of these commodities are also important. Physical characteristics of the commodities transported have a role to play, as agricultural goods, for instance, are perishable and require specialized more expensive storage facilities in comparison to commodities such as coal and iron ore. In general, storage, insurance and financial costs must be weighted against transportation costs in the decision of charterers of what consignment size to transport.
- Cargo consignments are proportional to transport distances, as economies of scale are important for the long-haul transportation of commodities. It is more economical then to use larger vessels to transport commodities over long distances.
- Transport system restrictions, such as limited draught, berth size and cargo handling facilities in ports, particularly in developing countries, and regulations in certain regions of the world influence the PSD. For instance, it is not possible for large gearless vessels with deep draughts to approach certain relatively shallow ports in developing countries, and as a consequence consignment sizes and vessels used in these trades are smaller.
- Vessel availability. Consignments of over 2,000-3,000 tons can fill a whole vessel (or hold of a vessel) rather than part of a vessel, and are transported in bulk. Smaller consignments, which fill only part of the vessel (or hold) move as general cargo.

Following the above observations, it can be said that bulk cargoes refer mainly to transportation of raw materials, which are transported on one-vessel one-cargo basis. They are further sub-divided into liquid cargo and dry cargo. Liquid cargo includes crude oil, oil products, chemicals (e.g. caustic soda), vegetable oils and wine. Dry cargo is broadly divided into three categories: (i) Majors; that is, iron ore, coal, grain, bauxite and phosphates; (ii) Minors; that is, steel, steel products, cement, sugar, gypsum, non ferrous metal ores, salt, sulphur, forest products, wood chips and chemicals; and (iii) Specialist bulk cargoes, requiring specific handling or storage requirements such as heavy lift, cars, timber, refrigerated cargo, etc.

The vessels involved in bulk cargo transportation are tankers, dry-bulk carriers, combined carriers (they carry either dry- or liquid-bulk) and specialist bulk vessels. Bulk cargoes constitute approximately 2/3 of seaborne trade movements, and are carried mainly by tramp vessels, which constitute about 3/4 of the world's merchant fleet. These are vessels which move around the world, seeking employment in any place/route of the globe. Bulk vessels usually carry one cargo in one vessel, at rates negotiated individually, between the shipowner and the charterer, for the service provided.

General cargo, is also dry cargo, in general, but is not transported in bulk. A large part of general cargo is transported in containers, multipurpose and other specialized vessels (RoRo, car carriers, etc.). General cargo, which constitutes 1/3 of seaborne trade, moves in either tramp vessels or liners; the latter provide a regular, scheduled, service transporting small cargo consignments at fixed tariff levels between areas of the world.

1.5.2. Bulk-Cargo Segmentation

For analysis, dry- and liquid-bulk cargoes may be further subdivided according to the PSD functions of the products carried. The PSD function depends on the maximum size delivery an industry is able or willing to accept at any one time. In some industries stockpiles are around 10-15 thousand tons, so a delivery of 50 thousand tons is too large. Physical limitations on vessel size draw a line between groups; for instance, Suezmax, Panamax, etc. are such groups. This is because size determines the type of trade the vessel will be involved in, in terms of type of cargo and route; this is a result of the different PSD's of commodities and the port and seaway restrictions for certain size vessels. Design features are important, such as, cargo handling gear (cranes), pumping capacity and segregation of cargo tanks in tankers; certain ports in developing countries cannot be used, for example, from vessels which do not have cargo handling gear. Also, coating of tanks and ballast spaces are distinguishing factors.

Tables 1.2 and 1.3 present the sub-markets that are distinguished for dry- and liquid-bulk. Capesize vessels [100,000-130,000 dead-weight tons (dwt)] transport iron ore, mainly from South America and Australia to Japan, West Europe and North America, and coal from North America and Australia to Japan and Western Europe. Panamax vessels (50,000-70,000 dwt) are used primarily to carry grain and coal from North America and Australia to Japan and West Europe. Handysize vessels (10,000-24,999 dwt) and Handymax vessels (25,000-49,999 dwt) transport grain, mainly from North America, Argentina and Australia to Europe and Asia, and minor bulk products – such as sugar, fertilizers, steel and scrap, forest products, non-ferrous metals and salt – virtually from all over the world.

As can be observed in Table 1.2, Capesize vessels are engaged in the transportation of three commodities, carrying mostly iron ore (70% of the iron ore trade), followed by coal (45% of the coal trade) and to a lesser extend grains (7% of the grains trade). Smaller size vessels are more flexible in the sense of carrying a larger number of commodities in more routes of the world. For example, Panamax vessels carry bauxite and alumina (45% of their trades), grain (43% of grains trade), coal (40% of the coal trade), iron ore (22% of the iron ore trade) and phosphate rock (20% of its trade). Similarly, Handymax and Handysize vessels carry phosphate rock (80%), bauxite and alumina (55%), grains (50%), coal (15%) and only 8% of iron ore trades. If there is a disturbance in one of the routes or in the economics of one of the commodities they carry, they are flexible enough to switch to other routes or to other trades. The operation of Capesize vessels, in terms of trading routes and ports they can approach, is restricted due to their deep draught and limited number of commodities that they can transport. Panamax vessels, due to the lack of cargo handling gears and deep draught, are not so flexible and are engaged in the transportation of few commodities. Finally, Handymax and Handysize vessels are mainly engaged in the transportation of grain commodities and minor dry-bulk commodities around the world. Due to their smaller size, relatively shallow draught and the existence of cargo handling gears on board, they are flexible to switch between shipping routes and types of commodities that they carry, should weak market conditions or other problems prevail on a trade that they serve.

Table 1.2. Cargo and Routes of Different Size Dry-Bulk Vessels

Class of Bulk Carriers	Commodities (percentage of total shipments)				
	Iron ore	Coal	Grain	Bauxite & Alumina	Phosphate Rock
Capesize	70%	45%	7%	-	-
Panamax	22%	40%	43%	45%	20%
Handy	8%	15%	50%	55%	80%
Major Routes					
	Iron ore	Coal	Grain	Bauxite & Alumina	Phosphate Rock
Capesize (100,000 – 180,000 dwt)	• Brazil to West Europe and Japan and China • W. Australia to West Europe, Japan and China	• E.Australia to Far East, Japan and West Europe • South Africa to West Europe and Far East	• Argentina and River Plate to Near East, and East Europe		
Panamax (50,000 – 79,999 dwt)	• Brazil to West Europe and Japan • Australia to West Europe and Japan	• North America to Japan and West Europe • E.Australia to Far East, Japan and West Europe	• North America to Far East, West Europe and Near East		
Handy (25,000 – 49,999 dwt)	• India to Japan, China and Korea • Canada to USA and Japan • Liberia and Mauritania to West Europe	• South Africa to Far East and Europe	• Australia to Far East, Japan and Middle East • North America to Africa and West Europe	• Caribbean to North America and West Europe • West Africa to West Europe and Japan • Australia to Japan and West Europe	• Morocco to West Europe • Russia to West Europe • The US to Japan and West Europe

Source: Fearnleys, World Bulk Trades, Lloyd's Shipping Economist and Baltic Exchange

Table 1.3. Cargo and Routes of Different Size Tanker Vessels

Class of Tankers	Commodities (percentage of total shipments)		
	Crude oil	Dirty Products	Clean Products
ULCC/VLCC	60%	-	-
Suezmax	30%	5%	0%
Aframax	10%	35%	20%
Panamax and Handy	0%	60%	80%
	Major Routes		
	Crude oil	Dirty Products	Clean Products
ULCC (320,000+ dwt) VLCC (200,000 – 319,999 dwt)	• Middle East to USEC, W.Europe and Far East		
Suezmax (120,000 – 199,999 dwt)	• Middle East to USEC, W.Europe and Mediterranean via Suez • Middle East to Far East • North Sea to USEC • West Africa to US and Europe	• Middle East to USEC, W.Europe and Far East	
Aframax (75,000 – 119,999 dwt)	• North Sea to USEC • West & North Africa to US and Europe • Indonesia to Japan • Venezuela to US Gulf	• Middle East to USEC, W.Europe and Far East • US Gulf to different destinations • Other routes around the world	• Middle East to USEC, W.Europe and Far East • US Gulf to different destinations • Mediterranean and West Europe • Other routes around the world
Panamax (50,000 - 74,999 dwt) Handy (10,000 - 49,999 dwt)		• Middle East to USEC, W.Europe and Far East • US Gulf to different destinations • Mediterranean and West Europe • Other routes around the world	• Middle East to USEC, W.Europe and Far East • US Gulf to different destinations • Mediterranean and West Europe • Other routes around the world

Source: Fearnleys, World Bulk Trades, Lloyd's Shipping Economist and Baltic Exchange

Therefore, there is a close relationship between vessel sizes and the transportation of specific commodities, as certain types of vessels are employed in the transportation of particular commodities on specific routes. Smaller vessels, such as Handysize and Handymax in the dry-bulk sector, are, in general, geared so that they can load and unload cargo in ports without sophisticated handling facilities. They can approach more ports compared to larger vessels. As ports of the world have developed Handymax vessels are carrying more and more of the trade the Handysize vessels carry. Even Handymax are now gradually superseded by the larger Supramax vessels.

The same is also true in the liquid-bulk sector. The very large ULCC and VLCC vessels trade in only 3-4 routes, as the draught restrictions in most ports and the storage facilities required ashore are very large to accommodate them and their cargoes. The smaller Suezmax, Aframax, Panamax and Handy vessels are more flexible in terms of routes and trades they are involved in, and the smaller the vessel size the greater is their flexibility. Table 1.3 shows that ULCC/VLCC vessels engaged in crude oil transport in three main routes, carrying 60% of the total crude oil trade; these routes are from Middle East to US East Coast, to West Europe and to Far East. Suezmax vessels carry 30% of the crude oil trades, from the Middle East to US East Coast, to West Europe and to Mediterranean ports. Also, they transport cargo from the North Sea and deliver it to the US East Coast and from West Africa to US and Europe. Suezmax vessels carry also approximately 5% of "*dirty products*" trades worldwide[8]; they transport cargos from the Middle East for delivery mainly to the US East Coast, to West Europe and to the Far East. Smaller size vessels, like Aframax, Panamax and Handy can carry, besides crude oil and "*dirty products*", "*clean products*" as well[9]. More specifically, Panamax and Handy vessels are mostly engaged in the transportation of "*clean products*" (80%), from the Middle East to the US East Coast, to West Europe and to the Far East, and also from the US Gulf to different destinations, and other routes around the world.

1.5.3. General (Dry) Cargo Segmentation

When general dry cargo is not moved by dry-bulk tramp vessels, it is transported by liners. The following distinctions are common. Container vessels, RoRo, Multi Purpose Vessels (Single-deck, Multi-deck, Semi-containers) and Barge Carrying Vessels (BCV), amongst others. Other specialized vessels include Refrigerated vessels (Reefers), Car-carriers, Cement carriers, Heavy lift, Ore carriers, Vehicle carriers, Liquefied Petroleum Gas (LPG) tankers, etc.

Table 1.4. Container Market Segmentation by Vessel Size

Vessel Type/Market	Vessel Size, TEU	Speed in Knots
Feeder	0 - 499	16.5
Feedermax	500 - 999	19.0
Handy	1,000 - 1,999	20.3
Sub-Panamax	2,000 - 2,999	21.0
Panamax	3,000 - 4,999	24.3
Post-Panamax	>5,000	25.9

Note: Standard 20' Container.

It should be mentioned here that within the liner trades there is a move towards containerization at the expense of non-unitized cargo, which used to be transported in

---

[8] "*Dirty*" vessels carry the "*black*" or "*dirty*" cargoes such as crude oil, heavy fuel oils, asphalt, etc.
[9] "*Clean*" vessels carry the refined "*white*" clean products such as gasoline, jet fuels, diesel oil, kerosene, naphtha, leaded and unleaded oil, etc.

Multi Purpose vessels. Containerships themselves have sub-markets according to size. These are shown in Table 1.4. One cannot fail to notice here the higher operating speeds for vessels of larger size. These larger container vessels carry relatively expensive goods in containers around the world, and require high speeds to reduce the opportunity cost of capital built into the high value commodities that they carry. Just as with dry-bulk, each of these sub-markets has its own economic characteristics, and the risks and rewards involved for the shipowner and the charterers are different.

1.6. Market Conditions in Shipping Freight Markets

The economics of general cargo and tramp markets are different. Oligopolistic conditions prevail in liner markets, as there are few suppliers of the freight service, organized through conferences. They produce and publish tariffs in a collusive oligopolistic manner, which shippers have to adhere to. Shippers, on the other hand, are many with relatively small cargo consignments to transport that occupy only part of the vessel. As a consequence, each individual shipper of a cargo does not have the power to negotiate freight rates.

In contrast, conditions of perfect competition prevail in tramp dry- and liquid-bulk markets. That is, there are many buyers and sellers of freight services, with no barriers to entry or exit, negotiating a relatively homogeneous product (the freight service) in well organised freight markets. The charterers, which include large trading companies, private and governmental exporters/importers, etc., compete between them to secure vessels which will carry their cargos. It can be safely assumed that in a particular route-trade there are no significant differences in the quality of the freight service offered; that is, the freight service is close to being homogeneous if not perfectly homogeneous, despite some minor differences in vessel characteristics and customer relations that may exist between shipping companies, aiming to differentiate their service. Similarly, there are many ship carriers, which include private and public shipowners, ship managers and state owned shipowning companies. They compete between them to secure employment for their vessels to transport cargos. These two counterparties come together through specialized brokers, who are based either in house or are independent brokerage houses. They secure the details and the freight rate in a charter party agreement. This is individually negotiated for each vessel and cargo carried. As mentioned before, such a fixture can take various forms, ranging from voyage charter, COA, time-charter of different durations, etc. – see Footnote 6.

The many buyers and sellers participating in the freight market can freely enter or exit the market, and their large number is by itself evidence of the ease of entering and exiting the market. It is true that the initial cost of buying a newbuilding or a second-hand vessel is high, but specialized departments in banks and specialized banks exist that are willing to finance these projects. True, significant collateral is needed to secure such financing, but then even smaller investors can participate in shipowning through the publicly listed shipping companies in stock exchanges. Exiting the industry is even simpler, as vessels may be sold in organised markets for second-hand vessels, or sent to scrap if this solution is better economically.

Furthermore, entry and exit (switching) of vessels into different trades/routes is not prohibited in any way, as long as the vessel has the appropriate technical specifications required to serve that trade/route. The same is also true for contracts of different duration, which are effectively distinct markets. In fact, this is what owners do; they consider the risk–return trade offs of operating vessels in particular routes of the industry and move their vessels accordingly. The same considerations are also taken into account when they decide on the type of fixture (voyage, 6-months time-charter, 12-months time-charter, etc.) to secure for their vessel. As is well-known, when such opportunities in a market are realized by market participants, the excess profits are eliminated through the joint movement of vessels towards the excess profit generating trade/route and/or type of fixture, to reap the profits. This mobility of vessels is an important characteristic that contributes to competition prevailing in freight markets, and is a property that doesn't exist in other industries, such as real estate. At the same time though there are costs involved in moving vessels between different lanes/trades, as vessel hulls may need to be cleaned or the vessel may have to travel in ballast to enter a different route than the one it trades at the moment. Moreover, switching between contracts of different duration involves certain costs, when agreements are broken, including penalties and loss of reputation in the market. These costs are insignificant in "*paper markets*", such as those involving derivatives, stocks, bonds and money instruments in general.

Finally, a few words are in order about the availability and the processing of information in freight markets. The Baltic exchange was formed in 1883 to bring together market participants wishing to buy and sell the freight service. This physical pooling of participants in an organised market is equivalent, amongst other things, to pooling of information, which helps discover prices and contributes towards the efficient working of markets. Since then a great number of developments have occurred, including technological innovations in communications and electronics. This has allowed shipbrokers possessing information generated in the market to exchange this information in the form of published reports, informed advises over the telephone, email, fax, or the web. In the age of information that we live it is not so important to gather around the pit of an exchange to trade the freight service. Specialized organizations and businesses have come to existence, which collect and disseminate relevant information on fixtures, prices, cargos and vessels available, to the market in various forms (paper or electronic), usually at a price. They include, the Baltic Exchange, Lloyds Maritime Information Services (LMIS), Lloyds Register of Shipping (LRS), Lloyds Shipping Economist, Lloyds list, Bloomberg, etc. This is all available to shipowners and charterers, who can utilize the available information to make informed decisions in freight markets, thereby contributing to the conditions of perfect competition.

1.7. Equilibrium Freight Rates in Tramp Freight Markets

Following the above discussion, freight rates in the shipping freight markets are determined at the interaction of demand and supply for freight services. Demand for freight services is a derived demand, in the sense that the demand from the shipper is not for the vessel, but for the service that it offers. Moreover, it is inelastic, due to the low value of the freight cost in relation to the final price of the good transported. Second, the supply of freight services has the shape observed in Figure 1.5; it is relatively flat when freight rates are low – that is, when the market is weak. In this case, the least efficient vessels are laid up and the fleet at sea is slow steaming. As freight rates rise, vessels are taken out of lay up and added to the active fleet. At the same time they start speeding up. As rates increase even further and the market becomes stronger, there is no lay up and vessels at sea are in full speed, in their effort to carry as many cargos as possible within specific periods of time. This is the almost vertical part of the supply curve.

In the longer-run, new vessels can be built and added to the fleet, shifting the entire supply curve to the right. Vessels may also be sent for scrap or lost through accidents. The net effect in the stock of the fleet depends on the balance between vessels delivered and vessels scrapped or lost. If deliveries exceed scrapping and losses, the entire supply curve shifts to the right, thereby reducing freight rates for a given level of demand. When scrapping and losses exceed deliveries, the supply curve shifts to the left, resulting in higher freight rates, *ceteris paribus*.

Figure 1.5. The Shipping Freight Market

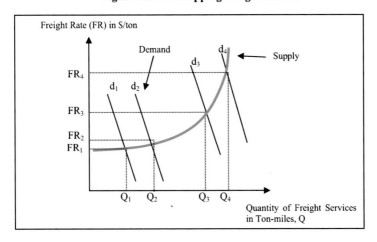

Equilibrium freight rates then are determined at each point in time, at the intersection of the demand and supply schedules in the market. This can be observed graphically in Figure 1.5. Say equilibrium freight rates are at FR_1 and freight services exchanged in the market are at Q_1, determined at the intersection of the demand schedule d_1 with the supply curve. Assume there is an increase in demand from d_1 to d_2. In this weak market, freight services exchanged in the market increase to Q_2, but freight rates only increase a little to FR_2. In contrast, in a strong market, where Q_3 freight services are exchanged in the market at freight rates FR_3, an equivalent (to the weak market) increase in demand from d_3 to d_4 raises freight rates significantly to FR_4. The same is also true when demand falls. Thus, at low freight rates – that is, under weak freight market conditions, declines or increases in the demand curve have a small influence on freight rates; that is, volatility in freight rates is low when the market is weak. At the top end of the supply curve, which represents a strong freight market, changes in demand for freight services bring about a large change in freight rates. Overall, it can be argued that:

- Under tight market conditions, changes in demand produce large variations in freight rates – that is, volatility and freight risks are high;
- Under weak market conditions changes in demand produce only small changes in freight rates - that is, volatility and freight risks are low. This is also shown to hold empirically in studies such as Kavussanos and Alizadeh (2001, 2002a).

It is important to realize that the freight market is not one. Instead, markets are segmented along the lines discussed above, with freight rates determined separately in each of these. That is, there is a separate market for Capesize vessels, another for

43

Panamax and so on. Moreover, different duration contracts within each vessel type constitute separate markets; that is, within the Capesize sector, there is a separate freight market for spot rates, another for 1-year time-charter rates, and so on. Of course, all markets are influenced by world economic activity, but there are factors, which are specific to each sub-market that determine rates separately in each of them. Thus, for analysis, these can be broadly classified according to the size/type of vessel used for transportation, or even by route a type of vessel is engaged in. Figures 1.6 and 1.7 show such equilibrium voyage (spot) freight rates in segments of the dry-bulk and tanker markets, and how they have evolved over time between 1990 and 2005. Notice that, rates in the dry-bulk sector are expressed in US$/ton, while tanker voyage rates are expressed in Worldscale (WS) units.

Figure 1.6. Voyage (Spot) Freight Rates for Different Size Dry-Bulk Vessels

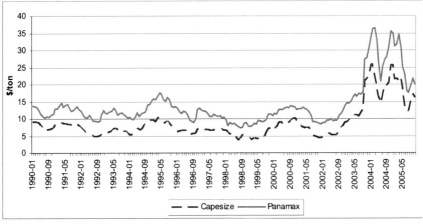

Source: Clarksons Research Studies

"Worldwide Tanker Nominal Freight Scale", more commonly known as *"Worldscale"*, was created in 1969, to assist the oil market to have an independent unit of measurement of rates. Market levels of freight rates are expressed as a percentage of the scale rates instead of a plus or minus percentage. Worldscale rates are derived assuming that a "nominal" tanker functions on round voyages between designated ports. The calculated schedule rate (which equates to different US$/ton equivalents for each different route combination) is referred to as *"Worldscale 100"* or *"Flat rate"*[10]. This method is known as *"Points of Scale"* and thus, Worldscale 100 means 100 points of 100 percent of the published rate or, in other words, the published rate itself. Against this Flat rate, an actual agreed percentage of this Flat rate is negotiated between shipowners and charterers. Thus, Worldscale 60 refers to 60% of the published Flat rate being applied to the actual voyage performed. From September 1969 until the end of 1988, Worldscale was regularly revised for changes in bunker prices and port costs but the fixed daily hire element of $1,800 remained constant. On 1st January 1989 the *"New Worldscale"* was introduced. It was agreed, that a standard vessel with a carrying capacity of 75,000 tonnes and a daily hire

---

[10] The Flat rate is expressed in $/mt of cargo carried between any two ports. The absolute value of the Flat rate depends on an assumed bunker price, and is based on a 75,000 dwt tanker with specific fuel consumption and speed. Port and cargo discharge dues are surveyed annually at every port, and the fuel costs for the voyage are estimated. In addition, a fixed notional daily hire is included in order to arrive at the Flat rate.

element of $12,000 is more representative. The Worldscale is the joint endeavour of two non-profit making organisations known as Worldscale Association (London) Limited and Worldscale Association (NYC) Inc. Each company is under the control of a Management Committee, the members of which are senior brokers from leading tanker broking firms in London and New York respectively (Worldscale Association, 2005).

Figure 1.7. Voyage (Spot) Freight Rates for Different Size Tanker Vessels

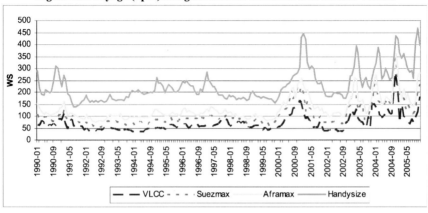

Source: Clarksons Research Studies

As can be observed, both in the dry-bulk and in the tanker markets, freight rates are distinct for each sub-sector. Rates seem to move together within the dry-bulk and the tanker sectors, driven by world demand for bulk trades. However, patterns of rates in each segment are also distinct. They are determined in their separate markets through their individual forces of supply and demand. These idiosyncratic patterns, which depend on the specifics of each segment as described earlier in this chapter, produce the patterns in freight rates that are observed in the figures. The aim of this book is to understand the volatilities observed in these rates, rather than the historical evolution. Rates seem to fluctuate considerably over time, thus affecting the revenue cash-flow of the shipping company, as well as the cost side of the charterer's cash-flow wishing to transport goods by vessels. These are the kind of fluctuations in freight rates that affect the income/costs of market participants in freight markets, that this book considers as freight risk, and proposes strategies for managing it.

1.7.1. Freight Rates for Different Duration Contracts
Continuing along the same lines discussed above, different duration contracts for the same type of vessel in the same route constitute distinct markets. Figure 1.8 shows three different supply curves on the same diagram, representing spot, 1-year and 3-year time-charter supply curves – effectively, three different markets are presented in the same diagram. As can be observed, the longer is the duration of the freight contract the flatter is the supply curve in the respective market. The flatter supply curve indicates that the supply of freight services, say for 1-year time-charter contracts, is less responsive to changes in freight rates compared to spot markets. This is because time-charter fixtures of longer duration are less flexible in comparison to ones with shorter duration. That is, suppliers of vessels assigned into longer time-charter agreements cannot be as responsive to changes in freight rates, in taking vessels in and out of these contracts to the extend that this is possible in the shorter

voyage contracts. Thus, the elasticity of supply of the longer duration contracts is lower in comparison to shorter duration ones, producing flatter shape supply curves, such as those observed in Figure 1.8.

Figure 1.8. Shipping Freight Markets for Different Duration Contracts

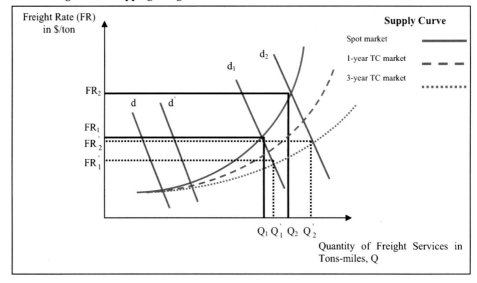

These observations have consequences for the reaction of freight rates of different duration contracts to changes in demand. As can be observed in the figure, the same change in demand from d_1 to d_2 brings about a larger reaction in spot freight rates (FR_1 to FR_2) in comparison to 1-year and 3-year time-charters ($FR_1^{'}$ to $FR_2^{'}$). Similarly 1-year time-charter rates react more to the same magnitude of changes in demand, in comparison to 3-year time-charter rates. Thus, in the figure, say demand increases from d_1 to d_2. In the spot market, freight rates increase from FR_1 to FR_2 as a consequence. In the 3-year time-charter market the increase in freight rates is much smaller, represented by the distance $FR_1^{'}$ to $FR_2^{'}$. As a consequence, volatilities in spot rates are expected to be higher, the shorter is the duration of the freight contract. This has been substantiated empirically in the studies by Kavussanos (1996a, 2003), which show this result for both the dry-bulk and tanker markets, by comparing the volatilities of freight rates in contracts of different duration.

Moreover, this reaction of freight rates to changes in demand varies according to the conditions of the market: In strong markets, the differences in volatilities of freight rates between contracts of different duration are much stronger than in weak markets. In the latter case, it may even be that the reaction of freight rates to changes in demand produces more or less the same weak effects between freight contracts of different duration. As discussed later in this chapter, at any point in time, fluctuations in freight rates may reflect the cumulative effect of cyclical, seasonal and random effects. It has been shown in the literature, see for instance Kavussanos (1996a) and Kavussanos and Alizadeh (2001, 2002a), that when considering only seasonal effects on volatilities, the same ranking is preserved; that is, longer duration freight contracts display lower seasonal volatility compared to ones with shorter duration.

Figure 1.9. One-year Time-charter Rates for Different Size Dry-Bulk Vessels

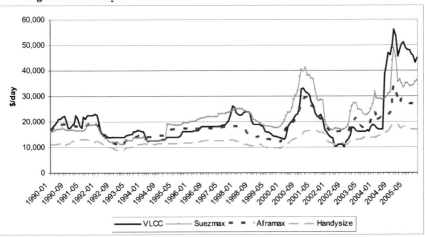

Source: Clarksons Research Studies

Figures 1.9 and 1.10 show historical values of the equilibrium freight rates for 1-year time-charter contracts as determined in the corresponding freight markets of each sub-sector of dry-bulk and tanker markets, respectively. They reflect the supply and demand balance for one year time-charter contracts in each market at each point in time. As can be clearly observed, the well-known cycles of the industry are reflected in the movements of these rates. Similarly, freight rates are determined in their respective markets in contracts of other durations, such as for 3-year time-charter contracts, etc.

Figure 1.10. One-year Time-charter Rates for Different Size Tanker Vessels

Source: Clarksons Research Studies

1.7.2. Term Structure of Freight Contracts

There is a fundamental relationship linking freight contracts of different duration. To see this, consider a shipowner who has the choice of hiring his vessel in the voyage (spot) market or letting it under a 1-year time-charter contract. Assuming that within the one year of the time-charter contract he could have hired the vessel for 12 consecutive monthly voyages, Equation (1.1) describes the relationship linking the two rates. It is based on the Expectations Hypothesis of the Term-Structure (EHTS) relationship. This states, that the sum of the discounted earnings (in \$/day) from an n period (say, 12 months) time-charter contract should be equal to the sum of the discounted expected earnings from a series of spot contracts with duration m (say, one month), within the life of the time-charter contract[11], plus a term-premium, $E_t\phi_t$. Mathematically:

$$\sum_{i=0}^{k-1}\frac{TC_t^n}{(1+r)^i}=\sum_{i=0}^{k-1}\frac{E_t(FR_{t+i}^m)}{(1+r)^i}+E_t\phi_t \quad ; \quad k=n/m \tag{1.1}$$

In its empirical form, the above relationship becomes:

$$TC_t^n=\theta\sum_{i=0}^{k-1}\delta^i E_t FR_{t+i}^m+E_t\phi_t+\varepsilon_t \quad ; \quad \varepsilon_t \sim IN(0,\sigma^2), \ k=n/m, \ \delta=\frac{1}{1+r}, \ \theta=\frac{1}{1-\delta^k} \tag{1.2}$$

where, TC_t^n is the n period (say, n = 12 month) earnings time-charter contract at time t, $E_t FR_{t+i}^m$ is the expected at time t, earnings of the spot charter contract, which lasts over m periods from t+i to t+(i+1), δ is the discount factor and θ is a coefficient of proportionality (for details, see Kavussanos and Alizadeh, 2002a). Also, k = n/m is a positive integer indicating the number of spot charter contracts in the life of a time-charter contract (say, 12 monthly contracts within a 1-year time-charter contract), $E_t\phi_t$ is a term measuring the price of risk; finally, ε_t is a stochastic error-term, which is very small and is sometimes positive, sometimes negative but on average is zero. It is uncorrelated with its past values and takes values from a normal distribution with mean zero and variance σ^2.

Assumptions underlying the above relationship include the following: first, that the duration of the trip (spot) charter is constant, m = 1 month;[12] second, that expectations are rational, in the sense that market participants utilize all the information available to them to obtain forecasts of relevant variables; and third, that the differences in risk levels between the spot and the time- charter contracts, is reflected in the term $E_t\phi_t$.[13] If $E_t\phi_t$ is zero, then the EHTS reduces to the "*Pure Expectations Hypothesis*", which posits that the long-term time-charter rates are solely determined as a weighted average of the expected future spot rates.

---

[11] Note that in order to test this relationship, spot and time-charter rates must be comparable; that is they should have the same units of measurement.

[12] Since we are using averages of monthly spot rates, the duration for a trip-charter is assumed to be one month.

[13] Apart from unemployment risk, there are other risks associated with the spot market operation, which are not present while the ship is on time-charter. Examples of these include the uncertainty of the freight rates that will prevail in the spot markets for the next 11 months, to the end of the time-charter contract; in contrast, in time-charter contracts, the payments that will be received during the period of the time-charter are agreed at the outset. Other factors that may make time-charter rates more attractive include the existence of higher administration costs involved in operating in the spot market compared to the time-charter, and the possible vessel relocation costs that may have to be paid for the commencement of a new trip-charter contract.

The relationship is instructive, in terms of the term-structure of freight rates one should expect to observe in practice, from different duration contracts. Thus, in their choice of whether to employ their vessel, say in a series of 12 monthly spot contracts or a 1-year time-charter contract, vessel owners consider the risk-return tradeoffs from each operating strategy and act accordingly. Thus, the choice to employ the vessel spot involves the extra risk emanating from the uncertainty of:

- The voyage freight rate that will prevail month after month within the one year duration of the time-charter contract,
- The voyage costs that will have to be paid in each trip – which are not the shipowner's responsibility in time-charter contracts,
- The vessel remaining unemployed during even small periods of time between the fixing of consecutive voyage contracts,
- The relocation costs, which will arise when the vessel does not find employment in the port where the cargo is discharged.

Moreover, there are extra administrative costs involved when employing the vessels in a series of 12 monthly fixtures, compared to only one fixture for the time-charter contract. Finally, time-charter fixtures are often preferred by banks as collateral, towards the advancement of loans to the company. All these "*risk factors*", contribute towards making the risk-premium in the relationship described by Equations (1.1) and (1.2) non-zero. In fact, Kavussanos and Alizadeh (2002a), using historical data and contracts for voyage, 1-year and 3-year duration, show that the risk-premiums are negative; that is, that time-charter rates are at a discount to voyage rates, and the longer is the duration of the contract the greater is the discount offered. The aforementioned reasons explain why.

Moreover, in a separate study Kavussanos and Alizadeh (2002b) show that this risk-premium varies by market condition. The rationale behind this finding is that, under strong freight market conditions – when rates are rising, owners are not willing to lock their vessel into a long-term time-charter, as they would like to take advantage of the rising freight rates by fixing their vessel at the rising rates prevailing month after month in the market. On the other hand, when the market is falling, owners wish to fix their vessel in longer-term time-charter contracts, in order to avoid the reduced income that will result month after month when fixing the vessel in spot markets. Naturally, in both cases, charterers with the same expectations as owners, regarding how freight markets will evolve, will not be so willing to offer these contracts. On the other hand, charterers with opposite expectations as to how the market will evolve (or charterers wishing longer-term security of their supply lines), will be willing counterparties to these owners.

A further consequence of the existence of risk-premia – that is, of the discrepancy between spot and time-charter rates – being non-zero and time-varying is that they can be used for investment/speculative purposes. For instance, when time-charters are under-priced in comparison to spot rates, vessels can be hired into a long duration contract and operated in the spot market, to obtain excess profits. Other strategies may also be formed according to the risk level investors are wiling to undertake.

1.7.3. Seasonality in Tramp Freight Rate Markets – Models
A further important issue that one must be aware of when dealing in bulk freight markets, is their seasonal behaviour. At any point in time, fluctuations in freight rates may be decomposed into a cyclical, a seasonal and a random component. It is

important to be aware of any seasonal characteristics in freight rates for risk management purposes.

A time-series, measured more than once a year (e.g. at monthly, quarterly or semi-annual intervals), is said to contain deterministic seasonal components when there are systematic patterns in the series at the measured points (seasons) within the year. This may be due to changes in the weather, the calendar, or the behaviour of market participants involved in decision-making. These systematic changes may or may not be regular due to different circumstances in which factors such as technology, politics, etc. can be influential. For instance, seasonal consumption of heating oil in the northern hemisphere, increases every winter and declines every summer.

In shipping, freight rate seasonality may arise because of factors that influence the demand for shipping services; that is, factors that influence the demand for international commodity transport. The demand for shipping services is a derived demand, which depends on the economics of the commodities transported, world economic activity and the related macroeconomic variables of major economies (see Stopford, 1997). These macroeconomic variables have been shown to have seasonal components in studies such as those of Osborne (1990) and Canova and Hansen (1995). The same is also true for trade figures in several commodities; for instance there are seasonal elements in the grain and petroleum trades (see, for example, Stopford, 1997 and Moosa and Al-Loughani, 1994). Kavussanos and Alizadeh (2001, 2002a) show that these seasonalities are transmitted to shipping freight rates. These are thought to be primarily the effect of weather conditions and calendar effects, such as the increase in heating oil consumption during the winter, and the increased demand for dry-bulk commodities by Japan before the change of their financial year every March.

The following empirical model is utilised to measure the seasonal variation in freight rates for each sub-sector of the dry-bulk and the tanker industry. The monthly growth rate of the freight rate, ΔX_t (where X_t is the natural logarithm of freight rates), is explained in terms of a constant (β_0) and a set of monthly seasonal dummy variables, as in Equation (1.3):

$$\Delta X_t = \beta_0 + \sum_{i=2}^{12} \beta_i Q_{i,t} + \varepsilon_t \quad ; \quad \varepsilon_t \sim IN(0,\sigma^2) \tag{1.3}$$

where, $Q_{i,t}$, $i=2,...,12$, are relative seasonal (monthly) dummies[14]; β_i are the corresponding parameters of interest measuring whether in a particular month of the year freight rates are significantly above or below their long-run average value; and ε_t is a white noise error-term taking values from a normal distribution with mean of zero and variance σ^2. Alternatively, one can regress the growth rate of the series, ΔX_t, on 12 seasonal dummies, $D_{i,t}$ where $i=1,...,12$. In such case, the significance of a dummy coefficient indicates a change in the series in that particular month compared to the previous month. The equation is estimated using historical data for freight rates. The

---

[14] Relative seasonal dummies are constructed as $Q_{i,t} = D_{i,t} - D_{1,t}$, $i=2,...,12$, where $D_{1,t},..., D_{12,t}$ are 12 articicially constructed or dummy variables, taking the values of 1 in a particular month and 0 for the rest of the months. In this case, the coefficient for the base month, January, can be calculated as

$$_1 = -\sum_{i=2}^{12} {}_i .$$

significance of each seasonal dummy indicates the existence of seasonality in the respective period; that is, it indicates a significant change in the dependent variable compared to its long-run mean, β_0.

Moreover, the studies consider whether seasonal effects vary under different market conditions. This is an important issue in the cyclical shipping freight markets since, as explained earlier in this chapter, the elasticity of supply is thought to be high during troughs and low in peaks of the shipping business cycle. As a consequence, seasonal increases or declines in demand are expected to influence freight rates differently. One way to answer this empirically is by using a modified version of Equation (1.3). The following two-state (weak vs. strong market) model may be used to estimate these varying seasonal effects.

$$\Delta X_t = \beta_{0,St} + \sum_{i=2}^{12} \beta_{i,St} Q_{i,t} + \varepsilon_{St,t} \quad , \quad S_t = 0,1 \tag{1.4}$$

where, S_t is a state variable taking the value of 1 in expansionary market conditions and the value of 0 in a contractionary/falling market state. Estimates of the parameters $\beta_{i,0}$ and $\beta_{i,1}$, $i=0,\ldots,12$ in Equation (1.4), provide measurements of differences in seasonal behavior of freight rate series under different market conditions. The state of the market may be distinguished in a number of different ways, including: use of Markov Regime Switching Seasonal regression (MRSS) model, which allows structural shifts in the behaviour of the time series over the estimation period (see, e.g. Hamilton, 1989, 1994), or by considering whether a 12-month moving-average of the dependent variable (that is, of monthly growth rates in freight rates) ΔX_t, is above or below 0, in what may be called a threshold switching model – see the studies by Kavussanos and Alizadeh (2001, 2002a) for further details.

1.7.3.1. Seasonality Patterns in Dry-Bulk Freight Rate Markets – Results
Significant monthly seasonal effects in freight rates, estimated for each sub-sector of dry-bulk shipping, for spot, 1-year and 3-year contracts, are aggregated for economy of space into four seasons (April, Summer, Autumn and Winter) and presented in Table 1.5. As can be observed:

Spot Market Seasonality
- Spot freight rates increase significantly during the spring months of March and April for all size vessels. The rise in freight rates in those months could be explained by the surge in demand from Japanese importers for all commodities (grain, coal, iron ore, etc.) because of the end of the fiscal (tax) year in Japan at the end of March. Market practitioners suggest that this is because Japanese importers try to stock up their inventories (inputs in production) before the end of the year so as to show them as expenses in their books. Also, the harvest season in the Southern Hemisphere (February to March in Australia and Argentina) increases the demand for Handysize and Panamax dry-bulk carriers (during March and April). Due to the shortage of storage facilities and the port structure in these countries, grains harvested are exported immediately, using mostly smaller vessels that can approach these relatively shallow ports. In contrast, large inventories of grains are held during the year in the Northern Hemisphere. These stock levels are reduced during March and April to make way for storage space required for the forthcoming harvest. Thus, the increase in demand for freight services in the Handy and Panamax sizes affect rates

positively. Capesize freight rates are also influenced positively by the shift of the Handysize and Panamax tonnage to grain transportation.

- During the autumn months of October and November Panamax spot rates show a combined increase of 14.4%. Since Panamax bulk carriers are heavily involved in coal and grain transportation from the US Gulf, this upsurge in their spot rates may be explained by the increase in US grain exports (harvested between June and October) as well as the increase in demand for coal to stock up for the winter requirements.
- During the summer months of June and July, there is a seasonal decline in spot rates across all three vessel sizes. This decline is more pronounced in July compared to June and in larger vessels compared to smaller vessels. The combined summer (June and July) decline in Capesize, Panamax and Handysize rates seems to be higher than the spring increase for all vessel sizes. The significant seasonal decline in the dry-bulk spot markets during mid summer is caused by the start of the summer holidays and the associated drop in the industrial output of the industrialized countries[15].

The weaker seasonal increase and decline in freight rates for smaller size vessels, in comparison to the larger ones, may be attributed to their flexibility, which enables them to switch between trades and routes more easily compared to larger vessels. In addition, most Capesize vessels are mainly engaged in long-term charter contracts, leaving relatively less tonnage to trade in the spot market. As a result *"shocks"* to spot rates have a much greater effect on Capesize rates compared to smaller vessels. These results are in line with the more general pattern (not only seasonality) of freight rate volatility discussed in the study by Kavussanos (1996a), which suggests that freight rates for larger vessels are more volatile than smaller ones.

Table 1.5. Quarterly Seasonal Percentage Changes in Dry-Bulk Freight Rates

	Voyage (Spot) Charter			1-Year Time-Charter			3-Year Time-Charter		
	Cape	Panamax	Handy	Cape	Panamax	Handy	Cape	Panamax	Handy
Spring	15.3	8.6	7.6	3.0	2.4	5.5	2.3	2.1	-
Summer	-26.0	-21.3	-13.8	-8.4	-9.7	-8.4	-4.2	-4.3	-4.9
Autumn	-	14.4	-	-	-	-	5.7	-2.1	-
Winter	-	-	-	-	-	-	-	-	-
R^2	0.11	0.15	0.14	0.07	0.11	0.16	0.08	0.09	0.07

Notes: Source: Kavussanos and Alizadeh, 2001
- Significant seasonal effects are presented in percentage changes.
- R^2 is the coefficient of determination, indicating the variation in freight rates explained purely by seasonal factors.

One-Year Time-Charter Seasonality
Consider next the findings for the 1-year time-charter rates. It is observed that:

- Rates for Handysize vessels show a significant rise of 5.5% during March and April, while the rates for Panamax and Capesize vessels show a significant increase of 2.4% in May and 3% in March, respectively. These are lower than the corresponding rises observed during spring in spot rates.
- Also, there is a significant summer decline in time-charter rates for all vessel sizes, of 8.4%, 9.7% and 8.4%, respectively. These are more or less the same between sectors. This decline in the time-charter rates during June and July may be due to: First, the reduction in the level of industrial production and

---

[15] The decrease in the level of industrial output in North America during June and July is also documented by Beaulieu and Miron (1991), amongst others.

trade in mid summer or switch of spot operators to time-charter operation after the end of the Japanese and harvest led spring upsurge, which causes an over-supply in the time-charter market. Also, since time-charter rates are linked to the current and expected spot rates, a drop in the spot market is transmitted to the time-charter market accordingly.

- In line with spot markets, the net seasonal effect on 1-year time-charter rates is negative for each sector, as the summer fall in rates is higher than the corresponding spring rises.

Three-Year Time-Charter Seasonality

The pattern of seasonal decline in 3-year time-charter rates for dry-bulk carriers is similar to 1-year rates. That is, there is a seasonal increase in 3-year time-charter rates during spring and decline in rates for all the sizes during June and July. For all vessel sizes, the combined decline in rates during the summer months is almost half of those for 1-year time-charter rates. Both the increase and the decline in 3-year time-charter rates are less pronounced compared to 1-year rates. Panamax rates also show a further decline of 2.1% during October, while rates for Capesize bulk carriers recover by a combined 5.5% during August and September. The seasonal fluctuations in 3-year time-charter rates for larger vessels during August and September coincide with the time that Japanese and Korean steel mills negotiate (or re-negotiate) and renew their long-term imports (iron ore and coal) and the associated charter contracts.

The seasonal movement of dry-bulk time-charter rates suggests that, on average, the levels of freight rates increase in certain months (March and April) and drop in others (June and July). Shipowners (and charterers) can base tactical operations on such movements, in order to maximize their revenue (minimize their transportation costs). For example, the best time for a shipowner to fix (renew) a dry-bulk time-charter contract or switch from spot to time-charter operation might be March and April. Taking such opportunity, he may well be able to "*ride the seasonal cycle*" until the next year. On the other hand, the best time for a charterer to fix a dry-bulk vessel for one year is June and July. Also, these regular seasonal movements in dry-bulk rates suggest that, if cleaning and repositioning costs permit, shipowners operating combined carriers might be able to switch between sectors (tanker and dry-bulk) in order to exploit these short-run fluctuations.

Seasonality Comparisons between Vessel Types and Contract Durations

Whether we focus on the spring rises or summer decline in rates, the results suggest that the degree of seasonal fluctuation of shipping freight rates varies across vessel sizes and duration of contract. Specifically, two results seem to prevail:

- Freight rate seasonality (whether increase or decrease) declines as the duration of the contract increases; the same arguments as those put forward when describing Figure 1.8 hold true here also.
- As one moves from spot to longer-term contracts, the seasonality effect on charter rates is more or less the same across different size vessels. That is, while for spot rates there is a marked difference in seasonality across vessel sizes in both the spring and the summer months, for 1-year and 3-year contracts the seasonal effects across vessel sizes are more or less equal.

Both these facts, the reduction in seasonality and the reduction in seasonality differences across vessels as the duration of contract rises are expected. This is because:

- One-year time-charter rates, say, are formed as the expected future spot rates over the year, as explained earlier in this chapter. Therefore, one would expect that 1-year time-charter rates would have already incorporated expected future seasonal variations and are smoother than spot rates. In addition, spot rate seasonalities are expected to be higher than time-charter rate ones, to incorporate possible periods of unemployment, as per our earlier discussion. As a consequence, differences in freight rate seasonalities between sectors are eliminated since they depend less on the idiosyncratic factors influencing rates in sub-markets and more on the length (type) of the contract involved. These arguments extend to longer duration time-charter contracts, as shown for the case of the 1-year time-charter contracts.
- The higher seasonal fluctuations of spot rates compared to time-charter rates may be further explained as the result of the chartering strategy of industrial charterers (e.g. power stations and steel mills). They use long-term charter contracts not only to fulfill their long-term requirements in terms of supply of raw materials, but also to secure and maintain their transportation costs at a relatively fixed level over a long period. They use the spot market then in order to meet their seasonal or cyclical requirements. Therefore, they may enter the spot market at certain seasons, which leads to an increase in demand and consequently in freight rates in the spot market at those periods.

Seasonality Patterns under Different Market Conditions
Finally, seasonality is compared between different market conditions. It is revealed, that in the spot market, although the pattern of seasonality remains broadly the same as before, seasonal fluctuations are or become significant in "*good*" market conditions when supply is inelastic – see Figure 1.8. In weak markets, rates display either lower or no significant seasonality in the flat portion of the supply curve of Figure 1.8. For 1-year and 3-year time-charter rates similar conclusions are reached. That is, seasonal fluctuations (positive or negative) are stronger for periods of market expansion as opposed to periods of market contraction. However, such differences become smaller as the duration of the contract rises from one to three years. For 3-year contracts it seems that seasonality is mainly attributable to periods of expansion, with the majority of seasonal coefficients becoming insignificant in depressed markets. This points to the conclusion that the supply for shipping services schedule is less and less steep (more and more elastic) at the top end of the curve as the contract duration rises. This supply curve is almost flat for 3-year time-charter rates in "*bad*" markets – see Figure 1.8.

1.7.3.2. Seasonality Patterns in Tanker Freight Rate Markets – Results
A similar study to the dry-bulk market has also been published for the tanker market by the same authors – see Kavussanos and Alizadeh (2002a). Once more, it is revealed that there are significant seasonal patterns in freight rates in the tanker sub-sectors of the shipping industry. They vary by market condition, being low or insignificant in weak markets, contrary to the results observed in strong markets where larger significant results are observed. Full details are in the study itself, with Table 1.6 reporting only the significant monthly coefficients for each submarket.

Significance of a t-statistic for β_i, $i=1,2,\ldots,12$, in the table is an indication of a significant increase or decrease in monthly freight rate growth at a particular month compared to the average over the sample period. The results indicate that freight rates in all size tankers experience a significant increase in November compared to the average monthly growth rate of zero ($\beta_0 = 0$) over the period. This increase is 6.6% for VLCC's, 10.5% for Suezmax, 11.0% for Aframax, 7.7% for Handysize rates. The increase in freight rates in early winter (November) is due to the increase in demand for oil by oil-importing countries (companies), which are in the process of building up sufficient inventory levels (crude oil) for winter[16]. Aframax spot rates continue to rise in December by 3.3% due to the increase in demand for small shipments, usually from short haul routes (such as from Venezuela and Mexico to the US), to satisfy any remaining inventory requirements for the winter months.

Table 1.6. Deterministic Seasonality in Tanker Freight Rate Series (01/1978 – 12/1996)

Month	Coef.	VLCC	Suezmax	Aframax	Handysize
Constant	β_0	0.004 (0.350)	0.004 (0.443)	0.003 (0.347)	0.002 (0.239)
January	β_1	-0.110 (-2.933)			
February	β_2	-0.067 (-1.695)	-0.049 (-2.034)	-0.030 (-1.900)	
March	β_3				
April	β_4		-0.048 (-2.056)	-0.041 (-2.662)	-0.059 (-2.701)
May	β_5				
June	β_6	0.105 (2.951)			
July	β_7			-0.052 (-3.068)	
August	β_8				
September	β_9				
October	β_{10}				
November	β_{11}	0.066 (1.847)	0.105 (4.321)	0.110 (4.725)	0.077 (4.894)
December	β_{12}			0.033 (1.832)	

Notes: Source: Kavussanos and Alizadeh, 2002a
- t-statistics, in parentheses, are corrected for Heteroskedasticity and serial correlation using the Newey-West method where appropriate.
- The coefficient for January dummies, β_1, are calculated as $\beta_1 = -(\beta_2 + ... + \beta_{12})$. Standard errors for January dummies are calculated from the variance-covariance matrix of the coefficients.

It seems that in January, VLCC rates decrease significantly by 11.0%, which may be attributed to the decline in the need for inventory building using large vessels after the cold season in the Northern Hemisphere. This decline in demand continues and leads to a further 6.7% drop in VLCC rates in February. The February dummy shows a significant 4.9% drop in Suezmax and 3.0% in Aframax rates. During April, Suezmax, Aframax and Handysize rates decline even further by 4.8%, 4.1% and 5.9%, respectively; this can be linked to the fall in the level of petroleum imports and trade activities during the spring months, and the routine maintenance program of refineries around the US Gulf and the Far East, which takes place during this period. VLCC rates show a significant rise of 10.5% in June. This is due to inventory building that takes place after the end of routine maintenance programs of refineries and terminals during April and May, the increase in Japanese imports, and to stock up for the US driving season from mid July to end of August. A decline of 5.2% in Aframax freight rates is observed in July. This is thought to be a result of the decline in demand for those vessels operating in the Mediterranean as well as annual maintenance in the North Sea terminals, which use primarily Aframax tankers.

---

[16] The coldest winter months are usually January and February; so excess demand for crude oil is generated sometime in November to give enough lead time for crude to be transported and refined (from the long haul, Middle East routes), which can take 6 to 8 weeks.

1.7.3.3. Seasonality Strategies

Following these results, shipowners may use this information on the seasonal movements of freight markets in order to make strategic decisions regarding the operation of their vessels. Specifically, they may follow the following non-exhaustive list of strategies to maximize return and/or reduce risk of their investments:

- Dry-dock vessels in seasons that rates are expected to fall (e.g. July and August).
- Adjust speeds to increase productivity during peak seasons. For instance, in the dry-bulk sector, increase vessel speeds during March, April and May and reduce speeds in the summer months.
- Maximise revenues, in the long-run, by fixing on time-charters during peak seasons (e.g. March and April in dry-bulk), rather than when time-charter rates are low (in the summer).
- Choose to invest in smaller vessels to reduce large seasonal effects in their cash-flows, provided they aim to use vessels in short-term spot freight markets. If a longer-term chartering policy is to be followed though, the choice of vessel is less important in terms of seasonality, as seasonal differences are eliminated amongst vessel sizes for larger duration contracts.
- Secure cash-flows (transportation costs for charterers) against seasonal movements by using freight derivatives contracts – examples of these are considered later in the book.

Thus, market agents operating in the tramp shipping freight markets may be able to use the information on the seasonal movements of freight rates in order to make better business decisions regarding; budget planning, dry-docking of vessels, vessel speeds, vessel repositioning to loading areas during peak seasons, etc. Charterers also can use the information derived here to optimize their transportation costs by timing, for instance, their inventory build up outside peak seasons.

1.8. Volatilities of Spot and Time-Charter Rates in Shipping Sub-markets

A number of regularities regarding freight markets have been described in the earlier sections of this chapter. They include, that tramp freight rates are determined, at any point in time, in a very competitive freight market, at the interaction of demand and supply for freight services and as a consequence, are highly volatile; that they are cyclical and seasonal; that seasonality is distinct between different submarkets of dry-bulk and tanker sectors, between contracts of different duration, and between different market conditions prevailing in shipping markets. This section puts these together to outline a number of issues relevant for risk management purposes.

More specifically, consider the information in Table 1.7, which presents mean values and relative volatilities[17] of monthly freight rate data for spot, 1-year and 3-year time-charter rates for different vessel sizes in the dry-bulk and in the tanker sector of the shipping industry, based on data collected over the period January 1990 to March 2005. Results are qualitatively the same as those first uncovered formally by Kavussanos in a series of studies – see Kavussanos (1997, 1998, 2003). These studies and Table 1.7 show that:

---

[17] Relative volatility of a variable is the term used here for the Coefficient of Variation, which is in turn defined as the standard deviation of the variable devided by its own mean value x 100. As a consequence, risk levels (that is, standard deviations) can be compared between different variables, which have different means.

a) Relative volatilities of spot (voyage) rates and of time-charter (period) rates are smaller for smaller size vessels, compared to those of larger ones: In the dry-bulk sector for instance, there is a clear ranking of volatilities in the spot and in the time-charter markets by vessel size, with the corresponding freight markets of the larger Capesize vessels displaying higher relative volatilities compared to the smaller Panamax ones, while Panamax volatilities are higher than those of the Handy ones. The same is also true in the tanker sector. In both the spot and in the time-charter markets the VLCC sector exhibits the highest volatility in rates compared to smaller sizes over the period examined. The Handy volatilities are the lowest in both markets compared to other sizes. The Aframax and the Suezmax sectors show significantly larger volatilities in comparison to the Handy sector and smaller ones compared to the VLCC in both the spot and the time-charter markets. As a consequence, possible diversification effects may be achieved for the shipowner by holding different size vessels in a portfolio of assets.

b) However, it seems that these differences in freight rate volatilities, by vessel sizes, are eliminated as we move into longer duration contracts, such as one-year and three-year time-charters.

c) As a consequence, owners that are interested to invest in vessels and operate them in spot markets will have to bear in mind the higher freight rate volatilities are involved in investments in the larger size vessels compared to those of the smaller ones in both the dry-bulk and the tanker sectors of the industry. However, if the intention is to operate the vessels in long-term time-charter (period) contracts, the differences in volatilities by vessel size are eliminated. Thus, investing in smaller vessels, for pure diversification effects is not a valid argument in this case.

d) Comparison of relative volatilities for each vessel size between the spot and the time-charter markets reveals that, spot rates are relatively more volatile compared to time-charter rates in all cases. The results seem to be consistent with *a-priori* expectations, in that the spot rates are much more exposed to the day-to-day market conditions in determining rates compared to time-charter rates. It seems that the risk involved in operating vessels in the spot markets is greater than in the time-charter markets and this seems to hold irrespective of vessel size. Several reasons for this relationship have already been put forward in earlier parts of this chapter, including the uncertainty of spot rates in relation to time-charters, the additive effect of bunker price risk, unemployment risk, etc. Yet another way to see this is by considering the nature of the relationship of spot and period time-charter rates, described earlier on in this chapter. The relationship is that, say, 1-year time-charter rates must be the sum of a series of expected (monthly) spot rates minus a risk-premium. Thus, time-charter rates, being an average of expected spot earnings, must be smoother compared single spot rates.

Table 1.7. Summary Statistics of Spot, 1-Year, and 3-Year Time-Charter Rates for Dry-Bulk and Tanker Vessels

Panel A: Dry-Bulk Vessels

	Voyage (Spot) Rates		1-Year T/C Rates		3-Year T/C Rates	
	Mean ($/ton)	Relative Volatility	Mean ($/day)	Relative Volatility	Mean ($/day)	Relative Volatility
Capesize	14.93	52.9	12,953	49.6	12,252	28.2
Panamax	7.87	49.8	10,979	48.6	10,021	24.3
Handy	6.97	39.7	8,097	38.4	8,070	19.3

Panel B: Tanker Vessels

	Voyage (Spot) Rates		1-Year T/C Rates		3-Year T/C Rates	
	Mean (WS)	Relative Volatility	Mean ($/day)	Relative Volatility	Mean ($/day)	Relative Volatility
VLCC	61.96	44.8	17,728	34.2	18,669	24.0
Suezmax	100.67	44.2	21,123	34.6	21,296	22.5
Aframax	130.05	39.8	17,557	23.0	18,010	13.6
Handysize	238.34	29.1	12,240	16.6	12,994	9.7

Notes:
- Sample covers January 1990 to March 2005.
- Mean is the arithmetic average.
- Relative Volatility is the standard deviation over the mean value x 100.
- WS stands for Worldscale rates.

1.8.1. Time-Varying Freight Rate Volatilities over Shipping Sub-sectors

The studies by Kavussanos, referred to above, move one step beyond the observations just discussed. They introduce in the shipping literature the concept of time-varying volatilities (risks) in freight rates – spot, 1-year and 3-year time-charter rates, and compare them between sub-sectors of shipping, but also between contracts of different duration[18]. It is shown there that freight rate risks are time-varying. That is, in each market, not only is the average value of freight rates affected by the state of the market, but also the risks (volatilities in rates) vary with changing market conditions.

Figure 1.11. One-Year Time-Charter Rate Volatilities for Different Size Tanker Vessels

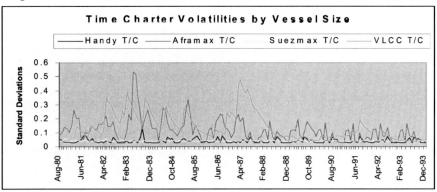

Source: Kavussanos, 1996b

---

[18] As discussed in later chapters of the book, the introduction in shipping research of ARCH (Auto Regressive Conditional Heteroskedasticity Models) and GARCH (Generalised ARCH) models, to investigate the properties of shipping variables, also provided very useful solutions in the provision of more efficient hedging techniques in shipping freight derivatives markets.

These risks are thought to be a combination of industry-market risk and idiosyncratic risk factors, relating for example to the individual vessel size properties. Idiosyncratic risk may be diversified by the shipowner, for instance, by choosing to use the spot instead of the time-charter market, or by deciding on alternative size vessels to invest upon. Figures 1.11 to 1.14 were produced in these studies to illustrate how the shipping industry is affected across markets, by estimating time-varying risks in the spot and in the time-charter markets for the tanker and dry-bulk sectors.

Figure 1.12. One-Year Time-Charter Rate Volatilities for Different Size Dry-Bulk Vessels

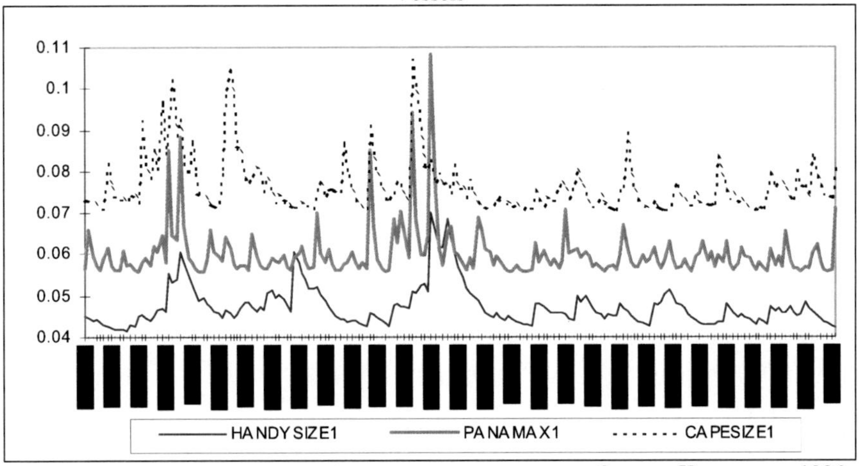

Source: Kavussanos, 1996a

This method of analyzing volatilities and examining them graphically has allowed inferences, such as that, for the dry-bulk sector: volatilities, and thus risks, vary over time and across sizes; in particular, volatilities are high during and just after periods of large imbalances and shocks to the industry. Thus, the 1980/81 oil crises, coupled with the decline in the demand for shipping services, due to the lower than expected growth in world demand following the second oil shock, the supply of oil restrictions imposed by the OPEC production ceiling in 1982/83, the targeting of vessels in the Gulf in 1984, the sharp decline in oil prices in 1986 with its lasting effect and the 1990/91 period of the Gulf War are particularly visible. It has also been shown that Panamax volatilities are driven by old *"news"*, while new shocks are more important in the Handy and Capesize markets. Also, conditional volatilities of Handy and Panamax vessel prices were found to be positively related to interest rates and Capesize volatilities to time-charter rates.

Shipping markets then tend to respond together to external shocks, and yet quite differently, implying market segregation between different size vessels. There are some common driving forces of volatilities in different size vessels, and yet there are idiosyncratic factors to each market that make each size – vessel volatility move at its own level and in its own way. These idiosyncratic factors relate to the type and number of routes each size vessel is engaged in. Thus, volatility for Handy and Capesize vessels has several hikes, while that for Panamax is smoother. Similar results are reached by considering the time-varying volatilities for the tanker sector. In addition, it was found that volatilities in the tanker sector and thus risks levels seem to be positively related to oil prices.

59

Figure 1.13. Voyage (Spot) Freight Rate Volatilities for Different Size Tanker Vessels

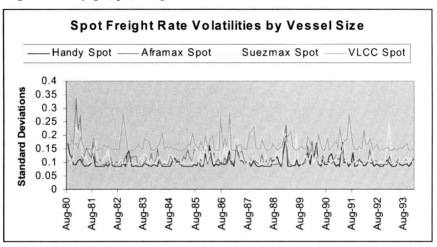

Source: Kavussanos, 1996b

The results suggest that freight rate risks in the larger sub-sectors of the tanker and dry-bulk sectors of the shipping industry may be mitigated by holding smaller vessels. Hence, risk-averse investors in shipping can diversify risks in their portfolios by heavier weighting towards smaller size vessels. Moreover, these risks are time-varying, and as a consequence, the mix of the investors' portfolios should be reviewed constantly to create optimal solutions that fit their risk-return profiles. It should also be mentioned that the availability of time-varying volatility estimates, as with other assets in the financial literature, may be used as inputs in pricing derivative instruments, such as options prices, etc.

Figure 1.14. Voyage (Spot) Freight Rate Volatilities for Different Size Dry-Bulk Vessels

Source: Kavussanos, 1996a

1.8.2. Time-Varying Freight Rate Volatilities for Contracts of Different Duration

Time-varying volatilities of 1-year time-charter and spot freight rates have also been published in the studies by Kavussanos (2003). Figures 1.15 – 1.18 show examples of the comparison of these volatilities for the VLCC and Suezmax sectors of the tanker industry and for the Capesize and Panamax sectors of the dry-bulk market. Broadly speaking, in line with the results presented in Table 1.7, volatilities in the time-charter markets are lower compared to spot volatilities for the period examined. The exception is the VLCC sector, which shows somewhat different results: Between 1982 and 1985 and between the summer of 1987 and that of 1988 time-charter volatility was mostly at a higher level than the spot one, with the reverse occurring during the rest of the period examined. For the post 1988 period time-charter risk (volatility) is lying constantly below the spot rate level of risk.

Figure 1.15. Spot vs. Time-Charter Volatilities (SD's): VLCC Sector

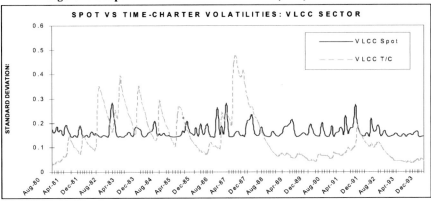

Source: Kavussanos, 1996b

It seems that when the market is at its low, time-charters can be more volatile than spot rates. This may be because time-charter rates reflect expectations of future events, which makes them more sensitive to changing perceptions of the future market. When the market is at the bottom and there is a feeling for a market upturn charterers rush to fix vessels on time-charter. This may result in time-charter rates moving more steeply upwards than spot rates. The opposite happens when the market is at its peak, where charterers fix in the spot market and the lack of demand for time-charters results in an abrupt drop in their values.

The example serves to illustrate the usefulness of such time-varying volatility estimates; when considering average volatility estimates of freight contracts calculated over a period of time, such as those presented in Table 1.7, the dynamics of the market risks may be missed. That is, while in the average estimates, there is a clear ranking of volatilities, with contracts of longer duration appearing to be less volatile than the shorter-term ones, it seems that this result may change as market conditions change, for the reasons explained above.

Figure 1.16. Spot vs. Time-Charter Rate Volatilities (SD's): Suezmax Sector

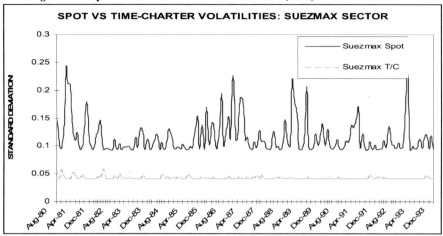

Source: Kavussanos, 1996b

Figure 1.17. Spot vs. Time-Charter Rate Volatilities (SD's): Capesize Sector

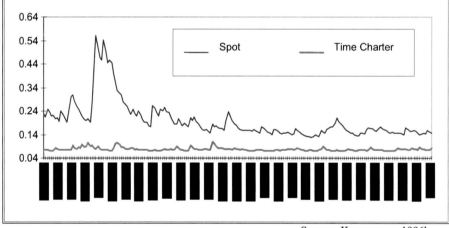

Source: Kavussanos, 1996b

From the above analysis, the following is a summary of strategies identified to deal with business risks in the shipping industry:

- Spot (voyage) operation vs. Time-charter (period) operation: In general, spot (voyage) rates are more volatile than time-charter (period) rates – owners are prepared to offer a discount for the relative security of period time-charter rates. As the duration of the contract increases, risk differences are eliminated.
- Large vs. Small vessels: Freight rates for larger vessels seem to show higher volatility than smaller ones – the portfolio risk is affected by the choice of vessels owned.
- Time-varying volatilities: Volatilities of shipping freight rates change over time depending on the expectations and uncertainty in the market – it is worth considering a continuous rebalancing of the mix of operational strategies as market conditions change.

Figure 1.18. Spot vs. Time-Charter Rate Volatilities (SD's): Panamax Sector

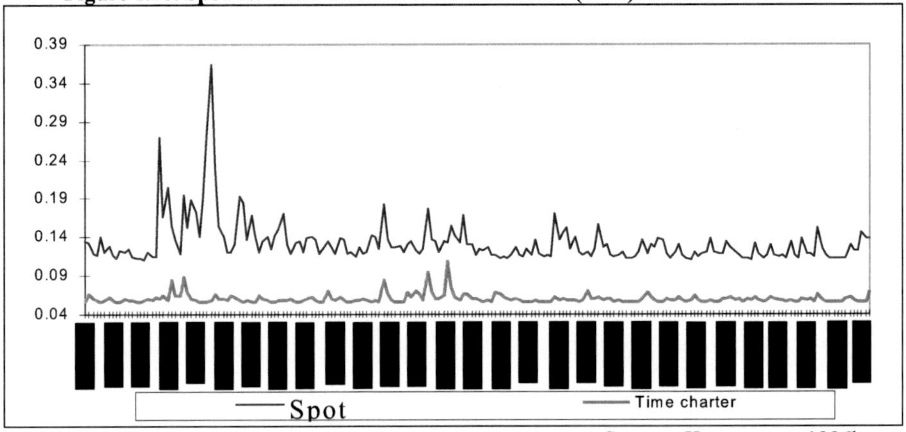

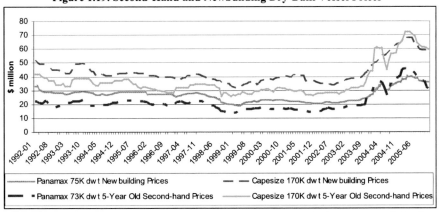

Source: Kavussanos, 1996b

1.9. Vessel Prices and Vessel Price Risks

1.9.1. Vessels as Capital Assets

As discussed earlier in this chapter, a large part of the fluctuations in the overall cash-flow position of the shipowner emanate from changes in the value of the asset that he holds in order to perform the shipping business. These changes in asset values can be observed in Figures 1.19 and 1.20, which show historical prices of 5-year old second-hand and newbuilding prices for a number of vessels in the dry-bulk and in the tanker sector of the shipping industry, respectively. One cannot help but notice the large fluctuations in prices, which are enticing to asset play. Just to take the latest period in Figure 1.19, Capesize five-year old vessels were trading at US$30 million in March 2003, whose value one year later was US$60 million, only to fall down to US$43 million six months later and up to US$72 million in June 2005. A large number of shipowners exploit these fluctuations to make hefty returns from buying and selling vessels. Often, the contribution of this asset-play to the balance-sheet is greater than the operation of the vessel itself. The timing of the investment decisions is extremely important. Wrong timing of purchasing or selling can turn the possibility of profits into heavy losses and to the closure of the business.

Figure 1.19. Second-Hand and Newbuilding Dry-Bulk Vessel Prices

Source: Clarksons Research Studies

Second-hand vessel prices of each type of vessel are determined in their respective second-hand market for vessels through the forces of supply and demand. Shipowners negotiate the transaction through specialist brokers, with the vessel being inspected in the process. The value of the asset depends on its condition; its age; its special characteristics, such as cargo handling gear, coated tanks, etc; its type, such as Capesize, VLCC, etc.; and the return that it is expected to provide to its owner by operating and reselling it in the future; moreover the return on the shipping asset must be compared to the return other assets would make for him, and accordingly decide on whether it presents an investment opportunity or not.

Figure 1.20. Second-Hand and Newbuilding Tanker Vessel Prices

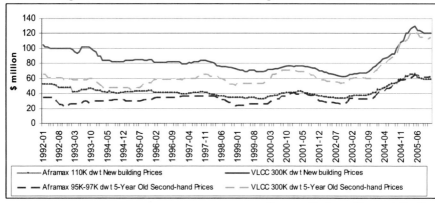

Source: Clarksons Research Studies

More specifically, a purchased vessel offers during its lifetime: A stream of profits/losses from operation, and a possible capital gain (or loss) by reselling it. Suppose the vessel is purchased at price P_t and is expected to be sold at P_{t+n}, n periods in the future. Then the expected capital gain (loss) from holding the asset is $(E_t P_{t+n} - P_t)$. During this period, the vessel provides a stream of expected profits (losses), as follows: $E_t \Pi_{t+1} + E_t \Pi_{t+2} + ... + E_t \Pi_{t+n}$, which, in turn, depend on expected freight revenues and costs. Thus, the expected return on the investment – the vessel – can be described by Equation (1.5):

$$E_t R_t = \frac{(E_t P_{t+n} - P_t) + \sum_{i=1}^{n} E_t \Pi_{t+n}}{P_t} \qquad (1.5)$$

It is higher, and as a result demand for second-hand vessels is higher: (i) the lower are vessel prices today – as both the income yield and the capital gain yield are larger in percentage terms when the vessel is bought at low values; (ii) the higher are prices expected to be in the future, as this will provide for a larger capital gain; and (iii) the higher the freight rates are expected to be, as this will provide a larger income stream from the operation of the vessel.

The decision to buy a vessel then depends on the current state of the market as reflected in vessel prices, and on expectations of future vessel prices and expected freight rates; both fluctuate widely over time and huge profits or losses may be made as a result. For transactions to take place there must be: (i) a discrepancy in

expectations regarding future developments in the market, between buyers and sellers
– the buyer believes that the prospects in the market are good, which is in contrast to
the seller's believes; or/and (ii) a possible cash-flow problem of the owner, in which
case a "*distress sale*" takes place.

Thus, vessel prices may be expressed as the present value of a stream of profits from
operation plus the present value of its terminal value (second-hand or scrap).
Mathematically, this can be written as:

$$P_t = \sum_{i=0}^{n-1} \frac{E_t \Pi_{t+1+i}}{(1+E_t R_{t+1+i})^{t+1+i}} + \frac{E_t P_{n-1}^{SC}}{(1+E_t R_{n-1})^{n-1}} \qquad (1.6)$$

where, E_t denotes expectations formed at time period t; Π_{t+1+i} are profits from
operations at time period $t+1+i$; $i=0, 1,..., n-1$, and hence $E_t\Pi_{t+1+i}$ are expected profits
at period $t+1+i$; P_{n-1}^{SC} is the terminal value of the vessel scrapped or resold in period
$n-1$; and R_{t+1+i} is the discount rate prevailing in period $t+1+i$.

1.9.2. Market Efficiency in the Markets for Vessels
The exact relationship presented in Equation (1.6) may fail because factors, such as
the age of the vessel, its condition, etc. may enter the equation. Also, it may be that
the market is not price efficient. Kavussanos and Alizadeh (2002c) examine formally
this relationship in these markets. Numerous other studies have tested the Efficient
Market Hypothesis (EMH) in various capital and financial markets[19], and a few
studies on real (physical) assets, such as the real estate market[20] or the market for
vessels. Ships are real assets with limited economic life and a significant residual
(scrapping) value. Apart from the aforementioned study, past studies in the literature
investigating the formation of ship prices include Vergottis (1998), Strandenes (1984),
Hale and Vanags (1992), Glen (1997) and Veenstra (1999). Results on the EMH are
mixed.

Kavussanos and Alizadeh (2002c) extend the Campbell and Shiller (1987 and 1988)
methodology to real assets with limited economic life and a significant terminal value.
The EMH in the market for dry-bulk vessels is rejected. This failure is explained by
relating excess returns to investors' perceptions of risk, and by examining the type of
participants in these markets. Specifically, it can be argued that investors in the
shipping industry can be divided in two main groups, depending upon their
investment strategies and horizons: The first group are the speculators or asset
players, and are those who participate in the sale and purchase market and rely more
on capital gains rather than on the operational profits of the vessels. These are
normally private investors or small shipping companies with a relatively short-term
investment horizon. On the other hand, there are investors who acquire vessels and
operate them for long periods. These types of investors are more interested in

---

[19] For example, Fama and French (1988) and Poterba and Summers (1988) examine long horizon
predictability of the US stock returns, Campbell and Shiller (1987 and 1988) examine the efficiency of
US stock prices using the present value relationship, Pesaran and Timmermann (1994) investigate the
predictability of excess returns in the UK (over one year, one quarter and one month) for the period
1954 to 1971, Cuthbertson *et al.* (1999) examine the EMH in different sectors of the UK stock market
for the period 1965 to 1992.
[20] For example, Case and Shiller (1989) investigate the efficiency of the market for family homes in the
U.S., and Meese and Wallace (1994) test the efficiency of house prices in San Francisco. Using
different methodologies and data sets, they all conclude that the real estate market is inefficient.

operating profits rather than capital gains and are normally larger public or state owned shipping companies with relatively long horizon investment strategies. The fact that investors may have heterogeneous behaviour and different investment objectives and horizons may contribute to the failure of the present value model and the EMH in the market for vessels. This is because investors may use different pricing models, discount factors or weights depending on their investment objectives and horizons.

Given the failure of the EMH, the study shows that this failure is due to the existence of time-varying risk-premia. Had this not been the case, arbitrage opportunities would be present. For example, if the market for vessels is found to be consistently inefficient and prices deviate from their rational values, then appropriate trading strategies can be devised to exploit excess profit-making opportunities. Thus, when prices are lower than their fundamental values, then buying and operating these vessels (or selling them when prices rise) might be profitable, since they are under-priced in comparison to their future profitability. On the other hand, when prices are higher than their corresponding rational values it might be profitable to charter vessels rather than buying them, since they are over-priced in comparison to their expected future profitability. Therefore, from the point of view of both asset players and long-term ship operators, it is important to understand the pricing mechanism as well as the efficiency of the market for vessels.

1.9.3. Volatilities (Risks) in Different Vessel Markets

The issue of what type vessels to invest on, if approached from the pure asset-play point of view, may be answered by considering the risk-return profiles of different size vessels. This issue was first investigated in Kavussanos (1996a,b, 1997, 2003), where it is shown that vessel size considerations are important since the sub-markets for each vessel type are distinct in terms of their risk/return profiles. As discussed above, vessel prices are the present value of the expected stream of cash-flows from their operation. As a result of this relationship, comparison of vessel price volatilities by vessel sizes is expected to reveal a similar relationship to that uncovered by examining freight rate volatilities for different size vessels. In fact, Table 1.8 computes mean and relative volatility measures for different types of newbuilding and five-year old second-hand vessels, as well as for their scrap prices and earnings for the dry-bulk and the tanker sectors, utilizing data over the period January 1990 to March 2005.

In line with earlier results, volatilities of earnings for larger vessels are higher than those of smaller ones, within the dry-bulk and tanker sectors. Moreover, newbuilding, second-hand and scrap prices for larger vessels seem to show higher relative volatilities than prices of smaller vessels. This observation is important in the decision of investors over the construction of their shipping portfolio of investments, in different sub-sectors of shipping. As discussed earlier in the chapter, the smaller size Handy vessels are, in general, geared so that they can load and unload cargo in ports without sophisticated handling facilities. In that sense and because of draught restrictions of larger vessels, they can approach more ports compared to larger vessels. Moreover, smaller vessels can switch between different trades more easily if required by economic or other circumstances. The same is also true in the tanker sector; the very large vessels trade in only 3-4 routes, as the draught restrictions in ports and the storage facilities required ashore must be very large to accommodate them and their cargoes. Since smaller vessels can approach more ports and can switch between more trades/routes they are more flexible for employment. Of course, smaller vessels operate at higher unit costs compared to larger vessels requiring higher freight rates, and this has to be born in mind when taking decisions.

Table 1.8. Risk Comparisons of Prices of Newbuilding, 5-year old, Scrap Prices and Earnings for Dry-Bulk and Tanker Vessels (January 1990 to March 2005)

Panel A: Dry-Bulk Vessels

	Capesize		Panamax		Handy	
	Mean	Relative Volatility	Mean	Relative Volatility	Mean	Relative Volatility
Earnings	19,684	75	11,388	65	10,789	54
Newbuilding Prices	35.74	20	26.42	16	23.00	14
Second-Hand Prices	30.29	35	20.57	28	17.95	22
Scrap Prices	3.60	40	2.30	37	1.33	25

Panel B: Tanker Vessels

	VLCC		Suezmax		Aframax	
	Mean	Relative Volatility	Mean	Relative Volatility	Mean	Relative Volatility
Earnings	33,770	68	24,750	67	21,456	58
Newbuilding Prices	82.67	18	54.15	15	42.55	12
Second-Hand Prices	62.15	21	41.53	20	33.52	18
Scrap Prices	6.32	38	4.53	35	3.21	35

Notes:
- Mean figures for Second-hand, Scrap and Newbuilding prices are in US million dollars.
- Figures for Earnings are in US$/day, calculated as daily Time-charter Equivalents (TCE) of voyage freight rates: Initially, the time taken on the voyage in days is estimated. Then, the net revenue earned on the voyage is calculated, after deducting total fuel/bunker costs, port costs and canal charges. The average earnings in $/day is computed by dividing net earnings by days on voyage. The calculated earnings are for a single voyage only and do not include any allowance for waiting time, delays or off-hire time.

Broadly speaking, risk-averse investors that wish to reduce their investment risk may wish to invest in smaller (larger) vessels, e.g. Panamax or Handysize (Capesize) if they want to reduce (increase) the risk in their portfolio of assets. The results are in line with the earlier discussion, of smaller vessels being more flexible as assets. They have lower risk of unemployment in adverse market conditions, as they can be switched more easily between routes and trades in order to secure employment. In addition, the cargo carrying capacity of larger vessels makes them less useful for charterers requiring transportation of smaller quantities. This makes the demand for these vessels less flexible, and vessels cannot switch between sea-lanes and charterers as easily as their smaller counterparts. If anything happens (e.g. a political or economic change) in one of the routes, large vessels operate, this will have a significant impact on freight rates in the market. As a consequence, the income streams from operations of smaller vessels and their prices, as present values of the expected future cash-flows, are subject to less fluctuations in comparison to those of larger vessels.

1.9.3.1. Time-Varying Volatilities of Different Vessel Sizes

Kavussanos (1996b, 1997, 2003), using GARCH type models, shows that standard deviations (risks) of vessel prices are time-varying and are affected, apart from their own past values and past values of shocks to long-run equilibrium in each market, by factors such as time-charter rates, interest rates and oil prices. Moreover, these variances, reflecting vessel price risks, are time-varying. Figures 1.21 and 1.22 present estimates from GARCH models, of these time-varying volatilities of vessel prices in the dry-bulk and in the tanker sector, respectively. Considering average volatilities of freight rates over a period of time (such as those presented in Table 1.8) as indicators of risk levels may be argued that it provides an incomplete picture of the risk/return profiles when portfolios of vessels are considered dynamically; this is because the mixture of vessels held by shipowners changes periodically, as volatilities (risks) are not constant over time. The patterns and relative levels of volatilities, at each point in time can be measured and compared between size vessels, reflecting thus better the changing market conditions.

Figure 1.21. Time-Varying Price Volatilities in the Dry-Bulk Sector

Price Volatilities in the Dry Bulk Sector

HANDYSIZE · · · · · · PANAMAX ━ ━ CAPESIZE

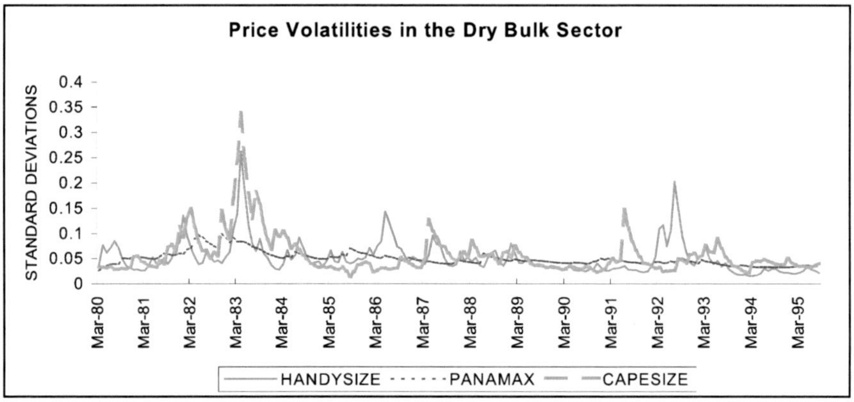

Source: Kavussanos, 1997

Just as in freight markets, risks emanating from vessel price fluctuations have a common trend but also have their idiosyncratic patterns, which are related to the factors affecting each market. These make each size-vessel volatility move in its own way. These idiosyncratic factors relate to the type of trade each size vessel is engaged in. Thus, volatility for Handy and Capesize vessels has several hikes, while that for Panamax is smoother. Regarding volatility levels, Capesize volatility lies in general above the volatilities of the other two sizes, except for two-three years in the mid-1980s. Similarly, the Panamax volatility is, in general, at a level above Handysize, which, however, is exceeded at times by the hikes in the Handysize volatility. Similar results hold for the tanker sector. In addition, volatilities in the tanker sector, and thus risk levels, are found to be positively related to oil prices.

The above approach recognizes that investors in the shipping sector are profit maximizing agents, who treat ships as capital assets. Investors are willing to hold them in their portfolios subject to certain rates of return. It can be argued that if investors are assumed to act as profit maximizing agents, then they should also be concerned about the risk involved in holding assets in conjunction with their returns. This is because rational and risk-averse investors maximize the return on their portfolio subject to a certain level of risk, or minimize risk subject to a certain level of return. Therefore, one would expect that investors foresee different types of risks involved in shipping investments, and incorporate them in their decision-making process, regarding pricing formulas and portfolio adjustments.

Figure 1.22. Time-Varying Price Volatilities in the Tanker Sector

Price Volatilities in the Tanker Sector

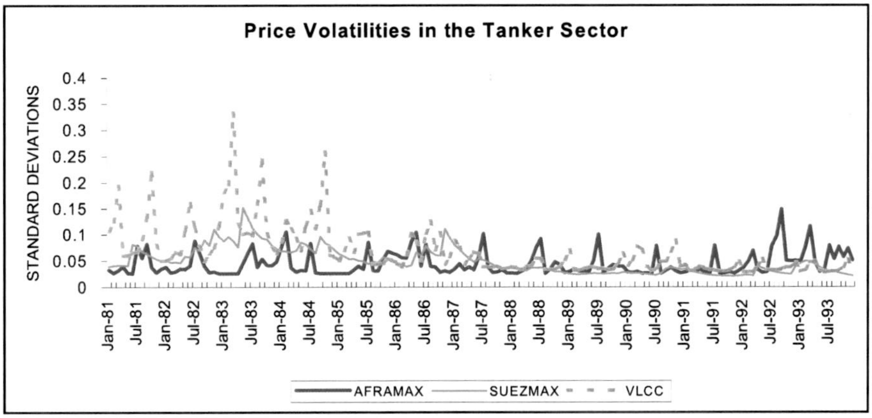

Source: Kavussanos, 1996b

It has been argued in the past that the risk involved in shipping can be much higher than other sectors of the economy (Stopford 1997), as investors in the shipping business experience sharp fluctuations in both freight rates as well as vessel prices. The current book concentrates in examining these risks. It documents that volatility of vessel prices varies over time and across vessel sizes; prices of larger vessels tend to fluctuate more than prices of smaller ones. Time-varying volatilities of vessel prices, in conjunction with the profit maximizing behaviour of investors, implies that investors should expect different returns on their investments at different points in time. Results indicate that returns on shipping investments are positively related to the time-varying variance of forecast errors, which is consistent with the capital asset pricing literature.

1.10.   Summary of Traditional Risk Management Strategies

The contribution of the above analysis is to point to real possibilities of risk reduction for investments, by choice of sub-sector within the dry-bulk and tanker sectors of the shipping industry. Risk-averse investors should opt for smaller vessels, while investors who wish to undertake higher risks in order to achieve higher returns within the shipping industry should invest in larger size vessels. In addition, the use of GARCH models to identify the existence of time-varying volatilities of vessel prices and of freight rates points to a strategy of dynamic revisions of assets which to include in a portfolio of vessels. No empirical analysis has been carried yet in the literature for the container sector, but one would expect similar conclusions regarding volatilities in rates of different vessel sizes. Yet another traditional strategy applied by market agents wishing to avoid risks emanating from fluctuations in vessel prices is to lease rather than buy the vessels. In that sense they become ship operators rather than owners, thus removing the capital gain/loss risk element appearing in the shipowner's cash-flow presented in Table 1.1.

Once the investments (vessels) have been acquired, shipowners have to make similar decisions of how to minimize risks from operations, subject to a required level of return that they wish to make on their shipping investments. Once again, the analysis so far has pointed to the possibility of using period contracts as ways of reducing risks in a portfolio of "*long*" positions on tonnage. Caution needs to be exercised though, say in a dynamic portfolio setting, to ensure that the relationship holds true in adverse market conditions, as time-charter volatility may rise above the spot one during certain situations. Of course, the seasonality results on freight rates and the associated strategies presented earlier in the chapter should also be borne in mind in the effort to reduce risks and increase return from ship operations.

Other risks for the shipping business identified in Table 1.1 include those emanating from fluctuations in currencies against the US$, and also from changes in interest rates. Not much can be done about the former type of risks, even though it is reported that certain shipping companies in an attempt to reduce the effects of adverse movements in the value of the US$ have drawn employee contracts in US$ rather than in local currency, such as the euro. This may work to a certain extend, particularly in businesses operating in developing countries, but can have a negative impact on personnel moral and effort if they are adversely affected by this situation. Adjusting the degree of financial leverage (that is, the debt to equity capital) of the business may also be argued to fall under the traditional strategies of reducing interest rate risks. Borrowing at fixed rates of interest than at floating ones, is also a way to manage interest rate risks, provided shipping companies can secure such deals.

1.11. Risk Management and the Use of Derivatives in the Shipping Industry

However, the strategies that the above sections point to are useful but may be proved to be expensive, non existent or inflexible, if not planned properly. For example, it costs to buy and sell vessels and to go in or out of freight contracts. This reduces the flexibility of the strategies. Long-term charters may be hard for owners to find when the market is in decline. The opposite is true for the charterers when the market is improving. In addition, when the conditions turn too much against one of the parties (owner or charterer) it may be that they decide to abandon the agreement. Moreover, it costs to buy and sell vessels, in order to switch between different segments of shipping for risk management purposes. Their prices can change very fast while negotiations take time, as vessels need to be inspected for their mechanical condition, their history, etc. It may be that prices must be reduced substantially in order to achieve a sale under falling markets, and this loss for the company may outweigh any benefits of diversification that may be achieved. Similar reservations may also be raised for other traditional strategies outlined in earlier sections of this chapter.

The existence of financial derivatives contracts has helped to alleviate these problems with respect to risk management in the business of shipping. They have made risk management cheaper, more flexible and readily available to parties exposed to adverse movements in freight rates, bunker prices, vessel prices, exchange rates, interest rates and other variables affecting the cash-flow position of the shipping company. Moreover, they allow entrepreneurs in the sector to get on with the business as they know it best, and yet manage their risks through this separate *"paper"* market.

Derivatives instruments are contractually created rights and obligations, the effect of which is to transfer risk to some other party willing to bear it. These contracts are determined by reference to or derived from (hence the word derivatives) underlying spot or physical markets. The classes of underlying assets, which a derivative instrument may derive its value from include physical commodities (e.g. agricultural products, metals, petroleum, etc.), financial instruments (e.g. debt, interest rate products, equity securities, foreign currencies, etc.), indices (e.g. securities prices, freight rates, etc.) or spreads between the value of such assets (Calvin, 1994).

The most basic derivatives contracts are: (i) **Forward contracts**, which are transactions in which the buyer and the seller agree upon the delivery of a specified quality and quantity of an asset at a specified future date and a certain price; (ii) **Futures contracts** are like forward contracts, only that they are standardized and are exchanged in organized markets rather than as private, Over-The-Counter (OTC)[21], agreements; (iii) **Swap contracts** involve the simultaneous buying and selling of a similar underlying asset or obligation of equivalent capital amount. This exchange of financial arrangements provides both parties to the transaction with more favourable conditions than they would otherwise obtain by resorting to markets on their own; and (iv) **Option contracts** confer the right, but not the obligation, to buy (call) or sell (put) a specific underlying instrument or asset at a specified price up until or on a specified date. The price to have this right is paid by the buyer of the option contract to the seller as a premium. These types of financial derivatives contracts can be arranged by the counterparties OTC by some financial institutions, or maybe exchanged through organized financial markets, such as derivatives exchanges. Each of these broad categories are described in detail in Chapter 2 of this book, while their application for the management of risks of the shipping business is explored in the rest of the chapters of the book.

They are important financial instruments for risk management as they allow risks to be separated and more precisely controlled. By using derivatives, market participants can secure (stabilize) their future income or costs and reduce their uncertainty and unforeseen volatility. In that sense, they shift elements of risk and therefore can act as a form of insurance. For example, assume that during January, gas oil market prices are at $145/ton and an oil producer believes that prices will be reduced in the next few months. In order to avoid the reduction in income this will bring about, he can sell today April gas oil futures contracts, available at New York Mercantile Exchange (NYMEX) or at the Intercontinental Exchange (ICE), at $144/ton, committing himself to sell at a certain price, at a certain time and at a certain quantity. Suppose that during April gas oil prices fall to $140/ton. The producer then, in order to close his futures position, buys futures contracts at $139/ton. In the physical (spot) market he realizes a loss of $5/ton (= $140/ton – $145/ton), while in the futures market he makes a gain of $5/ton (= $144/ton –$139/ton). Combining the physical with the derivatives positions the net result is zero, thus stabilizing his cash-flow at today's level.

In the 1970s and 1980s, derivatives expanded from commodities to financial markets, using as the underlying instruments fixed-income bonds, foreign exchange, stock-indices, equities, etc. Participants in the shipping industry were using currency swaps to secure foreign currencies for the payment of newbuildings, due to the fact that shipowners' income is in US dollars and payments for the shipyards are mostly in local currency, such as Japanese Yen. Shipping derivatives on freight rates started through the initiatives of the Baltic Exchange. Its origins can be traced back to the Virginia and Maryland Coffee House in 1744. It has been registered in London as a private limited company since 1900. Two-thirds of all the world's open market bulk cargo movement is at some stage handled by Baltic members. In addition, it is calculated that about half of the world's sale and purchase of vessels is dealt with through companies represented at the Baltic. The Baltic Exchange is responsible for providing the freight and vessel price indices, which are used as the underlying "*commodities*" of derivatives in the shipping industry. It has created an internal

---

[21] OTC markets are bilateral markets in which derivatives contracts are written on a tailor-made basis.

committee called the Freight Indices and Futures Committee (FIFC), which is responsible for appointing panellists, determining index and route composition, supervising all aspects of quality control and is responsible to the Board of the Baltic Exchange. In that effort, it collaborates with the Freight Market & Indices Users Group (FMIUG) and the Forward Freight Agreement Brokers Association (FFABA), as well as with other Baltic members. In addition to publishing various indices for the shipping market, the Baltic Exchange is publishing a daily fixtures report. All this is discussed in detail in Chapter 3 of this book.

The following list provides an overview of the important dates regarding developments of derivatives in shipping markets (Aury, 2003 and other market sources):

- **580 B.C:** Thales the Milesian purchased options on olive presses and made a fortune off of a crop in olives.
- **12th Century:** European trade fairs sellers sign contracts promising future delivery of the items they sold.
- **1634-1637:** Tulip bulb mania in Holland: Fortunes are lost, after a speculative boom in tulip bulb forward burst.
- **1650:** The first "*futures*" contracts are traced to the Yodoya rice market in Osaka, Japan.
- **Late 17th Century:** Dojima Rice Futures.
- **1848:** Chicago Board of Trade (CBOT) is formed. Trading starts in wheat, pork belly and copper futures.
- **1922:** The federal government makes its first effort to regulate the futures market with the Grain Futures Act.
- **1925:** The first futures clearing-house is formed at the CBOT.
- **Mid 1970's:** First currency swaps.
- **April 1973:** The Chicago Board Options Exchange opens.
- **1981:** First interest rate swap.
- **May 1985:** The Baltic Exchange starts to produce the Baltic Freight Index (BFI). Originally the BFI comprised Handy, Panamax and Capesize voyage routes. Also the London International Financial Futures and Options Exchange (LIFFE) launches the first freight futures contract, namely the Baltic International Freight Futures Exchange (BIFFEX), with settlement on values of the BFI.
- **1987:** First oil swap
- **October 1991:** BIFFEX Options introduced in LIFFE.
- **October 1992:** OTC Forward Freight Agreement (FFA) contracts introduced by Clarksons Securities Ltd., originally marketing them through their joint-venture company, Clarkson Wolff.
- **November 1992:** First dry-bulk FFA contract (Bocimar and Burwain in Route 2 of the BFI – US Gulf to Japan).
- **July 1995:** First Tanker FFA contract (Euronay and Worldwide on AG East based on the assessment of the London Tanker Panel).
- **June 1997:** The Baltic starts to publish the Baltic Handysize Index (BHI)
- **July 1997:** FFABA is created by members of the Baltic Exchange.
- **December 1998:** The Baltic starts to publish the Baltic Panamax Index (BPI). The major drawback of the BFI was its low correlation with the underlying market. Under pressure from the industry, the Baltic decided to produce a Panamax specific index.

- **April 1999:** The Baltic starts to publish the Baltic Capesize Index (BCI) for the same reason as for the BPI.
- **November 1999:** The BPI replaces the BFI as the underlying asset of BIFFEX.
- **April 2000:** The first internet-based electronic FFA trading platform, the FFAonline, is launched by Simpson Spence and Young (SSY).
- **October 2000:** The Baltic launches the Baltic Handymax Index (BHMI).
- **August 2000:** The Enron Online electronic FFA trading platform is created. Enron is the counterparty to all trades and in addition pledges to be a market maker. The platform was a success with 50 million tons of freight traded in the first 12 months. The system was easy to use, had narrow bid-offer spreads, and quotes were always available up to 12 months ahead.
- **August 2001:** Dirty and Clean Tanker Indices are launched under the Baltic International Tanker Routes (BITR) index.
- **October 2001:** The Baltic Exchange launches its own online FFA trading system for trading dry-bulk and tanker FFAs. The FFA trading system of the Baltic Exchange responded to an increased demand from market users to improve price transparency and credit risk management.
- **November 2001:**
  - o A web-based exchange for trading freight derivatives, the International Maritime Exchange (IMAREX), is launched. IMAREX uses the Norwegian Options and Futures Clearing-House (NOS) for the clearing of standardised listed futures and OTC derivatives.
  - o Enron and Bocimar enter the first ever zero-cost collar freight derivatives on the average of the four time-charter routes of the BCI with 5 years term to maturity[22]. The transaction had a floor supplied by Enron at $10,000 and a cap supplied by Bocimar at $15,000 with a start date 1st of January 2002.
- **April 2002:** LIFFE ends listing of the BIFFEX contract. Despite the early success of the BIFFEX contract, the trading volume during the last five years has been decreasing steadily, where in 2001 there were very few trades (2 to 4 lots per day) – see Figure 3.8 for volume of trading of BIFFEX.
- **January 2003:** The Baltic Exchange, the FFABA and the FMIUG sign a joint statement on working together to increase the liquidity of the FFA market.
- **March 2003:** The Baltic Exchange launches a new LPG route assessment.
- **May 2003:** The Baltic introduces a $25 per settlement fee. Due to continuous operating losses by the Baltic Exchange, the payment of $25 settlement fee was decided for contributing to the expenses related to the manufacturing of the shipping indices. Brokers are reporting to the Baltic the number of settlements for each of their principals every month and the Baltic, after aggregating the information from the various brokers, is invoicing the principals (talks are underway to make the invoicing quarterly instead of monthly and to create a cap for big users).
- **June 2003:** The Baltic Exchange starts to produce the first vessel value derivatives product, the Forward Ship Valuation Agreement (FoSVA), with an

---

[22] A zero-cost collar is an option trading strategy without premiums (a floor (min) and cap (max) zone is created). The motivation for the charterer (shipowner) is to get protected against possible rise (fall) in the cost of freight and buys (sells) the zero-cost collar. The zero-cost collar is created by a call and a put option with the same time to expiration, but with different strike prices, where the strike price of call is higher than the strike price of the put.

underlying asset the Baltic Ship Valuation Assessment (BaSVA). Four types of 5-years old vessels are assessed: VLCC, Capesize, Aframax, and Panamax (dry). BaSVAs are reported twice a month.

- **September 2003:** FoSVAs and BaSVAs are officially launched.
- **October 2003:** First ever FFA settlement over US$1 billion.
- **January 2004:**
  - IMAREX announces that all regulated members of the FFABA can clear their FFA trades through NOS.
  - IMAREX introduces an electronic screen trading of its derivatives products.
- **February 2004:** First bank loan extended against an FFA.
- **August 2004:**
  - The FoSVA is renamed to Sale & Purchase Forward Agreement (SPFA) and the BaSVA is renamed to Baltic Sale & Purchase Assessments (BSPA). BSPAs are reported four times a month (instead of just two) and two more vessel types are included: MR Motor TKR (Tanker) and Super Handy.
  - The Baltic Exchange begins to publish the Baltic Demolition Assessment (BDA).
- **April 2005:** Clarksons Securities Limited, Ifchor S.A. and Freight Investor Services announce than an on-line screen trading facility for FFA contracts, called C.I.F., is planned to be launched during the summer of 2005.
- **May 2005:** The New York Mercantile Exchange (NYMEX) launches nine tanker freight futures contracts on its NYMEX ClearPort(sm) electronic trading and clearing platform.
- **June 2005:**
  - The IMAREX launches the first cleared (mark-to-market) freight option contract on the tanker route TD3.
  - The Singapore Exchange (SGX) announces its intentsion to develop and implement an OTC FFA clearing facility.
- **September 2005:**
  - LCH.Clearnet launches a clearing service for FFA contracts.
  - The Shanghai Shipping Exchange is initiating talks with China's biggest exchange to explore the possibility of launching freight futures trading.
- **October 2005:** FFABA proposes a revised freight derivatives contract, named FFABA2005.
- **November 2005:** Clarksons announce that a hedge fund that will be investing in freight derivatives will be launched during 2006. The fund promises to produce returns in the range 15% to 20% and investors will have to place a minimum of $200 million to take part in this fund.
- **December 2005:** IMAREX launches an electronic screen market for bunker fuel oil derivatives.

1.12. Summary

This chapter of the book outlined the various sources of business risks that market agents in the shipping industry face in their decision-making process. It has presented old and new empirical evidence on the classification of these risks by sector and type of market, and outlined some traditional risk management strategies, which emanate from these observations, and which principals use to manage their business risks. The deficiencies of these strategies were discussed, followed by an introduction of how financial derivatives can provide solutions to these deficiencies and be used for the efficient management of risks in the sector. In that sense, this very important first chapter of the book has set the framework upon which to base the rest of the discussion in the book regarding the different aspects of risk management in the shipping industry. Some important results have been discussed in that process, including the market segmentation of the industry, the structure of its markets and the identification of the conditions of perfect competition, the cyclicality and the seasonality in freight ratesand vessel prices as the factors responsible for the high volatility we observe in the cash-flow of the businesses involved in the sector.

Chapter 2 of this book provides to the non-specialist an introduction to financial derivatives, knowledge of which is necessary to follow the rest of the chapters in the book. Readers who have already some knowledge of financial derivatives may omit chapter 2 and move straight into chapter 3 of the book.

CHAPTER 2. Introduction to Financial Derivatives

2.1. Introduction

Chapter 1 of this book provided some stylised facts regarding the structure and working of the shipping industry. Based on these observations, strategies for risk management were identified. These *"traditional"* strategies were deemed to be non-existent under certain conditions, but also relatively expensive or inflexible in comparison to the possibilities offered by financial derivatives. This chapter then aims to provide a brief but comprehensive introduction to financial derivatives instruments to the non-specialist, so as to be able to follow the rest of the chapters, where applications of financial derivatives in the shipping industry are considered. The chapter provides a good revision for readers who have followed a first course in financial derivatives before.

The core function of the financial system is to facilitate the allocation and development of economic resources, both spatially and across time, in an uncertain environment (Merton, 1990). The economic function of financial markets can be seen in three dimensions: time, risk, and information. The intertemporal (over time) nature of financial decisions implies uncertainty as to future outcomes of key variables, such as equity prices, foreign exchange rates, interest rates, commodity prices, freight rates, etc., and this constitutes risk, as it encompasses the prospect of a financial loss. For instance, an oil refinery does not know in August what price it will have to pay in October for crude oil, when it will need crude to continue its refining operations. The possibility of a rise in the crude's price over the period constitutes risk for the refinery, as it will increase its input costs. Money and capital markets provide a wide range of instruments or institutional arrangements to either diversify risks (hedge), i.e. to reduce or eliminate risks, or to (re)allocate the undiversifiable part of the risks among households and companies, from those who want to avoid it to those who are willing to accept it.

The origin of the term hedging is unclear, but it appears to derive from the use of hedges to form a protective or defensive barrier around property. In a business context, the term means *"to secure oneself against a loss on an investment by investing on the other side"* (Arditti, 1996). Hedging is insuring (protecting) against changes in the market, so that the buyer or seller in the market is protected against adverse changes in prices in the future[23]. Before implementing a hedge, various issues should be considered: Identification of the potential risk exposure, calculation of the risk exposure, selection of the appropriate hedging instrument, calculation of the size of the hedge, and finally monitoring of the hedge (Boland, 1999). The available methods of hedging rely upon the form of risk and investors' preferences. Companies and individual investors can use modern risk management instruments, such as financial derivatives, in order to hedge their risks.

---

[23] It should be noted that some risks cannot be hedged perfectly with derivatives instruments. They include: credit (default) risk, which is the risk for a participant that the other counterparty may default; quantity risk, which is the uncertainty about the quantity of the underlying commodity that will be sold or bought at some future date.

Financial derivatives are contracts which have a price. This price depends amongst other things, on the value of the underlying commodity upon which the contract is written. Hence the name derivative – its value derives from that of another "*commodity*", known as the underlying commodity. For instance, the value of a derivatives contract on crude oil depends on the current and expected price of crude oil.

2.1.1. The Economic Functions and Benefits of Financial Derivatives

Originally, producers and consumers of commodities used derivatives contracts to hedge prices and therefore reduce their risk. The growth in derivatives instruments has been attributed to their increasing use by governments, international corporations, and major institutional and financial investors. They use derivatives in order to lower international funding costs, to provide better rates of exchange in international markets, to diversify funding and improve risk management, and to hedge price risks, amongst others. Fite and Pfleiderer (1995) identify the following four roles of financial derivatives for traders. They allow traders to: (i) modify the risk characteristics of an investment portfolio, facilitating an efficient distribution of risks among risk bearers; (ii) enhance the expected return of a portfolio, depending on how efficiently risks can be shared among investors; (iii) reduce transactions costs associated with managing a portfolio; and (iv) circumvent regulatory obstacles.

To illustrate the above, consider the financial function of providing a well-diversified portfolio of equities for individual investors. At one time, this function was best served by buying shares on a stock exchange. However, transactions and monitoring costs as well as problems of indivisibilities, significantly limited the number of companies that could be held in almost any investor's portfolio. The innovation of pooling intermediaries, such as unit trusts greatly reduced those costs, provided for almost perfect divisibility, and thereby allowed individual investors to achieve vastly better-diversified portfolios. Subsequently, futures derivatives contracts were created on various stock indices. These exchange-traded contracts further reduced costs, improved domestic diversification, and provided expanded opportunities for international diversification. Moreover, these contracts gave the investor greater flexibility for selecting leverage and controlling risk. Further innovations that serve the diversification function have intermediaries using equity-return forward derivatives contracts, to create custom contracts with individual specifications of the stock index, the investment time horizon, and even the currency mix for payments.

From the point of view of the society as a whole, two traditional social benefits are associated with derivatives. First, derivatives are useful to manage risk. Second, trading financial derivatives generates publicly observable prices that provide information about future values of the underlying "*commodities*", upon which derivatives are written, known as price discovery. Society as a whole benefits substantially from derivatives markets in these two ways. Because derivatives are available for risk management, companies can undertake projects that might be impossible to undertake without advanced risk management techniques. Individuals in the economy also benefit from the risk transference role of derivatives. For example, most individuals who want to finance home purchases have a choice of floating rate or fixed rate mortgages. The ability of the financial institution to offer this choice to the borrower depends on the institution's ability to manage its own financial risk through the financial derivatives market.

Derivatives markets are instrumental in providing information to society as a whole. The existence of derivatives increases trader interest and trading activity in the derivatives instrument and in the cash market instrument from which the derivative stems. As a result of greater attention, prices of the derivatives and the cash market instrument will be more likely to approximate their true value. Thus, the trading of derivatives aids economic agents in discovering prices, because it increases the quantity and quality of information that prices incorporate. When parties transact based on accurate prices, economic resources are allocated more efficiently than they would be if prices poorly reflected the economic value of the underlying assets. Companies and individuals can use the information discovered in the derivatives market to improve the quality of their economic decisions, even if they do not trade derivatives themselves.

Table 2.1 provides a summary of the economic functions of derivatives transactions. As can be observed, the existence of derivatives improves risk management, the transparency and efficiency of markets, diversification, price discovery, provides for improved profit (and loss) margins for investors through leverage, improved volume and liquidity in markets, allows for arbitrage opportunities, better financial engineering and aids in completing financial markets.

Table 2.1. The Economic Functions of Derivatives Contracts

Hedging	Decreasing the risk exposure of the spot position.
Transparency of Markets	Reducing transactions costs, reducing bid-ask spread, promoting liquidity.
Efficiency of Markets	If traders with different risk preferences, expectations, and attitudes buy and sell the same instrument, information aggregation is stronger, and prices are more efficient in reflecting new information.
Diversification	Given that derivatives represent only a fraction of the cash investment, it is easier to diversify a given amount of capital across several assets.
Contract Standardisation	Allowing quick execution of transactions.
Price Discovery	Producing more information than the information that exists in the spot market.
Leverage	Requiring only a small fraction of the investment in the underlying securities.
Volume	Allowing traders to benefit from movements in the market as a whole.
Liquidity	Attracting new traders and new capital.
Arbitrage	Increasing liquidity and stabilising basis-risk.
Financial Engineering	New financial instruments can be created from the existing instruments.
Efficient Risk Allocation	Transferring risks from risk-averse traders (hedgers) to risk-takers (speculators).
Complete the Financial Markets	A market in which there is a distinctive marketable security for each and every possible outcome.
Access to Asset Classes	Which are not available as financial investments otherwise.

Source: Gibson and Zimmermann, 1994

In March 2004, the International Swaps and Derivatives Association (ISDA) conducted a survey, of finance professors, at the top 50 business schools worldwide to explore the perceptions of derivatives, as well as their impact on the global financial system. A total of 84 professors, at 42 academic institutions, provided responses. The major findings of the ISDA survey were the following: 98% of respondents agreed that managing financial risk more effectively is a way for companies to build shareholder value; respondents unanimously agreed that derivatives help companies manage financial risk more effectively; all respondents agreed that derivatives will continue to grow in use and application; over half the respondents agreed that derivatives have not created new types of risk – they simply allow existing risks to be managed better; 99% of respondents agreed that the impact of derivatives on the global financial system is beneficial; 81% of respondents agreed that the risks of using derivatives have been overstated; the use of derivatives by companies as a quick and efficient way to manage risks was commonly cited as a contribution to the stability of the global financial system; and the flexibility derivatives offer in customizing a company's risk profile was commonly cited as a benefit that these instruments offer to companies (ISDA, 2004).

There are also a number of questions about the actual economic impacts of derivatives trades: (i) do they make the underlying commodity markets more volatile? and (ii) do they lower the cost of capital or encourage investment? The impact of derivatives trading on the volatility of the underlying spot markets has been one of the most intensively studied subjects in the international economics literature. Mayhew (2000) reviews more than 150 published studies on the subject and concluded that the use of derivatives has either reduced or had no effect on the price volatility of the underlying spot markets. Moreover, companies, by hedging, can avoid financial distress or bankruptcy costs, as derivatives increase the profitability of investments. Allayannis and Weston (2001) report that hedging activity increases the value of the company, as after companies began (stopped) hedging, their market value increased (decreased). Thus, there is evidence that hedging increases the value of the company, and consequently, increases investment. .

Figure 2.1. Number of Companies using Derivatives

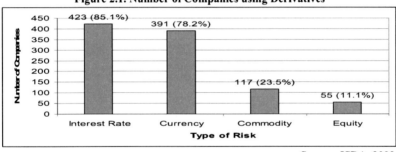

Source: ISDA, 2003

The number of different derivatives instruments and the volume of derivatives contracts traded are both increasing dramatically every year. ISDA carried out a survey in March 2003 of derivatives usage, by the world's 500 largest companies, ranked by revenues as of year-end 2001. In conducting the survey, ISDA examined publicly available information, including annual reports and regulatory filings. Companies, for which no disclosure is available, are counted, for purposes of the survey results, as not using derivatives. According to the survey, 85.1% of these companies use derivative instruments to manage and hedge their risks more effectively. The companies that use derivatives are located in 26 countries around the world and represent a broad variety of industries, ranging from aerospace to wholesalers of office and electronic equipment. Figure 2.1 presents the number of companies that use derivatives to manage particular types of risk. Of the companies that use derivatives, 85.1% use them to help manage interest rate risk; 78.2% of the companies use them to help manage currency risk; 23.5% utilize them to help manage commodity price risk; and 11.1% use them to help manage equity price risk. The survey demonstrates that derivatives contracts today are an integral part of corporate risk management among the world's leading companies (ISDA, 2003).

The Bank of International Settlements (BIS) conducted in April 2004 the triennial (2001-2004) central bank survey of derivatives market activity, where 52 central banks and monetary authorities participated. They collected data on turnover in OTC currency and interest rate derivatives contracts[24]. The major findings of the BIS survey were the following: Global daily turnover in foreign exchange and interest rate derivatives contracts rose by an estimated 74%, to $2.4 trillion, between April 2001 and April 2004. At constant exchange rates, the increase was 51%. Activity grew in both segments of the global OTC market, namely interest rate and currency products. Growth in the interest rate segment (up 110%) continued to exceed that in the foreign exchange segment (51%). In terms of total turnover, interest rate derivatives are now very close to exchange rate derivatives. Daily business in the two segments stood, as of end-April 2004, at $1,025 and $1,292 billion respectively, against $489 billion and $853 billion as of end-April 2001 (BIS, 2005).

According to the survey, the growth of business in exchange rate derivatives is related to the 57% expansion in turnover in traditional foreign exchange markets. Higher demand in both the traditional and the derivatives segments reflects the greater role that such products have recently been playing as an alternative investment class to equity and fixed income investments, as well as the larger role of hedge funds and asset managers. In addition, the large swing in the exchange rate of the dollar vis-à-vis other major currencies, between 2001 and 2004, may have increased hedging-related demand for currency derivatives. In the interest rate segment, activity was boosted by changes in hedging and trading practices in the US market, which contributed to turnover in the swap segment. Trading between reporting banks and other financial institutions, mainly hedge funds, mutual funds and insurance companies increased by 132%. However, business also rose substantially with non-financial customers, i.e. companies, by 77% (BIS, 2005).

2.1.2. The Risks Associated with Financial Derivatives

However, associated with the growth in the use of derivatives, there have been a few notable bank collapses and corporate losses involving billions of US dollars. In some cases the losses were incurred very rapidly, as in the case of the Barings Bank collapse, while others appear to have resulted from years of trading irregularities, as in the case of the Sumitomo Corporation. There have been organisations who have suffered losses due to poor financial controls and trading practices. For example, Orange County, California lost $1.7 billion in 1993, Mettallgesellschaft AG lost about $1.3 billion in 1993 in energy trading, Chile Copper Corporation (CODELCO) lost some $200 million in 1994 from irregular derivatives trading in copper and precious metals, Barings Bank collapsed in 1995 owning more than $1 billion on financial derivatives contracts by a single trader based in the bank's Singapore branch, the Federal Reserve Bank of New York organised a rescue of Long-Term Capital Management in 1998 in order to avoid disrupting international capital markets, and in 2001 Enron became at that time the largest bankruptcy in American History. All these cases raised significant concerns about counterparty (credit) risk and proper financial

---

[24] An OTC market is a decentralised market (as opposed to an exchange market) where geographically dispersed dealers are linked by telephones and computer screens. The market is for derivatives not listed on derivatives exchanges.

reporting. Unfortunately, there is still a lack of understanding of derivatives within the markets and losses can be huge.

Organisations then should carefully examine their risk management procedures, including the role that derivatives play in the financial positions of companies. It is of paramount importance that companies should define, in a clear way, limits to the financial risks that can be taken and proper monitoring procedures to ensure that they are followed. These limits should be applicable to the individuals responsible for managing particular risks. Daily reports, indicating the potential gain or loss, should be compared against the actual losses experienced to ensure that the valuation procedures are precise. Without daily reports, it is difficult to know whether a particular derivatives transaction is for hedging or speculative purposes. Even if a derivatives transaction, exceeding risk limits, results in a profit, the transaction should be controlled. The penalties for exceeding risk limits should be as great when profits result, as when losses result. Moreover, even if a trader has an outstanding track record, or appears good at predicting a particular market variable, it is likely to be a result of luck rather than superior trading skill, the trader's risk limits should not be increased and should not be left undiversified on just one market variable. Creative scenario analysis and stress testing should always accompany the calculation of risk measures (Hull, 2005).

More specifically, for financial institutions, it is important that all traders, even those making high profits, be fully accountable. The front-office, which consists of traders executing trades, the middle-office, which consists of risk managers monitoring the risks and the back-office, which consists of record keeping and accounting, should be kept separate. Models and computer systems should be reviewed and analysed at regular time intervals, to ensure correct and proper operation and function. In structured deals, where pricing of the derivatives product relies on the underlying model, inception profits should be recognized slowly, so that traders have the motivation to investigate the impact of several different models and several different sets of assumptions before committing themselves to a deal. Financial institutions should sell to their corporate clients appropriate products, irrespective of the appetite for the underlying risks of their clients. Trading strategies of large volumes of illiquid assets are dangerous, as illiquid assets often sell at a big discount to their fair values. Also, when many market agents are following the same trading strategy this may create a dangerous environment, where they are liable to unstable markets and large losses.

For non-financial institutions, it is important not to initiate a derivatives transaction which they do not fully understand. If a senior manager in a corporation does not understand a trade proposed by a subordinate, or if the company does not have the in-house capability to value a derivatives instrument, the trade should not be approved. Trader's positions should be controlled at all times and checked in terms of their purposes. Often, a derivatives transaction taken initially for hedging purposes, after a period of time alters to speculative purposes.

The aim of this chapter is to provide an introduction to financial derivatives products and to their use in the practice of business risk management and investment. It presents the types of participants in derivatives markets according to their aims, the types of derivatives products available, their specifications, their potential and practical examples of their uses. Armed with the material provided in this chapter the reader can then move on to later chapters of the book, where these issues are applied to the shipping industry. The rest of the chapter is organised as follows: Section 2.2 identifies the reasons for using financial derivatives and as a consequence classifies participants in three categories. Section 2.3 describes the basic derivatives instruments, including futures, forwards, swaps and options, discussing their specifications, characteristics, trading issues, pricing and their use for hedging and speculation purposes. Section 2.4 presents the accounting treatment of derivatives transactions and tax issues. Section 2.5 analyses the issue of credit risk in derivatives transactions and the use of credit derivatives. Section 2.6 presents the Value-at-Risk (VaR) model for measuring market risk. Finally, Section 2.7 concludes the chapter.

2.2. Types of Participants in Derivatives Markets

Market participants choose to use financial derivatives for various reasons – to satisfy different aims. Based on these aims, market agents can be generally categorised as hedgers, speculators or arbitrageurs:

- **Hedgers** are interested in reducing a price risk that they face by either transferring it to another hedger with an opposite position in the market, or to a party, such as a speculator, willing to accept and trade the risk. For instance, an oil producer is worried about a fall in the price of crude oil in the future, as this will reduce his future income. A refinery, on the demand side, is worried that the price of crude oil will increase in the future, thereby increasing its costs. The two parties have opposite positions in the physical market. Furthermore, they have opposite expectations regarding the future movements of crude oil prices in the market. They will thus be the counterparties in the derivatives hedge. In general, the hedger aims to stabilise income, costs or debt, or to get a better grip on cash management. By definition, hedgers are risk-averse; that is, they do not like risk.

- **Speculators** see financial derivatives as they see any other investment, which has a changing price, as determined by changing demand and supply conditions. They take positions in the market, which will result in a profit for them, when they predict correctly the directional changes in prices. They can be a counterparty to a hedger or to another speculator. They are less risk-averse than hedgers, betting that a price will go up or down; their motivation for trading is not to hedge any underlying physical position. A hedger accepts to sustain a loss on a derivatives contract, as it probably reflects profits from the underlying asset. The speculator does not have the underlying asset in his portfolio and seeks profits from the derivatives contract.

  Speculators are often viewed with suspicion. However, they are essential to the market's existence, as they are willing to take risks, thereby introducing capital to the market, thus increasing its liquidity. Speculators, relative to the spot market, benefit from leverage[25], low transaction costs, ease of opening and closing positions, narrow bid-ask spreads (prices) and the ability to *short* the market, as they typically take large in size trading positions. Without their presence, the market would tend to move violently, following demand or supply changes or shocks to the markets, reaching extreme values, as there

---

[25] As we see later, the operation of margin accounts and the mark-to-market clearing of positions in derivatives contracts allows manipulation of positions, much larger than the cash required to open these positions. As a consequence, the return on own equity is much larger compared to investments, where 100% of the value of the investment has to be cash financed. This is known as leverage.

would be less counterparties taking opposite positions and smoothing the fluctuations in prices.

- **Arbitrageurs** have a similar aim to speculators; they seek to make a profit. However, this profit is obtained without commitment of extra funds, and at no extra risk. They take advantage of temporary discrepancies in the prices of the same good trading in different markets, caused by time lags or temporary imbalances in demand or supply between the markets. This can be achieved by entering simultaneously into transactions in two or more markets, buying in the cheaper market and selling in the more expensive market the same good. In efficient markets, arbitrage opportunities occur infrequently or are eliminated very quickly when they appear.

2.3. Main Types of Financial Derivatives

Four main types of financial derivatives are considered: Forwards, futures, swaps, and options contracts. Consider each of them in turn.

2.3.1. Forward Contracts

A forward contract is a private OTC transaction under which the buyer and the seller agree upon the delivery of a specified quality and quantity of a "*commodity*" at a specified future date and at a specified price. The term commodity is used in a wider sense and may include gold, grains, exchange rates, interest rates, freight rates, etc. It is also referred to as the "*underlying*" (to the derivative) commodity. The forward contract is, as a consequence, a "*derivative*" to the underlying commodity, as its value derives from it. The specified underlying asset of the contract is not literally bought or sold, but the market price of that contract at maturity, compared to the contract price, determines whether the holder of the derivatives contract has made a profit or a loss.

A forward contract, by definition, involves a settlement at maturity, which results in a net cash outflow to one counterparty and a net cash inflow to the other counterparty. There is credit risk associated with a forward contract. That is, there is a possibility that one of the counterparties does not meet its obligations – it defaults the agreement. Two aspects of this risk warrant further consideration. Firstly, the credit risk implicit in a forward contract can be expressed as the risk that one party will not perform, on the settlement date, the obligations which the forward contract has imposed, relative to a change in the value of the forward contract from zero. If during the life of the forward contract spot prices continually mirror the forward price on which the contract is based, then there is negligible credit risk associated with the forward contract. The greater the deviation in spot prices from the forward price the greater the credit risk implicit in the forward contract, because the more probable it becomes then that one counterparty will owe a large settlement amount to the other counterparty at the maturity date of the contract. Secondly, the forward contract is a "*pure*" credit instrument in the sense that the only time a payment is made under a forward contract is at its maturity. There are no payments made at the initiation of the contract and none made during the life of the contract. The risk, therefore, that one party will not fulfill the settlement obligations required of him under the contract exists throughout the life of the contract and that risk increases the longer the maturity of the contract is.

2.3.2. Futures Contracts

A futures contract is similar to a forward contract, but with a significant difference in that it trades in an organised exchange. Its price is determined by demand and supply conditions in the market. The contracts are standardised in terms of quantity, quality, and delivery time of the underlying asset, so both counterparties know exactly what is being traded. Futures contracts are traded on currencies, on various kinds of interest bearing securities (e.g. US T-Notes and T-Bonds, UK gilts, Eurodollar deposits, bonds) and Fon various equity and stock indexes (e.g. Standard & Poors (S/P) 500 index, New York Stock Exchange (NYSE) composite index, Financial Times (FT) 100 index, Nikkei index, etc.). Major exchanges trading futures contracts include: the Chicago Board of Trade (CBOT), the Chicago Mercantile Exchange (CME), the Tokyo Stock Exchange (TSE), the London International Financial Futures and Options Exchange (LIFFE) and the EUREX (European Derivatives Exchange), amongst others.

Table 2.2. Contractual Differences between Futures and Forward Contracts

	Futures Contract	Forward Contract
Contract Specifications	Standardised specifications of unit, contract size, maturities and price of trading.	No standardisation, with individually agreed terms and prices.
Method of Trading	Open outcry auction on an exchange trading floor or electronic trading during specific trading hours.	OTC market between individual buyers and sellers, 24 hours per day.
Pricing	Same best price available at the time for all traders, regardless of transaction size.	The price varies with the size of the transaction and the credit risk involved. No guarantee that it is the best.
Daily Fluctuations Limit	There is a daily price limit for some contracts, e.g. +/- 200 basis points relative to previous day's settlement price.	There are no daily price limits.
Market Liquidity	High liquidity and ease of offsetting (closing) a position due to standardisation.	Limited liquidity and offset due to variable contract terms.
Payment Schedule	Interim payments during the life of the contract (mark-to-market).	A payment is made only on the maturity date and there is no initial cash-flow.
Clearing Operation	A clearing-house deals with the daily revaluation of open positions and cash payments.	There is no clearing-house function.
Security	A clearing-house assumes the credit risk and controls for default risk.	The trader's reputation and collateral control for default risk, and the participant bears the credit risk of the counterparty defaulting.
Delivery on Maturity	It is not the object of the transaction and only 2% of the contracts are delivered.	It is the object of the transaction and over 90% are delivered.
Delivery Procedure	- Specific maturity dates per year at approved locations. - Delivery on a particular day.	-Written with specific (individual agreed) times to maturity and locations. - Delivery at anytime during a certain period, with a few days notice of intention to deliver.
Publicity of Information	Information is publicly available.	Information is not disclosed to the public.
Regulation	Regulated by a government Agency (e.g. Capital Markets Commission)	Self-regulation.

Note: **Source:** Various Sources
- A basis point corresponds to 1/100 of a percentage point. For example, an interest rate futures of 5% is 50 basis points higher than an interest rate futures of 4.5%.

Table 2.2 presents the contractual differences between the OTC forward and the exchange traded futures contracts. They are very similar derivatives instruments, but there are substantial differences also. Which contract is used at the end of the day, depends on the preferences and the needs of the end user. For instance, as can be seen in the table, futures contracts are standardised in terms of size and maturity, while forward contracts are tailor made to the needs of the customer. Thus, if say futures contracts for a commodity trade in multiples of $250,000 for maturities of one-, two- and three-months, but the needs of a market agent is for a contract of $150,000 and a contract maturity of 45 days, a forward contract maybe more appropriate than a futures contract. As another example, consider a market agent who is worried about credit risk of the existing counterparties in the market. He will opt for a futures rather than a forward contract, as futures contracts clear on a mark-to-market basis, through a clearing-house associated with the exchange where the futures contract is trading.

2.3.2.1. Market Positions with Futures/Forward Contracts

Market agents, wishing to protect their investments, can participate in the derivatives markets and buy (sell) derivatives instruments in order to get protected against increasing (decreasing) market prices. Generally, the basic derivatives positions are long (buy derivatives), short (sell derivatives) and cross hedge. Consider each of these in turn.

Short Futures Hedge: Futures/forwards can be used to protect against a loss arising from a price decrease of a "*commodity*", which the market agent has in its possession. Suppose a company, say an investment bank, holds an inventory of bonds that it wishes to sell to its retail clients. It expects a rise in interest rates, which will reduce the bond's price. By shorting (selling) bond futures contracts the company will make money on them, as it will buy them back later at a lower price. This profit will offset the losses on its bond inventory. If interest rates fall, which will increase the price of bonds then the gain on its bond inventory is offset by its loss on futures.

For example, suppose that the current market price of bonds is $25, as shown in Figure 2.2. The bank enters a futures contract to sell bonds at $25, rather than at $15, or at any other price that may occur at the expiration of the futures contract. As the spot market price of bonds falls below $25, the investment bank begins making profits on the futures position. The lower the price of bonds, the lower will be the price of futures on these bonds and the higher will be the profit resulting from the short futures position. Thus, if the price falls to $15, the bank sells the bonds at $25, while they worth only $15, thus making a gain of $10 per bond. If the price falls to $10 it makes $15 per bond, and so on. On the other hand, if futures prices on bonds increase, the bank has agreed to sell at $25, bonds worth more, say $35 or $40, making $10 and $15 loss in each case. The higher the market price of bonds, the higher will be the loss in the futures position. The above profit/loss of the bank's position on the futures contracts can be seen graphically by the downward sloping, from left to right, solid line in Figure 2.2. The upward sloping dotted line, from left to right, on the same figure, shows the loss/profit of the bank from holding the actual bonds in its portfolio. It is exactly opposite in sign and magnitude from that of the futures position. In that sense, the losses in the underlying market are offset by the profits in the derivatives market. The overall spot-futures portfolio position is represented by the horizontal axis of Figure 2.2, as the net profit/loss is zero.

Figure 2.2. Short Futures Payoffs

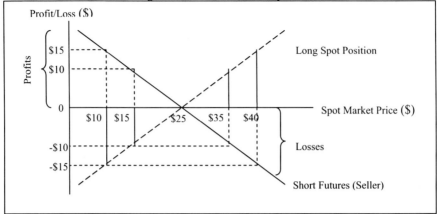

Long Futures Hedge: Futures may also be used to protect against a loss arising from a price increase of a *"commodity"*, which a market agent wishes to purchase in the future. Suppose that a money manager expects pension money to arrive in three months and intends to invest it in bonds. He is concerned that if long-term interest rates fall, the bonds will become more expensive, and this will reduce the rate of return of his portfolio.

Figure 2.3. Long Futures Payoffs

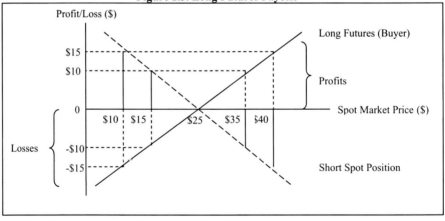

To offset this, he locks in today's bond interest rate by buying bond futures contracts. If interest rates are lower when the cash funds arrive, bonds and bond futures prices will be higher. As a consequence, he will be able to buy bonds at the agreed (lower) futures price and resell them at the prevailing higher spot price. These gains on his long bond futures position can be seen by the solid rising line from left to right in Figure 2.3. The higher the price of bonds, above the current price of $25, the higher is the profit from the long futures position. The opposite is true when prices fall below the agreed futures price of $25. The lower the price, the larger is the loss. This profit/loss position in the futures market offsets the loss/profit outcome in the spot market. This is evident from the falling, from left to right, dotted line in the figure, representing the spot bond market position. It is symmetrical to the solid line representing the futures position, with respect to the horizontal axis of the figure.

Thus, the losses/gains from one market offset those from the other, resulting in a net portfolio position of zero. In terms of the original problem of the money manager; he wishes to buy bonds in the future, he expects a higher spot price to prevail then and he buys bond futures contracts. The gain in the futures position exactly offsets the loss in the spot position.

Cross Hedge: This refers to the use of a futures contract to protect the value of a *"commodity"* for which there is no available futures contract. Suppose that there are two types of bonds trading: Grade 1 and Grade 2, but bonds futures contracts are available for Grade 1 only. Suppose also that the prices of the two bonds are highly correlated. The Grade 1 bond's futures price and Grade 2's price should also be highly correlated. Therefore, the Grade 1 bond futures contract could be used as a hedging instrument for Grade 2 bond. This is an example of cross hedge.

2.3.2.2. Clearing of Futures Contracts
We noted earlier that a forward contract has credit risk associated with it, because no collateral is held under the agreement and no payments are made until its maturity. In contrast, credit risk associated with futures contracts is eliminated by the fact that the exchange itself – or the clearing-house – interposes itself between the two parties to a futures contract, by functioning as the formal counterparty with each of the parties. Thus, it provides security to market agents, as it guarantees the financial settlement of all transactions in the event of default of any of the members. Both buyers and sellers, via their brokers, anonymously trade the same contract indefinitely, and the clearing-house stands in as the guarantor.

Specifically, with the initiation of a futures contract, the investor is required to place with the clearing-house a deposit (that is, to open a margin account), which acts as collateral for adverse price movements and the possibility of default. The initial deposit is payable immediately when trade begins and is returned upon closing out the position. Its size varies between 5% and 20% of the size of the position, depending on the volatility of the futures price, the liquidity of the contract and the creditworthiness of the client. This initial deposit, known as initial margin, is on a per contract basis, and is set at a size to cover the clearing-house against any losses which the new position of the investor might incur during the day.

A variation margin is also set, which is approximately 75% of the size of the initial margin. Variation margins are required to cover the extent to which a trading position shows a potential loss. Every night, the clearing-house compares the price of each contract with the official quotation at the final evening call (the closing price) and a new variation margin figure is calculated. If, as a result of fluctuations in the price of the futures contract, the funds held in the margin account fall below the variation margin, the investor receives a *"margin call"*, to deposit enough funds, so as to bring the sum held in the margin account back to its original level. Variation monies are usually required within 24 hours. Should the calculated figure show a profit, then this is credited to the client's account. Market players must have sufficient surplus funds in their accounts, to allow for such payments. Thus, a futures contract is much like a portfolio of forward contracts. At the close of each business day, in effect, the existing *"forward"* contract is settled and a new one is written. This daily settlement feature, combined with the margin requirement allows futures contracts to eliminate the credit risk inherent in forwards.

Example:

Table 2.3 presents an example of the mark-to-market procedure for a Brent crude oil futures contract trading at the Intercontinental Exchange (ICE) Futures (previously International Petroleum Exchange – IPE). Suppose on June 2nd a refinery wishes to purchase Brent crude oil in 17 days from today, but fears that its price will increase by then. It buys Brent crude futures to hedge its position. The futures contract is currently traded at $55 per 1,000 lots (barrels), having a value of $55,000 (= $55 x 1,000 barrels). The derivatives exchange sets a 5% initial margin per contract, that is $2,750, and a variation margin per contract of $2,000. Trading starts at $55. The second column of the table shows how futures prices evolve during the lifetime of the contract. The third column of the table calculates the daily change in the price of the contract. For instance, between June 2nd and 3rd the futures price change is -$0.5, as the price drops from $55 to $54.5. The fourth column of the table, uses this price change and the size of the position, to calculate the daily profit/loss in the margin account from this change in the price of the contract.

Table 2.3. Mark-to-Market Brent Crude Oil Futures Cash-flows

Date	Futures Price	Price Change	Daily Profit/Loss	Cumulative Profit/Loss	Initial Margin	Margin Call
June -02	$55.0				$2,750	
June -03	$54.5	-$0.5	-$500	-$500	$2,250	0
June -04	$54.2	-$0.3	-$300	-$800	$1,950	$800
June -07	$54.0	-$0.2	-$200	-$1,000	$2,550	0
June -08	$54.8	$0.8	$800	-$200	$3,350	0
June -09	$54.3	-$0.5	-$500	-$700	$2,850	0
June -10	$54.1	-$0.2	-$200	-$900	$2,650	0
June -11	$54.0	-$0.1	-$100	-$1,000	$2,550	0
June -14	$53.8	-$0.2	-$200	-$1,200	$2,350	0
June -15	$54.0	$0.2	$200	-$1,000	$2,550	0
June -16	$53.7	-$0.3	-$300	-$1,300	$2,250	0
June -17	$53.5	-$0.2	-$200	-$1,500	$2,050	0
June -18	$53.9	$0.4	$400	-$1,100	$2,450	0
June -21	$54.0	$0.1	$100	-$1,000	$2,550	0
June -22	$53.8	-$0.2	-$200	-$1,200	$2,350	0
June -23	$53.3	-$0.5	-$500	-$1,700	$1,850	$900
June -24	$53.0	-$0.3	-$300	-$2,000	$2,450	0
June -25	$53.5	$0.5	$500	-$1,500	$2,950	0

For instance, during the first day, the trading position incurred a loss of $500 (= -$0.5 x 1000 lots). When deducted from the initial margin, a sum of $2,250 (= $2,750-$500) remains in the account. This can be seen in the sixth column of the table. By the following day, June 4th, the price drops further to $54.2, resulting in a further loss of $300, presenting a cumulative loss from the start of trading of $800 (see column 5), further reducing the money held in the initial margin account to $1,950 (= $2,250 – $300). However, the money in the initial margin account now is bellow the $2,000 variation margin. As a consequence, a margin call of $800 is placed, as can be seen in the last column of the table, to restore the initial margin account back to its original level of $2,750. Thus, $800 must be paid to the clearing-house within 24 hours. A second margin call of $900 is also received on June 23rd. This mark-to-market procedure continues until the trading position is closed on June 25th. As can be seen in the table, the magnitude of the negative price changes and the corresponding losses is greater than those of the positive ones (see the third and the fourth columns of the table). As a consequence, the cumulative loss from futures trading, at the end of trading on June 25th, shown in the fifth column of the table, is $1,500.

2.3.2.3. Basis and Basis-Risk in Futures/Forward Contracts

The Basis (B_t) can be defined as the spot price of the underlying commodity (S_t) minus the price of the futures (forward) contract (F_t); that is, $B_t = S_t - F_t$. The basis is much more predictable than the individual level of spot and futures prices, and can provide more information about the market conditions (Sutcliffe, 1997). A narrowing (or strengthening) basis occurs when the basis moves towards zero and the absolute difference between spot and futures prices becomes smaller; that is, when spot and futures prices converge. On the other hand, a widening (or weakening) basis occurs when the basis moves away from zero and the absolute difference between spot and futures prices increases.

A feature of the basis, which is common to both futures and forward contracts, is its tendency to narrow when the expiration of the derivatives contract approaches. This is known as *basis convergence*, where at expiration the spot and the derivatives prices are equal. Figure 2.4 shows the path of futures and spot prices of a "*commodity*" during March 2005. It can be seen in the figure that at the beginning of March, spot prices are higher than derivatives prices; consequently, the basis is positive. This is called a market in **backwardation**. From mid-March onwards spot prices are lower than derivatives prices; consequently, the basis is negative. This is called a market in **contango** condition.

Figure 2.4. Contango and Backwardation Market Conditions

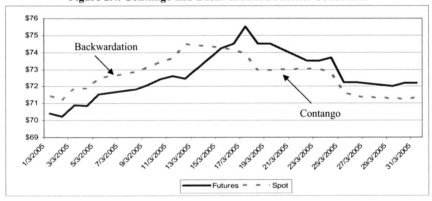

The main purpose of hedging is to eliminate or minimise the risk exposure that is caused by adverse price movements in a "*commodity*". This kind of exposure is called price risk and is due to the uncertainty of price levels in the future. Besides price risk, there is basis-risk, which occurs from changes of the derivatives prices in relation to the corresponding spot prices. When entering derivatives trades, market agents are willing to accept some small level of basis-risk in order to eliminate the price risk. In practice, the magnitude of the basis-risk depends mainly on the degree of correlation between spot and futures prices - the higher the correlation the less is the basis-risk. This becomes more clear by focusing on the definition of basis-risk, which is defined as the variance of the basis (B_t). That is:

$$\sigma^2(B_t) = \sigma^2(S_t - F_t) = \sigma^2(S_t) + \sigma^2(F_t) - 2\,\rho\,\sigma(S_t)\,\sigma(F_t) \qquad (2.1)$$

where, σ^2 = variance, σ = standard deviation, ρ = correlation coefficient between spot and futures prices, which takes values between -1 and +1.

The last equation reveals that if the correlation coefficient between spot and futures prices is low then there will be increasingly more basis-risk. The basis-risk should be significantly less than the price-risk in order for the hedge to be attractive. Since there is never a perfect correlation between spot and futures prices, hedgers always assume some basis-risk in order to reduce their exposure to price-risk[26]. The behaviour of the basis from the time a hedge is placed until the time it is lifted is of considerable importance to the hedger. The very essence of hedging involves an exchange of risk; that is, the exchange of price-risk for basis-risk.

Trading of the spread between a futures/forward contract and its underlying spot commodity is known as basis trading. Futures are usually priced at a premium to the spot market, with eventual convergence on expiration. This means that the longer the time remaining to expiration, the wider is the spread. Every day, traders calculate the "*theoretical basis*" based on models. When the basis trades outside the calculated "*theoretical*" area, a trading opportunity exists for arbitrage or spread trading. This type of analysis is useful for arbitrage and hedge management because it is in general preferable to sell futures contracts when they are "*rich to cash*" (market in contango) and buy futures contracts when they are "*cheap to cash*" (market in backwardation). Trading of the basis is done as follows: If the premium is too high (basis is widening) the trader sells the basis, by going short on spot and long on futures, and if the premium is too low (basis in narrowing) he buys the basis, by going long on spot and short on futures. Basis spreads are more frequently traded intraday rather than daily, because most trading occurs on a very short-term horizon. To see how basis trades work, consider the following example.

Example of Basis Trading

Table 2.4. Example of a Basis Trade

	Current Month	One-Month Out	Two-Months Out
Spot	$53	$55 (e)	$57 (e)
Futures	$57	$58	$59
Basis	-$4	-$3	-$2

Note: (e) stands for expected (forecasted) prices.

Assume that crude oil currently trades at $53 and it is forecasted that in one month and in two months it will trade at $55 and $57, respectively, as shown in the second row of Table 2.4. A crude oil futures contract is priced for the current month at $57 and for one-month and two-months out at $58 and $59, respectively, as shown in the third row of the same table. The basis (= spot price – futures price) for the current month, one-month out and two-months out is -$4 (= $53 – $57), -$3 (= $55 – $58), and -$2 (= $57 – $59), respectively, shown in the last row of the table. As the basis is narrowing, a trader could exercise a buy basis trade by buying crude oil at $53 and simultaneously selling a futures contract at $57, yielding a profit of $4, as the futures price is trading at a premium (overvalued). Moreover, the trader could also buy crude oil at $55 and sell a one-month out futures contract at $58, yielding a profit of $3, and/or buy crude oil at $57 and sell a two-months out futures contract at $59, yielding a profit of $2.

---

[26] Hull (2005) argues that hedging with futures and forward contracts works less than perfectly in practice for the following reasons: (i) the hedger may be uncertain as to the exact date when the asset will be bought or sold; (ii) the hedge may require the contract to be closed out well before its expiration date; and (iii) the asset whose price is to be hedged may not be exactly the same as the asset underlying the contract.

2.3.2.4. Advanced Hedging Strategies with Futures/Forward Contracts
2.3.2.4.1. Hedge Ratio Determination

As observed in the above examples, hedging of a spot position is performed through holding an equal but opposite position in the derivatives market, in order to "*neutralise*" the impact of adverse price level changes. Throughout the financial literature there is a plethora of research studies focusing on the hedging effectiveness of derivatives markets by estimating hedging ratios (see for example, Lindahl, 1992; Geppert, 1995; and Kavussanos and Visvikis, 2005, amongst others). The hedge ratio, h, is defined as the number of derivatives contracts that an agent must buy or sell for each unit of the spot position on which there is price risk.

Researchers and practitioners have concentrated on three hedging strategies: the traditional "*one-to-one*" (naïve) hedge; the beta hedge; and the conventional minimum variance hedge. The traditional naïve strategy involves hedgers adopting a derivatives position equal in magnitude but opposite in sign to the spot position, i.e. $h = -1$. Thus, an investor who is long in the spot market should sell one unit of a futures/forward contract today and buy the derivatives contract back when he sells the spot. Implicit in such a strategy is the view that derivatives and spot prices move closely together. Indeed, if proportionate price changes in one market exactly match those in the other market, then price risk is eliminated; that is, the hedge is perfect.

The beta hedge strategy is very similar, but recognises that the spot portfolio to be hedged may not match the portfolio underlying the derivatives contract. With the beta hedge strategy, h is calculated as the negative of the beta of the spot portfolio. Thus, beta is the coefficient of the independent variable in a regression of market returns on spot portfolio returns. For example, if the spot portfolio beta is 1.5, the hedge ratio will be -1.5, since the spot portfolio is expected to move by 1.5 times the movement in the derivatives contract. Where the spot portfolio is that which underlies the derivatives contract, the traditional strategy and the beta strategy yield the same value for h. In practice, price changes in the two markets do not move exactly together and, therefore, the traditional or beta hedge will not minimise risk.

The portfolio explanation of hedging, first presented by Johnson (1960), Stein (1961) and Ederington (1979) apply the Markowitz foundations of portfolio theory to show that the optimal hedge ratio strategy that minimises the risk of the spot position is given by the ratio of the covariance between spot and derivatives price changes over the variance of the derivatives price changes. The model of hedging ratios, developed by Johnson (1960) and Ederington (1979) assumes that hedger's interests are in minimising risk, and the covariance between spot and derivatives price changes as well as the variance of spot and derivatives price changes are known with certainty or are well-specified ex ante.

2.3.2.4.2. Calculation of the Optimal Hedge Ratio and Hedging Effectiveness
Johnson (1960) and Ederington (1979) assumed that market agents with a position in the physical market take a position in a futures/forward contract in order to hedge their risks. In particular, consider an investor who has a fixed long position of one unit in the spot market and a short position of $-h$ units in the derivatives market. The return of this portfolio of spot and futures positions, ΔP_t, between t-1 and t, can be written as:

$$\Delta P_t = \Delta S_t - h\,\Delta F_t \qquad\qquad (2.2)$$

where, $\Delta S_t = S_t - S_{t-1}$ is the logarithmic change in the spot position between periods t-1 and t; $\Delta F_t = F_t - F_{t-1}$ is the logarithmic change in the derivatives position between t-1 and t, and h is the hedge ratio (the proportion of the portfolio held in derivatives contracts)[27]. The variance of the returns of the hedged portfolio of Equation (2.2) is:

$$\mathrm{Var}(\Delta P_t) = \mathrm{Var}(\Delta S_t) + h^2 \mathrm{Var}(\Delta F_t) - 2h\mathrm{Cov}(\Delta S_t, \Delta F_t) \qquad (2.3)$$

where, $\mathrm{Var}(\Delta S_t) \equiv \sigma_S$, $\mathrm{Var}(\Delta F_t) \equiv \sigma_F$ and $\mathrm{Cov}(\Delta S_t, \Delta F_t)$ are, respectively, the unconditional variances and covariance of the spot and derivatives price changes[28]. The hedger must choose the value of h that minimises the variance of his hedged portfolio returns. That is, he wishes to $\min_h [\mathrm{Var}(\Delta P_t)]$. Taking the partial derivative of Equation (2.3) with respect to h, setting it equal to zero and solving for h, yields the conventional Minimum Variance Hedge Ratio (MVHR), h^*, as follows:

$$h^* = \frac{Cov(\Delta S_t, \Delta F_t)}{Var(\Delta F_t)} = \rho_{SF}\frac{\sigma_S}{\sigma_F} \qquad (2.4)$$

where, ρ_{SF} is the correlation coefficient between ΔS_t and ΔF_t, σ_S is the standard deviation of ΔS_t and σ_F is the standard deviation of ΔF_t[29]. As can be observed, $h^* = 1$ when $\rho_{SF} = 1$ and $\sigma_S = \sigma_F$. That is, the naïve hedge ratio is appropriate for hedging when there is perfect positive correlation between changes in the spot and futures prices, and at the same time the variation in futures prices is exactly equal to that in the spot market. As this is rarely the case in the practice, $h^* \neq 1$.

The MVHR takes into account the imperfect correlation between spot and futures markets and identifies the hedge ratio which minimises risk (as measured by the variance). Ederington (1979) argues that a portfolio approach to hedging is superior to both the traditional one-to-one risk minimising and Working's (1953) profit-maximising interpretations. However, Benninga et al. (1984) argue that unless there is an unbiased derivatives market, where the derivatives price is equal to the expected spot price, the conventional MVHR is not necessarily the optimal hedging strategy.

The MVHR may be estimated empirically as the slope coefficient, h^*, in the following regression:

$$\Delta S_t = h_0 + h^*\Delta F_t + \varepsilon_t \; ; \; \varepsilon_t \sim \mathrm{iid}(0, \sigma^2) \qquad (2.5)$$

---

[27] Note that, the proportion of the portfolio held in the spot commodity equals 1 by assumption.

[28] The variance of a variable has been defined in section 1.2 of Chapter 1. The covariance between variables, ΔS_t and ΔF_t with mean values $\overline{\Delta S}$ and $\overline{\Delta F}$, respectively, is defined as: $\mathrm{Cov}(\Delta S_t, \Delta F_t) \equiv$

$$\sigma_{SF} = \frac{\sum_{t=1}^{T}(\Delta S_t - \overline{\Delta S})(\Delta F_t - \overline{\Delta F})}{T-1}, \text{ calculated from a sample of data } T.$$

[29] The correlation coefficient between the variables ΔS_t and ΔF_t can be calculated as:

$$\rho_{SF} = \frac{\sigma_{SF}}{\sigma_S \sigma_F} = \frac{T\sum \Delta S_t \Delta F_t - \sum \Delta S_t \sum \Delta F_t}{\sqrt{\left[T\sum \Delta S_t^2 - \left(\sum \Delta S_t\right)^2\right]\left[T\sum \Delta F_t^2 - \left(\sum \Delta F_t\right)^2\right]}}.$$

where, ΔS_t and ΔF_t are changes in logarithmic spot and FFA prices, respectively, ε_t is a white noise independently and identically distributed with mean 0 and variance σ^2, h_0 and h^* are the regression parameters. The degree of variance reduction in the hedged portfolio achieved through hedging is given by the coefficient of determination (R^2) of the Ordinary Least Squares (OLS) regression Equation (2.5), since it represents the proportion of risk in the spot market that is eliminated through hedging; the higher the R^2 the greater is the hedging effectiveness of the minimum variance hedge.

It has also been argued in the literature (see Kroner and Sultan, 1993; and Kavussanos and Visvikis, 2005) that the variances in the spot and futures/forward markets and the covariance used to calculate the MVHR may not be constant over time. In this case, h^* must be time-varying and hedging strategies should allow for dynamic adjustments of the portfolio of spot and futures positions, as market conditions change. These issues are explored further in Chapter 3 of this book.

2.3.2.5. Pricing Futures/Forward Contracts
An important question when dealing with derivatives contracts is their correct pricing. It is important for both the market-maker[30], but also for the rest of the market participants to know the *"fair value"* of a derivatives product. Investors who are able to identify mispriced derivatives products can trade on this information, buying the undervalued ones and selling those which are overvalued. Arbitrage arguments may be used to derive the fair value of derivatives, which have investment assets as the underlying commodity. Investment assets include bonds, stocks, gold, etc. Moreover, sufficient number of investors holding an asset, which can be held for both investment and consumption purposes, such as gold[31], must be held for investment rather than for consumption purposes, for these arbitrage arguments to exist. Derivatives on commodities held for consumption purposes are not priced as precisely, as we see later on in this chapter. Before entering the subject of pricing it is useful to provide some definitions.

2.3.2.5.1. Short Selling
The concept of *"short selling"* is useful when undertaking arbitrage strategies, which involve futures and forward contracts. It refers to the sale of assets that the investor does not currently hold, but borrows them from another investor through his broker and sells them, with the obligation to purchase them back later, and return them to their owner. If the price of the asset declines, there is a profit, if it increases there is a loss. The broker is borrowing the assets from another client, who is willing to lend them and receive interest in return. The investor can be called at anytime the broker runs short of the asset in his inventory to close his position, irrespective of the prevailing market prices. If any income is generated by the asset during the period, it has to be returned to the owner of the asset through the broker.

To see how short selling works consider the following example, adapted from Hull (2005): Suppose an investor enters a short selling transaction of 100 stocks of Microsoft at $50 in March and closes the position in July, when the stock is trading at $47. Microsoft has paid $0.5/stock in dividends during June. The resulting cash-flow for the investor is: Income from the sale of stocks $5,000 = (100 x $50) minus the

---

[30] A market-maker maintains firm bid and offer prices in a given security, by standing ready to buy or sell lots at publicly quoted prices.
[31] Other examples of commodities held for consumption purposes include oil, cattle, sugar, etc.

dividends $50 (= 100 x $0.5) returned to the broker, minus the cost of purchase $4,700 (= 100 x $47), equals $250 profit.

2.3.2.5.2. The Time Value of Money
Another important concept is that of the time value of money; that is, the same sum of money received at different points in time has different value. Let r denote the interest rate that can be earned on an investment, t the number of years of the investment and m the frequency of compounding/discounting during the year.

Compounding the future value of a sum PV is calculated under the following three situations:
- **Simple Interest:** Future Value = PV $(1 + t \times r)$
    e.g.: €100 invested for 2 years with 10% annual interest will increase to:
        Future Value = €100 $(1 + 2 \times 0.1)$ = €120
- **Discretely compounded interest:** Future value = PV $(1 + r/m)^{m\,t}$
    e.g.1: with annual compounded interest:
        Future Value = €100 $(1 + 0.1/1)^{1 \times 2}$ = €121
    e.g.2: with monthly compounded interest:
        Future Value = €100 $(1 + 0.1/12)^{12 \times 2}$ = €122.04
- **Continuously compounded interest:** Future Value = PV $e^{r\,t}$, where e= 2.7182
    e.g.: €100 invested for 2 years with 10% continuously compounded interest will increase to:
        Future Value = €100 $e^{0.1 \times 2}$ = €122.14

As can be observed, the compound amount is higher when interest is compounded compared to simple interest payments. Moreover, the compound amount is higher the higher is the frequency of compounding (m) during the year.

Conversion of compounded rates from one frequency to another
Suppose that r_c is a rate of interest with continuous compounding and r_m is the equivalent rate with compounding m times per annum. From the above we have:
$$PV\, e^{r_c\,t} = PV\, (1 + r_m/m)^{m\,t} \Leftrightarrow e^{r_c} = (1 + r_m/m)^m$$
$$\Leftrightarrow r_c = m \times \ln(1 + r_m/m)$$
$$\Leftrightarrow r_m = m \times (e^{r_c/m} - 1)$$
These relationships can be used to convert a rate where the compounding frequency is m times per annum to a continuously compounded rate, and visa versa.

e.g.: Suppose that a lender quotes a continuously compounded lending rate of interest of r_c = 0.06 per annum, with interest paid quarterly. With m = 4 and r_c = 0.06, the equivalent rate with quarterly compounding is calculated as:
r_m = 4 x $(e^{0.06/4} - 1)$ = 0.0605 or 6.05% per annum.

Discounting
The present value of a sum to be received in the future can be obtained through discounting. Consider a sum of money FV, to be received t years in the future:
- **Discrete period discounting:** Present Value = FV $/ (1 + r/m)^{m\,t}$
    e.g.1: The present value of €100, received in 2 years, with quarterly discounting, where r = 10% per annum, is:
        Present Value = €100 $/ (1 + 0.1/4)^{4 \times 2}$ = €82.07
    e.g.2: with monthly discounting:
        Present Value = €100 $/ (1 + 0.1/12)^{12 \times 2}$ = €81.94

- **Continuous discounting:** Present Value $= FV\, e^{-r \times t} \equiv FV / e^{rt}$

   e.g.: The present value of €100, received in 2 years, with continuous discounting, where $r = 10\%$ per annum, is:

   Present Value $=$ €100 $e^{-(0.1 \times 2)} =$ €100 x 0.8187 = €81.87

As can be seen, the higher is the frequency of discounting the smaller is the present value of the future sum to be received today. The above formulas, which are used for the calculation of future values and present values of sums of money, will be used throughout this book.

2.3.2.5.3. The Cost-of-Carry Model

Let us turn next to the issue of pricing of futures/forward contracts. The following assumptions are made in order to simplify the analysis, with the results being qualitatively the same when these assumptions are modified. It is assumed that: (i) there are no transaction costs; (ii) the same tax rate applies to all participants in the market; (iii) there is no bid-ask spread; (iv) borrowers and lenders use the same risk-free interest rate; (v) markets are perfect, where all arbitrage opportunities are eliminated instantly; (vi) there are no restrictions on short selling; (vii) there is infinite divisibility of the assets. It has been shown by Cox et al. (1985) that futures and forward prices are identical under the assumption that interest rates are constant. Also, it must be noted that the daily settlement of futures (mark-to-market) does not have an effect on their relationship with forwards.

The following notation is utilised: T is the time to maturity of the contract, in years (e.g. three months $= 0.25$ years); S is the spot price of the underlying asset; F is the futures/Forward price; r is the annual risk-free interest rate, with continuous compounding, which expires on the delivery date (e.g. Treasury-Bill rate, LIBOR rate, etc.); and C is the cost-of-carry for the possession of the underlying asset over the maturity of the futures/forward contract.

The cost-of-carry model relates the futures/forward price (F) to the spot price (S) of the underlying asset. To understand the arguments behind the model, consider an investor who needs to possess a commodity in a future time period T, say, three months from now whose spot price today is S. He is faced with two alternatives: (i) borrow the required amount for three months at interest rate r and buy the commodity at the spot price (S) prevailing today, store it and have it available in three months time when needed; (ii) alternatively, buy a futures contract on the commodity, which promises to deliver this commodity in three months time, at a price F, agreed today. These alternative ways of obtaining the required commodity in three months time are equivalent for the investor, so they should cost the same.

Consider the alternative of obtaining the commodity through the spot market, in order to have it available in the future. The investor borrows at interest rate r, buys the commodity at the prevailing price S in the spot market, and stores it to have it available in three months. Thus, during the period he incurs interest, storage and insurance costs. For certain assets it is possible to receive income, such as dividends or interest payments during the period. Ignoring this for the moment, and denoting these costs to carry the commodity forward in time by C, this alternative costs him $S+C$; that is, the overall cost equals the sum of buying the commodity spot (S) and the financing and other costs (C). This way of obtaining the commodity must be equivalent in value to that of obtaining it through the futures/forward market. That is,

$F = S + C$. Assuming, for simplicity, that the only costs incurred are financial costs, this cost-of-carry model becomes

$$F = S + C = S (1 + r)^T = S e^{rT} \qquad (2.6)$$

Suppose now that market prices for futures/forwards are different from the theoretical one of $S (1 + r)^T$. Then arbitrage opportunities exist and risk-free profits may be made.

- More specifically, if $F > S (1 + r)^T$, then an investor could sell the expensive forward contract at F and borrow at r for a time period T, to buy the spot commodity at price S, creating thus a cash and carry arbitrage strategy. At the initiation of the trading position, the cash-flow needed is $+S -S = 0$. At the expiration of the forward contract, all obligations must be satisfied. Therefore, the investor delivers (sell) the underlying asset, and covers his debt $S (1 + r)^T$. Since he receives $F > S (1 + r)^T$, he pockets the difference $F - S (1 + r)^T > 0$, thus making a risk-free profit. If these arbitrage opportunities appear, in efficient markets, market agents will discover them and act in a similar manner to obtain the risk-free profits. Thus, the collective selling of forward contracts and the simultaneous purchasing of the underlying commodity will decrease forward prices and increase spot prices. This process continuous until $F=S(1+r)^T$, in which case the cash and carry arbitrage opportunities cease to exist and the forward contract trades at its fair value.
- Consider next the case when $F < S (1 + r)^T$; that is, the situation under which the forward price is below its fair value. In this case, an investor could buy the cheap forward contract at price F, short sell the spot commodity at S and invest the proceeds at rate r for T years, in what is known as inverse cash and carry arbitrage strategy. At the expiration of the forward contract, he has $S(1+r)^T$ in his bank account from the short sale, he pays F and takes delivery of the commodity under the terms of the forward contract and uses the commodity delivered to close his short position. Since $F < S(1 + r)^T$ he pockets the difference of $F - S (1 + r)^T > 0$, thus making a risk-free profit. The collective action of the arbitrageurs, to buy forward contracts and simultaneously sell the spot, increases F and reduces S until $F = S(1 + r)^T$; that is, until the forward contract trades at its fair value, $S(1 + r)^T$.
- Finally, when $F = S(1+r)^T$ no arbitrage opportunities exist and the forward contract trades at its fair value.

The following numerical examples illustrate the arbitrage strategies outlined above.

Example 1 – Contango Market: Derivatives Price Higher than the Spot Price
Suppose that gold in the spot market is traded at $456, a forward contract for gold for delivery in six months is traded as $467, the annual six-month risk-free interest rate is 4%. Initially, we consider whether the fair value of the six-month forward contract equals its price. According to the cost-of-carry model, its fair value is: $Se^{rt}=\$456e^{0.04 \times 0.5} = \$465.21$. Since there is a price discrepancy between the theoretical price ($465.21) and the actual forward price ($467), there are cash and carry arbitrage opportunities in the gold market. An investor can take advantage of these opportunities, by borrowing $456, at interest rate $r = 4\%$ for six months and financing in this way the purchasing of gold in the spot market today. At the same time he sells the forward contract in the derivatives market, agreeing to deliver gold in six months for $467. Six months later, at the expiration of the forward contract, the investor delivers the gold he purchased six months earlier in the spot market to the purchaser

of the forward contract and receives \$467. At the same time, he repays his loan which has grown by then to \$465.21 (= \$456 $e^{0.04 \times 0.5}$). The difference of \$1.79 (= \$467 − \$465.21) between his cash inflow from the derivatives position and the cash outflow from the spot position, consists of his risk-free profit. The above strategy, with the associated actions and cash-flows, is summarized in Table 2.5.

Table 2.5. Arbitrage Strategy in a Contango Market

Today:	
Borrow \$456 to buy gold in the spot market	−\$456.00
Sell a forward for delivery in six months at \$467	\$0.00
In 6 Months:	
Delivery of the gold	\$467.00
Repayment of loan	−\$465.21
Total Outcome of position	**\$1.79**

The possibility of obtaining risk-free profits by exploiting these arbitrage opportunities results in increased supply in the forward market, which leads to lower forward prices, *ceteris paribus*. Also demand in the spot market increases, leading to higher gold prices. These forces lead markets to equilibrium, the arbitrage opportunities disappear, and the six-months forward contracts for gold trade at their fair value; that is, at $S\,e^{r\,T} = \$465.21$.

Example 2 – Normal Backwardation: Derivatives Price Lower than the Spot Price

Consider the situation in the previous example, under which the six-months forward contract for gold is traded as \$450. In this case the forward price is lower than its fair value of \$465.21. A reverse cash and carry arbitrage strategy, to exploit this situation, is presented in Table 2.6. Thus, today the investor buys the six-months forward contract, agreeing to accept delivery of gold at \$450, which he has to pay upon delivery, in six-months time. Simultaneously, he is short selling gold in the spot market, at \$456 and invests the proceeds for six months at the annual interest rate of 4%. In six months time \$456 will grow to \$465.21 (= \$456 $e^{0.04 \times 0.5}$), which is used to pay \$450 for the delivery of gold. The remaining \$15.21 (= \$465.21 − \$450) consists of his risk-free profit, obtained through this reverse cash and carry arbitrage strategy. Once more the collective action of arbitrageurs will eliminate these opportunities and drive futures contracts to trade at their "*fair*" value.

Table 2.6. Arbitrage Strategy in a Normal Backwardation Market

Today:	
Proceeds of \$456 from the short sale of gold in the spot market	−\$456.00
Forward contract for the purchase of gold in six months	\$0.00
In 6 Months:	
Purchase of gold through the forward contract	−\$450.00
Proceeds from the sale of gold + Interest	\$465.21
Total Outcome of position	**\$15.21**

2.3.2.4.4. Pricing of Futures/Forward Contracts for Different Underlying "*Commodities*"/"*Assets*"

The pricing formula of futures/forward contracts varies according to the properties of the underlying asset. This is important to recognize as the identification of arbitrage opportunities by investors, for different asset classes, is based on knowledge of fair value pricing of futures/forward contracts. Consider a number of asset classes next.

Case 1 – Forward Price of Asset with No Income
Assets in this category include commodities, such as gold and silver, stocks with no dividends, bonds with no coupon payments (i.e. discount bonds). As shown earlier, for there to be no arbitrage opportunities, the market value of a forward contract on such assets must be equal to its fair value, which is:

$$F = S e^{rT} \qquad (2.7)$$

As can be observed, the forward price (*F*) is proportional to the spot price (*S*), the interest rate (*r*), and the time to maturity (*T*) of the contract. Increases in these variables lead to higher forward prices, *ceteris paribus*, and visa versa.

Case 2 – Forward Price of Asset with Income
Examples of assets in this category include stocks paying known dividends, coupon-bearing bonds, vessels fixed with a charterparty. As explained earlier, in the cost-of-carry model $F = S + C$, where *C* represents the cost of carrying the commodity forward in time. These costs are added to the spot price of the commodity to obtain the fair value of the forward contract and when the commodity/asset generates income, this must be subtracted in a relationship of the form $F = S + C - I$, where *I* denotes the present value of the expected income during the life of the forward contract. As a consequence, for there to be no arbitrage opportunities, the relationship between the forward price, *F*, and the spot price, *S*, for an income (*I*) generating asset becomes:

$$F = S e^{rT} - I e^{rT} = (S - I) e^{rT} \qquad (2.8)$$

The forward price (*F*) is proportional to the spot price (*S*), the interest rate (*r*) and the time to maturity (*T*), and inversely proportional to the present value of the income of the asset (*I*).

Example:
To see how arbitrage opportunities are eliminated if Equation (2.8) does not hold, consider an example, of a six-months forward contract on stock, whose spot price is S= €200, paying dividends of €0.80 in two and four months after the initiation of the contract. Annual risk-free rates stand at r = 8%. In this case, the theoretical – fair – value of the forward contract is:

$$F = (S - I) e^{rT} = [€200 - (€0.8\ e^{-0.08 \times 2/12} + €0.8\ e^{-0.08 \times 4/12})]\ e^{0.08 \times 6/12} = €206.53$$

If the actual forward price in the market is different, then arbitrage opportunities arise upon which market agents will act and will lead forward prices to their fair value of €206.53. Table 2.7 summarises the cash and carry and the reverse cash and carry arbitrage strategies that can be followed to obtain risk-free profits, when actual forward prices are larger and smaller, respectively than the fair price of €206.53.

- Consider the second column of the table showing an expensive forward market, of F = €210. In this case, an arbitrageur can purchase the asset in the spot market at S = €200, by borrowing this amount for six months at interest rate r = 8% and short (sell) the forward contract for delivery of one unit of the asset at F = €210 in T = 6/12 = 0.5 years from today. In six months time, at the expiry of the forward contract, the stock is delivered to the purchaser of the contract, receiving €210. During the six months, the stock has paid dividends of €0.80 in two months and €0.80 in four months, whose present value is €1.57 (= €0.8 $e^{-0.08 \times 2/12}$ + €0.8 $e^{-0.08 \times 4/12}$). The value of this amount in six months time is €1.63 (= €1.57 $e^{0.08 \times 6/12}$). At the end of the six months €208.2(=€200 $e^{0.08 \times 0.5}$) is paid to the bank for the repayment of the loan. The first two amounts are cash inflows while the last one is an outflow. On balance, they provide a risk-free profit of €3.43 to the investor.

- The final column of the table shows a case where the actual forward price in the market is less than its fair value of €206.53. The arbitrage opportunities can be exploited in this case by shorting the asset, investing the proceeds for six months at interest rate 8%, and taking a long position in the forward contract for the delivery of the stock at €190. Six months later, the amount in the bank from the short sale of the stock grows to €208.2 (= €200 $e^{0.08 \times 1/2}$), the stock is purchased for €190 under the terms of the forward contract and is returned to its owner as well as the future value (€1.63) of dividend payments of the stock. The net cash-flow from these transactions is €16.57 (= €208.2 − €190 − €1.63). As a consequence, when forward prices are above or below their fair value of €206.53 arbitrage opportunities arise, which bring the price back to this level. The only sustainable price is at €206.53.

Table 2.7. Forward Price of Asset with Income − Arbitrage Strategies

	Expensive Forward Market F = €210	Cheap Forward Market F = €190
Action in t = 0	Borrow €200 and purchase of 1 stock Short Forward contract for sale of 1 stock	Short sale of 1 stock for €200 and investment at 8% in the bank Long Forward contract for purchase of 1 stock for €190
Result in t = 6 months	Repayment of loan–amount: €208.2 (= €200$e^{0.08 \times 6/12}$) Sale of 1 stock and receipt of €210 Income from dividends: €1.63 (= $I e^{rt}$ = $(0.8e^{-0.08 \times 2/12} + 0.8e^{-0.08 \times 4/12})$ x $e^{0.08 \times 6/12}$)	Bank account grown to: €208.2 (= €200 $e^{0.08 \times 6/12}$) Purchase stock under forward at €190 Dividend payment to owner due to short sale −€1.63
Profit	€210 + €1.63 − €208.2 = **€3.43**	€208.2 − €190 − €1.63 = **€16.57**

Case 3 − Forward Price of Assets with Known Yield and Stock Indices
With certain assets, their yield is known; that is, their income expressed as a percentage of the price of the asset, rather than as cash income of a certain amount, is known. Assets in this category include stock indices. For there to be no arbitrage opportunities, the relationship between the forward price, and the spot price, for an asset generating income, which is expressed as a percentage of the price of the underlying asset (q), must be:

$$F = S\, e^{(r-q)\,T} \tag{2.9}$$

The forward price (F) is positively related to the spot price (S), the interest rate (r), and the time to maturity (T), and negatively related to the average yield per annum of the asset during the life of the forward contract (q).

Example 1: Forward price of a share with known yield
Table 2.8 presents an example which shows the strategies that can be followed to obtain risk-free profits when arbitrage opportunities arise; that is, when the forward

contract is mispriced. Consider a six-months forward contract on a stock, whose spot price is $S = \$50$ and its dividend yield is $q = 5\%$ per annum. Annual interest rates in the market are $r = 12\%$. According to Equation (2.9), the fair value of the forward contract is: $F = S\,e^{(r-q)\,T} = \$50\,e^{(0.12-0.05)\,\times\,0.5} = \$51.78$.

- If the actual forward price in the market is greater than $51.78, as shown in the second column of Table 2.8, an arbitrageur can borrow to buy the asset in the spot market for $50 and short a forward contract for delivery of the asset at $F=\$53$ in six months from today. In six months, a profit of $F - S\,e^{(r-q)\,T}=\$1.22$ is realised. This is achieved by selling the asset for $53, under the terms of the forward contract, and using the proceeds to repay the loan. A dividend income is also received during the six months period.

- If the actual forward price in the market is less than $51.78, as shown in the last column of Table 2.8, an arbitrageur can short sell the asset for $50, invest the proceeds in a bank account at 12%, and take a long position in the forward contract to take delivery of the asset in six months at $F = \$49$. In this case, after six months, a profit of $S\,e^{(r-q)\,T} - F = €2.78$ is realised. This is achieved by purchasing the stock under the forward contract for $49, returning the future value of the six-month dividend yield of $1.33 $\{=[\$50\text{x}0.05\text{x}(6/12)]e^{0.12\text{x}(6/12)}\}$ and the stock to its owner and financing all this through the compound amount $53.09 (= \$50\,e^{0.12\,\times\,0.5}$) of the receipts from the short sale of the stock.

Table 2.8. Forward Price of Asset with Known Yield – Arbitrage Strategies

	Expensive Forward Market $F = \$53$		Cheap Forward Market $F = \$49$
Action in $t = 0$	Borrow $50 for the purchase of 1 stock at $r = 12\%$		Short sale of 1 stock for $50 and investment of proceeds in bank account
	Short Forward contract for sale of 1 stock at $F = \$53$		Long Forward contract for purchase of 1 stock at $F = \$49$
Result in $t = 6$ months	Repayment of loan–amount: $53.09 ($= \$50\,e^{0.12\,\times\,6/12}$)		Receipts of $51.78 ($= \$50\,e^{(0.12-0.05)\,\times\,6/12}$): From bank investment $1.33 $\{=[\$50 \times 0.05 \times (6/12)]\,e^{0.12\,\times\,(6/12)}\}$ and return of dividends due to short sale $53.09 ($= \$50\,e^{0.12\,\times\,6/12}$)
	Future value of six-month income from dividends $1.33 $\{=[\$50 \times 0.05 \times (6/12)]\,e^{0.12\,\times\,(6/12)}\}$		
	Under forward contract, sale of 1 stock for $53		Under forward contract, purchase stock for $49
Profit	$\$53 - \$50e^{(0.12-0.05)\,\times\,0.5}$ $= \$53 - \$51.78 = \mathbf{\$1.22}$		$\$50e^{(0.12-0.05)\,\times\,0.5} - \$49$ $= \$51.78 - 49 = \mathbf{\$2.78}$

Example 2: Forward price of stock indices

Stock indices can be viewed as portfolios of stocks. The weighting of each stock in the index is a function of the capitalization of the company. Indices may be treated as assets that provide income (the dividends) as a percentage of their price, q. The fair value then a forward/futures contract is written on a stock index with known yield is given by Equation (2.9). As an example, consider a three-month futures contract on a stock index, whose spot price is $S = 2600$, its dividend yield is $q = 3\%$, while annual interest rates are $r = 5\%$. The fair value of a three-month forward contract on the stock index is:

$$F = S\,e^{(r-q)\,T} = 2600\,e^{(0.05-0.03)\,\times\,(3/12)} = 2600\,e^{0.02\,\times\,0.25} = 2613$$

Under similar reasoning to earlier cases, if market prices of forward contracts deviate from their fair value, arbitrageurs, by using similar strategies to those presented above, will force prices back to equilibrium.

Case 4 – Forward Price of Currency Contracts

The fair value of a forward/futures contract with a foreign currency as the underlying commodity reflects the interest parity relationship and is given by Equation (2.10):

$$F = S e^{(r - rf)T} \qquad\qquad (2.10)$$

where, r and r_f denote the domestic and foreign rates of interest, respectively.

As can be observed, the forward price of the contract (F) is proportional to the spot price (S), the domestic interest rate (r), the time to maturity of the contract (T) and inversely proportional to the interest rate of the foreign country (r_f). Comparing this equation to those describing the fair value of forward/futures prices for commodities with known yield and for stock indices, it can be observed that they are equivalent, with the foreign rate of interest (r_f) taking the role of the yield (q) in the relationship. Thus, a currency is like a yield paying asset.

If the price of a forward contract written on a currency is different to that presented in Equation (2.10) then arbitrage opportunities are exploited by market agents, thus forcing prices to the level determined by this equation. To see the arbitrage strategies that may be applied in such a case, consider the following example, which is also summarised in Table 2.9.

Example:

An American company needs to purchase €2,000,000. The exchange rate in the spot market is $S = \$/€\ 1.8$, the annual risk-free interest rate for six months deposits is $r=5\%$, while the Eurozone rates of interest are $r_f = 4\%$. According to Equation (2.10), the fair value of the foreign currency forward contract is:

$$F = S e^{(r - rf)T} = 1.8\ e^{(0.05 - 0.04)\ x\ 6/12} = 1.8\ e^{0.01\ x\ 0.5} = \$/€\ 1.81$$

- If the actual forward price in the market is greater than $\$/€\ 1.81$, as shown in the second column of Table 2.9, an arbitrageur can borrow dollars at $r = 5\%$ to purchase €2,000,000 at the spot rate of $\$/€\ 1.8$, and deposit the money at $r_f=4\%$. This grows to €2,040,403 (= €2,000,000 $e^{0.04\ x\ 0.5}$) in six months time. Simultaneously, he shorts a six-month forward contract for the sale of €2,040,403, at the forward rate of $F = \$/€\ 1.9$. Six months later the dollar loan of $3,691,134 (= $3,600,000 $e^{0.05\ x\ 0.5}$) is repaid from the proceeds of the receipts of $3,876,765 (= €2,040,403 / $\$/€\ 1.9$), which emanate from the agreement of the forward contract to sell the euro at the rate of $\$/€\ 1.9$. Thus, a risk-free profit of $185,631 is realised.
- If the actual forward price in the market is less than $\$/€\ 1.81$, as shown in the last column of Table 2.9, an arbitrageur can borrow €2,000,000 at the foreign exchange rate of $r_f = 4\%$, convert it at the current spot exchange rate of $S=\$/€1.8$, invest the proceeds at the domestic interest rate of $r = 5\%$, and take a long position in the forward contract agreeing to buy €2,040,403 in six months, at the prevailing forward rate of $F = \$/€\ 1.75$. Six months later $3,570,705.2 (= €2,040,403 x $\$/€\ 1.75$) is paid for taking delivery of the

€2,040,403 – which is used to repay the loan – and $3,691,134 is accumulated in the deposit account. Overall, a risk-free profit of $120,428.8 is realised.

Table 2.9. Forward Price of Currency Contracts – Arbitrage Strategies

	Expensive Forward Market $F = \$/\text{€ } 1.9$	Cheap Forward Market $F = \$/\text{€ } 1.75$
Action in $t = 0$	Borrow $3,600,000 at interest rate $r = 5\%$ for six months, buy €2,000,000 at exchange rate $\$/\text{€ } 1.8$ and deposit the money at $r_f = 4\%$	Borrow €2,000,000 at annual interest rate $r_f = 4\%$, convert it to $3,600,000 $(= €2,000,000 \times \$/\text{€ } 1.8)$, and deposit it at $r = 5\%$
	Short six-month forward contract for sale of €2,040,403 at $F = \$/\text{€ } 1.9$	Long forward contract to buy €2,040,403 in six months at $F = \$/\text{€ } 1.75$
Result in $t = 6$ **months**	Repayment of loan–amount: $3,691,134 (= \$3,600,000 \ e^{0.05 \times 6/12})$	Receive from the deposit account $3,691,134 (= \$3,600,000 e^{0.05 \times 6/12})$
	Receive €2,040,403 $(= €2,000,000 \ e^{0.04 \times 6/12})$ from deposit of €2,000,000	Payment of $3,570,705.2 $(= €2,040,403 \times \$/\text{€ } 1.75)$ for taking delivery of €2,040,403 and repayment of loan of €2,040,403
	Under the forward contract deliver euro at $\$/\text{€ } 1.9$: $3,876,765 $(= €2,040,403 \times \$/\text{€ } 1.9)$	
Profit	$3,876,765 – \$3,691,134 = **\$185,631**	$3,691,134 – \$3,570,705.2 = **\$120,428.8**

Case 5 – Forward Price of Commodities that are Held for Investment Purposes

The general form of the cost-of-carry model postulates that the forward price of an asset/commodity is given by the relationship $F = S + C - I$, where S is the spot price of the commodity, C denotes the finance, storage and insurance costs to carry the commodity forward in time, while I denotes the present value of the income generated by the commodity during the lifetime of the forward contract. So far we assumed that the only costs incurred when carrying the commodity forward in time are finance costs. We introduce next storage and insurance costs, as they are important, particularly for tangible commodities. We continue to assume that we are dealing with commodities which are held for investment purposes, such as gold and silver, and also that no income is generated from these commodities. The following equation describes the fair value of a forward contract on such a commodity:

$$F = S\,e^{rT} + U\,e^{rT} = (S + U)\,e^{rT} \tag{2.11}$$

where, U is the present value of the storage costs of the commodity.
In case where storage costs can be expresses as a percentage of the price of the commodity – say u – the equation takes the form:

$$F = S\,e^{(r + u)\,T} \tag{2.12}$$

In case the above relationships do not hold, arbitrage possibilities arise, which arbitrageurs realize and act on, which in turn will bring prices back to equilibrium. These strategies are illustrated through the following example.

Example:
Consider a one-year forward contract on gold, where the spot price of gold is $S=\$455$/ounce and the risk-free interest rate is $r = 6\%$ per annum. Suppose that it costs

$U=$ \$2/ounce per year to store gold, payable at the end of the storage period. In this case, the fair value of the forward contract on gold is:

$$F = (S + U) \, e^{r \, T} = [\$455 + (2e^{-0.06 \times 1})]e^{0.06 \times 1} = (\$455 + \$1.88) \, e^{0.06} = \$485.14$$

- If the actual forward price in the market is greater than \$485.14, as shown in the second column of Table 2.10, an arbitrageur can purchase gold in the spot market at $S =$ \$455/ounce, by borrowing $S + U =$ \$456.88 (= \$455 + \$1.88) at interest rate $r =$ 6%, store it for a year, and short a one year forward contract for the delivery of one ounce of gold to the counterparty at $F =$ \$490. At the end of the year, under the terms of the forward contract, one ounce of gold is delivered, receiving $F =$ \$490, storage costs of \$2 are paid and the loan amount of \$483.14 (= \$455 $e^{0.06}$) is repaid. On balance these cash-flows result in a profit of \$4.86 (= \$490 − \$483.14 − \$2). Furthermore, the collective action of the arbitrageurs will ensure that prices will adjust to satisfy Equatiuon (2.11).
- Consider next the case when the actual forward price in the market is less than its "*fair*" value of \$485.14. As shown in the third column of Table 2.10, an investor that already owns gold can sell one ounce of gold in the spot market at $S =$ \$455, and take a long position in the forward contract to buy one ounce of gold in one year at $F =$ \$475. One year later, the proceeds from the sale, having been invested in an interest bearing account become \$483.14(=\$455$e^{0.06}$), \$475 of which is paid to take delivery of gold under the terms of the forward contract. Thus, at the end of the year, a profit of \$8.14(=\$483.14 − \$475) plus \$2 from savings of storage costs is realised. Relative to the position the investor would have had in gold, he is \$10.14 better off.

Table 2.10. Commodities that are Held for Investment Reasons – Arbitrage Strategies

	Expensive Forward Market $F =$ \$490	Cheap Forward Market $F =$ \$475
Action in $t = 0$	Borrow \$455 at $r =$ 6% for the purchase and storage of 1 ounce of gold for one year	Sale of 1 ounce of gold in the spot market at \$455 Save of storage costs of \$1.88 (= \$2 $e^{-0.06}$)
	Short forward contract for delivery in one year of 1 ounce of gold	Long forward contract for delivery in one year of 1 ounce of gold at \$475
Result in t **=** T **months**	Repayment of loan – amount: \$483.14 (= \$455 $e^{0.06}$)	Cash-flow from short sale \$483.14 (= \$455 $e^{0.06}$)
	Payment of storage costs \$2	Storage costs savings of \$2
	Under forward contract, sale of 1 ounce of gold for \$490	Accept delivery of 1 ounce of gold at \$475
Profit	\$490 − \$483.14 − \$2 = **\$4.86**	\$483.14 − \$475 = **\$8.14** (+\$2 from savings of storage costs)

Case 6 – Forward Price of Commodities that are held for Consumption

Assets in this category include commodities like wheat, corn, crude oil, etc. According to the cost-of-carry model the price of the futures contract should always be greater than the underlying spot price. More specifically, we have seen that $F=S+C−I$, which for instance takes the form $F = (S + U) \, e^{r \, T}$ when only storage and finance costs exist and no income is generated by the commodity. It is observed then that $F > S$. There are instances however, when this is not the case. This situation may arise, not because the cost-of-carry model fails, but because there is a "*convenience yield*" in the market; that is, there are some benefits from holding the underlying asset now rather than waiting for it to be delivered under the terms of the forward contract. As a result, traders are willing to pay a premium in order to hold the physical asset now. For example, for wheat, convenience yields may exist because of supply disruptions due to congestions in ports or due to seasonal factors.

To see why convenience yields arise, consider a flourmill in Greece, which uses wheat as its input in the production process. It anticipates shortages of wheat in the market as port congestions are observed in the major exporting countries of South America during their harvest season. A long forward contract, which constitutes a "*promise*" to receive wheat in the future, is not equivalent to having the wheat in the warehouse. If the input – the wheat – to the production process is in storage, there is no danger of production stopping. Moreover, in this case, shortages in the market can be exploited for speculative purposes. As a consequence, under the circumstances, the flourmill is prepared to pay a premium to have the wheat in the warehouse.

In extreme cases, the market can be so far below the full carry price that futures prices may be below spot prices. This pattern in prices however, does not necessarily imply an opportunity for reverse cash and carry arbitrage (buying the futures contract and short selling the underlying asset). However, when the market has a convenience yield, short-selling the underlying asset is not possible; in this case, no one will lend the underlying asset without a cost, since they derive a benefit from holding it. Organisations hold reserves of commodities for their own consumption purposes (e.g. storage of corn by Kellogg, etc.). As a consequence of the above, $F < (S + U) e^{rT}$ for a consumption commodity. Moreover, if we denote the convenience yield by y then:

$$F e^{yT} = (S + U) e^{rT} \quad \Leftrightarrow \quad F = (S + U) e^{(r-y)T} \tag{2.13}$$

In case storage costs per unit are determined as a constant proportion (u) of the spot price, the above relationship becomes:

$$F = S e^{(r + u - y)T} \tag{2.14}$$

where, y measures the extent to which $F < (S + U) e^{rT}$ or $F < S e^{(r + u - y)T}$.

The lower the expected availability of the commodity the higher is the convenience yield. The opposite occurs when inventories are high, as there is a low possibility then of shortages arising in the market.

The cost-of-carry model is summarised in Equation (2.15):

$$F = S e^{(c - y)T} \tag{2.15}$$

where, c measures storage and insurance costs, the interest paid to finance the asset minus any income earned by the asset, y is the convenience yield, S is the spot price of the commodity, F is the value of the forward contract and T is its time to maturity. For consumption commodities the convenience yield (y) is positive, while it is zero for investment commodities. c takes values as follows:

$c = r$;   for assets with no income;

$c = r - q$;   for assets/stock indices with income expressed as a percentage of their value; that is, assets with known yield (q);

$c = r - r_f$;   for currencies, where r_f is the foreign interest rate, while r is the domestic rate of interest;

$c = r + u$;   for commodities with storage costs (u), which are expressed as a proportion of the price of the commodity.

Case 7 – Forward Price of Non-Storable Commodities

The cost-of-carry model is used to derive the price of forward/futures contracts for "*assets*"/"*commodities*", which are held for investment and consumption purposes. Arbitrage arguments are used to justify the forward price equation $F = S\ e^{(c\ -\ y)T}$, derived in the earlier parts of this chapter. For these arbitrage opportunities to be eliminated, strategies were developed based on the property of the "*assets*"/"*commodities*" examined, that they can be stored and carried forward in time. However, when "*commodities*" are not storable, the arbitrage arguments used to derive the fair value of the "*commodity*" are not valid. In this case, the relationship between spot and forward/futures prices is the following:

$$F_t = E_t(S_{t+i}) + \varepsilon_t \ \ ; \ \ \varepsilon_t \sim \text{iid}(0, \sigma^2) \tag{2.16}$$

where, F_t is the price of the forward contract at time t, with time to maturity i (e.g. $i=1, 2, \ldots$, for 1 month, 2 months maturity, etc.); E_t denotes expectations formed at time period t; S_{t+i} is the spot price of the "*commodity*" at period $t+i$; and ε_t is an independent and identically distributed stochastic error-term with a mean value of zero and variance σ^2.

This last term indicates that in the case of non-storable commodities the relationship between forward/futures and spot prices is not precise. Forward/futures prices at a certain period t of a contract with maturity i, are equal to the expected spot price of the "*commodity*" in period $t+i$ in the future - that is, at the expiry of the forward/futures contract - plus a stochastic error-term, which takes account of all the other factors, apart from expected spot prices, that may affect forward/futures prices of the "*commodity*". Market agents, when they consider the fair value of a forward contract, form expectations about how the spot market will evolve by the time the forward contract expires and set the forward price accordingly. It is the collective view of all participants in the market that determines forward prices then. They base their expectations on information available to them, which is obtained through market reports about factors that affect or will affect the spot market, but also on their own knowledge and analysis of the market. As new information becomes available, expectations about spot prices change and as a consequence forward/futures prices change to reflect this. "*Commodities*" that have this property of non-storability include freight services, hotel accommodation and energy. If a hotel or a vessel is not rented for a certain period, the value of the service for that period "*perishes*" – it cannot be stored and rented in a different time period. This relationship linking spot with futures prices of non-storable commodities is used later on in this book to examine the pricing of futures/forward contracts on freight rates.

2.3.3. Swap Contracts

A swap transaction is the simultaneous buying and selling of a similar underlying asset or obligation of equivalent capital amount, where the exchange of financial arrangements provides both parties to the transaction with more favorable conditions than they would otherwise expect.

The first public swap transaction, between the World Bank and IBM in 1981, was a currency swap. A swap is a single transaction in which the two counterparties agree to exchange or "*swap*" cash-flows. For example, an initial sum in US dollars is exchanged for its pound sterling equivalent and a reverse exchange takes place at the maturity of the swap. In the intervening period there is a regular exchange of payments, say on a monthly, semi-annual or quarterly basis. Credit risk is reduced by netting the flows that are periodically exchanged. The accounting impact is avoided because a contractual agreement to exchange cash-flows is treated as an off-balance-sheet transaction.

Consider the following example of a **currency swap**. A US company has receivables in Euro from a Belgian buyer; so it is looking for a Euro denominated liability to hedge the receivable. On the other hand, a Belgian company exports to the USA and has US$ denominated receivables; it needs a US$ liability to hedge receivables in US$. The two companies can agree the following:
- The US company borrows, say, $100,000 at 11%.
- The Belgian company borrows €80,000 (= $100,000 x €/$ 0.80) at 10%.
- The US company receives euros from its buyer and transfers it to the Belgian company so that it (Belgian) can repay its euro denominated loan.
- The Belgian company receives US$ from its buyer and give it to the US company so that it (US) can repay its US$ denominated loan.

Through this swap agreement both companies lock in the current spot rate for future payments of their obligations.

Another form of swap is the **interest rate swap**. Under the commonest form of an interest rate swap, a series of interest payments are calculated by swapping a fixed interest rate to a notional principal amount with a stream of payments, similarly calculated, but using a floating interest rate. This is a fixed-for-floating interest rate swap. Alternatively, both series of cash-flows to be exchanged could be calculated using floating rates but floating rates that are based upon different underlying indices.

Consider the following example of an interest rate swap. A portfolio manager currently holds $100 million par value of long-term bonds paying an average coupon rate of 6%. The manager believes that interest rates are about to rise. As a result, he enters into a swap agreement with a swap dealer to pay 6% on notional principal of $100 million and receive payment of the six-month LIBOR rate on that amount of notional principal. The participants to the swap do not lend each other money. They agree to exchange a fixed cash-flow (6%) for a variable cash-flow (LIBOR) that depends on the short-term interest rate. The difference between LIBOR and 6% is multiplied by the notional principal to determine the cash-flow exchanged by the parties. In other words, the manager swaps a payment of 6% x $100 million for a payment of LIBOR x $100 million. The manager's net cash-flow from the swap agreement is therefore (LIBOR – 6%) x $100 million.

Commodity swaps also have become increasingly popular over time. The way they work is presented through the following example. Suppose a refinery needs 200,000 barrels of oil per year and wants to secure its price for the next 10 years at its current market price, say, of $40 per barrel. It agrees to pay $8 million each year and in return to receive 200,000 x $40. Through the swap, the oil cost for the refinery is locked in at $40 per barrel. On the other hand, an oil producing company might agree to the opposite exchange. This would have the effect of locking in the price for its oil at $40 per barrel.

Swaps are used by a wide range of commercial banks, investment banks, non-financial operating companies, insurance companies, mortgage companies, investment vehicles and trusts, government agencies and sovereign states for one or more of the following reasons:
- To obtain lower cost of funding,
- To hedge their exposure in the physical market,
- To obtain higher yields in investment assets,
- To create types of investment assets not otherwise obtainable,
- To implement overall asset or liability management strategies,
- To take speculative positions in relation to future movements in interest rates.

Swaps, by exchanging cash-flows, have an amount of credit risk. However, there is no credit risk in respect of the amount of notional principal. Because the cash-flows to be exchanged under a swap on the settlement date are offset, what is paid or received represents the difference between fixed and floating rates. Under a loan, what is due is an absolute amount of interest, representing either a fixed or a floating rate of interest applied to the outstanding principal balance. The periodic cash-flows under a swap will be smaller than the periodic cash-flows due under a comparable loan. As a consequence, the credit risk of the swap is smaller.

2.3.3.1. Pricing of Swap Contracts
The difficulty in pricing a fixed-to-floating interest rate swap is that the future stream of floating interest rate payments, to be made by one counterparty, is unknown at the time the swap is being priced. However, capital markets possess a considerable body of information about the relationship between interest rates across different future periods of time.

2.3.3.1.1. Spot and Forward Yield Curves
In many countries there is a liquid market in interest bearing securities issued by the government. These securities pay interest on a periodic basis, they are issued with a wide range of maturities, where the principal is repaid only at maturity, and at any given point in time, the market values these securities to yield whatever rate of interest is necessary to make the securities trade at their par value.

It is possible to plot a graph of the yields of such securities, which reflect their varying maturities. This graph is known as the **yield curve**; it shows the relationship between future interest rates and time. Figure 2.5, presents the yield curve of Eurobonds from 1 year up to 30 years to maturity. The yield curve is derived by plotting values of the coupon yield across the years to maturity of the bond.

Figure 2.5. EuroBond Yield Curve in September 2005

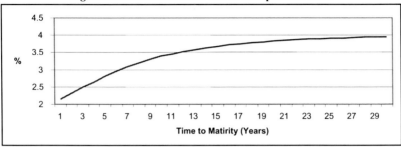

Source: Eurostat

A graph showing the yield of securities displaying the same characteristics as government securities is known as the **par coupon yield curve**. Figure 2.6 presents the par coupon yield curve of US Treasury-Bills. It can be seen that the yield curve is upward slopping (positive), indicating that long-term interest rates are higher than short-term interest rates.

Figure 2.6. The US Treasury-Bill Yield Curve in September 2005

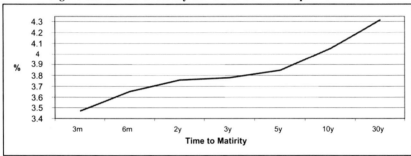

Source: Bloomberg

A different kind of security is the zero-coupon bond which does not pay interest at periodic intervals. Instead, it is issued at a discount from its par (face) value but is redeemed at par. A graph of the Internal Rate of Return (IRR) of zero-coupon bonds over a range of maturities is known as the **zero-coupon yield curve**. Figure 2.7 shows the Euro zero-coupon yield curve from 1 year up to 30 years to maturity. The yield curve is derived by plotting values of the zero-coupon yield across the years to maturity of the bond.

Figure 2.7. Euro Zero-Coupon Yield Curve in September 2005

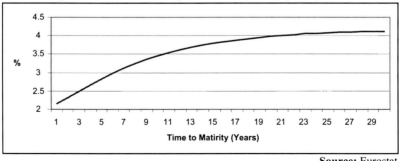

Source: Eurostat

Moreover, forward interest rates are quoted in the market. Consider an investor wishing to deposit an amount of money for six months and then reinvest that deposit, once it has matured, for a further six months. Financial institutions quote a rate today at which the investor can re-invest his deposit in six months time. The six-month forward deposit rate reflects a no-arbitrage relationship between current (spot) interest rates and forward interest rates. For example, if for an interest bearing asset the six-month spot interest rate (S_6) is 0.089 and the one-month spot interest rate (S_1) is 0.060, the forward rate of interest (F_6), that is implied by the two spot rates, for the period of time between the end of the first month and the end of the sixth month, is calculated as follows:

$$F_6 = S_6 \times [t_6 / (t_6 - t_1)] - S_1 \times [t_1 / (t_6 - t_1)] \qquad (2.17)$$
$$= 0.089 \times [6 / (6 - 1)] - 0.060 \times [1 / (6 - 1)]$$
$$= 0.0948$$

where, t_1 denotes period (month) 1 and t_6 denotes period (month) 6. The six-month forward interest rate is the rate of interest which eliminates any arbitrage profit. The investor should be indifferent as to whether he invests for six months and then re-invests for a further six months at the six month forward interest rate, or whether he invests for twelve months at today's twelve-month deposit rate. The **forward yield curve** shows graphically the relationship between forward rates of interest and time to maturity. Figure 2.8 utilizes the figures in Table 2.11 to present the forward yield curve graphically for a hypothetical asset. The forward interest rates are calculated in the last column of Table 2.11, using as inputs the time to maturity and the spot rates of the first and second columns in the table, per Equation (2.17).

Table 2.11. Calculation of the Forward Interest Rates

Maturity (Months)	Spot Rates	Forward Rates
1	0.060	-
2	0.070	0.0800
3	0.075	0.0825
4	0.080	0.0867
5	0.085	0.0913
6	**0.089**	**0.0948**
7	0.092	0.0973
8	0.096	0.1011
9	0.098	0.1028
10	0.100	0.1044

Figure 2.8. Spot and Forward Yield Curves

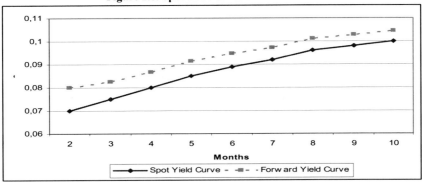

109

2.3.3.1.2. Pricing Interest Rate Swaps

The Net Present Value (NPV) of the aggregate set of cash-flows due under any swap is zero at inception. This becomes clear if we reflect on the fact that the NPV of any fixed rate or floating rate loan must be zero when that loan is approved. If this was not valid, it would be possible to make money by borrowing money. However, a fixed-to-floating interest rate swap is nothing more than the combination of a fixed rate loan and a floating rate loan, without the initial borrowing and subsequent repayment of a principal amount. Since the NPV of both the fixed rate payments and the floating rate payments in this type of swap is zero, the NPV of the swap must also be zero. Since the floating rate payments under the swap can be calculated using Equation (2.18), the fixed rate payments will be of such an amount that when they are deducted from the floating rate payments, and the net cash-flow for each period is discounted at the appropriate rate given by the zero-coupon yield curve, the NPV of the swap will be zero.

To see how the pricing of interest rate swaps works consider the following example. Suppose that it is now time zero and a financial institution receives fixed payments of k dollars at times t and makes floating payments at the same times. The value of the swap (V) to the financial institution is equivalent to the difference between the values of two bonds:

$$V = B_{fix} - B_{fl} \tag{2.18}$$

where, B_{fix} is the value of the fixed-rate bond of the swap; B_{fl} is the value of the floating-rate bond of the swap; and they refer to a nominal principal amount Q of the swap.

Assume that the cash-flows of the swap are discounted at LIBOR rates and that the swap has a value of zero. The zero-coupon yield curve defines the appropriate discount rates to use in Equation (2.19). Thus, the fixed coupon rate bond is valued as:

$$B_{fix} = \sum_{i=1}^{n} k e^{-r_i t_i} + Q e^{-r_n t_n} \tag{2.19}$$

B_{fl} is the value of the floating-rate bond, which after the payment date is always equal to the notional principal, Q. Between payment dates, B_{fl} will equal Q after the next payment date. If the next payment date is denoted as t_1, B_{fl} becomes:

$$B_{fl} = Q e^{r_1 t_1} + k^* e^{-r_1 t_1} \tag{2.20}$$

where, k^* is the floating-rate payment that will be made on the next payment date; that is, at time t_1.

In the situation where the financial institution is paying fixed and receiving floating, B_{fix} and B_{fl} are calculated in the same way, and the value of the swap for the institution becomes now:

$$V = B_{fl} - B_{fix} \tag{2.21}$$

Example:
Suppose a financial institution pays six-month LIBOR and receives 6% per annum (with semiannual compounding) on a swap with a notional principal (Q) of $200 million and the remaining payment dates are in 3 and 9 months. The swap has a remaining life of 9 months. The LIBOR rates with continuous compounding for three-months and nine-months maturities are 10% and 11%, respectively. The six-month LIBOR rate at the last payment date is 10.2% (with semiannual compounding). If $k=\$8$ million and $k^* = 10.2$ million, we have:

$$B_{fix} = 8\ e^{-0.1 \times (3/12)} + 208\ e^{-0.11 \times (9/12)} = 7.802 + 191.529 = \$199.33 \text{ million}$$

$$B_{fl} = 200\ e^{-0.1 \times (3/12)} + 10.2\ e^{-0.1 \times (3/12)} = 195.062 + 9.948 = \$205.01 \text{ million}$$

Thus, the value of the swap is:

$$V = \$199.33 \text{ million} - \$205.01 \text{ million} = -\$5.68 \text{ million}$$

If the financial institution had been in the opposite position, of paying fixed and receiving floating, the value of the swap would be +$5.68 million.

2.3.3.1.3. Pricing Currency Swaps
A currency swap, in the absence of default risk, can be decomposed into a position in two bonds, in a similar way to an interest rate swap. Suppose that a company is long a sterling bond that pays interest at 9% per annum and short a dollar bond that pays interest at 7% per annum. The value of the swap (V) to the party paying US$ interest rates is:

$$V = S\ B_F - B_D \tag{2.22}$$

Where, S is the spot exchange rate, expressed as number of units of domestic currency per unit of foreign currency, B_F is the value of the foreign-denominated bond of the swap, measured in foreign currency, and B_D is the value of the domestic, US$ bond, of the swap. Therefore, the value of the swap can be determined from the term-structure of interest rates in the foreign currency, and the spot exchange rate.

Example:
Suppose that the term structure is flat in both US and Japan. The US rate is 10% per annum and the Japanese rate is 5% per annum (both with continuous compounding). A bank receives from a three-year currency swap 6% per annum in yen and pays 9% per annum in dollars once a year. The principals are $20 million and ¥2,400 million. The current exchange rate is $1 = ¥117$. Therefore:

$$B_D = 1.8\ e^{-0.1 \times 1} + 1.8\ e^{-0.1 \times 2} + 21.8\ e^{-0.1 \times 3} = 1.63 + 1.47 + 16.15$$
$$= \$19.25 \text{ million}$$

$$B_F = 144\ e^{-0.05 \times 1} + 144\ e^{-0.05 \times 2} + 2,544\ e^{-0.05 \times 3} = 136.98 + 130.30 + 2,189.64$$
$$= ¥2,456.92 \text{ million}$$

The value of the swap in dollars is: $2,456.92 / 117 - 19.25 = \$1.749$ million

If the bank had been paying yen and receiving dollars, the value of the swap would have been -$1.749 million.

2.3.4. Options Contracts

Options contracts is another major class of financial derivatives products. An option contract confers to its holder the right, but not the obligation, to buy (call option) or sell (put option) an underlying asset or commodity at a specified price – the strike or exercise price at either: (i) a specified date – the expiry date (European option); or (ii) at a number of specified dates in the future (Bermudan option); or (iii) at any time up to the expiry of the option (American option). The price to have this right is paid by the buyer of the option contract to the seller as a premium.

In contrast to the forward and futures contracts, under which both parties must use the contract, option holders decide on whether to exercise the option to buy (for a call) or sell (for a put) the underlying commodity. The counterparties to a put or a call option, on the other hand, have to fulfill their obligations; if the holder of the call (put) option decides to buy (sell) the underlying commodity by exercising the option, the seller of the option must sell (buy). They trade both in organised exchanges and OTC.

If the strike price of the option is such that if it were exercised today it generates a profit for the holder, the option is said to be *"in-the-money"*; this is the case for call options when the market price is greater than the exercise price and for put options when the market price is less than the exercise price. If the reverse is true, the option is said to be *"out-of-the-money"*; this is the case for call options when the market price is less than the exercise price and for put options when the market price is greater than the exercise price. When the exercise price and the market price are equal the option is said to be *"at-the-money"*. In general, the more an option contract is in-the-money when it is entered into the higher is its premium. The premium – that is, the price paid for an option – is influenced by a number of other factors, which are analysed in section 2.3.4.5 of this chapter.

2.3.4.1 Options Contracts Payoffs
2.3.4.1.1. Call Options Payoffs

Consider the payoff of a call option under different prices of the underlying commodity. More specifically, let S_t be the spot price of the underlying commodity at time t, X the strike or exercise price of the option, and c its premium. The payoff for the buyer (holder) of the option is calculated as $\max(S_t - X, 0) - c$, while for the seller (writer) of the option it is $-\max(S_t - X, 0) + c$. As can be observed in Table 2.12, if at expiration $S_t > X$, the option is exercised and the holder's profit is $S_t - X - c$. This amount is paid by the writer of the option to the holder. If $S_t \leq X$, the option is not exercised by its holder; he has lost its premium c, which is the writer's profit. The game is zero sum, in the sense that the seller's gain (loss) is the buyer's loss (gain), summing the payoffs to zero.

Table 2.12. Call Option's Profit/Loss for the Holder and the Writer

	Holder's Profit/Loss	Writer's Profit/Loss
$S_t > X$	$S_t - X - c$	$-S_t + X + c$
$S_t \leq X$	-c	+c

Example:
Consider for instance a call option with an exercise price X = $50, whose premium is c = $5. Its payoffs for the holder and the writer of the option are shown in Figure 2.9

and the accompanying tables. The call option is exercised when $S_t > X$; that is, when $S_t > \$50$. Up to that point the option is out-of-the-money, and therefore it is not worth exercising it. For instance, when the price of the commodity is at $45 the payoff for the holder is $\max(\$45 - \$50, 0) - \$5 = \max(-\$5, 0) - \$5 = 0 - \$5 = -\$5$. Thus, there is a loss for the holder of the option of $5, which constitutes the gain of the writer. The option is not exercised – to buy the commodity at $50, as it can be bought in the spot market for $45. The payoff for the seller of the option is $-\max(-\$5, 0) + \$5 = +\$5$. The call option becomes at-the-money when the spot market price, S_t, equals the exercise price, $X = \$50$. When the spot price is greater than $50 the call option is exercised, as it is in-the-money. For instance, when the spot price is at $60 the payoff for the option holder is $\max(\$60 - \$50, 0) - \$5 = \$5$. The holder, by exercising the option, buys something worth $60 in the market, for $50; when the call premium is subtracted, he ends up with a profit of $5. For the option seller the payoff is $-\max(\$60 - \$50, 0) + \$5 = -\$5$.

The payoffs for a number of spot prices, for both the holder and the writer of the option, are shown in the two tables of Figure 2.9 and graphically in the figure itself. It can be seen that the option holder minimizes his losses from the expense of buying the option, between the values of $50 and $55 by exercising it, and starts making profits for spot prices above $55. The option writer still makes profits from the revenue of selling the option, between $50 and $55, which turn into losses for prices above $55. The payoffs for the option holder and writer are exactly symmetrical with respect to the horizontal axis of the graph; it is a zero-sum game. As can be seen, for prices up to the strike price of $50 the buyer's payoff is represented by the horizontal line at -$5, while that for the seller, is represented by a symmetrical horizontal line at +$5.

Figure 2.9. Call Option Payoffs, including the Call Premium

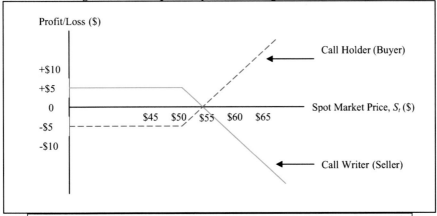

Call holder payoff table, including the call premium c = $5 – Exercise price X = $50								
Market Price, S_t	$35	$40	$45	$50	$55	$60	$65	$70
Call Holder Payoff; $\max(S_t - X, 0) - c$	-$5	-$5	-$5	-$5	0	+$5	+$10	+$15

Call writer payoff table, including the call premium c = $5 – Exercise price X = $50								
Market Price, S_t	$35	$40	$45	$50	$55	$60	$65	$70
Call Writer Payoff; $-\max(S_t - X, 0) + c$	+$5	+$5	+$5	+$5	0	-$5	-$10	-$15

2.3.4.1.2. Put Options Payoffs

A put option gives its holder the right to sell the underlying commodity/asset at its strike price, in return for a premium, p. The put is exercised by the holder when $S_t < X$ – that is, when it is in-the-money, otherwise it is either at- or out-of-the-money, and it is not exercised. The payoff, inclusive of the put's premium for the buyer, is calculated as $\max(X - S_t, 0) - p$. The payoff, for the option seller is exactly symmetrical and is calculated as $-\max(X - S_t, 0) + p$. As can be observed in Table 2.13, when the put option is exercised, the payoff for its holder is $X - S_t - p$, which he receives from the writer of the option. The last row of the table shows that when the option is not exercised by its holder, he has lost the put's premium of p, which constitutes the profit of the writer.

Table 2.13. Put Option's Profit/Loss for the Holder and the Writer

	Holder's Profit/Loss	Writer's Profit/Loss
$S_t < X$	$X - S_t - p$	$-X + S_t + p$
$S_t \geq X$	$-p$	$+p$

Example:

Figure 2.10. Put Option Payoffs

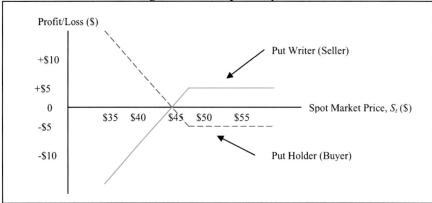

Put holder payoff table, including the put premium p = $5 – Exercise price X = $50							
Market Price, S_t	$35	$40	$45	$50	$55	$60	$65	$70
Put Holder Payoff; $\max(X - S_t, 0) - p$	+$10	+$5	0	-$5	-$5	-$5	-$5	-$5

Put writer payoff table, including the put premium p = $5 – Exercise price X = $50							
Market Price, S_t	$35	$40	$45	$50	$55	$60	$65	$70
Put Writer Payoff; $-\max(X - S_t, 0) + p$	-$10	-$5	0	+$5	+$5	+$5	+$5	+$5

Figure 2.10 and the corresponding tables presents the payoffs for the holder and the writer of a put option with a strike price of $50 and a premium of p = $5. The put buyer (holder) pays $5 premium to purchase this option from the seller (writer). It gives the right to the holder to sell a commodity for a price of $50, irrespective of its price. Consider for instance the situation when at the expiration of the European put option, the spot price is below its strike price of $50; more specifically, let S = $40. Then the holder will exercise the option and sell for $50 something which is worth in the market $40. Thus, the put option holder makes a profit of $\max(\$40 - \$50,0) - \$5 = +\$5$. This is the loss of the seller of the option, who has to pay this amount to the buyer. For spot values equal to or above $50 the put option is not exercised – it is out-

114

of-the-money; graphically, the payoff for the holder is shown by the horizontal line at -$5, while for the seller by the horizontal line at +$5. When $S_t < \$50$ the exercise of the put option by the holder minimizes his losses, between $45 and $50, and then produces profits, which are shown to be rising by the dotted line in the figure. The solid line in the same figure is exactly symmetrical to the dotted line, and shows the payoff for the writer of the put option. Notice the general property, that the lower is the spot price of the underlying commodity below $50 the higher is the profit for the option holder and the corresponding loss for the option writer.

Directional Investment Strategies with Options
Table 2.14 summarises the four directional option strategies, which an investor would take in options markets. They consist of either a long call, a short call, a long put or a short put. As can be observed in the table, the options position that the investor will assume depends on market and volatility expectations, on the time decay of the option, as well as on the profit and loss potentials. For example, for a long (short) call position, the expectations about the market are bullish (bearish) in the sense that it is expected that market rates will increase (decrease) in the future; rising volatility affects favorably (unfavorably) the option's value; the passage of time affects unfavorably (favorably) the option's value; the profit potential is unlimited, while the loss potential is limited in a short option position. The option strategies involving put options are also summarised in the last two rows of the same table. While this table provides a summary of the basic (plain vanilla) investment strategies that investors can assume by taking buy or sell positions in a single call or put option, other more complex strategies involving options can be created. They may involve combinations of options of different characteristics, and are examined further in section 2.3.4.10 of this chapter, in section 3.6.3 of Chapter 3 and in other chapter of the book.

Table 2.14. Options Directional Trading Strategies

Position	Market Expectation	Rising Volatility	Passage of Time	Profit Potential	Loss Potential
Long Call	Highly Bullish	Favourable	Unfavourable	Unlimited	Limited
Short Call	Somewhat Bearish	Unfavourable	Favourable	Limited	Unlimited
Long Put	Highly Bearish	Favourable	Unfavourable	Unlimited	Limited
Short Put	Somewhat Bullish	Unfavourable	Favourable	Limited	Unlimited

2.3.4.2. Hedging with Options Contracts
To see how market agents with long or short positions on a *"commodity"*, such as coffee, can use options to hedge, consider the following examples.

2.3.4.2.1. Hedging Long Positions in Physical Markets
Suppose a coffee producer, who will harvest and sell his coffee three months from now, expects a lower price compared to today's price. He wishes to hedge against this risk and at the same time exploit the possibility that coffee prices will rise. Assuming the price of coffee today stands at X, the spot (physical) position payoff is shown by the light solid line falling from right to left in Figure 2.11. If the spot price falls below X losses are incurred by the coffee producer. He can hedge against this risk by buying a put option, giving him the right to sell his coffee at the exercise price X, no matter what the price of coffee will be in three months time. The payoff of the put option, he bought for a premium p, is shown by the dotted line in the figure.

Figure 2.11. The Hedging Positions of the Coffee Producer

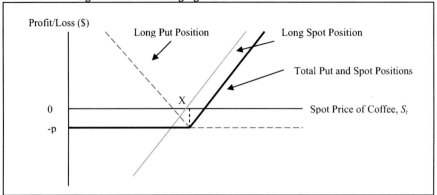

If the spot price falls below the exercise price ($S < X$) the put option is exercised and its payoff is $\max(X - S, 0) = X - S$; the producer is able to sell his coffee at price X, when the prevailing price of coffee in the spot market (S) is actually lower. As can be seen in the last row of the table and by the solid heavy line in the figure, the combined spot – put payoff in this case is constant. If the spot price (S) turns out to be greater or equal to the exercise price (X), the option is not exercised; its payoff is 0, as can be seen in the last column of Table 2.15. However, profits can still be made in the physical market, which are proportional to S. This is reflected in the rising solid line to the right of X, which shows the combined spot – option position of the coffee producer. It has cost $p to the coffee producer to buy this insurance.

Table 2.15. The Hedging Positions of the Coffee Producer, Ignoring Option Costs

	$S < X$	$S \geq X$
Long Put Payoff = max(X – S, 0)	$X - S$	0
Long Spot	S	S
Total	X	S

2.3.4.2.2. Hedging Short Positions in Physical Markets
Consider next the position of a coffee house owner wishing to purchase coffee in three months from now, anticipating a rise in the price of coffee. He can hedge his spot market position by buying a call option with exercise price X, at premium c. As we see below, this strategy protects him from a rise in the price of coffee, and at the same time allows him to benefit if coffee prices actually fall in three months. The solid light line, falling from left to right, in Figure 2.12 shows that, as the price of coffee rises, from today's price (X), the payoff of the coffee house owner declines, as he will have to pay higher amounts to purchase the coffee needed. If on the other hand, coffee prices fall below X, the coffee house pays less for coffee, as shown by the same line above the horizontal axis. In the call option position if at the expiration of the contract in three months time $S > X$, that is, if the spot price (S) rises above the exercise price (X) of the call option, the option is exercised it, buying coffee at X, despite its higher cost (S) in the spot market. Thus, a gain of $\max(S - X, 0) = S - X$ is made from the call option position. This is depicted by the rising dotted line, to the right of X.

Figure 2.12. The Hedging Positions of the Coffee House Owner

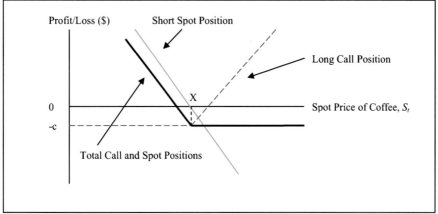

If the price of coffee does not rise above X the call option is not exercised; coffee can be bought in the market cheaper than X, at S. The combined spot–call position payoff is shown by the heavy solid line in the figure and the bottom row of Table 2.16. As can be observed, if the price of coffee actually rises the cost is stabilized at X (plus the cost of the call premium, c). If the price falls, the coffee house will pay the spot price prevailing in the market then, thus benefiting from this fall in prices. The coffee house owner has paid the amount $c as insurance for these payoffs.

Thus, for both the coffee producer and the coffee house owner, hedging through options stabilizes costs in case of adverse price movements, while at the same time allowing them to benefit from favorable price movements.

Table 2.16. The Hedging Positions of the Coffee House Owner, Ignoring Option Costs

	$S \leq X$	$S > X$
Long Call Payoff = max(S – X, 0)	0	$S - X$
Short Spot	-S	-S
Total	-S	-X

2.3.4.3. Hedging with Options vs. Hedging with Futures/Forwards
In general, an investor who is short on a "*commodity*" and wishes to be hedged against an expected rise in its prices can either:
  i.   purchase a futures/forward contract, which has unlimited profit and loss potential, as shown by the dotted line increasing from left to right in Figure 2.13;
  ii. purchase a call option, which has unlimited profit potential, but loss which is limited to the premium of the option, as shown by the dark solid line in the same figure;
  iii. write a put option, which yields a constant gain equal to the put's premium but unlimited loss, as shown by the light solid line in the same figure.

Suppose that the spot price rises above its current level of $25. The long futures/forward contract and the long call option contract have unlimited profits, while the short put option contract has limited profit equal to the premium (say, $5) of the options contract. Suppose next that the spot price falls below $25. The long futures/forward contract and the short put option contract have "*unlimited*" losses,

117

while the long call option contract has limited loss equal to the premium (say, $5) of the option contract.

Figure 2.13. Hedging Positions against Expected Rise in Spot Prices: Options vs. Futures

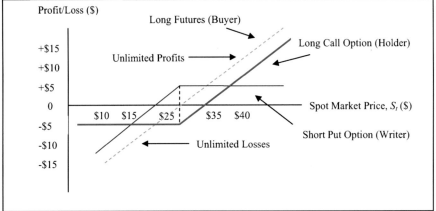

On the other hand, an investor who is long on a *"commodity"* and wishes to be hedged against an expected fall in prices can either:

i. sell a futures/forward contract, which has unlimited profit and loss potential, as shown by the dotted line decreasing from left to right in Figure 2.14;
ii. purchase a put option, which yields a potentially unlimited profit, but a loss which is limited to the premium of the put option, as shown by the light solid in the same figure;
iii. write a call option, which yields a limited gain, which is equal to the option's premium if the market falls, but unlimited loss if the market rises, as shown by the heavy solid line in the same figure.

Figure 2.14. Hedging Positions against Expected Fall in Spot Prices: Options vs. Futures

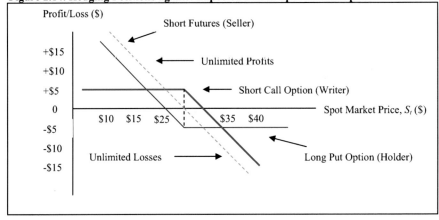

Suppose that the spot price rises above $25. The short futures/forward contract and the short call option contract have unlimited losses, while the long put option contract has a limited loss equal to the premium (say, $5) of the option contract. Suppose next that the spot price falls below $25. The short futures/forward contract and the long put

118

option contract have *"unlimited"* profits, while the short call option contract has limited profit equal to the premium (say, $5) of the option contract.

In Sum:
- Hedgers, when they use futures/forward contracts, neutralize risk, by fixing the price of the underlying *"commodity"* that they will pay or receive – see section 2.3.2.1 and Figures 2.2 and 2.3 therein. On the other hand, hedging through options provides insurance against adverse future price movements, but at the same time allows hedgers to benefit from favourable price movements.
- Another difference between hedging with forwards and hedging with options is that, it costs nothing to initiate a forward hedge, but hedgers will have to pay (for holders) or receive (for writers) a premium in an options transaction.
- For speculators also there is a similar difference between the use of forward/futures and options for investment purposes.
- The potential gain or loss is unlimited in a futures/forward speculative position. The potential loss however is limited to the value of the premium of the option, in an options speculative position, while the potential gain is unlimited.

2.3.4.4. Intrinsic and Time Value of Options
Another important concept of options is that of the value of an option's contract. This comprises two components; the intrinsic value and the time value:
- **Intrinsic value** is the in-the-money amount, which will result from exercising the option immediately. For a call option it is $\max(S_t - X, 0)$ and for a put option it is $\max(X - S_t, 0)$. Suppose the premium of a call option on a stock with three months to expiration is $c = \$5$, the strike price is $65, while the current spot price of the stock is $63. The intrinsic value of the option is $\max(\$65 - \$63, 0) = \$2$. That is, if the option was exercised immediately a payoff of $2 would result, making it an in-the-money option. If the price of the stock was $60, $\max(\$60 - \$65, 0) = 0$, the option is out-of-the-money and its intrinsic value becomes zero. As another example, consider a put option with three months to expiration, whose strike price is $70, its price is $8 and the current price of the stock is $60. The intrinsic value of the put is $\max(\$70 - \$60, 0) = \$10$.
- The **time value** of an option derives from the possibility of increases in the value of the option by the time it expires, due to favourable movements in the price of the underlying commodity. In the example considered above, for the call option, its price is $c = \$5$, while its intrinsic value is $2. The remaining $3, up to its price of $5 is its time value. Similarly, in the earlier example of the put, the put's price is $p = \$8$, its intrinsic value is $10, and as a consequence the time value of the put is $2 (= $10 – $8). Of course, the time value of the option is zero when either the option has reached maturity or it is best to exercise immediately.

Unlike futures, the holders of options are not allowed to buy them on margin, as there is substantial leverage involved when holding options. On the other hand, investors writing options are required by both the broker and the exchange to maintain a margin account, which reduces the risk of default. The Options Clearing Corporation (OCC) in the US has a similar role to the clearing-house of futures. Its existence is important as it eliminates credit risk.

Figure 2.15 combines the intrinsic and the time value of a call option. After adding time value, the relationship between the option's premium and the underlying price is represented by a smooth curve. Prior to expiration, a call option's relationship to the underlying asset is defined by this curve instead of the angular shape of the intrinsic value. The longer the period to expiration, the greater the price of the option and more straight is the shape of the curve. Only at expiration, when there is no time remaining, does the call option's profit/loss profile resemble an angular shape, and the price of the option is only determined by the prices of the underlying asset and the strike price.

Figure 2.15. Intrinsic and Time Value of Options Contracts

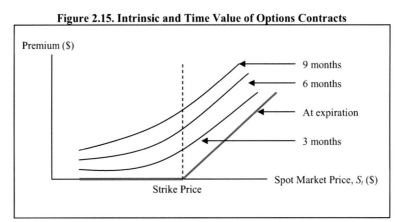

2.3.4.5. Factors Influencing Options Prices and the Greeks
When dealing with options it is important to know by what factors and to what extent their prices are affected. Factors which influence the prices of stock options contracts are the following:

- **Market price of underlying commodity – S**: We saw earlier that the payoff of a call is: max(S_t –X, 0). Thus, the value of a call is proportional to the price of the underlying commodity S_t. The payoff of a put is: max(X – S_t, 0). Thus, its value is inversely proportional to the price of the underlying commodity S_t.

  The sensitivities of options prices to changes in the factors affecting the underlying commodity are referred to as the Greeks – as Greek letters are used to denote these sensitivities. The rate of change of the option price in relation to changes in the market price of the underlying commodity, *ceteris paribus*, is known as **Delta**. Mathematically, it is the first partial derivative of the option's price with respect to a change in the price of the underlying asset. Thus, for a call $\frac{\partial c}{\partial S} > 0$, while for a put $\frac{\partial p}{\partial S} < 0$.

  In relation to Delta, another sensitivity is defined which is important; the **Gamma** of an option measures the sensitivity of Delta as the price of the underlying commodity changes. Mathematically, it is the first partial derivative of $\frac{\partial c}{\partial S}$ or of $\frac{\partial p}{\partial S}$, with respect to S, essentially being the second partial derivative of c and of p with respect to S.

$$\text{Gamma (call)} = \frac{\partial(delta\,c)}{\partial S} = \frac{\partial^2 c}{\partial S^2} \text{ and Gamma (put)} = \frac{\partial(delta\,p)}{\partial S} = \frac{\partial^2 p}{\partial S^2}$$

The Gamma of a put and of a call are identical and they can be positive or negative. Gamma tends to be large when the option is near-the-money, indicating that its Delta is highly sensitive to changes in the stock price. When an option is deep in-the-money its Delta is near one and is not sensitive to changes in the stock price, and hence Gamma will be low. A similar situation applies for options that are deep out-of-the-money. Gamma is high when an option is near-the-money.

- **Strike or Exercise price – X**: Given the payoff formulas for calls and puts, the value of a call is inversely proportional to the strike price X, while for a put its price is proportional to the strike price X. Thus, with respect to prices of the underlying commodity (S) and strike prices (X), put prices (p) and call prices (c) are affected in opposite ways.

- **Time to expiration – T**: For American type options, both put and call prices are proportional to the time to expiration of the option contract. To see this, consider two American options with time to expiration three and six months, respectively. The six-month option can give to its holder as many options as the three-month one, plus the possibility to exercise the option in the last three months of the six-month period. For European type options the relationship between time to expiration and the option price is uncertain. To see this, consider two European options on a stock with time to expiration two and four months, respectively. If a stock split is expected in three months time, this will decrease the price of the stock and make its four-month option price lower than the two-month one.

The sensitivity of the option's price in relation to time to expiration of the option is known as **Theta** (θ). Mathematically, it is measured by the first partial derivative of the option's price with respect to the time remaining until expiration. Thus, for an American call and put option Theta is $\theta_c = \dfrac{\partial C}{\partial T}$ and $\theta_p = \dfrac{\partial P}{\partial T}$, respectively. The tendency for options prices to change due, merely, to the passage of time is known as time-decay. Appropriate strategies may be formed to neutralize portfolios containing options from Theta effects on their value.

- **Price Volatility of the underlying commodity – σ**: High volatility of the price of the commodity underlying an option increases the probability that the option will have a high payoff with limited downside risk, *ceteris paribus*. For a call option, an increase in the price of the underlying stock due to its high volatility will increase its payoff, while the downside risk is limited to the call option's premium. Similarly for a put, low prices of the underlying commodity that will result from the high volatility produce high payoffs for the put option, with the downside risk limited to the put option's premium. As a consequence, a positive relationship is expected between the volatility of the underlying commodity and the call and put prices.

The sensitivity of options prices with respect to changes in the volatility of the price of the underlying commodity, *ceteris paribus*, is known as **Vega**. Mathematically, it is the first partial derivative of an option's price with respect to the volatility of the underlying stock, Vega(call) $=\dfrac{\partial c}{\partial \sigma}$ and Vega(put) $=\dfrac{\partial p}{\partial \sigma}$. The Vegas of calls and puts are identical and positive. Appropriate strategies may be formed to neutralize portfolios containing options from Vega effects on their value.

- **Risk-Free Interest Rate – r:** The effect of interest rates on options prices is ambiguous. Changes in interest rates may increase or decrease, say, call options prices, depending on the balance of two effects. These effects come through to options prices, as a consequence of interest rates affecting the underlying "*commodity*", say stock prices. Assume interest rates in the economy increase. This is expected to lead to higher prices for stocks, as rates of return in the economy are related. The second way interest rates may affect prices is through Net Present Values (NPV); for a company, higher rates of interest lead to lower NPV's and hence higher prices of the stock. Which of the two factors has a greater impact, in the sense of leading to higher or lower stock prices is not certain at the outset. As a consequence, the impact of interest rates on options prices is also uncertain. However, if it can be determined what impact interest rates will have on stock prices, then their effect on call and put options prices is the same as that described earlier on in this section, on the effect that changes in market prices the underlying commodity will have on options.

  The sensitivity of options to changes in interest rates, *ceteris paribus*, is known as **Rho**. Mathematically, it is the first partial derivative of the option's price with respect to the interest rate, that is, Rho(call) $=\dfrac{\partial c}{\partial r}$ and Rho(put)$=\dfrac{\partial p}{\partial r}$. In general, options prices are not very sensitive to interest rates. Rho changes as both the stock price and the time to expiration of the option change. It tends to be low for a call option that is deep out-of-the-money and high for a call option that is deep in-the-money, and vice versa for the Rho of put options. When an option is at- the-money Rho is at its most sensitive level to changes in stock prices. Rho for calls and puts change as time passes, and tends to zero as expiration approaches.

- **Dividends (on stocks):** The payment of dividends decreases the price of the stock. As we saw earlier on in this section, stock price decreases lead to reduction in call options prices and to increases in put options prices.

Each of the above sensitivities is calculated through specific formulas, which vary according to the options' pricing model used to value options. Such valuation models are discussed next, while the relevant formulas for the calculation of the Greeks can be found in standard derivatives textbooks, such as those refereed to in the last section of this chapter.

2.3.4.5.1. Utilizing the Greeks – A Delta Hedge Strategy

To see the usefulness of knowledge of the Greeks, these sensitivities of options prices to the factors affecting them can be utilized by market agents to form hedging strategies. For instance, an investor wishes to neutralize the effect of a change in the price of a non-dividend paying stock on his portfolio; that is, he wishes to construct a Delta Neutral Portfolio (Π_Δ). He can do that by buying Δ shares for each option sold. The value of the portfolio changes as stock prices change.

The Delta of this new portfolio is zero and so the portfolio will have become insensitive to changes in the price of the stock. The Delta of the portfolio of options on a stock whose price is S is $\dfrac{\partial \Pi}{\partial S}$, where Π is the value of the portfolio. If a portfolio consists of a quantity w_i of option i ($1 \leq i \leq n$), the Delta of the portfolio is given by:

$$\Delta = \sum_{i=1}^{n} w_i \Delta_i \qquad (2.23)$$

where, Δ_i is the Delta of the ith option. As stock prices change, the portfolio must be "*rebalanced*" periodically in order to maintain delta neutrality. By continually rebalancing we know that the portfolio has zero risk as a function of changing stock prices. In this way, we create a risk-free portfolio, which must (by definition) earn the risk-free rate.

Example:
Suppose a financial institution has three positions in options on a stock: (i) a long position in 1,000 call options, expiring in three months, with a strike price of $0.40. The Delta of each option is 0.622; (ii) a short position in 2,000 call options, expiring in five months, with a strike price of $0.41. The Delta of each option is 0.538; and (iii) a short position in 500 call options, expiring in two months, with a strike price of $0.41. The Delta of each option is -0.601. The Delta of the portfolio is:

$$1,000 \times \$0.622 - 2,000 \times 0.538 - 500 \times (-0.601) = -154$$

This means that the portfolio can be made Delta neutral by taking a long position of $154 stocks.

2.3.4.6. Options Pricing

A number of models have been developed for the correct pricing of options, each of which is appropriate under different circumstances. Commonly used models include the binomial model – see Cox *et al.* (1979) and the Black-Scholes-Merton model – see Black and Scholes (1973) and Merton (1973).

2.3.4.6.1. Binomial Model

The binomial model, introduced by Cox *et al.* (1979), involves the construction of a diagram – the binomial (or trinomial) tree – which represents the different possible paths that may be followed by the price of the commodity underlying an option. A number of distinct steps, usually at least 30, are assumed over the maturity of the options contract, and a number of assumptions are made regarding the probabilities of rise and fall in prices at each step, as well as the volatility of the price of the "*commodity*". Having such diagram in place, call and put options are priced at each "*node*" (starting from the end) of the tree, and as a result and at the current point in time, by considering the payoffs of these options in each node. As a point of reference, the complete set of equations used to build a binominal tree is:

$$u = e^{\sigma \sqrt{\delta t}}, \quad d = e^{-\sigma \sqrt{\delta t}}, \quad \text{and} \quad p = \frac{e^{rt} - d}{u - d} \tag{2.24}$$

where, σ is the volatility of the underlying *"commodity"* price, δt is the length of step in the tree, r is the risk-free interest rate, p can be interpreted as the probability of an up movement in price, while $(1 - p)$ is the probability of a down movement.

Also note that a *"risk neutral valuation principle"* is used in valuing options through the binomial tree approach. This approach assumes that the expected return from all traded securities equals the risk-free rate of interest, and the present value of future cash-flows can be obtained by discounting their expected values by the risk-free rate. Alternatively, the *"principle of no-arbitrage arguments"*, if used, leads to the same price for an option. This principle states that it is possible to set up a portfolio which consists of an option and the asset, which has no risk, thus earning the risk-free rate of interest. The principle, essentially, allows the option on the *"asset"*/*"commodity"* to be priced in terms of the asset's price.

Binomial models used for the estimation of options prices are useful, both for European options and when the option's holder has to decide on whether to exercise it early or not – that is, for American style options.

2.3.4.6.2. Monte Carlo Simulation
Monte Carlo simulation is another numerical procedure that may be used to derive options prices. It is useful when the payoff of the option depends on the (i) particular path followed by the spot price of the underlying commodity or when (ii) it is dependant only on its final price. The method is very flexible as any stochastic process followed by the price of the commodity underlying the option can be accommodated[32]. Also, albeit difficult, Monte Carlo methods have been developed that can accommodate path dependant American style options – see for instance Tilley (1993). The method is also appropriate when the payoff of the derivative depends on several underlying market variables. Drawbacks of the method include that it is computationally expensive.

2.3.4.6.3. Black-Scholes-Merton Model
The most commonly used options pricing model is the Black-Scholes model, developed by Black and Scholes (1973) and Merton (1973). It utilizes the no-arbitrage arguments discussed above to price options, by linking their price to the price of the underlying asset. The model also shows that by combining the underlying asset and a money market instrument a risk-less hedge can always be created that exactly replicates the payoff profile of the option to be hedged. This means that a portfolio formed by the combination of the option and its risk-less hedge must appreciate at the risk-free interest rate. By calculating the fair (theoretical) value of an option, the investor can determine whether the option is correctly priced. Option prices away from their fair value may present arbitrage and speculative opportunities in the market.

---

[32] A variable whose value changes over time in an uncertain way is known to follow a stochastic process.

Models for options prices make some assumptions regarding the stochastic process which is followed by the "*commodity*" upon which they are written. Besides the no-arbitrage arguments, the Black-Scholes model, in its basic form, assumes that the stock price of a non-dividend paying stock follows a Geometric Brownian Motion (GBM); that is, it can be described by the following equation:

$$dS = \mu S \, dt + \sigma S \, dz \quad \text{or} \quad \frac{dS}{S} = \mu \, dt + \sigma \, dz \quad ; \quad dz = \varepsilon \, dt \qquad (2.25)$$

where, dS denotes a small change in the spot price of the asset in a small (infinitesimal) time interval dt, μ is the expected return of the asset, σ is its volatility measured by its standard deviation, dz is known as a Weiner process (or Brownian motion), and is ε is a random variable taking values from a standard normal distribution – that is, $\varepsilon \sim N(0, 1)$.[33] The model states that the return of the stock $\left(\dfrac{dS}{S} \right)$, during a small period of time dt, equals its expected return μdt plus a stochastic component of this return, $\sigma \varepsilon \, dt$. The variance of the stochastic component, and as a consequence of the return, is $\sigma^2 dt$. Thus, by implication of the above, and making use of the Ito's lemma, it can be shown that the continuously compounded stock return per annum, $R_t = \ln\left(\dfrac{S_t}{S_{t-1}} \right)$, follows a normal distribution with mean value $(\mu - \sigma^2/2)$ and variance σ^2. That is:

$$\frac{1}{T} \ln\left(\frac{S_t}{S_{t-1}} \right) \sim N\left[\left(\mu - \frac{\sigma^2}{2} \right), \frac{\sigma^2}{T} \right] \qquad (2.26)$$

and hence $\ln S_t$ is normally distributed, as follows:

$$\ln S_t \sim N\left\{ \left[\ln S_{t-1} + \left(\mu - \frac{\sigma^2}{2} \right) T \right], \sigma^2 \not{t} \right\} \qquad (2.27)$$

By implication S_t has a lognormal distribution; that means that the logarithm of S_t follows a normal distribution. The expected value and variance of S_t can be shown to be, respectively:

$$E(S_t) = S_0 \, e^{\mu t} \quad \text{and} \quad \text{Var}(S_t) = S_0^2 \, e^{2\mu t} (e^{\sigma^2 T} - 1) \qquad (2.28)$$

Given the assumptions of: (i) no risk-less arbitrage opportunities; (ii) the stock price follows the GBM process described above; (iii) short sale of securities is allowed; (iv) no transactions costs or taxes; (v) securities are perfectly divisible; (vi) security trading is continuous; and (vii) the risk-free rate is constant and the same for all maturities, Black, Scholes and Merton have shown that for a non-dividend paying stock the prices of European call and put options are, respectively:

---

[33] A Weiner process is a particular type of Markov stochastic process with mean change of zero and variance rate of one per unit of time, say a year. A Markov stochastic process in turn, is one under which only the current value of a variable is relevant for forecasting future values. Past values of the variable are irrelevant for forecasting future values.

$$c = S\,N(d_1) - X\,e^{-rT}\,N(d_2) \tag{2.29}$$

$$p = X\,e^{-rT}\,N(-d_2) - S\,N(-d_1) \tag{2.30}$$

where, $d_1 = \dfrac{\left[\ln\left(\dfrac{S}{X}\right) + \left(r + \dfrac{\sigma^2}{2}\right)T\right]}{\sigma\sqrt{T}}$; $d_2 = \dfrac{\ln\left(\dfrac{S}{X}\right) + \left(r - \dfrac{\sigma^2}{2}\right)T}{\sigma\sqrt{T}} = d_1 - \sigma\sqrt{T}$;

c = Call option price; p = Put option price; S = Spot price of the underlying asset; X= Exercise price; T = Time to maturity in years; r = Risk-free interest rate; σ=Standard deviation of the spot price; e = 2.718; N(d) = Cumulative standard normal probability distribution function, measuring the probability that a standard normal variable will be less than a value d, and hence $N(d_1)$ = Probability that $S > X$, measuring the probability of unlimited profits; and $N(d_2)$ = Probability that $S < X$, measuring the probability of limited losses.

For an intuitive explanation of the model, consider Equation (2.29), which can also be written as: c = $e^{-rT}[S\,N(d_1)\,e^{rT} - X\,N(d_2)]$. $N(d_2)$ is the probability that the option will be exercised under risk neutrality. X $N(d_2)$ is the exercise price times the probability that this will be paid. S $N(d_1)$ e^{rT} is the expected value of a variable, which equals S_T if $S_T > X$ and zero otherwise. When S becomes very large, both d_1 and d_2 become very large and $N(d_1)$ and $N(d_2)$ tend to 1. In this case, the option is exercised and its payoff is c = $S - X\,e^{-rT}$. On the other hand, $N(-d_1)$ and $N(-d_2)$ tend to zero and the price of the put option, p, approaches zero.

Example:
To see how the Black-Scholes model is put in practice, consider the following example of a three-months European call option: Assume the current stock price is S=$100, the exercise price is X = $95, the time to maturity is T = 0.25 years (quarter), the risk-free interest rate is r = 0.10 per annum, and the volatility of the stock price is σ = 0.50. First, we obtain values for d_1 and d_2:

d_1 = [ln(100/95) + (0.10 + (0.5²/2) x 0.25)] / (0.5 x 0.25$^{1/2}$) = 0.43 and

d_2 = 0.43 − (0.5 x 0.25$^{1/2}$) = 0.18

From the standard normal distribution tables, which may be found in Appendix I of this chapter, we obtain the following values for $N(d_1)$ and $N(d_2)$: $N(d_1$ = 0.43) =0.6664 and $N(d_2$ = 0.18) = 0.5714. Substituting next into the Black-Scholes Equation (2.29), we obtain the price of the call option as:

$c = S\,N(d_1) - X\,e^{-rT}\,N(d_2)$ = ($100 x 0.6664) − ($95 $e^{-0.10 \times 0.25}$ x 0.5714) = $13.70

Using the same data as in the above example, consider the pricing of a three-month European put option with an exercise price X = $110. First, calculate d_1 and d_2 as:

d_1 = [ln(100/110) + (0.10 + (0.5²/2) x 0.25)] / (0.5 x 0.25$^{1/2}$) = -0.16

d_2 = 0.16 − (0.5 x 0.251/2) = -0.41

From the standard normal distribution tables, $N(-d_1) = N(0.16) = 0.5621$ and $N(-d_2) = N(0.41) = 0.6577$. Substituting in the Black-Scholes Equation (2.30), we obtain the following price of the put option:

$$p - X \, e^{-rT} N(-d_2) - S \, N(-d_1) = \$110 \, e^{-0.1 \times 0.25} \times 0.6577 - \$100 \times 0.5621 = \$7.94$$

European options prices can be calculated from the above Equations (2.29) and (2.30) when dividend payments or more generally when income is due during the lifetime of the option, by calculating the present value of the expected dividend payments, say I, and subtracting this present value from the current value, S, of the stock in the formulas. This has the effect of adjusting the stock price downwards, as dividend payments reduce the stock price on the ex-dividend date. Then simply use this adjusted spot price, $(S - I)$, in the Black-Scholes formulas to calculate the required call and put prices. With American options on stocks paying dividends, it can be shown that it is optimal to exercise them only at a time immediately before the stock goes ex-dividend. Variations of the Black-Scholes model are used to price options on other underlying assets, including foreign exchange futures, etc – see the books referenced in the last section of this chapter for further information. Research work that examines violations of the Black-Scholes model includes Heston (1991), Bates (1996) and Duffie *et al.* (2000), amongst others.

2.3.4.7. Price Limits of Options

We saw earlier on in this chapter that the payoffs for the holder of a call and of a put option are $\max(S - X, 0)$ and $\max(X - S, 0)$, respectively. The call is worth exercising when $S > X$, otherwise its value is zero, while a put is worth exercising when $S < X$, otherwise it has a zero value. It follows that the prices of calls and puts will fluctuate within certain limits. They are as follows:

For a non-dividend paying stock:

European call option: $\qquad \max(S - X \, e^{-rT}, 0) < c < S$

European put option: $\qquad \max(X \, e^{-rT} - S, 0) < p < X$

For a stock paying dividends with present value I, these limits become:

European call option: $\qquad \max(S - I - X \, e^{-rT}, 0) < c < S$

European put option: $\qquad \max(X \, e^{-rT} + I - S, 0) < p < X$

Notice that these limits are derived without making any assumptions about the volatility of the stock, as in the case of options' pricing models. When the price of a call or a put option moves outside these limits, then arbitrage opportunities arise for risk-less profits to be made. The following example illustrates how arbitrage strategies can be formed to exploit these opportunities.

Example:

To see an example of one such strategy, suppose that a European call on a non-dividend paying stock is worth \$4.00 and $S = \$30$, $X = \$27$, $r = 10\%$ and $T = 1$ year. The lower bound for this call is \$5.57 (= \$30 – \$27 $e^{-0.1}$). Since the market call price today is below the minimum, an arbitrageur can buy the call and short the stock, resulting in a cash-flow of $26 (= -$4 + $30). This can be invested for 1 year at 10% to grow to $28.73 (= $26 $e^{0.1}$). At the end of the year the call expires, and if $S > \$27$ it is exercised, thus buying the stock at $27, the short position is closed, resulting in a risk-free profit of $1.73 (= $28.73 – $27).

Similarly, arbitrage strategies exist when the call price is above its upper limit of S. In this case, an arbitrageur can buy the stock and sell the call and make a risk-less profit. For a put violating its upper bound of X, an arbitrageur can sell (write) the put option and invest the proceeds at the risk-free rate of interest. If it were the case that the market for the put violated its lower limit of $X e^{-rT} - S$, an arbitrageur could profit from the situation. He can borrow $p + S$ to buy the put and the stock today, and if at the expiry of the option $S < X$, exercise the put to sell the stock if $S < X$ and use the proceeds to repay the compound amount of the loan of $(p + S) e^{rT}$.

2.3.4.8. Put-Call Parity Relationship
An important relationship holds between the prices of European call and put options on a stock with the same strike price and maturity. For a non-dividend paying stock this relationship is:

$$c + X e^{-rT} = p + S \qquad (2.31)$$

For a dividend paying stock or more generally, when income (with present value I) is expected from the underlying asset during the lifetime of the option, the relationship becomes:

$$c + I + X e^{-rT} = p + S \qquad (2.32)$$

The relationship can be used to derive the value of a call option from the value of a put option, and visa versa. If the relationship does not hold arbitrage opportunities may exist, which allow market agents to make risk-free profits.

The above put-call parity relationship for European options does not hold for American options due to the possibility of early exercise. Arbitrage arguments though allow us to obtain upper and lower limits for the difference in prices on an American put (P) and call (C) with the same maturity and exercise price. For a non-dividend paying stock they are:

$$S - X \le C - P \le S - X e^{-rT} \qquad (2.33)$$

while for a dividend (income) paying stock (asset) the relationship becomes:

$$S - I - X \le C - P \le S - X e^{-rT} \qquad (2.34)$$

To see how these arbitrage opportunities can be exploited in practice, consider the arbitrage portfolios that were constructed by arbitrageurs trying to exploit the violation of the lower limits of European call and put options. More specifically, in the following examples consider the payoffs of two portfolios:
Portfolio A: One call option plus an amount of cash $X e^{-rT}$ from short sale of the underlying stock
Portfolio B: One put option plus long one share

Portfolio A	Portfolio B
1. One European call	1. One European put
2. Amount of cash X e^{-rT}	2. Long one share

Both are worth $\max(S_T, X)$ at expiration of the options. Because the options are European, they can be exercised only at the expiration date. Therefore, the portfolios must have identical values today and the put-call parity relationship of Equation (2.31) should hold. If Equation (2.31) does not hold, there are arbitrage opportunities. The following examples are used to demonstrate how the put-call parity relationship may be used to form arbitrage strategies.

Example 1:
Suppose a European call and a European put option are expiring in one year and are trading for $5 each, the exercise price is $50, while the stock price of the asset underlying the option is $50. The risk-free rate is 11.1% per annum. From the put-call parity relationship we have:

Portfolio A: $\qquad c + X\ e^{-rT} = \$5 + \$50\ e^{-0.111 \times 1} = \$49.75$

Portfolio B: $\qquad p + S = \$5 + \$50 = \$55$

Since $c + X\ e^{-rT} < p + S$, arbitrageurs can profit from this situation by buying the securities in Portfolio A and shorting the securities in portfolio B. The strategy involves buying the call and shorting both the put and the stock, producing a positive cash-flow of -$5 + $5 + $50 = $50. This can be invested at the risk-free rate, which will grow to $50 $e^{0.111 \times 1}$ = $55.87 by the end of the year. If, at expiration of the option, the stock price is greater than $50, the call will be exercised, while if it is less than $50, the put will be exercised. In either case, the investor buys one share for $50, which he can use to close out the short position. Therefore, the net profit is: $55.87 − $50 = $5.87.

Example 2:
Consider the same data as in example 1, only that the call price is $8 and the put price is $1. In this case portfolio A and B are:

Portfolio A: $\qquad c + X\ e^{-rT} = \$8 + \$50\ e^{-0.111 \times 1} = \$52.75$

Portfolio B: $\qquad p + S = \$1 + \$50 = \$51$

Since $c + X\ e^{-rT} > p + S$, arbitrageurs can profit from this situation by shorting the securities in Portfolio A and buying the securities in Portfolio B. The strategy involves shorting the call and buying both the put and the stock with an initial investment of: $50 + $1 − $8 = $43. Investing at the risk-free interest rate, at the end of the year a repayment of $48.05 (= $43 $e^{0.111 \times 1}$) is required. Also in this case, either the call or the put will be exercised. The short call and long put option position leads to the stock being sold for $50. Therefore, the net profit is: $50 − $48.05 = $1.95.

2.3.4.9. Asian Options
Asian options are options for which the payoff depends on the average price ($\bar{S}$) of the underlying asset over some period of time in the life of the "*asset*". Because of this fact, Asian options have a lower volatility and hence are cheaper than European or American options. Typically, they are written on "*commodities*" which have low

trading volumes and high volatility of the underlying price. Such commodities include crude oil, bunker prices, freight rates and futures/forward contracts on freight rates, amongst others. Thus, averaging of the spot price smoothens out the option payoff, in comparison to using the spot price on a particular date as is the case with conventional options. They were introduced in 1987 when Banker's Trust Tokyo office used them for pricing average options on crude oil contracts; hence the name "*Asian*" options.

The payoff of an average price Asian call is max($\overline{S}$ – X, 0) and that of an **average price Asian** put is max(X – $\overline{S}$, 0), where $\overline{S}$ is the average value of the underlying commodity calculated over a predetermined averaging period. If the payoff of a call option is calculated as max(S – $\overline{S}$, 0) and the payoff of a put as max($\overline{S}$ – S, 0) they are called **average strike call** and **put Asian** options, respectively. That is, the strike prices (X) of these options are an average of the spot prices of the underlying asset over a period of time. Average strike options can guarantee that the average price paid (received) for a commodity in frequent trading, over a period of time, is not greater (less) than the final price. Asian options can be either European style or American style.

There are no known analytical pricing formulas when options are defined in terms of arithmetic averages. This is because the distribution of the arithmetic average of a set of lognormal distributions does not have analytical properties and therefore, the lognormal assumptions collapse. Therefore, Asian options are either based on the average price of the underlying asset, or alternatively, they are the average strike type. There are three commonly used pricing models to price Asian options:

(i) Geometric Closed-Form
Kemma and Vorst (1990) proposed a closed-form pricing solution to geometric averaging price options, as the geometric average of the underlying prices follows a lognormal distribution, whereas under average rate options, this condition collapses[34]. The prices of the geometric averaging Asian calls and puts are:

$$c_G = S \, e^{(b-r)T} \, N(d_1) - X \, e^{-rT} \, N(d_2) \tag{2.35}$$

$$p_G = X \, e^{-rT} \, N(-d_2) - S \, e^{(b-r)T} \, N(-d_1) \tag{2.36}$$

where, $d_1 = \dfrac{\ln\left(\dfrac{S}{X}\right) + b + 0.5\sigma_A^2 T}{\sigma_A \sqrt{T}}$; $d_2 = \dfrac{\ln\left(\dfrac{S}{X}\right) + b - 0.5\sigma_A^2 T}{\sigma_A \sqrt{T}} = d_1 - \sigma_A \sqrt{T}$; $\sigma_A = \dfrac{\sigma}{\sqrt{3}}$;

$b = \dfrac{1}{2}\left(r - q - \dfrac{\sigma^2}{6}\right)$; $N(d)$ = Cumulative standard normal distribution function; σ=Standard deviation of spot price; r = Risk-free rate of interest; and q = Dividend yield.

Given the price of the geometric Asian (V_B) derived from the closed-form solution of Kemma and Vorst (1990), we can price the arithmetic Asian (V_A) as follows:

---

[34] For geometric averaging, the average value is the nth root of the sample values multiplied together: $Ave_G = \sqrt[n]{S_1 S_2 ... S_n}$.

$$V_A = V^*_A - V^*_B + V_B \qquad (2.37)$$

where, V^*_A is the estimated value of the arithmetic Asian through simulation and V^*_B is the estimated value of the geometric Asian through simulation.

(ii) Arithmetic Rate Approximation
As there are no closed-form solutions to arithmetic averages due to the inappropriate use of the lognormal assumption under this form of averaging, an approximation was proposed by Turnbull and Wakeman (1991) which suggests that the distribution under arithmetic averaging is approximately lognormal. The prices of the calls and puts under this approximation are:

$$c_{TW} = S e^{(b-r)T_2} N(d_1) - X e^{-rT_2} N(d_2) \qquad (2.38)$$

$$p_{TW} = X e^{-rT_2} N(-d_2) - S e^{(q-r)T_2} N(-d_1) \qquad (2.39)$$

where, $d_1 = \dfrac{\ln\left(\dfrac{S}{X}\right) + \left(b + 0.5\sigma_A^2\right)T_2}{\sigma_A \sqrt{T_2}}$; $d_2 = d_1 - \sigma_A \sqrt{T_2}$; $\sigma_A = \sqrt{\dfrac{\ln(M_2)}{T} - 2b}$;

$b = \dfrac{\ln(M_1)}{T}$; $M_1 = \dfrac{e^{(r-q)T} - e^{(r-q)t}}{(r-q)(T-t)}$;

$M_2 = \dfrac{2e^{(2(r-q)+\sigma^2)T} S^2}{(r-q+\sigma^2)(2r-2q+\sigma^2)T^2} + \dfrac{2S^2}{(r-q)T^2}\left(\dfrac{1}{2(r-q)+\sigma^2} - \dfrac{e^{(r-q)T}}{r-q+\sigma^2}\right)$; and

T_2 = Time remaining until maturity. If the averaging period has not yet begun, then $T_2 = T - t$, while if the averaging period has begun $T_2 = T$.

If the averaging period has begun, the strike price is adjusted as:

$$X_A = \frac{T}{T_2} X - \frac{(T - T_2)}{T_2} \overline{S} \qquad (2.40)$$

where, T = Original time to maturity; X = Original strike price; T_2 = Remaining time to maturity; and $\overline{S}$ = Average asset price

(iii) Another Arithmetic Rate Approximation
Levy (1992) proposed another analytical approximation, which, he argues, gives more accurate results than the Turnbull and Wakeman (1991) approximation. The prices of the calls and puts under this approximation are:

$$c_{Levy} = S_z N(d_1) - X_z e^{-rT_2} N(d_2) \qquad (2.41)$$

$$p_{Levy} = c_{Levy} - S_z + X_z e^{-rT_2} \qquad (2.42)$$

where, $d_1 = \dfrac{1}{\sqrt{K}}\left[\dfrac{\ln(L)}{2} - \ln(X_z)\right]$; $d_2 = d_1 - \sqrt{K}$; $S_z = \dfrac{S}{(r-D)T}\left(e^{-DT_2} - e^{-rT_2}\right)$

$$X_z = X - \overline{S}\,\frac{T-T_2}{T}; L = \frac{M}{T^2}; M = \frac{2S^2}{r-q+\sigma^2}\left\{\frac{e^{(2(r-q)+\sigma^2)T_2}-1}{2(r-q)+\sigma^2}\right\} - \frac{e^{(r-q)T_2}-1}{r-q}; \text{ and}$$

$$K = \ln(L) - 2[rT_2 + \ln(S_z)].$$

The aforementioned analytical approximations by Turnbull and Wakeman (1991) and Levy (1992) can be computed using Monte Carlo simulation, which gives relatively accurate prices for path dependent Asian options.

2.3.4.10. Exotic Options

The complex hedging needs of modern corporate and financial institutions often need more than the plain vanilla – traditional hedging products. Innovations in option pricing by financial engineers allow these institutions to customize hedging instruments in order to meet their market exposure. Therefore, several types of options contracts, known as exotic options, have been developed for hedging and investment purposes. Exotic options are tailor-made to meet the user's hedging or investment requirements and their payoffs and structures can be quite complex. Exotic options are mostly traded in OTC markets. In the pricing models of the plain vanilla options most of the variables (i.e. spot market price, strike price, risk-free rate, volatility of the underlying asset, time to expiry, etc.) are assumed to be constant during the life of the options, whereas in the case of exotic options, the values of these variables can be changed, depending on the kind of exotic option. Besides Asian options, other types of exotic options include – see also Hull (1995):

- **Barrier options**: Options where their payoffs depend on whether the price of the underlying asset reaches a certain level or not. For instance, the knock-out barrier option ceases to exist when the price of the underlying asset reaches a certain level (barrier). On the other hand, a knock-in option comes into existence only when the price of the underlying asset reaches a barrier.
- **Basket options**: Options where their payoffs depend on the price of the underlying portfolio (basket of assets).
- **Binary options**: Options where their payoffs are discontinuous. The payoff in the cash-or-nothing call is zero if the price of underlying asset does not reach the strike price, but the payoff is equal to a constant, say c, if it overcomes the strike price.
- **Chooser options**: Options where the holder can specify the type of the option (put or call). This right is given for a certain specified period of time.
- **Compound options**: Options on options. More specifically: call on a call, call on a put, put on a put and put on a call. They have two strike prices and two exercise dates.
- **Exchange options**: Options where one asset is exchanged for another (e.g. exchanging shares from the US with shares in the UK, this is called stock tender).
- **Forward Start options**: Options that will start some time in the future. It is usually expected that they start in-the-money, which is inscribed in the terms of the option.
- **Lookback options**: Options where their payoffs depend on the maximum or the minimum of the asset price, reached during their life.
- **Non-standard American options**: American option with extended features: (i) early exercise is restricted to certain dates – Bermudian option; (ii) early exercise is allowed only for certain part of the life of the option; and (iii) the strike price may change during the life of the option.

- **Packages**: Portfolio consisting of European put and call options.
- **Rainbow options**: Options which involve two or more underlying assets.
- **Shout options**: European style option where the holder "*shouts*" to the writer at one time during its life. The holder receives the payoff depending on the shout price or the price at the maturity, whichever make the profit greater.

2.4. Accounting Treatment of Derivatives Transactions and Tax Issues

In terms of accounting, a hedging transaction is a transaction entered into in the normal course of business to manage risk of price changes or currency fluctuation with respect to ordinary property that is held, or to be held by the taxpayer; or to manage risk of interest rate, or price changes, or currency fluctuations with respect to borrowings made or to be made, or ordinary obligations incurred or to be incurred, by the taxpayer. Every derivatives transaction is recorded in the balance-sheet as either an asset or liability measured at its fair value. Changes in the derivative's fair value must be recognised currently in earnings. A hedging transaction must be accounted for in a manner that clearly reflects income; in general, match timing of hedge profit/loss with profit/loss of the hedged item.

Positions in derivatives contracts are treated as if they are sold on the last day of the tax year. Any gains or losses on contracts are treated as capital gains/losses, whereas gains or losses on foreign currency contracts are treated as ordinary income/losses. In the US, capital gains are taxed at the same rate as ordinary income while the ability to deduct capital losses is restricted. For a corporate taxpayer, capital losses are deductible only to the extent of capital gains. A company can carry back a capital loss three years and forward five years. Gains or losses from hedging transactions are treated as ordinary income. The timing of the recognition of gains or losses from hedging transactions generally matches the timing of the recognition of income or deduction from the hedged items (Hull, 2005).

The Financial Accounting Standards Board's (FASB) statement No. 52, "*Foreign Currency Translation*", established in 1981 accounting standards in the US for foreign currency futures. FASB statement No. 80, "*Accounting for Futures Contracts*", established in 1984 accounting standards in the US for all other contracts. The two statements require changes in market value to be recognised when they occur unless the contract qualifies as a hedge. If the contract does qualify as a hedge, gains or losses are generally recognised for accounting purposes in the same period in which the gains or losses from the item being hedged are recognised.

Since then, there are a number of accounting issues related to derivatives that exist and have been debated for some time: (i) How should a derivative be accounted for when its value at inception may be very small or zero but may vary greatly over a potentially long period?; (ii) If the derivative is being used to hedge an underlying asset or commitment to buy or sell an underlying asset, how should such hedged positions be accounted for?; and (iii) What is the accounting methodology to use in valuing the derivative product once an accounting method has been selected?

During June 1998 the FASB issued Statement No. 133, "*Accounting for Derivative Instruments and Hedging Activities*". Statement No. 133 was subsequently amended by Statement No. 137 in June 1999 and Statement No. 138 in June 2000. The FASB identified four problem areas under previous accounting conventions: (i) the effects of derivatives were not transparent in financial statements, (ii) accounting guidance for derivative instruments and hedging activities was incomplete, (iii) accounting guidance for derivative instruments and hedging activities was inconsistent, and (iv) accounting guidance for derivatives instruments and hedging was difficult to apply (Energy Information Administration, 2002).

The FASB statements addressed each of the aforementioned issues. First, the visibility, comparability, and understandability of the risks associated with derivatives be reported as assets or liabilities and measured at fair value (mark-to-market). The guidance from Statement 133 on measurement of fair value states that, "*Quoted market prices in active markets are the best evidence of fair value and should be used as the basis for the measurement, if available*". When market prices are unavailable (as for example, in an OTC FFA contract) fair value should be estimated "... *based on the best information available in the circumstances*". Second, inconsistency, incompleteness, and the difficulty of applying previous accounting practice were reduced by the provision of guidance for all derivatives and hedging activities. Third, the statements included a range of hedge accounting practices by permitting hedge accounting for most derivatives instruments, including cash-flow hedges of expected transactions. Finally, the statements eliminated the requirement that an entity should demonstrate risk reduction on an entity-wide basis to qualify for hedge accounting. These changes have the result of reducing uncertainty about accounting requirements and therefore, encourage wider use of derivatives to hedge against risk.

2.5. Credit Risk in Derivatives Transactions and the Use of Credit Derivatives
2.5.1. Credit Risk
Potential defaults by counterparties in derivatives transactions give rise to significant credit risk for banks and other financial institutions. Credit risk is a significant element of the spectrum of risks facing the derivatives trader. There are different grades of credit risk. The most obvious one is the risk of default. Default means that the counterparty to which one is exposed will cease to make payments on obligations into which it has entered, because it is unable to make such payments. An intermediate credit risk occurs when the counterparty's creditworthiness is downgraded by the credit agencies, causing the value of obligations it has issued to decline in value.

The two aspects of credit risk are the market risk of the contracts into which we have entered with counterparties and the potential for some negative credit event, such as default or downgrade. One difficulty is to calculate the **probability of default** of a negative credit event. There are different methodologies to calculate default risk, such as the use of credit spreads observed in the corporate bond market, from historical default rates for a given class of credit, from financial statements and other public announcements of the counterparty's management, etc., the analysis of which is beyond the scope of the current book.

Another difficulty in assessing credit risk is estimating the **recovery rate**. Suppose that a bank defaults and that an investor has an outstanding swap with the bank, the market value of which is $5 million in his favor. After the end of the bankruptcy negotiations, normally the investor should be able to receive a partial payment. The recovery rate is the rate at which the investor will be paid in the event of a negative credit event. If the investor is paid $1 million then the recovery rate is 20%. In order to estimate the expected value, $E(V)$, of the swap to the investor before the bank defaults, suppose that the default probability is 6% and the recovery rate is 15%. Then, the expected value condition is straightforward.

$$E(V) = 0.94 \text{ x (\$5 million)} + 0.06 \text{ x (\$5 million x 0.15)} = \$4,745,000$$

It can be seen that the expected value of the swap is less than its current market value because of the possibility of default and less-than-total recovery of the value of the swap in the event of default.

Besides estimating the probability of default at different future times and the recovery rate, a company must estimate the **loss given default** (or credit exposure), which is the expected loss in the event that a default occurs. The expected loss is equal to the probability of default times the credit exposure. The loan given default on a loan made by a financial institution is:

$$\text{Loss Given Default} = V - R(L + A) \tag{2.43}$$

where, L is the outstanding principal on the loan; A is the accrued interest; R is the expected recovery rate; and V is the no-default value of the loan. For derivatives the estimation of the loss given default depends on the type of the derivatives contract:

- Derivatives that are always a liability to the investor and therefore, have no credit risk. If the counterparty goes bankrupt, there will be no loss (written option contract).
- Derivatives that are always an asset and therefore, always have credit risk. If the counterparty goes bankrupt, a loss is likely to be experienced (bought option contract).
- Derivatives that can be either an asset or a liability and therefore, may or may not have credit risk. When a company enters an interest-rate swap, it has a value equal to zero. As time passes, interest rates change and the value of the swap may become positive or negative. If the counterparty defaults when the value of the swap is positive, a claim will be made against the assets of the counterparty and a loss is likely to be experienced. If the counterparty defaults when the value of the swap is negative, no loss is made.

The **credit exposure** is equal to the greater of the current replacement value of the outstanding contracts plus the expected maximum increase in value of the contract over the remaining life of the contract for a given confidence interval or zero. This potential exposure can be calculated using VaR techniques. If the sum of those amounts is negative, then there is no exposure to the counterparty from a credit perspective because the financial institution is obligated to make payments to the counterparty.

The Basel Committee states that OTC off-balance-sheet contracts must be converted to on-balance-sheet contracts by calculating the **credit-equivalent amount.** The latter is equal to the **current exposure,** which reflects the current replacement cost of the contract (market or liquidation value of the contract at the time of evaluation) and can be calculated from forward rate curves plus the **potential exposure,** which reflects the future replacement cost of the contract.

However, there are some complicating issues implicit in this calculation of credit risk: (i) it is difficult to measure default probabilities; (ii) credit exposure is an increasing function of time, because of the potential increase in the value of the contract. The longer a contract's maturity, the greater the credit risk involved; (iii) as time passes and the counterparty makes cash-flow payments on contracts with a positive value, the credit risk of the contract is usually reduced; (iv) when an option is sold to a counterparty, there is no credit risk from the transaction other than settlement risk. For example, if the counterparty exercises a call by buying the underlying asset (say a stock), he must still deliver the funds for the stock. This delivery risk is called settlement risk; and (v) current positions may not represent future credit risks.

2.5.2. Credit Enhancements

Banks and dealers have worked with lawyers to develop techniques (called credit enhancements) that help mitigate the credit exposure inherent in derivatives transactions. **Credit enhancements** are modifications to credit transactions that improve the risk-reward relationship for credit providers. Enhancements can be real or merely perceived by the receiving party. Also, they can be tangible things like real estate and equipment or they can be intangibles like credit derivatives. Companies use credit enhancements to strengthen credit transactions and to improve pricing or terms. They may be used to entice credit providers to approve credit transactions that would otherwise be unacceptable because of the perceived risks. According to Wakeman (1996), credit enhancements usually fall within one of the following general categories: improvement in credit terms favouring the credit provider; additional collateral; guarantees, insurance or third party assurances; increased pricing, compensation or upside gain potential; or granting of specific rights or options.

The most commonly used credit enhancements, in order to minimise the impact of credit risk, in OTC financial transactions, are:

- **Master agreements:** They are credit support documents which offer protection against credit risk by introducing to the OTC transaction, default events, termination events, netting legislation, early termination payments,. The most popular is the 1992 ISDA master agreement (can be found at www.isda.org).
- **Credit rating:** Credit rating is evaluated using both qualitative and quantitative assessments. Going through both assessments of the company, will give a fair measurement of this company's credit risk (i.e. its chances to default and in case of default the level of the recovery rate).
- **Collateralisation of transactions**: Under such arrangement, a counterparty who owes an obligation to another counterparty posts collateral – typically consisting of cash or securities – to secure the obligation. In the event that the party defaults on the obligation, the secured party may seize the collateral. An arrangement can be unilateral with just one counterparty posting collateral. With two-sided obligations, bilateral collateralisation may be used. In that situation, both counterparties may post collateral for the value of their total obligation to the other.

In a typical collateral arrangement, the secured obligation is periodically marked-to-market, and the collateral is adjusted to reflect changes in value. The securing counterparty posts additional collateral when the market value has risen, or removes collateral when it has fallen. Suppose that a bank and an investor have swap contracts between them. Collateralization could require the investor to deposit collateral to the bank. The collateralization agreement would state that at any given time the collateral posted should be an amount greater than the positive value that the bank has in its outstanding swap contracts with the investor. If the investor is unable or unwilling to meet a demand for additional collateral, the collateralization agreement will state that the bank has the right to close out all outstanding swap contracts.

- **Third-party guarantee:** It can be given on behalf of the investor to the bank. The investor must find some other counterparty that will guarantee to pay the bank the difference between the market value of the contract before and after a negative credit event.
- **Credit insurance:** An insurance policy may provide for compensation in the event that a party defaults.
- **Letters of credit:** A form of guarantee of payment issued by a bank on behalf of a client that assures payments of principal amounts.
- **Downgrade triggers:** These are clauses in contracts with counterparties that state that if the credit rating of the counterparty falls below a certain level, then the contract is closed out using a pre-determined formula with one side paying a cash amount to the other side.
- **Netting:** It is the most commonly used technique which takes different forms, depending upon the institutions involved. Two forms of netting are widely employed in derivatives markets: (i) Payment netting reduces settlement risk: If counterparties are to exchange multiple cash-flows during a given day, they can agree to net those cash-flows to one payment per currency; (ii) Closeout netting reduces pre-settlement risk: If counterparties have multiple offsetting obligations to one another – for example, multiple swap contracts – they can agree to net those obligations. In the event that a counterparty defaults, or some other termination event occurs, the outstanding contracts are all terminated. They are marked-to-market and settled with a net payment. Suppose that a bank and a corporate investor have a number of outstanding interest rate swap contracts, some of which involve cash-flows on the same day. The bank and the investor have a netting agreement in place to net the cash-flows on any given delivery date into its root payment. For example, assume that during August the bank must pay $1 million to the investor and the investor must pay $1,300,000 to the bank. The net payment would be a $300,000 payment from the investor to the bank. Moreover, netting states that if a counterparty defaults on one contract with the financial institution then it must default on all outstanding contracts with the financial institution.
- **Use of other financial instruments**, such as credit derivatives.

2.5.3. Credit Derivatives

A credit derivative is a financial instrument used to mitigate or to assume specific forms of credit risk by hedgers and speculators. The payoff of credit derivatives depends on the creditworthiness of one or more commercial or sovereign entities. These products are particularly useful for institutions with widespread credit exposures.

The most popular form of credit derivatives is the credit default swap. A credit default swap is a contract that provides insurance against the risk of a default by particular company. The company is known as the reference entity. The buyer of the insurance obtains the right to sell a particular bond (called reference obligation) issued by the company for its par value (called the swap's notional principal) when a credit event occurs. The buyer of the credit default swap makes periodic payments to the seller until the end of the life of the swap or until a credit event occurs. The swap is settled

137

by either physical delivery, where the swap buyer delivers the bonds to the seller in exchange for their par value or in cash, where a mid-market price (Z) is calculated of the reference obligation some specified number of days after the credit event. The cash settlement is then $(100 - Z)\%$ of the notional principal.

Credit derivatives allow companies to manage their credit risk actively. Suppose that a bank had several hundred million dollars of loans outstanding to company A and is concerned about its exposure. It could buy a $100 million three-year credit default swap on the company A for $1.35 million per year. The bank, then, might want to exchange part of the credit exposure, for an exposure to a company (B), in a totally different industry. The bank could sell a three-year $100 million credit default swap for $1.25 million per year to company B, at the same time as buying a credit default swap on company A. The net cost of this strategy would be $100,000 per year.

Consider another case of credit default swaps between two banks. Suppose Bank A has made extensive loans in its corporate credit portfolio to a company. It is looking for some kind of insurance against a downgrade of the company by the major ratings agency. Bank A approaches bank B with the concept of a credit default swap. Bank A pays Bank B a premium, every six months, for the next five years, in exchange for which Bank B agrees to make payments to bank A, of a pre-set amount, should the company be downgraded. Bank B has exposure to bank A, a position they could not take directly because they are not part of Bank A's lending syndicate. Bank A has some degree of protection against a credit downgrade of the company. This reduction in their overall credit profile means that they do not need to hold as much capital in reserve, freeing the company up to take other business opportunities as they present themselves.

Another form of credit derivatives is the **total return swap**. A total return swap is an agreement to exchange the total return on a bond or other reference asset for LIBOR plus a spread. The total return includes coupons, interest, and the gain or loss on the asset over the life of the swap. Consider a three-year agreement with a notional principal of $100 million to exchange the total return on a 5% coupon bond for LIBOR+15 basis points. During the coupon paying dates, the payer pays the coupons earned on an investment of $100 million in the bond and the receiver pays LIBOR+ 15 basis points on a principal of $100 million. When the swap expires if the bond increased in value by 5% over the life of the swap, the payer pays $5 million (= $100 million x 5%) at the end of the three years. Alternatively, if the bond decreased in value by 5% over the life of the swap, the receiver is required to pay $5 million at the end of the three years. If there is a default on the bond, the swap is terminated and the receiver makes a final payment equal to the excess of $100 million over the market value of the bond.

Moreover, another way of packaging credit risk is the **credit spread options**, which are options where the payoff depends on either a particular credit spread or the price of a credit-sensitive asset. If the underlying asset defaults, credit spread options cease to exist.

Investors often use credit derivatives when entering in emerging markets for the ease of transaction in the same way that they use equity swaps. Fund managers can use credit derivatives to hedge against adverse movements in credit spreads. Companies can use credit swaps to hedge near-term issues of corporate bonds. Banks and other financial institutions can use credit derivatives to optimize the employment of their capital by diversifying their portfolio's credit risk.

2.6. Value-at-Risk (VaR) Models for Measuring Market Risk

Value-at-Risk (VaR) is a technique for measuring and reporting risk in a particular position or portfolio of instruments, such as cash instruments, derivatives instruments, and borrowing and lending. Financial institutions, corporate treasurers, fund/portfolio managers and companies, by VaR analysis have a rigorous and easily understood, by non-financial executives and regulators, method for reporting their risk. VaR is a single, summary, statistical number that expresses the maximum expected loss over a given time horizon, at a certain confidence interval and for a given position or portfolio of instruments, under normal market conditions, attributable to changes in the market price of the financial instruments. In other words, by using VaR, a manager can make the following statement: "*We are X percent certain that we will not lose more than V dollars in the next N days*", where V is the VaR of the portfolio, N is the time horizon, and X is the confidence level. In general, VaR is the loss corresponding to the $(100 - X)$th percentile of the distribution of the change in the value of the portfolio over the next N days. Assuming that the change in the value of the portfolio is normally distributed, VaR is shown graphically in Figure 2.16. The higher the level of confidence or the time horizon, the higher the VaR measure is, as more extreme outcomes have to be considered and greater uncertainty exists about the possible future market outcomes, respectively.

Figure 2.16. VaR and Probability Distribution of Changes in the Portfolio Value

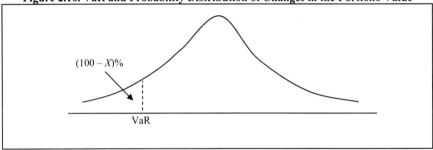

$(100 - X)\%$

VaR

Corporate Treasuries, Banks and Mutual Funds use VaR to obtain an idea of how their market exposures behave under normal market conditions. Suppose that a portfolio manager has positions of $100 million in foreign exchange, fixed income and equities. He needs a method to calculate the worst case for the position overnight with a 95% degree of confidence. An overnight-95% confidence interval VaR of $5 million would mean that the likelihood of that portfolio losing more than $5 million on the worst day is less than 5%.

Moreover, with VaR analysis, the riskiness of different portfolios can be compared. Suppose that two portfolio managers have $100 million each under management. Manager A makes a return of 20%, beating his target of 10%. Manager B makes a return of 10%, which is his target. In order to compare the performance of the two managers the risks of the portfolios should be assessed first. Further, suppose that the average overnight-95% VaR of Manager A is 6 million and of manager B is $2 million. The return on risk capital of Manager A is 333.33% (=$20million/$6millionx100) and of Manager B is 500%

(=$10million/$2millionx100). It could be reasonably argued that Manager B is a better portfolio manager, in that he used his risk capital more efficiently.

In comparing different portfolios, with the same VaR measure but different risk profiles, a more appropriate measure to use is the Conditional VaR (C-VAR). Whereas VaR asks the question *"How bad can things get?"*, C-VaR asks *"If things do get bad, how much can we expect to loose?"*. C-VaR is the expected loss during an N-day period, conditional on that we are in the $(100 - X)\%$ left tail of the distribution. For example, if X is 99 and N is 10, C-VaR is the average amount we lose over a 10-day period assuming that a 1% worst-case event occurs.

JP Morgan, during 1994, developed a methodology for calculating VaR for simple portfolios (i.e., portfolios that do not include any options), called RiskMetrics. RiskMetrics forecasts the volatility of financial instruments and their various correlations. Volatility is important because if the underlying markets are volatile, investments of a given size are more likely to lose money than they would if markets were less volatile. Volatility here refers to the distribution of the return around the mean. A volatile market is one in which the returns vary greatly around the mean while a stable market is one in which the returns vary little around the mean.

The correlation between the prices of the instruments of the portfolio is also important. A well-diversified portfolio, with financial instruments that move in different directions at different speeds, is less risky than a portfolio with financial instruments that move in the same direction. In the former portfolio we would expect to make money on some instruments and loose money on the remaining instruments whereas in the latter portfolio if all financial instruments move down, we will loose money on each of these instruments.

Currently VaR is adopted by most financial institutions, investment and commercial banks, institutional investors and regulators. In 1995, the Basle Committee on Banking Supervision and in 1996, the Capital Adequacy Directive (CAD) of the European Union, allowed banks to use their internal VaR models to calculate their capital requirements for market risk. The Basle II, still promotes the use of VaR models and extends their use in calculating capital requirements for credit risk.

2.6.1. Calculation of VaR
Most risk management methodologies are based on the analysis of a set of scenarios that describe possible future *"states"* of the world. Each of the methodologies makes different assumptions about the possible evolution of markets, but they follow a similar approach towards measuring market risk; they calculate a profit or revenue for each scenario, and then aggregate those results to form a distribution and extract the mean and variability of the profit, portfolio value, or revenue level for the set. There are three methodologies for calculating VaR: the variance-covariance (or analytic VaR), historical simulation and Monte Carlo simulation.

(i) Analytic VaR analyse the volatilities of, and correlation among, the different risk exposures of the company's portfolio. This method is a two-step process: Firstly, a selection of a set of market risk factors and a systematic measurement of the actual price levels, volatilities and correlations is made. Secondly, the company's exposures are put into a form that can be analysed using risk factor information. This is called *"cash-flow mapping"*. Examples of risk factors are typically, exchange rates, interest rates, equity prices, etc. The analytic VaR is based on the assumption that the underlying risk factors are normally distributed. To be compatible with the available risk factor data, every instrument in a portfolio needs to be reduced to a collection of cash-flows to derive a "synthetic" portfolio of assets held. The synthetic portfolio is made up of positions in the risk factors whose volatilities and correlations are known. The purpose is to find the "*best*" replication of a financial exposure in conjunction with the company's other exposures. Once the cash-flow mapping has been created, one need only perform basic matrix manipulation to calculate the VaR of a portfolio.

(ii) Historical simulation involves using past data in a very direct way as a guide to what might happen in the future and does not require assumptions about the statistical distributions of the underlying risk factors. To calculate VaR for a portfolio with one-day time horizon, a 99% confidence level and 400 days of data, the first step is to identify the risk factors affecting the portfolio. The next step is to collect historical prices of the risk factors over the most recent 400 days. Scenario 1 is where the percentage changes in the values of all factors are the same, as they were on the first day for which we have collected data; scenario 2 is where they are the same as on the second day for which we have data; and so on. For each scenario (1,…,400) we calculate the daily dollar change in the value of the portfolio. This defines a probability distribution for daily changes in the value of the portfolio. Define v_i as the value of a risk factor on day i and suppose that today is day t. The ith scenario assumes that the value of the risk factor tomorrow will be:

$$v_t \frac{v_i}{v_{i-1}} \qquad (2.44)$$

The fifth-worst daily change is the first percentile of the distribution, which loss represents the VaR estimate. The portfolio manager is now 99% certain that he will not take a loss greater than the VaR estimate. Each day, the VaR estimate is updated using the most recent 400 days of data. The advantages of the historical simulation method are that it does not use estimated variances and covariances, and does not assume anything about the distribution of portfolio returns. However, the disadvantage of the historical simulation is its assumption that future risks are much like past risks.

(ii) Monte Carlo simulation tries to calculate the probability of certain outcomes, by multiple trial runs, using random variables. Initially, the Monte Carlo simulation randomly selects values to create scenarios of a problem. Then these values are taken from within a fixed range and selected to fit a probability distribution. Monte Carlo is a sampling method because the input variables are randomly generated from probability distributions to simulate the process of sampling from an actual population. A distribution for the input variables is chosen, that most closely matches the data or best represents the current state of knowledge. In Monte Carlo simulation, the random selection process is repeated many times (e.g. 10,000 times or more) to create multiple scenarios. Each time a value is randomly selected, it forms one possible scenario and solution to the problem. Together, these scenarios give a range of possible solutions, some of which are more probable and some less probable. When repeated for many scenarios the average solution will give an approximate answer to the problem. Therefore, the hypothetical profits and losses of the company's portfolio under each scenario are converted into a histogram of expected profits and losses, from which VaR can be calculated. The accuracy of the VaR measure can be improved by simulating more scenarios. The accuracy of a Monte Carlo simulation is proportional to the square root of the number of scenarios used. One advantage of the Monte Carlo simulation is that it does not assume that portfolio returns are distributed normally. Another is that it is a forward-looking assessment of risk that takes into account options. However, the methodology requires the set of a correlation and volatility matrix to generate the random scenarios, and that makes it computationally intensive. It also requires the company to have pricing models for all the instruments in its portfolio.

2.6.2. Scenario Analysis and Back Testing
VaR calculates an expected maximum loss under normal market conditions and tends to ignore extreme (or abnormal) events. In case of abnormal market conditions, **scenario analysis** is used. Suppose that a portfolio manager has an overnight-95% VaR of $6 million on assets of $100 million. The VaR describes his expected loss under normal market conditions. In scenario analysis, the portfolio manager will simulate various hypothetical evolutions of events in order to determine their effect on the value of the portfolio. By determining the change in value of his portfolio under stressful conditions, a procedure called "*stress-testing*", the portfolio manager has a better perception of where the risks in his portfolio lie. By taking then appropriate trades, he can bring this risk to accepted risk levels. Without stress-testing, a portfolio manager may incur big losses if the worst case scenario occurs. Stress testing can be considered as a way of taking into account extreme events that do occur from time to time but that are virtually impossible to be captured by the probability distributions assumed for the risk factors.

Back testing considers how well the VaR estimates would have performed in the past. Suppose that a portfolio manager calculates a one-day 99% VaR. Back testing looks at how often the loss in a day exceeded the one-day 99% VaR calculated for that day. If this happened on about 1% of the days, the methodology used for calculating VaR is trustworthy.

2.6.3. Variations of VaR
There are various variations/extensions of the VaR measure, like Profit-at-Risk (PaR), Earnings-at-Risk (EaR) and Cash-Flow-at-Risk (CFaR), which are analysed in turn:

(i) Profit-at-Risk (PaR) assumes that positions will be taken through to delivery rather than closed out prior to the breakpoint. The PaR measure reflects the entire exposed profit of a portfolio position, not just the change expected in it for a period of time. PaR tests the entire range of risks affecting spot prices at the time of delivery. The Monte Carlo simulation calculates the change in the value of the portfolio using a sample of randomly generated price scenarios that are assumed to be equally probable. PaR requires making assumptions about market structures, the stochastic processes the prices follow, and the correlations between risk factors and the volatility of these factors.

Accounting rules prohibit companies with portfolios of physical assets from marking these assets to market. Nor can these companies liquidate or acquire their assets as quickly as companies with financial portfolios. In the **Earnings-at-Risk** (EaR) measure, profits are calculated as spot price revenues minus cost of production plus hedge payoffs prior to delivery plus hedge payoffs during delivery. A Monte Carlo simulation can provide an estimate of the distribution of the profit function. The distribution of profits captures the upside potential, as well as the downside risk, of variability of market prices, as well as the operational characteristics of physical assets. The EaR measure assesses the impact of derivative trading strategies on both tails of the profit distribution curve.

(ii) Cash-Flow-at-Risk (CFaR) is designed to forecast earnings volatility one quarter to one year ahead. CFaR is preferred by non-financial companies which are worried with managing the risks in the cash-flows and not changes in market values. CFaR answers the following question: *"What is the worst thing that can happen to the company financially in the next quarter or year?"*. The CFaR measure considers every type of risk to which a company can be exposed and produces a risk profile that can help answer the above question. CFaR measures the aggregate risk against a company's cash-flow. Because CFaR creates forward-looking probability distributions for a company's cash-flow, it provides a measure of the likelihood of negative events that could produce a significant drop in earnings. The CFaR model can be used by companies to enhance their financial strategy and investment planning, assess their capital structure and their credit-worthiness.

2.7. Summary
This chapter provided an introduction to financial derivatives products. It is by no means exhaustive. Its aim was to introduce the non-specialist to the possibilities offered by financial derivatives to market agents to profit and to control risks. The chapter started by presenting the different types of participants in derivatives markets, which are classified as hedgers, speculators, and arbitrageurs, based on the reasons for participation of each of them in these markets. Then, the main types of financial derivatives and their respective markets were described; namely forwards, futures, swaps, and options contracts and markets. In each case, a number of underlying *"commodities"* were considered, including storable commodities held for investment and for consumption purposes, non-storable commodities, where each of these categories can comprise *"commodities"* such as stocks, gold, oil, exchange indices, foreign exchange, interest rates and freight rates, amongst others. Issues involving the *"fair"* pricing of these *"commodities"* were analysed, and based on those arguments analytical formulas were provided – where possible – for the pricing of these financial derivatives products. Moreover, the chapter presented the accounting treatment of derivatives transactions and tax issues, and described the VaR model for measuring market risk, the issue of credit risk in derivatives transactions and the use of credit derivatives. Further issues on financial derivatives not discussed here are presented when the need arises in other chapters of this book. For readers interested in even further understanding of these products, there are excellent books in the market to refer to; they include, Hull (2005), Chance (2003), Kolb (2002) Stulz (2002), and Natenberg (1994), amongst others.

The next chapter of this book is probably the most important and most innovative part of the book. It discusses how freight risk can be managed much more effectively, compared to the traditional methods discussed in Chapter 1 of the book, by using a class of financial derivatives known as freight derivatives. It presents the most comprehensive discussion available in the literature in the subject matter.

APPENDIX I: Cumulative Standard Normal Distribution Table

Table of Cumulative Standard Normal Distribution Pr(X <= Z), from minus infinity to Z

Z =	0	0.01	0.02	0.03	0.04	0.05	0.06	0.07	0.08	0.09
0.0	0.5000	0.5040	0.5080	0.5120	0.5160	0.5199	0.5239	0.5279	0.5319	0.5359
0.1	0.5398	0.5438	0.5478	0.5517	0.5557	0.5596	0.5636	0.5675	0.5714	0.5753
0.2	0.5793	0.5832	0.5871	0.5910	0.5948	0.5987	0.6026	0.6064	0.6103	0.6141
0.3	0.6179	0.6217	0.6255	0.6293	0.6331	0.6368	0.6406	0.6443	0.6480	0.6517
0.4	0.6554	0.6591	0.6628	0.6664	0.6700	0.6736	0.6772	0.6808	0.6844	0.6879
0.5	0.6915	0.6950	0.6985	0.7019	0.7054	0.7088	0.7123	0.7157	0.7190	0.7224
0.6	0.7257	0.7291	0.7324	0.7357	0.7389	0.7422	0.7454	0.7486	0.7517	0.7549
0.7	0.7580	0.7611	0.7642	0.7673	0.7704	0.7734	0.7764	0.7794	0.7823	0.7852
0.8	0.7881	0.7910	0.7939	0.7967	0.7995	0.8023	0.8051	0.8078	0.8106	0.8133
0.9	0.8159	0.8186	0.8212	0.8238	0.8264	0.8289	0.8315	0.8340	0.8365	0.8389
1.0	0.8413	0.8438	0.8461	0.8485	0.8508	0.8531	0.8554	0.8577	0.8599	0.8621
1.1	0.8643	0.8665	0.8686	0.8708	0.8729	0.8749	0.8770	0.8790	0.8810	0.8830
1.2	0.8849	0.8869	0.8888	0.8907	0.8925	0.8944	0.8962	0.8980	0.8997	0.9015
1.3	0.9032	0.9049	0.9066	0.9082	0.9099	0.9115	0.9131	0.9147	0.9162	0.9177
1.4	0.9192	0.9207	0.9222	0.9236	0.9251	0.9265	0.9279	0.9292	0.9306	0.9319
1.5	0.9332	0.9345	0.9357	0.9370	0.9382	0.9394	0.9406	0.9418	0.9429	0.9441
1.6	0.9452	0.9463	0.9474	0.9484	0.9495	0.9505	0.9515	0.9525	0.9535	0.9545
1.7	0.9554	0.9564	0.9573	0.9582	0.9591	0.9599	0.9608	0.9616	0.9625	0.9633
1.8	0.9641	0.9649	0.9656	0.9664	0.9671	0.9678	0.9686	0.9693	0.9699	0.9706
1.9	0.9713	0.9719	0.9726	0.9732	0.9738	0.9744	0.9750	0.9756	0.9761	0.9767
2.0	0.9772	0.9778	0.9783	0.9788	0.9793	0.9798	0.9803	0.9808	0.9812	0.9817
2.1	0.9821	0.9826	0.9830	0.9834	0.9838	0.9842	0.9846	0.9850	0.9854	0.9857
2.2	0.9861	0.9864	0.9868	0.9871	0.9875	0.9878	0.9881	0.9884	0.9887	0.9890
2.3	0.9893	0.9896	0.9898	0.9901	0.9904	0.9906	0.9909	0.9911	0.9913	0.9916
2.4	0.9918	0.9920	0.9922	0.9925	0.9927	0.9929	0.9931	0.9932	0.9934	0.9936
2.5	0.9938	0.9940	0.9941	0.9943	0.9945	0.9946	0.9948	0.9949	0.9951	0.9952
2.6	0.9953	0.9955	0.9956	0.9957	0.9959	0.9960	0.9961	0.9962	0.9963	0.9964
2.7	0.9965	0.9966	0.9967	0.9968	0.9969	0.9970	0.9971	0.9972	0.9973	0.9974
2.8	0.9974	0.9975	0.9976	0.9977	0.9977	0.9978	0.9979	0.9979	0.9980	0.9981
2.9	0.9981	0.9982	0.9982	0.9983	0.9984	0.9984	0.9985	0.9985	0.9986	0.9986
3.0	0.9987	0.9987	0.9987	0.9988	0.9988	0.9989	0.9989	0.9989	0.9990	0.9990
3.1	0.9990	0.9991	0.9991	0.9991	0.9992	0.9992	0.9992	0.9992	0.9993	0.9993
3.2	0.9993	0.9993	0.9994	0.9994	0.9994	0.9994	0.9994	0.9995	0.9995	0.9995
3.3	0.9995	0.9995	0.9995	0.9996	0.9996	0.9996	0.9996	0.9996	0.9996	0.9997
3.4	0.9997	0.9997	0.9997	0.9997	0.9997	0.9997	0.9997	0.9997	0.9997	0.9998
3.5	0.9998	0.9998	0.9998	0.9998	0.9998	0.9998	0.9998	0.9998	0.9998	0.9998
3.6	0.9998	0.9998	0.9999	0.9999	0.9999	0.9999	0.9999	0.9999	0.9999	0.9999
3.7	0.9999	0.9999	0.9999	0.9999	0.9999	0.9999	0.9999	0.9999	0.9999	0.9999
3.8	0.9999	0.9999	0.9999	0.9999	0.9999	0.9999	0.9999	0.9999	0.9999	0.9999
3.9	1.0000	1.0000	1.0000	1.0000	1.0000	1.0000	1.0000	1.0000	1.0000	1.0000
4.0	1.0000	1.0000	1.0000	1.0000	1.0000	1.0000	1.0000	1.0000	1.0000	1.0000

CHAPTER 3. Freight Rate Derivatives and Risk Management

3.1. Introduction

Chapter 1 of this book identified all possible sources of business risk that exist in the maritime sector, outlined the traditional methods used by market participants for risk protection, and provided reasons for using derivatives products, as a solution to the inflexibilities, rigidities and higher costs involved in applying the traditional methods of risk management. Chapter 2 then introduced financial derivatives, in order to familiarise the non-specialist with this set of instruments, which provide an extra management tool to "*players*", in their effort to manage the risks that they face. The current chapter examines the management of, what is considered by most people as, the most important source of risk of all; namely the risk that emanates from freight rate volatility. The aim of this chapter then is to examine how freight derivatives can be used to manage freight rate risk. It provides a comprehensive discussion of the past and present use and the development of freight derivatives, designed to control fluctuations in freight rates. The issues involved are illustrated through many practical examples.

Just to remind our readers, freight derivatives contracts can be used for business decisions which include:

- **Risk management through hedging:** That is, they can be used to stabilise the cash-flow – income or cost, underlying a position (long or short) in the physical (or spot) market, up to three years ahead.
- **Investment/Speculation:** If a market agent has some convictions as to how the market will move in the future, and if the quoted price of a freight derivatives contract is cheap compared to its fair value, freight derivatives contracts can be bought in order to sell them in the future at the higher expected price. Freight derivatives contracts may also be shorted (sold) by speculators in anticipation of a market fall.
- **Spread play:** Based on historical data, if the freight derivatives price difference, observed currently, between two shipping routes is large, compared to their historical difference, a market agent can buy the cheap and sell the expensive in order to take advantage of an anticipated return to normal differentials. This can be done between freights in different regions, different vessel sizes, or types of trade.
- **Portfolio switching:** A market agent trading a particular route where he believes that the short-term volatility will be low, may sell freight derivatives contracts on the existing trade route and buy a matching volume on a different, more volatile route.
- **Portfolio management of existing time-charters:** A market agent using freight derivatives contracts can cover any unwanted positions that he may have in the physical market under time-charters.
- **Early access to newbuildings:** When a shipowner commits to a newbuilding, there is a lead-time before the vessel is delivered. The shipowner can bridge this gap by using freight derivatives contract to cover the period before his vessel is delivered. Thus, the shipowner, if his expectations are correct, can have a continuous cash-inflow from the freight derivatives trades until his vessel arrives.
- **A more flexible, less costly, less risky alternative to time-chartering or to COAs:** Buying (or selling) a freight derivatives contract is the same as time-

chartering in (out), without the physical risks involved in running the vessel itself. In addition to being less risky it is also a more flexible and less costly strategy, in terms of going in or out of freight market positions. Moreover, these freight derivatives positions may be closed or reversed earlier in a matter of minutes, if market conditions change.

- **Collateral against a bank loan:** It is reported that banks consider favorably loans when a potential customer has arranged security of freight through freight derivatives positions, just as it does when long-term time-charters are backing a vessel loan.
- **Price discovery:** Futures and forward contract prices can be used to discover current and futures prices in the spot market. Moreover, futures/forward contract prices lead the spot market in terms of information assimilation – see evidence presented in Kavussanos (2002) and Kavussanos and Visvikis (2004). These constitute *"free"* forecasts of spot rates, provided by the mere existence of efficient futures/forward markets.
- **Focused:** It helps market participants focus on specific segments of the market, on which they have an interest on.

It is evident then, that for all the above reasons it is very important for participants in freight markets to be aware of the possibilities offered by the existence of freight derivatives, but also to understand how they can use them under different circumstances, as well as the issues involved in the process. This chapter then provides the answers to these questions.

The rest of the chapter is organised as follows: Section 3.2 presents the underlying *"commodities"* of freight derivatives, upon which these derivatives are written; these *"commodities"* are freight indices, constructed by the Baltic Exchange and by Platts, on behalf of the ocean shipping industry. Section 3.3 introduces the first ever freight futures contract, the Baltic International Freight Futures Exchange (BIFFEX) contract. It provides an overview of its history, from its creation back in May 1985, until its termination in April 2002, showing examples of how it has been used by the industry to hedge freight rate risk. The same section presents the freight futures contracts, offered by the International Maritime Exchange (IMAREX) since 2001, and the New York Mercantile Exchange (NYMEX) since 2005. The freight forward contracts cleared by the London Clearing House Clearnet (LCH.Clearnet) are also discussed here. Section 3.4 presents the characteristics and specifications of Forward Freight Agreements (FFAs). It examines their use, their advantages, disadvantages and other relevant issues that their users must be aware of. They include: description of their characteristics, the interpretation of market information on FFAs, the negotiation of these contracts, as well as the credit risk issues involved with these OTC contracts. Section 3.5 provides a number of applications of freight futures and forwards trading positions. These applications are designed in such a way so as to demonstrate the relevant calculations assumed by freight derivatives positions under various circumstances. Thus, applications include freight derivatives trading in the dry-bulk and tanker sectors, non-cleared and cleared transactions, and voyage and time-charter applications, amongst others. Section 3.6 introduces freight options. Hedging, speculation and arbitrage strategies are presented through applications on freight rates. Having presented the range of derivatives instruments that may be used for freight rate risk management, section 3.7 takes another look at the traditional strategies which have been used for risk management in shipping and compares them to the flexible solutions provided by freight derivatives. Section 3.8 shows how Value-at-Risk (VaR) may be used to monitor freight market risks, which when combined with the preferences of the shipowner regarding risk, can become a decision tool on whether to use derivatives or not for freight risk management purposes. Section 3.9 discusses the important role of brokers in freight derivatives trading. Section 3.10 reviews the economics and presents the empirical evidence and published research on freight derivatives markets. Finally, section 3.11 concludes the chapter.

3.2. The Underlying Indices of Freight Rate Derivatives

As explained in Chapter 2 of this book, for financial derivatives contracts (e.g. futures, forwards, options, etc.) to be written on an underlying "*commodity*", a firm/independent price for this commodity must exist. This is important, in order to enable the derivatives contracts to be settled against this price. The Baltic Exchange, amongst others, has undertaken a central role, assisted by market brokers, in constructing such "*commodities*" for the shipping industry. The next important issue to be decided upon is how settlement of the forward contract will take place; that is, how the underlying commodity will be delivered? As freight services are a non-storable "*commodity*", which cannot be delivered, like gold or oil are, for instance, cash settlement against the value of a freight index provided the solution. Derivatives contracts then, written on the index, are cash settled against the price of the "*commodity*" – the index. The Baltic Exchange and Platts, amongst others, construct these freight rate indices and make them available to freight derivatives market-makers and to other freight market participants. This service to the industry is widely used by market-makers and users of freight derivatives; organizations, like the International Maritime Exchange (IMAREX), the New York Mercantile Exchange (NYMEX) and the London Clearing House Clearnet (LCH.Clearnet), described later on in this chapter, use the values of the indices to clear their derivatives contracts against them.

According to SSY Futures (2000), a freight index should be an accurate reflection of the real global spot market; must be trusted, rigorously computed and unbiased, published regularly and frequently (preferably daily, with conventional as well as electronic dissemination to the extent possible); it must be based on balanced and sufficiently expanded input, furnished by a representative and authoritative international panel; should be transparent and simple, audited and monitored by a recognised independent international body that must have proper procedures for dealing with complaints; finally, it should be low-cost and supported by the major participants in the market, as well as expressed in units familiar to the industry.

The Baltic Exchange freight rate indices, which are discussed in this section of the chapter, satisfy these properties. The Baltic Exchange appoints panel reporting companies, which are assigned the task of reporting freight rates to the exchange on a daily basis. These data are then used by the Baltic to build its freight rate indices, which it reports to the market. Obviously, the reliability of the freight rate indices depends greatly on the members of the panel. The Exchange, in its effort to produce quality indices selects the panel members in accordance with the following criteria: (i) the main business of panellists should be shipbroking. Principals, like shipowners or charterers, are not considered appropriate as panellists; (ii) they must be recognised as competent, professional firms, actively engaged in the markets they report, with adequate personnel to perform their role; (iii) panellists must be members of the Baltic Exchange, fulfilling all relevant membership criteria; (iv) they must agree to be bound by the standard terms set out by the Baltic Exchange; (v) an appropriate geographical spread of panellists is maintained; (vi) the Baltic Exchange seeks to avoid the appointment of panellists who are the exclusive representatives of charterers who are particularly influential in relevant trades; and (vii) panel reporting companies must nominate a "*principal*" or "*representative*" member of the Baltic Exchange as responsible for each index they report on (Baltic Exchange, 2005).

3.2.1. The Composition of Dry-Bulk Freight Rate Indices

In January 1985 the Baltic Exchange launched its Baltic Freight Index (BFI), in order to construct a "*barometer*" of how the world freight market moved, and at the same time provide the underlying "*commodity*" needed to write a futures contract on. The original composition of the BFI and its panelists, as they stood in 1985, can be seen, respectively, in panels A and B of Table 3.1.

Table 3.1. Routes, Vessels, Cargoes and Weights of the Baltic Freight Index (BFI), as of January 1985

Panel A: Index Composition				
Routes	Vessel Size (dwt)	Cargo	Route Description	Weights
1	55,000	Light cargo	US Gulf to ARA	20%
2	52,000	HSS	US Gulf to South Japan	20%
3	52,000	HSS	US Pacific Coast to South Japan	15%
4	21,000	HSS	US Gulf to Venezuela	5%
5	20,000	Barley	Antwerp (Belgium) to Red Sea	5%
6	120,000	Coal	Hampton Roads (US) to South Japan	5%
7	65,000	Coal	Hampton Roads (US) to ARA	5%
8	110,000	Coal	Queensland (Australia) to Rotterdam	5%
9	55,000	Coal	Vancouver (Canada) to Rotterdam (Netherlands)	5%
10	90,000	Iron Ore	Monrovia (Liberia) to Rotterdam (Netherlands)	5%
11	20,000	Sugar	Recife (Brazil) to US East Coast	5%
12	20,000	Potash	Hamburg (Germany) to West Coast India	2.5%
13	14,000	Phosphate	Aqaba (Jordan) to West Coast India	2.5%

Panel B: Panellists
Clarksons (UK), Galbraith's Ltd. (UK), E.A. Gibson Shipbrokers Ltd. (UK), Howard Houlder & Co. Ltd. (UK), Howe Robinson & Co. Ltd. (UK), Simpson Spence & Young Ltd. (UK), Arrow Chartering Ltd. (UK), John F Dillon & Co. (US), Yamamizu Shipping Co. Ltd. (Japan), Banchero-Costa & C (Italy), and Fearnleys A/S (Norway).

Notes: **Source:** Baltic Exchange
- The vessel size is measured by its carrying capacity (dwt – deadweight tonnes) and includes the effective cargo, bunkers, lubricants, water, food rations, crew and any passengers.
- HSS stands for Heavy Grain, Soya and Sorghum.
- ARA stands for Amsterdam, Rotterdam and Antwerp area.

It consisted of 13 major routes that dry-bulk vessels traded on, incorporating Handysize, Panamax, and Capesize spot freight rates. Each (major) route included in the BFI was given a number, 1 to 13, which is recorded in the first column of Table 3.1. It referred to a vessel size - shown in column 2; a certain cargo - presented in column 3; with the route description – appearing in column 4; while the weight assigned to each route is reported in the last column of the table. The weights assigned were set according to the importance of the route in the dry-bulk sector. We can see, for instance, that routes 1 and 2 (US Gulf to ARA and US Gulf to South Japan, respectively) were the most important ones, each of them with a weight of 20%, with route 3 (US Pacific Coast to South Japan) following in importance, as reflected by its weight of 15%. The remaining 45% of the index was represented by the other ten routes shown in the table. Each of their weights was either 2.5% or 5% of the value of the index. Thus, the contribution of route 12 or 13 to the index was eight times less than that of route 1, while the contribution of route 4, for instance, to the index was 4 times less than that of route 1, but twice that of route 12.

Provision was made that the composition of the BFI could be altered over time, in line with developments in the dry-bulk sector of the shipping industry, in order to continue to reflect changing trading patterns. If these modifications did not take place, the BFI would not track well the developments in freight markets. Specifically, at all times, the routes in the index were chosen carefully by analysis of the percentage revenue value of the main commodities on the spot voyage market, the total number and frequency of voyage fixtures by each commodity, and the balance of geographic origin and ton-mile contribution. Some provision was also made to give a balance of ship sizes. Time-charters were also included later, after careful consultation with market users, with the intention of including the element of net earnings of the shipowner together with the gross cost of moving cargo.

Table 3.2 presents the structural changes in the composition of the BFI since its inception. It can be seen, for instance, that by August 1990 time-charter routes 1A, 2A, and 3A were introduced, and route 5 was redefined from spot to being time-charter and from Antwerp – Jeddah it became South America – Far East; route's 11 definition changed in November 1988 from Victoria – China to Casablanca – West Coast of India and the commodity from pig iron became phosphate rock, with a corresponding drop in its weight from 5% to 2.5%. A similar change occurred in the same year in route 12; the Hamburg – West Coast of India, potash carrying 20,000 dwt vessel, was replaced with a 14,000 dwt vessel, carrying phosphate in the Aqaba – West Coast of India route. Finally, route 13 was removed from the BFI and the weightings changed. Broadly speaking, other major changes amounted to Handysize routes 4, 5, 11, and 12 being removed by November 1993. A further major restructuring took place in November 1999, removing the Capesize routes, thus, effectively leaving only Panamax routes in the index.

Following these restructurings of the BFI and the increasing recognition of the distinct segmentation of the dry-bulk sector of the industry, as well as of the tanker sector, along the lines discussed in Chapter 1 of this book, a number of distinct sectoral indices have been gradually launched by the Baltic to account for this situation. For instance, for the dry-bulk sector of the industry, these indices include the Baltic Handysize Index (BHI) introduced in 1997; the Baltic Panamax Index (BPI) launched in 1998; the Baltic Capesize index (BCI) introduced in 1999; the Baltic Handymax Index (BHMI) created in 2000, and from October 2000 officially replaced the Baltic Handy Index (BHI); and the Baltic Supramax Index (BSI) launched in 2005.

Table 3.2. Changes in the Composition of Baltic Freight Index (BFI)

Routes	Vessel Size (dwt)	Cargo	Route Description	1/01/85 – 3/11/88	4/11/88 – 3/08/90	6/08/90 – 4/02/91	5/02/91 – 4/02/93	5/02/93 – 2/11/93	3/11/93 – 5/05/98	6/5/98 – 29/10/99	From 1/11/99
1	55,000	Light Grain	US Gulf to ARA	20%	20%	10%	10%	10%	10%	10%	10%
1A	70,000	T/C	Trans-Atlantic Round (45-60 days)		10%	10%	10%	10%	10%	10%	20%
2	54,000	HSS	US Gulf to South Japan	20%	10%	20%	10%	10%	10%	10%	12.5%
2A	70,000	T/C	Skaw-Gibraltar to Taiwan-Japan (50-60 days)		10%		10%	10%	10%	10%	12.5%
3	54,000	HSS	US Pacific Coast to South Japan	15%	10%	7.5%	7.50%	7.50%	10%	10%	10%
3A	70,000	T/C	Trans-Pacific Round (35-50 days)			7.5%	7.50%	7.50%	10%	10%	20%
4	21,000	HSS	US Gulf to Venezuela	5%	5%	5%	5%	5%			
5	35,000	Barley	Antwerp (Belgium) to Jeddah (Saudi Arabia)	5%	5%	5%	5%	5%			
	38,000	T/C	South America to Far East								
6	120,000	Coal	Hampton Roads (US) to South Japan	5%	7.50%	7.50%	7.50%	7.50%	7.50%		
7	65,000	Coal	Hampton Roads (US) to ARA	5%	5%	5%	5%	5%			
	110,000	Coal	Hampton Roads (US) to ARA						7.50%	7.50%	
8	130,000	Coal	Queensland (Australia) to Rotterdam (Netherlands)	5%	5%	5%	5%	5%	7.50%		
9	55,000	Coke	Vancouver (Canada) to Rotterdam	5%	5%	5%	5%	5%			
	70,000	T/C	Japan-Korea to Skaw Passero (50-60 days)						10%	10%	15%
10	90,000	Iron Ore	Monrovia (Liberia) to Rotterdam	5%	5%	5%	5%	5%			
	150,000	Iron Ore	Tubarao (Brazil) to Rotterdam						7.50%	7.50%	
11	25,000	Pig Iron	Victoria (Brazil) to China	5%							
	25,000	Phosphate	Casablanca (Morocco) to West Coast India		2.50%	2.50%	2.50%	2.50%			
12	20,000	Potash	Hamburg (Germany) to West Coast India	2.50%							
	14,000	Phosphate	Aqaba (Jordan) to West Coast India		5%	5%	5%	5%			
13	14,000	Phosphate	Aqaba (Jordan) to West Coast India	2.50%							
14	140,000	Iron Ore	Tubarao (Brazil) to Beilun (China) and Baoshan (China)							7.50%	
15	140,000	Coal	Richards Bay (South Africa) to Rotterdam							7.50%	

Source: Baltic Exchange

Notes:

- The following minor amendments of the BFI are not presented in this table:
    1. As of May 6th 1998, Routes 2 and 3 refer to a 54,000 dwt Panamax Vessel
    2. Routes 1A, 2A, 3A and 9 were based on a 64,000 dwt Panamax Vessel for the period up to February 2nd 1996.
- Skaw Gibraltar refers to the area between Skaw (Skagerrak) in Scandinavia and the straights of Gibraltar.
- Skaw Passero refers to the area between Skaw (Skagerrak) in Scandinavia and Cape Passero in the south of Italy.
- T/C denotes time-charter routes.
- For further definitions see also notes in Table 3.1.

These developments reflect the recognition by the Baltic, and by the industry in general, of the concept of each of these sub-sectors of the dry-bulk shipping industry constituting a distinct market with its own distinct characteristics. These characteristics were discussed in Chapter 1 of this book and they include the employment of specific vessel categories, with corresponding cargo sizes, carrying particular commodities on specific trading routes. These characteristics, and the economies of each market, establish themselves into distinct patterns of freight rates, ship prices and volatilities in each sub-sector, as demonstrated first in Kavussanos (1996a, 1996b, 1997c, 1997) – see also Kavussanos (2002) for a review. Moreover, as demonstrated by Kavussanos and Nomikos (2000), the restructurings of the BFI index have had a positive impact on the hedging performance and other aspects of the freight derivatives contracts written on the BFI – again see Kavussanos (2002) and the discussion further down this chapter for a review; these results justify further the importance of treating the sub-sectors in the industry as distinct markets as this has also an impact on the performance of shipping derivatives.

Tables 3.3 to 3.7 show the compositions of the dry-bulk sector indices (BCI, BPI, BSI, BHMI, and BHI) and the corresponding panellists, appointed by the Baltic Exchange, as they stood in 2005. The routes included and the corresponding weights assigned to each route reflect the state of each sub-sector/market in 2005. As mentioned before, these routes and their weights are revised periodically to reflect the changing conditions in shipping markets; the definitions of the indices may be found at anytime in the website of the Baltic Exchange at www.balticexchange.com.

Table 3.3. Baltic Capesize Index (BCI) – Route Definitions and Panellists, 2005

Panel A: Index Composition				
Routes	Vessel Size (dwt)	Cargo	Route Description	Weights
C2	160,000	Iron Ore	Tubarao (Brazil) to Rotterdam (Netherlands)	10%
C3	150,000	Iron Ore	Turabao/Beilun and Baoshan (China)	15%
C4	150,000	Coal	Richards Bay (S. Africa) to Rotterdam	5%
C5	150,000	Iron Ore	W. Australia/Beilun-Baoshan	15%
C7	150,000	Coal	Bolivar (Columbia)/Rotterdam	5%
C8	172,000	T/C	Delivery Gibraltar-Hamburg range, 5-15 days ahead of the index date, transatlantic round voyage duration 30-45 days, redelivery Gibraltar-Hamburg range	10%
C9	172,000	T/C	Delivery ARA or passing Passero, 5-15 days ahead of the index date, redelivery China-Japan range, duration about 65 days	5%
C10	172,000	T/C	Delivery China-Japan range, 5-15 days ahead of the index date, round voyage duration 30-40 days, redelivery China-Japan range	20%
C11	172,000	T/C	Delivery China-Japan range, 5-15 days ahead of the index date, redelivery ARA or passing Passero, duration about 65 days	5%
C12	150,000	Coal	Gladston (Australia) to Rotterdam	10%

Panel B: Panellists

Arrow Chartering (UK) Ltd., Banchero-Costa & C (Italy), Clarksons (UK), Fearnleys A/S (Norway), E. A. Gibson Shipbrokers Ltd. (UK), Howe Robinson & Co Ltd. (UK), Ifchor S.A. (Switzerland), Ildo Chartering Corporation (South Korea), LSS (Lorentzen & Stemoco, Oslo; Sobelnord, Antwerp; and Socomet, Paris) (Luxemburg), Thurlestone Shipping (UK) and Simpson Spence & Young Ltd (UK).

Notes: **Source:** Baltic Exchange

- See also notes in Tables 3.1 and 3.2.
- Route C1, which involved a 120,000 dwt vessel carrying coal from Hampton Roads (US) to Rotterdam (Netherlands) was introduced on 1st March 1999, but ceased being published on 1st April 2004.

Thus, Table 3.3, panel A, shows the composition of the BCI. It comprises spot and time-charter routes, coded C2 to C12, involving vessel sizes, which range from 150,000 dwt to 172,000 dwt, carrying iron ore and coal in the routes described fully in the fourth column of the table. The latter correspond to the trade patterns examined in Chapter 1 of this book. Moreover, the weights assigned to each route, shown in the last column of the table, reflect the importance of the route in the composition of the index; for instance, route C10, involving a 172,000 dwt vessel, on a time-charter contract, delivery China – Japan range, on a round voyage, with duration 30-40 days and redelivery in the same area was assigned a 20% weight in 2005 – the highest in the index – as this reflected the market conditions at the time. The spot routes C3 and C5, involving iron ore trade imports in Beilun and Baoshan, China, from Turabao Brazil and from West Australia, respectively, are assigned 15% weighting each, for the same reason. In a period, where the world demand for imports of iron ore is driven by China, it is important to have this reflected in the composition of the index, as it is. As can be seen in the table, the weights of the remaining routes in the index are either 10% or 5%.

Table 3.4. Baltic Panamax Index (BPI) – Route Definitions and Panellists, 2005

Panel A: Index Composition				
Routes	**Vessel Size (dwt)**	**Cargo**	**Route Description**	**Weights**
P1	55,000	Light Grain	1-2 safe berths/anchorages US Gulf (Mississippi River not above Baton Rouge) to ARA	10%
P1A	74,000	T/C	Transatlantic (including East Coast of South America) round of 45/60 days on the basis of delivery and redelivery Skaw-Gibraltar range	20%
P2	54,000	HSS	1-2 safe berths/anchorages US Gulf (Mississippi River not above Baton Rouge) / 1 no combo port to South Japan	12.5%
P2A	74,000	T/C	Basis delivery Skaw-Gibraltar range, for a trip to the Far East, redelivery Taiwan-Japan range, duration 60-65 day	12.5%
P3	54,000	HSS	1 port US North Pacific / 1 no combo port to South Japan.	10%
P3A	74,000	T/C	Transpacific round of 35/50 days either via Australia or Pacific (but not including short rounds such as Vostochy (Russia)/Japan), delivery and redelivery Japan/South Korea range	20%
P4	74,000	T/C	Delivery Japan/ South Korea range for a trip via US West Coast – British Columbia range, redelivery Skaw Gibraltar range, duration 50/60 days	15%
Panel B: Panellists				
Arrow Chartering Ltd. (UK), Banchero-Costa & C (Italy), Braemar Seascope (UK), Clarksons (UK), Fearnleys A/S (Norway), E A Gibson Shipbrokers Ltd. (UK), Howard Houlder & Co. Ltd. (UK), Howe Robinson & Co. Ltd. (UK), J E Hyde & Co Ltd. (UK), Ifchor S.A. (Switzerland), John F Dillon & Co. (US), Lawrence (Chartering) Ltd (UK), Maersk Broker (Korea), Simpson Spence & Young Ltd. (UK), LSS S.A. (Lorentzen & Stemoco, Oslo; Sobelnord, Antwerp; and Socomet, Paris) (Luxemburg), Thurlestone Shipping (UK) and Yamamizu Shipping Co. Ltd. (Japan).				

- See also notes in Tables 3.1 and 3.2.   **Source:** Baltic Exchange

Panel B of Table 3.3 presents the panellists involved in the construction of the index. As can be seen, they are major independent shipbrokers, actively involved in the Capesize market and they are members of the Baltic Exchange. These conditions are important, as the panellists must be able to provide freight rate values for each route, which are trustworthy and unbiased and reflect the actual market rates in each route. If this is not the case, the quality of the constructed indices will not be accurate reflections of rates prevailing in freight markets. Moreover, freight derivatives contracts that may be written on the indices will be equally problematic, as they will be called to be settled against the values of an "*unreliable*" index. Once again, it should be mentioned that the composition of the panellists can change over time in order to ensure that members fulfill the conditions mentioned above.

The composition of the Baltic Panamax Index (BPI) and its correspond panellists are shown in Table 3.4. The panellists are partly the same as those of the BCI, but include also other shipbroking companies which are involved in the Panamax business. Just as with the BCI, the vessel sizes, the cargoes carried, the routes that the vessels engage in, in the transportation of the cargoes, as well as the weights assigned to each route, reflect the state of the Panamax market as it stood in 2005.

Table 3.5. Baltic Supramax Index (BSI) – Route Definitions, 2005

Routes	Vessel Size (dwt)	Route Description	Weights
S1A	52,000	Delivery Antwerp/Skaw range for a trip of 60/65 days redelivery Singapore/Japan range including China 5% commission total. Laycan (laydays cancelling) 5/10 days in advance	12.5%
S1B	52,000	Delivery passing Canakkale (Turkey) for a trip of 50/55 days redelivery Singapore/Japan range including China 5% commission total. Laycan 5/10 days in advance	12.5%
S2	52,000	Delivery South Korea/Japan range for 1 Australian or trans Pacific round voyage, for a 35/40 day trip, redelivery South Korea/Japan range 5% commission total. Laycan 5/10 days in advance	25%
S3	52,000	Delivery South Korea/Japan range for a trip of 60/65 days redelivery Gibraltar/Skaw range 5% commission total. Laycan 5/10 days in advance	25%
S4	52,000	Delivery Gibraltar/Skaw range for one trans-Atlantic round voyage of 45/50 days, redelivery Gibraltar/Skaw range, 5% commission. Laycan 5/10 days in advance	25%

Notes: **Source:** Baltic Exchange

- See also notes in Tables 3.1 and 3.2.
- Supramax vessels carry bulk cargos, grain and coal.
- Laycan refers to the time interval into which the vessel must be in port ready to pick up/deliver cargo.

Table 3.5 presents the composition of the Baltic Supramax Index (BSI), introduced by the Baltic Exchange on 1st July 2005. The BSI values are published both in US dollars and as an index, to enable direct comparison with other Baltic dry market indices. It is based on one size vessel with the following specifications: Standard "*Tess 52*" type vessel, with grabs, as follows: 52,454mt dwt, self trimming, single deck, bulk carrier on 12.02m ssw (summer salt water), 189.99m LOA (length over all) 32.26m Beam 5ho/ha (hold hatch) 67,756cum (cubic meters) grain 65,600cum bale[35], 14L (laden)/14.5B (ballast) on 30mt (380cst) no mdo (marine diesel oil) at sea, with Cr 4 x 30mt with 12 cum grabs, maximum age 10 years. The BSI was introduced by the Baltic Exchange in order to capture the trend in the industry of vessels in the Handysize/Handymax sector gradually increasing from 43,000 dwt and 45,000 dwt, respectively, to approximately 52,000 dwt. The Supramax vessels (as well as the Handysize and Handymax vessels) are categorised as multi cargo/purpose vessels which can carry in the different routes all bulk cargoes, grains, coal, and iron ore. Also, typically Handysize vessels can carry steel products as well.

---

[35] Bale measures the cubic capacity of the cargo space in the holds of the vessel, while allowing for broken stowage.

Table 3.6. Baltic Handymax Index (BHMI) – Route Definitions and Panellists, 2005

Panel A: Index Composition			
Routes	**Vessel Size (dwt)**	**Route Description**	**Weights**
HM1A	45,500	Delivery Antwerp/Skaw range for a trip about 60/65 days redelivery Singapore/Japan range including China	12.5%
HM1B	45,500	Delivery passing Canakkale for a trip about 50/55 days redelivery Singapore/Japan range including China	12.5%
HM2	45,500	Delivery South Korea/Japan for 1 Australian or trans Pacific round voyage, one laden leg, redelivery South Korea/Japan range	25%
HM3	45,500	Delivery South Korea/Japan range for a trip about 60/65 days redelivery Gibraltar/Skaw range	25%
HM4A	45,500	Delivery Antwerp/Skaw range for a trip about 30/35 days redelivery US Gulf	12.5%
HM4B	45,500	Delivery US Gulf for a trip about 30/35 days redelivery Skaw/Passero	12.5%

Panel B: Panellists
Anchor Cross Shipbrokers Ltd. (Australia), Angus Graham & Partners (UK), Clarksons (UK), L. Dens (Shipbrokers) Ltd. (UK), Fearnleys, A/S (Norway), Galbraith's Ltd. (UK), Howe Robinson & Co Ltd. (UK), J E Hyde & Co Ltd. (UK), John F Dillon & Co. (US), Maersk Broker (UK), A N Petersen A/S (Denmark), Simpson Spence & Young Ltd. (UK), and Yamamizu Shipping Co. Ltd. (Japan).

Notes: **Source:** Baltic Exchange
- See also notes in Tables 3.1 and 3.2.
- Handymax vessels carry bulk cargos, grain and coal.

The predecessor of the BSI was the Baltic Handymax Index (BHMI). Its composition and panellists are shown in Table 3.6. It replaced the Baltic Handysize Index (BHI) in October 2000, and remained in existence until December 2005, when itself was replaced by the BSI. Finally, the composition of the BHI is shown in Table 3.7. It was introduced in 1997 and was replaced by the BHMI in October 2000.

Table 3.7. Baltic Handy Index (BHI) – Route Definitions and Panellists, 2005

Panel A: Index Composition			
Routes	**Vessel Size (dwt)**	**Route Description**	**Weighs**
H1	43,000	Delivery Antwerp/Skaw range trip, duration about 60/65 days, to Far East, redelivery Singapore/Japan range (including China)	25%
H2	43,000	Delivery South Korea/Japan range for 1 Australian or transpacific round voyage one laden leg redelivery South Korea/Japan range	30%
H3	43,000	Delivery Singapore time-charter trip 65/70 days duration via Australia redelivery Gibraltar/Skaw range	15%
H4	43,000	Delivery Skaw/Passero range 1/1 laden legs via US Atlantic, US Gulf or South Atlantic, 50/60 days duration, redelivery Skaw/Passero	30%
TR2	43,000	1 safe port Brazil/1 safe port Lisbon-Hamburg range (excluding UK/France)	-

Panel B: Panellists
Same panellists as in Table 3.6

Notes: **Source:** Baltic Exchange
- See also notes in Tables 3.1 and 3.2.
- Handysize vessels carry bulk cargos, grain, coal and steel products.

3.2.2.   The Composition of Tanker Freight Rate Indices

The Baltic Exchange launched in January 1998 the Baltic International Tanker Route (BITR) index, in an effort to create an independent index for the tanker freight markets also. Besides providing a "*barometer*" of how tanker freight rates changed over time, the BITR and its constituent route indices could serve the role of the underlying asset, upon which tanker freight derivatives could be settled. Table 3.8

shows the composition of the BITR as it stood when it was launched, and how it was modified up until 30th September 2001, in order to make it more representative of the tanker sector. The routes in the table are equally weighted at all times.

The index included tanker vessels which were involved both in "*Dirty*" and in "*Clean*" trades. The "*dirty*" vessels carry the "*black*" or "*dirty*" cargoes such as crude oil, heavy fuel oils, asphalt, etc. The "*clean*" vessels carry the refined "*white*" clean products such as gasoline, jet fuels, diesel oil, kerosene, naphtha, leaded and unleaded oil, etc. Chemical carriers would also fall into the "*clean*" category. It should be noted here that because of the strict tank inspection requirements for clean products, most proprietary vessels or those on long-term charter, do not routinely change their trading patterns from clean to dirty or vice versa. However, market requirements and charter economics do require vessels to sometimes slip in and out of these clean and dirty trades.

As can be seen in the table, five equally weighted (20% each - see fifth column of the table) "*dirty*" routes, involving crude oil transportation, composed the index at its inception, on 27th January 1998. The route descriptions and the vessel sizes involved can be seen in the third and second columns of the table, respectively. In order to make the index more representative, in terms of vessel sizes and routes on which tanker cargoes moved, a number of changes were made in its composition. In column six of the table, for instance, we see that less than three months later, on 31st March 1998, routes 6 and 7, involving 70,000 dwt and 30,000 dwt vessels transporting clean oil products in Middle East to Japan and Caribbean to USAC (US Atlantic Coast), respectively, joined the BITR. As a consequence, the weights of each route in the BITR fell from 20% to 14.28%, as can be seen in the corresponding column of the table. Routes 8, 9, 10 and 11, representing one "*clean*" and three "*dirty*" tanker routes, were added to BITR in August of the same year. Each route's contribution to the index now fell to 9.09%, as can be seen in the seventh column of the table.

In April 1999, in the "*clean*" route 6 (Middle East to Japan) the vessel size changed from 70,000 dwt to 75,000 dwt, and in the "*clean*" route 8 (Continent to USAC) the vessel size changed from 35,000 dwt to 33,000 dwt, as can be seen in column eight of the table. An age limit of twenty years was introduced in April 2000 for routes 1, 2, 3, 4, 6, 8 and 9. In May 2000 "*dirty*" route 9 changed from Middle East Gulf to Continent, to Middle East Gulf to US Gulf (Ras Tanura to Loop – Louisiana Offshore Oil Port), and the "*dirty*" route 12 (Cross Mediterranean: Siri Kerrir, Egypt to Lavera, France) was added. As a consequence, the weights of each route fell from 9.09% to 8.33%, as can be seen in the last column of the table.

On 10th July 2000 the routes of the BITR were renumbered from 1, 2,...,12 to T3, T4,...,T6, etc., in order to be sorted in descending order, based on vessel sizes; that is, they were sorted from the largest vessel to the smallest vessel, as can be seen in the first column of Table 3.9. A subsequent "*recoding*" took place one year later, on 1st August 2001, to distinguish more clearly the "*dirty*" from the "*clean*" routes; thus, "*dirty*" route T3 became TD3, route T10 became TC1, etc.

Table 3.8. Changes in the Composition of the Baltic International Tanker Route Index (BITR) (27 January 1998 – 30 September 2001)

Routes	Vessel Size (mt)	Route Description	Product	27/01/98 – 30/03/98	31/03/98 – 02/08/98	03/08/98 – 14/04/99	15/04/99 – 02/05/00	03/05/00 – 09/07/00	10/07/00 – 30/07/01	01/08/01 – 30/09/01
1 T3 TD3	250,000	Middle East AG to Japan	Dirty	20%	14.28%	9.09%	9.09%	8.33%	8.33%	
2 T4 TD4	260,000	West Africa to US Gulf	Dirty	20%	14.28%	9.09%	9.09%	8.33%	8.33%	8.33%
3 T5 TD5	130,000	West Africa to USAC (US Atlantic Coast)	Dirty	20%	14.28%	9.09%	9.09%	8.33%	8.33%	8.33%
4 T7 TD7	80,000	North Sea to Continent	Dirty	20%	14.28%	9.09%	9.09%	8.33%	8.33%	8.33%
5 T9 TD9	70,000	Caribbean to US Gulf	Dirty	20%	14.28%	9.09%	9.09%	8.33%	8.33%	8.33%
6 T10 TC1	70,000 75,000	Middle East to Japan AG to Japan	Clean		14.28%	9.09%	9.09%	8.33%	8.33%	8.33%
7 T12 TC3	30,000	Caribbean to USAC (US Atlantic Coast)	Clean		14.28%	9.09%	9.09%	8.33%	8.33%	8.33%
8 T11 TC2	35,000 33,000	Continent to USAC (US Atlantic Coast)	Clean			9.09%	9.09%	8.33%	8.33%	8.33%
9 T1 TD1	280,000	Middle East Gulf to Continent Middle East Gulf to US Gulf (Ras Tanura to Loop)	Dirty			9.09%	9.09%	8.33%	8.33%	8.33%
10 T2 TD2	260,000	Middle East Gulf to Singapore	Dirty			9.09%	9.09%	8.33%	8.33%	8.33%
11 T8 TD8	80,000	Kuwait to Singapore	Dirty			9.09%	9.09%	8.33%	8.33%	8.33%
12 T6 TD6	130,000	Cross Mediterranean: Siri Kerrir (Egypt) to Lavera (France)	Dirty					8.33%	8.33%	8.33%

Table 3.9. Changes in the Composition of the Baltic Dirty Tanker Index (BDTI) and Baltic Clean Tanker Index (BCTI) (01 October 2001 – 14 July 2005)

Routes	Vessel Size (mt)	Route Description	01/10/01 – 04/02/02	04/02/02 – 14/07/03	14/07/03 – 04/10/04	04/10/04 – 12/10/04	12/10/04 – 04/01/05	04/01/05 – 01/03/05	01/03/05 – 13/06/05	13/06/05 – 14/07/05
Panel A: Baltic Dirty Tanker Index (BDTI)										
TD1 (9)	280,000	AG to US Gulf	11.11%	10.00%	9.09%	9.09%	8.33%	8.33%	8.33%	8.33%
TD2 (10)	260,000	AG to Singapore	11.11%	10.00%	9.09%	9.09%	8.33%	8.33%	8.33%	8.33%
TD3 (1)	250,000	AG to Japan	11.11%	10.00%	9.09%	9.09%	8.33%	8.33%	8.33%	8.33%
TD4 (2)	260,000	W. Africa to US Gulf	11.11%	10.00%	9.09%	9.09%	8.33%	8.33%	8.33%	8.33%
TD5 (3)	130,000	W. Africa to USAC	11.11%	10.00%	9.09%	9.09%	8.33%	8.33%	8.33%	8.33%
TD6 (12)	130,000	Cross Mediterranean	11.11%	10.00%	9.09%	9.09%	8.33%	8.33%	8.33%	8.33%
TD7 (4)	80,000	N. Sea to Continent	11.11%	10.00%	9.09%	9.09%	8.33%	8.33%	8.33%	8.33%
TD8 (11)	80,000	Kuwait to Singapore	11.11%	10.00%	9.09%	9.09%	8.33%	8.33%	8.33%	8.33%
TD9 (5)	70,000	Caribbean to US Gulf	11.11%	10.00%	9.09%	9.09%	8.33%	8.33%	8.33%	8.33%
TD10	50,000	Caribbean to USAC		10.00%	9.09%	9.09%	8.33%	8.33%	8.33%	8.33%
TD11	80,000	Cross Mediterranean			9.09%	9.09%	8.33%	8.33%	8.33%	8.33%
TD12	55,000	ARA to US Gulf					8.33%	8.33%	8.33%	8.33%
TD 14	80,000	Indonesia to Japan				On Trial				
TD15	260,000	W. Africa to China							On Trial	On Trial
TD16	30,000	BlackSea to Med								
Panel B: Baltic Clean Tanker Index (BCTI)										
TC1 (6)	75,000	AG to Japan	33.33%	25.00%	20.00%	20.00%	16.67%	16.67%	16.67%	16.67%
TC2 (8)	33,000	Continent to USAC	33.33%	25.00%	20.00%	20.00%	16.67%	16.67%	16.67%	16.67%
TC2_37	37,000									
TC3 (7)	30,000	Caribbean to USAC	33.33%	25.00%	20.00%	20.00%	16.67%	16.67%	16.67%	16.67%
TC3_38	38,000									
TC4	30,000	Singapore to Japan		25.00%	20.00%	20.00%	16.67%	16.67%	16.67%	16.67%
TC5	55,000	AG to Japan			20.00%	20.00%	16.67%	16.67%	16.67%	16.67%
TC6	30,000	Algeria/Euromed					16.67%	16.67%	16.67%	16.67%

Notes:

- The numbers in parentheses after the names of the routes indicate the previous numberings of the routes under the BITR.
- The term trial refers to tanker routes being on trial, which at the time of writing, are not formally adopted.
- See also Table 3.8.

157

Moreover, by 1st October 2001 the BITR was split into two separate indices; the Baltic Dirty Tanker Index (BDTI) and the Baltic Clean Tanker Index (BCTI), bundling separately the "*dirty*" and the "*clean*" routes, respectively. This modification came in recognition of the fact that "*dirty*" and "*clean*" markets are separate entities, and must be treated accordingly. Table 3.9 shows the composition of these two indices when they were introduced and the subsequent changes up to the time of writing. Thus, the fourth column of the table shows that up to February 3rd 2002 the BDTI was constructed from nine equally weighted routes (11.11% each), covering VLCC, Suezmax and Aframax vessels. Panel B of the same table indicates that the BCTI started with the three "*clean*" routes, TC1, TC2, and TC3, each contributing 33.33% to the value of the index. Using the same principle described earlier on, the indices have been revised periodically to make them more representatives of the "*dirty*" and "*clean*" tanker trades they purport to describe. These changes are clearly visible in the table.

In the interest of clarity Tables 3.10 and 3.11 present the BDTI and the BCTI compositions as they stood in 2005. The panellists assigned to report freight rates on each of the routes of the indices are shown in panel B of Table 3.10. They are selected by the Baltic using the same criteria as those for the dry-bulk sector, described earlier on in this chapter. The aim is to obtain reliable, unbiased and secure daily freight rates, upon which to base the construction of route indices and of the overall BDTI and BCTI values. Then freight derivatives can be written, as they do, on these values.

Table 3.10. Baltic Dirty Tanker Index (BDTI) – Route Definitions and Panellists, 2005

Routes	Vessel Size (mt)	Type of Vessel	Route Description
Panel A: BDTI Routes			
TD1	280,000	VLCC	Middle East to US Gulf: Ras Tanura (South Arabia) to Loop (US)
TD2	260,000	VLCC	Middle East Gulf to Singapore: Ras Tanura to Singapore
TD3	260,000	VLCC	Middle East Gulf to Japan: Ras Tanura to Chiba (Japan)
TD4	260,000	VLCC	West Africa to US Gulf. Off Shore Bonny (Nigeria) to Loop
TD5	130,000	Suezmax	West Africa to USAC. Off Shore Bonny to Philadelphia (US)
TD6	135,000	Suezmax	Black Sea / Mediterranean
TD7	80,000	Aframax	North Sea to Continent. Sullom Voe (UK) to Wilhelmshaven (Germany)
TD8	80,000	Aframax	Kuwait to Singapore. Mena al Ahmadi (Kuwait) to Singapore
TD9	70,000	Panamax	Caribbean to US Gulf. Puerto La Cruz (Venezuela) to Corpus Christi (US)
TD10	50,000	Panamax	Caribbean to USAC. Aruba (Antilles) to New York
TD11	80,000	Aframax	Cross Mediterranean/Danias (Syria) to Lavera (France)
TD12	55,000	Panamax	ARA to US Gulf. Antwerp (Belgium) to Houston (US)
TD14	80,000	Aframax	On Trial - Indonesia to Japan
TD15	260,000	VLCC	On Trial - West Africa to China
TD16	30,000	Handysize	On Trial - Black Sea to Mediterranean
Panel B: Panellists			
ACM Shipping Ltd. (UK), Barry Rogliano Salles (France), Bassoe (PF) A/S & Co. (France), Braemar Seascope Ltd. (UK), Bravo Tankers s.r.l. (Italy), Capital Shipbrokers Ltd. (UK), Clarksons (UK), Clarksons (Asia), Eastport Chartering Ltd. (Singapore), Fearnleys A/S (Norway), Galbraith's Ltd. (UK), E A Gibson Shipbrokers Ltd. (UK), Island Shipbrokers (Singapore), Mallory Jones Lynch Flynn & Assoc. Inc. (US), McQuilling Brokerage Partners Inc. (US), McQuilling Brokerage Partners (Singapore), Odin Marine Inc. (US), and Simpson Spence & Young Ltd. (UK).			

Notes: **Source:** Baltic Exchange

- The routes are equally weighted; each of the first 12 routes has a weight of 8.33%.
- Routes TD14, TD15, and TD16 are on trial at the time of writing.

Table 3.11. Baltic Clean Tanker Index (BCTI) – Route Definitions and Panellists, 2005

Routes	Vessel Size (mt)	Type of Vessel	Route Description
Panel A: BCTI Routes			
TC1	75,000	Aframax	Middle East Gulf to Japan. Ras Tanura to Yokohama (Japan)
TC2_37	37,000	Handysize	Continent to USAC. Rotterdam to New York
TC3_38	38,000	Handysize	Caribbean to USAC. Aruba to New York
TC4	30,000	Handysize	Singapore to Japan. Singapore to Chiba (Japan)
TC5	55,000	Panamax	Middle East to Japan. Ras Tanura (South Arabia) to Yokohama
TC6	30,000	Handysize	Algeria/Euromed. Skikda (Syria)/Lavera (France)
Panel B: Panellists			
Same panellists as in Table 3.10			

Note: **Source:** Baltic Exchange
- The routes are equally weighted; each of the 6 routes has a weight of 16.67%.

For the record, a joint effort to produce a tanker freight index was also made by the London Tanker Brokers' Panel (LTBP) based in London, in conjunction with the Association of Shipbrokers and Agents Tanker Brokers' Panel (ASBA) based in New York. Daily hires for time-charter rates and Worldscale rates for voyage assessments were calculated for each route and an average of these was taken to produce the index[36]. The composition of the International Tanker Freight Index (ITFI) is shown in Table 3.12, panel A. It included six equally weighted routes, covering VLCC, Suezmax, Aframax and Panamax tankers. Its panellists were six members of the LTBP plus four brokers in the US and are shown in panel B of the same table. ITFI was launched in February 1998 but was only available on subscription, unlike the BITR assessment, which was free. However, no users were prepared to pay the fees suggested and finally ITFI stopped being produced on 3rd of August 1999.

Table 3.12. International Tanker Freight Index (ITFI) – Route Definitions and Panellists, 1999

Panel A: Index Composition		
Routes	Vessel Size (dwt)	Destinations
1	250,000	Persian Gulf to Japan, 20 to 30 days notice periods.
2	280,000	Persian Gulf to US Gulf, 20 to 30 days.
3	80,000	Persian Gulf to Singapore, 10 to 15 days.
4	130,000	West Africa to US Atlantic Coast, 20 to 30 days.
5	50,000	Caribbean to US Atlantic Coast, 7 to 10 days.
6	70,000	Caribbean to US Gulf, 7 to 10 days.
Panel B: Panellists		
Clarksons (UK), Galbraith's Ltd. (UK), E.A. Gibson Shipbrokers Ltd. (UK), Howard Houlder Ltd. (UK), Jacobs and Partners (UK), and Seascope Shipping (UK), McQuilling Brokerage Partners (US), Odin Marine (US), Poten and Partners (US), and Charles R. Weber Company (US).		

Note: **Source:** London Tanker Brokers' Panel
- The routes are equally weighted, each of the 6 routes has a weight of 16.67%.

Finally, it is worth mentioning here that the Baltic Exchange launched a Liquefied Petroleum Gas (LPG) route assessment during March 2003. The Baltic LPG route is a stand-alone assessment, based on the following criteria: 44,000mt, 5 per cent, 1 to 2 grades fully refrigerated LPG. Ras Tanura to Chiba, laydays 10/40 days in advance, laytime 96 hours total, maximum vessel age 20 years. The panellists, as of 2005, are: Braemar Seascope Ltd. (UK), Clarksons (UK), Fearnleys A/S (Norway), E. A. Gibson Shipbrokers Ltd. (UK), Inge Steensland A/A (Norway), Lorentzen & Stemoco A/S (Norway), and Poten & Partners (UK) Ltd. Such an index provides the potential for a freight derivatives contract to be written on it.

---

[36] Notice that Worldscale rates are US$/ton equivalents for each route, which are derived assuming that a nominal tanker operates on round voyages between designated ports.

159

3.2.3. The Formation of Freight Rate Indices and their Historical Performance

The discussion so far in this section of the chapter presented the different freight rate indices that exist in the cargo carrying sector of the shipping industry. It has discussed the composition of the indices and the way that this composition has evolved over time, to reflect the prevailing market conditions. Moreover, it has presented the panel members of each index, which play a central role in the construction of these indices. More specifically, for the BPI, for instance, whose composition is presented in Table 3.4, panel A, freight rate assessments on the individual routes are reported to the Baltic Exchange on a daily basis, by the panel of independent shipbrokers, presented in panel B of the table. Each member of the panel submits its daily view of the freight rate of each route of the index at 11:00 a.m. London time. These rates are based on actual fixtures, or in the absence of an actual fixture they represent the panelist's view of what the rate would be on that day if a fixture had been agreed. Then the Baltic Exchange, for each route, takes an arithmetic average and converts these values into indices for the routes. A constant Weighting Factor, unique for each route, is then used to calculate the overall average of the index[37]. The Baltic reports the route indices, as well as the overall indices to the market at 13:00 p.m. (dry) and 16:00 p.m. (tankers) London time.

Figure 3.1. Baltic Freight Index (BFI) Daily Prices (January 1985 – January 1998)

Source: SSY Futures Brokers

Figure 3.1 is a sample outcome of this process. It shows a series of daily values of the BFI for the period January 1985 to July 1998. Each value of the index is produced as a weighted average of the values of the individual routes of the index shown in Table 3.1, with the weights presented in the table reflecting the contribution of each route to the BFI. As shown in Table 3.2, the routes and the weights used were modified periodically to reflect the changing market conditions in the dry-bulk sector of shipping. These changing compositions were used at any point in time to build the values of the index. The BFI then, in a single figure, gives the prevailing level of freight rates in the market each business day, while a plot of a sequence of these figures over time reflects how the market changed during the period. This historical performance of the BFI is shown in Figure 3.1. It reflects the changing state of the dry-bulk shipping market over time. The index started at 1000 in January 1985, fell to

---

[37] Up until mid 2004 the highest and lowest assessments of the panellists for the day were excluded before calculating the average.

its all time low of 554 points in July 1986, during the great depression of the shipping sector in the mid-1980's, picked up since then and fluctuated significantly over the period, at any time reflecting the balance of demand and supply conditions, as determined by various events affecting the sector. Some of these historical events that determined the level of freight rates are registered on the graph by SSY Futures Brokers and are reproduced here.

The break down of the BFI into separate indices did not stop the Baltic continue to produce an index which reflects the overall freight rates earned in the sector. This index, which can be thought of as a continuation of the BFI, is called the Baltic Dry Index (BDI). Figure 3.2 presents the BDI for the period January 1985 to September 2005. As mentioned, the index is an overall composite of the Capesize, Panamax and Handymax indices and continues to provide a "*barometer*" for the dry-bulk sector of the shipping industry. As an example, one can easily observe the unprecedented freight rates in the dry cargo sector between the autumn of 2003 and the spring of 2005, but also the very high volatility in rates accompanying the high earnings. These rates earned, is well-known to be a consequence of the very sharp changes in imports from China over this period.

Figure 3.2. Baltic Dry Index (BDI) Daily Prices (January 1985 – September 2005)

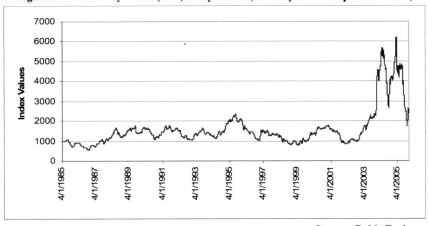

Source: Baltic Exchange

Separate indices for the sub-sectors of dry-bulk are built in a similar way, with the underlying structure of these indices presented earlier, in Tables 3.3, 3.4, and 3.6, for the BCI, BPI and BHMI, respectively. Thus, Figure 3.3 shows a time-series of freight rates for the BPI over the period May 1998 to September 2005. Each value of the index is a weighted average of the freight route values constituting the index. Thus, changes in the BPI in the figure represent how market conditions in the Panamax sector of the shipping industry changed over time. We can observe, for instance, the low earnings in the market in the summer of 1998, the improving market from the spring of 1999, until the spring of 2001, the declining market and the low freight rates that followed that up until the summer of 2002, the tremendous rise in rates with their peak reaching levels in March 2004 and their explosive fluctuations that followed this rise.

Figure 3.3. Baltic Panamax Index (BPI) Daily Prices (May 1998 – September 2005)

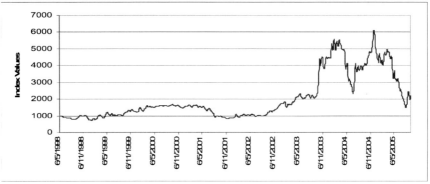

Source: Baltic Exchange

As mentioned before, indices for each of the routes constituting the BPI are also made available to the market, but are not shown here for economy of space. However, the availability of these indices, for routes of the BPI as well as for the BPI itself is important for the existence of freight rate derivatives. As we see later on in this chapter, freight derivatives have developed, which use the values of these indices as the underlying "*commodity*".

Figure 3.4. Baltic Capesize Index (BCI) Daily Prices (March 1999 – September 2005)

Source: Baltic Exchange

Figure 3.4 shows the BCI over the period March 1999 to September 2005, reflecting the average freight rates earned by Capesize vessels over the period. One way to think of the index then is that it reflects a "*basket*" of freight rates that would be earned by a shipowner with a fleet of vessels simulating the composition of the BCI and employed in the trades/routes of the BCI – see Table 3.3. From the charterer's point of view, the index represents a "*basket*" of rates that must be paid to transport a set of cargoes in the routes constituting the index. Of course if owners do not have the exact fleet of vessels matching the composition of the BCI and charterers do not have the exact set of cargoes matching the BCI, as is usually the case, there is a need for freight rate derivatives to be written on the routes of the index rather than on the index itself. If such freight derivatives on the individual route indices are not available, cross hedging problems arise and the effectiveness of the hedges is questionable. We come back to this point later on in this chapter.

Figure 3.5. Baltic Handymax Index (BHMI) Daily Prices (September 2000 – Sept. 2005)

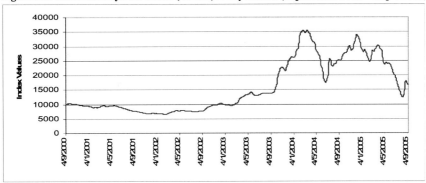

Source: Baltic Exchange

In the meantime, in order to see how freight rates have changed, on average, in the rest of the sub-sectors of the shipping industry, Figure 3.5 presents the BHMI over the period September 2000 to September 2005, while Figures 3.6 and 3.7 present the BDTI and the BCTI, respectively, over the period August 1998 to September 2005. These last two indices show how freight rates evolved in the dirty and clean sectors of the tanker industry, respectively.

Figure 3.6. Baltic Dirty Tanker Index (BDTI) Daily Prices (August 1998 – Sept. 2005)

Source: Baltic Exchange

In order to see how closely related the sub-sectors of dry-bulk shipping are, we consider the correlation coefficients of the daily logarithmic prices of the BCI, the BPI, and the BHMI over the period 4th September 2000 to 8th September 2005: The BPI and the BCI have a correlation coefficient of 98.5%, the BPI and the BHMI have a correlation coefficient of 98.0%, while the BCI and the BHMI have a correlation coefficient of 96.1%. These coefficients are reduced to 51.7%, 51.5% and 43.7% when logarithmic first-differences (that is, when daily changes) of freight rates are considered. These results indicate that rates in the three sub-sectors of dry-bulk are trending together – driven by a common variable, the world trade, but the daily changes in their values are much less correlated, as each sub-sector has its own characteristics which may be distinct from the rest. This is justified from the earlier observation that the three sub-sectors of Capesize, Panamax, and Handymax are distinct markets, driven by their own idiosyncratic factors. That is, it is justified to produce separate indices for the sub-sectors of the dry-bulk sector of shipping, as they are distinct markets. By bundling them together, as they were under the BFI *"something"* was missed.

Figure 3.7. Baltic Clean Tanker Index (BCTI) Daily Prices (August 1998 – September 2005)

Source: Baltic Exchange

The story is similar in the tanker trades; we constructed *"portfolios"* of rates for VLCC, Suezmax, Aframax, and Panamax dirty trades from the individual route indices of the BDTI. Then we computed correlation coefficients between pairs of freight rate levels and of daily logarithmic first-differences for these artificially created sub-sectoral indices of the *"dirty"* tanker sector. These coefficients range in the former case between 72.6% and 88.8%, while in the latter case this range becomes 7.1% to 32.9%. We also constructed *"portfolios"* of rates out of the BCTI route indices for Aframax, Panamax and Handysize clean trades. In this case, the correlation coefficients between pairs of logarithmic freight rate levels range between 77.7% and 97.4%, while for logarithmic first-differences these coefficients range between 32.5% and 69.8%. It seems that within the BDTI index there are distinct sub-sectors, which however are not represented separately through distinct indices. The story is similar for the BCTI index. Perhaps this will be done in the future.

3.2.4. Platts Price Assessments

As we see in later sections of this chapter, tanker freight rate indices produced by Platts are also used for settlement of freight derivatives contracts, which exist on some of the shipping tanker routes. Platts is providing energy news, price benchmarks, energy intelligence and decision-support services to the industry. From 14 offices worldwide, it covers the petroleum, petrochemical, electricity, natural gas, coal, metals, nuclear power, bunker fuels and freight rate markets. Its products range from real-time news and pricing services to newsletters and magazines, market reports and in-depth studies, databases, electronic directories, and research services. Its customers include producers, traders, market-makers, refiners and analysts.

Regarding pricing formation, Platts offers independent, accurate price assessments for all of its markets. It collects data from market participants, such as traders, principals, brokers and others, from around the world, and verifies them prior to their use. It assesses the open market rates for the chartering of both *"dirty"* and *"clean"* tankers for a number of key shipping regions, presented in Table 3.13. Using the geographical areas shown in this table, it provides daily price assessments for the *"clean"* and *"dirty"* trades, presented in Table 3.14 panels A and B, respectively. The figures in the cells of the table indicate the typical cargo size/vessel type carried/used on the route.

Platts tanker assessments for each route are published at 4:00 p.m. London time, through the daily Dirty Tankerwire and Clean Tankerwire newsletters as well as the Oilgram price report[38]. These assessments are derived from both fixtures concluded and market levels talked in the period since the previous set of assessments was published. The aim of these assessments is to: (i) provide a reflection of market activity (i.e. fixtures, vessels put on subjects, bids and offers) heard since publication of the previous set of freight assessments and (ii) publish an indication of the level at which Platts believes chartering activity could occur, given the movements in other markets. Given that for some routes several days can pass by without any significant activity, either actual chartering or bids/offers, the tanker assessments are adjusted up or down on the basis of broader market trends and a survey of the market is made to determine their views on a relative value of a vessel charter for a particular route (Platts, 2003).

Table 3.13. Platts Shipping Regions and Geographical Descriptions, 2005

Regions	Descriptions
R. Sea	All ports in the Red Sea
AG	All ports in the Arabian Gulf, up to the Straits of Hormuz
Indo	All ports in Indonesia
S. Korea	All ports in South Korea
USWC	Seattle to Los Angeles
USGC	Pascagoula, Mississippi to Corpus Christi
USAC	North of Cape Hatteras to Portland, Maine
Australia	All ports in Australia
HK	All ports in Hong Kong
UKC	Bilbao (Spain) to Hamburg (Germany), but not including Portugal. Designation includes Southern Sweden and Western Norway
Med	Everything from Gibraltar to Istanbul
Black Sea	All ports in Black Sea
Caribean	Venezuela and the islands
India	All ports in India
E. Africa	From the African horn south to Durban, South Africa
EC Canada	Atlantic coast, as well as shipments into the St. Lawrence
Japan	All ports in Japan

Source: Platts

Platts tanker assessments are primarily expressed as a percentage of the annual Worldscale Flat rate that is being agreed upon in open market transactions to charter a vessel. For example, if the Worldscale annual Flat rate – that is, the Worldscale 100 – is set at $10.00/mt for a specific route, a Platts' assessment of 50 for that route would mean that the class of vessels being assessed is being chartered for $5/mt of freight on that voyage. In some "*clean*" tanker markets, some routes are assessed on a lump sum, expressed in US$/mt, for the cost of chartering a vessel of the specified size. The markets that are assessed on that basis have historically traded in US$/mt, and Platts' assessment of a lump sum rather than Worldscale rate simply follows the practice. There are no "*dirty*" tanker assessments done on a lump-sum basis. The tonnage specified in the assessments represents the weight of the cargo carried. Platts considers charters of different, yet approximate sizes, when making its assessments, pro-rating the market rates to the size of the vessel in the assessment. Assessments are typically based on double-hull/double-bottom vessels, under 20 years of age or typically under 15 years for voyages involving a European load or destination port.

---

[38] Platts Oilgram price report is a daily report that covers market changes, market fundamentals and factors driving prices. Platts Oilgram price report also brings an array of Platts international prices for crude oil products, crude oil postings, market commentary, spot tanker rates and futures settlements.

Table 3.14. The "*Clean*" & "*Dirty*" Tanker Routes of the Platts Price Assessments, 2005

Panel A: Clean Tanker Routes

East of Suez

From	To											
	UKC	Med	AG	India	Sing	Japan	S.Korea	HK	Austr	USWC	USAC	E.Africa
R.Sea	35, 55	35, 55	35	35	35, 55	35, 55	35, 55			35	35	35
AG	30, 55 75	30, 55, 75	30	30, 55	30, 55 75	30, 55 75	30, 55 75			30, 75	30, 55 75	30
Sing				30, 55	30	30, 55	30, 55	30, 55	30	30		
India					30	30	30					
S.Korea					30	30		30		30	30	

West of Suez

	UKC	Med	India	Sing	Japan	USAC	USGC	USWC	S.America	W.Africa	UKC	Med
UKC	30, 60	60		30		30, 60	30, 60		30	30		
Med	30, 55	30	30	30	30, 55	30, 55	30, 55		30, 55	30		
B.Sea	30	30	30						30		30	30
Car	30, 40	30	30			30, 40	30, 40	30	30			
USMC			30	30	30				30			

Panel B: Dirty Tanker Routes

West of Suez

From	UK Cont	EC Can	USAC	US Gulf	Med	USWC	East	Car
UKC	27.5, 30 80, 135	80, 135, 270	80, 135, 270	55, 80, 135, 270	27.5, 30, 55, 80, 135, 270			135
Med	80, 135, 260	80, 135, 260	80, 135, 260	80, 135, 260	27.5, 80, 135, 260			135
B.Sea			135	135	30, 80 135			
Car	50, 130	50	50, 130	50, 130	50, 130	50		
Balt	100	100						
WAF	130, 260	260	130, 260	130, 260	130, 260		130, 260	130, 260

East of Suez

	East	Sing	R.Sea	Japan	S.Korea	Austr	USAC	US Gulf	USWC	UK Cont	Med
AG	80, 260, 130	260	80, 260, 130	260	260		80, 130	80, 260, 130	80, 260, 130	80, 260, 130	80, 260, 130
Indo		80		80	80	80					

Note: **Source:** Platts

- For regions notation and full description refer to Table 3.13.
- Figures in the cells indicate cargo sizes. E.g. In panel A, cell R.Sea to UKC, 35, 55 means that the freight rate assessments are for 35,000 and 55,000 metric tonnes of clean cargos, which are carried in the Red Sea to UK Continent route.

Platts also converts its Worldscale and lump-sum rates into $/mt equivalent assessments. It determines $/mt freight rates based on a basket of Worldscale Flat rates on several key routes between the two regions noted. For example, the UKC-USG $/mt assessment would be based on such routes as Sullom Voe-Houston. Platts' spot Worldscale assessments are applied against this basket, to produce the assessment for a $/mt rate. The basket is updated annually, when the Worldscale Association establishes new Flat rates for the year. For those routes which are assessed on a US$ lump-sum, the $/mt assessment is calculated by dividing the lump-sum total by the size of the cargo assessed.

Having considered the freight rate indices built by the Baltic Exchange and by Platts, which provide reliable values of freight rates to the market on a daily basis, we turn next to the issue of freight derivatives contracts that can be written on the values of these indices. It is instructive to consider the first effort, which was made in 1985 by writing a futures contract on a basket of dry-bulk freight rates; this "*basket*" was the newly created BFI, which was used as the underlying commodity of the Baltic International Freight Futures (BIFFEX) contract.

3.3. Freight Futures on Organised Derivatives Exchanges
3.3.1. The Baltic International Freight Futures Exchange (BIFFEX) Contract

The buyer or seller of the BIFFEX (futures) contract would settle it, against the value the BFI would have at the expiry of the futures contract. The BIFFEX contract was introduced by the London International Financial Futures and Options Exchange (LIFFE) on May 1st 1985 and traded up to April 2002.[39] The London Clearing-House (LCH) provided the services for the clearing of BIFFEX contracts. The contract provided protection of potential income loss for shipowners and against higher freight costs for charterers, emanating from fluctuations in freight rates. This was achieved by taking a freight futures position, which was opposite to the exposure in the physical market (Gray, 1986, 1987, 1990).

An owner, say, with a 55,000 dwt vessel likely to trade in the US Gulf to ARA (route 1) region, would sell BIFFEX contracts in order to protect himself against the possibility of a fall in freight rates in the route. At the same time he would be hoping that the prices of the BIFFEX contract would follow the freight rates in that route and as a consequence, that the evolution in rates of the route would follow that of the BFI (upon which BIFFEX was trading), and all that would provide for an effective hedge. No futures contracts were available on individual routes at the time, in order for the shipowner to use a futures contract on route 1 for his hedging purposes. As a consequence, users of the contracts were exposed to cross hedging problems of the type just described; that is, of problems, of whether BIFFEX prices would follow closely changes in the freight rates of the route that the shipowner had his vessel on.

Table 3.15. Summary of BIFFEX Contract Details

Unit of Trading	Valued at $10 per Index point.
Delivery Months	The current month, the following two consecutive months and January, April, July, October for up to eighteen months forward such that eight delivery months are available for trading.
Last Trading Day	Last market day of the delivery month (in the case of December the 20th day) at 12:00 London time (if not a business day then the first business day immediately proceeding).
Settlement Day	The first business day after the Last Trading Day of the delivery month.
Settlement Price	The average of the Index on the last trading day and the six preceding market days of the delivery month.
Tick Size (Value)	One full Index point ($10).
Trading Hours	10:15 – 12:30 and 14:30 – 16:40 London time.

Source: LIFFE

By definition, a futures market must trade a uniform, standardised contract, in standard quantities, for delivery on specified dates in the future, with good price availability (transparency of pricing). These conditions were satisfied in the BIFFEX market. A summary of the specifications of the contract is presented in Table 3.15. BIFFEX contracts were originally (August 1985 – July 1988) traded for quarterlies; that is, for delivery in January, April, July and October. In 1988 *"spot"* and *"prompt"*

---

[39] In May 1985, another derivatives instrument was created for the dry-bulk industry, by the International Futures Exchange (INTEX) in Bermuda. It was similar to the BIFFEX contract (had BFI as the underlying asset), but failed due to lack of interest from the industry. In February 1986, an attempt was made in London to create a similar instrument for the tanker industry, the Tanker International Freight Futures Exchange (TIFFEX) contract, but again failed due to lack of interest. The TIFFEX was a freight futures contract on the average of the nine routes of the Baltic Tanker Index. Its contract specifications were the following: the contract multiplier was $10, the minimum price movement was 0.5 index points, it was trading for the three prompt months and then March June, September and December, up to one year ahead.

months (i.e., the current and the following month, respectively) were introduced, with a second prompt month included in October 1991. Thus, the months traded were the current month, the following two months and January, April, July and October, for up to 18 months ahead. The contracts were traded every business day between 10.15 – 12.30 and 14.30 – 16.40hrs. Expectations of market agents regarding the prevailing future state of the physical market determined demand and supply for BIFFEX contracts. In turn, BIFFEX prices for the different contract months were determined by these prevailing demand and supply conditions (Veldhuizen, 1988).

The BIFFEX bids and offers were quoted in *"Value Points"* of the BFI and prices were a whole number multiple of the minimum price fluctuation (i.e. of one Value Point). One Value Point was 1.0 and had a value of US$10 per lot. One contract at par value was worth $10,000, the par being equal to 1,000. A bought or sold contract could either be offset by selling or buying, respectively, at any time on the BIFFEX market, or could be taken to *"settlement"*, that is, until the contract stopped trading and was settled against values of the BFI then. The Exchange Delivery Settlement Price (EDSP) for BIFFEX contracts, for a particular delivery month, was the average of the BFI values over the last seven trading days of that month. All BIFFEX trades were conducted via the LCH; it administered and regulated the paying of deposits and trades between market members, who were essentially the brokers on the trading floor. LCH acted as the middleman – the counterparty - between buyers and sellers of BIFFEX contracts. As a consequence, they were released from any obligations to each other, which were transferred to LCH. As the LCH guaranteed all contracts there was no credit risk involved in BIFFEX transactions. That is, there was no risk of non-payment should the counterparty to the transaction defaulted.

Figure 3.8. Yearly Volume (Num. of Contracts) of BIFFEX Contract (1985:05–2002:04)

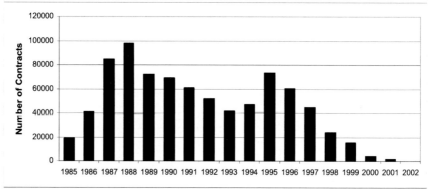

Source: LIFFE

BIFFEX contracts, while serving the industry between 1985 and 2002, did not produce overly effective hedges – see Kavussanos (2002) for a review. The unsatisfactory hedging effectiveness, lack of liquidity towards the end of BIFFEX's life, coupled with the inception, since 1992, of the FFA OTC, tailor-made contracts to satisfy the needs of the shipowners and the charterers, contributed to the decline in the volume of trading of the BIFFEX contracts to levels which did not make it sustainable to trade at LIFFE anymore[40]. This is demonstrated in Figure 3.8, which shows the

---

[40] Cullinane (1991), during the early days of the introduction of derivatives in shipping, in an effort to explain the use of the BIFFEX contract by the shipping fraternity, performed a behavioural and

steep rise in the use of BIFFEX contracts in the first four years of its life, up until 1998, and the ups and downs in its volume of trading. Since 1995 though the volume of trading declined gradually to such low levels in 2000 and 2001, that LIFFE withdraw the contract from its trading floor.

3.3.2. Freight Derivatives at the International Maritime Exchange (IMAREX)

The Oslo-based International Maritime Exchange (IMAREX) utilizes mostly the indices built by the Baltic Exchange but also some indices from Platts, to write freight rate derivatives upon. IMAREX is a professional freight derivatives exchange for the global maritime industry, founded in spring 2000, as a joint venture by Herman W. Michelet, a former Platou Shipbrokers partner and Frontline, I.M Skaugen ASA, RS Platou AS and NOS Holding ASA, all Norwegian public limited companies. It is accepted by the US Commodity Futures Trading Commission (CFTC) to operate an electronic trading facility as an Exempted Commercial Market (ECM). It is not regulated in the UK, but can offer its services to professional companies as defined in the Financial Services Act (FSAct) (IMAREX, 2005)[41].

Following extensive market consultation, the company launched a complete marketplace for freight derivatives and partnership agreements on technology and exchange operation were established. It started operating on 2nd November 2001. Its focus during the first half of 2002 was to establish a critical mass of trading and clearing members in the tanker segment. Later on, in the same year, operations extended to the dry cargo market (IMAREX, 2005). In partnership with the Norwegian Options and Futures clearing-house (NOS) – offering its clearing services – IMAREX has become an authorised and regulated marketplace for trading and clearing shipping freight derivatives. Its trading hours are during all business days, from 11:00 to 18:00 UK time. Registration of orders can take place before trading starts, from 09:00 to 11:00 UK time. IMAREX is closed for trading on UK public holidays. Trading can be facilitated directly on the IMAREX trading screen (www.imarex.com), via their broker teams in Oslo, Singapore and New York or via an authorised third-party freight derivatives broker (e.g. Clarksons, SSY, FIS, GFI, etc. – see Table 3.40 shown later in the chapter).

Someone wishing to trade at IMAREX, can obtain either a direct membership account or get access to the IMAREX marketplace through a financial intermediary, which is called a General Clearing Manager (shipping derivatives broker or shipping lending bank). In a direct membership structure, principals enter into membership agreements both with IMAREX and NOS. With IMAREX a Trading Membership Agreement (see Appendix I – www.imarex.com) must be filled, while for NOS a Clearing Membership Agreement (see Appendix II – www.nos.no) and a Margin and Settlement Account Agreement (see Appendix III – www.nos.no) must be filled. Upon receipt of the membership agreements, IMAREX and NOS will complete

---

attitudinal survey of shipowners from Britain, Greece, Hong Kong and Norway. From the 85 usable responses, he concluded that there is great scope for improving the acceptability of the market amongst shipowners, particularly as a hedging tool.

[41] IMAREX is neither an authorised person nor an exempt person under the Financial Services and Markets Act (FSMA). Under the FSMA, IMAREX may, as an "*overseas person*", arrange trades in freight derivatives in accordance with paragraph 72 of the Regulated Activities Order 2001 without falling within the scope of the FSMA if it does not contravene section 21 of the FSMA, which broadly restricts IMAREX from engaging in financial promotion other than to investment professionals. Accordingly, IMAREX will engage in marketing in the UK only in accordance with section 21 of the FSMA.

internal compliance check-lists and initiate a dialogue with relevant back-office or risk management personnel to secure that operational procedures are sorted out before trading starts. It takes around 2 to 4 weeks from the time agreements are received to the time an account can be opened, depending on the corporate structure of the member.

According to IMAREX's website, a trading environment is provided to the shipping market by offering trading systems and rules, guaranteed settlement through the NOS clearing-house, anonymous trading, flexible and tailored contracts, firm trading prices, professional exchange systems, and a Market Place Service (MPS) to facilitate trading of freight derivatives products not-listed at IMAREX. Each member of IMAREX has a dedicated member of the IMAREX MPS support who they can contact and refer to at all times. In Oslo the MPS support consists of a full tanker and a dry-bulk team. In Singapore, the MPS support consists of a tanker team and a smaller dry-bulk team. Both are fully dedicated to providing instant support by telephone, email and instant messenger.

An objective of IMAREX is to increase freight derivatives liquidity through: market-maker agreements with professional companies, attracting as members the largest existing freight derivatives players; increasing the trading volumes of committed IMAREX shareholders, trading on expectations on future freight market directions; and offering extensive customer training and support. Customer segments include international shipping companies, energy companies and refiners, commodity trading houses, and financial trading houses. Other potential areas of expansion include bunkers and second-hand tonnage. The main users registered on IMAREX, and which are actively trading are: AEP, EDF Trading Limited, Bocimar, Armada, Swiss Marine, BP Shipping, Goldman Sachs, Frontline and Morgan Stanley. Most of the leading players in tanker freight derivatives signed up for membership in the first four years of its operation. IMAREX trading volumes have grown substantially, both as a result of considerable market growth but also due to market share growth. From inception until August 2005, IMAREX has handled over 250 million tonnes of tanker freight, representing 30% of the world wide tanker derivatives market.

Table 3.16 provides an indication of the number of transactions, number of lots in days and value of transactions in US$ million for the tanker, dry-bulk and combined (tanker and dry-bulk) freight derivatives trades for the first eight months of 2005. The last column of the table shows the total figures up to August 2005. Out of 3,790 transactions, 245 were in dry-bulk, while 3,545 were in tanker trades. The total value equivalent of the 3,790 transactions was US$2,116 millions, $1,363 of which came from tanker freight derivatives, while $753 was from dry-bulk freight derivatives.

Table 3.17 presents the "*Dirty*" and "*Clean*" tanker freight futures (listed), Forward Freight Agreements (non-listed) and options (non-listed) contracts offered by IMAREX at the time of writing. Freight derivatives on other freight routes are also offered upon demand by negotiation, but do not appear on the table. As can be observed, the IMAREX derivatives products have as the underlying commodity (that is they use for settlement) the route freight indices constructed by either the Baltic Exchange or Platts. Market agents can select either contracts that are listed at IMAREX or non-listed contracts, which are available for trading through its MPS. Both are cleared through NOS.

Table 3.16. Trade Volumes Conducted on IMAREX (January 2005 – August 2005)

Total	Jan	Feb	Mar	Apr	May	Jun	Jul	Aug	Total
Number of Transactions	603	527	547	335	379	422	378	599	3,790
Number of Lots	22,257	13,631	15,904	11,395	13,015	14,659	17,847	17,411	126,119
Value ($ million)	$390	$245	$301	$228	$212	$228	$233	$279	$2,116
Tankers	**Jan**	**Feb**	**Mar**	**Apr**	**May**	**Jun**	**Jul**	**Aug**	**Total**
Number of Transactions	573	503	517	311	353	390	337	561	3,545
Number of Lots (1,000mt)	18,190	10,990	12,207	7,310	8,890	9,245	11,826	13,290	91,948
Value ($ million)	$265	$175	$197	$122	$119	$131	$145	$210	$1,363
Lots/Transactions	32	22	24	24	25	24	35	24	208
Dry-Bulk	**Jan**	**Feb**	**Mar**	**Apr**	**May**	**Jun**	**Jul**	**Aug**	**Total**
Number of Transactions	30	24	30	24	26	32	41	38	245
Number of Lots (days)	4,067	2,641	3,697	4,085	4,125	5,414	6,021	4,121	34,171
Value ($ million)	$125	$71	$104	$106	$93	$97	$89	$69	$753
Lots/ Transactions	136	110	123	170	159	169	147	108	1,122

Source: IMAREX

Table 3.18 summarises the contract details of IMAREX tanker futures derivatives, which exist on the routes of Table 3.17, and upon demand on other routes. As can be observed in Table 3.18, for each route, IMAREX members can trade derivatives contracts in 12 different periods; these are the front 4 months, the front 6 quarters and the front 2 calendar years, thus, providing for hedge coverage of freight rates for a period which extends up to two years ahead. In other words the futures/forward derivatives products offered are "*Month*", "*Quarter*" and "*Year*". They are periods, which start on: the first index day of the month and run up to the last index day of the month; the first index day of the quarter up to the last index day of the quarter and; the first index day of the year up to the last index day of the year, respectively, as per the Baltic Exchange or Platts index days.

The minimum contract size for 1 Month lot is 1,000mt, for 1 Quarter lot it is 3,000mt, and for 1 Year lot it is 12,000mt. For each contract route the settlement price is calculated as the average of all Baltic Exchange or Platts spot price assessment prices over the number of index days in the delivery period. The derivatives products written on TD3, TD4, TD5, TD7, TD9 and TC2 routes are settled against Baltic Exchange spot quotes, while those written on TC1, TC4 and TC5 routes are settled against Platts spot quotes. All contracts are priced in Worldscale points. The minimum price fluctuation in any contract is 0.25 Worldscale point. The value of each contract is calculated as: the Number of Lots in a contract x the Worldscale Flat Rate applicable for the delivery period x the Number of Worldscale Points in the price divided by 100.

At the time of writing, there were four single-route freight futures contracts, written on the dry-bulk routes produced by the Baltic Exchange. These are shown in Table 3.19, panel A. They involve the Capesize voyage routes C4 and C7 and the Panamax time-charter routes P2A and P3A, as these routes attract most of the dry-bulk freight derivatives trading, both at IMAREX and in OTC markets.

Table 3.17. IMAREX Dirty and Clean Tanker Derivatives, 2005

Routes	Sector	Route Description	Cargo Size (mt)	Cargo Size (barrels)	Settlement	Type of Contract	Settlement Index
Panel A: Dirty Tanker Derivatives							
TD3	VLCC	AG – East	260,000	1,925,000	Baltic	Listed – Futures, Asian Option	Baltic
TD4	VLCC	West Africa – USG	260,000	2,002,000	Baltic	Listed – Futures	Baltic
TD5	Suezmax	West Africa – USAC	130,000	1,001,000	Baltic	Listed – Futures	Baltic
TD7	Aframax	North Sea – UK/Cont	80,000	616,000	Baltic	Listed – Futures	Baltic
TD9	Aframax	Caribs – USG	70,000	539,000	Baltic	Listed – Futures	Baltic
TD8	Aframax	AG – Singapore (FO)	80,000	616,000	Baltic	Non-Listed – FFA	Baltic
TD10	Panamax	Caribs – USAC	50,000	385,000	Baltic	Non-Listed – FFA	Baltic
TD12	Panamax	ARA – USG	55,000	423,500	Baltic	Listed – Futures and Non-Listed – FFA	Baltic
Panel B: Clean Tanker Derivatives							
TC1	LR 2	AG – Japan	75,000	577,500	Platts	Listed – Futures	Platts
TC2	MR	Cont – USAC	37,000	254,100	Baltic	Listed – Futures	Baltic
TC4	MR	Sing – Japan	30,000	231,000	Platts	Listed – Futures	Platts
TC5	LR 1	AG – Japan	55,000	423,500	Platts	Listed – Futures	Platts
TC6	MR	Algeria/Euromed	30,000	–	Baltic	Listed – Futures	Baltic

Notes: Source: IMAREX

- LR 1 refers to Long Range Product Carriers between 55,000mt – 85,000mt.
- LR 2 refers to Long Range Product Carriers over 85,000mt.
- MR refers to Middle Range Product Carriers between 25,000mt – 55,000mt.
- The trading unit is Worldscale (WS) prices.

Table 3.18. Summary of Contract Details of IMAREX Tanker Derivatives, 2005

Delivery	Cash settled against Baltic indices
	Cash settled against Platts (for routes TC1, TC4 and TC5)
Pricing	Worldscale points
Minimum Tick	0.25 Worldscale point
Trading Period	Month, Quarter, Calendar
Minimum Lot Size	1 Month lot = 1,000mt, 1 Quarter lot – 3,000mt, 1 Year = 12,000mt
Contract Value	Number of lots x lot size x WS Flat rate x WS points / 100
Expiry	Last business day of expiring month
Daily Margining	Marked-to-market at end of every day against prices supplied by the Baltic Exchange (routes TD3, TD4, TD5, TD7, TD9 and TC2) or Platts (routes TC1, TC4 and TC5)
Final Settlement	The average of all Baltic (for routes TD3, TD4, TD5, TD7, TD9 and TC2) or Platts (for routes TC1, TC4 and TC5) spot price assessment prices over the number of index days in the delivery period
Contract Series	Front 4 Months, front 6 Quarters, front 2 Calendar Years
Clearing Fee	0.4% of Contract Value (for both listed and non-listed products)s
Settlement Fee	0.05% of Contract Value

Source: IMAREX

Besides the futures contracts written on the Baltic single route indices, Table 3.19, panel B, shows the three time-charter "*basket*" futures contracts, which are listed and traded at IMAREX. These "*baskets*" of time-charter rates are constructed from the Baltic dry-bulk route indices of the Capesize, Panamax and Handymax markets' routes, shown in Tables 3.3, 3.4 and 3.6, respectively. Thus, the four time-charter values of routes C8, C9, C10 and C11 of the BCI in Table 3.3, are used to calculate CS4 T/C, representing the average time-charter rate that could be earned in the Capesize sector. Similarly, the average of the four Panamax time-charter routes (P1A, P2A, P3A and P4) of the BPI produces the PM4 T/C, while the HM6 T/C is the average of the six Handymax routes (HM1A, HM1B, HM2, HM3, HM4A and HM4B) of Table 3.6. In this way, three more underlying indices are created by IMAREX, as "*baskets*" of time-charter rates, which are earned in these three sub-sectors of dry-bulk shipping. Given these indices, futures contracts are written by IMAREX, with the values of the indices used for settlement. These freight derivatives products could serve, for instance, "*principals*" that employ vessels on all time-charter routes of the BCI, say, and need to protect themselves against anticipated adverse movements in these time-charter rates.

Table 3.19. IMAREX Single Route and T/C "*Basket*" Dry-Bulk Derivatives, 2005

Routes	Sector	Route Description	Cargo Size (mt)	Type of Contract
Panel A: Single Route Dry-Bulk Derivatives				
C4	Capesize	Richards Bay – Rotterdam	150,000	Listed – Futures
C7	Capesize	Bolivar – Rotterdam	150,000	Listed – Futures
P2A	Panamax	T/C Skaw Gibraltar – Far East	74,000	Listed – Futures
P3A	Panamax	T/C S.Korea – Japan Pacific R/V	74,000	Listed – Futures
Panel B: T/C Basket Dry-Bulk Derivatives				
CS4 T/C	Capesize	Capesize 4 T/C routes Average	n/a	Listed – Futures
PM4 T/C	Panamax	Panamax T/C routes Average	n/a	Listed – Futures
SM5 T/C	Supramax	Supramax T/C routes Average	n/a	Listed – Futures

Note: For definition of routes refer to section 3.2.1.   **Source:** IMAREX

Table 3.20. Summary of Contract Details of IMAREX Dry-Bulk Derivatives, 2005

Delivery	Cash settled against Baltic indices
Lot Size	1,000 metric tons/lot (for voyage routes) and 1 day/lot (for T/C routes)
Pricing	US$/ton (for voyage routes) and US$/day (for T/C routes)
Minimum Tick	$0.05 (for voyage routes) and $25 (for T/C routes)
Trading Period	Month, Year (for single routes) Quarter, Half Year, Calendar (for T/C basket routes)
Contract Value	Number of lots x lot size x price
Expiry	Last business day of expiring month
Daily Margining	Marked-to-market at end of every day against prices supplied by the Baltic Exchange
Final Settlement	The average of all Baltic spot price assessment prices over the number of index days (or monthly weighted over the number of calendar days in each month for T/C basket routes) in the delivery period
Contract Series	Front 12 Months, front 3 Calendar Years (for single routes) Front 4 Quarters, front 2 Half Years, front 3 Calendar Years (for T/C basket routes)
Clearing Fee	0.3% of Contract Value
Settlement Fee	0% of Contract value

Source: IMAREX

Table 3.20 summarises the contract details of IMAREX dry-bulk derivatives contracts, issued on the single routes and time-charter "*baskets*" of Table 3.19. The lot size for Capesize contracts (C4 and C7) is: 1 lot = 1,000mt; the price quotations are in US$ per metric ton; while the minimum price fluctuation is $0.05 (5 cents). The lot size for the two Panamax routes (P2A and P3A) and for the time-charter "*basket*" routes (CS4 T/C, PM4 TC and HM6 T/C) is: 1 lot = 1 voyage day; the price quotations are US$ per day; while the minimum price fluctuation is $25.00. Single route freight futures can be traded for "*Months*" (minimum 1 lot) or "*Years*" (minimum 4 lots), while time-charter "*basket*" freight futures can be traded for "*Quarters*", "*Half Years*" or "*Years*". The value of both single and "*basket*" of time-charter dry-bulk freight futures contracts is calculated as follows: Number of lots x Lot size x Price. Settlement prices are calculated as the average of the corresponding Baltic spot price assessment prices: (a) over the number of index days in the delivery period for single route products or (b) in the delivery period monthly weighted over the number of calendar days in each month for time-charter "*basket*" products. Examples of each of these are shown later on in this chapter.

3.3.2.1. The NOS Clearing Services
When it comes to counterparty security, IMAREX has addressed the issue by providing a central clearing service. Trading is executed through an online trading system, with the NOS, as the counterparty to transactions completed, providing full financial clearing and settlement services. NOS was established in 1987 and is licensed by the Norwegian Ministry of Finance, under the Norwegian Stock Act of 2000, to conduct clearing. It is supervised by the Banking, Insurance and Securities Commission of Norway (Kredittilsynet). It is a limited company, owned by about 80 shareholders, including banks, securities companies, insurance companies, financial investors and private persons. NOS is both the clearing-house for the marketplace for standardised financial derivatives at Oslo Stock Exchange, as well as a clearing-house for clearing of OTC derivatives contracts and securities loans. Moreover, NOS provides clearing services to Nord Pool, the Nordic Power Exchange, since the introduction of their derivatives marketplace, in 1995. Handling of transactions and funds relating to clearing is carried out by Norway's largest commercial bank, Den Norske Bank (DNB) New York. NOS is also the provider of the exchange trading system through its partnership with Cinnober Financial Technology (CFT) and delivers system operation and support services to IMAREX.

Shipping companies and other market participants can use the clearing facilities of NOS through one of the following alternative procedures: (i) through an IMAREX broker, (ii) through the trading platform of IMAREX and (iii) through their own derivatives broker (as from January 2004). All the three trading procedures will clear the trade through NOS. The freight derivatives contracts listed at IMAREX are cleared by NOS, and NOS will in turn ensure that the counterparties of the contracts can meet their obligations through collecting collateral from both contract parties. The clearing system of NOS, also shown graphically in Figure 3.9, consists of:
- **End-User Clearing**: Each trading member of the IMAREX marketplace will have to also become a clearing member of NOS in order to be able to trade, requiring the deposit of dedicated funds on an interest-paying US$ margin account (at DnB NOR Bank, NY), with transfer of title to NOS. NOS has a right to draw funds for settlement and in case of default. The account is in the customer's name and earns interest on it. As a clearing member, each market participant will only be responsible for his own positions on IMAREX. Since there is no mutual responsibility between the clearing members, the clearing model of NOS requires that the obligation of each clearing member be fully covered by margins; the margin levels are set to cover 99.8% of possible market price fluctuations. The margin is set at this level to ensure that NOS has sufficient collateral to cover its contractual obligations in case of member default, even under the most adverse market conditions, thus minimising credit risk. As shown graphically in Figure 3.9, the margin consists of the base

collateral ($150,000), which is a mandatory minimum deposit and enough cash or letters of credit in favour of NOS to cover daily margin calls.

- **Real-Time Margining**: The real-time margining system built into the exchange is named *"The SPAN On-The-Fly"* and it entails that the calculation of required margin by each clearing member is performed real-time, continuously through the trading day, each time an order is placed[42]. The trading system does not allow contracts to be entered unless the clearing member is covered by sufficient collateral. The total provided collateral is divided into two modes, the utilisation mode and the control mode. The level between these two modes is decided by each member and is called the Control Mode Level. As long as the total margin requirement is within the utilisation mode, the member is free to place new orders. The control mode equals the maximum order size. This means that a member will not be able to place any new order that will result in a margin requirement exceeding the total provided collateral (IMAREX, 2004). With the above systems, NOS is covered against default risk amongst its clearing members.

Figure 3.9. NOS Clearing System

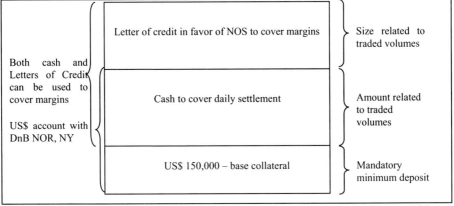

Source: NOS

- **Capital Structure and Default Guarantees**: As an additional security, NOS also maintains a capital structure and default guarantees to ensure that its contractual obligations will be fulfilled. Therefore, NOS maintains net assets to cover its commitments and continuously reviews this requirement in terms of market exposure.

---

[42] Standard Portfolio Analysis of Risk (SPAN), created by the Chicago Mercantile Exchange's (CME), is a widely used method for calculating margins on commodity derivatives, which has no impact either on the methods of settlement of contracts or on the methods employed by clearing members to cover their liabilities. The method produces a margin requirement, which is a function of the market volatility, time to settlement of the derivatives contract and liquidity in the particular route. The higher the volatility and the maturity to settlement and the lower the liquidity, the higher the margin requirement is, and visa versa. More information can be obtained at the website of the London Clearing House – www.lch.com).

To see how the aforementioned procedure works in practice, consider the following example (adapted from IMAREX), which also summarized in Table 3.21: As mentioned before, for a trading member to start trading, a base collateral of US$150,000 must be deposited with DnB NOR Bank, NY.

- During the first day of trading, a tanker futures contract is bought on TD3 (VLCC Middle East Gulf – Japan) at WS100 for December, with a contract size of 20,000mt. The trade value of the contract is $262,200 (=20,000mtx$13.11/mt x WS100 / 100), where $13.11/mt is the Flat rate for the route. This is shown on the third column of the table. To guarantee settlement of the contract on behalf of the client, NOS calculates, using SPAN, the collateral (margin) to be 12% of the trade value or $31,464 (=$262,200x12%), shown on the fourth column of the table. Thus, the client, in order to initiate trading, must deposit $150,000 (base collateral) and $31,464 in the form of letters of credit or cash. The total sum in the clients account is shown in the last column of the table, while the column before shows the change in cash-flows from the previous day.

- Suppose that during the second day of trading the futures value of the December contract rises to WS105. The trade value based on the new level (closing price) is $275,310 (= 20,000mt x $13.11/mt x WS105 / 100). The client has gained WS5 points or $13,110 (= $275,310 – $262,200), which will be credited to his account. This brings up the total sum in the clients account to $194,574. Thus, the 12% margin, which is dynamically calculated every day, amounts to $33,037.20 (= $275,310 x 12%).

- Suppose next that during the third day of trading the futures value of the December contract falls to WS98, thus losing WS7 points. The trade value, based on the new level is $256,956 (= 20,000mt x $13.11/mt x WS98 / 100). The client has lost $18,354 (= $275,310 – $256,956), which will be debited to his account. Thus, the 12% margin amounts to $30,834.72 (= $256,956 x 12%). The total sum deposit in the customers account now falls to $176,220 (=$194,574 – $18,354).

Table 3.21. IMAREX Margin System – Example

Day	WS	Trade Value	12% Margin Request	Day's Cash-flow on clients account	Total Sum on clients account
1	100	$262,200 (= 20,000mt x $13.11/mt x WS100 / 100)	$31,464 (– $262,200 x 12%)	+$181,464 (= $150,000 + $31,464)	$181,464 (= 150,000+$31,464)
2	105	$275,310 (= 20,000mt x $13.11/mt x WS105 / 100)	$33,037.20 (= $275,310 x 12%)	+$13,110 (= $275,310–$262,200)	$194,574 (= $181,464+$13,110)
3	98	$256,956 (= 20,000mt x $13.11/mt x WS98 / 100)	$30,834.72 (= $256,956 x 12%)	-$18,354 (=$256,956–$275,310)	$176,220 (= $194,574–$18,354)

As can be observed, the total sum in a clients account, together with the margin requirement, change on a daily basis, and they depend on the volatility of freight rates. It is not difficult to imagine situations, when, following a market upturn, the market has moved violently in the opposite direction for a prolonged period of time. There is a real danger then that companies with open positions in futures markets will see their profits eliminated and their cash reserves exhausted very quickly. If there is enough liquidity in the company, they may well run out of cash very quickly and be forced to liquidate other more tangible assets in order to satisfy the margin calls for cash from the clearing-house. It is also possible that in a derivatives market with low liquidity, they cannot find a counterparty immediately to close out positions, which will exacerbate the problem. At the extreme, the company may be declared in default and be forced to close down altogether. It is important, therefore, to consider carefully the derivatives trades open, in conjunction with the capabilities of the company to draw cash in case of difficulties, and to monitor derivatives positions and market changes constantly. Scenario analysis, with evaluation of extreme situations (fluctuations in prices) will help understand the potential dangers. Also, VaR methods, discussed in Chapter 2 of this book and also further down this chapter, can help monitor these risks.

3.3.3. Freight Futures at the New York Mercantile Exchange (NYMEX)

Since May 2005, the New York Mercantile Exchange (NYMEX) started offering freight derivatives. NYMEX is the world's largest physical commodity futures exchange and the trading forum for energy and precious metals. Transactions executed on the exchange avoid credit risk because its clearing-house acts as the counterparty to every trade. Trading is conducted through two divisions, the NYMEX Division, home to the energy, platinum, and palladium markets; and the Commodity Mercantile Exchange (COMEX) Division, on which all other metals trade. The exchange pioneered the development of energy futures and options contracts since 1979, as means of bringing price transparency and risk management to this vital market.

The wide array of trading markets provided by the Exchange include futures and options contracts for crude oil, gasoline, heating oil, natural gas, electricity, gold, silver, copper, aluminium, and platinum; futures contracts for coal, propane, and palladium; and options contracts on the price differentials between crude oil and gasoline, crude oil and heating oil, Brent and West Texas Intermediate (WTI) crude oil, and various futures contract months (calendar spreads) for light, sweet crude; Brent crude; gasoline; heating oil; and natural gas. The Exchange also lists e-miNY energy futures (50% of the size of the standard-sized contracts) on light sweet crude oil and natural gas that offer smaller investors and traders the opportunity for an efficient means of participating in energy markets. The contracts trade via the Chicago Mercantile Exchange's (CME) GLOBEX electronic trading system and clear through the NYMEX clearing-house.

NYMEX introduced nine tanker freight futures contracts on its NYMEX ClearPort(sm) electronic trading and clearing platform[43], beginning on May 16th 2005. These futures contracts are very similar in principle to those trading at IMAREX. They use as underlying commodities the Baltic Exchange or the Platts indices. More specifically, Table 3.22 presents the specifications of the underlying indices; they are the five "*dirty*" tanker routes TD3, TD5, TD7, TD9 and TD10, shown in panel A of the table, and the four "*clean*" tanker routes TC1, TC2, TC4 and TC5, presented in panel B of the same table.

---

[43] The NYMEX ClearPort(sm) internet-based system provides a market gateway to trading and clearing services. The system lets market participants take advantage of the financial depth and security of the Exchange clearing-house along with access to more than 130 energy futures contracts. ClearPort(sm) gives market participants flexibility to either trade derivatives through the trading system or, to conduct their own transactions off-exchange, negotiate their own prices, and still take advantage of the financial depth and integrity of the Exchange clearing-house by submitting the transactions through ClearPort clearing.

Table 3.22. NYMEX Listed Dirty and Clean Tanker Futures in 2005

Baltic Routes	NYMEX Coding	Sector	Route Description	Cargo Size (mt)	Type of Contract	Settlement Index
Panel A: Dirty Tanker Futures						
TD3	TL	VLCC	Middle Eastern Gulf to Japan	260,000	Listed – Futures	Baltic
TD5	TI	Suezmax	West Africa – USAC	130,000	Listed – Futures	Baltic
TD7	TK	Aframax	North Sea – Europe	80,000	Listed – Futures	Baltic
TD9	TN	Panamax	Caribbean to US Gulf	70,000	Listed – Futures	Baltic
TD10	TO	Panamax	Caribbean to USAC	50,000	Listed – Futures	Baltic
Panel B: Clean Tanker Futures						
TC1	TG	LR 2	Ras Tanura to Yokohama	75,000	Listed – Futures	Platts
TC2	TM	MR	Europe to USAC	37,000	Listed – Futures	Baltic
TC4	TJ	MR	Singapore to Japan	30,000	Listed – Futures	Platts
TC5	TH	LR 1	Ras Tanura to Yokohama	55,000	Listed – Futures	Platts

Source: NYMEX

Table 3.23 summarizes the specifications of the NYMEX freight futures contracts. The following can be observed in the table:

- **Contract Quantity and Value**. The contract quantity (trading unit) is 1,000 metric tons. Each contract is valued as the contract quantity (1,000mt) multiplied by the settlement price.
- **Trading Months**. Listed for 36 consecutive months forward, from the current month.
- **Trading Hours (New York time)**. The contracts are available for trading on the NYMEX ClearPort(sm) trading platform from 7 PM Sundays through to 2:30 PM Fridays, with a 45-minute break each day between 2:30 PM and 3:15 PM.
- **Prices and Fluctuations**. Prices are quoted in U.S. dollars and cents per metric ton. The minimum price fluctuation is $0.0001 per metric ton. There is no maximum price fluctuation.
- **Margin Requirements**. Margins are required for open futures positions. These are shown in the last box of the table, for non-members and for members. They vary according to the status of the trader and also fees are different between the routes.
- **Termination of Trading**. Trading ceases on the last business day of the contract month.
- **Contract Fees**. The fees, including the final cash settlement fee, are $5.00 per lot for non-members and $4.00 per lot for members.
- **Final Settlement**. Delivery under the contract is by cash settlement. Final settlement, following termination of trading for a contract month, is based on the Floating Price. The final settlement price will be the Floating Price calculated for each contract month.
- **Floating Price**. The Floating Price for a particular route and each contract month is equal to the arithmetic average of the rates for each business day over the contract month. The tanker rates used are those published by the Baltic Exchange, for routes TD3, TD5, TD7, TD9, TD10 and TC2, and those published in the Platts Oilgram price report, for routes TC1, TC4 and TC5. If for any reason the Baltic Exchange or Platts cannot provide any rate required for establishing the Floating Price, then the Forward Freight Agreement

Brokers Association (FFABA) may be instructed by either party to form a panel to establish any rate which will be binding on both parties.

Table 3.23. Summary of Contract Details of NYMEX Tanker Futures, 2005

Unit of Trading	1,000 metric tons		
Trading Months	36 consecutive months		
Trading Hours	7:00 PM Sundays to 2:30 PM Fridays, with a 45-minute break each day between 2:30 PM and 3:15 PM New York time		
Price Quotes	US dollars and cents per ton		
Minimum Price Fluctuations	$0.0001 per ton (10 cents per contract)		
Termination of Trading	Trading ceases on the last business day of the contract month		
Financial Settlement	The price of each contract is equal to the arithmetic average of the rates for each business day of the respective route as published by the Baltic Exchange (for routes TD3, TD5, TD7, TD9, TD10 and TC2) or Platts Oilgram Price Report (for routes TC1, TC4 and TC5)		
Margin Requirements	**Non-Members Initial**	**Members Initial**	**Maintenance Margin**
	TG $2,025	$1,650	$1,500
	TM $1,620	$1,320	$1,200
	TJ $1,350	$1,100	$1,000
	TH $2,363	$1,925	$1,750
	TL $810	$660	$600
	TI $1,283	$1,045	$950
	TK $675	$550	$500
	TN $1,013	$825	$750
	TO $1,013	$825	$750

Note: **Source:** NYMEX

- TG, TM, TJ, TH, TL, TI, TK, TN and TO are the trading symbols of the Tanker Route TC1 (Ras Tanura to Yokohama), Tanker Route TC2 (Europe to U.S. Atlantic Coast), Tanker Route TC4 (Singapore to Japan), Tanker Route TC5 (Ras Tanura to Yokohama), Tanker Route TD3 (Middle East Gulf to Japan), Tanker Route TD5 (West Africa to U.S. Atlantic Coast), Tanker Route TD7 (North Sea to Europe), Tanker Route TD9 (Caribbean to US Gulf) and Tanker Route TD10 (Caribbean to USAC) freight futures, respectively.

3.3.4. Freight Forwards at the London Clearing House Clearnet (LCH.Clearnet)

The London Clearing House (LCH) Limited, founded in 1888, during 22nd of December 2003 merged with Clearnet S.A. to form the "*LCH.Clearnet*" Group, with 120 members and a default fund of about sterling £580 million. The LCH.Clearnet launched, during 13th September 2005, a recording, clearing and settlement service for OTC Freight Forward Agreements (FFAs). According to LCH.Clearnet, the clearing service that it will provide will have all the benefits of broadly based central counterparty services. They include the elimination of counterparty credit risk, multi-lateral transaction netting, and improved operational and capital efficiency across multi-market positions.

Potential members can establish a relationship with a LCH.Clearnet clearing member, for the management of margin and cash-flows, agreeing the commercial terms bilaterally, with the counterparty risk lying between the client and the clearing member. Alternatively, potential members can sign up to LCH.Clearnet as a clearing member; this requires the member to contribute to a default fund with a minimum of £100,000, based on volume, making it no longer necessary to purchase a LCH.Clearnet share. Moreover, the company is required to have the equivalent of a minimum of £5 million in net capital, and the counterparty risk lies with the clearing-house.

Table 3.24. Listed Dirty and Clean Tanker Forwards at LCH.Clearnet, 2005

Routes	Sector	Route Description	Cargo Size (mt)
Panel A: Tanker Forwards			
TD3	VLCC	Middle Eastern Gulf to Japan	260,000
TD5	Suezmax	West Africa – USAC	130,000
TD7	Aframax	North Sea – USAC	80,000
TC2	MR	Continent to USAC	37,000
Panel B: Dry Voyage Forwards			
C3	Capesize	Tubarao/Beilun and Baoshan	150,000
C4	Capesize	Richard Bay/Rotterdam	150,000
C5	Capesize	West Australia/Beilun-Baoshan	150,000
C7	Capesize	Bolivar/Rotterdam	150,000
Panel C: Dry Time-charter Basket Forwards			
CTC	Capesize	Capesize 4 T/C routes Average	–
PTC	Panamax	Panamax 4 T/C routes Average	–
STC	Supramax	Supramax 5 T/C routes Average	–
Panel D: Dry Trip Time-Charter Forwards			
P2A	Panamax	Skaw – Gibraltar/Far East	–
P3A	Panamax	Transpacific Round - Japan	–

Note: Source: LCH.Clearnet
- Freight forward contracts in panel A, B, and D are written on single routes from either the tanker or the dry-bulk sector, while freight forwards in panel C are written on "*baskets*" of time-charter routes from the dry-bulk sector.

Table 3.24 presents the underlying indices upon which the freight forward contracts, which are cleared at LCH.Clearnet are based. They include 4 tanker FFAs (crude and refined products), presented in panel A of the table; 4 dry voyage FFAs (dry-bulk commodities), presented in panel B of the table; 3 "*baskets*" of dry time-charter FFAs, shown in panel C of the table; and 2 dry trip time-charter FFAs, shown in panel D of the table. In the tanker sector, forwards are written on the "*dirty*" TD3, TD5, TD7 routes and the "*clean*" TC2 route. In the dry-bulk sector, forwards are written on the Capesize voyage routes C3, C4, C5 and C7; on Capesize, Panamax, and Handymax time-charter "*baskets*" (same products as IMAREX – see Table 3.19); and on the Panamax time-charter P2A and P3A routes.

Table 3.25. Summary of Tanker Forward Contract Details at LCH.Clearnet, 2005

Delivery	Cash settled against Baltic indices
Lot Size	1,000 metric tons
Pricing	Worldscale points
Minimum Tick	US$0.0001
Trading Period	Month, Quarter, Calendar
Contract Value	Number of lots x lot size x Flat rate x WS points / 100
Expiry	Last business day of expiring month
Daily Margining	Marked-to-market at end of every day against prices supplied by the Baltic Exchange
Final Settlement	The average of all Baltic WS rate spot price assessment prices during the expiring month x Flat Rate / 100 – to 4 decimal points
Contract Series	Front 6 Months, front 4 Quarters, front 2 whole Calendar Years (out to a maximum of 36 months)
Clearing Fee Per/Lot	$4/lot for TD3, TD5, TD7 and TC2
Cash Settlement Fee/Lot	$2/lot for TD3, TD5, TD7 and TC2

Source: LCH.Clearnet

The specifications of the freight forward contracts are summarised in Tables 3.25 to 3.28, respectively. The initial margin is approximately 0.025% of the contract value (compared with 0.125% of NOS). The clearing and settlement fees are expressed as

US\$/lot and vary between the types of contracts, as shown in the last box of each table. Settlement fees are set at 50% of the clearing fees.

Table 3.26. Summary of Dry Voyage Forward Contract Details at LCH.Clearnet, 2005

Delivery	Cash settled against Baltic indices
Lot Size	1,000 metric tons
Pricing	US\$/mt
Minimum Tick	US\$0.0001
Trading Period	Month, Quarter, Calendar
Contract Value	Number of lots x lot size x price
Expiry	Last business day of expiring month
Daily Margining	Marked-to-market at end of every day against prices supplied by the Baltic Exchange
Final Settlement	The average of the last 7 Baltic spot price assessment prices during the expiring month – to 4 decimal points
Contract Series	C4 and C7 - Front 6 Months, following 2 Quarters registered as Front Month (Jan, Apr, Jul or Oct), front 2 Calendars Years (out to a maximum of 36 months) C3 and C5 – Front 3 Months, following 3 Quarters registered as front month of each quarter (out to 12 months)
Clearing Fee Per/Lot	\$5/lot for C4 and C7, \$8/lot for C3, \$4/lot for C5
Cash Settlement Fee/Lot	\$2.5/lot for C4 and C7, \$4/lot for C3, \$2/lot for C5

Source: LCH.Clearnet

Table 3.27. Summary of Dry T/C Basket Forward Contract Details at LCH.Clearnet, 2005

Delivery	Cash settled against Baltic indices
Lot Size	1 day
Pricing	US\$/day
Minimum Tick	US\$0.0001
Trading Period	Month, Quarter, Half Year, Calendar
Contract Value	Number of lots x lot size x price
Expiry	Last business day of expiring month
Daily Margining	Marked-to-market at end of every day against prices supplied by the Baltic Exchange
Final Settlement	The average of all daily Baltic spot price assessment prices for every trading day in the expiring month – to 4 decimal points
Contract Series	Front 1 or 2 Months, front 4 quarters, front 2 Half Years, front 3 Calendar Years (out to a maximum of 45 months)
Clearing Fee Per/Lot	\$7/lot for HTC and PTC, \$15/lot for CTC
Cash Settlement Fee/Lot	\$3.5/lot for HTC and PTC, \$7.5/lot for CTC

Source: LCH.Clearnet

Clearing of OTC freight contracts is open to all clearing members who meet the minimum criteria set out in the clearing-house's rulebook and have been approved by the clearing-house. Those members wishing to clear OTC freight contracts should request, for completion, the "*Clearing Extension Agreement*" and the "*Static Data Form*", which includes details of the static data required by the clearing-house for its systems. Clearing is open from 08:00 to 17:00 hours, Monday to Friday. OTC freight brokers must input trade details within 30 minutes of execution of the trade. Clearing members must either accept or reject the trade within a further 30 minutes of the input. All contracts are margined through the London SPAN system.

The development of allowing FFA contracts to be settled through a clearing-house, in order to eliminate credit risk, is in response to calls from the industry. Potential market participants have always voiced their concern in relation to counterparty risk. These "*hybrid*" FFAs seem to combine the best of futures and forwards into one contract. That is, counterparty risk is removed and yet they retain their flexibility in terms of adjusting their terms according to the needs of the counterparties.

Table 3.28. Summary of Dry Trip T/C Forward Contract Details at LCH.Clearnet, 2005

Delivery	Cash settled against Baltic indices
Lot Size	1 day
Pricing	US$/day
Minimum Tick	US$0.0001
Trading Period	Month
Contract Value	Number of lots x lot size x price
Expiry	Last business day of expiring month
Daily Margining	Marked-to-market at end of every day against prices supplied by the Baltic Exchange
Final Settlement	The average of the last 7 Baltic spot price assessment prices during the expiring month – to 4 decimal points
Contract Series	Front 6 months
Clearing Fee Per/Lot	$8/lot for P2A and P3A
Cash Settlement Fee/Lot	$4/lot for P2A and P3A

Source: LCH.Clearnet

3.3.5. Practical Applications of Freight Futures Contracts

Having considered the various exchanges which offer the opportunity to the market participants to trade freight derivatives, this section demonstrates through some practical examples, how these derivatives contracts may be used in practice. To aid in the decision of whether to buy or sell freight futures/forwards, Table 3.29 presents the buy or sell positions that potential users of freight futures/forwards would take. For instance, charterers (shipowners) in order to hedge a potential rise (fall) in the market buy (sell) freight futures/forwards contracts; speculators believing that currently it is a cheap (expensive) market in comparison to future levels of rates buy (sell) freight futures/forwards contracts; shipbrokers in order to hedge their commission income in a falling market may sell freight futures/forwards contracts; and operators and fund managers may buy or sell freight futures/forwards contracts depending on their exposure in the spot market.

Table 3.29. Summary of Freight Futures/Forwards Trading Positions for Potential Market Agents

	BUY	SELL
Charterer – Hedging against potential rise in the market	X	
Shipowner – Hedging against potential fall in the market		X
Speculator – Believing the market will move up or that it is cheap	X	
Speculator – Believing the market will move down or that it is expensive		X
Shipbroking Company – Hedging commission income against a falling market		X
Operator – Hedging risk for cargoes and vessels	X	X
Fund Managers – Reacting to patterns of trade regardless of physical market	X	X

Source: Clarksons Securities Ltd.

3.3.5.1. BIFFEX Example

To see how BIFFEX contracts have been used for hedging in practice by the potential counterparties, the principals as they are known in shipping, consider the following example. Suppose today is 1/2/2000 and the current freight rate in route P2 (US Gulf to South Japan) of the BPI is $25/ton grain, with the BPI standing at 1500 points.

BIFFEX futures contracts for April 2000 are available at 1450 points, which translate to a contract value of $14,500 (= 1450 points x $10). Thus, futures contracts trade at a discount of 3.33% [= (1450 / 1500) – 1], relative to the spot market, which reflects the market's view that spot freight rates are likely to fall by April. That is, the market expects that freight rates in route P2 will fall to $24.17/ton [= $25/ton x (1 – 0.0333)]. A shipowner knows that his vessel (54,000 dwt) will be available on 1st of April 2000, in the US Gulf area to pick up a cargo of 51,400mt. On the other side, there is a charterer with a 51,400mt cargo of grain to transport from the US Gulf to Japan, also at the beginning of April. If the freight rate does not change, the shipowner's (charterer's) freight revenue (cost) would be $1,285,000 (= 51,400mt x $25/ton). This amount represents the freight risk exposure of the shipowner and of the charterer.

The shipowner (charterer) fears that freight rates may fall (rise) in early April, thereby reducing (increasing) his income (cost). His chartering assistant suggests selling (buying) April BIFFEX contracts. He decides to open a BIFFEX position, which matches exactly the spot position. Thus, the number of contracts to sell (buy) is calculated as: (51,400ton x $25/ton) / (1450 x $10) = $1,285,000 / $14,500 = 88.6 ≈89 BIFFEX contracts. The shipowner (charterer) contacts his broking company, which has a representative broker at LIFFE who executes the transaction to sell (buy) 89 contracts. For this service the shipowner (charterer) is charged $15 per contract per *"round trip"*, which is the fee for selling (buying) and then buying back (selling) the contract. The fee of $1,335 (= $15 x 89 contracts) is paid to the broker by the shipowner (charterer) at the completion of the transaction, when he would have bought back (sold) the 89 contracts. The buyer (seller) of the BIFFEX contracts could be a charterer (shipowner) who fears that freight rates will rise (fall), but might have been a speculator who also anticipates higher (lower) rates in April. Trading BIFFEX contracts, just like with any futures contracts, involved opening a margin account with the London Clearing House (LCH), which was cleared on a mark-to-market basis – see chapter 2 for details.

Table 3.30. The Two Possible Outcomes of BIFFEX Hedging

February 2000	
Spot (Physical) Market	**BIFFEX Market**
BPI: 1500	BIFFEX February price 1450
Freight rate: $25/ton	Shipowner sells 89 (= $1,285,999/$14,500) contracts
Cargo size: 51,400mt	Charterer buys 89 contracts
Freight income/cost: $1,285,000 (=51,400mt x $25)	Value of BIFFEX: $1,290,500 (= 1450 x $10 x 89)
First scenario: Freight rates decrease	**Second scenario: Freight rates increase**
April 2000: Spot Market	
BPI: 1150	BPI: 1750
Freight rate: $20/ton	Freight rate: $30/ton
Cargo size: 51,400mt	Cargo size: 51,400mt
Freight income/cost: $1,028,000 (=51,400mt x $20)	Freight income/cost: $1,542,000 (=51,400mt x $30)
The shipowner (charterer) loses (gains) $257,000	**The shipowner (charterer) gains (loses) $257,000**
April 2000: BIFFEX Market	
BPI (settlement price): 1150	BPI (settlement price): 1750
Value of BIFFEX: $1,023,500 (= 1150 x $10 x 89)	Value of BIFFEX: $1,557,500 (= 1750 x $10 x 89)
The shipowner (charterer) gains (loses) $267,000	**The shipowner (charterer) loses (gains) $267,000**
Portfolio of Spot and BIFFEX Positions	
Net gain (loss) for shipowner (charterer): $10,000 (= $267,000 – $257,000)	**Net loss (profit) for shipowner (charterer): $10,000** (= $257,000 – $267,000)
Transactions Costs: $1,335 (= $15 x 89 contracts)	

Table 3.30 summarises the two possible outcomes of hedging, two months later, in April, under two alternative scenarios.

- Under the first scenario, presented in the first column of the table, freight rates decrease to $20/ton, corresponding to a fall in the BPI to 1,150 points. The shipowner (charterer) receives (pays) $1,028,000 (= 51,400ton x $20/ton) in the spot market. Thus, the shipowner (charterer) loses (gains) $257,000(=$1,028,000 – $1,285,000) in the spot market in comparison to the February rates. In the BIFFEX paper market he realises a gain (loss) of $267,000 (=$1,290,500 – $1,023,500) as he buys (sells) the BIFFEX contracts at the lower price of 1,150. Combining the spot with the paper position results overall in a net inflow (outflow) of $10,000. The gain of the shipowner is the loss of the charterer – it is a zero-sum game. When transactions fees are incorporated, the net profit for the shipowner is $8,665 (= $10,000 – $1,335) while the loss for the charterer becomes $11,335 (=$10,000 + $1,335). If the shipowner did not participate in the BIFFEX market to hedge his freight rate risk, he would have lost $257,000 of income due to the fall in freight rates. Opening the BIFFEX position produced a combined spot – BIFFEX result of $8,665 profit. Essentially, he stabilised his income at more or less today's levels. The result for the charterer is also to stabilise his costs at today's levels, despite the fact that he would have been better off if he did not enter the BIFFEX position; his costs would have been lower in the spot market and would not have made losses in the paper market – but then his expectations regarding future movements of freight rates did not materialized.
- Under the second scenario, presented in the second column of the table, freight rates increase to $30/ton, corresponding to a rise of the BPI rise to 1750 points. The shipowner (charterer) gains (loses) $257,000 (= $1,542,000 – $1,285,000) in the spot market, in comparison to February's rates. In the BIFFEX paper market he realises a loss (gain) of $267,000 (= $1,557,000 – $1,290,500), as he has to buy the BIFFEX contracts at the higher price of 1750. Combining the spot with the paper position it results in a net loss (gain) for the shipowner (charterer) of $10,000. When transactions costs are taken into account the net loss for the shipowner is $11,335, while the net gain for the charterer is $8,665.

3.3.5.2. IMAREX Example

The example presented above on BIFFEX is typical of a hedge that may be taken on by a shipowner or a charterer wishing to minimize their freight rate risk exposure. As the BIFFEX contract ceased trading since April 2002, IMAREX was for three years the only exchange able to provide futures contracts on freight. Since 2005 NYMEX joined the market. To see how IMAREX can be used by market agents, for freight rate risk management or for speculation, consider the following example adopted from IMAREX (2005).

The Hedger's point of view

Suppose a shipowner receives a 130,000 dwt Suezmax newbuilding at the beginning of April. He decides to employ the vessel for the next nine months on route TD5 of the BDTI that is, on the West Africa – USAC route, and the market is strong at the moment, but a fall in freight rates is expected during the nine months period. The shipowner decides to hedge his freight rate risks and uses IMAREX to sell freight futures contracts on TD5 to cover the next nine months as follows: He sells 130 lots of each of April, May and June monthly contracts, 390 lots of each of quarter 3 (Q3) and quarter 4 (Q4) contracts, at the WS rates quoted by IMAREX, and presented in Table 3.31. Thus, the April contract is sold at WS165, the May one for WS162, etc. Multiplying these WS rates with the vessel tonnage of 130,000 dwt and the Flat rate for the route of $10.28/mt, obtained from the Worldscale organisation publications, produces the opening position amount for each futures contract. Thus, the futures contract position opened for April is $2,205,060 (= 130 lots x 1,000 mt/lot x $10.28/mt x WS165/100); the derivatives position for May is $2,164,168 (=130 lots x 1,000 mt/lot x $10.28/mt x WS162/100) and so on for June, Q3 and Q4 contracts. In total, he has sold 1,170 lots (=130 x 3 + 390 x 2), worth $18,335,408 (= $2,205,060 + $2,164,968 + $2,138,240 + $6,214,260 + $5,612,880). On the other side of the transaction may be a refinery, which needs the Suezmax vessel to transport one crude oil cargo per month, for the next nine months, on route TD5. The refiner does not wish to take on a vessel on time-charter. Instead, he uses the more flexible paper market and becomes the buyer of the futures contracts that the shipowner sold. His freight futures transactions can be seen in the second column of Table 3.31.

The counterparties conduct their brokers at IMAREX and pay brokerage fees of $5,512.7 (= 0.25% x $2,205,060) for the April contract, $5,412.4(=0.25%x$2,164,968) for the May contract, $5,345.6 (= 0.25% x $2,138,240) for the June contract, $15,535.7 (= 0.25% x $6,214,260) for the Q3 contract and $14,032.2 (=0.25% x $5,612,880) for the Q4 contract. The clearing fees for tanker contracts at IMAREX are 0.4% of the contract value and the settlement fees for tanker contracts are 0.05% of the contract value. Therefore, the clearing and settlement fees combined are $9,922.8 (= 0.45% x $2,205,060) for the April contract, $9,742.4(=0.45%x$2,164,968) for the May contract, $9,622.1 (= 0.45% x $2,138,240) for the June contract, $27,964.2 (= 0.45% x $6,214,260) for the Q3 contract and $25,258.0 (=0.45% x $5,612,880) for the Q4 contract. The total transactions costs are $15,435.5 (=$5,512.7 + $9,922.8) for the April contract, $15,154.8(=$5,412.4+$9,742.4) for the May contract, $14,967.7(=$5,345.6+$9,622.1) for the June contract, $43,499.9 (= $15,535.7 + $27,964.2) for the Q3 contract and $39,290.2 (=$14,032.2+$25,258.0) for the Q4 contract. Over all contracts, the counterparties have to pay $128,348 (= $15,435.5 + $15,154.8 + $14,967.7 + $43,499.9 + $39,290.2).

Each of the futures contracts, sold by the shipowner and bought by the refiner, is closed at expiry. The settlement prices used come from the Baltic Exchange. They are the averages of the BDTI prices for route TD5 over the number of index (business) days in the contract period. Thus, for the April monthly contract the settlement price is WS181.5, which is obtained as the average WS rates published by the Baltic over the month of April. Similarly, for the Q3 contract the settlement price of WS144, that can be seen in the table, is obtained as the average of the WS rates of the Baltic TD5 index over the three months period. Given a Flat rate of $10.28/mt, and the cargo size of 130,000 dwt, the total settlement amount can be calculated by multiplying the WS rate/100 with these numbers. Thus, for the April contract, the settlement amount is $2,425,566 (= 130 lots x 1,000 mt/lot x $10.28/mt x WS181.5 / 100). The contract was sold by the shipowner for WS165, i.e. for $2,205,060 (= 130 lots x 1,000 mt/lot x $10.28/mt x WS165 / 100). As a consequence, the shipowner made a loss on this futures April contract of $220,506. This is the difference between the settlement amount and the amount for which the contract was sold. As can be seen in the second column of the table, the position for the refinery is exactly opposite. That is, the refiner has made a profit of $220,506 on this contract, as he bought at WS165 and settled (sold) at WS181.5.

The gain/loss for the rest of the futures contracts for both the shipowner and the refinery are also calculated in the table. As can be observed, for the April, May and June monthly contracts and for the quarterly Q4 contract the shipowner made a loss in the futures position, as the WS rates increased during these periods. The losses of the shipowner were the gains of the refiner, the shipowner's counterparty; it is a zero-sum game. For Q3, WS rates fell, from WS155 to WS144, producing a profit of $441,012 for the shipowner and a corresponding loss for the refiner of the same amount. Over all contracts, the shipowner lost $334,100, which has been the refiner's profit. When the futures positions are combined with the spot positions, the net effect for the shipowner and for the refiner is to stabilize their cash-flows; the gains made in the spot market are offset by the losses in the paper market. When transactions costs are included, the shipowner lost $462,448 (= $334,100 + $128,348) and the refiner gained $205,752 (= $334,100 – $128,348).

The main advantage of using the derivatives markets rather than the time-charter market, in order to reduce the exposure to freight rate risk, is the flexibility and lower cost that they offer. For instance, it is much easier in terms of time and cost to close a paper trade position, simply by selling or buying the contract, compared to going in or out of time-charter contracts. Thus, if, say, in June, the shipowner revises his expectations, due to new information obtained, and thinks that the freight market will improve, he can unwind his Q3 and Q4 positions by buying back the contracts earlier. He would then have no paper trade and would simply take advantage of the rising WS rates obtained in the spot market. He can close these positions instantly and at very little cost. On a time-charter though, he would suffer loss of reputation, perhaps a law suit and will pay for personnel time to carry all this through.

Once more, it should be noted that the NOS clearing-house is the counterparty to the shipowner and to the refiner for all these transactions. It employs the mark-to-market clearing mechanism, thus settling the contracts on a daily basis, based on the way futures prices moved from day to day. Effectively, this eliminates credit risk; that is, the counterparty risk of default that would exist in a bilateral derivatives contract agreement, between the shipowner and the refinery, is eliminated.

The Speculator's/Investor's point of view
It should be noted here that the cash-flows shown on Table 3.31 could have been those of a speculator rather than a hedger. Thus, it may have concerned the cash-flows of positions taken by a market player with no underlying exposure to the freight market; that is, without owning a vessel which he needs to hire in the case of a shipowner, or without the need to hire in the freight service in the case of a charterer. The speculator would simply bet on the potential future movements of freight rates and take long or/and short positions in futures contracts in order to benefit from the volatility of freight rates. Thus, a speculator, for instance, that is fairly confident about his ability to forecast the freight market for the next nine months will trade freight futures. If he forecasts a decline in freight rates in route TD5 he will sell one or more futures contracts at IMAREX, such as those observed in the first column of Table 3.31. If he expects freight rates to rise, he will buy freight futures contracts, such as those in the second column of the table, in order to sell them back later on at the higher price he forecasts and make a profit. He may even create a portfolio of short

and long freight futures positions, if he can predict freight market turnings from high to low and vise versa; for instance, the speculator may expect a fall in rates in April but a rise in rates in June. He could sell April futures and buy June futures to benefit from this forecast of the volatility.

The way IMAREX futures contracts work, as demonstrated through the above examples and also through the BIFFEX example, is similar for all listed futures contracts on freight rates. At the moment IMAREX and NYMEX provide the market for freight futures contracts, where the prices of those contracts are determined at any point in time, based on the balance of demand and supply. The corresponding clearing-house becomes the counterparty to the principals on behalf of the exchange, undertaking the clearing of the contracts and as a consequence, eliminates credit risk. A class of derivatives contracts exists that are negotiated directly between the counterparties, through their brokers. These are forward contracts; they are not exchange-traded and do not use a clearing-house – settlement is made at the end of the contract's life, based on the difference between the negotiated price and the market price prevailing at the expiry of the contract. Freight Forward Agreement (FFA) contracts, examined next, fall under this category.

Table 3.31. Shipowner and Refiner Tanker Hedging at IMAREX

Shipowner	Oil Refiner
Spot Market	**Spot Market**
The owner had the advantage of a strong spot market for the first three months. The market dropped during the third quarter but again increased during the fourth quarter.	The refiner had the advantage of the weak spot market during the summer (third quarter). For the other periods, the losses from a high spot market were compensated by a profit on the futures positions.
IMAREX Market	**IMAREX Market**
Lots sold: 130	Lots bought: 130
April sold: 130 lots x 1,000 mt/lot x $ 10.28/mt x WS165/100 = $2,205,060	April bought: 130 lots x 1,000 mt/lot x $10.28/mt x $165/100 = $2,205,060
Avg. BDTI TD5: 130 lots x 1,000 mt/lot x $10.28/mt x WS181.5/100 = $2,425,566	Avg. BDTI TD5: 130 lots x 1,000 mt/lot x $10.28/mt x WS181.5/100 = $2,425,566
Loss on Futures: = **-$220,506**	Gain on Futures: = **$220,506**
Lots sold: 130	Lots bought: 130
May sold: 130 lots x 1,000 mt/lot x $10.28/mt x WS162/100 = $2,164,968	May bought: 130 lots x 1,000 mt/lot x $10.28/mt x WS162/100 = $2,164,968
Avg. BDTI TD5: 130 lots x 1,000 mt/lot x $10.28/mt x WS168/100 = $2,245,152	Avg. BDTI TD5: 130 lots x 1,000 mt/lot x $10.28/mt x WS168/100 = $2,245,152
Loss on Futures: = **-$80,184**	Gain on Futures: = **$80,184**
Lots sold: 130	Lots bought: 130
June sold: 130 lots x 1,000 mt/lot x $10.28/mt x WS160/100 = $2,138,240	June bought: 130 lots x 1,000 mt/lot x $10.28/mt x WS160/100 = $2,138,240
Avg. BDTI TD5: 130 lots x 1,000 mt/lot x $10.28/mt x WS165.5/100 = $2,211,742	Avg. BDTI TD5: 130 lots x 1,000 mt/lot x $10.28/mt x WS165.5/100 = $2,211,742
Loss on Futures: = **-$73,502**	Gain on Futures: = **$73,502**
Lots sold: 390	Lots bought: 390
Q3 sold: 390 lots x 1,000 mt/lot x $10.28/mt x WS155/100 = $6,214,260	Q3 bought: 390 lots x 1,000 mt/lot x $10.28/mt x WS155/100 = $6,214,260
Avg. BDTI TD5: 390 lots x 1,000 mt/lot x $10.28/mt x WS144/100 = $5,773,248	Avg. BDTI TD5: 390 lots x 1,000 mt/lot x $10.28/mt x WS144/100 = $5,773,248
Gain on Futures: = **$441,012**	Loss on Futures: = **-$441,012**
Lots sold: 390	Lots bought: 390
Q4 sold: 390 lots x 1,000 mt/lot x $10.28/mt x WS140/100 = $5,612,880	Q4 bought: 390 lots x 1,000 mt/lot x $10.28/mt x WS140/100 = $5,612,880
Avg. BDTI TD5: 390 lots x 1,000 mt/lot x $10.28/mt x WS150/100 = $6,013,800	Avg. BDTI TD5: 390 lots x 1,000 mt/lot x $10.28/mt x WS150/100 = $6,013,800
Loss on Futures: = **-$400,920**	Gain on Futures: = **$400,920**
Conclusion	**Conclusion**
By selling freight futures the owner hedged his exposure to a weaker spot market and achieved a predictable revenue stream.	By buying freight futures the oil refiner has managed the freight exposure and obtained a predictable freight element in his refinery margins for the rest of the year.
Total loss for shipowner from all transactions: -$334,100 (= -$220,506 - $80,184 - $73,502 + $441,012 - $400,920)	
Total gain for refiner from all transactions: +$334,100	
Total Brokerage, Clearing and Settlement fees: $128,348 (= $15,435.5 + $15,154.8 + $14,967.7 + $43,499.9 + $39,290.2)	

Source: Adapted from IMAREX

3.4. Forward Freight Agreements (FFAs)

In 1992 OTC FFA contracts became available to market agents, as an alternative to BIFFEX contracts for hedging freight rate risks. They were introduced through the leadership of Clarksons, amongst others, with the collaboration of the Baltic Exchange, as a response to the needs of the industry to achieve better hedges than those obtained from BIFFEX contracts. They are principal-to-principal "*Contracts for Differences*" (CFDs), between a seller and a buyer to settle a freight rate in a future period, for a specified quantity of cargo or type of vessel, for one, or a combination, of the major trade routes of the dry-bulk and liquid-bulk shipping sectors[44]. Notice that, unlike BIFFEX contracts whose underlying "*commodity*" was the BFI index, FFA contracts were written on individual route indices of the BFI. In that sense, they became a more precise alternative to the only existing futures contract at the time, namely the BIFFEX.

Figure 3.10. Yearly Volumes of Dry-Bulk FFA Contracts (January 1992 – Sept. 2005)

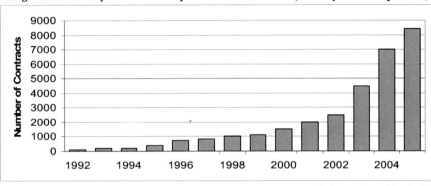

Source: Clarksons Securities Ltd.

Up until November 1st 1999, the underlying assets of FFA contracts were one (or a combination) of the routes of the BFI. The two counterparties to the contract, through the market-maker (e.g. Clarksons, FIS, SSY, etc.), agreed a freight rate for a particular cargo size, e.g. 52,000 tons of HSS, on a specified trade route, e.g. US Gulf to Japan, for a designated settlement date in the future, e.g. four months from now. Negotiations are very similar to those carried in the physical market to fix a vessel, only that here, specialised brokers are involved. Following a renaming of the BFI into BPI in November 1999 and the introduction of the BCI and the BHI indices, apart from FFA contracts on routes of the BPI, FFA contracts were also issued on routes of these indices, representing the Capesize and Handy sectors, respectively, as presented in Tables 3.3 and 3.6. Tanker FFA contracts appeared since mid-1997 on routes of the BITR, and since October 2001 on routes of the BDTI and BCTI.

Since their introduction, FFA deals in both value and volume terms have grown substantially. Figures 3.10 and 3.11 show, respectively, the volume (number of contracts) and market value (in US$ billion) of dry-bulk FFA transactions from inception until 2005. The volume/value of trading has followed an exponential rise,

---

[44] The term Contracts for Differences (CFDs), refers to the way the forward contract is initiated and settled. More specifically, a price for the forward contract is agreed at the initiation of the contract. When the contract is closed the settlement price is compared with the agreed price and the difference is paid to or received from the counterparty, based on the difference between these two prices; hence, the term CFD. Notice that, unlike futures contracts which operate on a daily mark-to-market margining system, no money changes hands in a forward contract until the termination of the contract.

189

particularly since 2000, when interest on BIFFEX receded, but particularly so after the BIFFEX's withdrawal in April 2002. Thus, the volume of 1,500 contracts which traded in 2000, increased to 8,400 in 2005, with a market value of more than US$29 billion.

Figure 3.11. Yearly Market Values of Dry-Bulk FFA Contracts (Jan. 1992 – Sept. 2005)

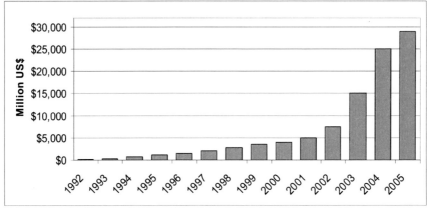

Source: Clarksons Securities Ltd.

Figure 3.12. Seaborne Dry Cargo Trades and Freight Covered by FFAs

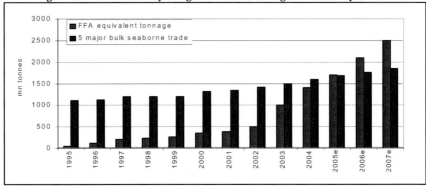

Note: **Source:** Freight Investor Services (FIS)
- The 5 major bulk trades are: Iron ore, Coking coal, Steam coal, Grain (including soyabean) and Bauxite alumina.

Figure 3.12 compares the metric ton equivalent of FFAs on dry-bulk cargoes, with the volume of the physical cargoes transported, between 1995 and 2007. The seaborne dry-bulk trades of the five major commodities (Iron ore, Coking coal, Steam coal, Grain and Bauxite alumina) constitute the majority of dry-bulk seaborne trade and re representing of the route that FFAs are written on. It is evident from the figure that by 2005 dry-bulk FFA contracts in million tonnes surpassed the volume of trading in the physical market. The trend is expected to continue, with FFA trading covering increasingly larger proportions of the underlying market. In other more mature markets, the futures/forward trading may be more than ten times that of the underlying commodity. This reflects the potentials in the freight derivatives market. The exponential rise in FFA trading, the increasing liquidity and transparency of the market creates a virtuous circle and will hopefully attract more and different types of market participants with an interest in shipping markets.

Figure 3.13. Physical Capesize Route C4 and FFA C4 Volumes (in million mt)

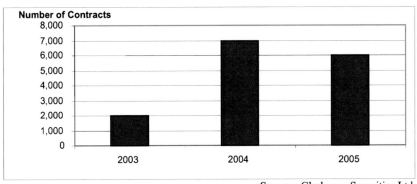

Source: SwissMar

Figure 3.13 provides a comparison of the volume of trading (in million mt) in the underlying physical trade on Capesize Route C4 with the corresponding FFA volume for the period 2001 to 2005. As can be seen in the figure, in 2001 the FFA volume surpassed the physical volume of trading in this route by approximately 30%. FFA trading has grown approximately to three times that of the physical market by 2005. As route C4 is one of the most liquid ones in dry-bulk trades, it can be taken as an indicator of how the FFA market for the rest of the dry-bulk routes will also develop. In the tanker markets, the volume and value of FFA trading for the period 2003 – 2005 are shown in Figures 3.14 and 3.15, respectively. The volume of trading in 2005 stood at 6,000 contracts, with a market value of US$12 billion.

Figure 3.14. Yearly Volumes (Number of Trades) of Tanker FFA Contracts (January 2003 – September 2005)

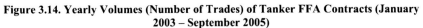

Source: Clarksons Securities Ltd.

Figure 3.15. Yearly Market Values of Tanker FFA Contracts (Jan. 2003 – Sept. 2005)

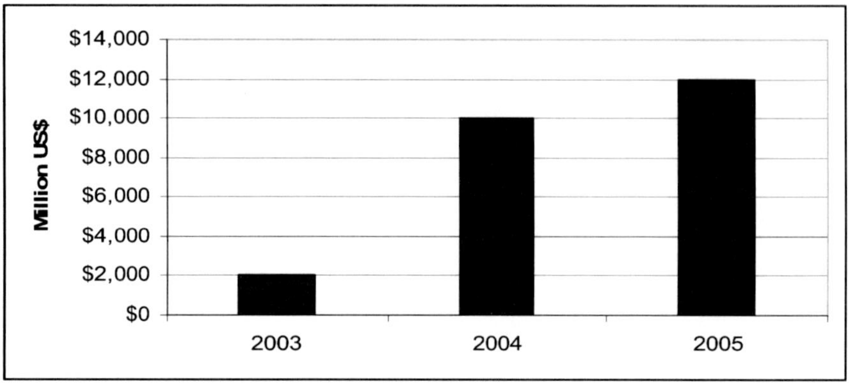

Source: Clarksons Securities Ltd.

Table 3.32 shows some FFA market statistics for 2005 compiled from information obtained from Freight Investor Services (FIS) and Clarksons Securities Ltd. Thus, according to this information, market agents that use FFA contracts are from all sectors of the shipping industry. They are shipowners (20%), charterers and operators (fleet managers/freight traders) (30%) trading companies (grain, coal, electricity, oil traders) (40%), financial houses and banks (10%). Capesize vessels seem to attract most of the trades, almost twice that of the Handymax vessel trades.

Table 3.32. FFA Statistics (Estimated Breakdown of Trades for 2005)

Intention of Use: - Hedging 30% - Speculation 70%	**Major FFA brokers:** - Clarksons (30%) - SSY (20%) - FIS (20%) - Others (30%)
Regional FFA trading: - Europe 50% - USA 20% - Asia 30%	**Types of Market Agents:** - Shipowners 20% - Charterer – Operators 30% - Trading Companies (coal, grain, electricity, oil) 40% - Financial houses and banks 10%
Capesize Trades (40%): - 75% Route C4 (RB/Rott) - 10% Route C7 (Bolivar/Rott) - 10% T/C average - 5% Other **Capesize Major Players:** American Electric Power, EDF, Cargill, Coeclerici, Armada, BHP Biliton, Morgan Stanley, Bocimar, Glencore	**Panamax Trades (37%):** - 60% T/C average - 15% Route P2A (Skaw/Far East) - 15% Route P3A (Transpacific round) - 10% Other **Panamax Major Players:** Cargill, Armada, TMT (Taiwan Marine Transport), Navios, Coeclerici, Klaveness, Dreyfus, D'Amato, AWB (Australian Wheat Board), Glencore
Handymax Trades (23%): - 75% T/C average - 10% Route M1A (Antwerp/Skaw) - 10% Route M2 (South Korea/Japan) - 5% Other	
Tanker Trades: - 38% VLCC - 38% Suezmax - Aframax - 24% MR/LR	**Major Tanker Players:** Arcadia, BP, Ceres, Euronav, Frontline, Goldman Sachs, Hetco, Morgan Stanley, Shell, Trafigura, Worldwide

Source: Freight Investor Services (FIS), Ltd. and Clarksons Securities Ltd.

Regional FFA trading reveals that 70% of the trades are from Europe and the US, and the remaining 30% is from Asia. The value of trading for speculation is more than twice that for hedging, being 70% and 30%, respectively. It should be noted here that in mature markets, speculative and arbitrage trades surpass those intended for hedging purposes by several times. Speculative and arbitrage trades provide liquidity to the market, and if supervised appropriately will help the functioning of the FFA market. The most active routes can also be deduced from the table; for instance, 60% of the Panamax FFA trades are on T/C average, followed by routes P2A and P3A representing Skaw – Far East and Transpacific round trip, respectively. In the Capesize market, 75% of FFA contracts are on route C4 (Richards bay to Rotterdam), while 10% of FFAs are on route C7 (Bolivar to Rotterdam) and 10% on the average basket of time-charter rotes. In the tanker FFA trades, VLCC vessels attract most of the trades with a 38% market share, while another 38% is shared between Suezmax and Aframax vessels.

Figure 3.16. FFA and Spot Prices in BPI Route P2; Daily Data (16/01/97 – 12/05/04)

Figure 3.17. FFA and Spot Prices in BPI Route P2A; Daily Data (16/01/97 – 20/04/05)

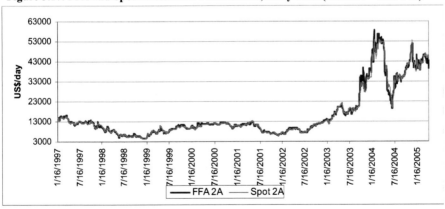

Figures 3.16 and 3.17 present the near-month FFA prices against the Baltic index spot prices in the Panamax voyage route P2 (16/01/1997 to 12/05/2004) and time-charter route P2A (16/01/1997 to 20/04/2005), respectively. In both routes, the FFA and spot freight rates move closely together, which is also confirmed by the values of their correlation coefficients as they stand at 0.996 and 0.995, respectively. Such a close

relationship between spot and futures/forward prices is a prerequisite for effective hedges. For instance, as discussed in Kavussanos (2002) the hedging effectiveness of BIFFEX contracts has been very low due to cross hedging problems, explaining partly the decline of interest on them. The FFAs became a substitute for hedging, for the shipping industry, and these high correlation coefficients provide a justification for that.

Figure 3.18. FFA and Spot Prices in BDTI Route TD3; Daily Data (27/09/04 – 12/09/05)

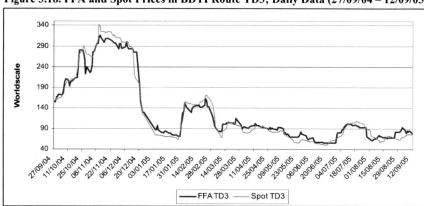

Figures 3.18 and 3.21 present the near-month FFA prices against the Baltic tanker index spot prices (in Worldscale) in the VLCC route TD3, Suezmax route TD5, Aframax route TD7 and Handysize route TC4 (27/09/2004 to 12/09/2005), respectively. Again, in all routes, the FFA and spot freight rates move closely together, which is also confirmed by the values of their correlation coefficients as they stand at 0.987, 0.978, 0.963 and 0.943, respectively.

Figure 3.19. FFA and Spot Prices in BDTI Route TD5; Daily Data (27/09/04 – 12/09/05)

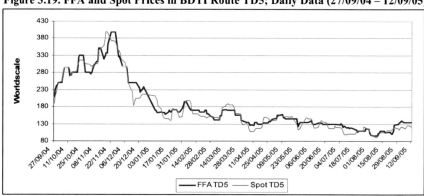

Figure 3.20. FFA and Spot Prices in BDTI Route TD7; Daily Data (27/09/04 – 12/09/05)

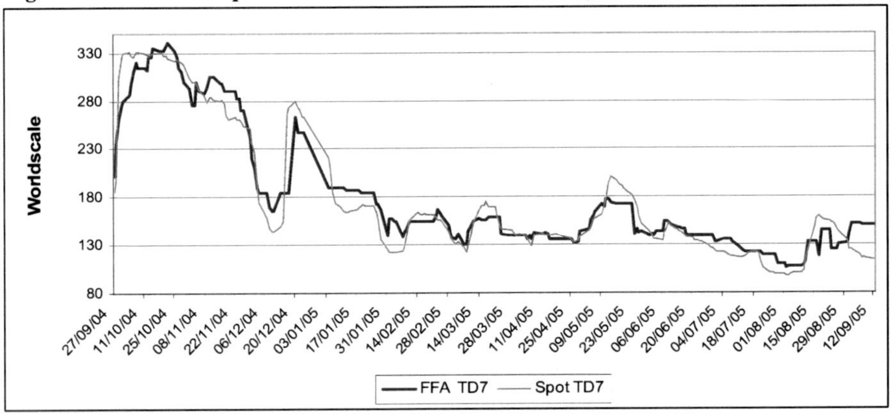

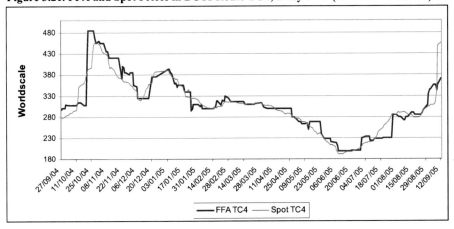

Figure 3.21. FFA and Spot Prices in BCTI Route TC4; Daily Data (27/09/04 – 12/09/05)

3.4.1. Characteristics of FFA Contracts

As FFA contracts are not exchange traded, they are not standardised. They are negotiated individually between the two counterparties, and as a consequence they can be tailor-made to their needs. For instance, for route C4 of the BCI, referring to a 150,000 dwt Capesize vessel, carrying coal from Richards Bay to Rotterdam, a FFA contract can allow for variations in the size of the contract, its maturity or its settlement price, amongst others. Thus, it may be that the FFA is drawn to refer to a part cargo of 100,000 tons, with time to maturity 75 days, arranging for settlement to take place in the first week of the month, with the settlement price to be calculated as the average over the last 15 days of the contract's life. All these are non-standard terms, which are not possible to negotiate in futures contracts of freight rates traded at NYMEX or IMAREX. On the other hand, FFAs must be carried to maturity as there is no secondary market to close positions; if markets turn against the position of a counterparty it cannot close its position to avoid losses.

A further worry with FFA contracts is the credit risk that the other counterparty will default. As this issue has been a major worry for market participants in these trades "*hybrid*" FFAs have evolved. These are FFAs, which are cleared for a fee through clearing-houses, such as the NOS for contracts traded at IMAREX, and since

September 2005 at LCH.Clearnet. The FFAs registered through a clearing-house for clearing are contracts negotiated OTC, but use the clearing-house simply to eliminate credit risks. In that sense, they retain the flexibility of OTC contracts in terms of size, duration, and other terms, which may be important to a counterparty and which are not there in standardised exchange-traded futures contracts, while at the same time eliminating the credit risk that exists in typical OTC forward contracts, but which futures contracts do not have.

3.4.2. Market Information on FFA Contracts

An important question for a newcomer say, a principal or a charterer to the field of freight rate derivatives, is where to obtain information about the FFA products available in the market and their prices and other information about these products? They will need to contact a broker offering FFAs, such as Clarksons, which would typically send a report on a daily basis, of the type included in Appendix VI – dated September 8th, 2005. As can be observed, the report starts by presenting the day's index levels of the BPI, the BDI and the BCI standing, respectively, at 2203, 2561, and 3624. Also, the price changes between the previous day and the current day values for each of the above indices are shown in the next row.

Further down, the first column of the table shows the FFA contracts, which are offered on a number of routes and "*baskets*" of routes of the Baltic Exchange. They are monthly contracts for the current month of September, for October, November, December and January – that is, monthly contracts are offered up to five months ahead, including the current month. These monthly FFA contracts may be used as hedges against one voyage. For instance, for a shipowner, a vessel becomes available for hire in December, and he wishes to hedge his exposure to freight rate risks. He will sell December contracts. If he has another vessel that will come out of a time-charter and will become available for hire in January he will also sell January FFAs. As can be seen in the report, FFAs are also available for the fourth quarter of 2005 (Q4 05) and for the first two quarters of 2006, namely Q1 06 and Q2 06. The Cal 06, Cal 07 and Cal 08 are annual contracts for 2006, 2007 and 2008, respectively. They are useful for long-term hedging of freight rates, and can possibly serve as hedges against a time-charter contract or a COA.

The report provides information for most popular monthly FFA contracts; these are, route P3A Pac RV, route P2A TCT East and route P1A TARV – refer to Table 3.4 for details. A bid and an ask price is quoted against each contract for every route. The bid price of $17,000/day for the September contract refers to the price that the buyer of the contract, e.g. the charterer, is asked to pay to buy the FFA, while the $19,000/day ask price of the same contract is the price that the seller of the contracts, e.g. the shipowner, will receive. The difference between these two prices is known as the bid-ask spread. It represents a gain for the market-maker, but it is a cost to the counterparties, as at settlement they have to reverse their FFA positions, by selling FFAs for charterers and buying FFAs for shipowners. The higher the spread the larger is the cost to the principals. Competitive brokers are those which are able to offer, apart from low brokerage fees, narrow bid-ask spreads. Brokers are often chosen on the basis of bid-ask spreads offered, as low brokerage fees may be more than eliminated by high bid-ask spreads[45]. In competitive, liquid, efficiently functioning

---

[45] Batchelor, Alizadeh and Visvikis (2005) examine the relationship between expected volatility and bid-ask spreads in routes P1, P2, P1A and P2A of the BPI. The results indicate that there is a positive relationship between bid-ask spreads and expected price volatility in routes P1, P2, and P2A, after

markets bid-ask spreads are lower/narrower, compared to markets with low liquidity, generally less mature.

Going back to the report, on the last row of the boxes where the FFA prices are quoted, the value of the Baltic route is also reported. Thus, vessels on route P3A earn on September 8th \$15,533/day, while the rates earned in route P2A are \$21,314/day. The price of each FFA contract is determined at the balance of demand and supply for the particular contract. If, for instance, demand for October FFA contracts is high relative to supply for the contract, prices will be high, and visa versa if demand is lower relative to supply. The FFA prices then reflect the consensus in the market and they change constantly as market conditions change. This situation can be inferred from the commentary on the Panamax market which appears half way through the report.

The FFA contract prices for the next months can be seen to be higher than the rates prevailing today. More specifically, for September the mid price for route P2A is 22,500/day, for October, November and December mid prices stand at \$24,250/day, which drop to \$21,000/day in January. Kavussanos and Visvikis (2004), using data over the period January 1996 to December 2000, show that FFA prices for the next one, two and three months are on average correct in predicting the freight rates that will prevail in the spot market in one, two and three months time. Thus, one can assume that there is very high probability that rates on the route will increase in the next months. More specifically, for October, November and December the market expects spot freight rates to rise by 13.77% [= (\$24,250 / \$21,314) − 1], in comparison to September's levels. Apart from the Panamax FFA prices for each route, FFA monthly, quarterly and calendar prices for a basket of the 4 BPI time-charter routes are also reported. These FFA contracts are quite popular and are useful, for instance, to charterers with sets of cargoes to transport or to shipowners with a fleet of vessels to run.

The report, provides also the Capesize FFA bid and ask prices for voyage routes C7 and C4 of the BCI, for the current FFA contract (Sep), and monthly contracts up to January 2006 and finally calendars 2006, 2007 and 2008 contracts, expressed in \$/ton. Again, the most liquid, in terms of trading, routes are shown, but FFAs on other Capesize routes are also available. The spot prices of the underlying markets can be found below the FFA prices; on September 8th 2005 they stood at \$13.815/ton for route C7 and \$13.135/ton for route C4. Considering FFA prices, the market seems to think that rates will rise in the next few months, but they are expected to fall in the years ahead.

A number of spreads between routes are also shown in Clarksons' market report. For instance, the difference in FFA prices for each contract, between Routes P3A and P2A is reported, as well as the difference between the "*basket*" of the BPI 4 T/Cs and the Handy mid price. These are used by speculators for spread play strategies – an example is presented further down this chapter.

---

other factors are controlled. Market agents using the information of the behaviour of the bid-ask spreads can have a better insight about the timing of their FFA transactions and the future direction of the FFA market, as a widening bid-ask spreads corresponds to an anticipation of increased future volatility.

The report concludes by presenting the price levels of the constituent routes of the BPI, of the BCI and the average of the 4 time-charter routes of the BPI and BCI. Thus, the average of the BPI 4 T/Cs is calculated from the figures reported in the time-charter routes of the BPI; that is, from P1A, P2A, P3A and P4. The rest of the spot prices on all routes are also available as they represent price levels underlying the FFA contracts. It should be noted that similar reports are produced for the Handy market.

3.4.3. Negotiating and Writing FFA Contracts

A typical application of a FFA would be for a charterer who needs a vessel to transport his cargo in the future, say in four months, anticipates a rising freight rate in the route and would like to protect himself against this risk of rising costs. He would contact a FFA broker, such as Clarksons, SSY, etc., who would in turn find a shipowner with opposite expectations regarding the future move of freight rates, who is willing to be the counterparty to the transaction. The shipowner will sell FFA contracts while the charterer would buy these contracts. FFA's are settled in cash. If freight rates fall below the agreed rate, the charterer pays the difference between the agreed FFA price and the settlement spot price; if rates increase, then the charterer receives the difference. Voyage-based dry-bulk contracts are settled on the difference between the contracted price and the average price of the spot route selected in the index over the last seven working days of the month, while time-charter-based contracts are settled on the difference between the contracted price and the average price of the business days of the month[46, 47].

The names of the counterparties in a FFA transaction initially remained confidential until a deal was virtually concluded, but nowadays they are revealed from the beginning of the negotiations. All terms and conditions can be tailor-made and are negotiable between the two parties, though the basic contract form is rarely altered. The most common contracts are the FFABA 2000 contract, a sample of which is presented in Appendix IV[48], the new FFABA 2005 contract, a sample of which is presented in Appendix V and the adapted International Swap & Derivatives Association (ISDA)[49] contract, which can be downloaded from the ISDA website (www.isda.org). The FFABA 2000 and 2005 contracts are short and easy to understand and are typically used by shipowners and charterers, while the ISDA contract is typically used by banks and big trading houses (around 30% of FFA

---

[46] As mentioned before, these standard terms and conditions may be individually negotiated.

[47] Up until November 1999, the settlement price for voyage contracts was calculated over the last five days.

[48] There are currently three FFABA contracts used: (i) the FFABA 2000 contract (a four pages contract in its last version dated 2000, which is very simple but with no language on credit issues like the event of default, margin calls, netting etc.); (ii) the FFABA 2002 contract, drafted by Brian Perrot, an ex in-house lawyer of Cargill from Hill Taylor Dickinson, at the request of the FFABA, with credit support language. After a promising start the FFABA 2002 contract found some resistance. The FFABA 2000 contract is the most used contract these days, with around 70% of the contracts made using this form; and the FFABA 2005 contract which closely resembles the original FFABA contract but incorporates the ISDA master agreement in order to address (and reduce) the risks not otherwise dealt with by the original FFABA contract and to promote liquidity.

[49] There are currently two ISDA contracts used: (i) the Full ISDA master agreement with attached schedule. This approach was pioneered by energy merchant companies like Duke and Enron and is followed today by AEP, EDF Trading, and Morgan Stanley, amongst others. There are very few full master agreements in place as they are unknown to the shipping business community and they are long and costly and (ii) the ISDA flavoured long form confirmation. This type of contract, which is halfway between the FFABA contract and a full master agreement, is becoming popular nowadays.

trades). Once the route and settlement period are established, negotiations are very quick over the phone (instant messenger systems like MSN or Yahoo messengers are getting very popular to start negotiations), with the price and volume being talked about. Providing all terms are agreed, the deal has to be confirmed within minutes.

Assuming the deal is confirmed, the contract becomes binding and the broker issues a confirmation (recap) through a fax or an email and later on a full contract for the parties to sign it. At settlement, the broker sends a note to both parties with the settlement price, the amount due and the name of the party owing and monitoring the payment. At the same time the broker sends his commission invoice, normally 0.25% of the nominal amount to each of the parties of the forward contract. For instance, for a deal of $1,000,000 the commission is $2,500. The party that is owed monies at settlement produces an invoice with all bank details included. Payment between the two parties is made by money transfer in US dollars within five business days following the settlement date. FFA contracts are traded in OTC derivatives markets. The market-makers, that is, the institutions that facilitate this market are major shipbrokers, investment banks, and other financial intermediates in the fund management industry.

As we referred to the FFABA 2000 and 2005 forms as the standard contract forms being used by the industry, a few words are due about FFABA. The association was formed in 1997, as an independent body, by FFA brokers, members of the Baltic Exchange, under its auspices. According to the Baltic Exchange the association was formed in order to:

- Promote the trading of FFA contracts and the high standards of conduct amongst market participants;
- Ensure the production of high quality indices;
- Provide a forum for brokers and principals to resolve problems as they arise;
- Develop and promote the use of standard contracts;
- Develop the use of other OTC and Exchange traded derivatives products for freight risk management;
- Not only provide tools for the freight derivatives market but also to provide credible barometers of the freight market for physical users.

The members of FFABA in 2005 are shown in Table 3.33.

Table 3.33. Members of the FFABA as of 2005

Banchero-Costa & C (Italy)	Clarksons Securities Ltd. (UK)
Bernd von Blomberg Schiffsmakler GmbH (Germany)	McQuilling Brokerage Partners (Singapore)
Bravo Tankers (Italy)	GFI Brokers Ltd. (UK)
BRS Futures Ltd. (UK)	Global Freight Forwards (UK)
P F Bassoe A/S & Co. (Norway)	Freight Investor Services (FIS) (UK)
Ifchor S.A. (Switzerland)	Mallory Jones Lynch Flynn (USA)
Simpson Spence & Young (SSY) Ltd. (UK)	Yamamizu Shipping Co. Ltd. (Japan)
ICAP Hyde Ltd. (UK)	Prebon Energy (UK)
Pasternak Baum & Co Inc. (USA)	Braemar Spectron (UK)
Traditional Financial Services (TFS) Ltd. (UK)	

3.4.4. Applications of FFAs and Cleared FFAs

This section of the chapter demonstrates how FFAs and "*hybrid*" cleared FFAs may be used in practice by principals, to hedge their freight rate exposures in the physical market.

3.4.4.1. Voyage Dry-Bulk OTC FFA Non-Cleared Hedge

Suppose it is 18th of May. A charterer, with a cargo size of 51,400 tons of Heavy Grain, Soya and Sorghum (HSS) to move from US Gulf to Japan (BPI route P2) on 30th of July, wants to lock his costs at the prevailing forward rate of $15/ton. A shipowner, with a Panamax vessel of 54,000 dwt is aware of the seasonality results presented in Chapter 1 of this book, that freight rates are likely to be significantly lower in July. Thus, he is willing to sell July OTC FFAs for similar dates, at $15/ton, in order to get protected against the expected drop in freight rates. The size of the physical exposure for both parties is $771,000 (= $15/ton x 51,400tons). Thus, the shipowner is the seller of July FFA contracts and the charterer is the buyer of July FFAs. The contract is issued by a provider of OTC FFAs, such as Clarksons, SSY or FIS, who secures the agreement, going through the relevant paperwork. The price is fixed at $15/ton, and brokerage fees are agreed to be paid by both parties to the broker; that is, $1,927.5 (= 0.25% x $771,000) is paid by the charterer and $1,927.5 is paid by the shipowner, amounting to $3,855 (= $1,927.5 x 2) income to the broker, which is paid at settlement.

Suppose on 30th of July, when the FFA contract expires, its seven-day average settlement price is $18.1964/ton. Since the settlement price is higher than the fixed price, the shipowner pays $3.1964/ton to the charterer. That is, $165,295(=$51,400x$3.1964) is paid by the shipowner to the charterer. Moreover, for the calculation of his total cash outflow, $3,855, that is paid in fees to the broker, must be added, resulting in a net cash outflow for the shipowner from the OTC FFA deal of $169,150 (= $165,295 + $3,855). The charterer's total cash inflow from the OTC FFA deal amounts to $161,440 (= $165,295 – $3,855). The charterer's expectations about the future market move proved correct, so he gains from the FFA deal. This gain is the loss of the FFA counterparty, the shipowner, who made a mistake in his forecast about future movements of freight rates. The gain of the charterer in the FFA market is used to offset the loss in the physical market, where he will have to pay the higher rates. Overall, the charterer would have stabilized his costs at today's levels. Similarly, the shipowner's loss in the FFA market is offset by the gain that he makes in the physical market as a result of the increased freight rates.

3.4.4.2. Voyage Dry-Bulk OTC "*Hybrid*" FFA Cleared at LCH.Clearnet Hedge

Suppose it is 8th of July. The chief executive of a European electricity producer, with a 144,900 tons of coal commitment in September, decides to import coal from Richards Bay to Rotterdam. He wishes to get protected against freight rate increases and therefore, buys September FFA contracts through his broker. Since he wants to eliminate credit risk, he advises his broker to clear the FFA transaction through LCH.Clearnet; that will cost him $7.5/lot in total, comprising a $5/lot clearing fee plus $2.5/lot settlement fee payable to LCH.Clearnet. A shipowner with a Capesize vessel of 150,000 dwt, which will be in the US Gulf at the end of September wishes to hedge against potential declining rates in the Capesize sector and sells September FFA contracts. The agreed price, fixed through the broker, is $15/ton. The size of the deal $2,173,500 (= $15/ton x 144,900 tons). Brokerage fees are paid by both parties to the broker as agreed. That is, $5,433.75 (= 0.25% x $2,173,500) is paid by the buyer and $5,433.75 is paid by the seller, totaling $10,867.50 of fees to the broker from the deal. Each counterparty pays the LCH.Clearnet a clearing fee of $724.5(=$5/lotx144,900mt / 1,000mt lot size) and a settlement fee of $362.25(=$2.5/lotx144,900mt / 1,000mt lot size), totaling $1,086.75 of fees to LCH.Clearnet. This is the amount paid extra by each counterparty in order to avoid the credit risk that the OTC transaction entails – as a proportion of the size of the FFA deal this is a very small amount indeed. The total transactions costs (brokerage, clearing and settlement fees) for each of the counterparties comes to: $6,520.5(=\$5,433.75 + \$724.5 + \$362.25)$.

Suppose that when the FFA contract expires on 31st of September, the seven day average settlement price is \$14.5526/ton. This price is lower than the agreed price of \$15/ton, so the charterer pays the difference of \$0.4474/ton to the shipowner. That is, \$64,828 (= 144,900tons x \$0.4474/ton) is paid by the charterer to the shipowner. Moreover, for the calculation of his total cash outflow, the transaction costs of \$6,520.5, that are paid to the broker and to LCH.Clearnet, must be added, resulting in a net cash outflow for the charterer from the FFA deal of \$71,348.5(=\$64,828+\$6,520.5). Correspondingly, the shipowner's total cash inflow from the FFA deal comes to \$58,307.5 (= \$64,828 – \$6,520.5). Of course, in a hedge, both charterer and shipowner must consider, as in the previous example, the overall cash-flows from the portfolio position involving both the physical and the FFA trades; the overall effect is for both market participants to stabilise their costs/revenues at the prevailing market freight rates.

3.4.5. Credit Risk in OTC FFA Contracts

As mentioned before, an issue with OTC derivatives contracts is the counterparty or credit risk, which is present when opening positions in these contracts. The potential solutions to the problem were discussed in Chapter 2 of this book. The problem prevails with OTC freight derivatives contracts also. The sums involved in FFA transactions are large and a number of bids/asks come from principals, which may not be large, well-known companies, with publicly available information on character and other characteristics which are important to assess their creditworthiness. As a consequence, this is a big worry for a counterparty, particularly when there is no background information on the other party they will be dealing with. This worry has been expressed by potential market participants on several occasions. As a response, the industry has considered several solutions to address the issue, which include:

- Improve the terms and conditions of the contract form, to include default clauses;
- Develop a credit rating system, specifically for the market agents of the shipping industry;
- Develop an electronic trading system, which can then clear FFAs through a clearing-house on a margin, mark-to-market system, like the one of LCH.Clearnet. We consider each of these next.

The first strand of solutions refers to the revision of the terms and conditions of the FFABA contract form. In August 2002, the FFABA 2000 contract was revised, in order to include clear definitions of a default event, default procedures, and rights and remedies to net and offset against physical freight that may exist between counterparties or their affiliates. However, market agents never really adopted it and kept on using the FFABA 2000 contract, which at the time of writing is used by almost 70% of the market. During 1st October 2005, the FFABA contract was again revised, in order to include events of default, netting of payments, close-out netting, two way payments, and to enhance representation, settlement dates, payment procedures and law and jurisdiction, which ties in the existing law and jurisdiction clause with that of the ISDA master agreement. Table 3.34 presents the major revisions/enhancements between the provisions of the FFABA 2000 and the FFABA 2005 contracts.

Table 3.34. Changes between the FFABA 2000 and FFABA 2005 Contracts

Provision	Original FFABA 2000	New FFABA 2005	Comments
Events of Default	X	✓	The provision for Events of Default gives the parties greater freedom to identify what constitutes a default. It also permits the parties to establish a clear contractual procedure in the event of such a default. This is an improvement on the common law of most jurisdictions, which would (usually) otherwise disadvantage the innocent party.
Netting of Payments	X	✓	Netting of payments is a practical and beneficial tool utilised in most financial contracts. It is designed to simplify (and in many cases) speed up payment.
Close-Out Netting	X	✓	It permits a party to net payments in the event of the other party's insolvency. This will help prevent an innocent party from having to make payment without offset to an insolvent party.
Two Way Payments	X	✓	On close-out following default, this provides for a balanced position between the parties in a trading environment.
Representations	Partially Dealt With	✓	The warranties in the original FFABA 2000 contract were not broad enough. The new proposals expand these provisions, giving greater comfort to an innocent party.
Settlement Date(s)	Partially Dealt With	✓	The proposed provisions clarify when payments should be made in the context of weekends and month ends.
Payment Procedures	Partially Dealt With	✓	This provision does not alter when payment should be made – but instead clarifies when a payee should produce an invoice.
Law and Jurisdiction	✓	✓	This clause ties in the existing law and jurisdiction clause with that of the ISDA Master Agreement

Source: FFABA

Some companies, particularly banks and financial institutions, favour the ISDA master agreement instead of the FFABA 2000, the FFABA 2002 and the FFABA 2005 contracts. Some of the potential difficulties on the implementation of the ISDA agreement are that the contract is complex and not easily readable and the contract can be too long when combined with annexes. However, the ISDA master agreement is internationally recognised among the financial trading community and has an excellent default system; they include events of default, early exposure termination, overall position netting, margin/credit facility, etc.

The second strand of solutions refers to assessing the creditworthiness of the FFA counterparties. This is particularly important in this industry, where a large number of companies are not public and as a consequence do not have the obligation to disclose their financial information. More specifically, it is now generally acknowledged, by financial services regulators, financial services providers and corporate users alike, that a key component of a robust framework for the management of the risks attached to OTC derivatives business is a strong structure of risk management controls within companies active in this business. Prior to FFA trading, administrative controls must be created. They include trading procedures and controls/limits by traders, "*accepted*" counterparty list, corporate net long/short position, financial tools to calculate market exposure, and in-depth market analysis. Then, the FFA trading should be integrated in the corporate structure of the management, and the physical and derivatives functions, within the company, should be separated. Moreover, physical traders should be fully knowledgeable of the FFA market and visa versa. However, it should be stressed here that risk management control mechanisms are not a substitute for adequate capital. The control structure that should be established, and the practices that should apply, in the case of any particular institution, must be appropriate to that institution relative to the scale, the risk profile and the complexity of its OTC derivatives activities. A number of high profile aberrations in performance within the dry-bulk FFA sector (according to market estimates, by 2005, around 30 companies defaulted from FFA inception) has led to the need of a system of financial regulation for OTC contracts.

In order for market agents in the shipping industry to safeguard their positions, it is important to have information regarding the adequacy of the management control systems put in place, if any, by the counterparty they will be dealing with. Market participants must adopt a qualitative approach and check their counterparty's business profile, geographical location, management profile, trading track record, business history, and financial flexibility. Moreover, each company should ensure that their counterparty has the power to enter into a proposed transaction, is represented by an officer with actual or ostensible authority, is creditworthy, and has access to appropriate payment systems. Derivatives brokers have incentives to monitor customers' use of derivatives. Brokers often have access to information about counterparty characteristics that mitigates the information asymmetry concerning the motive behind the OTC derivatives. Specifically, the broker may know the "*direction*" of the counterparty's operating exposure to the underlying risk factor, based on which it can infer whether the OTC derivative contract is meant to be a hedge or not. Moreover, it is possible to implement the simple accept/reject decision rule based on observed counterparty credit rating (certain investment grade threshold level) that guarantees the exclusion of some over risky speculative contracts.

The third strand of solutions considered by the industry is to have FFA contracts cleared through a clearing-house. This solution has been provided since September 2005 by LCH.Clearnet, for a number of actively traded routes, in both dry-bulk and tanker trades – see Table 3.35. Following extensive consultations with market participants and market-makers, it offers the possibility to have FFA contracts cleared on a margin mark-to-market system. In this case, LCH.Clearnet becomes the central counterparty to each transaction. Thus, for a FFA contract, agreement is between LCH.Clearnet and each of the counterparties separately. As a result, they do not have to worry now about each other's credit risk, the burden of which falls on LCH.Clearnet. In turn, the latter has in place, a set of procedures set out in its Rulebook and calculates, using its SPAN system, appropriate margin requirements (see www.lchclearnet.com). The fees charged in 2005 for offering this facility are presented for each route in Table 3.35, while examples of their calculation for real cargo sizes were presented earlier on in this section. Thus, for a relatively "*small*" fee, which reflects the credit risk of the position, principals can get rid of this risk present in FFA trading. These "*hybrid*" FFAs still retain the advantages of forward contracts in terms of their flexible terms and conditions, and have credit risk eliminated by allowing them to go through the clearing system of LCH.Clearnet. IMAREX also provides the option to have FFAs cleared through NOS, for the reasons discussed above. Its fees are also presented in Table 3.35. For comparison, the NYMEX fees of the futures contracts cleared through its Clearport system are also shown in Table 3.35. During 2005, the Shanghai and Singapore exchanges have also announced their plans to introduce clearing systems for FFA transactions.

Finally, another solution, which is generally followed in markets to eliminate credit risk, is through the introduction of credit derivatives. These are derivatives instruments whose value derives from the existence of credit/counterparty risk, which is present when opening a non-cleared FFA position. Credit derivatives are discussed in section 2.5.3 of this book. At the time of writing, no freight credit derivatives have been traded in the industry. However, freight credit derivatives could be used in the same ways as they are in other financial markets

Table 3.35. Clearing and Settlement Fees at NOS, NYMEX and LCH.Clearnet

Exchange	Tanker			Routes/ Baskets	Dry-Bulk		
	Clearing	Settlement	Total		Clearing	Settlement	Total
NOS	0.4%	0.05%	0.45%		0.3%	0.0%	0.3%
NYMEX	$5/lot for members		$5/lot		–	–	–
	$4/lot for non members		$4/lot		–	–	–
LCH.Clearnet	$4/lot	$2/lot	$6/lot	C4,C7	$5/lot	$2.5/lot	$7.5/lot
				C3	$8/lot	$4/lot	$12/lot
				C5	$4/lot	$2/lot	$6/lot
				HTC, PTC	$7/lot	$3.5/lot	$10.5/lot
				CTC	$15/lot	$7.5/lot	$22.5/lot
				Trip T/C	$8/lot	$4/lot	$12/lot

3.5. Applications of FFAs and Freight Futures Contracts

This section presents further a number of examples of how freight futures and forward contracts may be used in practice to hedge and speculate in both the dry-bulk and the tanker sector, covering voyage as well as time-charter positions.

3.5.1. Voyage Dry-Bulk OTC FFA Non-Cleared Hedge vs. Cleared NOS Hedge

Suppose in September a shipowner knows that he will have a 54,000 dwt vessel open in the Pacific at the end of November. Rates in the Pacific are weak, so he intends to ballast through to the US North Pacific to take advantage of the current attractive rates for a trip to the East. Fearing that rates might ease by November he decides to hedge this risk through the FFA market. He chooses to sell a November BPI Route P3 (US North Pacific/South Japan) FFA contract at the prevailing FFA price of $32. The bid may come from a charterer, with a freight service requirement from US North Pacific to South Japan in November, who wishes to cover himself against the possibility of rising freight rates. By entering into this *"paper"* contract both parties maintain the flexibility to achieve the best possible rate in the spot market. Also, they may close their paper trade position very quickly if their sentiment changes about how the market will evolve. The counterparties agree on a cargo size of 51,400mt for their FFA trade, which amounts to a FFA position of $1,644,800 (= 51,400mt x $32/ton). The counterparties conduct their brokers for this OTC FFA trade. Therefore, each counterparty has to pay $4,112 (= 0.25% x $1,644,800) in brokerage fees.

Table 3.36 summarises the positions for the owner and for the charterer, in both the spot and the paper markets, under two alternative scenarios; a market rise and a market fall in rates. Under the first scenario, shown in the first column of the table, spot freight rates increase to $32.5/ton by November. In this case, the shipowner (charterer) gains (loses) $25,700 (= $1,670,500 – $1,644,800) in the spot market, while in the FFA market he realises a loss (gain) of $51,400 (= $1696,200 – $1,644,800). Thus, by opening a paper trade to hedge the physical (spot) position, the shipowner and the charterer have opened up a portfolio of two positions. In a hedge, what is of interest is the total outcome from the positions. Thus, the net loss (profit) of this portfolio for the shipowner (charterer) is $25,700 (= $25,700 – $51,400). When FFA transactions costs are also taken into account these payoffs become for the shipowner and the charterer, respectively, $29,812 (= $25,700 + $4,112) and $21,588(= $25,700 – $4,112). Compared to not taking a FFA position the charterer is $25,700 better off. The aim of the hedge is to stabilise revenue/costs of the original position at today's levels – not to make profits. A speculator of FFA's on the other hand, with no exposure on the spot market aims to make profits from FFA trades.

Table 3.36. The Two Possible Outcomes of Voyage Hedging

September	
Physical (Spot) Market Cargo size: 51,400mt, Route P3 Freight rate: $32/ton Freight income/cost: $1,644,800 (= $32/ton x 51,400mt)	**FFA Market** FFA September price: $32/ton Value of FFA: $1,644,800 (= $32/ton x 51,400mt)
First scenario: Freight rates increase	**Second scenario: Freight rates decrease**
November: Spot Market	
Freight rate: $32.5/ton Freight income: $1,670,500 (= $32.5/ton x 51,400mt)	Freight rate: $31.5/ton Freight income: $1,619,100 (= $31.5/ton x 51,400mt)
The shipowner (charterer) gains (loses) $25,700	**The shipowner (charterer) loses (gains) $25,700**
November: FFA Market	
FFA November price: $33/ton Value of FFA: $1,696,200 (= $33/ton x 51,400mt)	FFA November price: $31/ton Value of FFA: $1,593,400 (= $31/ton x 51,400mt)
The shipowner (charterer) loses (gains) $51,400	**The shipowner (charterer) gains (loses) $51,400**
Portfolio of Spot and FFA Positions	
Net loss (profit) for shipowner (charterer) : $25,700	**Net profit (loss) for shipowner (charterer): $25,700**
Brokerage fees: $4,112 (= 0.25% x $1,696,200)	

Under the second scenario, shown in the second column of the same table, freight rates fall to $31.5/ton. In this case, the shipowner (charterer) loses (gains) $25,700(=$1,619,100 – $1,644,800) in the spot market, while in the FFA market he realises a gain (loss) of $51,400 (= $1,593,400 – $1,644,800), giving a net profit (loss) of $25,700. Thus, the net profit (loss) of this portfolio for the shipowner (charterer) is $25,700 (= $25,700 – $51,400). When FFA transactions costs are also taken into account these payoffs become for the charterer and the shipowner, respectively, $29,812 (= $25,700 + $4,112) and $21,588 (= $25,700 – $4,112).

Route P3 of the BPI can be offered upon demand for clearing, say at NOS of IMAREX. The shipowner (charterer) in order to hedge his spot market exposure should sell (buy) 52 lots (≈ 51,400mt / 1,000mt lot size) of freight futures, with a freight futures value of $1,664,000 (= 52 lots x 1,000mt lot size x $32/ton). The IMAREX clearing fee is $4,992 (= 0.3% x $1,664,000) for each counterparty; there is no settlement fee for dry-bulk freight futures on IMAREX. Under the first scenario, the shipowner realises a net loss of $34,804 (= $51,400 – $25,700 + $4,992 + $4,112) and the charterer receives a net profit of $16,596 (= $25,700 – $51,400 – $4,992 – $4,112). Under the second scenario, the shipowner receives a net profit of

$16,596(=\$51,400 - \$25,700 - \$4,992 - \$4,112)$ and the charterer realises a net loss of $34,804 (= \$51,400 - \$25,700 + \$4,992 + \$4,112)$.

3.5.2. T/C Dry-Bulk FFA OTC FFA Non-Cleared Hedge vs. Cleared NOS Hedge

This example illustrates how to perform calculations when a FFA hedge is fixed on a time-charter route. Suppose in December a shipowner sees FFA rates at higher levels than initially anticipated. Knowing that he has a vessel coming open at the end of February, the owner is keen to lock into an attractive bid of $20,000/day in the February FFA market for a Skaw – Gibraltar/Far East time-charter (BPI Route P2A) for 45 days. His exposure is $700,000 (= \$20,000/day x 45 days)$. The bid is from a charterer aiming to manage his risk of rising freight rates on the same route. Brokerage fees of $1,750 (= \$700,000 x 0.25\%)$ are agreed to be paid by both parties to the broker.

Table 3.37 summarises the two possible outcomes, two months later, in February. Under the first scenario, presented in the first column of the table, freight rates increase against the shipowner's expectations to $20,500/day. In this case, the shipowner (charterer) gains (loses) $22,500 (= \$922,500 - \$900,000)$ in the physical time-charter market, while in the FFA market he realises a loss (gain) of $27,000(=\$900,000 - \$927,000)$. Thus, the net loss (profit) of this portfolio for the shipowner (charterer) is $4,500 (= \$22,500 - \$27,000)$. When FFA transactions costs are also taken into account, the shipowner's loss becomes $6,250 (= \$4,500+ \$1,750)$, while the charterer's gain is reduced to $2,750 (= \$4,500 - \$1,750)$.

Under the second scenario, shown in the second column of the same table, the shipowner's expectations are correct; freight rates fall to $19,250/day. In this case, the shipowner (charterer) loses (gains) $33,750 (= \$866,250 - \$900,000)$ in the spot market, while in the FFA market he realises a gain (loss) of $36,000 (= \$900,000 - \$864,000)$. Thus, the net profit (loss) of this portfolio position, of spot and FFA trades, for the shipowner (charterer) is $2,250 (= \$36,000 - \$33,750)$. When FFA transactions costs are also taken into account, the shipowner's gain is reduced to $500(= \$2,250 - \$1,750)$, while the charterer's loss is increased to $4,000(=\$2,250+\$1,750)$. Compared to not opening the FFA paper trade, where the shipowner would have lost $33,750 in income, he has made a profit of $500 from the overall portfolio position of physical and FFA trades. From the charterer's point of view, who opened the FFA trade to hedge his costs exposure in the spot market, in anticipation of higher freight rates, his expectations did not materialize. Thus, he makes a loss in the combined physical – FFA trade of $4,000 (= \$2,250 + \$1,750)$. Compared to not opening the paper trade – that is, compared to just using the physical market to charter the vessel – where he would have paid $33,750 less – he is worse off. Yet, the net outcome is to stabilize his costs at more or less today's levels.

Suppose next that the counterparties were worried about credit risk; that is, that the other parry in the OTC FFA transaction may not honour its obligations to pay at settlement. The FFA transaction then could be backed up by a clearing service mechanism. This is now possible in the market. For instance, apart from LCH.Clearnet, IMAREX is offering this service through its partnership with NOS. Thus, the two counterparties could approach NOS and IMAREX, and use a freight futures cleared contract on P2A. The shipowner (charterer), in order to hedge his spot market exposure, sells (buys) 45 lots (= 45 days x 1 day lot size) of freight futures, with a freight futures value of $900,000 (= 45 lots x 1 day lot size x \$20,000/day)$.

The NOS clearing fee would be $2,700 (= 0.3% x $900,000) for each counterparty. Thus, this extra fee is paid by each counterparty to eliminate credit risk; It is the value of credit risk on the $900,000 paper transaction. Notice that, there is no settlement fee for dry-bulk freight futures at NOS. At the time of writing these fees were waved, in order to promote IMAREX trading on dry-bulk trades.

Table 3.37. The Two Possible Outcomes of Period T/C Trip Hedging

December	
Physical (Spot) Market Freight rate: $20,000/day Cargo size: 51,400mt, Route P2A Freight income/cost: $900,000 (= $20,000/day x 45 days)	**FFA Market** FFA December price: $20,000/day Value of FFA: $900,000 (= $20,000/day x 45 days)
First scenario: Freight rates increase	**Second scenario: Freight rates decrease**
February: Physical (Spot) Market	
Freight rate: $20,500/day Freight income: $922,500 (= $20,500/day x 45 days)	Freight rate: $19,250/day Freight income: $866,250 (= $19,250/day x 45 days)
The shipowner (charterer) gains (loses) $22,500	**The shipowner (charterer) loses (gains) $33,750**
February: FFA Market	
FFA February price: $20,600/day Value of FFA: $927,000 (= $20,600/day x 45 days)	FFA February price: $19,200/day Value of FFA: $864,000 (= $19,200/day x 45 days)
The shipowner (charterer) loses (gains) $27,000	**The shipowner (charterer) gains (loses) $36,000**
Portfolio of Spot and FFA Positions	
Net loss (profit) for shipowner (charterer): $4,500	**Net profit (loss) for shipowner (charterer): $2,250**
Brokerage fees: $1,750 (= 0.25% x $700,000)	

Consider how the cash-flows of the charterer and the shipowner evolved in the example above, under the two scenarios. Under the first scenario, the shipowner would realise a net loss of $8,950 (= $27,000 – 22,500 + $2,700 + $1,750) and the charterer would receive a net profit of $50 (= $27,000 – 22,500 – $2,700 – $1,750). Under the second scenario, the shipowner would receive a net loss of $2,200(=$36,000 – 33,750 – $2,700 – $1,750), while the charterer realizes a loss of $6,700 (= $33,750 – $36,000 + $2,700 + $1,750).

By comparing the OTC trade and the cleared trade, it can be seen that, under the first scenario, in the OTC trade the shipowner (charterer) loses (gains) $6,250 ($2,750), while in the cleared NOS trade the shipowner (charterer) loses (gains) $8,950 ($50). Under the second scenario, in the OTC trade the shipowner (charterer) gains (loses) $500 ($4,000), while in the cleared NOS trade the shipowner (charterer) loses (loses) $2,200 ($6,700). The differences in the amounts are marginal, under both scenarios, and therefore, clearing the trades seems to be a much more preferred alternative, since the credit risk is eliminated.

3.5.3. 12-Month Period T/C Dry-Bulk OTC FFA Hedge: Non-Cleared vs. Cleared at NOS

This example illustrates how FFAs written on a "*basket*" of freight rates on time-charter routes can be used for hedging freight risks. As we discussed earlier, market-makers offer futures and FFAs on these "*baskets*". Consider a shipowner, who in March 2004, is awaiting delivery of a newbuilding in October 2004. He sells a 12-month period "*basket*" T/C FFA contract, which consists of the average of the four

T/C routes of the BPI, to hedge against the possibility of a fall in freight rates during the first year of operation of the newbuilding. By using an average of the routes the shipowner ensures that the vessel is hedged against a worldwide delivery/redelivery basis. The four period T/C routes of the BPI are: Route P1A – Trans-Atlantic Round; Route 2A – Ska*w*/Passero to Taiwan/Japan; Route 3A – Trans-Pacific Round; and Route 4 – Far East to Europe.

Assume the owner sells the 12-month period T/C FFA at $35,000/day, with monthly settlement. The 12-month period runs from 1st October 2004 to 30th September 2005. The settlement price is calculated as follows: The average of the four BPI T/Cs is calculated daily from the data published by the Baltic. Then, the monthly average of these figures is calculated using the number of business days in a month. This, is shown in the third column of Table 3.38. Given the number of calendar days in a month, shown in the second column of the table, the freight risk exposure in the physical market is calculated in the fourth column of the table. Finally, for settlement, the number of calendar days in a month is utilized. Given this, the monthly profit/loss is calculated as (FFA Price – Settlement Price) x No. of calendar days in a month. These calculations, for the monthly payoff of the shipowner are shown on the sixth column of the table. For instance, for October the shipowner loses on the FFA trade $147,715 (= ($35,000 – $39,765) x 31 days); this is because he sold FFAs and the settlement price for the month is below the agreed price. The FFA payoffs for the rest of the period are shown in the remaining rows of this column.

As can be observed, during the first six months the shipowner is experiencing a loss, since the settlement price is higher than the agreed FFA price in all cases. From the seventh month onwards, the shipowner starts making profits; since spot rates have declined, the settlement price is lower than the agreed FFA price month after month until the expiry of the contract. Over the 12 month period the overall profit for the shipowner, excluding transactions costs, from the FFA trade is $1,644,222. This should offset the physical (spot) market exposure of $11,130,778 of the newbuilding shown in the last row of the fourth column of the table.

Suppose the trade goes through an OTC FFA broker, charging a brokerage fee of 0.25%. The seventh column of the table calculates the brokerage fee for each month as: Contract value (= $35,000/day x No. of days in a month) x 0.25%. Thus, for October 2004 the brokerage fee is $2,713 (= $35,000 x 31 days x 0.25%), while the total fee for the whole period is shown in the last row of the table. The brokerage fee must be subtracted from the shipowner's gross payoff in order to calculate the payoff net of brokerage fees. This figure is shown for each month and over the whole period in the eight column of the table. As can be observed the net profit over the period becomes $1,612,285. Suppose next that the counterparties wish to eliminate credit risk and decide to clear the FFA trade, say through NOS. A clearing fee of 0.3% times the contract value (=$35,000/day x No. of days in a month) is charged by NOS. Column nine of the table calculates the clearing fees for each month, as: 0.3% x ($35,000/day x No. of calendar days in the month). That is, for October, the clearing fee is $3,255[=0.3%x($35,000 x 31 days)]. Taking these into account, as well as the brokerage fees, the net profit per period for the shipowner is shown in the last column of the table. Thus, for instance, the net profit for the period becomes $1,573,960. The difference of $38,325 (= $1,612,285 – $1,573,960) represents the extra cost, the shipowner pays to NOS, in order to eliminate his credit risk.

Table 3.38. Calculation of Payoffs of Period T/C FFA Hedge

Month	No. of Calendar Days	Settlement Price	Spot Market Exposure	FFA Price	Shipowner's Gross Payoff	OTC Brokerage Fee (0.25%)	Shipowner's Net OTC Payoff	NOS Clearing Fee (0.3%)	Shipowner's Net NOS Payoff
Oct-04	31	$39,765	$1,232,715	$35,000	-$147,715	$2,713	-$150,428	$3,255	-$153,683
Nov-04	30	$51,011	$1,530,330	$35,000	-$480,330	$2,625	-$482,955	$3,150	-$486,105
Dec-04	31	$35,974	$1,115,194	$35,000	-$30,194	$2,713	-$32,908	$3,255	-$36,162
Jan-05	31	$51,011	$1,581,341	$35,000	-$496,341	$2,713	-$499,054	$3,255	-$502,309
Feb-05	28	$37,960	$1,062,880	$35,000	-$82,880	$2,450	-$85,330	$2,940	-$88,270
Mar-05	31	$37,991	$1,177,721	$35,000	-$92,721	$2,713	-$95,434	$3,255	-$98,689
Apr-05	30	$25,547	$766,410	$35,000	$283,590	$2,625	$280,965	$3,150	$277,815
May-05	31	$24,363	$755,253	$35,000	$329,747	$2,713	$327,035	$3,255	$323,780
Jun-05	30	$18,608	$558,240	$35,000	$491,760	$2,625	$489,135	$3,150	$485,985
Jul-05	31	$12,987	$402,597	$35,000	$682,403	$2,713	$679,691	$3,255	$676,436
Aug-05	31	$15,637	$484,747	$35,000	$600,253	$2,713	$597,541	$3,255	$594,286
Sept-05	30	$15,445	$463,350	$35,000	$586,650	$2,625	$584,025	$3,150	$580,875
Total	365		$11,130,778		$1,644,222	$31,938	$1,612,285	$38,325	$1,573,960
Average	30	$30,525				$2,661		$3,194	

3.5.4. Voyage Dry-Bulk Trend FFA Hedge Cleared at NOS

Suppose in March the freight market is at a very high level, say at $75/ton. A shipowner that runs a Panamax vessel on route P2 (US Gulf to South Japan) of the BPI, with a cargo of 51,400 tons of HSS, forecasts a downward trend in freight rates in the future months. He observes high values of FFA prices. More specifically, as can be observed in Table 3.39 route P2 FFA contract prices for the following months are the following: April FFA price $76.5/ton; July FFA price $74.5/ton; October FFA price $73.5/ton. He can sell FFA contracts in order to cover the specific vessel for the period up to October. If over time, the spot market rises above his hedge level, he will lose on the FFA positions but gain on his tonnage due to higher freight received in the spot market. If the spot rate falls below his hedge line he will profit from his derivatives positions, which will compensate for the diminishing earnings on his vessels. The shipowner is a member of IMAREX and can trade on his won account. To hedge his freight rate risks he sells 52 lots ($\approx$ 51,400mt / 1,000mt lot size) of P2 FFA contracts for each month, with a FFA value of $3,900,000 (= 52 lots x 1,000mt lot size x $75/ton). NOS, upon approval of the company of the shipowner, can clear FFA contracts. In order to have his derivatives positions cleared, the shipowner pays to NOS $11,700 (= 0.3% x $3,900,000) for each FFA settlement.

Table 3.39 summarises the outcomes of the trend hedge, in April, July and October. Suppose that during this period freight rates in the spot market evolved as follows: March freight rate $75/ton, April freight rate $78/ton, July freight rate $74/ton, October freight rate $72/ton. The corresponding freight incomes for these months are also shown in the table, as well as the loss/gain in relation to March, based on how rates have moved during this period.

- Under the first settlement, the April FFA contract, which was sold at $76.5/ton, generates a loss in the FFA position of $77,100(=$1.5/tonx51,400mt). In the spot market, the shipowner gains $154,200(=$4,009,200 – $3,855,000). Thus, the net profit of this portfolio for the shipowner is $77,100 (= $154,200 – $77,100). When FFA transactions costs are also taken into account this payoff becomes for the shipowner $65,400 (=$77,100 – $11,700).
- Under the second settlement, the July FFA contract, which was sold at $74.5/ton, provides a gain of $25,700 (= $0.5/ton x 51,400mt). In the spot market, the shipowner loses $51,400 (= $3,803,600 – $3,855,000). Thus, the

net loss of this portfolio for the shipowner is $25,700 (= $25,700 – $51,400). When FFA transactions costs are also taken into account this payoff becomes for the shipowner $37,400 (= $25,700 + $11,700).

- Finally, under the third settlement, the October FFA contract, which was sold at $73.50/ton, produces a gain of $77,100 (= $1.5/ton x 51,400mt). In the spot market, the shipowner loses $154,200 (= $3,700,800 – $3,855,000). Thus, the net loss of this portfolio for the shipowner is $77,100 (= $77,100 –$154,200). When transactions costs are also taken into account this payoff becomes for the shipowner $88,800 (= $77,100 + $11,700).

Table 3.39. The Two Outcomes of FFA Trend Hedge

Physical (Spot) Market	FFA Market
March 15ˢᵗ	
Cargo size: 51,400mt, Route P2 Freight rate: $75/ton March freight income/cost: $3,855,000 (= $75/ton x 51,400mt)	FFA April price: $76.5/ton FFA July price: $74.5/ton FFA October price: $73.5/ton Value of FFA: $3,855,000 (= $75/ton x 51,400mt)
Clearing fees for each settlement: $11,700 (= 0.3% x $3,900,000)	
1ˢᵗ Settlement April 30ᵗʰ: Freight rates are at $78/ton	
Freight rate: $78/ton April freight income/cost: $4,009,200 (= $78/ton x 51,400mt)	FFA April price: $76.5/ton Value of FFA: $3,932,100 (= $76.5/ton x 51,400mt)
The shipowner gains $154,200 [= ($78/ton – $75/ton) x 51,400mt]	**The shipowner loses $77,100** [= ($75/ton – $76.5/ton) x 51,400mt]
Net profit for shipowner: $77,100 (= $154,200 – $77,100), instead of $154,000	
2ⁿᵈ Settlement July 31ˢᵗ: Freight rates are at $74/ton	
Freight rate: $74/ton July freight income/cost: $3,803,600 (= $74/ton x 51,400mt)	FFA July price: $74.5/ton Value of FFA: $3,829,300 (= $74.5/ton x 51,400mt)
The shipowner loses $51,400 [= ($74/ton – $75/ton) x 51,400mt]	**The shipowner gains $25,700** [= ($75/ton – $74.5/ton) x 51,400mt]
Net loss for shipowner: $25,700 (= $51,400 – $25,700), instead of $51,400	
3ʳᵈ Settlement October 31ˢᵗ: Freight rates are at $72/ton	
Freight rate: $72/ton October freight income/cost: $3,700,800 (= $72/ton x 54,000mt)	FFA October price: $73.5/ton Value of FFA: $3,777,900 (= $73.5/ton x 51,400mt)
The shipowner loses $154,200 [= ($72/ton – $75/ton) x 51,400mt]	**The shipowner gains $77,100** [= ($75/ton – $73.5/ton) x 51,400mt]
Net loss for shipowner: $77,100 (= $154,200 – $77,100), instead of $154,200	
Total Outcome of the trend hedge: -$25,700 (= $77,100 – $25,700 – $77,100)	

When combining the results of the three portfolio positions, it yields a loss of $25,700 instead of a loss of $51,400, which would have resulted if the shipowner did not enter the FFA market at all. During the first two months of his hedge, the forward position on April did not improve his cash-flow, as the physical market remained very strong. But, as the market turned downwards at the end of July, his trend hedge started to work as his July and October FFA positions resulted in gains.

3.5.5. OTC FFA Hedge vs. BIFFEX Hedge

This example is used to demonstrate the difference in the hedging outcome that may result from hedging with a forward contract written on a specific route of the BPI versus a futures contract which is written on the index (e.g. BIFFEX). Suppose that today is 18th of May 2000 and a charterer is interested in transporting HSS from the US Gulf to Japan under a voyage charterparty, two months from today on 31st of July. Had the charterer been able to charter the vessel immediately it would have cost him $1,187,340 (= $23.1/ton x 51,400mt), representing his risk exposure in the spot market. In order to protect himself from adverse freight rate movements which may occur by the day of the physical fixture (30th of July), the charterer decides to sell FFA contracts. He approaches his FFA broker and gives the following contract specifications: (a) route P2 (US Gulf-Japan) of the BPI, (b) cargo size 51,400mt HSS, (c) contract date 31st July 2000, and (d) forward price $21.8/ton. The broker searches for a suitable counterparty a shipowner, say with the same contract specifications but with opposite expectations. If the shipowner is willing to sell forward freight for similar dates at $21.8/ton then the agreement is reached and the FFA contract is drafted. The value of the FFA contract is $1,120,520 (= $21.8/ton x 51,400mt).

The second column of Table 3.40 summarises the outcome of the FFA hedge, two months later, in July 2000. At the expiration day of the FFA contract (31st of July) suppose that the FFA settlement price is $23.788/ton. The settlement price is higher than the fixed price, so the shipowner pays $102,183 [= ($23.788/ton – $21.8/ton) x $51,400mt] to the charterer. Combining the loss in the spot market, as can be seen in the first column of the table, of $35,363 (= $1,222,703 – $1,187,340) with the gain in the forward market gives an overall profit (loss) of $66,820 for the charterer (shipowner). The brokerage fees, agreed to be paid by both parties to the broker, are $2,801.3 (= 0.25% x $1,120,520). When these fees are also taken into account the payoffs become: For the shipowner, loss of $69,621.3 (= $66,820 + $2,801.3) and for the charterer profit of $64,018.7 (= $66,820 – $2,801.3).

With BIFFEX contracts the same market agents would have traded the underlying asset BPI (basket of seven routes) instead of just route P2, as futures contracts on routes of the BFI and later of the BPI did not exist. Thus, as can be seen in the third column of the table, the charterer buys BIFFEX contracts for delivery on 31st July 2000, at the current price of 1455 points, which represents a monetary value of $14,550 (= 1455 x $10/point). Based on this, he calculates the number of BIFFEX contracts to buy as 82 (≈ $1,187,340 / $14,550). Therefore, the value of his BIFFEX position is $1,193,100 (= $14,550 x 82 contracts). For this service the shipowner (charterer) is charged $15 per contract per "*round trip*". The clearing fee of $1,230 (=$15 x 82 contracts) is paid to LIFFE by the shipowner and by the charterer. Moreover, the counterparties pay a brokerage fee of $2,982.8 (=0.25%x1455x$10x82) at the completion of the transaction.

The third column of Table 3.40 summarises the outcome of the hedge, two months later, in July. The July BIFFEX contract stands at 1570 points, with a monetary value of $15,700 (= 1570 x $10/point). The charterer unwinds his hedge, selling back 82 contracts, representing a total amount of $1,287,400 (= $15,700 x 82 contracts). His futures position generates a profit of $94,300 (= $1,287,400 – $1,193,100). Combining the loss in the spot market with the gain in the futures market gives an overall profit (loss) of $58,937 for the charterer (shipowner). When transactions costs (clearing and brokerage fees) are also taken into account these payoffs become for the shipowner and the charterer, respectively, \$63,149.8 (= \$58,937 + \$1,230 + \$2,982.8) and \$54,724.2 (= \$58,937 − \$1,230 − \$2,982.8).

The difference in the end results, say for the charterer, between the FFA hedge (\$66,820) and the BIFFEX hedge (\$58,937) can be justified on the grounds that the specifications and the design of the two derivatives products are different. FFA contracts are route specific, while the BIFFEX contracts were a cross-hedge.

Table 3.40. FFA vs. BIFFEX Hedges

18th May 2000		
Physical (Spot) Market	**FFA Market**	**BIFFEX Market**
BPI: 1617	FFA May price: \$21.8/ton	BIFFEX May price: 1455
Cargo size: 51,400mt, Route P2	Value of FFA: \$1,120,520	Shipowner sells 82
Freight Rate: \$23.1/ton	(= \$21.8/ton x 51,400mt)	(= \$1,187,340 / \$14,550) contracts
Freight income: \$1,187,340		Charterer buys 82 contracts
(= \$23.1/ton x 51,400mt)		Value of BIFFEX: \$1,193,100
		(= 1455 x \$10 x 82)
31st July 2000		
BPI: 1730	FFA July price: \$23.788/ton	BIFFEX July price: 1570
Freight rate: \$23.788/ton	Value of FFA: \$1,222,703	Value of BIFFEX: \$1,287,400
Freight Income: \$1,222,703	(= \$23.788/ton x 51,400mt)	(= 1570 x \$10 x 82)
(= \$23.788/ton x 51,400mt)		
The charterer (shipowner) loses (gains) \$35,363	The shipowner (charterer) loses (gains) \$102,183	The shipowner (charterer) loses (gains) \$94,300
	Combined Spot-FFA Profit (loss) for charterer (shipowner): \$66,820	**Combined Spot-BIFFEX Profit (loss) for charterer (shipowner): \$58,937**
	Brokerage fees: \$2,801.3 (= 0.25% x \$1,120,520)	**Brokerage fees: \$2,982.8** (= 0.25% x 1455 x \$10 x 82) **Clearing fees: \$1,230** (= \$15 x 82 contracts)

3.5.6. Voyage Tanker OTC FFA Non-Cleared Hedge

Consider next an example of a hedge on a voyage tanker route using FFAs, in order to demonstrate the calculations using worldscale quotations. Suppose that in September 30th a Suezmax tanker owner notes that the October FFA market for a voyage of 130,000mt crude oil on the WAF/USAC TD5 route of the BDTI is quoted around WS105, where the Flat rate for the route is \$4.02/mt.[50] His market intelligence tells him that the rate on this route will most probably fall. His vessel will be open in WAF in mid-October so he decides to hedge against the risk of a possible market downfall by selling FFA contracts for 130,000mt on that route at WS105. An oil trader who is interested in transporting his crude cargo also in mid October notices the forward offer of the owner and expects, on the basis of his experience, that the market for that route might well rise. Both parties contact their broker and fix a contract for 130,000mt on route TD5 at WS105, with a settlement date of October 30th. The brokerage commission, that each counterparty has to pay is \$1,371.8(=0.25%x\$548,730).

Table 3.41 summarises the possible outcomes of the hedge for the two participants, one month later, in October 30th with the market, as per route TD5 of the BDTI, to be valued at WS120. The shipowner must forward within seven working days to the

---

[50] Flat rates for each route may be obtained from Worldscale publications and are revised every year. They are used to calculate the freight hire rate for a tanker vessel by multiplying the flat rate for the route with the vessel's tonnage and the prevailing WS rate obtained from the market.

trader the difference between the contractual "*fixed*" rate and the settlement rate, multiplied by the Flat rate and quantity of cargo. Therefore, the FFA contract difference value is $78,390 [=130,000mt x $4.02/mt x (WS120 – WS105) / 100]. The shipowner would aim to recover the notional paper loss through being able to fix his vessel at a higher rate in the spot market. When transactions costs are also taken into account, the shipowner realises a loss on his tanker FFA paper trade of $79,761.8 (=$78,390 + $1,371.8). The oil trader, by using a tanker FFA trade, managed to cover the losses from the spot market of $78,390, by receiving $78,390 from the shipowner. When FFA transactions costs are taken into account, the oil trader's gain on his tanker FFA paper trade is reduced to $77,018.2 (= $78,390 – $1,371.8).

Table 3.41. Tanker OTC Non-Cleared FFA Hedge

Physical (Spot) Market	FFA Market
September 30th	
Freight rate: WS105 Cargo size: 130,000mt, Route TD5 Flat rate: $4.02/mt Freight income/cost: $548,730 (= 130,000mt x $4.02/mt x WS105 / 100)	FFA October price: WS105 FFA Value: $548,730 (= 130,000mt x $4.02/mt x WS105 / 100)
October 30th	
Freight rate: WS120 Cargo size: 130,000mt Flat rate: $4.02/mt Freight income/cost: $627,120 (=130,000mt x $4.02/mt x WS120 / 100)	FFA October price: WS120 FFA Value: $627,120 (= 130,000mt x $4.02/mt x WS120 / 100)
The shipowner (oil trader) gains (loses) $78,390	**The shipowner (oil trader) loses (gains) $78,390**
Brokerage fees: $1,371.8 (= 0.25% x $548,730)	

3.5.7. Voyage Tanker Freight Futures Cleared at NYMEX Hedge

Suppose that during March a tanker owner has an Aframax vessel (80,000 dwt) trading in route TD7 (N. Sea-UK/Cont) and currently spot rates are at WS180, where the Flat rate for the route is $3.37/mt. The shipowner believes that the market will fall during June and would like to fix a rate at the current market levels. He sells June freight futures contracts at the prevailing rate of WS180. A charterer notices the offer of the shipowner and buys the contracts.

NYMEX ClearPort(sm), which clears freight futures on route TD7, charges the shipowner (and the charterer) $5/lot as clearing and settlement fee, being a non-member of the exchange (for members the fee is $4/lot). Thus, the shipowner (charterer) in order to hedge his spot market exposure sells (buys) 80 lots (=80,000mt/1,000mt/lot) of freight futures, with a freight futures value of $485,280 (= 80 lots x 1,000mt/lot x $3.37/mt x WS180 / 100). Therefore, the NYMEX ClearPort(sm) clearing and settlement fee is $400 (= 80 lots x $5/lot) for each counterparty.

Table 3.42 summarises the possible outcomes of the hedge for the two participants, three months later, on June 30th, when the BDTI route TD7 has risen to WS104.212. The oil trader must forward to the shipowner $210,387 [= 80,000mt x $3.47/mt x (WS180 – WS104.212) / 100]. He would aim to recover the notional paper loss through being able to fix the vessel at a lower rate in the spot market. When freight futures transactions costs are also taken into account, the oil trader realises a loss in his tanker freight futures paper trade of $210,787 (= $210,387 + $400). The shipowner, by using a tanker paper trade, managed to cover the losses from the spot market of $210,387, by receiving $210,387 from the oil trader. When transactions costs are also taken into account, the shipowner receives a gain in his tanker paper trade of $209,987 (= $210,387 – $400). The net spot – FFA portfolio effect for both is to stabilize revenues/costs at the current level.

Table 3.42. Tanker NYMEX ClearPort(sm) Cleared Futures Hedge

Physical (Spot) Market	NYMEX Market
March 31st	
Freight rate: WS180 Cargo size: 80,000mt, Route TD7 Flat rate: $3.47/mt Freight income/cost: $499,680 (= 80,000mt x $3.47/mt x WS180 / 100)	Futures October price: WS180 Futures Value: $499,680 (= 80,000mt x $3.47/mt x WS180 / 100)
June 30th	
Freight rate: WS104.212 Cargo size: 80,000mt Flat rate: $3.47/mt Freight income/cost: $289,293 (= 80,000mt x $3.47/mt x WS104.212 / 100)	Futures October price: WS104.212 Futures Value: $289,293 (= 80,000mt x $3.47/mt x WS104.212 / 100)
The shipowner (oil trader) loses (gains) $210,387	**The shipowner (oil trader) gains (loses) $210,387**
Clearing and settlement fees: $400 (= 80 lots x $5/lot)	

3.5.8. Period T/C Tanker OTC "*Hybrid*" FFA Cleared Hedge at LCH.Clearnet

Suppose a European oil major has a contract to deliver 130,000mt of crude oil each quarter, over a 12 months period, starting on January 1st. In order to avoid the physical commitment of a time-charter, he decides to place a bid to buy a FFA T/C contract at WS95 (Flat rate $9.50/mt), for each of the four quarters, on route TD5 (Bonny/Philadelphia) of the BDTI. A shipowner, in order to retain full control of his vessels, decides to run them spot (instead of time-chartering them) and be able to take advantage of the expected market peaks. He therefore, agrees to sell the FFA T/C contracts to the oil major. The four quarters are the following: 1st Quarter – 1st January to 31st March; 2nd Quarter – 1st April to 30th June; 3rd Quarter – 1st July to 30th September; and 4th Quarter – 1st October to 31st December. The settlement of each FFA contract on the TD5 is the average of the route TD5 values over the number of working days of the quarter.

Table 3.43 presents the outcome of the hedge for each of the four quarters. In the 1st quarter, the TD5 route settlement price is WS95, so neither party owes each other any money. In the 2nd Quarter, the TD5 settlement price is WS95. The shipowner (seller) receives $37,050 (= 130,000mt x $9.50/mt x (WS95 – WS92) / 100) from the charterer (buyer). In the 3rd Quarter, the TD5 settlement price is WS88. The shipowner receives $86,450 (= 130,000mt x $9.50/mt x (WS95 – WS88) / 100) from the charterer. Finally, in the 4th Quarter, the TD5 route settlement price is WS99.5. The charterer (buyer) receives $55,575 (= 130,000mt x $9.50/mt x (WS99.5 – WS95) / 100) from the shipowner (buyer). The overall gain (loss) for the shipowner (charterer) in the FFA market is $67,925 (= $37,050 + $86,450 – $55,575). The gains/losses in the spot market per quarter are shown in the first column of the table. Overall, the shipowner (charterer) has lost (gained) in the spot market $67,925 (= -

$37,050 - \$86,950 + \$55,575$). The loss (gain) in the spot market for the shipowner (charterer) is offset by the gain (loss) in the FFA market.

Table 3.43. Tanker FFA T/C "*Quarterlies*" Hedge

Physical (Spot) Market	FFA Market
January 1ˢᵗ	
Freight rate: WS95 January freight income/cost: $1,173,250 (= 130,000mt x $9.50/mt x WS95 / 100)	FFA January price for each "quarterly", Q1, Q2, Q3 and Q4: WS95 Value of FFA: $1,173,250 (= 130,000mt x $9.50/mt x WS95 / 100)
Brokerage fees for each settlement: $2,933.1 (= 0.25% x $1,173,250) **Clearing and Settlement fees for each quarterly: $780 (= $6/lot x 130 lots)**	
1ˢᵗ Quarter March 31ˢᵗ: The Worldscale rate remains the same at WS95	
March freight income/cost: $1,173,250 (= 130,000mt x $9.50/mt x WS95 / 100) **The shipowner/charterer gains/loses $0**	FFA March settlement price: WS95 The settlement price equals the FFA price, so no exchange of cash takes place
2ⁿᵈ Quarter June 30ᵗʰ: The Worldscale rate decreases to WS92	
June freight income/cost: $1,136,200 (=130,000mt x $9.50/mt x WS92 / 100) **The shipowner (charterer) loses (gains) $37,050**	FFA June settlement price: WS88 Value of FFA: $1,136,200 (= 130,000mt x $9.50/mt x WS92 / 100) **The shipowner (charterer) gains (loses) $37,050**
3ʳᵈ Quarter September 30ᵗʰ: The Worldscale rate decreases to WS88	
September freight income/cost: $1,086,800 (= 130,000mt x $9.50/mt x WS88 / 100) **The shipowner (charterer) loses (gains) $86,450**	FFA September settlement price: WS88 Value of FFA: $1,086,800 (= 130,000mt x $9.50/mt x WS88 / 100) **The shipowner (charterer) gains (loses) $86,450**
4ᵗʰ Quarter December 31ˢᵗ: The Worldscale rate increases to WS99.5	
December freight income/cost: $1,228,825 (= 130,000mt x $9.50/mt x WS99.5 / 100) **The shipowner (charterer) gains (loses) $55,575**	FFA December settlement price: WS99.5 Value of FFA: $1,228,825 (= 130,000mt x $9.50/mt x WS99.5 / 100) **The shipowner (charterer) loses (gains) $55,575**
Total gains/losses	
The shipowner (charterer) loses (gains) $67,925 (= –$37,050 – $86,950 + $55,575)	**The shipowner (charterer) gains (loses) $67,925** (= $37,050 + $86,450 – $55,575)

Of course in all the above there are transactions costs, which must be taken into account in the calculation of the net cash-flow(s) from these trades. Since the size of the FFA deal is $1,173,250 (= 130,000mt x $9.50/mt x WS95 / 100), the brokerage fees, paid by each party to the broker, are as follows: $2,933.1 (= 0.25% x $1,173,250). Over the four quarterlies they come to $11,732.4 (= $2,933.1 x 4). Moreover, suppose that the shipowner wishes to eliminate credit risk. He advises his broker to clear the FFA transaction through LCH.Clearnet; that will cost him $6/lot in total, comprising $4/lot clearing fee plus $2/lot settlement fee, payable to LCH.Clearnet. Thus, each counterparty pays to LCH.Clearnet a clearing fee of $520(=$4/lotx130,000mt/1,000mt) and a settlement fee of $260 (= $2/lot x 130,000mt / 1,000mt lot size), totaling $780 in fees to LCH.Clearnet. Thus, it costs $3,120(=$780x 4) to eliminate credit risk from the four FFA trades. Brokerage and LCH.Clearnet fees per quarter come to $3,713.1 (= $2,933.1 + $780). Overall, for the four settlement periods, each of the two counterparties has to pay $14,852.4(=$3,713.1 x 4 settlements) for brokerage, clearing and settlement services.

3.5.9. Application of the Optimal Hedge Ratio in the FFA Market

Chapter 2 of this book outlined how optimal hedge ratios (Minimum Variance Hedge Ratios, MVHR) can be calculated and used to achieve more efficient hedges in futures/forward contracts. More specifically, the MVHR, h^*, is obtained through the following formula: $h^* = \dfrac{Cov(\Delta S_t, \Delta F_t)}{Var(\Delta F_t)} = \rho_{SF} \dfrac{\sigma_S}{\sigma_F}$, where $Cov(\Delta S_t, \Delta F_t)$ is the covariance between changes in spot rates, ΔS_t, and changes in futures/forward rates, ΔF_t, $Var(\Delta F_t)$ is the variance of changes in ΔF_t, ρ_{SF} is the correlation coefficient between ΔS_t and ΔF_t, σ_S is the standard deviation of ΔS_t and σ_F is the standard deviation of ΔF_t: Thuong and Vischer (1990), Haralambides (1992b), Kavussanos and Nomikos (2000) and Kavussanos and Visvikis (2005) show that greater risk reduction in the BIFFEX and FFA trades can be achieved by using the constant MVHR to calculate optimal rather than naïve, one-to-one, hedges, of the type shown in the previous examples of this chapter. That is, it is suboptimal to initiate paper trades, which are exactly equal in magnitude to the exposure a shipowner or a charterer has in the physical (spot) market. The conventional one-to-one hedge ratio would be optimal in case the variation in the physical (spot) market is exactly equal to that of the futures/forward market.

This is evident from the MVHR formula, as $Cov(\Delta S_t, \Delta F_t) = Var(\Delta F_t)$ when $\Delta S_t = \Delta F_t$; that is, when changes in rates in the spot market match exactly the changes in rates in the futures/forward market. Evidently, this does not happen in freight markets, as shown in the aforementioned studies. Moreover, Kavussanos and Nomikos (2000) and Kavussanos and Visvikis (2005) show that the MVHR is time-varying in BIFFEX and FFA contracts, respectively. That is, the variation in spot and futures/forward rates change over time, which in turn imply that h^*, the MVHR is time-varying. If this is the case, as it is in a number of freight markets, use of the constant MVHR or even worse, use of conventional one-to-one hedge ratios (MVHR = 1) leads to suboptimal hedges. Figure 3.22 illustrates this issue. Using weekly spot and FFA prices in Panamax route P2 of the BPI from 16 January 1997 to 31 December 2001, the optimal MVHR is calculated to be $h^* = 0.51$. This is a value which is 51% of the value of the conventional hedge ratio of 1. The value of 0.51 indicates that only 51% of the physical position should be initiated in FFA contracts to obtain a full hedge. That is, if the exposure to the freight market is $1,000,000, a paper trade of $510,000, rather than a FFA position of $1,000,000, is sufficient to fully cover the risk exposure. This overhedging is clearly a waste of resources for the principal, which moreover constitutes a speculative trade of $490,000 (not matched by an opposite physical position).

Using GARCH type models the variance and the covariance terms entering the calculation of h^* in the formula are allowed to vary and thereby produce a time-varying MVHR, h^*. Its values are shown graphically in Figure 3.22. The changing values of the hedge ratio are a consequence of new information arriving in the market, over time. Clearly, using a time-varying hedge ratio, that is, adjusting the number of FFA contracts held over time in a dynamic portfolio setting, allows for better hedges than if the constant hedge ratio of 0.51 is used over the whole period. This can be seen by the value of the time-varying hedge ratio, which is at times well away from the constant value of 0.51 and even further away from 1 (in case a one-to-one hedge is used). For instance, if 51% of the spot position is hedged in observation 105, when the hedge ratio stands at 0.41, there is a 10% overhedging on the particular date. Similarly, on observation 125 the dynamic hedge ratio stands at 0.575, 6.5% above the constant one. In this case, the spot position is not fully covered by the FFA trades calculated through the constant hedge ratio.

Figure 3.22. Constant vs. Time-Varying Hedge Ratios for Spot & FFA Prices, Route P2

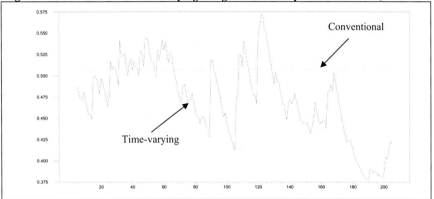

The following example demonstrates how the constant MVHR ratios may be calculated in the FFA market. The calculation of time-varying hedge ratios requires more advanced techniques, such as those applied in Kavussanos and Visvikis (2005), and is beyond the scope of this book. However, further details on this may be found in this last reference. Suppose a shipowner has in his possession the daily spot (S_t) and FFA (F_t) prices for route P2A of the BPI (Skaw-Gibraltar to Taiwan-Japan) from 1st to 31st of March 2005, shown in Table 3.44. Ideally, the sample period should be equal to the hedging period; in the example it is assumed that the hedging period is one month. In order to calculate the hedge ratio, h^*, he takes the logarithmic price changes of spot (ΔS_t) and FFA (ΔF_t) prices, calculates the standard deviations of ΔS_t (σ_S) and ΔF_t (σ_F), and the correlation coefficient between ΔS_t and ΔF_t, ρ_{SF} – see section 2.3.2.4 in Chapter 2 of this book. The results are shown in Table 3.44. These numbers are used in Equation (2.4) to obtain the optimal hedge ratio: $h^*=0.3145\text{x}0.0087/0.0158 = 0.173$. The estimated hedge ratio h^* of 0.173 implies that the shipowner should sell $0.173 worth of FFA contracts for each US$ of freight rate income[51]. Assuming that the size of the spot position to be hedged (N_S) is $1,000,000, the shipowner then calculates the size of his FFA position (N_F) in monetary terms as follows: $N_F = h^*$ x N_S = 0.173 x $1,000,000 = $173,000. Therefore, in order to hedge himself against freight rate risk in route P2A he has to sell $173,000 worth of FFA contracts. If he sells FFAs worth $1,000,000 instead, then he has hedged $827,000(=$1,000,000 – $173,000) more than he has to. This $827,000 of "*over-hedging*" represents a speculative position for the shipowner.

---

[51] An alternative estimation method is for the shipowner to run the regression of Equation (2.19), where the coefficient h^* represents the optimal hedge ratio.

Table 3.44. Daily FFA and Spot Prices of BPI Route 2A (01/03/05 – 31/03/05)

Date	FFA Price (F_t) ($/ton)	Natural Logarithm of F_t, $\ln(F_t)$	$\Delta F_t =$ $\ln(F_t) - \ln(F_{t-1})$	Spot Price (S_t) ($/ton)	Natural Logarithm of S_t, $\ln(S_t)$	$\Delta S_t =$ $\ln(S_t) - \ln(S_{t-1})$
01/03/05	43,625	10.683		41,615	10.636	
02/03/05	44,500	10.703	0.020	41,638	10.637	0.001
03/03/05	44,500	10.703	0.000	41,712	10.639	0.002
04/03/05	45,250	10.720	0.017	42,244	10.651	0.013
07/03/05	45,250	10.720	0.000	42,787	10.664	0.013
08/03/05	45,750	10.731	0.011	43,232	10.674	0.010
09/03/05	46,375	10.745	0.014	43,944	10.691	0.016
10/03/05	46,375	10.745	0.000	45,016	10.715	0.024
11/03/05	46,375	10.745	0.000	45,618	10.728	0.013
14/03/05	46,375	10.745	0.000	45,764	10.731	0.003
15/03/05	45,500	10.725	-0.019	45,815	10.732	0.001
16/03/05	45,500	10.725	0.000	45,545	10.726	-0.006
17/03/05	46,750	10.753	0.027	45,576	10.727	0.001
18/03/05	46,250	10.742	-0.011	45,757	10.731	0.004
21/03/05	46,500	10.747	0.005	46,243	10.742	0.011
22/03/05	45,500	10.725	-0.022	46,688	10.751	0.010
23/03/05	44,500	10.703	-0.022	46,856	10.755	0.004
24/03/05	44,500	10.703	0.000	46,631	10.750	-0.005
29/03/05	44,750	10.709	0.006	46,563	10.749	-0.001
30/03/05	43,125	10.672	-0.037	46,188	10.740	-0.008
31/03/05	42,500	10.657	-0.015	45,776	10.732	-0.009
Standard Deviations			0.0158			0.0087
Correlation Coefficient between ΔS_t and ΔF_t, ρ_{SF}			0.3145			

Note: Route P2A is the Skaw Passero-Gibraltar to Taiwan-Japan time-charter route of the BPI.

3.5.10. OTC Spread Speculation Trades

According to market sources, freight derivatives are described as the *"missing link"* between disparate markets in the underlying commodities, creating hedging and arbitrage opportunities. To see how such arbitrage opportunities may arise, consider some examples:

The differential between the Brent and WTI may be used for spread trades; oil markets are linked together by several Europe and North Sea/US East Coast tanker routes. Likewise, Atlantic and Pacific coal markets are linked together by chartered Capesize vessels. For instance, there may be arbitrage possibilities between CIF (Cost, Insurance, Freight) and FOB (Free On Board) Richards Bay coal prices, as the CIF element is included in the commodity (coal) trade price, while the FOB freight prices are paid separately. Traders can lock in the implied freight element between the two prices and then switch out through a FFA trade.

The differential between the All Publications Index, API 2 CIF (coal delivered into northwest Europe – ARA) and API 4 FOB (coal loading price at Richards Bay, South Africa) swap contracts can be traded against the cost of the C4 (Capesize, Richards Bay/Rotterdam) FFA contract. The fact that coal can be shipped from multiple origins into Rotterdam causes the differential between delivered coal (API 2) versus FOB Richards Bay (API 4) to deviate, at times, from the price of freight on the C4 freight route. A typical trade is where an arbitrageur sells the implied freight differential of the two coal swaps (API 2 minus API 4) and buys the FFA on the C4 route. The inflows of coal from other origins can lower the delivered price in Rotterdam, enabling a trader to gain on the short position in implied freight, while the FFA price remained unchanged. Besides geographical reasons, there are also technical reasons for the existence of arbitrage opportunities. They include (i) the settlement of the two API contracts and the FFA are based on quotes from different market sources. For instance, settlement of API 2 is based on information from Argus[52], for API 4 from Argus, the McCloskey Group[53] and the South African Coal Report and for FFA settlement information comes from the Baltic Exchange); (ii) Capesize refers to vessels hauling 130,000mt to 180,000mt of bulk cargo; (iii) lot sizes differ. For both API 2 and API 4, the lot size is 5,000mt for nearby months. The contracts typically trade in quarterly blocks (or 15,000mt). The lot size of the IMAREX and LCH.Clearnet C4 FFA contract is 1,000mt lots, while OTC C4 FFA contracts typically trade in 25,000mt or 75,000mt. All these discrepancies create basis risk. Therefore, there is a trend towards an even more integral relationship between the freight and coal businesses, as freight rates may determine a trader's choice of where to buy coal from.

Consider next a numerical example of a spread strategy. Suppose that a trader believes that during the following months freight rates will increase and wishes to get advantage of it by entering the FFA market. During 10th of October, Q1 is trading at $32,000/day, Q2 is trading at $32,850/day and Q3Q4 is trading at $26,000. As shown in Table 3.45, the trader buys the cheap Q3Q4 (184 days) contract at $26,000/day and simultaneously sells Q2 (91 days) at $32,850/day. During 30th of December he sells Q3Q4 at $31,000 and buys Q2 at $39,000. The outcomes of these transactions are the following: On the Q3Q4 position there is a profit of $920,000 [= ($31,000/day − $26,000/day) x 184 days], while on the Q2 position there is a loss of $560,000 [=$32,850 − $39,000) x 91 days]. Combining the two positions results a net profit of $360,000.

Table 3.45. FFA Quarters Spread Speculation Strategy

Action	Cash-flows	Profit/Loss
October Buy Q3Q4 (184 days): $26,000	Cost of Q3Q4: $4,784,000 (= $26,000 x 184 days)	
Sell: Q2 (91 days): $32,850/day	Receipt from Q2: $2,989,350 (= $32,850/day x 91 days)	
December Sell Q3Q4 (184 days): $31,000	Receipt from Q3Q4: $5,704,000 (= $31,000 x 184 days)	Profit from Q3Q4: $920,000 [= ($31,000/day − $26,000/day) x 184]
Buy Q2 (91 days): $39,000	Cost from Q2: $3,549,000 (= $39,000 x 91 days)	Loss from Q2: $560,000 [= ($32,850 − $$39,000) x 91]
Total Profit		**+$360,000**

Consider yet another example. Suppose that during May a corn producer has fixed a deal with a shipowner on an unpriced contract for November and that the October FFA settlement of route P2 of the BPI will establish the cost of this vessel's freight. As shown in Table 3.46, today (May) the corn producer buys a Q4 (92 days) at $23,500/day. During July the producer sells freight (55,000mt) at $55/mt for

[52] Argus is a privately held UK-registered company, which provides an oil and gas price reporting service and OTC market prices and analysis for European natural gas, US and European power, and US and international coal trading and transportation. Argus publishes a broad range of newsletters in which it reports international industry developments and analyses emerging trends in the energy sector. Its newsletters cover natural gas and power in Asia-Pacific, Europe and Latin America. Argus information is available online on its website: www.argusonline.com.

[53] The McCloskey Group is a provider of news, analysis, and prices on the international coal industry. All McCloskey Group information is available online on its website: www.mccloskeycoal.com.

November. On 1st of September, he sells (closes out) his Q4 position at $30,000/day and buys a route P2A (60days) FFA at $35,000/day. Finally, on 31st of October he sells a route P2A FFA at $41,000/day and buys freight, by fixing a vessel, at $64/mt. The outcomes of these transactions are the following: On the Q4 position there is a profit of $598,000 [= ($30,000/day – $23,500/day) x 92 days]. On the P2A FFA there is a profit of $360,000 [= ($41,000/day – $35,000/day) x 60]. And on the spot freight position there is a loss of -$495,000 (= ($55/mt – $64/mt) x 55,000mt). Combining the three positions, results in a net profit of $463,000.

Table 3.46. Spot and FFA Spread Speculation Strategy

Action	Cash-flow	Profit/Loss
May Buy Q4 (92 days): $23,500/day Buy unpriced freight for November	Cost of Q4: -$2,162,000 (= $23,500/day x 92 days)	
July Sell freight for November: $55/mt	Receipt from freight: +$3,025,000 (= 55,000mt x $55/mt)	
September Sell Q4 (92 days): $30,000/day Buy P2A FFA (60 days): $35,000/day	Receipt from Q4: +$2,760,000 (= $30,000/day x 92 days) Cost of P2A: -$2,100,000 (= $35,000/day x 60 days)	From Q4: +$598,000 [= ($30,000/day – $23,500/day) x 92]
October Sell P2A FFA (60 days): $41,000/day Buy freight: $64/mt	Receipt from P2A: +$2,460,000 (= $41,000/day x 60 days) Cost of freight: -$3,520,000 (= 55,000mt x $64/mt)	From FFA P2A: +$360,000 [= ($41,000/day – $35,000/day) x 60] Loss from freight: -$495,000 [= ($55/mt – $64/mt) x 55,000mt]
Total Profit		**+$463,000**

3.5.11. Various Strategies for Banks

A new type of market agent that is slowly appearing in the FFA market is the shipping-bank player. Potential strategies for banks using FFA contracts for hedging include:

i.   Vessel lending portfolios. That is, to look at ship lending as a long position on freight services and to hedge it against market falls. As discussed in Chapter 1 of this book, vessel prices, as the discounted stream of expected cash-flows from operating the vessel, are positively correlated with vessel prices. Declining freight rates lead to lower vessel values, and visa versa. Freight derivatives then may be used to hedge exposures in a bank lending portfolio comprising vessel loans.

ii. Moreover, a bank could impose on a shipowner to use derivatives as a condition to obtain a loan or as a condition to obtain better conditions for the loan (Aury, 2003). If a shipping company has a stream of cash-flows from a vessel that fluctuates with the market conditions, and it has borrowed to finance a vessel, the cash-flows to repay the loan will also move with the market. If the company does not hedge, it may end up with a default situation in a weaker market. The question needs to be asked whether banks should undertake deals that could potentially go wrong in the event of a weak market. Banks should be aware of the cash-flows of any owner before a loan is made.

iii.   Another case for using freight derivatives exist is when banks try to hedge against a time-charter. Time-charters are becoming rarer because grain houses, such as Cargill, are using FFAs to manage price risk. If time-charters are not so readily available, banks will be keen to finance ships with a hedge in place. According to FFA market sources, some shipping banks accept FFA contracts, whereby a shipowner, purchasing a second-hand vessel, is able to lock in two – three years worth of revenue. Instead of assigning a period time-charter to a bank, the shipowner can execute a FFA commitment to receive two – three years worth of cash inflows, settled monthly at levels tied to one of the four time-charter routes of the BPI. A number of shipping banks acknowledge that they allow shipowners to use FFA's instead of time-charters, as part of a security package tied to financing the purchase of vessels.

iv.   FFA contracts may be used for hedging shipping sensitive portfolios. Electricity generation and mining portfolios or portfolios of shares of shipping companies are examples of portfolios which are sensitive to freight rate risk and need hedging. The idea that banks should want to incorporate hedges into deals has started to become more acceptable (Aury, 2003).

v.   Another strategy for banks is to use FFA contracts for intermediary activities. Banks have been faced with increased demand from their customers to supply them with energy related price risk management tools. Most energy related commodities have got a freight element embedded. Banks can intermediate between two shipping parties (for example, its own shipping customers and counterparties on the FFA market) for "*sleeving*" purposes, which can occur for credit or legal reasons. For example, Company A deals only on FFABA documentation and Company B deals only on ISDA documentation and therefore cannot trade together. The deal will be sleeved by Company C (bank) which can trade with both A and B and accept to take the risk on the difference between the contracts against a margin.

vi.   FFA contracts may also be used by banks for speculative trading activities which include: (a) a directional play, using technical and fundamental analysis; (b) arbitrage, identified by taking positions in a voyage fixture against a time-charter one[54]; (c) actual against implied FFA rates; (d) between markets such as between the IMAREX and the OTC market and between NYMEX and IMAREX; and (e) market-making: in efficient markets, market-makers are making their money from the bid-offer spread as a reward for being last resort liquidity providers (Aury, 2003).

In 2005, banks that were active in FFA trading were: Morgan Stanley, Goldman Sachs (through its subsidiary commodity company J. Aron) and Deutsche Bank. Morgan Stanley is active on a daily basis in both the dry and tanker markets, whereas J. Aron and Deutsche Bank are only dealing in tanker freight derivatives. The Royal Bank of Scotland (RBS), ABN Amro Holding NV, JP Morgan, Soc Gen, AIG (through its hedge fund Framework), Barclays Capital, BNP Paribas, DVB, NIB,

---

[54] It is possible to calculate a voyage rate from a time-charter, the outcome being called a Time-Charter Equivalent (TCE) rate. Arbitrage possibilities occur when the implied rate is not the same with the real rate. If the real voyage rate is higher (lower) than the TCE, then taking a long (short) TCE position and a short (long) voyage position. These positions will eventually equalise the real voyage and the implied TCE rates, as a result of the collective actions of market participants trading.

Standard Bank and a few other banks and hedge funds, have shown interest and are actively researching the FFA market. Some other potential new players are big Japanese operators. Companies like K Line, MOL, NSS (Nippon Steel Shipping), NYK have entered the FFA market. At the time of writing none of the Chinese operators are trading on the FFA market, possibly due to credit issues, regulatory issues, documentary issues, and the relationship between physical exposure and route availability. Moreover, not a single traditional integrated steel mill has ever done a FFA trade. The Capesize market is dominated by the steel industry (iron ore and coking coal) and therefore, a move from the steel industry into the FFA market will be a major boost to the number of players.

3.6. Freight Options Contracts

Besides futures and forward contracts, options contracts are another derivatives tool available to principals for risk management, speculation or arbitrage purposes. This type of financial derivatives contracts has been used extensively in finance on a number of underlying instruments, including exchange rates, interest rates, etc. An introduction to options is provided in Chapter 2 of this book. Their payoffs, terminology, the factors affecting their prices, pricing models and the hedging outcomes achieved are considered there. Moreover, interesting comparisons of their payoffs with futures/forward contracts were considered and strategies for hedging were outlined. It is often argued that options should be thought of as buying insurance, for a premium, rather than as derivatives trading. This is because the maximum loss is the premium of the option, while the gain is proportional to the adverse movement in the price of the underlying commodity. This section extends that discussion and shows how options can be used in freight rate markets. A number of examples are considered, outlining simple and more complex strategies for hedging.

3.6.1. The Freight Options Market

Freight options contracts were introduced in 1991 with a European options contract on BIFFEX, trading at LIFFE. Trading on these contracts never became popular and they, like BIFFEX, ceased trading in April 2002. According to market sources, Enron and Bocimar, in November 2001, negotiated the first ever OTC zero-cost collar freight option on the average of the 4 T/Cs of the BCI, with five years term to maturity. OTC Asian options contracts are now available on individual routes of the Baltic dry and tanker indices, as well as on baskets of time-charter routes of the indices and on the FFA contracts available on them. They are offered by the same brokers that trade FFA contracts – see Table 3.72. According to Clarksons Securities Ltd., the most active freight options market is on the twelve-month contracts (or longer), on the arithmetic averages of the time-charter routes of the Handy, Panamax and Capesize sectors, and on Capesize South Africa to Rotterdam (C4) and Bollivar/Rotterdam (C7) routes. They represent about 10%-20% of the total freight derivatives market. Accordingly, it seems that market agents are mostly interested in hedging with options medium- to long-term average vessel earnings rather than short-term route-specific vessel earnings, which has been the focus of the FFA market.

During 1st June 2005 the first cleared tanker IMAREX Freight Option (IFO) contract was launched, on route TD3 (VLCC AG – East), cleared through NOS. The IFOs are available for trading and clearing for all IMAREX and NOS members, are structured as monthly call and put Asian style options (see Chapter 2 for details), with monthly, quarterly and yearly maturities and with a minimum contract size of 5 lots. IFOs are settled against the arithmetic average of the Baltic Exchange quotes for all index days of the settlement month. The total clearing and settlement fee for the IFOs is 2% of the options premium. IFO contracts on a route are offered for a number of strike prices, which are moving in steps of WS10 points (e.g. WS70, WS80, WS90, etc.).

The standard freight option contract is either a freight put option (floor) or a freight call option (cap), where their settlement is similar to that of FFAs; freight options contracts settle the difference between the average spot rate over a defined period of time and an agreed strike price (that is, they are Asian options)[55]. Settlement prices for the tanker routes (measured in Worldscale points) and time-charter dry-bulk routes (measured in US$/day) are calculated as the arithmetic average across all trading days in a calendar month and those for dry-bulk voyage routes (measured in US$/ton) are calculated as the average price over the last seven working days of the month. For freight options (as well as for FFAs) with durations longer than one month, such as the quarterly and calendar year contracts, intermediate settlements occur at the end of each calendar month for the duration of the contract. Thus, long-term freight options are either floorlets or caplets, settled on a rolling monthly basis as average price Asian options. Shipowners wishing to hedge against freight rate decreases may buy put options. Charterers wishing to hedge against freight rate increases may buy call options. They buy "*insurance*" against adverse price movements. If their expectations materialize they exercise the options. If not, they let the options expire worthless, costing them the initial options premium.

3.6.2. Options Strategies for Freight Hedging Purposes
The following examples illustrate how freight options contracts may be used in practice for hedging purposes by the potential counterparties in the shipping industry.

3.6.2.1. Dry-Bulk Plain Vanilla Freight Options Hedges
Suppose that during October a commodity trading house sold 51,400mt of HSS to receivers in Japan. Shipment, with a Panamax vessel of 54,000 dwt in route P2 of the BPI (US Gulf to South Japan), will take place in late January and the seller will be responsible for transportation costs. The current freight rate is $38.62/ton. Had the charterer been able to charter a vessel immediately his freight cost would have been $1,985,068 (= $38.62/ton x 51,400mt). This would have been the income of the shipowner who had a Panamax vessel available for hire immediately. In order for the charterer (shipowner) to hedge his freight rate costs (income) he decides to buy a January call (put) option for route P2 of the BPI.

The options position that a party, which is short or long in the physical market, needs to create to hedge his exposure to price risk of the underlying commodity, is shown by the dotted lines of Figures 2.12 and 2.11, respectively, in Chapter 2 of the book. The payoffs of the physical and the combined physical–derivatives positions are also shown in the same figures. The same graphs are reproduced, for convenience, in Figures 3.23 and 3.24. They show the payoffs for the shipowner and the charterer, respectively. Thus, the broker of the charterer (shipowner) advises him that there is a suitable counterparty (such as, a bank or a financial institution), willing to "*write*" him a January call (put) option with a strike price of $55.5/ton at a premium of 70 cents/ton. Therefore, the total premium that the charterer (shipowner) will pay to the seller of the call (put) is $35,980 (=$0.70/ton x 51,400mt). Brokerage fees are agreed

---

[55] Asian options are often used in thinly traded commodity markets to avoid problems with price manipulation of the underlying commodity near or at maturity.

to be paid by the charterer (shipowner) to the broker. That is, $7,131.80[=0.25%x($55.5/ton x 51,400mt)] is paid by the charterer (shipowner).

Figure 3.23. The Trading Positions in Buying a Protective Put (or Floorlet)

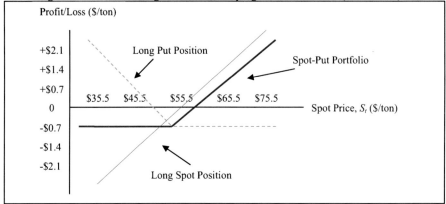

Figure 3.24. The Trading Positions in Buying a Protective Call (or Caplet)

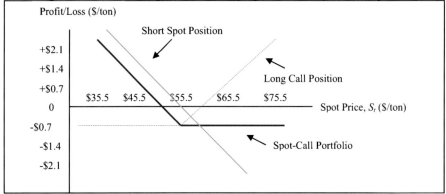

Before we consider the actual outcome of these hedges for the shipowner and the charterer. it is worth referring back to Figures 2.13 and 2.14 in Chapter 2 of the book. These outline the potential payoffs of the physical (spot), the options, and the combined spot–options positions from both the party long in the underlying commodity (the coffee producer) and the party short in the underlying commodity (the coffee house). They correspond to the shipowner and the charterer, respectively, in the freight market. Thus, in Figure 2.13 and in the accompanying Table 2.15, we observe that if coffee prices fall the coffee producer stabilizes the payoff (income) of his portfolio but is able to receive the benefits of increased coffee prices in case they rise. These same positions are observed in Figure 3.23 and the accompanying Table 3.47, for the shipowner wishing to hire his vessel in the freight market. Similarly, the coffee house, as can be observed in Figure 2.14 and in the accompanying Table 2.16, stabilizes the payoff of his portfolio (his costs) in case coffee prices rise, but is able to reduce his costs in case coffee prices turn out to be lower. In the freight market, the charterer is short in freight. He is worried about freight rate increases. In line with the buyer of coffee, his positions are presented in Figure 3.24 and the accompanying Table 3.48. Abstracting from brokerage fees, the cost to the shipowner is the put's premium, while for the charterer the cost is the call's premium.

224

3.6.2.1.1. The Shipowner's Options Hedge (Buying a Protective Put or a Floorlet)

Table 3.47. Shipowner's Dry-Bulk Freight Options Hedge

Three-Months Hedge Using Options (31st October – 30th January)	
Physical (Spot) Market	**Freight Options Market**
31st October	
Freight rate: $38.62/ton Cargo size: 51,400mt, route P2 Freight income: $1,985,068 (= $38.62/ton x 51,400mt)	Action: Buy January put option Put strike price: $55.5/ton Options premium: 70 cents/ton Options cost: $35,980 (= $0.7/ton x 51,400mt)
30th January: Rising Market	
Freight rate: $70.44/ton Freight income: $3,620,616 (= $70.44/ton x 51,400mt)	Strike price ($55.5/ton) < Spot price ($70.44/ton) Action: Put option is not exercised
Gain in the spot market: $1,635,548 (= $3,620,616 – $1,985,068)	Option's payoff: -$35,980 (premium)
Total Freight Income (including options premium): $3,584,636 (= $3,620,616 – $35,980)	
30th January – Alternative Scenario: Falling Market	
Freight rate: $35.32/ton Freight income: $1,815,448 (= $35.32/ton x 51,400mt)	Strike price ($55.5/ton) > Spot price ($35.32/ton) Action: Exercise the put option
Loss in the spot market: $169,620 (= $1,815,448 – $1,985,068)	Option's payoff: $1,001,272 (= ($55.5/ton – $35.32/ton) x 51,400mt – $35,980)
Total Freight Income (including options premium): $2,816,720 (= $1,815,448 + $1,001,272)	
Brokerage fees: $7,131.80 [= 0.25% x ($55.5/ton x 51,400mt)]	

Coming back to our example, consider first the position of the shipowner, which is summarised in Table 3.47 and Figure 3.23. Consider two scenarios:

- Suppose that freight rates increased to $70.44/ton in January. The shipowner experiences gains in the spot market of $1,635,548 (= $3,620,616 – $1,985,068). Since the spot price is higher than the strike price the put option is not exercised. A loss of $35,980, results in the paper market, which is equivalent to the option's premium. It represents the cost of the "*insurance*" he bought, but never used, as the market did not turn against him.

- Consider the alternative scenario, presented in the table, under which freight rates decreased to $35.32/ton. As a consequence, the shipowner experiences a loss in the spot market of $169,620 (= $1,815,448 – $1,985,068). Because the spot price is lower than the strike price, the put option is exercised giving a brokerage fee and premium adjusted payoff of $994,140 [= ($55.5/ton – $35.32/ton) x 51,400mt – $35,980 – $7,131.80]. Combining the freight income of $1,815,448, received in the physical market, with the profit of $994,140 made in the options market, results in an overall physical – paper cash-flow for the shipowner of $2,809,588. This is $994,140 better off compared to not using the options market.

As can be observed from these outcomes, if the freight market moves against the shipowner – that is, if freight rates fall – by buying the put option, he reduces his losses in the physical market by a substantial amount. If the freight market remains favourable the put option is not exercised and his cash-flow is simply reduced by $35,980; that is, by the amount paid to purchase the put option.

3.6.2.1.2. The Charterer's Options Hedge (Buying a Protective Call or a Caplet)

Table 3.48. Charterer's Dry-Bulk Freight Options Hedge

Three-Months Hedge Using Options (October 31st – January 30th)	
Physical (Spot) Market	**Freight Options Market**
31st October	
Freight rate: $38.62/ton	Action: Buy January call option
Cargo size: 51,400mt, route P2	Call strike price: $55.5/ton
Freight cost: $1,985,068	Options premium: 70 cents/ton
(= $38.62/ton x 51,400mt)	Options cost : $35,980 (= $0.7/ton x 51,400mt)
January 30th: Rising Market	
Freight rate: $70.44/ton	Strike price ($55.5/ton) < Spot price ($70.44/ton)
Freight cost: $3,620,616	Action: Exercise the call option
(= $70.44/ton x 51,400mt)	
Loss in the spot market: $1,635,548	Option's payoff: $731,937
(= $1,985,068 – $3,620,616)	[= ($70.44/ton – $55.5/ton) x 51,400mt – $35,980]
Total Freight Cost (including options premium): $2,888,679 (= $3,620,616 – $731,936)	
January 30th – Alternative Scenario: Falling Market	
Freight rate: $35.32/ton	Strike price ($55.5/ton) > Spot price ($35.32/ton)
Freight cost: $1,815,448	Action: Call option is not exercised
(= $35.32/ton x 51,400mt)	
Gain in the spot market: $169,620	Option's payoff: -$35,980 (premium)
(= $1,985,068 – $1,815,448)	
Total Freight Cost (including options premium): $1,851,428 (= $1,815,448 + $35,980)	
Brokerage fees: $7,131.80 [= 0.25% x ($55.5/ton x 51,400mt)]	

Consider next the positions of the charterer, summarised in Table 3.48 and Figure 3.24. The charterer buys a protective call, which protects him against freight rate rises but allows him to gain if freight rates fall in the spot market. Consider two possible outcomes:

- Suppose that freight rates increased to $70.44/ton on January 30th. The charterer is experiencing a loss in the spot market of $1,635,548 (= $1,985,068 – $3,620,616). In the paper market, since the spot price ($70.44/ton) is higher than the strike price ($55.5/ton), the call option contract is exercised, providing a payoff of $731,937 [= ($70.44/ton – $55.5/ton) x 51,400mt – $35,980]. Therefore, it will cost $2,888,679 (= $3,620,616 – $731,937) to the charterer to transport his cargo, instead of $3,620,616, which he would have paid had he not used the options market to hedge his position in the physical market. When brokerage fees are also taken into account this payoff becomes $2,895,810.80 (= $2,888,679 + $7,131.80).
- Consider an alternative scenario under which freight rates fall to $35.32/ton by January 30th. As shown in the same table, the charterer realises a gain of (saves) $169,620 (= $1,985,068 – $1,815,448) in the spot market. In the call options market, since the spot price is lower than the strike price, the option is not exercised. He lost the call option premium of $35,980. The overall cost to the charterer is the sum of the actual freight cost, the call option cost and the

226

option's brokerage fee. That is, $1,858,559.8 (= $1,815,448 + $35,980 + $7,131.80) in this case.

Figure 3.24 shows graphically the profit/loss of the short physical (light solid line), the long call option (dotted line) and the combined spot-option (heavy solid line) positions of the charterer for a range of prices of freight rates.

3.6.2.1.3. Options versus Futures/Forwards for Hedging Purposes

For comparison purposes, suppose next that the charterer or the shipowner, instead of using the freight options market to hedge their positions, choose to use the OTC FFA market. The charterer buys January FFA contracts for route P2 of the BPI, while the shipowner sells January FFA contracts for the same route and the same maturity. January FFA prices stand at $55.5/ton. Each party has to pay brokerage fees of $7,131.80 [= 0.25% x ($55.5/ton x 51,400mt)]. We illustrate the comparison of these outcomes between using options and FFAs from the charterer's point of view only; conclusions are similar for the shipowner.

Table 3.49. Charterer's Dry-Bulk FFA Hedge

Three-Months Hedge Using FFAs (October 31st – January 30th)	
Physical (Spot) Market	**FFA Market**
31st October	
Freight rate: $38.62/ton Cargo size: 51,400mt, route P2 Freight cost: $1,985,068 (= $38.62/ton x 51,400mt)	FFA January price: $55.5/ton Value of FFA: $2,852,700 (= $55.5/ton x 51,400mt)
January 30th: Rising Market	
Freight rate: $70.44/ton Freight cost: $3,620,616 (= $70.44/ton x 51,400mt) Loss in the spot market: $1,635,548 (= $1,985,068 – $3,620,616)	Freight rate: $70.44/ton Freight income: $3,620,616 (= $70.44/ton x 51,400mt) Gain in the FFA market: $767,916 [= ($70.44/ton – $55.5/ton) x 51,400mt]
Total Freight Cost: $2,852,700 (= $3,620,616 – $767,916)	
January 30th – Alternative Scenario: Falling Market	
Freight rate: $35.32/ton Freight cost: $1,815,448 (= $35.32/ton x 51,400mt) Gain in the spot market: $169,620 (= $1,985,068 – $1,815,448)	Freight rate: $35.32/ton Freight income: $1,815,448 (= $35.32/ton x 51,400mt) Loss in the FFA market: $1,037,252 [= ($35.32/ton – $55.5/ton) x 51,400mt]
Total Freight Cost: $2,852,700 (= $1,815,448 + $1,037,252)	
Brokerage fees: $7,131.8 [= 0.25% x ($55.5/ton x 51,400mt)]	

Table 3.49 summarises the positions for the charterer, in both the spot and the FFA paper markets, under the two alternative scenarios considered earlier; a market rise and a market fall in rates.

- Under the first scenario, spot freight rates increase to $70.44/ton by January. In this case, the charterer loses $1,635,548 (= $1,985,068 – $3,620,616) in the spot market, while in the FFA market he realises a gain of $767,916 [=$70.44/ton – $55.5/ton) x 51,400mt]. Thus, the net loss of this portfolio of spot and FFA positions for the charterer is $2,852,700 (= $3,620,616 – $767,916).

- Under the second scenario, freight rates fall to $35.32/ton. In this case, the charterer gains $169,620 (= $1,985,068 – $1,815,448) in the spot market, while in the FFA market he realises a loss of $1,037,252 [= ($35.32/ton – $55.5/ton) x 51,400mt], giving a net loss of $2,852,700 (=$1,815,448+$1,037,252).

Thus, under both scenarios, with the FFA contract the charterer faces a freight rate cost of $2,852,700. With the freight call option contract, when freight rates rise, the charterer exercises the option and faces a freight rate cost of $2,888,679. However, under the second scenario, where the freight rate market falls, the charterer does not exercise the freight call option and benefits fully in the physical market from the falling freight rates. In this case, his freight rate cost is only $1,851,428, approximately $1 million less compared to using FFAs. The example illustrates the flexibility of freight options contracts in comparison to FFAs. With FFAs (and freight futures) contracts, irrespective of the direction of the freight market, *"exercise"* is obligatory. This is not the case with options, allowing thus better payoffs, in case of favourable movements in prices.

3.6.2.1.4. The Shipowners Hedge – Writing a Covered Call

As we saw in the example presented in section 3.6.2.1.1, the shipowner can hedge his long freight position by buying a (protective) put option. Alternatively, he can write (i.e. sell) a (covered) call. In this case, his portfolio consists of a long position in the freight market and a short call option on freight with a strike price X = $55.5/ton, sold at a premium of c = $0.7/ton. Figure 3.25 depicts graphically the payoffs of these positions. As can be seen by the solid line, representing the payoff of his portfolio, profits are limited to the option's premium, in case freight rates rise. In case they fall by more than the option's premium, the shipowner is not covered by the option's position and makes losses. Thus, for a decrease in freight rates, higher than the amount of the premium, the shipowner is not covered by this strategy.

Figure 3.25. The Trading Positions in Writing a Covered Call

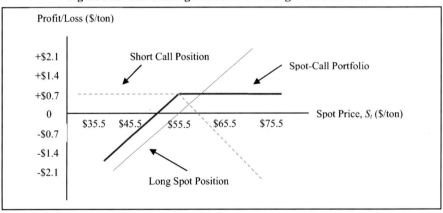

The shipowner may select this strategy over the protective put one if, for instance, strike prices for long puts on freight rates are not readily available or long puts are deeply out-of-the-money; this would not make them so attractive hedging instruments, as the probability of exercise is low. Moreover, if long puts are deeply in-the-money, this would make them very expensive hedging instruments. Under the covered call strategy, the short position in the call covers the long position in the spot market against a decrease of its price below the strike price. In this case, the options premium is received, as the option is not exercised by the holder of the call option.

3.6.2.1.5. The Charterer's Hedge – Writing a Covered Put
As we saw in the example presented in section 3.6.2.1.2, the charterer, who wishes to be covered against a rise in freight rates, can hedge his position by buying a (protective) call. Alternatively, he could write a (covered) put. In this case, his portfolio consists of a short spot position and a short put option on freight, with a strike price X = $55.5/ton, sold at a premium of p = $0.7/ton. Figure 3.26 depicts graphically the payoffs of these positions. If freight rates increase, the put option is not exercised by the put option's holder and losses in the spot market are reduced for the charterer by receiving the option's premium p = $0.7/ton. For a decrease in freight rates below its exercise price, the put option is exercised by its holder. The losses in the put option position for its writer counterbalance the gains in the short spot position. Overall, as can be observed, the portfolio profit is limited to the option's premium. These two outcomes, for a range of prices, can be seen by the heavy solid line in Figure 3.22.

Figure 3.26. The Trading Positions in Writing a Covered Put

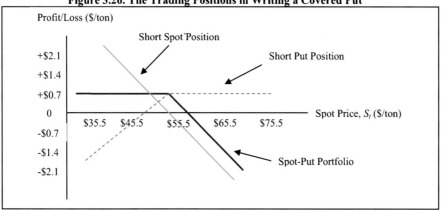

3.6.2.2. Shipowner's Tanker Freight Options Hedge at IMAREX
Suppose that during the end of September a shipowner expects to have in December a 260,000 dwt VLCC vessel open in the Middle East Gulf area. An oil producer sold 240,000mt of crude oil to receivers in Japan, to be transported in December. The current Worldscale rate in route TD3 of the BDTI (Middle East Gulf to Japan) is WS96 and the Flat rate of this route is $12.76/mt. The shipowner believes that freight rates will fall by December and would like to hedge his position in the physical market. He buys TD3 December put IMAREX Freight Options (IFOs) contracts with a strike price of WS96, at a premium of WS10/mt; that is, at a premium of $1.276/mt(= $12.76/mt x WS10/mt / 100). The total premium, therefore, is $306,240(=$1.276/mt x 240,000mt). NOS, which clears freight options on route TD3, charges the shipowner 2% of the option's premium as clearing fee; that is $6,125(=$306,240 x 2%).

Table 3.50 summarises two possible outcomes of the hedge for the shipowner, three months later, on December 31st. Assume the BDTI route TD3 has risen to WS120.

- The shipowner experiences gains in the spot market of $734,976 (=$3,674,880 – $2,939,904). Since the spot price is higher than the strike price the put option is not exercised. A loss of $312,365 (= $306,240 + $6,125), in the options market results, which is equivalent to the option's premium plus the clearing fees. Combining the freight income of $3,674,880, received in the physical market, with the loss of $312,365, made in the options market, results in an overall physical–paper cash-flow for the shipowner of $3,362,515.
- Suppose that freight rates decreased to WS85, instead. As can be seen in the table, the shipowner experiences a loss in the spot market of $336,864(=$2,603,040 – $2,939,904). Because the spot price is lower than the strike price, the put option is exercised, giving a, clearing fee and premium adjusted, payoff of $24,499 {= [(WS96 – WS85) / 100] x $12.76/mt x 240,000mt – $306,240 – $6,125}. Combining the freight income of $2,603,040 received in the physical market, with the profit of $24,499, made in the options market, results in an overall physical – paper cash-flow for the shipowner of $2,627,539.

Table 3.50. Shipowner's Tanker Freight Options Hedge

Three-Months Hedge Using Options (30th September – 31st December)	
Physical (Spot) Market	**Freight Options Market**
30th September	
Freight rate: WS96	Action: Buy December put option
Cargo size: 240,000mt, route TD3	Put strike price: WS96
Flat rate: $12.76/mt	Options premium: WS10/mt ($1.276/mt)
Freight income: $2,939,904	Options value: $306,240
(= 240,000mt x $12.76/mt x WS96 / 100)	(= 240,000mt x $12.76/mt x WS10/mt / 100)
31st December: Rising Market	
Freight rate: WS120	Strike price (WS96) < Spot price (WS120)
Freight income: $3,674,880	Action: Put option is not exercised
(= 240,000mt x $12.76/mt x WS120 / 100)	Option's payoff: -$306,240 (premium)
Gain in the spot market: $734,976	
(= $3,674,880 – $2,939,904)	
Total Freight Income (including options premium): $3,368,640 (= $3,674,880 – $306,240)	
31st December – Alternative Scenario: Falling Market	
Freight rate: WS85	Strike price (WS96) > Spot price (WS85)
Freight income: $2,603,040	Action: Exercise the put option
(= 240,000mt x $12.76/mt x WS85 / 100)	Option's payoff: $30,624 {= [(WS96 – WS85) /
Loss in the spot market: $336,864	100] x $12.76/mt x 240,000mt – $306,240}
(= $2,603,040 – $2,939,904)	
Total Freight Income (including options premium): $2,633,664 (= $2,603,040 + $30,624)	
Clearing fees: $6,125 [= 2% x (240,000mt x $12.76 x WS10 / 100)]	

3.6.2.3. Calendar Hedges for Charterers and Shipowners

This section provides examples of how freight rate risk can be hedged for periods of time longer than a single voyage, and for combinations of routes.

3.6.2.3.1. Charterer's Calendar Hedge, with Freight Call Options

It is end of the year and a charterer has a series of cargo commitments for the whole of the following year. He anticipates that freight rates will increase during the year and wishes to get protected from such rises, but at the same time exploit favourable freight rate movements that may occur. He buys a calendar-year call option on the basket of the 4 T/C BCI routes, with a strike price of $64,000/day, at a premium of $1,100/day. Settlement takes place on a monthly basis.

Table 3.51 presents the monthly settlement schedule of the contract over the year. Columns two and three of the table show the strike price and the average of the 4 T/C BCI rates used for settlement. The settlement prices for each month are calculated as the average over the number of business days of the "*basket*" of the 4 T/C BCI routes. If the (average of the 4 T/C BCI) settlement prices in a calendar month exceeds the strike price of $64,000/day, the charterer exercises the option contract and receives the difference between the settlement spot and the strike price. If the settlement price in a calendar month is below the strike price, the charterer does not exercise the respective options contracts and he just loses the up-front paid premium of $1,100/day. These monthly payoffs are shown in the fourth column of the table. For instance, during January the average of the 4 T/C BCI rates is $89,962, which is higher than the strike price of $64,000. The charterer exercises the option, which gives him a payoff of $25,962 (= $89,962 – $64,000). In order to calculate the total payoff for each month, the monthly payoff, shown in the fourth column of the table, is multiplied by the number of calendar days in the month, shown in the fifth column, to obtain the overall monthly profit, calculated in the last column of the table. Thus, January's profit is $804,822 (= $25,962 x 31 days), and so on. At the end of the year, the charterer received a cumulative total of $3,016,267, while the premium he paid was $401,000 (= $1,100/day x 365 days), resulting in a net payoff of $2,615,267(=$3,016,267 – $401,000).

Table 3.51. Monthly Settlement of a Calendar-Year Freight Option Contract

Months	Strike Price ($/day)	Average 4 T/C BCI Rates ($/day)	Monthly Profit ($/day)	No. of Days in Month	Settlement Profit ($/day)
January	$64,000	$89,962	$25,962	31	$804,822
February	$64,000	$75,799	$11,799	28	$330,372
March	$64,000	$66,814	$2,814	31	$87,234
April	$64,000	$57,306	-	30	-
May	$64,000	$45,149	-	31	-
June	$64,000	$43,551	-	30	-
July	$64,000	$65,724	$1,724	31	$53,444
August	$64,000	$66,837	$2,837	31	$87,947
September	$64,000	$67,311	$3,311	30	$99,330
October	$64,000	$77,635	$13,635	31	$422,685
November	$64,000	$97,648	$33,648	30	$1,009,440
December	$64,000	$67,903	$3,903	31	$120,993
Total			$99,633	365	$3,016,267

3.6.2.3.2. Shipowner's Calendar Hedge, with Freight Put Options

Suppose, in 2005, a shipowner is interested in purchasing two new Capesize vessels but his banker is nervous about the freight market in 2006 and only provides credit for one vessel. To resolve the issue, the banker proposes to the shipowner to buy a Cal06 put option on the 4 T/C BCI routes with a strike price of $35,000/day and term to maturity one year, at a premium of $1,000/day. This will cost for the whole calendar year $365,000 (= $1,000/day x 365 days). Settlement takes place on a monthly basis. The payoff of this option for the shipowner can be seen in Figure 3.27. If settlement freight rates fall below $35,000/day, the put option is exercised by the shipowner with a payoff of max(X – S, 0). For instance, if rates fall in January to $30,000/day the shipowner exercises the put option making max($35,000/day – $30,000/day, 0) =$5,000/day, which comes to $155,000 (= $5,000/day x 31 days). The payoff of the put option counterbalances the losses in the physical market where the vessel is hired at the lower rate of $30,000/day. As long as freight rates each month are below the exercise price of $35,000/day the shipowner exercises the put option, resulting in cash inflows, otherwise the option in not exercised.

This is the kind of risk, emanating from the freight market fall that the shipowner's banker was worried about. He successfully advised his client to hedge his freight income, for the first year of his loan, thus reducing the probability of not honoring his loan obligations. Thus, freight rate options may be viewed as insurance against falling freight rates; a premium is paid to buy the put option, in order to get compensated, in case freight rates turn against the holder of the option.

Figure 3.27. The Trading Positions of a Freight Put Option

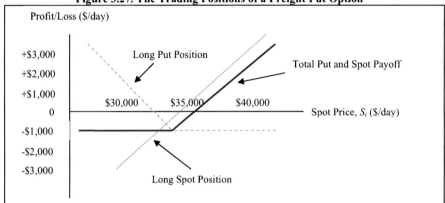

3.6.3. Freight Options Strategies for Investment Purposes
A great number of investors use options without having an exposure in the underlying "*commodity*"/"*asset*". That is, they use options not for hedging but for investment purposes. This section of the chapter considers the payoffs that may be obtained from investment strategies with options. It is assumed that the options positions taken involve options on the same underlying "*commodity*"/"*asset*". A distinction is made between strategies which involve options of the same type (e.g. two or more calls or two or more puts) known as spread strategies, and combinations of options of different type (e.g. both calls and puts on the same underlying asset). Moreover, it is assumed that the options used in the strategies we discuss are European. American options may lead to slightly different outcomes because of the possibility of early exercise. One of the attractions of options is that they can be used to create a wide range of different payoff functions. The most widely used options strategies for investment purposes are outlined next.

3.6.3.1. Options Spread Strategies
Spread strategies involve portfolios of options of the same type with either different strike prices or different expiration dates.
- **Bull and Bear Spreads**: involve two or more calls (or puts) with different strike prices and the same time to expiration.
- **Butterfly Spreads**: involve three call or three put options with three different strike prices and the same time to expiration.
- **Calendar (or Time) Spreads**: involve either call or put options with the same strike price but different times to expiration.

- **Diagonal Spreads**: involve options with different strike prices and different times to expiration.

Applications of these strategies are considered next.

3.6.3.1.1. Bull Call Spreads (or Supercaps)

Bull call spreads can be constructed by buying a call option on an "*asset*" at premium c_1, with a strike price X_1 and selling a call option at premium c_2, with a strike price X_2, where X_2 is greater than X_1. The time to expiration of the two calls is the same. Figure 3.28 shows the profits/losses of each call option and of the overall portfolio (solid line) position. Since call premiums (prices) are inversely proportional to their strike prices, $c_1 > c_2$, which means that the strategy requires a net investment of c_1-c_2. As can be observed in the figure, the strategy produces a certain level of profits, when the price of the underlying asset increases. Also, losses are limited when the price of the underlying asset falls, as can be seen by the position of the solid line, lying below the horizontal axis. The profits/losses of these positions are also shown in Table 3.52.

Figure 3.28. The Trading Positions in a Bull Call Spread

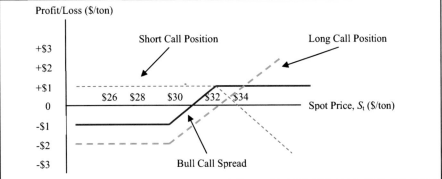

To see why an investor would use a bull strategy, consider a charterer who bought a freight call option at a premium $c_1 = \$2/\text{ton}$ with a strike price $X_1 = \$30/\text{ton}$, in order to protect himself against a freight rate rise. He may be willing to limit his profit potential by selling a call option at a premium $c_2 = \$1/\text{ton}$ with a strike price $X_2=\$32/\text{ton}$. In return for limiting his profit potential to $(X_2 - X_1) + (c_2 - c_1) = \$2/\text{ton} - \$1/\text{ton} = \$1/\text{ton}$, he receives the call's premium of $c_2 = \$1$. The maximum loss that may arise from this strategy is also limited to $c_2 - c_1$, that is, to $\$1/\text{ton}$. Notice that the payoffs from this strategy depend on how much in-the-money or out-of-the-money are the options which are used. That is, when both calls are initially in-the-money they are expensive and the potential profit and loss is high. When one call is in-the-money and the other is out-of-the-money the profit margins are narrower, and they narrow even further when both calls are initially out-of-the-money. Thus, whenever investors expect prices to increase, they can put a floor under their potential losses and simultaneously a ceiling over their potential profits.

Table 3.52. Profits under a Bull Call Spread

Freight Rate	Long Call Profit	Short Call Profit	Total Profit
$S_T \geq X_2$	$S_T - 30 - 2$	$32 - S_T + 1$	$(32 - 31) + (1 - 2)$
$X_1 < S_T < X_2$	$S_T - 30 - 2$	$+1$	$(S_T - 31) + (1 - 2)$
$S_T \leq X_1$	-2	$+1$	$1 - 2 = -1$

Note: $X_1 = \$30/\text{ton}$, $X_2 = \$32/\text{ton}$, $c_1 = \$2/\text{ton}$ and $c_2 = \$1/\text{ton}$.

Alternatively, investors can create a bull spread with puts. This can be observed in Figure 3.29. They can write a put with a higher strike price (X_2) receiving a premium p_2 and buying a put with a lower strike price (X_1), paying a premium p_1, where $p_2 > p_1$. The difference between a vertical bull spread with calls and the one with puts is that the latter results in net income, as the bought put is less expensive than the written put.

Figure 3.29. The Trading Positions in a Bull Put Spread

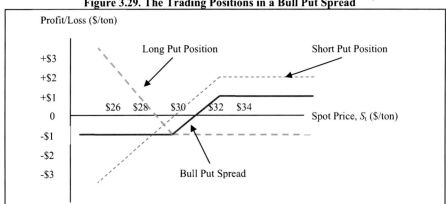

3.6.3.1.2. Bear Call Spreads (or Superfloors)

Investors who expect prices to fall can create bear call spreads by writing a call, say with a strike price $X_1 = \$30$/ton, at a premium of $c_1 = \$2$/ton and buying a call with a strike price $X_2 = \$32$/ton, at a premium of $c_2 = \$1$/ton. The profit/loss from this strategy can be seen in Figure 3.30. The strategy involves an initial cash inflow, as the call bought is cheaper than the one sold. Under this strategy, the maximum profits and losses are limited and investors get protected from a fall in the market. Table 3.53 presents the profits/losses and the positions of the bear call spread. To see why an investor would enter such strategy, consider a charterer who bought a freight call option at $X_2 = \$32$/ton, in order to get protected against freight rate increases. His expectations change due to new information that becomes available to him and sells a freight call option at a strike price of $X_1 = \$30$/ton. If prices fall, he ends up with a profit from his option's positions.

Table 3.53. Profits under a Bear Call Spread

Freight Rate	Long Call Profit	Short Call Profit	Total Profit
$S_T \geq X_2$	$S_T - 32 - 1$	$30 - S_T + 2$	$-(32 - 30) + (2 - 1)$
$X_1 < S_T < X_2$	-1	$30 - S_T + 2$	$-(S_T - 30) + (2 - 1)$
$S_T \leq X_1$	-1	$+2$	$2 - 1 = +1$

Note: $X_1 = \$30$/ton, $X_2 = \$32$/ton, $c_1 = \$2$/ton and $c_2 = \$1$/ton.

As another example, consider a shipowner who sold a call option with a strike price $X_1 = \$30$/ton, receiving $c_1 = \$2$/ton as premium, in order to get protected against freight rate decreases in the physical market. He buys a call with a strike price $X_2 = \$32$/ton at a premium of $c_2 = \$1$/ton. An initial cash inflow results, due to the difference in call option premiums. The strategy protects the shipowner against a freight rate decrease but at the same time limits his potential profits. As can be seen in Table 3.53, maximum profits of $(c_1 - c_2) = \$1$/ton are received when freight rates (S)

234

are lower than $X_1 = \$30$/ton. The losses from the options positions are also limited to $(X_1 - X_2) + (c_1 - c_2) = -\$1$, and are incurred when $S > X_2 = \$32$/ton.

Figure 3.30. The Trading Positions in a Bear Call Spread

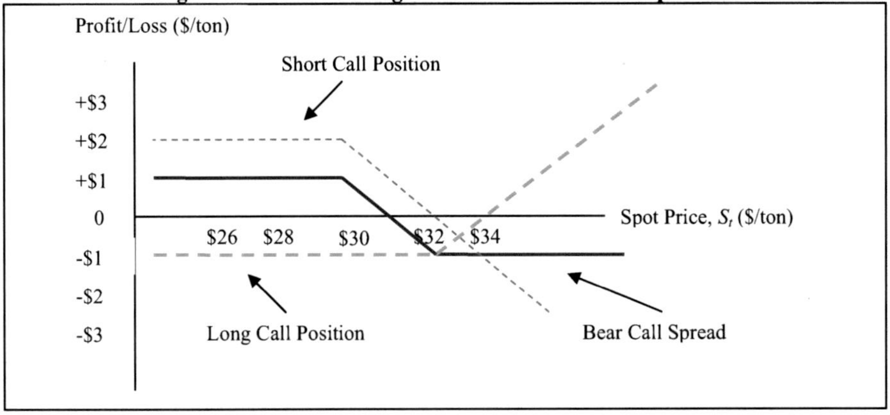

Profit/Loss ($/ton)

Short Call Position

Long Call Position

Bear Call Spread

Spot Price, S_t ($/ton)

Alternatively, investors can create a vertical bear spread with puts. They can buy a put at premium p_2, with a strike price X_2 which is higher than the strike price X_1 ($X_1 < X_2$) of the written put. The premium of the latter is p_1, where $p_2 > p_1$. The payoffs of the bear spread, created with puts, can be observed in Figure 3.31. The difference between a bear spread with calls and one with puts is that the latter results in net costs, as the put bought is more expensive than the one sold.

Figure 3.31. The Trading Positions in a Bear Put Spread

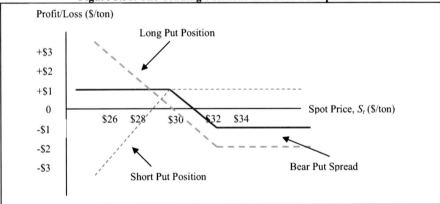

Profit/Loss ($/ton)

Long Put Position

Short Put Position

Bear Put Spread

Spot Price, S_t ($/ton)

3.6.3.1.3. Butterfly Spreads

Investors, who are uncertain about the direction of the spot market, expect low volatility in prices of the underlying commodity and want to limit the unlimited loss potentials on both the upside and the downside, can create a butterfly spread. The strategy involves the purchase of two call options with strike prices X_1 and X_3, where $X_3 > X_1$, at prices, say, c_1 and c_3, respectively, and the sale of two call options at premium c_2, with a strike price $X_2 = (X_1 + X_3)/2$.

Figure 3.32 and Table 3.54 show the profit/loss outcomes for a shipowner or a charterer, from such a strategy, where $X_1 = \$30$/ton, $X_2 = \$31$/ton, $X_3 = \$32$/ton, with premiums $c_1 = \$2/ton$, $c_2 = \$1.2/ton$ and $c_3 = \$1/ton$, all with duration of six months. Maximum profit is obtained when $S = X_2 = \$31/ton$, which is $\$0.4/ton$. Maximum loss is incurred when $S < X_1 = \$30/ton$ or when $S > X_3 = \$32/ton$, which is $(c_1 - 2 \times c_2 + c_3)$ $= \$0.6/ton$.

Figure 3.32. The Trading Positions in a Long Call Butterfly Spread

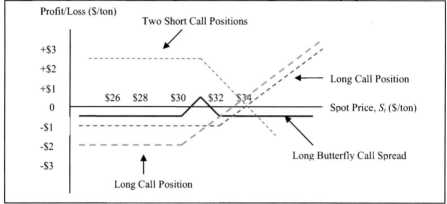

Table 3.54. Profits under a Long Call Butterfly Spread

Freight Rate ($/ton)	Long Call Profit ($/ton) $X_1 = \$30/ton$	Two Short Calls' Profit ($/ton) $X_2 = \$31/ton$	Long Call Profit ($/ton) $X_3 = \$32/ton$	Total Profit ($/ton)
$S_T \leq 30$	-2	$+2.4$	-1	-0.6
$30 < S_T \leq 31$	$S_T - 30 - 2$	$+2.4$	-1	$S_T - 30 - 0.6$
$31 < S_T \leq 32$	$S_T - 30 - 2$	$-2(S_T - 31) + 2.4$	-1	$32 - S_T - 0.6$
$S_T > 32$	$S_T - 30 - 2$	$-2(S_T - 31) + 2.4$	$S_T - 32 - 1$	-0.6

Note: $X_1 = \$30/ton$, $X_2 = \$31/ton$, $X_3 = \$32/ton$, $c_1 = \$2/ton$, $c_2 = \$1.2/ton$, $c_3 = \$1/ton$.

Butterfly spreads can also be constructed by buying two put options with exercise prices X_1 and X_3, where $X_3 > X_1$, and selling two puts with a strike price $X_2 = (X_1 + X_3)/2$. As can be seen in Figure 3.33, the butterfly put spread has the same profits/losses as the butterfly spread created with calls.

Figure 3.33. The Trading Positions in a Long Put Butterfly Spread

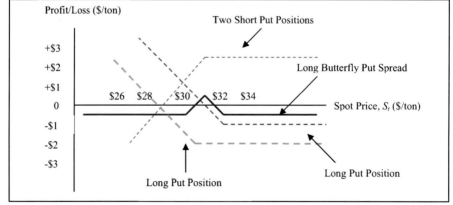

Say market conditions change within the six months period of the options maturity. That is, say the volatility in the freight market is expected to rise. The butterfly spread can be sold by reversing the initial positions. That is, call options with strike prices $X_1=\$30$/ton and $X_3 = \$32$/ton are sold and two call options with exercise price $X_2=\$31$/ton are bought. If there is a significant movement in the prices of freight rates, the strategy can produce a profit. This can be seen in Figure 3.34.

Figure 3.34. The Trading Positions in a Short Call Butterfly Spread

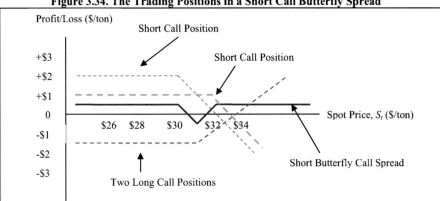

3.6.3.1.4. Calendar Spreads

There are three different kinds of calendar spreads:
  a) neutral calendar spreads, which are constructed with either call or put options, with strike prices very close to the underlying spot price;
  b) bullish calendar spreads, which are constructed with either call or put options that have strike prices which are higher than the underlying spot price; and
  c) bearish calendar spreads, which are constructed with either call or put options that have strike prices which are lower than the spot price of the asset.

The profit patterns these strategies produce are very similar to those of the butterfly spread. Thus, they are appropriate when volatility in the price of the underlying commodity is expected to be low, up until the expiration of the strategy.

Figure 3.35. The Trading Positions in a Calendar Call Spread

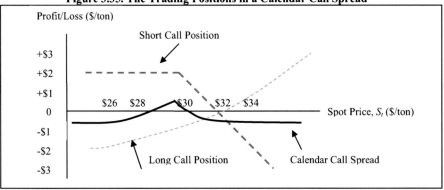

As can be observed in Figure 3.35 and Table 3.55, the strategy can be created by writing a call with time to expiration T_1 and buying a call with time to expiration T_2, where $T_2 > T_1$. The longer the maturity of the call contract, the higher is its price. Thus, the premium c_1 of the short call is smaller than the premium of the long call, c_2, requiring an initial cash outflow to set up the strategy. Maximum profit is received when the write call expires and the position that remains (the long call with time value ε – where ε is a small number) will give higher long-term profits, the higher is S in comparison to X. Maximum loss is incurred before the write call expires (before T_1) and the loss is limited if S is away from X in any direction. After the write call expires (after T_1), the loss is the cost of the strategy $(c_1 - c_2)$.

Table 3.55. Profits under a Calendar Call Spread

Freight Rate	Long Call Profits	Short Call Profits	Total Profits
$S_T > X$	$S_T - X + \varepsilon - c_1$	$-(S_T - X) + c_2$	$\approx \varepsilon + (c_2 - c_1)$
$S_T \leq X$	$\approx -c_1$	$\approx +c_2$	$\approx +(c_2 - c_1)$

Calendar spreads may also be constructed by buying a put option with exercise price X and maturity T_2, and selling a put option with the same strike price but lower maturity T_1, where $T_1 < T_2$. The profit/loss patterns of the calendar put strategy are displayed in Figure 3.36.

Figure 3.36. The Trading Positions in a Calendar Put Spread

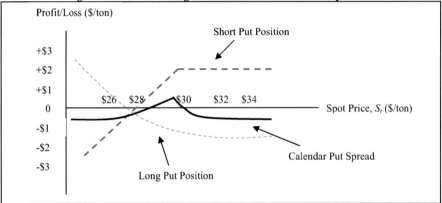

3.6.3.2. Options Combination Strategies
Combination strategies involve portfolios of options of different types, with the same or different strike prices and the same or different expiration dates. The most common ones are:

- **Bottom Straddles (or straddle purchases)** involve the simultaneous buying of a call and a put, with the same time to expiration and the same strike price. Investors applying this strategy expect significant volatility in spot prices, but have no feeling about the direction (up or down) of the move in prices.
- **Top Straddles (or straddle write)** involve the simultaneous selling of a call and a put, with the same time to expiration and the same strike price. Investors applying this strategy expect small movements in prices of the underlying commodity.
- **Bottom Strips** involve the simultaneous buying of one call and two puts with the same strike price and expiration date. A bottom strip strategy may be used by investors who expect a large spot price movement, but believe that a decrease in spot prices is more likely than an increase; as a result, they buy more put than call options.

238

- **Top Strips** involve the simultaneous selling of one call and two puts with the same strike price and expiration date. A top strip strategy is used when spot prices are expected to fluctuate in a narrow range, but if they move beyond the range, they would move upward; thus, they sell more put than call options.
- **Bottom Straps** involve the simultaneous buying of two calls and one put, with the same strike price and expiration date. A bottom strap strategy may be used by investors who expect that an increase in spot prices is more likely than a decrease, so they buy more call than put options.
- **Top Straps** involve the simultaneous selling of two calls and one put, with the same strike price and expiration date. A top strap strategy may be used by investors who expect the spot prices to fluctuate in a narrow range, but also believe that in case spot prices move beyond the range, they would move downward; thus, they sell more call than put options.
- **Bottom Strangles (or bottom vertical combination)** involve the simultaneous buying of a call and a put with the same time to expiration and different strike prices. Investors applying this strategy expect significant volatility in spot prices, but have no feeling about the direction (up or down) of the move in prices.
- **Top Strangles (or top vertical combination)** involve the simultaneous selling of a call and a put, with the same time to expiration and different strike prices. Investors, expecting some volatility in spot prices, where prices are expected to stay within a certain range, apply this strategy.

Table 3.56 summarises the combination strategies of straddles, strangles, strips and straps in terms of the market expectation, volatility, and time decay.

Table 3.56. Summary of the Straddles, Strangles, Strips and Straps Options Strategies

Strategy Type	Market Expectation	Rising Volatility	Passage of Time	Profit Potential	Loss Potential
Long Straddle / Strangle Long Strip / Strap	Volatile	Favourable	Unfavourable	Unlimited	Limited
Short Straddle / Strangle Short Strip / Strap	Stagnant	Unfavourable	Favourable	Limited	Unlimited

The following examples illustrate how the above combination strategies may be applied in the shipping industry.

3.6.3.2.1. Bottom (or Long) Straddles (or Straddle Purchases)
In a long (or bottom) straddle investors buy calls and puts, which have the same at-the-money strike price and expire on the same date. This strategy is used when significant volatility of the underlying spot price is expected, but the direction of the move in prices is uncertain. As can be observed in Figure 3.37 and in Table 3.57, which display the profit/loss of the strategy, the maximum loss is limited to the sum of the premiums of the call and the put. The maximum profit is unlimited if S moves away from X in either direction.

Table 3.57. Profits of the Shipowner's Bottom Straddle

Freight Rate	Long Call Profit	Long Put Profit	Total Profit
$S_T > X$ (large rise in freight rates)	$S_T - X - c$ $= S_T - 30 - 2$	$-p = -1.4$	$S_T - X - (c + p)$ $= S_T - 30 - 3.4$
$S_T \leq X$ (large fall in freight rates)	$-c = -2$	$X - S_T - p$ $= 30 - S_T - 1.4$	$X - S_T - (c + p)$ $= 30 - S_T - 3.4$

Note: X = $30/ton, c = $2/ton, p = $1.4/ton.

Consider a situation, under which the current freight rate on the voyage route P2 of the BPI stands at $S = \$30$/ton, and a shipowner believes that freight rates will change substantially during the next two months, but does not know in which direction. In order to take advantage of the situation he purchases a long straddle. That is, he buys a call with time to expiration two months with a strike price $X = \$30$/ton, trading at a premium of $c_1 = \$2$/ton and a put option with the same maturity and strike price, trading at $p_1 = \$1.4$/ton. As can be observed in the table and the figure, the strategy results in a profit if freight rates are much lower or much higher than \$30/ton. In the first case, the profit is $\$[30 - S - (c + p)]$/ton, with the put option being exercised. When S is much higher than $X = \$30$/ton, the call option is exercised and the profit becomes $\$[S - 30 - (c + p)]$/ton. The maximum loss from this strategy occurs if freight rates in two months time are equal (or near) to \$30/ton. In this case, the loss is the sum of the option's premiums; that is, \$3.4/ton (= \$2/ton + \$1.4/ton).

Figure 3.37. The Trading Positions in a Bottom (Long) Straddle

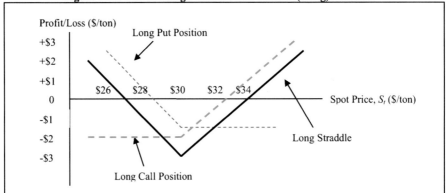

3.6.3.2.2. Top (or Short) Straddles (or Straddle Writes)

A short (or top) straddle or straddle write strategy is employed, when small movements of the underlying price are expected. In this case, investors write a call and a put with identical at-the-money strike price (X) and the same time to expiration. As can be observed in Figure 3.38 and Table 3.58, short straddles produce profits in a stable underlying market with low volatility in prices. The maximum profit is the sum of the premiums of the call and the put received. The danger with this strategy is that losses are "*unlimited*", when prices turn out to be well away from the exercise price at the expiration of the contracts.

Table 3.58. Losses of the Shipowner's Top Straddle

Freight Rate	Short Call Loss	Short Put Loss	Total Loss
$S_T > X$ (rise in freight rates)	$-(S_T - X) + c$ $= -(S_T - 30) + 2$	$+p = +1.4$	$-(S_T - X) + (c + p)$ $= -(S_T - 30) + 3.4$
$S_T \leq X$ (fall in freight rates)	$+c = +2$	$-(X - S_T) + p$ $= -(30 - S_T) + 1.4$	$-(X - S_T) + (c + p)$ $= -(30 - S_T) + 3.4$

Note: $X = \$30$/ton, $c = \$2$/ton, $p = \$1.4$/ton.

Consider a situation, under which the current freight rate on the voyage route P2 of the BPI stands at $S = \$30$/ton, and a shipowner believes that freight rates will not change substantially during the next two months. In order to take advantage of the situation he purchases a short straddle. That is, he sells a call with time to expiration two months with a strike price $X = \$30$/ton, trading at a premium of $c_1 = \$2$/ton and a put option with the same maturity and strike price, trading at p_1 = $1.4/ton. As can be observed in the table and the figure, the strategy results in a loss if freight rates are much lower or much higher than $30/ton. In the first case, the loss is $[-(30 − S) + (c+p)]/ton, with the short put option being exercised. When S is much higher than X=$30/ton, the short call option is exercised and the loss becomes $[-(S − 30) + (c+p)]/ton. The maximum profit from this strategy occurs if freight rates in two months time are equal (or near) to $30/ton; In this case, the profit is the sum of the option's premiums; that is, $3.4/ton (= $2/ton + $1.4/ton).

Figure 3.38. The Trading Positions in a Top (Short) Straddle

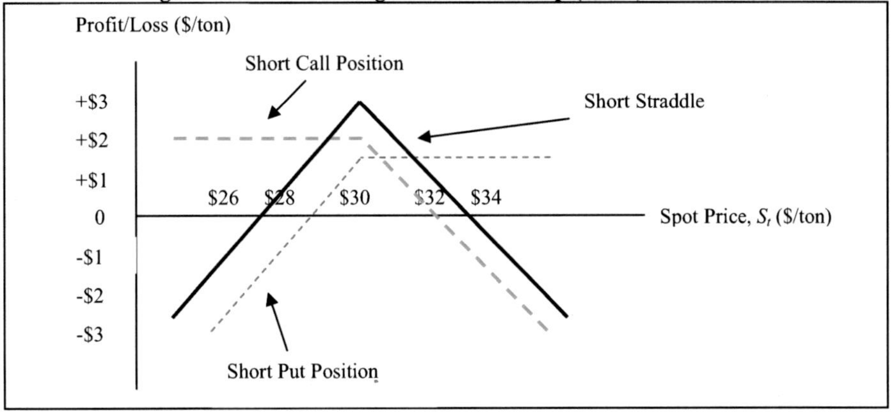

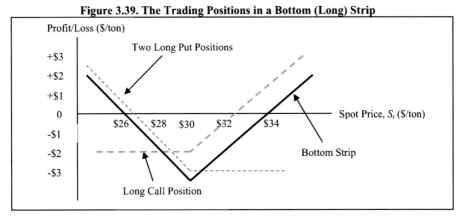

3.6.3.2.3. Bottom (or Long) Strips

In a bottom strip investors buy one call and two puts, which have the same at-the-money strike price and expire on the same date. This strategy is used when significant spot price movements are expected, but a decrease in spot prices is more likely than an increase. As can be observed in Figure 3.39 and Table 3.59, which display the profit/loss of the strategy, the maximum loss is limited to the sum of the premiums of the option positions. The maximum profit is unlimited if S moves away from X in either direction, but it is higher if spot prices decrease.

Figure 3.39. The Trading Positions in a Bottom (Long) Strip

Consider a situation, under which the current freight rate on the voyage route P2 of the BPI stands at S = $30/ton. A shipowner believes that freight rates will change substantially during the next two months, but a decrease in freight rates is more probable than an increase. In order to take advantage of the situation he purchases a bottom strip. That is, he buys a call with time to expiration two months, with a strike price X = $30/ton trading at premium c = $2/ton. He also buys two put options with the same maturity and strike price as the call, trading at p = $1.4/ton. As can be observed in the figure and in the table, the strategy results in a profit if freight rates are much lower or much higher than $30/ton, but the profit is higher in case freight rates are much lower than $30/ton. When S is much lower than X = $30/ton, the two put options are exercised, producing a profit of $[2(X − S_T) − (c + 2p)]/ton = $[2(30 − S_T) − 4.8]/ton. When S is higher than X = $30/ton, the call option is exercised and the profit becomes $[S_T − X − (c + 2p)]/ton = $[S_T − 30 − 4.8]/ton. The maximum loss from this strategy occurs if freight rates in two months time are equal (or near) to $30/ton. In this case, the loss is the sum of the options premiums; that is, $4.8/ton (=$2/ton + 2 x $1.4/ton).

Table 3.59. Profits of the Shipowner's Bottom Strip

Freight Rate	Long Call Profit	Two Long Puts' Profit	Total Profit
$S_T > X$ (large rise in freight rates)	$S_T − X − c$ = $S_T − 30 − 2$	$−2p = −2.8$	$S_T − X − (c + 2p)$ = $S_T − 30 − 4.8$
$S_T \leq X$ (large fall in freight rates)	$−c = −2$	$2(X − S_T) − 2p$ = $2(30 − S_T) − 2.8$	$2(X − S_T) − (c + 2p)$ = $2(30 − S_T) − 4.8$

Note: X = $30/ton, c = $2/ton, p = $1.4/ton.

3.6.3.2.4. Top (or Short) Strips

A top strip is employed, when movements of the underlying price are expected to stay in a narrow range, but if prices move beyond the range, they are likely to move upwards. In this case, investors write a call and two puts with identical at-the-money strike price (X) and the same time to expiration. As can be observed in Figure 3.40 and Table 3.60, top strips produce profits in a stable underlying market with low volatility in prices. For up movement in prices, for the solid line to fall below the horizontal axis (i.e. results in losses) it needs a larger increase in prices, in comparison to a fall in prices with the resultant fall of the left tail of the solid line below the horizontal axis. The maximum profit is the sum of the premiums of the call and the two puts received. The danger with this options strategy is that losses are *"unlimited"*, in case prices turn out to be well away from the exercise price at the expiration of the contracts.

Figure 3.40. The Trading Positions in a Top (Short) Strip

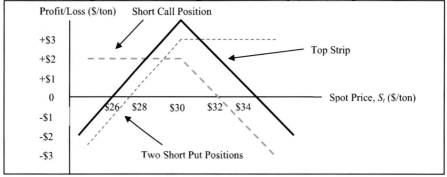

Consider a situation, under which the current freight rate on the voyage route P2 of the BPI stands at $S = \$30$/ton. A shipowner believes that freight rates will not change substantially during the next two months, but an increase in freight rates is more probable than a decrease. In order to take advantage of the situation he purchases a top strip. That is, he writes a call with time to expiration two months, with a strike price $X = \$30$/ton trading at premium $c = \$2$/ton. He also writes two put options with the same maturity and strike price as the short call, trading at $p = \$1.4$/ton. As can be observed in the figure and in the table, the strategy results in a loss if freight rates are much lower or much higher than 30/ton. When S is much lower than $X = \$30$/ton, the two short put options are exercised, producing a loss of $\$[-2(X - S_T) + (c + 2p)]$/ton = $\$[-2(30 - S_T) + 4.8]$/ton. When S is higher than $X = \$30$/ton, the short call option is exercised and the loss becomes $\$[-(S_T - X) + (c + 2p)]$/ton = $\$[-(S_T - 30) + 4.8]$/ton. The maximum profit from this strategy occurs if freight rates in two months time are equal (or near) to 30/ton. In this case, the profit is the sum of the options premiums; that is, $\$4.8$/ton (=$\$2$/ton + 2 x $\$1.4$/ton).

Table 3.60. Losses of the Shipowner's Top Strip

Freight Rate	Short Call Loss	Two Long Puts' Loss	Total Loss
$S_T > X$ (rise in freight rates)	$-(S_T - X) + c$ $= -(S_T - 30) + 2$	$+2p = +2.8$	$-(S_T - X) + (c + 2p)$ $= -(S_T - 30) + 4.8$
$S_T \leq X$ (fall in freight rates)	$+c = +2$	$-2(X - S_T) + 2p$ $= -2(30 - S_T) + 2.8$	$-2(X - S_T) + (c + 2p)$ $= -2(30 - S_T) + 4.8$

Note: $X = \$30$/ton, $c = \$2$/ton, $p = \$1.4$/ton.

3.6.3.2.5. Bottom (or Long) Straps
In a bottom strap investors buy two calls and one put, which have the same at-the-money strike price and expire on the same date. This strategy is used when significant spot price movements are expected, but an increase in spot prices is more likely than a decrease. As can be observed in Figure 3.41 and Table 3.61, which display the profit/loss of the strategy, the maximum loss is limited to the sum of the premiums of the option positions. The maximum profit is "*unlimited*" if S moves away from X in either direction, but is higher if spot prices increase.

Figure 3.41. The Trading Positions in a Bottom (Long) Strap

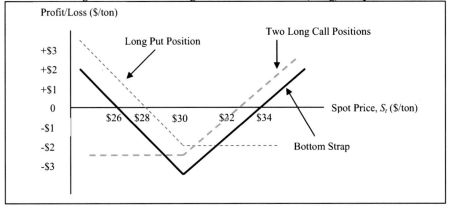

Consider a situation, under which the current freight rate on the voyage route P2 of the BPI stands at $S = \$30$/ton, and a charterer believes that freight rates will change substantially during the next two months, but an increase in freight rates is more probable than a decrease. In order to take advantage of the situation he purchases a bottom strap. That is, he buys two calls with time to expiration two months with a strike price X = $30/ton trading at a premium of c = $1.4/ton and a put option with the same maturity and strike price, trading at p = $2/ton. As can be observed in the figure and in the table, the strategy results in a profit if freight rates are much lower or much higher than $30/ton, but the profit is higher in case freight rates are much higher than $30/ton. That is, the solid line intersects the horizontal axis at a point to the right of X, which is further away from X than the point of intersection to the left of X. When S is lower than X = $30/ton, the profit is $[X − S − (2c + p)]/ton = $(30 − S − 4.8)/ton, with the put option being exercised. When S is higher than X = $30/ton, the two call options are exercised and the profit becomes $[2(S − X) − (2c + p)]/ton = $[2(S − 30) − 4.8]/ton. The maximum loss from this strategy occurs if freight rates in two months time are equal (or near) to $30/ton; In this case, the loss is the sum of the options premiums; that is, $4.8/ton (= $2/ton + 2 x $1.4/ton).

Table 3.61. Profits of the Shipowner's Bottom Strap

Freight Rate	Long Calls Profit	Long Put Profit	Total Profit
$S_T > X$	$2(S_T − X) − 2c$	$−p = −2$	$2(S_T − X) − (2c + p)$
(large rise in freight rates)	$= 2(S_T − 30) − 2.8$		$= 2(S_T − 30) − 4.8$
$S_T ≤ X$	$−2c = −2.8$	$X − S_T − p$	$X − S_T − (2c + p)$
(large fall in freight rates)		$= 30 − S_T − 2$	$= 30 − S_T − 4.8$

Note: X = $30/ton, c = $1.4/ton, p = $2/ton.

3.6.3.2.6. Top (or Short) Straps

A top strap is employed, when movements in prices of the underlying commodity are expected to be in a narrow range, but in case prices move beyond the range, they are more likely to move downwards than upwards. In this case, investors write two calls and one put with identical at-the-money strike price (X) and the same time to expiration. As can be observed in Figure 3.42 and Table 3.62, top straps produce profits in a stable underlying market with low volatility in prices. The left tail of the solid line cuts the horizontal axis further out to the left of the strike price of the options than the right tail does. The maximum profit is the sum of the premiums of the two calls and the put received. The danger with this strategy is that losses are "*unlimited*", in case prices turn out to be well away from the exercise price at the expiration of the contracts.

Figure 3.42. The Trading Positions in a Top (Short) Strap

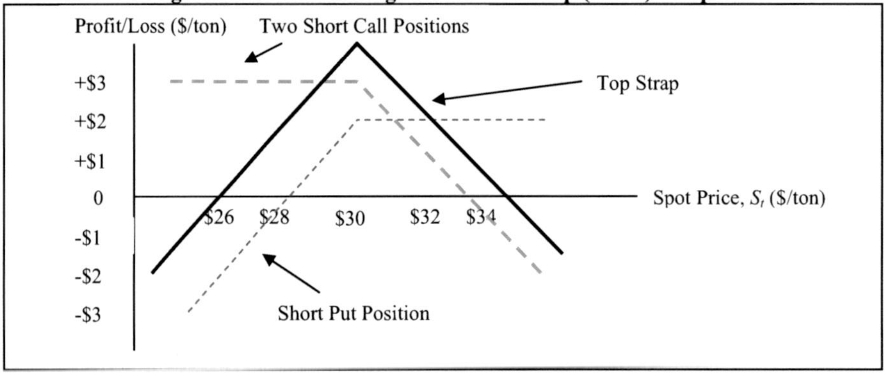

Consider a situation, under which the current freight rate on the voyage route P2 of the BPI stands at S = $30/ton, and a charterer believes that freight rates will not change substantially during the next two months, but a decrease in freight rates is more probable than an increase. In order to take advantage of the situation he purchases a top strap; that is, he writes two calls with time to expiration two months with a strike price X = $30/ton trading at a premium of c = $1.4/ton and a put option with the same maturity and strike price, trading at p = $2/ton. As can be observed in the figure and in the table, the strategy results in a loss if freight rates are much lower or much higher than $30/ton. When S is lower than X = $30/ton, the loss is $[– (X – S) + (2c + p)]/ton = $[– (30 – S) + 4.8]/ton, with the short put option being exercised. When S is higher than X = $30/ton, the two short call options are exercised and the loss becomes $[–2(S – X) + (2c + p)]/ton = $[–2(S – 30) + 4.8]/ton. The maximum profit from this options strategy occurs if freight rates in two months time are equal (or near) to $30/ton. In this case, the profit is the sum of the option's premiums; that is, $4.8/ton (= $2/ton + 2 x $1.4/ton).

Table 3.62. Losses of the Shipowner's Top Strap

Freight Rate	Short Calls Loss	Short Put Loss	Total Loss
$S_T > X$ (large rise in freight rates)	$-2(S_T - X) + 2c$ $= -2(S_T - 30) + 2.8$	$+p = +2$	$-2(S_T - X) + (2c + p)$ $= -2(S_T - 30) + 4.8$
$S_T \leq X$ (large fall in freight rates)	$+2c = +2.8$	$-(X - S_T) + p$ $= -(30 - S_T) + 2$	$-(X - S_T) + (2c + p)$ $= -(30 - S_T) + 4.8$

Note: X = $30/ton, c = $1.4/ton, p = $2/ton.

3.6.3.2.7. Bottom (or Long) Strangles (or Bottom Vertical Combination)

In a long (or bottom) strangle or bottom vertical combination, investors buy an out-of-the-money call, with a strike price, say X_2 = $32/ton, and an out-of-the-money put, with a strike price, say X_1 = $30/ton, where $X_1 < X_2$, and the same time to expiration T. The profits/losses from this strategy are presented in Figure 3.43 and the associated Table 3.63. As can be observed, investors make profits out of this strategy when freight rates move substantially, below the lower strike price X_1 or above the higher strike price X_2. In between they make losses. Thus, investors undertaking this strategy expect high volatility of the underlying spot price but do not know the direction of the change in price. In that sense, the strategy is similar to a long straddle. The difference is that here a higher volatility in prices is expected and this is reflected in the wider opening of the sides of the strangle; the larger the difference in the strike prices, X_1 and X_2, the larger this opening can be, and reflects expectations of higher volatility levels. Also, as can be observed in the same figure, the downside of a strangle, which occurs when spot prices turn out to be between the strike prices, is larger, compared to a straddle.

Figure 3.43. The Trading Positions in a Long Bottom (Long) Strangle

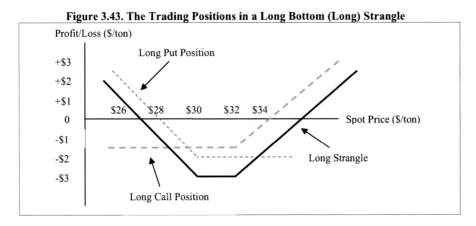

Table 3.63. Profits/Losses Under a Bottom Strangle

Freight Rate	Long Call	Long Put	Total Outcome
$S_T \leq X_1$	$-c$	$X_1 - S_T - p$	$(X_1 - S_T) - (c + p)$
$X_1 < S_T < X_2$	$-c$	$-p$	$-(c + p)$
$S_T \geq X_2$	$S_T - X_2 - c$	$-p$	$(S_T - X_2) - (c + p)$

Note: $X_1 = \$30$/ton, $X_2 = \$32$/ton.

3.6.3.2.8. Top (or Short) Strangle (or Top Vertical Combination)

Similar to a straddle, a short (or top) strangle or top vertical combination may be assumed by investors, who expect stable prices with low volatility of the underlying freight rates. They can sell an out-of-the-money call with a strike price X_2 and an out-of-the-money put with a strike price X_1, where $X_2 > X_1$. The profits/losses from this strategy are presented in Figure 3.44 and the associated Table 3.64. At expiration, if the underlying price lies in between the put's lower strike price and the call's higher strike price, profit is at its maximum and is equal to the sum of the call and the put premium received through the sale of these options. However, the maximum loss is "*unlimited*", when volatility turns out to be high and prices move well above or below the exercise prices of the call and the put, respectively.

Figure 3.44. The Trading Positions in a Top (Short) Strangle

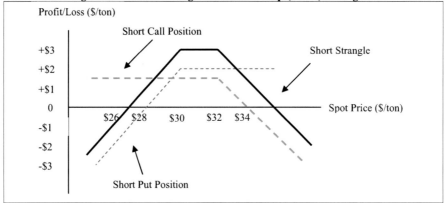

Table 3.64. Profits/Losses Under a Top Strangle

Freight Rate	Short Call	Short Put	Total Outcome
$S_T \leq X_1$	$+c$	$-(X_1 - S_T) + p$	$-(X_1 - S_T) + (c + p)$
$X_1 < S_T < X_2$	$+c$	$+p$	$+(c + p)$
$S_T \geq X_2$	$-(S_T - X_2) + c$	$+p$	$-(S_T - X_2) + (c + p)$

Note: $X_1 = \$30$/ton, $X_2 = \$32$/ton.

3.6.4. Freight Options Strategies for Arbitrage Purposes

The term arbitrage denotes strategies providing a return that is higher than the risk-free rate of interest, without taking extra risks and without committing extra capital. Arbitrage may take the form of the simultaneous purchase and sale of the same underlying asset, which is quoted at different prices in different markets. The underlying asset is bought at the market with the cheaper price and, at the same time, sold at the market with the higher price. The difference is locked in as a risk-free profit. In a perfectly efficient market it would be impossible to earn a risk-free return that is higher than the risk-free interest rate. Arbitrage takes advantage of the existence of price discrepancies and continues to be utilized by market agents until the price discrepancies have been eliminated. This type of transactions can be carried out only if transactions costs (including taxes) and opportunity costs are low.

A risk-free position may be created through the purchase and sale of positions characterised by the same rights and obligations if these positions are traded at different prices. This is mostly done by creating synthetic positions with the use of the put-call parity relationship, investigated in Chapter 2 of this book. The ability to create synthetic positions implies that if at any time options prices become mispriced, traders will buy the undervalued position and sell the equivalent overvalued position. There are three commonly used arbitrage options strategies: the **conversions**, the **reversals**, and the **boxes**. These are examined next.

3.6.4.1. Conversions
The conversion arbitrage options strategy is constructed by buying the underlying asset using an actual FFA contract and selling it at the same time by means of a synthetic FFA contract (with the use of the put-call parity relationship), which consists of a purchased put and a written call. Arbitrage is possible when the underlying can be sold at a price that is higher than the price at which is bought; that is, when the synthetic FFA price is higher than the actual FFA price. In effect, arbitrage occurs because the physical underlying position is bought at a fair price and the synthetic position is sold at an overvalued price, locking in a risk-free return. Taking into account the costs of the transactions and capital opportunity costs, the relationship is:

[(Call option premium + Interest up to expiration) > [FFA price + (Transactions costs − (Put option premium + Interest up to expiration)   + Interest up to expiration)] + Strike price]

Example:
Suppose that the freight rate on route P3 of the BPI is $65.5/ton and the three-month (90 days) FFA contract is trading at $66/ton. In the market a $64.5/ton freight call option on route P3 is trading at a cost of $10/ton and a $64.5/ton freight put option on the same route is trading at a cost of $4/ton. The expiration of the two options is in 90 days, while the risk-free interest rate is 12%. The FFA contract is bought at the same time the call is written and the put is purchased. The proceeds from the options' trades are $6/ton (= $10/ton − $4/ton), which by the expiration date of the contracts become $6.18/ton [= $6/ton x $e^{0.12 \times (90/360)}$].

Table 3.65. Results of the Conversion Arbitrage Options Strategy, in $/ton

Freight Rates ($/ton)	Short Call, X = $64.5/ton	Long Put, X = $64.5/ton	Long FFA, Price = $66/ton	Options Income Compounded	Net Result
61.5	0	+3	-4.5	6.18	4.68
62.5	0	+2	-3.5	6.18	4.68
63.5	0	+1	-2.5	6.18	4.68
64.5	0	0	-1.5	6.18	4.68
65.5	-1	0	-0.5	6.18	4.68
66.5	-2	0	+0.5	6.18	4.68
67.5	-3	0	+1.5	6.18	4.68
68.5	-4	0	+2.5	6.18	4.68

Table 3.65 and Figure 3.45 present the results of the conversion strategy at the expiration date, for a number of possible freight rate prices, shown in the first column of the table. Columns two, three and four of the table show for each level of freight rates the payoffs from the short call, the long put and the long FFA positions, respectively. The fifth column of the table shows the compound amount of the $6/ton received from the options' transaction, while the last column of the table records the overall cash-flow from these positions. As can be observed, by the horizontal straight line in the figure, on the expiration date the net profit is $4.68/ton, regardless of where the freight rates stand. The example does not take into account transactions costs. For the conversion strategy to be profitable transactions costs must not be higher than $4.68/ton.

Figure 3.45. The Trading Positions in a Conversion

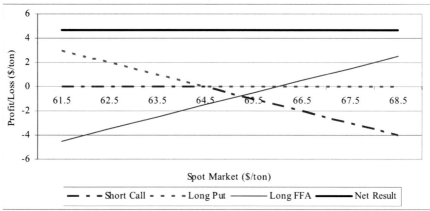

3.6.4.2. Reversals
The reversal arbitrage options strategy is the opposite of the conversion strategy. In this case, the underlying asset is sold through an FFA contract and, at the same time, purchased by means of a synthetic FFA contract, which consists of a purchased call and a written put. Arbitrage is possible when the synthetic FFA contract is cheaper than the actual FFA contract. For example, this may be the case when the underlying asset can be bought at a price that is lower than the price at which it is sold. Taking into account transactions costs and the opportunity cost of capital, the relationship is:

Actual FFA price > (Call option premium + Interest up to expiration)
– (Put option premium + Interest up to expiration)
+ Strike price
+ (Transactions costs + Interest up to expiration)

Example:
Suppose that the freight rate on route P3 of the BPI is $65.5/ton and the relevant 90 day FFA contract is trading at a price of $66/ton. In the market, a $64/ton freight call option on route P3 is trading at a cost of $8/ton and a $64/ton freight put option on route P3 is trading at a cost of $6.5/ton. The expiration of the two options is in 90 days, while the risk-free interest rate is 12%. The FFA is sold at the same time at which the put is written and the call is purchased. This generates a cash outflow of $1.5/ton (= 8/ton – $6.5/ton). Assuming that the investor does not have the $1.5/ton and has to borrow funds, say from a bank, the compound amount due by the

repayment date is $1.55/ton [= $1.5/ton x $e^{0.12 \times (90/360)}$]. Table 3.66 and Figure 3.46 display the results of the reversal strategy at the expiration date of the options for a number of possible outcomes of freight rates. As can be observed, by the horizontal straight line in the figure, on the expiration date the net result is $0.45/ton, regardless of where freight rates stand. This example does not take into account transactions costs, which if they are less than $0.45/ton make worth the reversal arbitrage strategy.

Table 3.66. Results of the Reversal Arbitrage Options Strategy, in $/ton

Freight Rates ($/ton)	Long Call, X = $64/ton	Short Put, X = $64/ton	Short FFA, Price = $66/ton	Option Outlay Compounded	Net Result
61.5	0	-2.5	4.5	-1.55	0.45
62.5	0	-1.5	3.5	-1.55	0.45
63.5	0	-0.5	2.5	-1.55	0.45
64.5	0.5	0	1.5	-1.55	0.45
65.5	1.5	0	0.5	-1.55	0.45
66.5	2.5	0	-0.5	-1.55	0.45
67.5	3.5	0	-1.5	-1.55	0.45
68.5	4.5	0	-2.5	-1.55	0.45

Figure 3.46. The Trading Positions in a Reversal

Figure 3.46. The Trading Positions in a Reversal

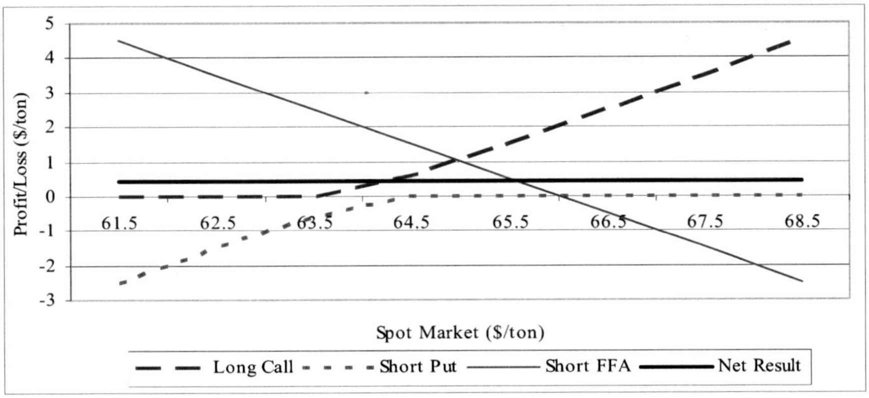

3.6.4.3. Boxes

The box arbitrage options strategy is constructed through a synthetic long FFA position, which consists of a purchased call option and a written put option, and a synthetic short FFA position, which consists of a written call option and a purchased put option.

A **long box** strategy is constructed when the synthetic long FFA position consists of options with a strike price that is lower than the strike price of the options used in setting up the synthetic short FFA position. The long box requires an initial investment to set up, as the options purchased (call with the lower strike price and put with the higher strike price) are more expensive than the options written (call with the higher strike price and put with the lower strike price). On the expiration date, income is realised in an amount equivalent to the difference between the option strike prices as follows:

(Net costs – Interest up to expiration < Proceeds at expiration) = Difference between strike prices

The **short box** strategy generates income when it is set up, as the options written (call with the lower strike price and put with the higher strike price) are more expensive than the options bought (call with the higher strike price and put with the lower strike price). On the expiration date, costs are incurred in an amount equivalent to the difference between the option strike prices:

(Net costs + Interest up to expiration > Costs at expiration) = Difference between strike prices

The following examples demonstrate the construction of short and long box strategies.

Example 1: Short Box Strategy
Suppose that the freight rate on route P3 of the BPI is $65.5/ton. In the market, the following options are available on route P3: A $64/ton freight call option, trading at a premium of $8/ton; a $64/ton freight put option, trading at a premium of $3/ton; a $66/ton freight call option, trading at a premium of $6/ton; and a $66/ton freight put option, trading at a premium of $7/ton. Options expire in 90 days, while the risk-free interest rate is 12%.

Table 3.67. Results of the Short Box Arbitrage Options Strategy, in $/ton

Freight Rates ($/ton)	$64/ton Short Call ($/ton)	$64/ton Long Put ($/ton)	$66/ton Long Call ($/ton)	$66/ton Short Put ($/ton)	Options Income Compounded ($/ton)	Net Result ($/ton)
61.5	0	2.5	0	-4.5	6.18	4.18
62.5	0	1.5	0	-3.5	6.18	4.18
63.5	0	0.5	0	-2.5	6.18	4.18
64.5	-0.5	0	0	-1.5	6.18	4.18
65.5	-1.5	0	0	-0.5	6.18	4.18
66.5	-2.5	0	0.5	0	6.18	4.18
67.5	-3.5	0	1.5	0	6.18	4.18
68.5	-4.5	0	2.5	0	6.18	4.18

Route P3 $64/ton freight options (lower strike price) are used to set up the synthetic short FFA position, by writing a $64/ton call and buying a $64/ton put. Route P3 $66/ton freight options (higher strike price) are used to set up the synthetic long FFA position, by writing a $66/ton put and buying a $66/ton call. This produces an income of $6/ton (= $8/ton − $3/ton − $6/ton + $7/ton), which, compounds to $6.18/ton[=$6/ton x $e^{0.12 \text{ x } (90/360)}$]. The profit is $4.18/ton (= $6.18/ton − $2/ton), where $2/ton denotes the difference between the strike prices ($66/ton − $64/ton). Table 3.67 and Figure 3.47 present the results of the short box strategy for a number of possible freight rates at the expiration date of the options. As can be observed, by the horizontal straight line in the figure, on the expiration date, no matter what the level of freight rates are a risk-free profit of $4.18/ton is produced. If transactions costs are lower than this amount the arbitrage strategy is worth undertaking.

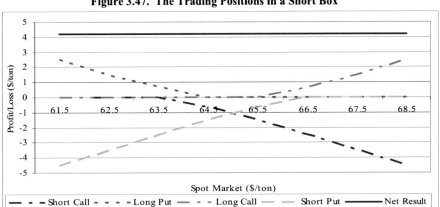

Figure 3.47. The Trading Positions in a Short Box

Legend: — - - Short Call   - - - - Long Put   — - - Long Call   — — Short Put   ———— Net Result

Example 2: Long Box Strategy

Suppose that the freight rate on route P3 of the BPI is $65.5/ton. In the market, a $66/ton freight call option is trading at a premium of $4/ton; a $66/ton freight put option is trading at a premium of $6/ton; a $69/ton freight call option is trading at a premium of $3/ton; and a $69/ton freight put option is trading at a premium of $7/ton. The expiration of the options is in 90 days, while the risk-free interest rate is 12%.

Table 3.68. Results of the Long Box Arbitrage Options Strategy, in $/ton

Freight Rates ($/ton)	$66/ton Long Call ($/ton)	$66/ton Short Put ($/ton)	$69/ton Short Call ($/ton)	$69/ton Long Put ($/ton)	Cost ($/ton)	Net Result ($/ton)
61.5	0	-4.5	0	7.5	-2.06	0.94
62.5	0	-3.5	0	6.5	-2.06	0.94
63.5	0	-2.5	0	5.5	-2.06	0.94
64.5	0	-1.5	0	4.5	-2.06	0.94
65.5	0	-0.5	0	3.5	-2.06	0.94
66.5	0.5	0	0	2.5	-2.06	0.94
67.5	1.5	0	0	1.5	-2.06	0.94
68.5	2.5	0	0	0.5	-2.06	0.94
69.5	3.5	0	-0.5	0	-2.06	0.94
70.5	4.5	0	-1.5	0	-2.06	0.94
71.5	5.5	0	-2.5	0	-2.06	0.94

Route P3 $66/ton freight options (lower strike price) are used to set up the synthetic long FFA position, by buying a $66/ton call and writing a $66/ton put. Route P3 $69/ton freight options (higher strike price) are used to set up the synthetic short FFA position, by writing a $69/ton call and buying a $69/ton put. This requires a net investment of $2/ton (= -$4/ton + $6/ton + $3/ton – $7/ton), which if financed with a 90 day (3 month) loan at 12% rate of interest amounts to a compounded amount in 90 days of $2.06/ton [= $2/ton x $e^{0.12 \times (90/360)}$]. The net profit from this strategy is $0.94/ton (= $3/ton – $2.06/ton), where $3/ton is the difference between the strike prices ($69/ton – $66/ton). Table 3.68 and Figure 3.48 present the results of the long box strategy at the expiration date of the options, for a number of possible freight rates. A net risk-free profit of $0.94/ton results in every case, which, if greater than the transactions costs, make the arbitrage strategy worth executing.

Figure 3.48. The Trading Positions in a Long Box

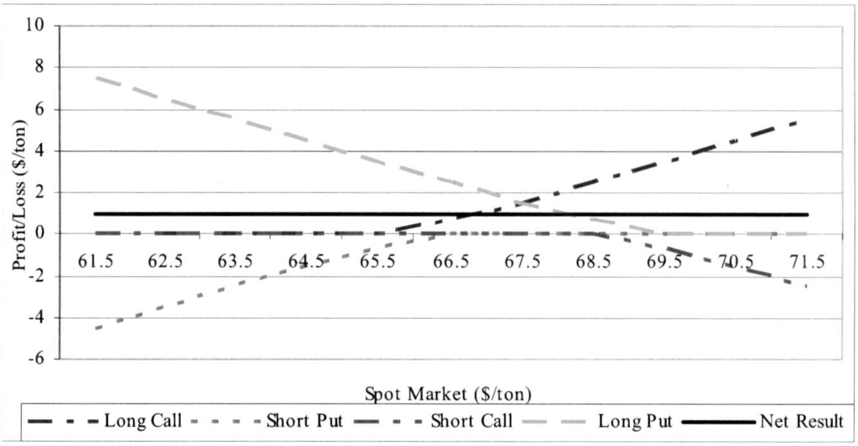

Spot Market ($/ton)

— - - Long Call - - - - Short Put — - - Short Call — — Long Put ———— Net Result

3.6.5. Summary of Investment and Arbitrage Freight Options Strategies

Table 3.69 panel A summarizes the **directional** (long call, short call, long put and short put) options strategies for hedging purposes, while panel B summarizes the **spread** (bull spread and bear spread), **combination** (long straddle, short straddle, long strangle, short strangle long strip, short strip, long strap and short strap) and **arbitrage** (conversion, reversal, long box and short box) options strategies for investment purposes. The second column of the table presents the names of the strategies, while the third and fourth columns present the options positions needed to construct the strategies and the market expectations regarding the direction and the price volatility of the underlying physical (spot) market, respectively.

For instance, investors, who want to use options for hedging purposes, who expect a raise (fall) in the price of the underlying market in the future, can buy a protective call or write a covered put (buy a protective put or write a covered call). Investors, who want to use options strategies for investment purposes, who expect a raise (fall) in the price of the underlying market in the future, can use a bull call spread or a bull put spread (a bear call spread or a bear put spread). On the other hand, investors, who expect a raise (fall) in the volatility of the underlying market in the future, can use a short call or put butterfly spread (a long call or put butterfly spread). Morover, investors, who expect a raise (fall) in volatility but they are uncertain of the direction of the physical market in the future, can use a bottom straddle or a bottom strangle (a top straddle or a top strangle). Investors, who expect a raise in the volatility of the market in the future, but believe that a decrease (increase) in spot prices is more likely than an increase (decrease), can use a bottom strip (bottom strap) options strategy. Investors, who expect a fall in the volatility of the market in the future, but believe that a decrease (increase) in spot prices is more likely than an increase (decrease), can use a top strap (top strip) options strategy. Finally, investors, who want to use options for arbitrage purposes, can use the conversion, the reversal or the box strategies. It should be mentioned here that these investment strategies are the most widely used options strategies that exist for investment purposes, as there are others, not very popular, that are not mentioned here.

Table 3.69. Summary of Options Strategies for Hedging, Investment and Arbitrage Purposes

Panel A: Options Strategies for Hedging Purposes

	Strategy Name	Options Positions	Market Expectations
Directional	Buying Protective Put	Long Put (Long Spot Market)	Falling Market
	Buying Protective Call	Long Call (Short Spot Market)	Raising Market
	Writing Covered Call	Short Call (Long Spot Market)	Falling Market
	Writing Covered Put	Short Put (Short Spot Market)	Raising Market

Panel B: Options Strategies for Investment Purposes

Spreads	Bull Call Spread	Long Call (X_1), Short Call (X_2)	Raising Market
	Bull Put Spread	Long Put (X_1), Short Put (X_2)	Raising Market
	Bear Call Spread	Short Call (X_1), Long Call (X_2)	Falling Market
	Bear Put Spread	Short Put (X_1), Long Put (X_2)	Falling Market
	Long Call Butterfly Spread	Long Call (X_1), Two Short Calls (X_2), Long Call (X_3)	Falling Volatility
	Long Put Butterfly Spread	Long Put (X_1), Two Short Puts (X_2), Long Put (X_3)	Falling Volatility
	Short Call Butterfly Spread	Short Call (X_1), Two Long Calls (X_2), Short Call (X_3)	Raising Volatility
	Short Put Butterfly Spread	Short Put (X_1), Two Long Puts (X_2), Short Put (X_3)	Raising Volatility
	Calendar Call Spread	Long Call (T_2), Short Call (T_1)	-
	Calendar Put Spread	Long Put (T_2), Short Put (T_1)	-
Combinations	Bottom Straddle	Long Call, Long Put (same X)	Raising Volatility
	Top Straddle	Short Call, Short Put (same X)	Falling Volatility
	Bottom Strips	Long Call, Two Long Puts (same X)	Raising Volatility Falling Market
	Top Strips	Short Call, Two Short Puts (same X)	Falling Volatility Raising Market
	Bottom Straps	Long Put, Two Long Calls (same X)	Raising Volatility Raising Market
	Top Straps	Short Put, Two Short Calls (same X)	Falling Volatility Falling Market
	Bottom Strangle	Long Put (X_1), Long Call (X_2)	Raising Volatility
	Top Strangle	Short Put (X_1), Short Call (X_2)	Falling Volatility

Panel C: Options Strategies for Arbitrage Purposes

Arbitrage	Conversion	Long Forward, Long Put Short Call	-
	Reversal	Short Forward, Long Call Short Put	-
	Long Box	Long Call (X_1), Short Put (X_1), Short Call (X_2), Long Put (X_2)	-
	Short Box	Short Call (X_1), Long Put (X_1), Long Call (X_2), Short Put (X_2)	-

Note: $X_1 < X_2$, $X_2 = (X_1 + X_2)/2$ and $T_1 < T_2$.

3.7. Freight Derivatives vs. Other Risk Management Strategies

As mentioned, on a number of occasions, before in this book, freight derivatives provide real gains for market agents, compared to traditional strategies of freight risk management. Now that we have discussed how these tools work in practice, we provide an overview of the benefits of using freight derivatives contracts as well as the issues involved with these trades. Thus, freight derivatives contracts, compared to time-chartering a vessel, are beneficial to both shipowners and charterers. Thus, a shipowner retains operational control of his vessel and at the same time is benefiting from favourable spot market conditions. A charterer is free from any operational risks, which are present in a time-charter agreement. Commissions payable to brokers are lower in freight derivatives compared to chartering agreements. Broadly, they are 0.5% of the fixed price (principal sum), as opposed to 1.25% payable by the seller if the deal was physical[56]. The low commission structure implies that it is cheaper to trade in and out of a freight derivatives position prior to the settlement month than trading in and out of a spot position, where the commissions are higher. Moreover, as Drewry Shipping Consultants (1997) note, the simple nature of a freight derivatives contract makes it easier to trade in and out of a position, compared to contracts on physical cargo.

Freight derivatives allow the market to respond quickly to changing needs and circumstances by developing new variations of old contracts. There is no physical delivery involved with freight derivatives. They simply become a cash settlement upon conclusion of the agreed terms. In case the contracts are traded OTC, there are not any cash deposits (initial guarantee) and margin calls like in futures contracts, although they can be negotiated into FFAs if the counterparties agree that this additional financial security is appropriate or agree to trade the freight derivatives contracts in one of the clearing-houses providing this service, such as at IMAREX or LCH.Clearnet. Finally, freight derivatives trades are subject to the accounting implicit in International Accounting Standard (IAS) statement No. 39, applying to countries in the EU, and to Financial Accounting Standards Board's (FASB) statement No. 133 in the United States, making them easy to be incorporated in the accounting treatment system of the companies.

Table 3.70 presents some recent statistics for the overall OTC (FFA) and cleared (freight futures) freight derivatives market, as well as for the dry-bulk and tanker paper markets. These statistics, taken from Carnegie, are based on estimates from press clippings, FFABA statements, polls and IMAREX trading statistics.

Table 3.70. The Freight Derivatives Market (as of November 2005)

	2003	2004	2005
Overall physical market (wet and dry)	US$80 billion	US$90 billion	US$90 billion
Overall paper market			
Market size US$	US$17 billion	US$32 billion	US$36 billion
Market growth		88%	20%
Paper Multiple of physical	21%	36%	40%
Dry-bulk market share	95%	78%	60%
Tanker market share	5%	16%	40%
Dry-bulk			
Nominal trade value	US$15 billion	US$25 billion	US$30 billion
Contracts/Transactions	4,500	7,000	8,400
Lots	607,500	945,000	1,134,000
Market growth (transactions)		56%	20%
OTC market share	97%	95%	90%
Cleared futures market share	3%	5%	10%
Tanker			
Nominal trade value	US$2 billion	US$7 billion	US$6 billion
Contracts/Transactions	2,000	10,000	12,000
Lots	70,800	370,500	741,000
Cargo tons	50 million	250 million	300 million
Market growth (transactions)		400%	20%
OTC market share		40%	35%
Cleared futures market share		60%	65%

Source: Carnegie

---

[56] According to market sources, a number of players have got deals with zero commission above a certain number of trades per month or for intra-week trading. Moreover, many players and banks are pushing for commission to be a fixed amount and not a percentage and some brokers are pushing to see commission payable upon doing the deal rather than upon settlement.

Thus, once more, the major benefits of freight derivatives contracts can be summarised as follows:

- Risk management, by stabilising cash-flows for up to three years forward.
- There is no window of time on re-delivery as in the time-charter spot market. The period of time from the conclusion of a time-charter contract until the actual redelivery of the vessel to its owner may be one – two months. During this period revenue is forgone for the shipowner. The issue is non-existent with freight derivatives trading.
- Buy/Sell positions prior to expiry, thereby providing flexibility.
- Easy to fix and close out positions.
- Price Discovery, as the freight derivatives market is forward looking and as a consequence, leads the spot market and provides a market insight.
- No physical performance with its associated risks; it is a purely financial transaction.
- No restrictions to physical operation are required. Control of the vessels and of specific types of cargos is retained.
- Easily understood (simplicity) and quickly traded (immediacy).
- No re-negotiations from parties are needed, as in the physical market.
- No re-letting of the vessel to other parties is required, as in the physical market.
- An additional market for banks and financial institutions to add to their trading or loan portfolios of traded instruments.

Some other issues in the OTC freight derivatives market are:

- The possible manipulation of the market. In order to overcome this the settlement period could be altered from the average of the last 7 business days to 14 business days or even better to a monthly settlement period.
- Not real and firm bids and offers. This has changed since the Enron days as many players have realised the benefit of increased liquidity created by the willingness of the players to trade. At the same time the bid-ask spread is narrowing and, at the time of writing, is typically around $0.50/ton on voyage routes and about $250/day average on time-charter routes.
- There is no secondary market in OTC contracts, which may enable the FFA and options positions to be closed before the expiry of the contract.
- Liquidity is low in some routes, and this can make it difficult to find counterparties. Also, low liquidity does not enhance transparency and market efficiency, which can lead to manipulated prices as a result.
- It is not easy, in some thinly traded routes, to close (unwind) an open position by reversing the initial position for the same settlement month. In this case, the opposite trade will most likely be carried out with a different counterparty and therefore the settlement obligations remain open with the two separate counterparties. Thus, although through this strategy of reversing the initial derivatives position, to counteract the changed market, thereby eliminating the risk regarding market movements, there is still credit risk left in OTC contracts.
- Credit risk or counterparty risk is an issue in shipping markets, where a large number of principals are privately owned companies, which are not obligated to disclosure information to the public.
- Finally, FFA contracts can produce large cumulative gains or losses in comparison to futures contracts, as there is no daily mark-to-market settlement, as is the case with futures.

3.8. VaR in Freight Markets

The management of risk should be an integral part of the economic decision process of market participants in freight rate markets. Through the practice of risk management, market agents can reduce uncertainty in their economic activities and optimize investment decisions by setting limits, mitigating losses through diversification and by optimizing the timing of their investments. Corporate threats such as catastrophic losses, misallocation and underutilization of resources can be minimised with the use of risk management techniques.

Regardless of the risk exposure, risk management should perform the following three tasks: estimate, control and manage risk. An approach for assessing market risk is Value-at-Risk (VaR), presented in Chapter 2 of this book. VaR is a summary measure of downside risk, which describes in a single number the maximum loss that a portfolio may sustain, with certain confidence and for a determined holding period, due to market risk. In other words, for a certain exposure, VaR provides an upper bound for the potential loss that may result due to adverse market fluctuations.

It is an easy to understand risk metric of the extent to which a company is exposed to market risk. Moreover, it is considered as a more representative measure of risk than other parameters, such as the standard deviation, the variance, the semi-variance or the expected absolute deviation. VaR is not limited only to the monitoring or estimation of risk but it can also be a valuable tool for controlling and managing it. For instance, investors may use VaR to limit their risk, while maximizing expected utility by constraining to maintain the VaR of a target horizon to a specific level. This level depends on the utility function of the investor and it is usually set below some "*floor*", which corresponds to a sustainable level of loss.

Assume that a shipowner is exposed to market risk stemming from freight rate fluctuations. In order to monitor freight rate risk, the shipowner should estimate VaR for a certain confidence level (or many confidence levels, to obtain the risk profile of the freight market) for the terminal horizon of the freight fixture and the tonnage of interest. For instance, for an average voyage of 15 days, the 15 days and the 1 day freight market VaR can be estimated as:

$$VaR_{1-a} - X \, x Z_a \, x \sigma_L \tag{3.1}$$

and

$$VaR_{1-a} = \sqrt{15} x \, X \, x \, Z_a \, x \sigma_d \tag{3.2}$$

where, VaR_{1-a} is the VaR with a confidence level of 100 x (1 - a)%, Z_a the ath quantile of the standard normal distribution and σ_L, σ_d the conditional forecasts of volatility for 15 days and one day freight rates, respectively. Notice that the square root of time ($\sqrt{15}$) rule entails the additional binding assumptions that logarithmic price differences are normally and independently distributed and volatility is identical across all time periods.

VaR estimated by Equations (3.1) or (3.2) expresses the maximum 15 days or 1 day loss (or more coherently the maximum decline in the revenues) that a shipowner may suffer under normal market conditions. The term "*normal market conditions*" is closely related to the confidence level of interest. For example, for a 95% confidence level VaR, normal market conditions correspond to 95 out of 100 cases (or days).

Under extreme market conditions stress testing should be performed for the estimation of extreme quantiles, that is, for the estimation of the expected shortfall of the exposure.

After estimating VaR, the next issue in the practice of risk management concerns the risk preferences of agents involved in the freight market, and reduces to a utility maximization problem. Limits for VaR based projected losses are set and hedging strategies are drawn, either traditional or through freight derivatives. For instance, diversification, by choosing a mix of voyage and time-charter contracts or by including other vessels in their portfolio, may be used by shipowners to increase their "*portfolio*" opportunity set. In such a multivariate setting, which corresponds to a more realistic situation, where many vessels are owned, incremental VaRs can be estimated and limits can be set for every category of vessels separately. In such a multivariate VaR analysis account must be taken of the correlations and co-variances between the freight rates in different markets.

To see how VaR analysis may be used to monitor and mitigate freight rate risks consider the following example. For the sake of simplicity, assume that a shipowner owns only one Panamax vessel of 75,000 dwt. He is exposed to freight risk, stemming from Panamax freight rate fluctuations. Figure 3.49 displays the daily Panamax freight prices for the period September 2000 to May 2005. As can be observed, historical prices fluctuate substantially in small periods of time; we see for instance the large drop of 15% in freight rates during the first two weeks of October 2003 and the dramatic decline in rates by approximately 40% for the April-May 2004 time period. These declines, when combined with other adverse market movements (for instance, possible hikes in oil prices), may lead to substantial losses and negative pressures on the cash-flow position of the shipping company. Notice that for a charterer, the situation is exactly the opposite. He would be worried about high levels in freight rates, as these will increase his freight costs.

Figure 3.49. Panamax Freight Rates

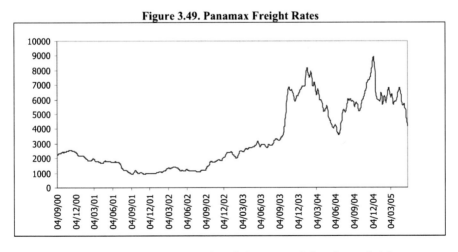

Descriptive statistics of logarithmic first-differences of the above freight rates are presented in Table 3.71. The mean is not statistically different from zero, a high standard deviation of 15%, significant asymmetry and excess kurtosis, as well as non-normality (Jarque-Bera test) of the distribution, are characteristics of these data.

Table 3.71. Descriptive Statistics on the Logarithmic Differences of Daily Panamax Freight Rate Prices (04/09/2000 – 26/05/2005)

N	Mean	STD	Min	Max	Skew	Kurt	J-B
1,771	0.005	0.151	-0.723	0.770	0.146	4.298	915.737
	(0.004)				[0.039]	[0.000]	[0.000]
	[0.217]						

Notes:
- N is the number of observations.
- Mean and STD are the sample mean and sample standard deviation of the series.
- Max and Min are the maximum and minimum values of the series.
- Skew and Kurt are the estimated skewness and excess kurtosis of the data.
- J-B is the Jarque-Bera (1980) test for normality, distributed as $\chi^2(2)$.
- The standard error of the sample mean is in parentheses.
- Figures in square brackets are exact significance levels (or p-values).

Practically, a convenient method to monitor risk is to calculate VaR on a daily basis by employing a VaR model through a recursive or sliding window technique. The holding period for the estimation of VaR may be set equal to the average fixture time of the vessel. For instance, if the vessel is operated in the market, this may be a 15 day period.

Figure 3.50 displays the daily Panamax freight rate returns (that is, the logarithmic differences of freight rates) along with the recursive out-of-sample daily VaR forecasts that are generated from a GARCH(1,1) model. These VaR forecasts are produced under the simplifying assumption of capacity of 1 unit (ton). That is,

$$VaR^{\alpha}(\text{for one unit}) = Z_{\alpha} \times \sigma + \mu$$

where, VaR^{α} is the $100 \times (1-\alpha)\%$ VaR, σ is the conditional out-of-sample forecast of the standard deviation, Z_a is the ath quantile of the standard normal distribution and μ the forecasted mean.

Figure 3.50. Panamax Returns and VaR

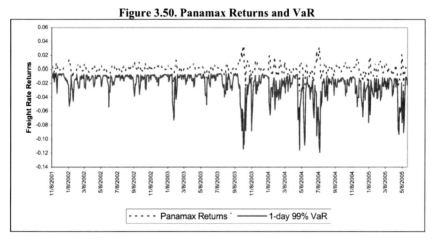

The solid line in the figure represents the daily loss (or the cut off point) for one ton of freight service, for which we are confident that it is not going to be exceeded at 99% of the cases. The VaR for the specific vessel can be obtained by multiplying the one unit VaR of the specific date with the tonnage of the vessel, assuming a zero expected mean. For example, according to Figure 3.50, if the VaR forecast for one unit on 13th

258

October 2003 is equal to -0.069, then the shipowner may estimate the VaR for the Panamax vessel by multiplying the tonnage of the vessel with the forecasted unit VaR number. Thus:

$$\text{VaR} = \text{tonnage x VaR(for one unit)} = 75,000 \text{ dwt x } (-0.069) = -\$5,175$$

That is, the maximum next day's loss, with 99% confidence, for the shipowner is equal to $5,520. The question that needs to be addressed here is whether the shipowner is willing to take his chances on losing this sum or not. If he is not, then he should hedge in order to mitigate unwanted potential losses. This can be done by entering the freight derivatives markets or by diversifying his operational strategies towards time-chartering or COA, or by investing into other sectors of shipping or even investing into other industries, in order to benefit from possible negative correlations (if any) between the cash-flows of investments. Of course, if the shipowner considers this loss as the potential downside to undertaking the market risks of employing his Panamax vessel in the voyage market he takes no further action.

We can, therefore, infer, that the use of VaR could make shipowners more proactive and forward looking by rationalizing their economic activity (specifically their investment or hedging decisions), in accordance with their utility function in the risk-return space. The procedure, which has been proposed here for the first time in the shipping finance literature, can be extended to more realistic cases, where ownership of many vessels is involved. In this case, incremental VaRs for each vessel can be calculated and the total risk exposure can be obtained by aggregating the incremental VaRs for each vessel.

3.9. The Role of Brokers in Freight Derivatives Trading

In many organised exchanges, trading of "*commodities*"/"*contracts*" takes place through brokers, whose role is to bring together market agents wishing to buy with those wishing to sell the "*commodity*"/"*contract*". The role of a broker then is to act as an intermediary between the two counterparties to a contract, whether they are shipowners and charterers in the chartering market, or buyers and sellers in the sale and purchase vessel market, or hedgers or speculators in the freight derivatives paper market. The Federation of National Associations of Ship Brokers and Agents (FONASBA) is represented in some 49 counties. Despite the large number of shipbrokers in the physical freight market, only a few provide freight derivatives services. The most active, in the dry-bulk sub-sector, are Clarksons Securities Ltd., Freight Investor Services (FIS) and Simpson Spence and Young (SSY), while in the tanker sector the most active ones are at IMAREX. Table 3.72 presents the major freight derivatives brokers around the world. As can be seen in the table, most of the freight derivatives brokers are situated in the UK, followed by the US, with representations in other countries, such as Italy, France, Norway, Germany, and Switzerland.

Table 3.72. Major Freight Derivatives Brokers, 2005

Clarksons Securities Ltd. (UK)	Banchero-Costa & C (Italy)
Freight Investor Services Ltd. (UK)	Fearnleys (Norway)
Simpson Spence and Young Ltd. (UK)	GFI Brokers Ltd. (UK)
IMAREX (Norway)	Ifchor S.A. (Switzerland)
Galbraith's Ltd. (UK)	Marsoft (US)
E. A. Gibson (UK)	Pasternak & Baum & Co Inc. (US)
Howard Houlder (UK)	McQuilling Brokerage Partners (US)
Howe Robinson (UK)	Yamamizu Shipping Co. Ltd. (Japan)
Arrow Chartering (UK)	SwissMar (Switzerland)
J.F. Dillon (US)	Mallory Jones Lynch Flynn (US)
Tradition Financial Services Ltd. (UK)	Bernd von Blomberg Schiffsmakler GmbH (Germany)
Barry Rogliano Salles Futures Ltd. (France)	

An important question that market participants in freight derivatives markets face is whether to use a broker or not in their freight derivatives trade. Currently, principals interested in freight derivatives have the opportunity to trade on their own account if they become members of IMAREX or NYMEX. In that sense, they can avoid paying the brokerage fees which, as we saw in the examples presented earlier in the chapter, must be part of their calculations regarding their net cash-flow positions from freight derivatives trades. Just to take the example of principals trading through IMAREX on their own account, the extra costs that they face, compared to using a broker, involve membership fees and fees to obtain access to the IMAREX trading screen – in 2005 the fees was $300 – $400 per month. Also, one has to consider the hidden costs of the losses that may be incurred, as a result of not having available the advice of the broker. They have to weight these costs against the brokerage fees, which they pay to the freight derivatives broker, essentially, as compensation for providing a service, which includes:

- Market information, which is disseminated in the market by the exchange of reported fixtures and freight derivatives trades between brokers on a daily basis. The knowledge brokers acquire, through direct and third-party reports of freight derivatives transactions allows them to be well informed.
- Information on counterparty risk, which is assessed based on the experience brokers have, in terms of the background of principals and knowledge of the details of freight derivatives contract forms.
- Specialist financial advise regarding derivatives and risk management issues. The principals, e.g. shipowners and charterers, usually have experienced personnel to collect and analyse data and market information of interest on the physical market – this is what they do best. Derivatives trading requires different skills.
- Derivatives brokers have a web of contacts of potential counterparties and the state of the market, which principals do not have. This may include liquidity of trading in specific routes, direction of trading, etc.
- Brokers can advise on best course of action under different circumstances, according to the needs of the clients. This may involve advise on magnitude of positions, the best course of action to take when there is a sudden change in the market trend, etc.
- Advise on risk exposures of principals if they do not have specialised, experienced personnel.

Assuming that market participants decide to use a broker for their freight derivatives trades, an important question that they face is how to select their broker amongst a number of alternatives. As one market participant put it to us; "*the answer is, shop around*". To do this effectively, the following qualitative and quantitative criteria are presented below to assist in answering this question. Notice that some of these may also be thought of as additional reasons (to the list above) for using brokers for derivatives trading, rather than trading on their own account without involving a broker.

Qualitative criteria; Freight derivatives brokers should:
- Provide value-added services. Clients increasingly expect investment advice, statistical analysis, administrative and operational back-up. It is the ability of a broker to identify opportunities that can prove extremely beneficial to their clients.
- Be involved in the stages of the deal, particularly in non-standardized OTC contracts: negotiating the main terms of the freight derivatives contract, finalizing the details of the contract and following the deal through to its conclusion.
- Have an established web of contacts and relationships to ensure that they have access to all trades.
- Create personal relationships with their clients, in a climate of trust. Relationships between shipbrokers and clients take considerable time to develop, being established on reliable, trustworthy advice and service from the broker.
- Provide quality and true knowledge and opinion, like a consultant, beyond market insight, on the past, present and future state of both the freight derivatives and the physical markets.
- Possess the relevant skills to time the market, as entering such a volatile market a day too early or a day too late can have a significant impact on the derivatives position.
- Enhance the flow of market information, validate its accuracy, and have the information available on a real-time basis.
- Be proactive on all issues and tasks that their clients have difficulties in dealing with.
- Have separate physical and freight derivatives broking desks.
- Have all the required knowledge of physical levels.
- Have a clear understanding on all technical details and issues of freight derivatives trading.
- Be a team player with the principal, where the broker and the principal have equal input and appreciation of each other.
- Provide a continuous broking service to their clients, with no delays, mistakes, repetitions, etc.

Quantitative criteria; Freight derivatives brokers should:
- Offer competitive and firm freight derivatives prices for all different contract types and durations.
- Offer relatively small freight derivatives bid-ask spreads, as their difference represents a cost that their clients must pay for utilizing their services.
- Provide competitive freight derivatives brokerage fees.
- Provide easily measurable advices and solutions on the various risk exposures of their clients.

- Provide daily reports, drafted from various sources of information; e.g. from market analysts and consultants, from traders and principals, from the internet and market reports and from other brokers.
- Offer tailor-made solutions to each of their clients.
- Have a liquid, in terms of number of contracts, freight derivatives trading desk, for their clients to close any unwanted freight derivatives positions quickly and efficiently.
- Specialize in individual market sectors and/or geographical areas, as some freight derivatives brokers are good in dry-bulk and some others in tanker sub-sectors, while some brokers are good in Atlantic trades and some others in Pacific trades.
- Have the appropriate IT systems in place.

It should be noted in all the above that as derivatives markets mature, with high liquidity and depth, there is a tendency for them to move into electronic trading. This has been shown in the literature to be beneficial to the working of the market in terms of improved information flow, transparency and efficiency, amongst others (see for instance, Kavussanos and Phylaktis, 2001). Freight derivatives trading moves in that direction. Freight derivatives are more adaptable for electronic trading in contrast to chartering, which involves settlements resulting in physical transactions. Freight derivatives transactions are concluded by financial settlements, which make it more conducive for electronic trading. The strengths of an electronic trading system lie in its ease of use, clarity and installation, its security which should be optimal, its anonymity, but most importantly in the fact that each user, whilst seeing all bids and offer prices on the system, should only be presented with firm trading prices from counterparties that have received their prior clearance. An electronic screen-trading facility for freight derivatives contracts was launched at the beginning of 2006. This clearing service is jointly provided by Clarksons Securities Limited (CSL), Ifchor S.A. and Freight Investor Services (FIS). The online trading platform is marketed under the name C.I.F. to reflect the joint cooperation and its trades are cleared through the LCH.Clearnet.

As part of the advise that freight derivatives brokers should give to market participants, wishing to enter this market, is the following list of trading steps which they should follow before they engage in derivatives trading:
- Assign commercial staff of the company and train them in freight derivatives.
- Start receiving daily reports from market-makers.
- Start comparing freight derivatives pricing and make it a daily routine.
- Start comparing freight derivatives and spot prices.
- Start calling freight derivatives brokers for prices and/or become members of exchanges offering freight derivatives.
- Learn the market terminology.
- Simulate the buying and selling of freight derivatives contracts for a period of time and review the outcomes.
- Liquidate the positions.
- Evaluate the outcomes.
- Do it again.
- Start trading for real.

3.10. Economics and Empirical Evidence on Freight Derivatives Markets

As discussed on a number of occasions before in this book freight derivatives contracts appeared since 1985 with the introduction of the exchange-traded (at LIFFE) freight futures BIFFEX contract written on the BFI index, playing the role of the derivatives instrument that could be used for hedging freight rate risks in the shipping industry. Options on BIFFEX contracts also came into the scene in 1991 but ceased trading, along with the withdrawal of BIFFEX, in April 2002. Forward OTC contracts (FFAs) appeared in 1992 and gradually replaced the not-so-well-functioning BIFFEX contracts. Hybrid versions of FFAs, which trade OTC but are cleared through a clearing-house mechanism, have also entered the scene in order to address the worries of market agents about the credit risk prevalent in these OTC contracts. Moreover, OTC and exchange-cleared freight options contracts have become available to interested parties since 2001 for hedging and investment purposes.

A number of researches have put their efforts into examining a number of issues which make freight derivatives contracts different from other derivatives contracts. Part of the reason for this situation has been the lack of availability of data, which could be used to support empirical work in these markets. In the early days, research work had to rely on short samples of data, often involving primary data collected from surveys (see for example, Cullinane, 1992) or from freight derivatives brokers' records (e.g. Kavussanos and Visvikis 2004, 2005), often meeting the reluctance of agents in the *"secretive"* shipping industry to provide data and information for research. Things are getting better, and can only get better if published work can help provide answers to real business problems.

For instance, special features of freight derivatives markets and the contracts traded involve: The recognition that the *"commodity"*/*"asset"* traded is a service, whose need emanates from the need to transport goods around the globe, thus constituting a derived demand. Moreover, the freight service that the vessel can provide is *"perishable"*, in the sense that if it is not used at the time it is available, it is *"gone"* for ever. Thus, the *"commodity"* freight service, is non-storable and cannot be carried forward in time. It cannot be delivered in its physical form. It is also important to recognize the significant sums involved in hiring vessels, but also the high cyclicality and volatility in freight rates. Furthermore, the structure of the industry and the parties involved in trading the freight service and its derivatives instruments are often private companies whose creditworthiness characteristics are not always transparent to the market. All the above properties provide a flavour of the issues that must be taken into account when designing derivatives contracts, which have freight rates as the underlying *"commodity"*.

Take for instance the problem of pricing freight futures and forward contracts. It is recognized that freight futures prices in shipping are based on expectations, which are themselves highly fickle and heavily influenced by the level of spot freight rates. Unlike physical commodities, which are stored in their physical form, freight derivatives contracts, have the price of a service as the underlying *"commodity"*, and as a consequence they cannot be stored and carried forward in time (see Kavussanos and Visvikis, 2004). The theory governing the relationship between spot and derivatives prices of continuously storable commodities is developed in Working (1970) amongst others, while that of non-storable commodities is examined in studies such as Eydeland and Geman (1998), Geman and Vasicek (2001), Bessembinder and Lemmon (2002) in the electricity derivatives markets and by Kavussanos (2002) and

Kavussanos and Visvikis (2004) in freight derivatives markets. The non-storable nature of the freight derivatives market implies that spot and derivatives prices are not linked by a cost-of-carry (storage) relationship, as in financial and agricultural derivatives markets. The arbitrage strategies required to enforce the cost-of-carry relation include purchasing the asset at the spot price and storing it for subsequent sale at the forward price (see MacKinlay and Ramaswamy, 1988). Since this strategy cannot be executed in freight markets, freight derivatives prices need not conform to the cost-of-carry relation. Thus, inter-dependence between spot and derivatives prices may not be as strong as it is for storable commodities. Thus, following the arguments put forward in Kavussanos and Visvikis (2004) freight derivatives prices must reflect expectations of where the rates will be at the time of settlement.

The success or failure of a derivatives contract is determined by its ability to perform its economic functions efficiently, and therefore, to provide benefits to economic agents, over and above the benefits they derive from the spot market. These economic functions are price discovery and risk management through hedging. If the derivatives market does not perform one or both of these functions satisfactorily, then market agents have no reasons to trade in the derivatives market, which eventually leads to loss of trading interest. This section of the chapter considers empirical work that has appeared in the literature on these and other issues pertaining to freight rate derivatives. They include, surveys of the use of futures/FFA market by principals, the impact of the introduction of the FFA markets on the volatility of freight rates, the relationship between FFA bid-ask spreads and expected volatility, the forward freight rate dynamics and the pricing of freight options. The results of this empirical work are presented next[57].

3.10.1. Pricing and Price Discovery Function of Freight Futures and FFAs

The impossibility of storing the freight service and delivering it for settlement meant that clearing of a freight futures or forward contract on the freight service had to be cash settled. Moreover, the usual cost-of-carry relationship, presented in section 2.3.2.5 of Chapter 2, does not hold, as the usual arbitrage relationships do not apply in this case. As discussed in earlier sections of this chapter and in Chapter 2, futures/forward prices on freight rates are driven by the expectations of market agents regarding the spot prices that will prevail at the expiry of the contract. This pricing relationship, which is discussed as case 7 in section 2.3.2.5.3 of Chapter 2, is called the "*unbiasedness hypothesis*", since it implies that futures/forward prices are unbiased forecasts of the realised spot prices.

As discussed in Kavussanos and Nomikos (1999) and Kavussanos (2002), examination of the unbiasedness hypothesis in the BIFFEX market indicates that futures prices one- and two-months from maturity provided unbiased forecasts of the realised spot freight prices, while Haigh (2000) also finds the three-months BIFFEX contracts to be unbiased forecasts of the BFI spot prices. Moreover, it seems that BIFFEX prices provided better forecasts of future spot rates in comparison to a number of other statistical models, like the Autoregressive Integrated Moving Average (ARIMA) and exponential smoothing models (for further discussion, see Kavussanos, 2002).

---

[57] For a comprehensive survey of the empirical studies on the FFA market see Kavussanos and Visvikis (2006), where mathematical equations are used to describe the relevant relationships more analytically.

In addition to revealing information about expected spot prices, futures prices also provide information about current spot prices. The investigation of the lead-lag relationship (price discovery) in the BIFFEX market indicates that there is a bi-directional causal relationship between the BIFFEX contracts and spot prices, with the relationship being stronger from BIFFEX to spot prices. The latter is thought to be a consequence of higher transactions costs that prevail in the spot market in comparison to those in the freight futures market. Moreover, univariate and multivariate forecast models when applied to data from the BIFFEX market indicate that a Vector Error-Correction Model (VECM) generates significantly the most accurate forecasts of BFI prices, for a period up to 15 days ahead, and therefore, BIFFEX prices help in improving the forecasting performance of spot prices. For the BIFFEX prices however, the increase in forecasting performance, through the VECM, is insignificant across all the forecasting horizons. This suggests that the prior of market efficiency is reasonable (for further discussion, see Kavussanos, 2002).

Kavussanos, Visvikis and Menachof (2004) and Kavussanos and Visvikis (2004) investigate the unbiasedness hypothesis and the lead-lag relationship in returns and volatilities between spot and FFA prices, respectively. They examine the following constituent routes of the BPI: (a) the Atlantic voyage route P1 (US Gulf/Antwerp-Rotterdam-Amsterdam); (b) the Atlantic time-charter route P1A (Transatlantic round to Skaw-Gibraltar range); (c) the Pacific voyage route P2 (US Gulf/Japan); and (d) the Pacific time-charter route P2A (Skaw Passero-Gibraltar/Taiwan-Japan). They find that FFA prices one- and two-months prior to maturity are unbiased predictors of the realised spot prices in all investigated routes. FFA prices for contracts with three-months evidence is mixed, with FFA prices on routes P2 and P2A being unbiased estimators, while FFA prices for routes P1 and P1A seem to be biased estimators of the realised spot prices. Thus, it seems that unbiasedness depends on the market and type of contract under investigation. For the investigated routes and maturities for which unbiasedness holds, market agents can use the FFA prices as predictors of the future course of spot prices, in order to guide their physical market decisions.

Moreover, the Kavussanos and Visvikis (2004) study investigate the lead-lag relationships between forward and spot markets, both in terms of returns and volatility – which represent the second dimension of the price discovery role of derivatives markets. A VECM model is used to investigate the short-run dynamics and the price movements in the spot and the FFA markets. Causality tests and impulse response analysis indicate that there is a bi-directional causal relationship between FFA and spot markets in all routes, implying that FFA prices can be equally important as sources of information as spot prices are in commodity markets. Further tests on the unrestricted VECM models, suggest that causality from FFA to spot returns runs stronger than the other way in routes P1 and P2A, while for routes P1A and P2 causality runs stronger from spot to FFAs than from FFAs to spot. Volatility spillovers between spot and FFA markets are also investigated through an extended bivariate VECM-Generalised Autoregressive Conditional Heteroskedasticity Model (GARCH) model. The results indicate that the FFA market volatility spills information to the spot market volatility in route P1. In route P1A no volatility spillovers prevail in either market. In routes P2 and P2A there is a bi-directional relationship, as each market transmits volatility into the other. Differences in findings between the routes are attributed to the liquidity differences that exist between the routes. The results, in routes P1 and P2A, indicate that informed agents are not indifferent between trading in the FFA or in the spot market, as new market information disseminates faster in the FFA market compared to the spot market. Thus, it seems that FFA prices in those routes contain useful information about subsequent spot prices, beyond that already embedded in the current spot price and, therefore, can be used as price discovery vehicles.

3.10.2. The Hedging Effectiveness of Freight Derivatives
The second important function that futures and forward contracts are expected to fulfill is that of hedging effectiveness. This is discussed in section 2.3.2.4 of Chapter 2 of this book. Market agents, when using these contracts, aim to neutralize the possibility of adverse price change of the underlying commodity. This function has been investigated in the case of BIFFEX contracts for each period there was a major change in the composition of the BFI, by Kavussanos and Nomikos (2000). Broadly speaking, changes in the composition of the BFI made it gradually more homogeneous, a result of which was to improve the hedging effectiveness of the BIFFEX contract. This hedging effectiveness, measured by the variance reduction in the portfolio of BIFFEX with individual routes of the BFI, was shown to range from 4% to 19.2%. Moreover, it was shown in the same study that time-varying hedge ratios perform much better in improving hedging effectiveness in such routes as 1, 1A, 3A, 7, 8 and 10 of the BFI, in comparison to other strategies.

However, BIFFEX contracts failed to reduce the risk of the physical position to the extent found in other markets in the literature. For instance, for the Canadian interest rate futures the hedging effectiveness is 57.06% (Gagnon and Lypny, 1995), for the corn and soybean futures the hedging effectiveness is 69.61% and 85.69%, respectively (Bera, Garcia and Roh, 1997), for the FTSE/ASE-20 and FTSE/ASE Mid-40 stock index futures the hedging effectiveness is 94.62% and 96.02%, respectively (Kavussanos, Visvikis and Alexakis, 2004).

Kavussanos and Visvikis (2005) investigate the risk management function of the FFA market. They examine the effectiveness of time-varying hedge ratios (estimated from bivariate VECM-GARCH models), in reducing freight rate risk in four routes of the BPI. In-sample and out-of-sample tests indicate that in voyage routes (P1 and P2) the relationship between spot and FFA prices is quite stable and market agents can use simple first-difference regression models in order to obtain optimum hedge ratios. In contrast, in time-charter routes (P1A and P2A), it seems that the arrival of new information affects the relationship between spot and FFA prices, and therefore, time-varying hedge ratios should be preferred. Also, the hedging effectiveness varies from one freight market to the other. This is because freight prices, and consequently FFA quotes, are affected by different regional economic conditions. The relatively low trading volume, the way that shipbrokers estimate their FFA quotes, and the lack of the cost-of-carry arbitrage relationship, that keeps spot and derivatives prices close together, may provide explanations about the finding that spot price fluctuations of the investigated trading routes are not accurately tracked by FFA prices.

3.10.3. The Forecasting Performance of Freight Derivatives
A number of authors have examined the issue of forecasting freight futures/forward prices. The issue is interesting, as accurate forecasting of prices help market agents plan ahead and make better decisions. The first effort to forecast freight futures was made by Cullinane (1992) who build a univariate ARIMA model for forecasting BIFFEX. He concludes that an Autoregressive (AR) model outperforms the other specifications for forecasts up to 7 days ahead, while for greater lead times, the Holt-Winters model provides superior forecasts. His exercise was repeated in Cullinane *et*

al. (1999) with more updated data. Chang and Chang (1996) also examine the forecasting ability of BIFFEX and suggest that forecasts of the BFI can be employed to develop a strategy for speculation. The last and most comprehensive study on forecasting the BIFFEX – see Kavussanos (2002) for details – shows that BIFFEX prices indicate that BIFFEX prices across all maturities outperform a number of alternative models for predicting realised spot prices – such as VECM, ARIMA, exponential smoothing and random walk. This implies that market participants receive accurate signals from BIFFEX prices and can use them as indicators of the future course of spot index prices.

Batchelor, Alizadeh and Visvikis (2003) compare the performance of multivariate and univariate time-series models in generating short-term forecasts of spot freight rates and FFA prices. They create independent non-overlapping forecast sets by generating *N*-period ahead multiple forecasts, constructed from recursively estimated model parameters. Results indicate that, while conditioning spot returns on lagged FFA returns, generates more accurate forecasts of the spot prices for all forecast horizons (1–20 days ahead), conditioning FFA returns on lagged spot returns enhances forecast accuracy only up to 4 days ahead. For longer forecast horizons (up to 20 days ahead), simple univariate ARIMA models seem to be the best models for forecasting FFA prices. Thus, FFA prices seem to be able to enhance the forecasting performance of spot prices.

3.10.4. Impact of Freight Derivatives Trading on the Volatility of the Underlying Markets

Kavussanos, Visvikis and Batchelor (2004), using a Glosten, Jagannathan, and Runkle (1993) GJR-GARCH model, investigate the impact of FFA trading and the activities of speculators on spot market price volatility. The results suggest that the onset of FFA trading has had (i) a stabilising impact on the spot price volatility in all routes; (ii) a reduction in the asymmetry of volatility and market dynamics in routes P2 and P2A; and (iii) substantially improved the quality and speed of information flow in routes P1, P1A and P2. After including in the conditional variance equation other explanatory economic variables that may affect spot volatility, the results indicate that only in voyage routes P1 and P2 the reduction of volatility may be a direct consequence of FFA trading. The results do not present a clear answer as to whether the reduction in spot freight rate volatility, in time-charter routes P1A and P2A, is a direct consequence of FFA trading. We conjecture that by attracting more, and possibly better informed, participants into the market, FFA trading has assisted in the incorporation of information into spot prices more quickly. Thus, even those market agents who do not directly use the FFA market have benefited from the introduction of FFA trading.

3.10.5. Forward Freight Rate Dynamics

Koekebakker and Adland (2004) investigate the forward freight rate dynamics by modelling them under a term-structure model. They transform time-charter rates into average based forward freight rates. They then assume that there exists a continuous forward freight rate function that correctly prices the average based forward freight rate contracts. For their analysis, they use time-charter rates for a Panamax 65,000 dwt vessel under three different time-charter maturities; six-months, one-year and three years. These data are then used to construct, each day, a forward rate function using a smoothing algorithm in order to investigate the factors governing the dynamics of the forward freight rate curve.

Results show that the volatility of the forward curve is bumped, with volatility reaching a peak for freight rates with roughly one-year to maturity. Moreover, correlations between different parts of the term-structure are in general low and even negative. They conclude that these results are not found in other markets. Such a forward freight rate model provides the necessary tool to perform freight rate derivatives valuation and hedging. However, the authors argue that the empirical results of their study must be interpreted with care, since building a term-structure based on only 3 T/C rates is somewhat limited and further research in needed.

3.10.6. The Relationship between Expected Volatility and Bid-Ask Spreads in Freight Derivatives

Batchelor, Alizadeh and Visvikis (2005) examine the relationship between expected volatility and FFA bid-ask spreads. The results indicate that there is a positive relationship between bid-ask spreads and expected price volatility (derived from a well-specified GARCH model) in routes P1, P2, and P2A, after other factors are controlled. In contrast, in route P1A a significant relationship is not observed between bid-ask spreads and expected volatility. This finding may be explained by the thin trading of the FFA contracts in the latter route. Overall, these results provide a better understanding of the movements of FFA prices, and the consequent effect in transactions costs. Market agents using the information of the behaviour of the bid-ask spreads can have a better insight about the timing of their FFA transactions and the future direction of the FFA market, as widening bid-ask spreads are indicators of increased future volatility. More specifically, traders, speculators, hedgers, and arbitrageurs alike are interested in extracting information from the bid-ask spreads in order to be used in predicting future prices.

3.10.7. Pricing of Freight Options

The correct pricing of derivatives contracts is important for market agents concerned. As mentioned before, the special features present in the underlying commodity – the freight rate – must be taken into account when pricing derivatives contracts on them. For instance, we saw earlier in this section of the chapter and in Chapter 2 of this book that Kavussanos (2002) and Kavussanos and Visvikis (2004) show that freight futures and forward contracts are priced in terms of the expected values of freight rates, as a result of the feature of non-storability of freight services. The model is shown to work well in practice. Similarly, with freight options, Tvedt (1998) derives a pricing formula for European freight options on BIFFEX, recognizing the special features related to the freight rate market. Two main characteristics make his formula different from the futures option formula of Black (1976). Due to the possible lay-up of vessels, the BFI is never close to zero. Therefore, it is assumed that the BFI, and also the futures price process, are restricted downward by an absorbing level above zero. Secondly, it is recognized that freight rates are reverted downward if they are above average and upward if they are below average. This log-normal mean reversion property is due to frictional capacity adjustments to changes in the demand for shipping services, and it influences the valuation of the futures options.He argues that the option pricing formula may also be applicable to other futures markets (e.g. electricity), after some adjustments.

Koekebakker *et al.* (2005) propose a mathematical framework for Asian freight options modelling. Assuming lognormal spot freight dynamics, they argue that FFAs are lognormal prior to the settlement period, but this lognormality breaks down in the settlement period. They suggest an approximate dynamics in the settlement period for the FFA, leading to closed-form option pricing formulas for Asian call and put options written on the spot freight rate indices in the Black (1976) framework. However, they admit that the accuracy of their approximation is questioned as other dynamics, than the lognormal, have to be investigated. Moreover, despite aknowledging that freight services are non-storable, and as a consequence standard arbitrage arguments do not hold, it is not evident how this is taken into account in the pricing framework they propose.

While sea transportation is a continuous supply of the freight rate service, the freight rate is fixed and set when a vessel is fixed on the spot freight market. Consequently, the freight revenue for a vessel in the spot freight market is given by discretely sampled prices, at stochastic intervals. As discussed earlier in this chapter, freight options belong to the family of path-dependent contingent claims called Asian options, which have a payoff based on an average of freight rates. While an Asian option with geometric averaging has a closed-form solution in a standard geometric Brownian pricing framework, exact pricing formulas for arithmetic average options do not exist, since the distribution of the arithmetic average of a lognormal process is unknown (Kemma and Vorst, 1990). According to Tvedt (1998), European BIFFEX futures options were informally valued using the analytical pricing formulas of Black (1976) and Black and Scholes (1973), with implied volatility having an important role in the pricing of options. This practice continues for the Asian style freight options traded today. Koekebakker *et al.* (2005) argues that, while unjustifiable from a theoretical and mathematical point of view, these well-known option pricing formulas are fast, easy to use and familiar to traders.

3.10.8. Market Surveys on the Use of Freight Derivatives
There have been three studies known to us in the literature that investigate the perceptions of market agents in shipping, as to the use of freight derivatives. Cullinane (1991) surveys the attitudes and behaviour of shipowners with respect to BIFFEX. The survey includes questionnaire replies from 85 shipowners in four countries (Britain, Greece, Hong Kong and Norway). The results of the survey suggest that the shipping community was fully aware of the existence of BIFFEX and that shipowners were reasonably aware of how to make use of this facility. However, he concludes that a problem existed, in that BIFFEX was not accepted as a viable hedging mechanism by the vast majority of the sample.

Dinwoodie and Morris (2003) survey the attitudes of tanker shipowners and charterers towards freight hedging and their risk perceptions of FFAs. The survey includes questionnaire replies from seven countries over 22 shipowners and 8 charterers. They argue that although FFAs were widely viewed as an important development, some respondents were unaware of their function and the majority had not used them. Most of the participants in this survey were concerned about the risk of payment default on settlement. Many shipowners also feared that FFAs might expose their risk management policies to counterparties. The link between freight hedging activity and participants' risk aversion was not clear-cut, but they argue that improved "*technical*" education is essential for widespread acceptance.

Kavussanos, Visvikis and Goulielmou (2005) conducted a questionnaire survey with 31 replies, to investigate the importance of hedging freight rate risk through derivatives for the Greek shipowners. The results indicate that: (i) risk management and shipping derivatives are in early development and understanding in the Greek shipping market, although participants in the sample seem to know about them; (ii) the traditional ways of thinking must be changed and replaced with modern risk management concepts, which should be part of the general business strategy of the company; (iii) liquidity and credit (counterparty) risk are considered to be major obstacles in the use of shipping derivatives; (iv) in line with the findings of Dinwoodie and Morris (2003), they consider education to be of paramount importance for them; and finally (v) there seems to be a positive view of the future of shipping derivatives in Greece, especially if the banks endorse them.

3.11. Summary

This chapter presented how freight rate derivative tools, such as futures, forwards and options can be used to hedge freight rate risks in the dry- and liquid-bulk sectors of the shipping industry. Speculation and arbitrage strategies were also considered. The chapter started by presenting the underlying indices of freight rate derivatives, which are constructed by the Baltic Exchange and Platts. These indices and their constituent routes provide the underlying commodities for freight rate derivatives to be written upon.

As freight services are non-storable, non-deliverable commodities, cash settlement takes place on the values of the indices the derivatives are written on. Settlement varies, according to the maturity of the contract (one month, one quarter or one year), the type of contract (voyage, time-charter, etc.) and the sector (dry-bulk, tanker). Exchange-traded, OTC and cleared-OTC freight derivatives have been examined and compared under different situations. It is argued here that freight rate derivatives can be thought of as a third market which provides the flexibility that traditional methods of risk management are not able to provide to companies. All these issues have been demonstrated through many practical examples. Furthermore, critical discussion of the issues involved in derivatives trading has been provided in order to understand the pros and cons of using freight derivatives, and at the end of the day allow the reader to make an informed choice about how to use these instruments effectively for risk management purposes. Finally, the economics underlying the freight derivatives markets and the empirical evidence related to it have been presented in this chapter.

The next chapter of the book considers another source of risk identified in chapter one of this book as affecting the balance-sheet of the shipowner and of the charterer under time-charter agreements; that is, bunker price risk. It shows how derivative instruments may be used to control this cost side of the balance-sheet of the business. Given the fluctuations of bunker fuel prices it represents an important element of risk management for companies.

APPENDIX I: IMAREX Trading Membership Agreement

 **NOS**

TRADING MEMBERSHIP AGREEMENT

This Trading Membership Agreement ("**Agreement**") is entered into on the .... between

A. **THE INTERNATIONAL MARITIME EXCHANGE AS ("IMAREX"),** a limited company incorporated under the laws of Norway, with Reg. No: 981 999 460 in the Norwegian Register of Business Enterprises; and

B. .... (**"Company"),** established under the laws of ....with postal address .... and Reg. No:............................in the *(name of company register)*........................ ....

(together the "**Parties**").

1. Subject to the terms and conditions of this Agreement and the Rulebook, the Trading Member may trade Listed Products and Non-Listed Products at IMAREX.

2. By signing this Agreement the Trading Member:

(a) acknowledges and accepts the terms of the Rulebook; and

(b) agrees to be bound by and observe such terms as amended from time to time.

3. The Trading Member represents and shall represent on a continuing basis for the duration of this Agreement:
   (a) that it fulfils the Trading Membership Requirements;

   (b) that all information that it has provided or will provide to IMAREX with respect to its financial position and qualification to be a Trading Member is true, accurate and correct as at the date of this Agreement or, if later, as at the date of its provision;

   (c) that this Agreement and the Rulebook constitute its legal, valid and binding obligations of the Trading Member, enforceable against it in accordance with their respective terms;

   (d) that it has all necessary power and authority to execute this Agreement and perform and comply with its obligations hereunder and that the individual signing this Agreement is duly authorised to do so;

   (e) that the execution and performance of this Agreement does not violate any law, rule, or regulation, or any agreement, document or other instrument binding on or applicable to it: and

   (f) it has any and all licences, consents, registrations, authorisations or other similar approvals which are required under applicable laws or regulations in order to enable it to participate as a Trading Member in accordance with the Rules, execute Contracts in Non-Listed Products through IMAREX and perform its obligations to its counterparties pursuant to such Contracts.

4. Subject to the Rules, this Agreement may be terminated by either of the Parties upon one month's written notice, such notice to be given in accordance with the User Guide.

5. The provisions of the Rules shall apply to this Agreement as if incorporated in this Agreement.

6. Defined terms in this Agreement shall bear the meaning ascribed to them in the Rules.

7. Save as provided by the Rules, a person who is not a Party may not enforce any of its terms under the Contracts (Rights of Third Parties) Act 1999 and IMAREX shall be under no obligation to enforce the Rules against any such person.

8. The provisions of the Rules as to governing law, submission to jurisdiction and dispute resolution shall apply as if incorporated in this Agreement.

9. This Agreement may be executed in two counterparts. Such execution shall have the same effect as if the signatures of the counterparts were on a single copy of this Agreement.

10. If at any time any provision of this Agreement becomes illegal, invalid or unenforceable in any aspect under the law of any relevant jurisdiction, neither the legality, validity or enforceability of the remaining provisions of this Agreement nor the legality, validity or enforceability of such provision under the law of any other jurisdiction shall in any way be affected or impaired thereby.

11. The Trading Member may not assign or transfer any rights or obligations under this Agreement without the prior written consent of IMAREX.

Oslo, ... 2005

....

The International Maritime Exchange AS

....(Company)

(place) (date).......................... 2005

.... Signature

....

Repeat signature in block letter

APPENDIX II: IMAREX Clearing Membership Agreement

 **NOS**

CLEARING MEMBERSHIP AGREEMENT

This Clearing Membership Agreement ("**Agreement**") is entered into on .... between

A. THE NORWEGIAN FUTURES AND OPTIONS CLEARING HOUSE (NOS CLEARING ASA) ("NOS"), a public limited company incorporated under the laws of Norway, with postal address P.O. Box 246 Sentrum, 0103, Oslo, and Reg. No: N 981 119 487 in the Norwegian Register of Business Enterprises; and

B. ....("**Company"),** established under the laws of .... with postal address ....
.... and Reg. No:
.... in the *(name of company register)*................................,

(together the "**Parties**").

1. Subject to the terms and conditions of this Agreement and the Rulebook, the Clearing Member may Clear in NOS, Contracts in Listed Products and Non-Listed Products on the International Maritime Exchange AS ("**IMAREX**").

2. By signing this Agreement the Clearing Member:

    (a) acknowledges and accepts the terms of the Rulebook; and

    (b) agrees to be bound by and observe such terms as amended from time to time.

3. The Clearing Member must hold a Trading Membership with IMAREX to be able to enter Cleared Contracts. If the Clearing Member is not a Trading Member, it acknowledges that this Agreement shall not commence until IMAREX has notified it of its successful application for Trading Membership.

4. The Clearing Member represents and shall represent on a continuing basis for the duration of this Agreement:

    (a) that it fulfils the Trading Membership Requirements;

    (b) that it fulfils the Clearing Membership Requirements;

    (c) that all information that it has provided or will provide to IMAREX with respect to its financial position and qualification to be a Trading Member or otherwise in accordance with the Rules is true, accurate and correct as at the date of this Agreement or, if later, as at the date of its provision;

    (d) that all information that it has provided or will provide to NOS with respect to its financial position and qualification to be a Clearing Member or otherwise in accordance with the Rules is true, accurate and correct as at the date of this Agreement or, if later, as at the date of its provision;

    (e) that this Agreement and the Rulebook constitute legal, valid and binding obligations of the Clearing Member, enforceable against it in accordance with their respective terms;

    (f) that it has all necessary power and authority to execute this Agreement and perform and comply with its obligations hereunder and that the individual signing this Agreement is duly authorised to do so;

(g) that the execution and performance of this Agreement does not violate any law, rule, or regulation, or any agreement, document or other instrument binding on or applicable to it: and

(h) it has any all licences, consents, registrations, authorisations or other similar approvals which are required under applicable laws or regulations in order to enable it to participate as a Clearing Member in accordance with the Rules, execute Contracts in Cleared Contracts through IMAREX and perform its obligations to its counterparties (including NOS) pursuant to such Contracts.

5. The Clearing Member has been allocated the following clearing account(s) with NOS:
(Will be supplied by NOS later).
Clearing Account: ....
Clearing Account: ....

6. Subject to the Rules, this Agreement may be terminated by either of the Parties upon one month's written notice, such notice to be given in accordance with the Rulebook chapter 9.

7. The provisions of the Rules shall apply to this Agreement as if incorporated in this Agreement.

8. Defined terms in this Agreement shall bear the meaning ascribed to them in the Rules.

9. Save as provided by the Rules, a person who is not a Party may not enforce any of its terms under the Contracts (Rights of Third Parties) Act 1999 and NOS shall be under no obligation to enforce the Rules against any such person.

10. The provisions of the Rules as to governing law, submission to jurisdiction and dispute resolution shall apply as if incorporated in this Agreement.

11. This Agreement may be executed in two counterparts. Such execution shall have the same effect as if the signatures of the counterparts were on a single copy of this Agreement.

12. If at any time any provision of this Agreement becomes illegal, invalid or unenforceable in any aspect under the law of any relevant jurisdiction, neither the legality, validity or enforceability of the remaining provisions of this Agreement, nor the legality, validity or enforceability of such provision under the law of any other jurisdiction shall in any way be affected or impaired thereby.

13. The Clearing Member may not assign or transfer any rights or obligations under this Agreement without the prior written consent of NOS.

Oslo, ... 2005

....
NOS Clearing ASA

(place)(date) 2005

.............................Signature

...........................(Company)
....
Repeat signature in block letters

274

APPENDIX III: IMAREX Margin and Settlement Account Agreement

NOS

MARGIN AND SETTLEMENT ACCOUNT AGREEMENT

This Margin and Settlement Account Agreement ("Agreement") is entered into as of [   ] between

A. [   ] (the "Member"); and

B. THE NORWEGIAN FUTURES AND OPTION CLEARING HOUSE (NOS CLEARING ASA) ("NOS"),

(together the "Parties").

The Parties agree as follows:

1. Reference is made to the Rulebook for Trading at IMAREX - The International Maritime Exchange and Clearing with NOS - The Norwegian Futures and Options Clearing House (NOS Clearing ASA) (as amended from time to time, the "Rulebook"). The provisions of the Rulebook (including without limitation Clause 8) shall apply to this Agreement, and capitalized defined terms not defined in this Agreement have the meanings given to them in the Rulebook.

2. NOS has established in its name a deposit account (the "Account") with the bank identified a separate letter from NOS to the Member (the "Settlement Bank"). Clearing Members shall deposit funds into the Account to provide for margin in the form of cash collateral and for settlement requirements for contracts on Non-Listed Products and Listed Products on IMAREX.

3. The Settlement Bank has agreed to maintain on its books and records a sub-account for each Clearing Member. A Clearing Member's sub-account will record the funds received from that Clearing Member as well as disbursements made to the Clearing Member from the Account at NOS's direction and withdrawals and deposits made by NOS.

4. With the Member's authorization and agreement, NOS has directed the Settlement Bank to establish a sub-account (the "Sub-account") for the Member. The Sub-account does not constitute a separate account at the Settlement Bank and the Member does not have a depositor or other contractual relationship with the Settlement Bank or the right to make withdrawals from the Sub-account or the Account. Only NOS has the right to make withdrawals from the Account and to debit the Sub-account. The Member has the right to request that NOS direct the Settlement Bank to make disbursements to the Member under the circumstances described in Clause 6.4.2 of the Rulebook. The Member authorizes NOS to hold the Member's funds in the Account and to commingle those funds with funds received from other Clearing Members.

5. In a separate letter from NOS to the Member, there is set forth (a) the identity and address of the branch of the Settlement Bank at which the Account and the Sub-Account are maintained, (b) the account number of the Account, and (c) the sub-account number of the Sub-account. In making deposits, the Member must reference both this account number and sub-account number. All deposits must be made in immediately available funds.

6. The Member bears all risk of loss with respect to funds held on its behalf in the Account with the Bank. NOS shall not be responsible for any loss suffered by the Member as a result of the insolvency of the Bank, the Bank's failure to make any payment, any moratorium or any other event whatsoever. The member recognizes and acknowledges that neither the account nor the sub-account is insured by any governmental agency or private entity.

7. The Member authorizes NOS to disclose such information concerning the Member as the Settlement Bank shall reasonably request, including without limitation the information contained in the Member's

Trading and Clearing Membership Application Form and Appendix A: Commodity Exchange Act Compliance Questionnaire.

8. The Sub-account constitutes the Member's "Margin and Settlement Account" for purposes of the Rulebook and corresponds to the Clearing Account No. [ ] held by the Member with NOS for clearing of contracts in Non-Listed and Listed Products on IMAREX.

9. By signing this Agreement the Member acknowledges and accepts the terms of the Rulebook and agrees to be bound by and observe its terms, as amended from time to time. Without limiting the generality of the foregoing, the Member agrees to provide margin and pay settlements amounts when due in accordance with the provisions of the Rulebook.

10. The Member represents and warrants and shall represent and warrant on a continuing basis for the duration of this Agreement:

(a) that this Agreement and the Rulebook constitute legal, valid and binding obligations of the Member, enforceable against it in accordance with their respective terms;

(b) that it has all necessary power and authority to execute this Agreement and perform and comply with its obligations hereunder and that the individual signing this Agreement is duly authorized to do so;

(c) that the execution and performance of this Agreement does not violate any law, rule, or regulation, or any agreement, document or other instrument binding on or applicable to it;

(d) it has any and all licenses, consents, registrations, authorisations or other similar approvals which are required under applicable laws or regulations in order to enable it to participate as a Clearing Member in accordance with the Rulebook, execute Transactions in Cleared Contracts through IMAREX and perform its obligations to its counterparties (including NOS) pursuant to such transactions; and

(e) no person or entity other than the Member will have any interest in the Sub-account or the Pledged Cash (as defined below).

11. The Member pledges to NOS and grants NOS a security interest and right of set-off in all cash which is at present, or will in the future be, deposited in or credited to the Sub-Account (including interest) (the "Pledged Cash") to secure payment of margin and any settlement amounts in accordance with the Rulebook. For purposes of this pledge, the Members assigns to NOS any rights it may now have or later acquire to claim these cash deposits from the Settlement Bank.

12. The Member agrees that NOS has the right to withdraw funds from the Account and debit the Sub-account without notice to the Member for the purposes and to make the payments described in the Rulebook. NOS may apply the Pledged Cash in payment of margin and any settlement amounts owing by the Member in accordance with the Rulebook without notice to the Member and in such order as NOS sees fit. The Member agrees that NOS alone has the right to give instructions to the Settlement Bank with respect to the Account and the Sub-account and further agrees that it will not give or attempt to give the Settlement Bank instructions with respect to the Account or the Sub-account.

13. Interest shall accrue on the Sub-account to the extent, if any, provided a separate letter from NOS to the Member.

14. The Member agrees that all confirmations and account statements received by it from NOS or the Settlement Bank shall be conclusive and binding on it unless the Member sends a written objection to NOS within [3] days after receipt.

15. The Member authorizes NOS to disclose such information concerning NOS, the Member and its relationship and transactions with NOS as any regulator, regulatory authority or similar body may request.

16. The Member agrees to indemnify NOS and hold NOS harmless from and against any and all liabilities, losses, damages, reasonable costs and expenses (including attorneys' fees) incurred by NOS in the performance of its obligations or the enforcement of its rights under this Agreement or in

connection therewith or because of any default or breach by the Member of any of its obligations under this Agreement or in connection therewith, except to the extent that the same is incurred through the gross negligence, willful default or fraud of NOS. The Member also agrees to pay promptly to NOS all losses, damages, reasonable costs and expenses (including attorneys' fees) incurred by NOS in the enforcement of any provisions of this Agreement. This indemnity is additional to any other rights or remedies available to NOS.

17. This Agreement may be amended only by a writing signed by both Parties. This Agreement shall be binding on the Parties and their respective successors and permitted assigns. The Member may assign or transfer its rights or obligations under this Agreement only with the prior written consent of NOS, and any transfer in violation of the foregoing shall be void and of no effect.

18. This Agreement will be governed by and construed in accordance with the laws of the State of New York. With respect to any suit, action or proceedings relating to this Agreement, Chapter 10 of the Rulebook shall apply. The Parties irrevocably waive their rights to a trial by jury of any dispute or claim relating to this Agreement.

19. Neither this Agreement, nor the establishment of the Account or the Sub-account, nor the deposit of funds in accordance with this Agreement establishes any fiduciary relationship, relationship of trust or agency or similar relationship between the Parties; and NOS shall have no fiduciary or similar duties to the Member. NOS shall have no responsibility or liability for the acts or omissions of third parties, including, without limitation, the Settlement Bank.

20. This Agreement contains the entire agreement between the Parties with respect to the matters to which it relates, and supersedes all prior commitments, agreements and understandings, whether written or oral, with respect to those matters.

21. This Agreement shall terminate only at such time as the Member has terminated its Clearing Membership Agreement and has fully discharged all its obligations to pay margin and settlement amounts in accordance with the Rulebook.

22. This Agreement may be executed in counterparts, all of which taken together shall constitute one and the same original.

The Parties intending to be legally bound have executed and delivered this Agreement as of the date first above written.

[Member]
By: _____
Signature: _____
Repeat in block letters: _____
Title: _____

The Norwegian Futures and Option Clearing House (NOS Clearing ASA)
By: _____
Name: _____
Repeat in block letters: _____
Title: _____

APPENDIX IV: FFABA 2000 Contract

FFABA 2000 ™ 1 August 2000

FORWARD FREIGHT AGREEMENT BROKERS ASSOCIATION ("FFABA")
FORWARD FREIGHT 'SWAP' AGREEMENT

File Ref:

Contract Date:

This Forward Freight 'Swap' Agreement is made this   day of   2000 in London between:

("the Buyer")

and

("the Seller")

on the following terms and conditions.

1) Contract Route:
    As per Route .. of the Baltic .... Index as defined on the Contract Date including any relevant official forthcoming amendments published at the Contract Date which will become effective prior to the settlement of this Agreement.

Contract Rate ("fixed rate"): USD per ton

3) Contract Quantity:

4) Contract Month:

5) Settlement Date:

6) Settlement Rate ("floating rate"):

The Settlement Rate shall be the average of the rates for the Contract Route published by the Baltic Exchange over the Settlement Period defined as the last seven Baltic Exchange Index publication days of   the   Contract   Month   up   to   and   including   the   Settlement   Date. If for any reason the Baltic Exchange cannot provide any rate required for establishing the Settlement Rate, then the Forward Freight Agreement Brokers Association ("FFABA") may be instructed by either party to form a panel to establish any rate which will be binding on both parties. In this event, the parties hereto agree to indemnify and hold harmless this panel, the Baltic Exchange, the FFABA and their members against all actions, claims, demands, liabilities, damages, costs and expenses consequential to the panellists' decision.

7) Settlement Sum:
The Settlement Sum is the difference between the Contract Rate and the Settlement Rate multiplied by the Contract Quantity. If the Settlement Rate is greater than the Contract Rate, the Seller shall pay the Buyer the Settlement Sum. If the Settlement Rate is less than the Contract Rate, the Buyer shall pay the Seller the Settlement Sum.

8) Payment Procedure and Obligations:
a) Payment of the settlement sum is due on the [each] settlement date and must be received within (5) London banking days after the settlement date. the parties are obliged to provide each other with their respective bank remittance details, and invoice if requested, in order to facilitate timely payment. Payment shall be made telegraphically in full in United States Dollars without any deduction or set off unless agreed by the buyer and seller in writing. The costs incurred in effecting the payment shall be for the account of the payer. The payment may only be effected directly between the parties.

A payment is "received" for the purposes of clause 8(a) when the settlement sum has been received into the bank account designated by the payee and the payee has been notified.

If receipt of payment is delayed beyond the five day period referred to in clause 8 (a) above solely as a result of clerical and/or bank error then the payee shall give the payer written notice forthwith upon discovery of the error granting the payer three clear banking days to rectify the error. If payment has not been received within the three clear banking day period, the payor shall be in default and payee may take enforcement action.

Where the agreement calls for more than one settlement, it is clearly understood that any default in payment of any settlement in accordance with this agreement will be a repudiatory breach of the entire agreement and the innocent party may elect to terminate this agreement (without prejudice to any claim he may have for sums due to him under this agreement, interests and costs), or may deduct any arrears then due to him from any adequate subsequent settlement due by him under this agreement.

9) Capacity and Goodstanding:
Each party warrants (which warranty will be continuing) that:
a) It is duly incorporated and validly exists under the laws of its domicile and is solvent and in goodstanding;
b) It has the power to execute, deliver and perform this Agreement;
All governmental and other consents that are required to have been obtained by it with respect to this Agreement have been obtained and are in full force and effect and all conditions of any such consents have been complied with.
In the event that either party to this Agreement is a person domiciled in the United States, or a corporation incorporated in the United States [or a body [[corporation]] with its principal place of business in the United States], that party represents to the other party that its is an 'eligible swap participant' as defined by the United States Commodities Futures Trading Commission in C.F.R., paragraph 35-1 (b) (2) or similar regulations as may be applicable.

10) Commission:
Each of the parties agrees to pay brokers' commission as agreed within five days of the payment of the Settlement Sum against invoice.

11) Non-Assignability:
This Agreement is non-assignable unless otherwise agreed in writing between the Buyer and the Seller.

12) Law and Jurisdiction:
This Agreement shall be governed by and construed in accordance with English law and subject to the non-exclusive jurisdiction of the High Court of Justice in London, England. Proceedings may be validly served upon either party by sending the same by ordinary post and/or by fax to the addresses and/or fax numbers for each party given above.

Entire Agreement:
This Agreement constitutes the entire understanding and agreement between the parties and there are no representations, understandings or agreement, oral or written, which are not included herewith.

Signed for the Buyer by........................   Signed for the Seller by..........................
[printed name]   [printed name]

Duly authorised signatory   Duly authorised signatory

APPENDIX V: FFABA 2005 Contract

FFABA 2005 ™ 1 October 2005

FORWARD FREIGHT AGREEMENT BROKERS ASSOCIATION ("FFABA")

FORWARD FREIGHT SWAP AGREEMENT (DRY)

Trade Ref: [•]
Contract Date: [•]

The purpose of this confirmation is to state the terms and conditions of the forward freight swap agreement entered into between:

[•] (hereafter, "**Seller**")
Attention: [•]
Postal Address: [•]
Street Address: [•]
Telephone No.:   [•]
Facsimile No.:   [•]
Email Address: [•]

       and

[•] (hereafter, "**Buyer**")
Attention: [•]
Postal Address: [•]
Street Address: [•]
Telephone No.:   [•]
Facsimile No.:   [•]
Email Address: [•]

This agreement between the parties as constituted by this confirmation is referred to as the "**Agreement**".

Until superseded by notice information in a subsequent confirmation or other communication, the above addresses are hereby recognized as the correct addresses to which any notification under this Agreement may be properly served.

The terms of this Agreement are as follows:

1)   **Contract Route(s):**

       [•] as defined on the Contract Date including any relevant official forthcoming amendments published at the Contract Date which will become effective prior to the settlement of this Agreement.

2)   **Contract Rate ("fixed rate"):**

       [•]

3)   **Contract Quantity:**

       [•]

4)   **Contract Month(s):**

       [•]

5)   **Contract Period:**

[●]

6) **Settlement Date:**

The last Baltic Exchange Index publication day of each Contract Month.

7) **Settlement Rate:**

(a) The Settlement Rate shall be the average of the rates for the Contract Route(s) published by the Baltic Exchange over the Settlement Period defined as [●] Baltic Exchange Index publication days of the Contract Month(s) up to and including the Settlement Date.

(b) If for any reason the Baltic Exchange cannot provide any rate required for establishing the Settlement Rate, then the current chairman of the FFABA may be instructed by either party to form a panel comprising of a minimum of three independent brokers (the "**Panel**") to determine an appropriate rate, which determination will be final and binding on both parties.

(c) Each party shall bear its own costs and expenses in connection with any determination made pursuant to this clause 7.

(d) The parties shall severally indemnify and hold harmless each of the members of the Panel, the Baltic Exchange and its members and the FFABA and its members (the "**Indemnified Persons**") against all liabilities, actions, demands, costs and expenses incurred by any of them arising directly or indirectly out of or in connection with the formation of the Panel and any determination made by the Panel.

(e) As between the parties, each party shall have a right of contribution against the other party in respect of any indemnity payment made pursuant to the preceding paragraph so that their respective liabilities pursuant to that paragraph shall be equal.

8) **Settlement Sum:**

The "**Settlement Sum**" is the difference between the Contract Rate and the Settlement Rate multiplied by the Contract Quantity. If the Settlement Rate is greater than the Contract Rate, the Seller shall pay the Buyer the Settlement Sum. If the Settlement Rate is less than the Contract Rate, the Buyer shall pay the Seller the Settlement Sum.

9) **Payment Procedure and Obligations:**

(a) Payment of the Settlement Sum is due on the later of two (2) London business days after presentation of payee's invoice (with complete payment instructions) or five (5) London business days after the Settlement Date and for this purpose a "**London business day**" means a day (other than a Saturday or Sunday) on which commercial banks are open for business in London) . The Settlement Sum will be deemed "paid" when it has been received into the bank account designated by the payee.

(b) Payment of the Settlement Sum shall be made telegraphically, in full, in United States dollars. The costs incurred in effecting payment shall be for the account of the payer. Payment may only be effected directly between the parties. The Settlement Sum shall be paid without any deduction or set off unless agreed by the Buyer and the Seller in writing.

10) **ISDA Master Agreement:**

This Agreement incorporates by reference the 1992 ISDA® Master Agreement (Multicurrency – Cross Border) (without Schedule) as if it were fully set out in this Agreement and with only the following specific modifications and elections:

(a)   Section 2(c)(ii) shall not apply so that a net amount due will be determined in respect of all amounts payable on the same date in the same currency in respect of two or more Transactions;

(b)   Seller is the Calculation Agent;

(c)   the most current published set of ISDA® Commodity Definitions and ISDA® Definitions shall apply;

(d)   Credit Event Upon Merger is applicable to both parties;

(e)   for the purposes of payments on Early Termination, Loss will apply and the Second Method will apply;

(f)   the Termination Currency is United States dollars;

(g)   the Applicable Rate shall mean the one month USD-LIBOR plus 2%, reset daily and compounded monthly; and

(h)   Local Business Day or banking day shall each refer to such a day in London,

(such form, as modified, the "**Standard Agreement**") and this Agreement, including the incorporated Standard Agreement, shall govern the transaction referred to in and constituted by this Agreement except as expressly modified by this Agreement.

11)   Capacity and Good Standing:

In addition to the representations contained in Section 3 of the Standard Agreement, each party warrants that:

(a)   it is duly organized and validly existing under the jurisdiction of its organization or incorporation, and is solvent and in good standing;

(b)   it has the power to execute, deliver, and perform this Agreement;

(c)   all governmental and other consents that are required to have been obtained by it with respect to this Agreement have been obtained and are in full force and effect and all conditions of any such consents have been complied with;

(d)   in the event that a party to this Agreement is a person organized under, domiciled in, or having its principal place of business in, the United States, each party represents to the other party that it is an "eligible contract participant" as defined in § 1a(12) of the Commodity Exchange Act (7 U.S.C. § 1a(12), as amended)

12)   Telephone Recording:

Each party consents to the recording of telephone conversations in connection with this Agreement.

13)   Commission:

Each of the parties agrees to pay brokers' commission to any broker (a "**Broker**") as agreed with any Broker.

14)   Non-Assignability:

Except as provided in Section 7 of the Standard Agreement, this Agreement is non-assignable unless otherwise agreed in writing between the parties to this Agreement.

15)   **Principal To Principal:**

This is a principal to principal agreement with settlement directly between the two parties. Both parties agree that any Broker shall be under no obligation or liability in relation to this Agreement. Both parties agree jointly and severally to indemnify and hold harmless any Broker against all actions, including but not limited to all claims, demands, liabilities, damages, costs and expenses both from the two parties and any third party. Claims, demands, liabilities, damages, costs and expenses suffered or incurred are to be settled directly by or between the two parties.

16)   **Law and Jurisdiction:**

Pursuant to Section 13(b) of the Standard Agreement, this Agreement shall be governed by and construed in accordance with English law and shall be subject to the exclusive jurisdiction of the High Court of Justice in London, England. The terms of Section 12(a) of the Standard Agreement notwithstanding, proceedings may be validly served upon either party by sending the same by ordinary post and/or by fax to the addresses and/or fax numbers for each party given above.

17)   **Entire Agreement:**

This Agreement constitutes the entire agreement and understanding of the parties with respect to its subject matter and supersedes all oral communication and prior writings with respect thereto.

18)   **Payment Account Information:**

For Seller: For Buyer:
Bank address: Bank address:

Aba: Aba:
Swift address: Swift address:
Account no.:   Account no.:
Sort code: Sort code:

19)   **Third party rights**

(a)   Unless provided to the contrary in this Agreement, a person who is not a party to this Agreement has no rights under the Contracts (Rights of Third Parties) Act 1999 to enforce or enjoy the benefit of any term of this Agreement.

(b)   Any Indemnified Person and any Broker shall have the right to enjoy the benefit of and enforce the terms of clause 7(d) in the case of any Indemnified Person and clause 13 in the case of any Broker.

(c)   Notwithstanding any term of this Agreement, the consent of any person who is not a party to this Agreement is not required to rescind or vary this Agreement.

20)   **Inclusion of historical FFAs under Master Agreement**

(a)   Unless the parties to this Agreement specifically agree otherwise in writing, this clause 20 shall apply in accordance with its terms.

(b)   This clause 20 applies to this Agreement and to every agreement entered into between the parties to this Agreement (and no other persons) before the date of this Agreement:

        (i)   that is expressly stated to be subject to, or is subject to substantially the same terms as, either the FFABA 2000 terms or the FFABA 2005 terms, (excluding for the avoidance of doubt terms as to the Contract Route(s), Contract Rate, Contract Quantity, Contract Month(s), Contract Period and Settlement Date), with or without amendment; and

(ii)   that does not incorporate a clause substantially in the same form as this clause 20.

(c)   Each agreement to which this clause 20 applies shall be treated as a confirmation (each a "**Confirmation**") under a master agreement (the "**Master Agreement**") constituted by the Standard Agreement as modified by, and in the form as incorporated in, this Agreement pursuant to clause 10 as if such agreement had been entered into between the parties on the terms of the Master Agreement on the date of the first such Confirmation.

(d)   If there is any inconsistency between the provisions of any agreement constituted pursuant to paragraph (c) above and the agreement constituting a transaction to which this clause 20 applies, the provisions of the agreement constituting the transaction to which this clause 20 applies will prevail for the purposes of the transaction under such agreement.

(e)   This clause 20 shall not affect any rights or obligations of the parties under any transaction accrued before the date of this Agreement.

(f)   This clause 20 is effective notwithstanding any entire agreement clause or similar provision in any such agreement relevant to any such transaction.

21)   Inclusion of subsequent FFAs under Master Agreement

(a)   Unless the parties to this Agreement specifically agree otherwise in writing, this clause 21 shall apply in accordance with its terms.

(b)   This clause 21 applies to every agreement entered into between the parties to this Agreement (and no other persons) after an agreement incorporating a Master Agreement (as defined in and pursuant to a clause substantially in the same form as and equivalent to clause 20) has been entered into by them.

(c)   This Agreement shall constitute a Confirmation under the Master Agreement on the terms of clauses 20 (c), (d), (e) and (f) as if they were incorporated and fully set out in this clause 21 with appropriate and necessary modifications for such incorporation.

Signed for the Seller by   Signed for the Buyer by

....
Duly Authorized Signatory   Duly Authorized Signatory

APPENDIX VI: Clarkson FFA Report

CLARKSON
SECURITIES LIMITED

FFA Report   8 Sep 2005

BPI	BDI	BCI	Euro/USD	USD/Yen	UK/USD	180CST Rdam	380CST Rdam
2203	2561	3624	1,2397	110,43	1,8382	320	292
+ 111,00	+ 81,00	+ 124,00	- 0,00	+ 0,37	+ 0,00	+ 11,00	+ 3,00

	Route 3A Pac RV		Route 2A TCT East		Spread Diff	Route 1A TA RV	
Sep	17.000	19.000	21.500	23.500	4.500	15.000	16.000
Oct	18.500	20.000	23.500	25.000	5.000	17.000	18.500
Nov	18.500	20.000	23.500	25.000	5.000	17.000	18.500
Dec	18.500	20.000	23.500	25.000	5.000	17.000	18.500
Jan	16.500	18.500	20.000	22.000	3.500	15.000	17.000
	BPI 15.535		**BPI 21.314**			**BPI 16.639**	

	Average of the 4 BPI TCs		Handy Mid Price	Diff	Cape Mid Price	Diff
Sep	15.000	16.000	17.250	1.750	38.000	22.500
Q4 05	21.000	21.500	19.350	-1.900	38.500	17.250
Q1 06	20.000	20.500	18.000	-2.250	36.250	16.000
Q2 06	19.500	20.000	17.700	-2.050	35.750	16.000
Cal 06	19.000	19.500	16.000	-3.250	35.000	15.750
Cal 07	14.000	15.000	12.600	-1.900	25.500	11.000
Cal 08	11.500	13.250	11.450	-925	23.000	10.625
	BPI 4TC 16.785					

Panamax
The morning brought further buying interest and q4 back above 22000 once more, and cal 06 nudged back towards the upper 19s. As the day moved on, bids became harder to find and prices declined back to the starting levels. The physical market seems to have further upward momentum, but still stands some way under the levels traded on q4.

Cape
A curious day; the index was expected well up, and it performed. Geneva took a day off to watch the first session of the last Ashes match for 2005. Not a lot of trading interest around.

	Route 7 Bolivar/Rdam	
Sep	13,50	14,50
Oct	13,75	14,50
Nov	13,75	14,50
Dec	13,75	14,50
Jan	13,75	14,50
Cal 06	13,25	14,00
Cal 07	11,50	12,50
Cal 08	10,50	12,00
	BCI 13,815	

	Route 4 Rbay/Rott	
Sep	13,00	13,75
Oct	13,25	14,00
Nov	13,25	14,00
Dec	13,25	14,00
Jan	13,25	13,90
Cal 06	12,75	13,25
Cal 07	10,75	12,00
Cal 08	10,25	11,50
	BCI 13,135	

Baltic Exchange Indices:			Cape Index (BCI)	3.624	+ 124
Baltic Pmax Index (BPI)	2.203	+ 111	2. Tub/Rotterdam	13,430	+ 0,205
1. US Gulf/Cont	20,479	+ 0,621	3. Tub/Beilun + Bao	25,273	+ 0,528
1A. TA Round Voyage	16.639	+ 1018	4. Rbay/Rotterdam	13,135	+ 0,505
2. US Gulf/Japan	37,883	+ 1,047	5. W Aust/Beilun + Bao	9,740	+ 0,335
2A. Skaw-Gib/Twn-Japan	21.314	+ 1102	7. Bolivar/Rotterdam	13,815	+ 0,280
3. NoPac/Japan	23,227	+ 0,791	8. TA Round Voyage	42.170	+ 1495
3A. TP Round Voyage	15.535	+ 901	9. ARA-Pass/China-Jpn	55.273	+ 2023
4. Japan-SK/Skaw-Gib	13.653	+ 962	10. TP Round Voyage	31.864	+ 2091
			11. China-Jpn/Cont	22.591	+ 959
			12. Glad/Rdam (Trial)	16,714	+ 0,278
Average 4 TCs	16.785	+ 995	**Average 4TCs**	37.975	+ 1642

CHAPTER 4. Bunker Price Derivatives and Risk Management

4.1. Introduction

The previous chapter concentrated on the risks to the owner and the charterer that emanate from the volatility of freight rates. It was demonstrated how the use of freight derivatives can mediate these risks. Shipowners (when the vessel is under a voyage contract) and charterers (when the vessel is operated under a time-charter contract) are not only exposed to the risk of changes in freight rates, but they are also affected by fluctuations in expenses, particularly operating costs, when operating the vessel[58]. Operating costs (including voyage costs) include fuel, manning, repairs and maintenance, stores and lubes, insurance, administration, broking commission, fuel costs, port charges, tugs, canal dues, etc. However, they are dominated by fuel costs, which according to Stopford (1997), account for around 50%-60% of the total cost base of the running expenses of the vessel. Moreover, the rest of the costs are fairly predictable as they rise in line with inflation. Thus, the bunker price is the important variable to control on the cost side for risk management purposes, as changes in this variable could damage the cost side of shipowners' cash-flow. Given the volatility that is observed in bunker prices (see Figures 4.2 and 4.3 and later discussion in this chapter), it is important that this source of risk also is not ignored by market agents. It is often easy to forget about bunker costs in a strong freight market when revenues are high, but if the cost of bunkers also is controlled, it contributes to a better overall management of the cash-flow.

For instance, a fully operational ULCC vessel consumes around 180 tons of bunker fuel daily, when laden with cargo, and about 160 tons in ballast. For one of its major voyage routes – say Arabian Gulf to Europe – it will take about 40 days in normal weather conditions. Approximately, 8,000 tons of bunker fuel (including the fuel for the diesel generator) will be required for this voyage. At the time of writing (April 2005) bunker prices in Rotterdam were at $214.5/mt, which creates a substantial cash exposure of around $1,716,000. For the same voyage two months earlier the bunker fuel price was $164.5/mt and three months earlier the fuel price was $141.5/mt. Thus, the bunker cost would have been $1,316,000 ($400,000 less) and $1,132,000 ($584,000 less), respectively. This example illustrates the substantial sums involved as well as the large fluctuations in these sums that the high volatility of bunker prices can bring about in a very short period of time.

Still, there is a view that hedging bunker prices may be useful for those involved with COAs, for liner operators and some tanker owners. For owners who do not have a regular pattern of bunker lifting (e.g. those in the tramp market or owners with only small volumes) the potential gains are marginal (Drewry Shipping Consultants, 1997).

Historically, there has been substantial volatility in energy prices. Figure 4.1 shows these fluctuations in the prices of Brent Crude Oil from January 1990 to April 2005. Crude prices in 2000 nearly quadrupled from their 1998 lows, primarily as a result of OPEC production cutbacks, and they remained volatile in 2001 despite OPEC's efforts to keep prices into a $22/bbl to $28/bbl band. OPEC's cutbacks and

---

[58] When a vessel is delivered on a period time-charter, it is conventional for the charterer to purchase the bunkers remaining on board from the shipowner at an agreed price. Upon the vessel's redelivery at the end of the time-charter, the shipowner purchases back from the charterer the bunkers remaining on board at that time.

subsequent easing of production curbs, as crude prices soared to as high as $35/bbl-$38/bbl, had a big impact on fuel oil availability and led to a very volatile fuel oil market in 1999 and 2000. OPEC's attempt in 2001 to control crude prices has been broadly successful; the price of the cartel's *"basket"* has deviated little from the $25/bbl price – that is, the middle of the desired band. But, product markets have remained volatile. However, the post 2001 period has seen an explosion in oil prices, with an equally high volatility.

Figure 4.1. Brent Crude Oil Prices ($/bbl) (January 1990 – April 2005)

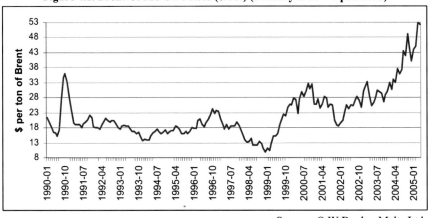

Source: O.W Bunker Malta Ltd.

Bunker prices generally tend to move in line with crude oil prices. In practice, fuel prices can fluctuate wildly with little correlation to crude. The past few years have been amongst the most volatile on record, as can be seen in Figures 4.2 and 4.3. During the period 2000 – 2005, bunker prices in Rotterdam swung between $109/mt and $190/mt, Singapore bunkers have ranged from $113/mt up to $209/mt, while prices in Houston fluctuated between $97/mt and $229/mt.

This chapter outlines the use of bunker derivatives for hedging these fluctuations in bunker prices. The rest of the chapter is organised as follows: Section 4.2 presents a historical overview of the bunker market. Section 4.3 considers the economic variables affecting bunker prices. Section 4.4 describes the alternative bunker derivatives products, including forward bunker agreements, petroleum futures contracts, bunker swaps, and bunker options. Section 4.5 presents the empirical evidence of these markets/products. Finally, Section 4.6 concludes the chapter.

4.2. The Bunker Market

Bunker fuel is the final product of a simple distillation of Crude Oil. It is a residue after all of the higher components, such as Gasoline, Aviation spirit, Butane, Kerosene and Naphtha, have been evaporated or boiled off. It is a dark viscous liquid, almost solid at room temperature and it is difficult to ignite. There are two basic grades of bunker Intermediate Fuel Oil (IFO); the IFO180cst (centistokes) and the more widely used, IFO380cst. The distinction between the two grades is the distillate content; Grade 180 has 7-15% distillate content, while Grade 380 has 2-5% distillate content. The higher the distillate content, the more energy the fuel has. According to Marine Fuels Yearbook (2002) 60% of the world trade in bunkers is in IFO380cst, 30% is in IFO180cst and other grades, with the remaining 10% covered by Marine Diesel Oil. As technology is progressing, the vessels with engines that run on IFO180cst have decreased over time, as the more modern engines are designed to run on IFO380cst.

Although, marine bunkers are bought and sold at almost every port in the world, the world bunker market can be broadly divided into three major regional markets, in which the bulk of physical bunkering activities take place. These markets are Singapore, Rotterdam and Houston[59]. Singapore has long flourished as a transshipment centre due to its strategic geographical location. The Singapore bunker market is by far the largest marine fuel market in the world, and is duly considered a prime benchmark for the industry. The heart of Europe's bunker market is the ARA (Amsterdam – Rotterdam – Antwerp) region, being an industrial and cargo handling region and a major refining and oil storage centre. ARA is extremely competitive, with major oil companies and independents fighting for market share. Prices are quoted for a wide array of products, including Gas Oil and Marine Fuels, among others. Products in the ARA region are generally quoted as "*barges Free on Board (FOB) Rotterdam*", quoted on an FOB export basis[60]. The biggest bunkering market in the US Gulf coast is Houston, which has refining capacity to match its status as the world's energy and oil capital. However, as plants have become more efficient, little or no ready-made fuel is available at the refinery gates and suppliers mostly blend themselves (see Alizadeh, Kavussanos and Menachof, 2004). The high level of competition in this area, combined with developed offshore supply business and a good access to fuel oil supplies, usually makes the area the cheapest US market.

Figure 4.2. Bunker Fuel IFO380 Prices in Three Major Ports (Jan. 1992 – Feb. 2005)

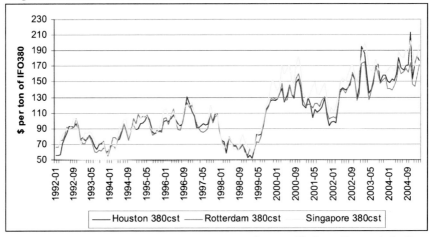

Source: Clarksons Research Studies

Figures 4.2 and 4.3 show the historical fluctuations in prices for IFO380cst and IFO180cst bunker fuel in the three major ports from January 1992 to February 2005, respectively. It can be observed than bunker prices move together, indicating that they are driven by a common variable – that is the world oil price. Yet, there are

---

[59] The average volume of bunker fuel in these ports, in 2004, is the following: in Singapore 16 million tonnes per annum, in Rotterdam 8 million tonnes per annum, and in Huston 5.5 million tonnes per annum.

[60] Generally, the "*barges FOB*" quotation, indicate that barging costs are included in the given prices. Alternatively, the quotation of the price would indicate that barging costs must be added.

differences in fluctuations in prices between ports, as local market conditions determine prices in each location. These observations can also be substantiated through the correlation coefficients of the first price-differences between Houston and Rotterdam, Houston and Singapore, and Rotterdam and Singapore for the IFO180cst market, which are 0.832, 0.663, and 0.754, while for the IFO380cst market the corresponding coefficients are 0.816, 0.627, and 0.755, respectively. There seems to be high correlation in prices between the regional markets, with the highest ones observed between Houston and Rotterdam and Rotterdam and Singapore, while the lowest correlation coefficient is between Houston and Singapore.

Figure 4.3. Bunker Fuel IFO180 Prices in Three Major Ports (Jan. 1992 – Feb. 2005)

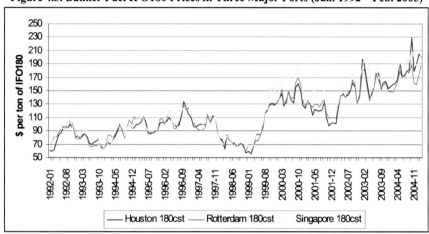

Source: Clarksons Research Studies

The demand for bunkers comes from shipowners and vessel operators, including charterers, who have a vessel on a time-charter agreement. On the supply side, bunker providers are major oil companies and independent companies as well as refineries. In a market with high volatility bunker suppliers are very reluctant to close deals for periods exceeding one week ahead.

4.3. Economic Variables affecting the Bunker Market

In order to assess the bunker market, analysts require not only intimate knowledge of supply and demand in a wide range of ports, but also an in-depth understanding of the petroleum industry and related business. Prices for oil products are determined by supply and demand factors for each specific oil product, as well as by the price and availability of substitutes. For example, fuel oil prices are affected not only by the demand for power and the capacity to generate it, but also by the price of alternative sources of energy, such as Natural Gas. Several factors can come into play for any particular oil product: economic conditions, weather effects (e.g. El Nino) and the political stability of oil producing countries (see for instance, Montepeque, 2003). To operate in the bunker market it is of vital importance to understand what the economic variables that influence this market are and the possible sources of volatility in this market. These are analysed next:

- **Oil markets:** Factors which influence the price of Crude Oil will usually have a knock-on effect in the bunker market. When the Crude Oil price rises, so will the prices of products derived from Crude Oil. Even though the bunker market follows the general swings of the crude market in the long- and medium-term, there are times in the short-term when bunker prices may deviate from these trends. Activity in the wider High Sulphur Fuel Oil (HSFO) market has a profound influence on bunker prices. This is because bunker suppliers derive bunker fuel from this market and so the price of the HSFO cargoes provides the base-line from which bunker suppliers start. Bunker prices in different parts of the world will usually follow trends in the nearest oil cargo market centre (Stewart, 2001). For example, bunker prices in north-west European ports follow trends in the Rotterdam HSFO market. Likewise, Mediterranean ports are linked to the Italian market and Far Eastern ports to the Singapore market. Factors which influence the HSFO market include available storage capacity, the level of a country's fuel reserves, freight rates, the weather and manipulation by financial institutions (Marine Fuels Yearbook, 2002).

- **Changes in bunker stock levels:** A reduction in stock levels raises prices, ceteris paribus, and can be the result of many factors. They include: a refinery shut-down, the discovery of off-specification material from a local refinery or an incoming cargo, a delay in replacement cargoes of fuel, a sudden increase in local inland demand or in demand for bunkers or a lack of available supply barges or traffic congestion within a port. Marine fuel shortages may be deliberately created by suppliers with the intention of forcing prices up. When this happens, such price surges are often followed by an equally dramatic slump, contributing to high volatility in the market. When suppliers, within a competitive and price-sensitive port, such as Rotterdam, Singapore or Houston, all recognise the potential for a rising market, they will sometimes withhold stocks in anticipation of higher prices. This practice results in temporary shortages, which serves to accelerate the price rises. However, when one supplier finally decides to offer bunkers on the market, the resulting fall in prices is often quite dramatic (Cockett, 1997).

- **Refinery practices:** Although marine fuel is extremely important to the shipowner, to the refiner is often the least important market he deals with. Marine fuels represent less than 5% of the value of all petroleum products traded worldwide. There are often many other *"demands"* on a refiner's fuel oil output, demands, which may be more profitable and easier to deal with. As a result, it is often difficult for bunker suppliers in many ports to guarantee a regular supply of bunker fuel throughout all grades, which satisfy an operator's quality criterion, at a predictable price.

- **Changes in overseas competition:** This is often seen when a neighboring port, for its own reasons, may be attracting new bunker business with low prices, or alternatively, shedding it with high prices. The reaction of nearby ports is usually to do the opposite, as the start-up of a new bunkering station or the demise of an existing one can be a stimulus to prices elsewhere. The effects of these types of changes can be very far ranging. A fall in prices in Singapore can influence the prices in Rotterdam and vice versa. Both Rotterdam and Singapore prices can affect the prices offered in Saudi Arabian ports, and Singapore can have a profound influence on bunker prices throughout the Pacific region, including South Korea and Japan (Marine Fuels Yearbook, 2002).

- **Changes in local markets:** The collapse or withdrawal of a bunker supplier from the local market can raise prices as competitors take advantage of the increased market influence. Conversely, the entry into the market of new players may lower prices, offering low, or even loss-making, prices for fuel in order to attract customers away from the established suppliers.

- **Delivery methods:** The final price, which the operator pays, can also be significantly affected by the method of delivery. In some ports, vessels at berth can take deliveries directly from the storage tanks, although this can be expensive if a vessel only requires bunkers, but is forced to pay port fees to take up a berth space. However, usually bunkering is made by barge at the vessel's berth or at anchorage within the approaches to the port, though also sometimes offshore on the high seas. For example, several barge operators have built up successful businesses by supplying fuel by tanker to fishing fleets far from shore. The extra costs linked to barge delivery vary widely and depend upon the number of barge operators in an area and, thus, the competitiveness of the barge market. The quality of the barge and the operating standards of the crew will also play a part in the delivery cost (Cockett, 1997).

- **Unpredictable factors:** Weather incidents, port delays, field shut downs, political events, army coups in sensitive producing areas, OPEC decisions, Russian production, refinery run levels, storage availability, industry decisions from the American Petroleum Institute (API) and the US Department of Energy (DOE) (for example for the US) can all influence bunker prices.

4.4. Bunker Derivatives Contracts
Shipowners, vessel operators and charterers can use the following instruments to manage bunker price risk: forward bunker agreements, energy futures contracts, bunker swaps, and bunker options. These instruments are analysed in turn next.

4.4.1. Forward Bunker Agreements
A forward bunker contract is an OTC agreement between a seller and a buyer to exchange a specified quantity of bunker of certain quality, at an agreed price, at a certain delivery location and time in the future. Settlement is made on the difference between the forward price and the price of bunkers at the delivery point, although physical delivery is also possible. Since the contracts are OTC, each party accepts credit risk from the other party. Institutions providing these contracts include investment banks (e.g. Morgan Stanley) and bunker traders (e.g. Bunkerfuels and O.W. Bunker Malta) and receive a commission on the total amount payable for their services, which is typically included in the quoted prices.

To see how these work, consider the following example, which is also summarised in Table 4.1. Suppose that today is 4th of May and a shipowner has fixed a voyage charter (US Gulf to Rotterdam) for 30th of June, for which it is expected to need 5,000 tons of IFO380cst bunker fuel to be loaded at Houston. The current spot bunker price is $162/mt at Houston. As can be seen in the first column of Table 4.1, if he bought the fuel in June at today's prices, he would pay $810,000 (= $162/mt x 5,000 tons). However, he expects bunker prices to increase by 30th June. In order to protect himself from this increase he decides to buy a forward bunker contract. The forward bunker seller can be a financial institution which provides OTC products in commodity markets. The forward bunker price is negotiated and fixed at $165/mt at Houston. Through the agreement he has fixed the price of the fuel the vessel needs for the trip to $165/mt, which fixes his bunker fuel costs to $825,000(=$165/mtx5,000tons).

Let us see the position of the shipowner in June. Assume the settlement price of bunkers at Houston during 30th of June is $170/mt. That is, the shipowner's expectations about a price increase are fulfilled. Because the settlement price of $170/mt is higher than the forward price of $165/mt, the forward seller pays $25,000(= $5/mt x 5,000 tons) to the shipowner. That is, in the forward market, the owner closes his bunker position by selling forward contracts for $825,000(=$165/mtx5,000 tons), making a gain in this market of $25,000. In the spot market the shipowner bought the bunkers for $850,000 instead of $810,000 he would have paid today, amounting to an extra cost of $40,000. Overall, the portfolio of the spot and the forward position makes a loss of $15,000, instead of a $40,000 loss he would have made had he not utilized derivatives. The cash-flow positions of the bunker seller and the bunker's derivatives seller are exactly opposite to those of the shipowner.

Consider next, the scenario that the shipowner made an error in his forecast that bunker prices will increase in June, as can be seen in the second column of Table 4.1. Because the settlement price of $160/mt is lower than the forward price of $165/mt, the shipowner pays $25,000 (= $5/mt x 5,000 tons) to the forward seller. Thus, in the forward market he makes a loss of $25,000. In the spot market the shipowner bought the bunkers for $800,000 instead of $810,000 he would have paid today, amounting to a gain of $10,000. Overall, the portfolio of the spot and the forward position makes a loss of $15,000, instead of a $10,000 profit he would have made had he not utilized derivatives.

Table 4.1. The Two Possible Outcomes of Forward Bunker Hedging Voyage Charter Bunker Requirements; US Gulf to Rotterdam: 5,000 tons

May 4th	
Spot Market	**Forward Market**
Bunker price at Houston: $162/mt	Action: Buy forward contracts
Bunker cost: $810,000	Bunker forward May price: $165/mt
(= $162/mt x 5,000 tons)	Value of forward: $825,000
	(= $165/mt x 5,000 tons)
First scenario: Bunker rates increase	**Second scenario: Bunker rates decrease**
June 30th: Spot Market	
Bunker price at Houston: $170/mt	Bunker price at Houston: $160/mt
Bunker cost: $850,000 (= $170/mt x 5,000 tons)	Bunker cost: $800,000 (= $160/mt x 5,000 tons)
The shipowner (bunker seller) loses (gains) $40,000	**The shipowner (bunker seller) gains (loses) $10,000**
June 30th: Forward Market	
Action: Sell forward contracts	Action: Sell forward contracts
Bunker forward June price: $170/mt	Bunker forward June price: $160/mt
Value of forward: $850,000	Value of forward: $800,000
(= $170/mt x 5,000 tons)	(= $160/mt x 5,000 tons)
The shipowner (forward seller) gains (loses) $25,000	**The shipowner (forward seller) loses (gains) $25,000**
Portfolio of Spot and Forward Positions	
Net loss in portfolio position for shipowner: $15,000, instead of $40,000 loss	**Net loss in portfolio position for shipowner: $15,000**, instead of $10,000 profit

4.4.2. Energy Futures Contracts

Despite the high trading volume in the global and regional bunker markets and the high volatility of bunker prices, which directly affect shipowners' and shipping companies' profit margins, the number of instruments available to shipowners and operators to minimise their exposure to bunker price fluctuations are limited. With the exception of financial institutions, offering tailor-made OTC derivatives products, since the 1980s, such as forward, swap and option contracts, up until 5th December 2005, there was no tradable futures contract for bunkers.

During 5th December 2005, IMAREX launched an electronic screen market for trading and clearing (through NOS) bunker fuel oil futures, which is available to all its trading and clearing members. IMAREX offers bunker futures contracts on: (i) Rotterdam 3.5% Sulphur Barges FOB[61]; (ii) Northwestern Europe (NWE) 1.0% Sulphur Barges FOB; (iii) Singapore IFO180cst FOB; (iv) Singapore IFO380cst FOB; and (v) Fujairah IFO380cst FOB. IMAREX quotes prices for contract durations of 6 months, 6 quarters and 2 calendar years. The price quotation is US$/mt, 1 lot = 1,000mt, the minimum volume is 0.1 lot (= 100mt), while the maximum volume is 999 lots (= 990,000mt). The settlement price is determined by Platts and Bunkerworld and the settlement period is the average of the month. After just one month of trading at IMAREX, a total of 23 bunker derivatives transactions were traded, covering 260,000mt of bunker fuel with a nominal trade value of all trades of US$ 57 million, while the average number of lots traded per transaction was 11.

Before that, in the absence of bunker futures contracts, hedging against bunker price fluctuations using futures involved the search for alternative futures contracts that could be available on "*commodities*" whose prices are closely related to bunker prices. Good candidates for these are energy futures contracts, where this process of hedging is known as cross-hedging[62].

There are two derivatives exchange markets trading oil contracts: the New York Mercantile Exchange (NYMEX)[63] and the Intercontinental Exchange Futures (ICE Futures), formerly known as the International Petroleum Exchange (IPE)[64,65]. In London, the energy futures market grew mainly with the creation of the IPE. During 26th October 2005, the IPE was renamed to ICE Futures. The ICE Futures is a futures and options exchange that lists futures and options contracts for energy products, such as Brent Crude and Gas Oil. It is the second largest energy futures exchange in the world, listing futures contracts that represent the pricing benchmarks for two thirds of the world's Crude Oil and the majority of middle distillate traded in Europe. The contracts listed by the ICE Futures are used by producers, refiners, traders, consumers and institutional investors across the world to either manage their inherent price risk, to speculate on outright price changes in oil and/or to balance their portfolio of risk exposure. Most of the oil futures contracts have adopted a delivery procedure to

---

[61] 3.5% Sulphur means that 1 ton of IFO has 35kg Sulphur.

[62] Some of the advantages of futures contracts over forward contracts include: (a) The leverage effect, which due to the mark-to-market clearing does not require holding of the full monetary amount of the position, as profit/losses are marked daily. With forwards the trader must hold the full monetary amount since there is only a single payment at settlement; (b) The existence of a secondary market, which enables easier exit compared to forward markets; and (c) No credit risk exists in futures markets, due to the operation of the mark-to-market system, operated by the central counterparty – the clearing-house.

[63] The energy derivatives products of NYMEX are: Light, Sweet Crude Oil (futures and option), Natural Gas (futures and option), Heating Oil (futures and options), Unleaded Gasoline (futures and options), Brent Crude Oil (futures and options), Propane (futures), and Coal (futures).

[64] The energy derivatives products of ICE Futures are: Brent Crude (futures and options) and Gas Oil (futures and options).

[65] The Singapore Exchange (SGX) had launched an energy derivatives product, the Middle East Crude Oil (MECO) futures, which was trading until October 2004.

match as closely as possible the local physical market conditions. For example, the ICE Future's Gas Oil contract is based on the barge market in North-West Europe and all the nomination procedures and quality checks are as similar as possible.

In both exchanges, once the futures contract has expired, the relevant clearing-house matches up the buyers and sellers with outstanding positions. Buyers must then take delivery from the sellers to whom they have been allocated under the rules of the exchange concerned. There are two exceptions to this system: the Alternative Delivery Procedure (ADP) and the Exchange for Physicals (EFP). Under an ADP, the buyer and seller, having been matched up by the exchange, can agree to deliver under different conditions such as in a different place, or even to deliver a different product. In this case, they notify the exchange that they are doing an ADP and their delivery can then take place as agreed between them. However, under an ADP, the exchange and the clearing-house will not guarantee the fulfillment of the contract. Under an EFP, the buyer and seller again agree to a physical delivery outside the rules of the exchange, but in this case, they make the arrangements. Before they are matched by the exchange, they notify the exchange that the agreement has been made. Their futures' positions are then closed by the exchange and, again, the clearing-house no longer guarantees the futures contracts.

None of the abovementioned exchanges trade bunker futures contracts. The SGX in 1998 launched a bunker futures contract and the IPE in 1999 launched a similar contract in London. However, both contracts failed to attract trading interest by market participants and were eventually withdrawn from the market due to low trading volume. One of the justifications of this is the nature of the bunker market, since physical bunker is traded in different geographical locations around the world, whereas futures contracts are for the delivery of bunker fuel in specific locations. Consequently, futures prices do not follow accurately the movement of bunker fuel prices in different locations, which in turn affects the hedging effectiveness of the contract (see Alizadeh, Kavussanos and Menachof, 2004).

Given the situation, Alizadeh, Kavussanos and Menachof (2004) searched for the possibility of using energy futures contracts as substitutes for the absent bunker futures contracts. More specifically, they examine the effectiveness of hedging marine bunker price fluctuations in Rotterdam, Singapore and Houston, from 30/06/98 to 09/11/00, using different Crude Oil and petroleum futures contracts traded at NYMEX and IPE. When analysing the hedging effectiveness of those oil futures contracts, using both constant and time-varying hedge ratios, the results indicated that the hedging effectiveness is different across regional bunker markets. The most effective futures instrument for out-of-sample hedging of spot bunker prices in Rotterdam is the IPE Crude Oil futures, with 43% hedging effectiveness; for Singapore is the NYMEX Gas Oil futures, with 15.9% hedging effectiveness; while for Houston is the IPE Gas Oil futures, with 14% hedging effectiveness. It is argued in the study that differences in hedging effectiveness across regional markets are attributed to the varying regional supply and demand factors in each market. However, in comparison to other markets, the cross-market hedging effectiveness investigated in the bunker market is low.

The degree of hedging effectiveness for a futures contract is proportional to the correlation coefficient of the first-difference in its price with that of the first-difference in the spot bunker price. Table 4.2 presents the correlation matrix of spot bunker prices in three major ports and oil futures contracts traded in IPE and NYMEX markets from 12th September 2003 to 27th May 2005. It can be seen that the highest correlation for the Rotterdam IFO380cst is with NYMEX Crude Oil futures (32.90%), for the Singapore IFO380cst is with NYMEX Crude Oil futures (40.10%), and for the Houston IFO380cst is with IPE Crude Oil futures (32.60%).

Table 4.2. Correlation matrix of Spot Bunker Prices in Three Major Ports and Oil Futures Contracts

	Rotterdam IFO380	Singapore IFO380	Houston IFO380	NYMEXHO	NYMEXCO	NYMEXGO	IPECO	IPEGO
Rotterdam IFO380	1.000	-	-	-	-	-	-	-
Singapore IFO380	0.683	1.000	-	-	-	-	-	-
Houston IFO380	0.537	0.596	1.000	-	-	-	-	-
NYMEXHO	0.244	0.274	0.247	1.000	-	-	-	-
NYMEXCO	**0.329**	**0.401**	0.312	0.856	1.000	-	-	-
NYMEXGO	0.197	0.204	0.155	0.716	0.744	1.000	-	-
IPECO	0.281	0.316	**0.326**	0.875	0.922	0.754	1.000	-
IPEGO	0.267	0.212	0.185	0.917	0.797	0.667	0.843	1.000

Notes:
- Sample Period is 12/09/03 to 27/05/05.
- The spot bunker and futures prices are in logarithmic first differences format.
- NYMEXCO, NYMEXGO, NYMEXHO, IPECO, and IPEGO represent NYMEX crude oil, NYMEX gas oil, NYMEX heating oil, IPE crude oil, and IPE gas oil futures contracts, respectively.

Menachof and Dicer (2001) compare the effectiveness of the Bunker Adjustment Factor (BAF) with oil commodity futures contracts[66]. Through the BAF a shipowner is able to transfer the risk of fuel price fluctuation to the shipper. This and other surcharges are generally undesired by shippers who must pay this fee. Menachof and Dicer provide an alternative method of bunker risk management. They show that the strategic use of oil commodity futures (Gas Oil futures) contracts, in the North Atlantic route, is a much more effective method for hedging the risk arising from fluctuating bunker prices, and therefore, the BAF surcharge should be eliminated by liner shipping companies.

Table 4.3. The Hedging Outcome of a Petroleum Futures Hedge for 5,000 tons Bunkers

	Spot Price	Futures Price	Result in Spot Position	Result in Futures Position
1st April	$107.00	$24.00	+$535,000	-$552,000
1st July	$120.50	$27.22	-$602,500	+$626,060
Net Result	-$13.50	+$3.22	-$67,500	$74,060

Despite the benefits of hedging bunker price risk, only a limited number of shipping and bunker supplier companies actually hedge this risk. According to market sources, the convention is to hedge between 40% and 60% of their exposure over the current

---

[66] Liner shipping companies have acted in concert to establish oligopolistic control over rates and service in many trade lines of the world. Using this market control, liner companies have been able to pass many costs of doing business to the shipper, with the major variable factors listed as separate charges, such as the BAF. Surcharges, designed to compensate carriers for sudden, temporary changes in costs, have been a part of the liner shipping industry for the last 28 years. A definition of surcharges put forth by the United Nations describes surcharges as "*general rate increases applied to all commodities transported on a particular liner tariff*". The bunker fuel surcharge was introduced in 1974, following the first oil crisis. The magnitude of this surcharge varied by conference, but generally has amounted to 10-15% of the basic freight rate (Menachof and Dicer, 2001).

financial year plus one. The main reason that companies put forward for hedging only a fraction of their bunker risk is that they want to benefit should the market moves in their favor, but also because they are worried of being left at a disadvantage to their competitors if they do nothing about this market risk.

Following the implications of the results we observe in Table 4.2, NYMEX Crude Oil futures contracts should be used to hedge bunker price fluctuations, when loading in Rotterdam. The following example, which is also summarised in Tables 4.3 to 4.5, illustrates the calculations. Suppose that today is April 1st and a shipowner expects to load 5,000 tons of bunkers in Rotterdam for the next trip on July 1st, and is worried that bunker prices will increase by then. The total value of bunkers on April 1st is $535,000 (= $107/mt x 5,000 tons). One NYMEX Crude Oil futures contract costs $24,000 (= 1,000 trade size x $24.00). Therefore, in order to hedge his exposure he needs to purchase $23 \approx 22.29$ (= $535,000 / $24,000) futures contracts. During April 1st, the shipowner buys 23 futures contracts for $552,000 (= 23 x $24,000). On July 1st, the shipowner buys the bunkers in the spot market for $602,500(=$120.5/mtx5,000 tons) and closes his derivatives position by selling the futures contracts for $626,060 (= 23 contracts x $27.22). The shipowner has made a gain of $6,560 (=$74,060 – $67,500) instead of a loss of $67,500, that he would have made had he stayed unhedged.

Consider next, the scenario under which the shipowner made a mistake in his forecast that bunker prices will increase between April and July. Instead, the settlement price of bunkers at Rotterdam during 1st of July falls to $93.50/mt. As can be seen in Table 4.4, the shipowner makes a loss of $69,000 on the derivatives position as bunker prices fell, but makes a gain in the spot position of $67,500 as he pays less for his bunker requirements. Overall, combining the spot with the derivatives positions he makes a loss of $1,500.

Table 4.4. An Alternative Hedging Outcome of a Petroleum Futures Hedge for 5,000 tons Bunkers

	Spot Price	Futures Price	Result in Spot Position	Result in Futures Position
1st April	$107.00	$24.00	+$535,000	-$552,000
1st July	$93.50	$21.00	-$467,500	+$483,000
Net Result	+$13.50	-$2.00	+$67,500	-$69,000

Consider yet another scenario, under which again the shipowner makes a mistake in his forecast, but less severe. That is, the settlement price of bunkers at Rotterdam during 1st of July falls to $100/mt. As can be seen in Table 4.5, in this case the shipowner makes a loss of $23,000 on the derivatives position, but saves $35,000 in the spot market. The net result is a profit of $12,000.

Table 4.5. Another Alternative Hedging Outcome of a Petroleum Futures Hedge for 5,000 tons Bunkers

	Spot Price	Futures Price	Result in Spot Position	Result in Futures Position
1st April	$107.00	$24.00	+$535,000	-$552,000
1st July	$100.00	$23.00	-$500,000	+$529,000
Net Result	+$7.00	-$2.00	+$35,000	-$23,000

In either case, one must remember that entering a derivatives transaction in order to hedge a spot position is aimed at eliminating losses of the spot position through gains in the derivatives trade. That is, the aim is to have a net portfolio effect of zero or close to zero, rather than to make a profit.

4.4.3. Bunker Swap Agreements

Following the introduction of swaps, in the mid-1980's, the energy derivatives market has become an important mechanism for hedging oil price risk[67]. The bunker swap market is used by many suppliers and bunker purchasers to lock in their bunker prices[68]. A simple bunker swap contract (plain vanilla) is an agreement whereby a floating price for bunkers is exchanged for a fixed price for bunkers, over a specified period (divided into sub-periods), for a defined volume per period (and sub-periods). Using the swap, the buyer exchanges a floating price for a fixed price (see Figure 4.4). A swap contract can be considered as a portfolio of forward contracts, i.e. a series of consecutive forward contracts agreed at the same time. This is an OTC arrangement, which involves no transfer of the physical commodity. Credit risk is an important issue. On bunkers, swaps are typically written against assessments of the spot bulk market supplying the relevant bunkering ports. The difference between the floating price (usually Platts' rates) and the fixed price is settled in cash. The net result, when combined with transactions in the physical market, is the outcome of hedging through the swap market.

Figure 4.4. Swap Transactions

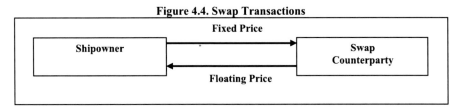

However, as with futures/forward contracts, it must be remembered that while hedging in this way limits bunker price risk, it also limits the profit potential. A point to remember is that in the key price-setting centres of Houston, Singapore and Rotterdam, bunker prices are highly responsive to changes in the bulk spot freight market. That is, expected increases in the demand for freight cargo will lead to higher levels of demand for fuel and visa versa.

To see how bunker swaps work, consider the following example, which is also summarised in Tables 4.6 and 4.7. Suppose that a shipowner, during December, has fixed a COA for the transportation of 1.2 million tons of coal at $10/mt from New Orleans to Hamburg for a German Electricity company. The contract is for 12 shipments over the next year, one each month. The freight rate is fixed through the COA. The shipowner is interested in securing his exposure to adverse bunker price movements. The current bunker price at New Orleans is $125.8/mt. The owner enters a bunker swap contract with a financial institution, which provides such OTC

---

[67] Crude swaps are OTC contracts traded in London, Singapore, and New York. Brent is the most actively traded contract, followed by West Texas Intermediate (WTI), Dubai and Tapics. Crude swaps are traded up to ten years ahead, but the most liquid markets, like Brent, are traded up to four years forward. The US oil product swaps are Gasoline, Jet/Diesel, and Residual fuel. The Asian oil product swaps are Naphtha, Jet/Gas Oil, and Fuel oil. The European oil product swaps are Gasoline, Naphtha, Jet, and Fuel oil.

[68] Financial institutions, which are closely involved with the oil industry (providing letters of credit or financing long-term ventures), use oil swaps in combination with other financial indices, such as London InterBank Offer Rates (LIBOR), in order to hedge their risks.

products. The swap contract is for 12 lots of 2,000 tons of bunker at the end of each calendar month. A fixed price of $130/ton is agreed against the floating bunker prices prevailing at the last business day of each month in New Orleans.

Table 4.6. Bunker Cost for the Shipowner in the Physical Market

Months	(1) Bunker Purchased	(2) Spot Bunker Price	(3) = (1) x (2) Bunker Cost
	Mt	$/mt	US$
January	1,850	129.00	238,650
February	1,950	129.63	252,779
March	2,150	135.10	290,465
April	1,740	128.75	224,025
May	2,200	131.00	288,200
June	1,850	141.20	261,220
July	1,920	137.25	263,520
August	2,320	132.88	308,282
September	1,820	139.50	253,890
October	1,780	145.88	259,666
November	2,150	142.00	305,300
December	1,960	130.10	254,996
Total	23,690		3,200,993

Consider the bunker requirements of the shipowner during the 12 months of the next year, as expressed in Table 4.6. He makes 12 shipments, one per month, requiring the bunker tonnage shown in column 1 of Table 4.6. The bunker price prevailing for each month is shown in column 2 of the table, while column 3 shows the total bunker cost per month. Finally, the last row of the table shows the total volume of bunkers purchased as well the total cost incurred. Thus, during December of the next year, in the spot freight market the shipowner has fulfilled the contract (12 shipments of coal 100,000mt each) and the total freight collected over the 12 months is $12,000,000 (=12 x 100,000mt x $10/mt). Over the year, the shipowner had to pay $3,200,993 in order to buy 23,690 tons of bunker fuel.

Figure 4.5. The Bunker Swap Agreement (Fixed price $130/mt)

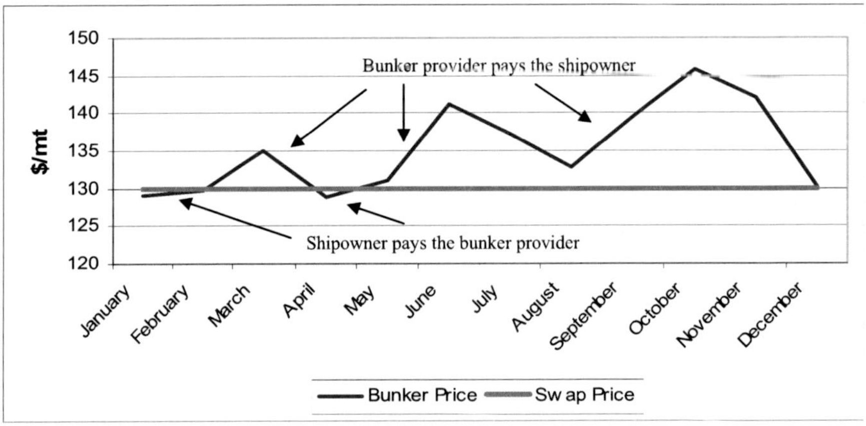

Suppose the owner decides to enter a bunker swap agreement in order to manage bunker price risk for the 12 months ahead. The settlement each month is calculated as the difference between the floating (spot) price and the fixed (swap) price times the

agreed – fixed – quantity of bunkers, say 6,000 tons in this case. Figure 4.5 shows that when the settlement is negative (positive) the shipowner (swap provider) pays the swap provider (shipowner) to compensate for the difference between the physical and the swap price.

The relevant calculations can be seen in Table 4.7, which assume a fixed (swap) price of $130/mt (column 4) and a contract size of 2,000 tons (column 1). Thus, for January, the difference between the spot price of $129/mt and the swap price of $130/mt, of 1$/mt, is multiplied with the contract size of 2,000 tons, to arrive at the settlement figure of -$2,000, which appears in column 6. That is, the owner pays to the bunker provider $2,000. This is because the spot price is lower than the agreed swap price. The opposite occurs in March, when the spot price stands at $135.10/mt, $5.10/mt above the swap price of $130/mt. That is, the owner receives a net cash inflow of $10,200. Over the 12 month period, the shipowner, by using the bunker swap, has paid $3,120,000 and received $3,244,580 from the counterparty. This gives him a net profit of $124,580 over the whole period. Overall, he managed to decrease his bunker cost by $124,580, to $3,076,413 (= $3,200,993 – $124,580) instead of paying $3,200,993, which he would have to pay had he not used the bunker swap market. Of course, if spot prices had a different pattern, e.g. on average over the 12 month period lower than the swap price, then the swap would result in a loss for the shipowner.

Table 4.7. The Bunker Swap Transactions from the Shipowner's Side

Months	(1) Contract Size	(2) Spot Bunker Price	(3) = (1) x (2) Bunker Cost	(4) Swap Price	(5) = (1) x (4) Swap Cost	(6) = (3) – (5) Settlement (Shipowner)
	mt	$/mt	US$	$/mt	US$	US$
January	2,000	129.00	258,000	130	260,000	-2,000
February	2,000	129.63	259,260	130	260,000	-740
March	2,000	135.10	270,200	130	260,000	10,200
April	2,000	128.75	257,500	130	260,000	-2,500
May	2,000	131.00	262,000	130	260,000	2,000
June	2,000	141.20	282,400	130	260,000	22,400
July	2,000	137.25	274,500	130	260,000	14,500
August	2,000	132.88	265,760	130	260,000	5,760
September	2,000	139.50	279,000	130	260,000	19,000
October	2,000	145.88	291,760	130	260,000	31,760
November	2,000	142.00	284,000	130	260,000	24,000
December	2,000	130.10	260,200	130	260,000	200
Total			**3,244,580**		**3,120,000**	**124,580**

4.4.4. Bunker Options Contracts

As explained in Chapter 2, an option contract gives the right to buy or sell an asset, within a specified period of time, at a predetermined strike (exercise) price. The holder of options can benefit from advantageous price movements, but enjoy the security of a hedge in case prices moved against him. In the latter situation, by exercising the option he can buy or sell at the predetermined strike price. Options are traded in OTC and exchange based markets[69]. However no exchange presently trades

---

[69] Several of the leading exchanges offer oil options, including NYMEX and IPE. NYMEX began trading crude oil WTI options in November 1986, three and a half years after introducing its first energy futures contract. IPE followed with Gas Oil options in July 1987, having launched its Gas Oil contract six years earlier. No exchange is currently trading Heavy Fuel Oil contracts. The options market has seen dramatic growth. NYMEX recorded a 61.7% increase in the volume of options traded between 1994 and 1998. Exchange traded options are exercised into futures

bunker options. These options are only available in OTC markets. For agents wishing to use exchange-traded options, they could use energy options as proxies for the non-existent bunker options. This would involve cross-hedging with options. Energy options exist in exchanges, suh as NYMEX and ICE Futures. The option contracts of NYMEX and ICE Futures are American type options, while most of the OTC bunker options are Asian[70], though a few American or European options also exist. Asian options are popular within bunker hedging, because the averaged settlement moderates short-term fluctuations and price spikes, common within the bunker market. OTC options, like OTC swaps, are generally settled in cash.

Suppose a shipowner wants to protect himself against rising bunker prices, and at the same time he wants the flexibility to buy bunkers at a lower price should they actually fall. He buys a call option, giving him the right to buy bunkers in the future at the predetermined exercise price of the option. He pays a premium for this right. Likewise, bunker suppliers may want to protect themselves against a drop in bunker prices, but also wish to retain the flexibility to capitalise on price increases. By buying a put option they secure the right to sell at a predetermined strike price. Most shipping and bunkering companies will find it easier to buy rather than write (sell) options. This is a matter of credit rating. To buy an option requires an upfront premium to be paid (usually 3% - 4%) one or two business days after buying the option. The option buyer therefore poses a lower credit risk than the option seller, who settles his obligation in full on exercise of the option.

To see how bunker options work, consider the following example, which is also summarised in Table 4.8. It is late October 2003 and a US commodity trading house sold 51,400mt of light grain to receivers in the ARA region (that is, route 1 of the BPI – US Gulf to ARA). Shipment, with a Panamax vessel of 54,000mt, will take place late December 2003. The Panamax vessel will need 5,000 tons of fuel oil. The current bunker fuel price at Houston is \$160/mt. The shipowner expects that bunker prices at Houston will increase by December 2003, and therefore decides to hedge his bunker costs with a call option contract, with the following specifications: strike price \$165/mt, option premium \$2/mt, and maturity date 25th December 2003. Thus, the shipowner, at a cost of \$10,000 = \$2/mt x 5,000 tons, buys the right but not the obligation to purchase 5,000 tons of bunker oil at \$165/mt on 25th December 2003.

Suppose bunker prices increases to \$170/mt in December 2003. The shipowner is experiencing a loss in the spot market of \$50,000 (= 800,000 – 850,000). However, since the spot price (\$170/mt) is higher than the strike price (\$160/mt), the call option contract is exercised, giving a payoff of \$15,000 (= (\$170/mt – \$165/mt) x 5,000 tons – \$10,000). Therefore, the shipowner's combined spot and options position is \$835,000, instead of \$850,000, which he would have had he not used the options market. Consider the alternative scenario, under which the bunker price decreases to \$155/mt. The shipowner is realising a gain of \$25,000 (= \$800,000 – \$775,000) in the spot market. Because the spot price is lower than the strike price, the option is not

---

contracts. If held until maturity, these futures can be exchanged for the physical delivery of the product. An exception is the cash-settled Brent Crude Oil contract offered by the IPE.

[70] An Asian (or Average Rate) option is settled, on maturity, against an average price for the underlying asset over a certain period. When the average market price over some period prior to maturity is used as exercise price, the option is called "*average strike option*". When the average spot price over a certain period prior the maturity is used as spot price, then the option is called "*average price option*".

exercised, giving a loss of $10,000, the option premium. The overall bunker cost to the shipowner is $785,000.

Table 4.8. Shipowner's Bunker Options Hedge

Two-month Hedge using Bunker Options (31st October 2003 – 25th December 2003)	
Physical (Spot) Market	**Options Market**
31st October 2003	
Bunker price: $160/mt Bunker cost: $800,000 (= $160/mt x 5,000 tons)	Action: Buy December 2003 call options Call strike price: $165/mt Options premium: $2/mt Options cost: $10,000 (= $2/mt x 5,000mt)
25th December 2003: Rising Market	
Bunker Price at Houston: $170/mt Bunker cost: $850,000 (= $170/mt x 5,000 tons)	Strike price ($165/mt) < Spot price ($170/mt) Action: Exercise the call option
Loss in Physical Market: $50,000 (= $800,000 – $850,000)	Option's profit: $15,000 [= ($170/mt – $165/mt) x 5,000mt – $10,000]
Total Bunker Cost (including options premium): $850,000 – $15,000 = $835,000	
25th December 2003: Falling Market	
Bunker Price at Houston: $155/mt Bunker Cost: $775,000 (= $155/mt x 5,000 tons)	Strike price ($165/mt) > Spot price ($155/mt) Action: Call option is not exercised
Gain in Physical Market: $25,000 (= $800,000 – $775,000)	Option's payoff: -$10,000 (options premium)
Total Bunker Cost (including options premium): $775,000 + $10,000 = $785,000	

4.4.4.1. Bunker Collars (or Cylinder Options)
(i) Zero-Cost Collars or Range Forwards or Tunnels

Investors wishing to avoid paying an initial premium when taking a long call or a long put position, may employ a zero-cost collar, which, as its title implies, has no upfront cost requirement. However, the term zero-cost is only applicable to the upfront premium. There are significant costs if the price moves excessively against the predicted direction. With the collar option strategy, investors bracket the value of their portfolio between two bounds.

Example 1:

To see how zero-cost collars work, consider a shipowner that expects bunker prices to rise from their current level of $85/mt, and wishes to hedge this risk exposure. He buys a call option (cap) at a strike price of $90/mt. The option comes with an upfront premium of $2.7/mt (3%). The shipowner wants to avoid this cost, but still stay protected from bunker risk. To that effect, he writes (sells) a put option (floor) with a strike price of $80/mt, with a premium equal to the long call option and the same time to expiration as the call option. Thus, the premium received by selling the put cancels out the premium paid to purchase the call. Consider the three different outcomes that may occur under this zero-cost collar strategy:

- If the bunker price at settlement rises above the exercise price of the call option of $90/mt, say to $95/mt, then the shipowner exercises the call and receives $5/mt from the writer (seller) of the collar.
- If the bunker price at settlement is between the two exercise prices of the put and call, that is between $80/mt and $90/mt, then the net cash-flow is zero. For example, if the bunker price is $85/mt then the shipowner will benefit from the lower bunker prices without incurring the loss of the upfront premium.
- If the bunker price at settlement falls to $75/mt, the shipowner will have to pay $5/mt to the writer of the collar.

When combined with the spot position, the shipowner observes the following payoffs.
- When bunker spot prices fall below the exercise price of the put option, his costs are constant and equal to the strike price of the put; in this case $80/mt.
- When bunker prices rise above the strike price of the call, the bunker cost to the shipowner is the call's exercise price of $90/mt.
- For prices in between and inclusive of the strike prices the payoff – the cost – from his combined spot-derivatives position equals the spot price.

Thus, a collar or a range or a tunnel of prices has been created through this strategy. It protects against bunker price rises and neutralises the costs of the derivatives positions needed to achieve this protection.

The general zero-cost collars' payoffs, which combine the spot, the long call and the short put positions are summarized in Table 4.9. A range of spot prices are shown in the first row of the table, in columns two, three and four. Each row represents the payoffs from the three markets, the spot, the put and the call. The final row of the table shows the payoff from the combined spot-derivatives positions for the shipowner. As can be seen, for $S < X_p$, the cost is X_p; for $X_p \leq S \leq X_c$, the cost is S; for $S > X_c$, the cost is X_c; moreover, the derivatives costs are neutralised.

Table 4.9. Payoff Table of a Collar Strategy for the Bunker Consumer

	Case A: $S < X_p$	Case B: $X_p \leq S \leq X_c$	Case C: $S > X_c$
Spot Market Cost: S	$-S$	$-S$	$-S$
Gain/(Loss) on Options			
Put Payoff: $-\max(X_p - S, 0)$	$-(X_p - S)$	0	0
Put Premium: P	$+P$	$+P$	$+P$
Call Payoff: $\max(S - X_c, 0)$	0	0	$(S - X_c)$
Call Premium: C	$-C$	$-C$	$-C$
Total Gain/(Loss) of Derivatives Position	$-(X_p - S)$	0	$(S - X_c)$
Cost of Bunkers	$-X_p$	$-S$	$-X_c$

Note: It is assumed that P = C.

Example 2:
Consider another example. Suppose that an industrial Natural Gas consumer is exposed to rising fuel costs and needs to set a cap. The Natural Gas spot price is currently at $3.85. He wishes to neutralize the premium of $0.20 for a $4.25 call option (long cap) and therefore, writes a $3.00 put option (short floor) for $0.20. That is, a long zero-cost collar of $3.00 to $4.25 is set. The cash inflow from writing the put offsets the cash outflow from buying the call.

Table 4.10 presents the possible outcomes of this collar strategy for the Natural Gas consumer, assuming three possible scenarios for the spot price at the expiration of the contracts. Specifically, let the spot price fall below the put's exercise price of $3.00, say to $2.50. The second and third columns of the table show that: In the spot market, the Natural Gas consumer pays $2.50; in the derivatives positions, the put option is exercised with a payoff of $-\max(X_p - S, 0) = -\max(\$3.00 - \$2.50, 0) = -\max(\$0.50,0)$ = -$0.50; the call option is not exercised. The $0.2 cash outflow paid to buy the call option is offset from the $0.2 inflow received from selling the put. The overall derivatives position payoff, taking into account the premiums, is a loss of $0.50. Combining this with the spot position results an overall cost to the Natural Gas consumer of $3.00. Actually, as can be seen at the bottom row of the table, this $3.00=$X_p$ is the exercise price of the put option and provides the floor, below which the bunker cost will not fall. When the spot price is between or equal to the two exercise prices of $3.00 and $4.25, neither option is exercised, with the two premiums canceling each other out. The fourth column of the table, for instance, shows the payoffs from a hypothetical spot price of $3.85; the bottom cell of this and the fifth column of the table indicates that for the range of prices between the two exercise prices of $3.00 and $4.25, the payoff equals the spot price. The last two column of the table show the payoffs when the spot price is above the call's exercise price of $4.25; such as when the price is at $5.00. It can be seen that only the call is exercised, giving a combined spot-derivatives payoff of $4.25 = X_c. That is, the exercise price of the call option (X_c) provides the upper limit, beyond which the bunker cost will not rise.

Table 4.10. Payoff Table of a Collar Strategy for the Natural Gas Consumer

	Case A: $S < X_p$ e.g. $S = \$2.50$		Case B: $X_p \le S \le X_c$ e.g. $S = \$3.85$		Case C: $S > X_c$ e.g. $S = \$5.00$	
Spot Market Cost: S	-$2.50	-S	-$3.85	-S	-$5.00	-S
Gain/(Loss) on Options						
Put Payoff: $-\max(X_p - S, 0)$	-$0.50	$-(X_p - S)$	0	0	0	0
Put Premium: P	$0.20	$+P$	$0.20	$+P$	$0.20	$+P$
Call Payoff: $\max(S - X_c, 0)$	0	0	0	0	$0.75	$(S - X_c)$
Call Premium: C	-$0.20	$-C$	-$0.20	$-C$	-$0.20	$-C$
Total Gain/(Loss) of Derivatives Position	-$0.50	$-(X_p - S)$	0	0	$0.75	$(S - X_c)$
Cost of Natural Gas	-$3.00	$-X_p$	-$3.85	-S	-$4.25	$-X_c$

Note: It is assumed that $P = C$.

The situation is shown graphically in Figure 4.6. The heavy dotted lines show the payoffs of the long $4.25 call and the short $3.00 put, with the heavy solid line indicating the combined derivatives position for the range of spot prices. Specifically, we observe this combined position to give a zero payoff in the range between and inclusive of the two strike prices, as the premiums and the payoffs cancel each other out. When the spot price falls below the put's exercise price, losses appear, while the opposite occurs - for spot prices above the call exercise price. This is also obvious when considering the second row from the bottom of Table 4.10. What is of interest though, is the total spot–derivatives position. The light continuous line emanating from zero and falling towards the bottom right of the diagram represents the increasing (negative payoff) cost of gas to the consumer as its spot price rises. Combining the solid derivatives line, which shows the total derivatives position, with that of the light solid line representing the payoff of the spot market, gives the light dotted line at the bottom of the diagram. This shows clearly, what the gas consumer achieved through his derivatives positions: He has created a tunnel for his costs, which now lie between the two exercise prices: his costs are equal to the constant $3.00 when the price of gas falls below this exercise price of the put option; his costs are also constant and equal to the exercise price of the call option when prices rise above this exercise price of $4.25; finally, when spot prices range between the two exercise prices the combined spot - derivatives position payoff equals the spot price. All this is also apparent in the last row of Table 4.10.

303

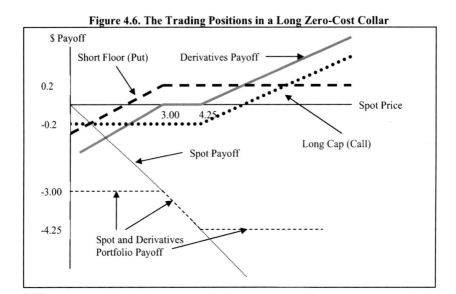

Figure 4.6. The Trading Positions in a Long Zero-Cost Collar

$ Payoff

Short Floor (Put)   Derivatives Payoff

0.2

Spot Price

3.00   4.25

-0.2

Long Cap (Call)

Spot Payoff

-3.00

-4.25

Spot and Derivatives
Portfolio Payoff

Example 3:
As another example, consider next the other side of the market of example 2. A Natural Gas producer is exposed to falling prices and wishes to protect himself against this. He can buy a put option (long floor) at a premium of $0.20 and an exercise price of $3.00. At the same time he wishes to neutralize the cost of the put option premium and writes a call (short cap) with an exercise price of $4.25 at a premium of $0.20. Thus, a short zero-cost collar of $4.25 to $3.00 is set.

Table 4.11. Payoff Table of a Collar Strategy for the Natural Gas Producer

	Case A: $S < X_p$ e.g. $S = \$2.50$		Case B: $X_p \leq S \leq X_c$ e.g. $S = \$3.85$		Case C: $S > X_c$ e.g. $S = \$5.00$	
Spot Market Income	$2.50	$+S$	$3.85	$+S$	$+\$5.00$	$+S$
Gain/(Loss) on Options						
Put Payoff: max($X_p - S$, 0)	$0.50	$(X_p - S)$	0	0	0	0
Put Premium: P	-$0.20	-P	-$0.20	-P	-$0.20	-P
Call Payoff: -max($S - X_c$, 0)	0	0	0	0	-$0.75	$-(S - X_c)$
Call Premium: C	$0.20	+C	$0.20	+C	$0.20	+C
Total Gain/(Loss) of Derivatives Position	$0.50	$(X_p - S)$	0	0	-$0.75	$-(S - X_c)$
Income of Natural Gas	**$3.00**	X_p	**$3.85**	S	**$4.25**	X_c

Note: It is assumed that P = C.

Table 4.11 presents the possible outcomes of this collar strategy for the Natural Gas producer, assuming three possible scenarios for the spot price at the expiration of the contracts. When the spot price falls below the put's exercise price of $3.00, say to $2.50 the put option is exercised, with a payoff of ($X_p - S$), which is $2.50 in this case; the call is not exercised; the call premium cancels that of the put; the spot position gives an income of S; resulting in an the constant overall payoff of X_p, which in this case is $3.00 – this is equal to the put's exercise price. Thus, the gas producer has set a floor to his income; no matter how much prices fall, his income will not fall below X_p. These outcomes can be seen in columns two and three of Table 4.11. Columns four and five of the same table show the payoffs when spot prices take values between or equal to the two exercise prices. In this case, income is proportional to the spot price, S. For spot prices above the call's exercise price, the producer's income is also a constant and equal to X_c, that is, the upper limit equals the call's strike price.

This situation is also shown graphically in Figure 4.7. The heavy dotted lines show the payoffs of the short $4.25 call and the long $3.00 put, with the heavy solid line indicating the combined derivatives position for the range of spot prices. The light continuous line emanating from zero and rising towards the top right of the diagram represents the increasing income of the gas producer. The combined spot – derivatives position is shown by the light dotted line at the top of the diagram. It shows that the income of the producer will not fall below $3.00, no matter how much prices fall, but will also not rise above $4.25. In fact, the payoff will be equal to the spot price when prices are between $3.00 and $4.25. This overall position can also be seen in the last row of Table 4.11.

Figure 4.7. The Trading Positions in a Short Zero-Cost Collar

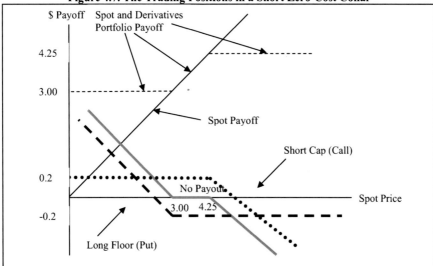

(ii) Participating Collars (or Participating Forwards)
A variation of the zero-cost collar is the participating collar. To create a participating collar, an at-the-money put option is sold and an out-of-the-money call option, of the same quantity and maturity, is purchased. However, an at-the-money option is of greater value. Thus, under this strategy, investors receive a greater premium than they pay. To make the participating collar a zero-cost collar using the above options, requires the purchase of an out-of-the-money call option for a greater quantity of fuel than sold as an at-the-money put option.

Example:
Suppose a shipowner wants to construct a zero-cost participating collar, using an at-the-money put option and an out-of-the-money call option, in order to get protected against future bunker price increases. At the same time he wishes to avoid the cost of the options' premiums. The current IFO380cst price is $90/mt. He buys an out-of-the-money call option on 5,000 tons at a strike price of $95/mt, paying a premium of

$2.85/mt and at the same time he sells an at-the-money put option with a strike price of $90/mt, for a premium of $4.70/mt. In order to make it a zero-cost collar, the quantity sold of the put option should be lower, so that the total premium for both the put and the call options is the same. In the market, a put option with a premium of $2.85/mt exists. It is sold to cover the quantity of 3,265mt.

Consider the three different outcomes that may occur under this zero-cost collar strategy:

- If the bunker price at settlement rises above the exercise price of the call option of $95/mt, say to $100/mt, then the shipowner exercises the call and receives $25,000 (= $5/mt x 5,000 tons) from the writer (seller) of the collar.
- If the bunker price at settlement is between and including the two exercise prices of the put and call, that is, between $90/mt and $95/mt, then the net cash-flow is zero. For example, if the bunker price is $93/mt then the shipowner will benefit from the lower bunker prices without incurring the loss of the upfront premium.
- If the bunker price at settlement falls to $80/mt, the shipowner will have to pay $32,650 (= $10/mt x 3,265mt) to the writer of the collar.

The shipowner receives the full benefit of a favourable movement in bunker prices, and in case of an adverse movement in bunker prices pays only 65.3% of the amount normally due.

4.4.5. Swaptions
A swaption is an option with a swap as the underlying asset. The holder of a swaption has the right to exercise it to purchase a swap at a predetermined exercise price.

Example:
Suppose that the bunker broker of a shipowner believes that bunker prices will follow an upward trend in the next three to fifteen months and advises his client to hedge this bunker price risk exposure with a swap in three month from now. However, the shipowner can get from his broker a better price for the swap today. Therefore, he decides to buy a call swaption, maturing in three months. The option is for a twelve month swap for Rotterdam IFO180cst barges, at an exercise price of $95/mt.

Assume that at the expiration of the option's contract, the price of a Rotterdam IFO180cst barges swap is $100/mt. The shipowner exercises the call option and buys the swap at $95/mt. As with a normal call option, the shipowner has to pay an upfront option premium to purchase the swaption. If the price of the swap on expiration of the option was $92/mt the shipowner would not exercise it, loosing only his upfront option premium. The shipowner would instead purchase a swap at the price prevailing in the market then. With the swaption, the shipowner has hedged his bunkers requirements for the next three to fifteen months.

4.5. Summary
This chapter examined the most important source of risk which affects the cost side of the vessel operations of shipowners and/or charterers; namely bunker rate fluctuations. After presenting and analysing the most important bunker markets around the world, their characteristics and the economic variables affecting them, modern risk management derivatives instruments used to hedge bunker rate fluctuations, were presented. Bunker derivatives include: forward bunker agreements,

which are traded in OTC markets; exchange traded energy futures contracts, which involve cross-hedging bunker fuels with futures contracts that have energy products as the underlying commodities; bunker swaps, which are traded in OTC markets; and bunker options, which are traded both in OTC and exchange-based markets. In each case, practical hedging examples were given. The next chapter presents two of the newest derivatives instruments introduced in the shipping industry; forward contracts designed to hedge vessel value and scrapping price risks.

CHAPTER 5. Vessel Value Derivatives and Risk Management

5.1. Introduction

Chapter 1 of this book emphasized the importance of the fluctuations of vessel prices in contributing to the fluctuations in the cash-flow position of the shipowner. It is argued that because vessels are the main asset which shipowners hold in order to provide their freight service to the market, and since the sums involved in holding these assets are the largest item in the shipowner's cash-flow, changes in their values can make all the difference in terms of ending up with a profit or loss from their investments in the shipping sector. Often the contribution of asset play to the balance-sheet is greater than the operation of the vessel itself. The timing of the investment decisions is extremely important. Investors which have exercised successfully the "*buy low – sell high*" principle in the vessel markets have ended up with hefty bank balances at the end of the day. A large number of shipowners/companies rely on these (vessel) transactions to make a profit in the sector. Others make a loss and fall spectacularly out of business, as the sums involved are large.

Figure 5.1. Second-Hand and Newbuilding Dry Cargo Vessel Prices

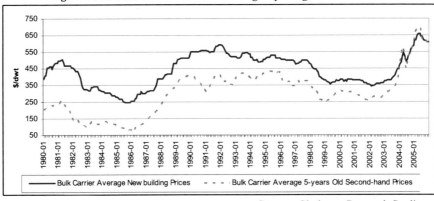

Source: Clarksons Research Studies

Vessel prices fluctuate substantially, as can be seen in the historical average newbuilding and second-hand prices for the bulk carrier and and tanker sectors presented in Figures 5.1 and 5.2, respectively. This is expected, as vessel prices, at any point in time, can be thought of as the present value of the expected cash-flows from operating the vessel over its lifetime, plus the present value of the expected scrap value of the vessel at the end of its lifetime, say 25 years after being built - see Kavussanos and Alizadeh (2002) for a formal analysis of this relationship. Expected cash-flows in turn, are determined by expected freight rates, costs and discount (interest) rates. The largest contributor to the cash-flows and as a consequence in vessel values are expected freight rates. Expected discount rates (used to calculate the present values) and expected operating costs are relatively constant (with the exception of bunker prices), as discussed in Chapter 4 of this book. Beenstock and Vergottis (1993) for instance show that second-hand vessel prices are positively related to expected discounted profits, to discounted newbuilding prices and to a wealth over the stock of the fleet variable; the latter two factors reflecting the state of the market for vessels as well as the wealth/income effect of investors. Kavussanos (1996b, 1997), using GARCH type models, shows that the second moments (the variances) of vessel prices are time-varying and are affected by factors such as time-charter rates, interest rates and oil prices. Moreover, these variances, reflecting vessel price risks, are time-varying.

Figure 5.2. Second-Hand and Newbuilding Tanker Vessel Prices

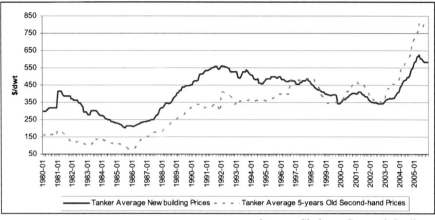

Source: Clarksons Research Studies

Returning to our investor's problem, who is interested in asset play, in the absence of the possibility of short selling vessels and of a derivatives market for vessels, investors are only able to exploit correct anticipations of market upturns in the vessel value market. Thus, they would buy a vessel at a certain time period and wait until vessel prices increased to sell the vessel at a higher price. If prices fall they would make a loss. Moreover, highly volatile vessel values, combined with a lengthy Sales & Purchase (S&P) process and relatively low liquidity in the physical market, can make market timing difficult and have adverse effects on the Return on Equity (ROE). The existence of a derivatives market for vessel prices allows investors to exploit market downturns, as well as upturns in the market. This is important in order to have a more complete market and helps in price discovery and the smoothing out of asset value fluctuations. During September 2003, the Baltic Exchange, in collaboration with Clarksons Securities Limited, launched vessel value derivatives contracts. These are based on the second-hand value of selected types of vessels. The aim of this chapter is to present the risk management of vessel values and scrapping prices of vessels, through the use of derivatives products.

The rest of the chapter is organised as follows: Section 5.2 describes the specification of vessel value derivatives contracts. Section 5.3 presents, through practical examples, how vessel value derivatives can be used for hedging purposes. Section 5.4 puts forward a pricing formula which allows calculation of the *"fair"* value of forward contracts on vessel values and applies this to a real-world example. Section 5.5 describes how the risks emanating from fluctuations in vessel demolition prices can be hedged using scrapping derivatives for bulk carriers and tankers. Finally, Section 5.6 concludes the chapter.

5.2. Sale & Purchase Forward Agreements (SPFAs)

The Forward Ship Valuation Agreements (FoSVAs) are OTC forwards contracts which cover both the dry-bulk and the tanker markets. These contracts are settled in cash against the Baltic Ship Valuation Assessments (BaSVAs). From 2nd of August

2004, the Baltic Exchange renamed both the FoSVAs and the BaSVAs, to Sale & Purchase Forward Agreements (SPFAs) and Baltic Sale & Purchase Assessments (BSPAs), respectively. The BSPA was established by a number of the Baltic Exchange member companies and has been tested by the Baltic Exchange, with simulation trades, since May 2003. It is described by the Baltic Exchange as "*A brand new concept for the industry, providing independent assessments on the market value of six vessel types*" (Baltic Exchange, 2004). These vessel values, provided they are reliable, provide the underlying commodity upon which vessel value derivatives can be written on.

Table 5.1 panel A presents the six types of vessels (three tanker and three dry), while panel B presents the vessel characteristics, which form the BSPA and are the underlying assets of the SPFA derivatives contracts. All the valuations are made on five-year old vessels and based on professional assessments made by ten panellists, presented in Table 5.1 panel C. The BSPAs are reported every week (four per month, every Tuesday, as from 2nd of August 2004), and are calculated using the same procedures developed by the Baltic Exchange for the dry and tanker freight indices – see Chapter 3, section 3.2.1 for a description of this procedure. Before 1st of August 2004 the BSPA was reported only twice a month. The reason for reporting BSPAs every week and not on a daily basis, as with freight rate indices, is that the physical market for second-hand vessels is less liquid and less volatile in comparison to the freight rate market. Figure 5.3 presents the BSPA prices for the six vessel types, of Table 5.1, from 16 September 2003 until 05 September 2005. They reflect fully the developments in the second-hand vessel markets during this period.

Figure 5.3. BSPA Prices of Six Vessels (16/09/03 – 05/09/05)

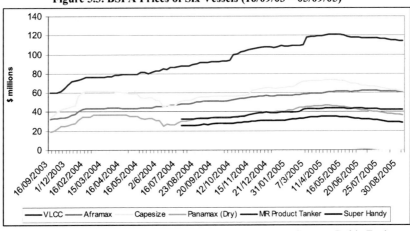

Source: Baltic Exchange

The SPFAs can be tailored by principals, according to their needs, in terms of agreed settlement period and maturity. As usual, for a forward contract, no money changes hands at the time of purchase. Even though large sums change hands in the physical sale and purchase of vessels, it is less likely that someone will want to take a paper position in a full VLCC, with the potential multi-dollar exposure and the corresponding credit risk, which are present in an emerging derivatives market (Abeal and Adland, 2003). To address this concern, the SPFAs are traded in multiple of lots, where one lot represents 5% of the vessel's value, where one vessel represents 20 lots of 5% each. Table 5.2 shows a break down for these contracts for a Capesize vessel with a value of $35 million. As seen in the table, a 20 lots hedge represents 100% of the vessel's value; that is, $35 million. A 5 lots hedge represents 25% of the vessel's value; that is, $8.75 million. A 2 lots hedge represents 10% of the vessel's value; that is, $3.5million, and a 1 lot hedge represents 5% of the vessel's value, which is $1.75 million.

According to Abeal and Adland (2003), this unitisation achieves at least three things: (i) it lowers the barrier to entry in the market, thereby hopefully improving liquidity in the early stages of the development of these markets, (ii) it lowers the risk and the credit exposure, which is always a concern in an OTC market, and (iii) it facilitates the hedging of values for vessels of different ages (and therefore, of different vessel values than the underlying asset) or vessels of different size (e.g. the hedging of Handymax values for which a derivative contract is not available, using the available Panamax forward contract).

Table 5.1. The Products of the Baltic Sale & Purchase Assessments (BSPA) – Vessel Definitions and Panellists, 2005

Panel A: BSPA Products		
Vessel Type	**Description**	**Vessel Size (dwt)**
VLCC	Double Hull – Max 5 Years Old	305,000
Aframax	Double Hull – Max 5 Years Old	105,000
MR Product Tanker	Double Hull – Max 5 Years Old	45,000
Capesize	Max 5 Years Old	172,000
Panamax (Dry)	Max 5 Years Old	74,000
Super Handy	Max 5 Years Old	52,000

Panel B: BSPA Vessel Characteristics
VLCC: built in "*first class competitive yard*", European standard B&W main engine, about 15.5 knots service speed laden on about 90.0 tons, loa (length overall load) about 332m, beam about 58m, non coated, not ice classed.
Aframax: built in "*first class competitive yard*", European standard B&W main engine, about 15.5 knots service speed laden on about 50.0 tons, loa about 248m, beam about 42m, non coated, not ice classed.
Medium Range Products Tanker: built in "*first class competitive yard*", European standard B&W main engine, about 14.5 knots service speed on about 35/32.8mt fuel oil (laden/ballast), loa about 182m, beam about 32m, draft about 12m, coated, not ice classed.
Capesize: built in "*first class competitive yard*", 190,000cbm (cubic meter) grain, max loa 289m, max beam 45m, draft 17.75m, 14.5 knots laden, 15.0 knots ballast on 56mts fuel oil, no diesel at sea, non coated, not ice classed.
Panamax: built in "*first class competitive yard*", 89,000cbm grain, max loa 225m, draft 13.95m, 14.0 knots on 32/28 fuel oil laden/ballast and no diesel at sea, non coated, not ice classed.
Super Handy: built in "*first class competitive yard*", European standard B&W main engine, 66,500 cbm grain, loa 190m, beam 32.25m, draft 12.05m, 14.5 knots on average 30.5mt fuel oil (laden/ballast) and no diesel at sea, 5 holds/5 hatches, 4x30t cranes, non-coated, not ice classed.

Panel C: BSPA Panellists
ACM Shipping Ltd. (UK), Arrow Chartering Ltd. (UK), Banchero-Costa & C s.p.a. (Italy), Barry Rogliano Salles (France), Clarksons (UK), Fearnleys A/S (Norway), Lorentzen & Stemoco A/S (Norway), Mallory Jones Lynch Flynn & Associates Inc. (US), Optima Shipbrokers Ltd. (Greece), RS Platou Shipbrokers A/S (Norway), Simpson Spence & Young Ltd. (UK) and Yamamizu Shipping Co. Ltd. (Japan).

Notes: **Source:** Baltic Exchange
- All vessels have the following characteristics: Prompt delivery (2-3 months), Special Survey (SS) passed, Charter free and 2% total commission.

Settlement of the SPFA contracts is against the four-week average of the BSPA prices of the expiration month of the contract. For example, a February 2006 SPFA will settle against the average of the four BSPA assessments, published during February 2006. The typical length of these contracts, according to market sources, is two to three years.

Table 5.2. SPFA Contract Size for a Capesize Vessel with a Value of $35 million

Number of Lots	Percentage of Vessel's Value	Proportion of Vessel's Value
20 lots	100%	$35 million
5 lots	25%	$8.75 million
2 lots	10%	$3.5 million
1 lot	5%	$1.75 million

Asset prices have traditionally been highly volatile, and this new product has huge potential as a tool for shipowners, providing amongst others: greater leverage and security against loans; paper based asset play opportunities without the risk of operating in the physical market); for shipyards, allowing them to hedge against newbuilding options; for lending banks, it provides security and maturity matching against the shipping loan portfolio, and developing of proprietary trading desks[71]; and for asset underwriters, which are considered the natural sellers of these products. Traditional shipping "*asset players*", charterers (hedge against inventory movements, purchase options with correlation to long-term charters), non-shipping investors (seeking exposure to the shipping industry without having to buy the steel), and investors looking for a commodity that correlates strongly with the state of the world economy and industrial production, are considered the natural sellers of these products.

Abeal and Adland (2003) present the possible SPFA positions that shipowners may take: They can take short positions in the SPFA market in order to hedge their long positions in the physical market (owning the vessel), thereby protecting the asset values in the company against a potential decline. Shipowners can leverage off their commercial market knowledge and speculate on the future value of vessels without the operational risks of actually owning the vessel. Moreover, shipowners do not need to have operating expertise, but can invest in market sectors outside the current core business areas. Another example is the owner who wants to purchase a vessel but lacks funds, who therefore is exposed to the risk of increasing values before a purchase can be made. Thus, the shipowner can take a short-term long SPFA position, as he has a short position in the second-hand market. Another example is the large shipping company, with a diversified fleet that is concerned about being "*over weighted*" in one sector, (e.g. VLCCs) and "*under weighted*" in another sector (e.g. Aframax tankers). Instead of entering physical transactions of buying and selling vessels, the company could rebalance its portfolio of vessels by taking long positions or short positions on SPFAs, on Aframax and VLCCs, respectively. Speculators could play the market irrespective of its direction by the successful timing of long and short positions in SPFAs, whereas until now "*asset play*" has only been possible during a market upswing.

The advantages of the SPFAs are: (i) the size of the contracts ranges between 5% to 100%, as opposed to 100% in physical transactions; (ii) the maturity of the contracts is customized to take positions to hedge or arbitrage along the time curve, as opposed to only short dated trades in physical trades; (iii) the absence of operational risks inherent in vessel ownership, as a paper trader (speculator or arbitrageur) do not have to posses any vessel; (iv) the trading of vessel price spreads is possible, by trying to locate mispricings, using arbitrage arguments, between two values of the same type of

---

[71] The introduction of Basel II makes it important for banks to manage their exposures to asset risks. For instance, financial institutions may wish to incorporate the cost of a put option in the cost of a loan, thereby ensuring that vessel values do not fall below a level that the bank is comfortable with (Abeal and Adland, 2003).

vessel; (v) the market of the underlying asset (vessel) can be shorted for the first time, as this is not possible in the physical market; (vi) the speed of execution of the contracts, as a SPFA trade can be concluded in just a day, as opposed to physical trades which may take several months; (vii) the cost efficient nature of the transactions, by having firm BSPA quotes by the Baltic Exchange; and (ix) that the deals are structured, following the conventional wisdom of derivatives brokers.

The main issues in this market are: (i) the low liquidity, which can be assisted by proper marketing and promotion actions. Thin trading may result in poor price discover and quotes, given by brokers, which are limited to short hedge time periods in the future (2 with 3 years forward); (ii) the existence of basis-risk, which should be properly modeled through analysis and simulations. Severe deviations between the BSPA and SPFA prices may result to low hedging effectiveness of the derivatives contracts; and (iii) the existence of credit risk, which can be minimised with the use of bank guarantees, credit language in the contract, or even with the use of credit derivatives.

A new independent advisory group was formed during 2004, to enhance the emerging market for vessel asset derivatives. The group consists of key users, derivative brokers and physical panelists and will act as an information gatherer and advisor to the marketplace. The group is actively seeking views from the market regarding these assessments. The group consists of: Barry Rogliano Salles (France), Banchero-Costa & C (Italy), Cargill International (UK), Clarksons Capital (UK), Freight Investor Services (UK), Fortis Bank, Oceanbulk Maritime (Singapore), Simpson, Spence & Young (UK), Thenamaris Ships Management (Greece), and Torvald Klaveness Group (Norway).

5.3. Applications of the Use of SPFA Contracts
The following examples of the use of SPFA contracts illustrate the concepts already discussed:

5.3.1. Hedging a Capesize Vessel with a Single Maturity SPFA Contract
Suppose that a shipowner buys, during 1st July 2003, a Capesize vessel, which he intends to keep and operate until 30th June 2006. He wishes to protect himself against future falls in vessel values. He can hedge his exposure to vessel price risk by selling SPFA contract(s), each contract representing a percentage of the risk he wishes to manage. He decides to sell 10 Cape SPFA lots, representing 50% of the vessel's value, at $30 million, with contract duration of 3 years. The settlement price, during 30th of June 2006, is the average of the four weekly BSPA rates of the settlement month.

Table 5.3 summarizes the information and presents the outcome of two alternative scenarios; a vessel value decrease and an increase in the market for vessel prices. Assume that by 30th June 2006 vessel values decrease to $28 million. Thus, the shipowner bought the vessel at $30 million, which is now worth $28 million, amounting to a $2 million loss in the physical market. On the other hand, the SPFA position gives him a gain of $1million (= 50% x $2 million). The net result is: $1million – $2 million = $1 million loss, instead of $2 million, which would have occurred if the SPFA market was not used for hedging. Under an alternative scenario, of a market rise in vessel prices, presented in the second column of Table 5.3, assume that the value of Capesize vessels rise to $32 million. The shipowner loses $1 million

313

on the SPFA contract(s), but covers his paper losses from the physical sale of his Capesize vessel in the open market. In the former market he loses $1 million, but gains $2 million in the physical market, resulting in an overall gain of $ 1 million.

Table 5.3. The SPFA Part Hedge

1st July 2003	
Physical Market	**SPFA Market**
Capesize vessel value: $30 million	SPFA price: $30 million
	Action: Sell 10 SPFA contracts, representing 50% of the vessel's value
	SPFA Contract value: $15 mil. (= $30 mil. x 50%)
First scenario: Vessel values decrease	**Second scenario: Vessel values increase**
30th June 2006: Physical Market	
Capesize vessel value: $28 million	Capesize vessel value: $32 million
The shipowner loses $2,000,000	**The shipowner gains $2,000,000**
30th June 2006: SPFA Market	
SPFA price: $28 million	SPFA price: $32 million
Action: Buy 10 SPFA contracts	Action: Buy 10 SPFA contracts
SPFA Contract value: $14 mil. (= $28 mil. x 50%)	SPFA Contract Value: $16 mil. (= $32 mil. x 50%)
The shipowner gains $1,000,000	**The shipowner loses $1,000,000**
Portfolio of Physical and SPFA Positions	
Net Loss: $1,000,000, instead of $2 million	**Net Profit: $1,000,000**, instead of $2 million

5.3.2. Hedging a Capesize Vessel with a SPFA Contract with Two Maturities

Suppose that a shipowner buys a Capesize vessel during 1st October 2003 at $35 million, but needs some protection against possible falls in vessel values in years 2005 and 2006. The situation is presented in Table 5.4. He part hedges his exposure by selling 10 Cape SPFA lots, representing a 50% share of his total risk, at $35 million for 2005 and $34 million for 2006, with a contract duration of 3 years. Notice that the shipowner is free to sell his vessel anytime during this period. The two settlement prices, during December 2005 and December 2006, are calculated as the average of the four weekly BSPA rates of the respective settlement months.

Let us assume that by 31st December 2005 vessel values decrease to $33 million, while by 31st December 2006 vessel values increase to $34.5 million. Thus, by December 2005 he makes a loss of $2 million in the physical market due to the fall in prices. The SPFA position gives him a profit of $1 million (= 50% x $2 million). By the time of the second settlement of the SPFA contract in December 2006, the shipowner would have bought the vessel in the physical market at $34 million, which during December 2006 is worth $34.5 million, resulting in a $0.5 million profit in the physical market. The SPFA position results in a loss of $250k (= 50% x $0.5 million). The overall outcome of the two SPFA settlements is: $1 million – $250k = $0.75 million profit in the forward market. If the shipowner did not use the SPFA market he would have lost $2 million in 2005 and gained $0.5 million in 2006. The net result in the physical market would have been $1.5 million loss. In the SPFA trade he chose a 50% hedging strategy and made a profit of $0.75 million. Overall, his combined portfolio of the physical and the derivatives position reduces his loss from $1.5 million to $0.75 million.

Table 5.4. SPFA, 50% Hedge in Oct. 2003, with Two Settlements, Dec. 2005 & Dec. 2006

1st October 2003, Capesize vessel value: $35 million	
Physical market, 31st December 2005	**Physical market, 31st December 2006**
Capesize vessel value $33 million	Capesize vessel value $34.5 million
The shipowner loses $2,000,000	**The shipowner gains $500,000**
Net loss in the physical market: $2,000,000 – $500,000 = $1,500,000	
SPFA market, 1st October 2003	
Capesize SPFA Prices, for Settlement 31st December 2005: $35 million	Capesize SPFA Prices, for Settlement 31st December 2006: $34 million
Action: Sell 10 SPFA lots, representing 50% of vessel's value – worth $17,5 million (= $35 million x 50%)	Action: Sell 10 SPFA lots, representing 50% of vessel's value – worth $17 million (= $34 million x 50%)
SPFA Market, 31st December 2005	**SPFA Market, 31st December 2006**
SPFA price: $33 million	SPFA price: $34.5 million
Action: Buy 10 SPFA lots – worth $16,5 million (= $33 million x 50%)	Action: Buy 10 SPFA lots – worth $17,25 million (= $34.5 million x 50%)
The shipowner gains $1,000,000	**The shipowner loses $250,000**
Net profit in the SPFA market: $1,000,000 – $250,000 = $750,000	
Net result of combined physical and SPFA positions: $0.75 million loss, instead of $1.5 million in physical	

5.4. SPFA Pricing

As we saw in section 2.3.2.5, the pricing of forward contracts is important for market participants in derivatives markets. If market participants can determine the "*fair*"/theoretical value of the forward contract, with the vessel value as the underlying commodity, then they can develop trading strategies, according to whether the observed market value is above or below this "*fair*" value. If the actual forward price in the market is greater (less) than the theoretical value, arbitrageurs can purchase (short) the vessel in the spot market and take a short (long) position in the corresponding SPFA forward contract, thus making a risk-free profit. These arbitrage opportunities shouldn't exist for long in well functioning markets, as the collective action of market agents should bring prices back to their 'correct' levels.

In view of the above, this section proposes a model which allows us to calculate the "*fair*" value of a forward contract – the SPFA – written on the value of a vessel. More specifically, vessels are assets which provide an income over their lifetime. We saw in Chapter 2 that the price of a forward contract on this type of income generating assets is obtained through the following formula:

$$F = (S - I) e^{r T} \qquad (5.1)$$

where F is the forward value of the contract, S is the spot price of the vessel, I is the present value of the income of that the vessel generates over the lifetime of the forward contract, r is the risk-free interest rate with the same maturity as the forward contract, T is the time to maturity of the contract, while e is the number 2.718. Following the arguments of section 2.3.2.5, and given the assumptions outlined therein, the above pricing formula is used in the example that follows to calculate the "*fair*" price of a two-month SPFA contract on a Suezmax vessel.

Assume today is 3rd February 2005 and the market value of a five-year old Suezmax vessel is $68mil. The two-month time-charter rate is $55,000/day, paid every 15 days (= 1/24 years). Therefore, the 15 days income from the time-charter is:

$55,000/day×15 days = $825,000. Based on market sources, total expenses from operating the vessel, can be assumed to be around $7,000/day. Therefore, the 15 days' expenses for the time-charter are: $7,000/day x 15 days = $105,000. As a result, the net income from the time-charter for the 15 days period is: $825,000 – $105,000 = $720,000. The first time-charter payment is received in advance. The annualized risk-free (Treasury-Bill) interest rates for 15, 30, 45 and 60 days are: 2.305%, 2.330%, 2.355% and 2.38%, respectively.

The sum of the present values of the four payments is:

$$I = \$720,000 + \$720,000\ e^{-0.02305 \times (1/24)} + \$720,000\ e^{-0.0233 \times (2/24)} + \$720,000\ e^{-0.02355 \times (3/24)}$$
$$= \$720,000 + \$719,309 + \$718,603 + \$717,884 = \$2,875,796$$

Utilising the formula presented earlier, the theoretical value of a SPFA contract is calculated as:

$$F = (S - I)\ e^{r\,T} = [\$68,000,000 - \$2,875,796] e^{0.0238 \times (2/12)} = \$65,383,043$$

If the actual forward price in the market is greater than $65,383,043, say $69 million, as in the first column of Table 5.5, arbitrageurs can follow the strategy outlined next and make a risk-free profit. Purchase the vessel in the spot market at S = $68 million, by borrowing this amount for two months at the annualized interest rate of r = 2.38%, and short the SPFA forward contract for delivery of the asset at F = $69 million in T=2/12 years from today. In two months from today, the loan amount of $68,270,269[= $68million $e^{0.0238 \times (2/12)}$] is repaid, the vessel is sold through the forward contract at $69 million and a cash-flow of $2,887,226 has resulted from the operation of the vessel during the two months. The net cash-flow from these transactions is a risk-free profit of $3,616,957.

If the actual forward price in the market is less than the theoretical price of $65,383,043, as in the second column of Table 5.5, an arbitrageur can make a risk-free profit as follows: Short the value of the vessel, invest the proceeds in an interest bearing account and take a long position in a SPFA two month forward contract. As can be seen in the second column of the table, after two months, a profit of $(S - I)\ e^{r\,T}$ – F = $1,383,043 is realised.

These arbitrage opportunities are discovered by market agents who act upon them and through their collective actions eliminate them, in the process forcing prices to be at their "*fair*" level. In fact, for the cheap forward market scenario, under which the shorting of the vessel is part of the arbitragers' strategy, this shorting is not necessary for the "*fair*" forward values to be "*discovered*". It is sufficient that enough shipowners sell their vessels, for prices to reach their "*fair*"/theoretical level. It can be argued then that the above analysis provides us with a methodology which enables us to calculate the "*fair*" value of forward contracts that have vessel values as the underlying assets.

Table 5.5. Forward Price of Vessel with T/C Income

	Expensive Forward Market (SPFA) $F = \$69$mil	Cheap Forward Market (SPFA) $F = \$64$mil
Action in $t = 0$	Borrow $68mil for the physical purchase of the vessel	Short sale the vessel for $68mil and investment of proceeds in interest bearing account for two months.
	Short SPFA for the sale of the vessel at $69mil	Long SPFA for the purchase of the vessel at $64 mil
Result in $t = 2$ **months**	Repayment of loan – amount: $\$68,000,000 e^{0.0238 \times (2/12)} = \$68,270,269$	Receipts of $\$68,000,000 e^{0.0238 \times (2/12)}$ $= \$68,270,269$
	Sale of the vessel and receipt of $69mil	Purchase of the vessel at $64mil
	Net Income from T/C earnings: $Ie^{rT} = [(\$720,000 + \$720,000\, e^{0.02305 \times (1/24)}$ $+ \$720,000\, e^{0.0233 \times (2/24)} + \$720,000$ $e^{0.02355 \times (3/24)}]\, e^{0.0238 \times (2/12)} = \$2,887,226$	T/C earnings payment to be returned to the owner of the vessel (due to short sale) -$2,887,226
Risk-free **Profit**	$69,000,000 + $2,887,226 –$68,270,269 = **$3,616,957**	$68,270,269 – $64,000,000 – $2,887,226 = **$1,383,043**

Adland *et al.* (2004) consider the applicability of the above pricing relationship for the SPFAs. Due to lack of sufficient data, in order to price a SPFA contract with any given maturity, they derive a term-structure function of freight rates (implied vessel forward prices) from January 1990 to March 2003 for the Aframax and Panamax sectors and from December 1991 to March 2003 for the VLCC and Capesize sectors. They examined whether the unbiasedness hypothesis holds between "*implied*" vessel forward prices and realised spot rates, and report that the unbiasedness hypothesis is rejected for all sectors and all horizons investigated. Moreover, it is argued that this result can be justified through the existence of a risk-premium. However, this relationship remains to be tested at some stage, when there are longer time series of actual data that could be actually used for the empirical examination of the relationship.

5.5. Vessel Scrapping Price Derivatives
5.5.1. Baltic Demolition Assessments (BDAs)
With the creation of a derivative contract for hedging second-hand vessel values, the industry turned into the design of a derivatives product for hedging vessel scrapping prices. The launching, by the Baltic Exchange, of an independent benchmark on the demolition values of bulk carriers and tankers, for the first time, enables the development of a derivatives product, which offers protection against the fluctuating values of vessel scrapping prices. Figure 5.4 presents the considerable fluctuations in scrap prices of VLCC and Capesize vessels from November 1995 until October 2005.

Testing of the data for the BDAs begun on 12th July 2004 and were officially launched during August 2004. The available BDAs, shown in Table 5.6 panel A, are based on the following specifications:
- Per long ton light displacement derived from a Dirty Tanker (D/TKR) of between 15,000 and 25,000 light weight, gas free for man entry. Delivery China (15/30 days), as is, under own power, cash price, basis standard commission.
- Per long ton light displacement derived from a Dirty Tanker (D/TKR) of between 15,000 and 25,000 light weight, gas free for man entry. Delivery

Subcontinent (15/30 days), as is, under own power, cash price, basis standard commission.

- Per long ton light displacement derived from a Product Tanker (C/TKR) of between 6,000 and 10,000 light weight, gas free for man entry. Delivery China (15/30 days), as is, under own power, cash price, basis standard commission.
- Per long ton light displacement derived from a Product Tanker (C/TKR) of between 6,000 and 10,000 light weight, gas free for man entry. Delivery Subcontinent (15/30 days), as is, under own power, cash price, basis standard commission.
- Per long ton light displacement derived from a Bulk Carrier (B/C) of between 7,000 and 12,000 light weight. Delivery China (15/30 days), as is, under own power, cash price, basis standard commission.
- Per long ton light displacement derived from a Bulk Carrier (B/C) of between 7,000 and 12,000 light weight. Delivery Subcontinent (15/30 days), as is, under own power, cash price, basis standard commission.

Figure 5.4. Scrap Prices of VLCC and Capesize Vessels (11/1995 – 10/2005)

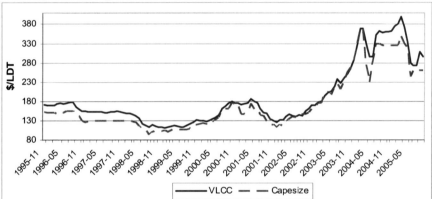

Note: LDT is Light Displacement Ton.   **Source:** Clarksons Research Studies

The assessments are published on a weekly basis and are based on reported prices from the vessel demolition broker's panel Whose members in 2005 are shown in Table 5.6 panel B. The assessments are expressed in US dollars and are subject to the same auditing procedures as other Baltic Exchange assessments, described earlier in this book. Figure 5.5 presents the BDA prices of the six vessel types from 13th July 2004 until 9th May 2005. As can be seen, demolition prices vary considerably over time, contributing to the riskiness of the cash-flow of the shipowner/investor, as discussed in Chapter 1 of this book. These fluctuations in BDA prices provide a justification for the use of derivatives to hedge scrapping price risks. The strategies to use in this case are very similar to the ones presented in other parts of the book for futures and forward contracts.

Table 5.6. The Products of the Baltic Demolition Assessments (BDAs) – Vessel Definitions and Panellists, 2005

Panel A: BDA Products		
Vessel Type	**Description**	**Vessel Size (dwt)**
D/TKR China	Del China (15/30 days)	15,000 - 25,000
D/TKR Subcon	Del Subcontinent (15/30 days)	15,000 - 25,000
C/TKR China	Del China (15/30 days)	6,000 - 10,000
C/TKR Subcon	Del Subcontinent (15/30 days)	6,000 - 10,000
B/C China	Del China (15/30 days)	7,000 - 12,000
B/C Subcon	Del Subcontinent (15/30 days)	7,000 - 12,000
Panel B: Panellists		
ACM Shipping Ltd. (UK), Clarksons (UK), Compass Maritime Services LLC (USA), Galbraith's Ltd. (UK), Optima Shipbrokers Ltd. (Greece), JV Shipping Ltd. (UK) and Simpson Spence & Young Ltd. (UK).		

Notes: **Source:** Baltic Exchange
- D/TKR, C/TKR, B/C are Dirty Tanker, Product Tanker, and Bulk Carrier, respectively.

5.5.2. Description and Economic Principles of the Scrapping Industry

As with any other derivatives market, in order to make correct investment decisions, it is important to understand the market and its characteristics of the underlying commodity. To that effect, a few words about the scrapping industry are in order. The scrapping tonnage in terms of dwt is important if one wants to measure the fleet removed permanently from service; this is because dwt scrapped, together with vessel losses and newbuildings, reflect the changes in the long run supply of freight services in the industry. In terms of the scrapping industry, though, what is interesting is the steel and other materials content in the vessel. Light Displacement Tonnage (LDT) is the unit of measurement in this case. It includes the hull, engines, spare parts, etc. The scrapping industry is a low technology industry, with a beach, with close to basic facilities, often being sufficient to operate; It is labour intensive, since very little capital is needed - breaking is done manually. Large metal structures, such as masts, pipes, deck equipment, the main engine, decks, the propeller, metal structures, etc. are removed one by one. The remainder of the vessel is taken ashore and cut into large sections. The availability of a quay or dry-dock can improve efficiency and safety. It is an environmentally dirty industry, as it pollutes the surrounding area.

Figure 5.5. The BDA Prices of the Six Vessels; Daily Data (13/07/04 – 05/09/05)

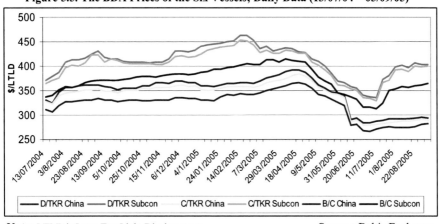

Note: LTLD is Long Ton Light Displacement.   **Source:** Baltic Exchange

Panels and sections of the broken vessel are cut into smaller pieces, using manually operated acetylene cutters, scrap assembled and transported to the final destination. Steel scrap is heated and rolled into rods, which are used in the construction industry, in sewage projects, in metal roads and in agriculture amongst others. The Far East and the Indian continent provide most of the demand for the output of the industry. In developed countries scrap is completely melted down to make fresh steel. The non-ferrous items on ships amount for a large part of the returns; thus, cranes, diesel engines, generators, compasses, clocks and furniture are resold, especially in developing countries.

A ship-breaker has to provide an evaluation to the owner and a contract has to be drawn to agree on the sale. This evaluation takes into account factors such as: The type of vessel offered for scrap – as specified in the plate configuration, with special features taken into account in the evaluation; The age of the vessel is important as this determines its steel content and design features; The building details determine the quality and content of the steel; The condition of the hull is taken into account; The equipment and spares on board; The bunkers on board; The location of the vessel in relation to the scrapyard is also important as it determines the costs of bringing it to the yard. The negotiation of a vessel for scrap is usually handled by scrap specialist brokers, who negotiate with the breakers. The breaker in turn sells his products to steelmakers and non-ferrous scrap buyers. Equilibrium scrapping prices are determined by supply and demand factors.

The supply for scrap depends on: The second-hand value of the vessel relative to scrap values – the higher the scrap price in relation to the value of the vessel, the more vessels will be supplied for scrap; Expectations of future freight rates and vessel prices – if the freight market remains strong with good prospects for strong freight rates then less vessels are supplied for scrap, shipowners delaying the scrapping decision for as long as possible in order to exploit the good freight market; Scrap prices (in relation to second-hand prices) – the higher the price of scrap the more vessels will be turned in for scraping, ceteris paribus; The higher the age of the fleet, the greater is the proportion of vessels that will be turned in for scraping. The scraping age though can vary according to the prevailing economic conditions and past maintenance levels of the vessel - strong freight markets delay the decision to scrap, as well as good maintenance level of the vessel during its life time; Technological obsolescence, as new technology is being used in newly built vessels, leads more ships to scrapyards; Regulatory changes, such as OPA90 (The 1990 Oil Pollution Act) requiring double hulls has led proportionally more vessels to scrapyards; Shifts in trade patterns and order quantities, requiring for example larger vessels, different vessel designs and improved efficiency will increase the supply o vessels for scrap; Imminent special surveys and major repairs may be costly and make them uneconomical to retain the vessel in service, thus leading to increases in scraping. Ultimately, the value of the vessel is compared to scrap prices to decide whether to keep or scrap. When the value of the vessel falls below the scrap value the vessel is scrapped – in that sense scrap prices provide a floor for second-hand prices. As mentioned before, scrap prices are determined at the intersection of demand with supply and are quite volatile, just like second-hand prices – see Figure 5.5.

5.6. Summary

This chapter presented the vessel value derivatives contracts - the SPFAs - introduced by the Baltic Exchange and Clarksons, and which are based on the second-hand values of selected types of vessels. Their uses, characteristics and practical examples were presented. Asset prices have traditionally been highly volatile, and this new product has good prospects as a tool for greater risk management of asset values for the market agents involved in the shipping industry. To manage the risks associated with fluctuations in the terminal value of the vessel, demolition price derivatives have also been introduced. They are based on BDA prices reported by the Baltic Exchange.

When a market agent operating in the shipping industry has to convert one currency for another one in a future time period, he is faced with foreign exchange risk. For instance, income for a European shipping company maybe in US$ but a large part of its expenses are in Euro. In order to pay for these expenses the US$ have to be converted to Euro. The purpose of the next chapter is to consider exchange rate risks and to demonstrate the use of foreign exchange rate derivatives products (such as currency futures, forwards, swaps, and options) to minimise this risk for shipping companies.

CHAPTER 6. Foreign Exchange Derivatives and Risk Management

6.1. Introduction

Another source of risk, identified in Chapter 1 as a factor affecting the shipowner's cash-flow, is the exchange rate risk. Foreign exchange (forex) risk emanates from fluctuations in the value of an asset or a liability as a consequence of changes in exchange rates. The forex risk comprises:

- **Transaction Exposure**: The risk that the domestic cost or proceeds of a transaction may change. Hedging them insulates the company against exchange rate changes.
- **Translation Exposure**: The risk that the translation of the value of foreign-currency denominated assets is affected by exchange rate changes. Changes in the company's balance-sheet will generally have little effect on its ongoing operations. The cash-flows are ignored and the balance-sheet entries are measured in terms of the book values. The only possibility, of an impact on the operations of the company in terms of changes in the balance-sheet, is the tax gain/loss asymmetry. If the company operates in a high inflationary environment, it may find that the translation adjustment, reported in the income statement, is taxed more when positive than credited when negative. Likewise, a company may find that changes in foreign borrowing are subject to asymmetric treatment of capital gains/losses.
- **Economic Exposure**: The risk that exchange rate changes may affect the present value of future income streams. Economic exposure is ultimately what the company should be concerned with. Investors are concerned with the value and riskiness of the company itself. Indeed, even transaction exposures should be evaluated in terms of whether they are associated with an underlying economic exposure. When considering hedging a known outflow or cost, the company needs to evaluate the revenue side operations; and when considering a known inflow or revenue, the company needs to evaluate the cost side. For whenever the currency movement affects revenues and costs equally, only the profit margin is truly exposed.

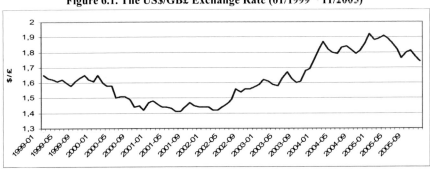

Figure 6.1. The US$/GB£ Exchange Rate (01/1999 – 11/2005)

In the shipping industry, because of its global nature, cash-flow transactions involve more than one currency somewhere. Consider the following examples: Payments to a Japanese yard for a newbuilding vessel are in Yen but reserves of the shipowner are in US$; The payment of a loan, for a vessel acquisition, may be issued in a different currency than the shipowner's reserves; management costs may be paid in domestic currency, whereas revenues are in US$; commissions of brokers are in US$, but they operate in the UK, say. Figures 6.1 – 6.4 show the US$/GB£, JP¥/US$, Won (South Korea)/US$ and US$/€ exchange rates, respectively, from January 1999 to November 2005, which represent some of the most commonly used currencies in the shipping business. As can be seen from the figures, the large fluctuations in the exchange rates provide a considerable source of risk for the market agents operating in the shipping industry. Therefore, the aim of this chapter is to show how exchange rate risk can be managed for companies in the sector, through both traditional methods and more modern forex derivatives instruments. Before setting into this task it is important, just like with other risk factors considered earlier in this book as affecting the shipping company, to say a few words about the most important economic influences of foreign exchange rates between two countries.

Figure 6.2. The JP¥/US$ Exchange Rate (01/1999 – 11/2005)

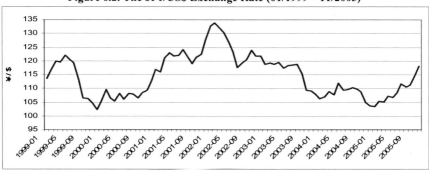

They are the following – see for instance Grauwe (2005): Interest rate and inflation rate differentials between the countries; monetary policy in each country; trade surpluses or deficits in each country; economic growth levels in each country; intervention tactics by central banks; the level of political, social, business security and stability in each country, and expectations regarding the future direction of currency values.

Figure 6.3. The Won/US$ Exchange Rate (01/1999 – 11/2005)

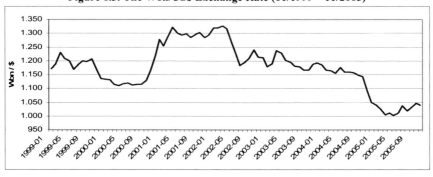

Figure 6.4. The US$/€ Exchange Rate (01/1999 – 11/2005)

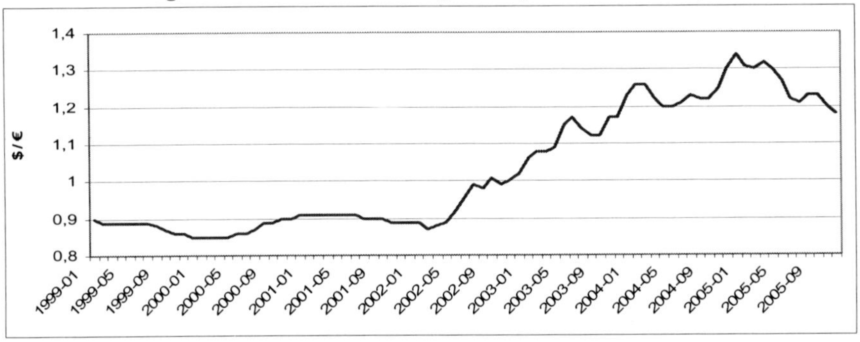

Each row of Table 6.1 summarizes the impact of each of the aforementioned economic factors on forex rates, separately, assuming that other factors are held constant in the process - *ceteris paribus*. For instance, as seen in the first row of the table, lower (higher) domestic interest rates will lower (increase) forex rates, *ceteris paribus*; lower (higher) inflation at home will increase (decrease) forex rates, *ceteris paribus*; a budget deficit (surplus) will lead forex rates to decrease (increase), *ceteris paribus*; central bank open market operations to buy (sell) the domestic currency will increase (decrease) forex rates, *ceteris paribus*; political instability (stability) at home will decrease (increase) forex rates and trade surplus (deficit) will increase (decrease) forex rates, *ceteris paribus*.

Table 6.1. Impact of Economic Factors on Forex Rates of the Home Country

Economic Factors for the Home Country, *Ceteris Paribus*	Increase in Forex Rates	Decrease in Forex Rates
Lower Interest Rates		√
Less Inflation	√	
Budget Deficit		√
Central Bank Buys Currency	√	
Political Instability		√
Trade Surplus	√	

The rest of this chapter is organised as follows: Section 6.2 presents the currency derivatives contracts available to market agents wishing to hedge or speculate in the currency market. Section 6.3 compares the performance of these financial products in hedging foreign exchange rate risk. Finally, section 6.4 concludes the chapter.

6.2. Currency Derivatives Contracts
There are a number of financial instruments that can be used to hedge forex risk:
- **Money Market Hedges:** Borrowing and lending in the money markets. It is considered flexible, but depends on whether the company has equal access to domestic and foreign credit markets.
- **Currency Forwards:** They are tailor-made contracts, with quantities and time to maturity matched to the needs of the company. Forward contracts are typically quite costly over longer horizons, as the market becomes highly illiquid.
- **Currency Swaps:** They offer companies the ability to borrow against long-term foreign currency exposures when direct access by the company to foreign debt markets is costly.

- **Currency Futures:** These derivatives contracts are traded on exchanges, which are commonly highly liquid. They have the benefit that there is a secondary market, which allows for positions to be closed before the maturity date of the contract. As a result, futures contracts are particularly useful for hedging exposures whose maturity is uncertain. On the other hand, futures contracts are standardised in terms of time to expiration and contract sizes, and this results in less than perfect hedges for the company exposures.
- **Currency Options:** Plain vanilla options allow companies to hedge against currency movements in one direction while retaining exposure in the other. There are strategies with combinations of options that can cover many other situations of course. Options are particularly useful in hedging exposures that are highly uncertain with respect to timing and magnitude.

Each of the above is illustrated next with examples.

6.2.1. Money Market Hedges

Two situations are distinguished: One, when an inflow of foreign currency is anticipated in the future and the recipient is worried that depreciation of the home currency will reduce the amount of "*home*" money to be received in the future. The second is when an outflow of foreign currency is anticipated in the future and the debtor company in the home country is worried that the home currency will depreciate, thus costing the home company more in "*home*" currency than it would have cost today. We consider next how to 'insulate' each of these exchange rate risks using the money markets, with examples illustrating the particular gains in each situation. It should be mentioned here that offshore currency deposits or Eurocurrency deposits are the main money market hedge instruments for these transactions.

When an inflow of foreign currency is anticipated, and it is expected that the home currency will depreciate in terms of the foreign currency, a typical series of transactions using money market hedges are the following:
- Borrow the present value of the foreign currency at a fixed interest rate and convert it into home currency.
- Deposit the home currency at the fixed interest rate prevailing at home.
- When the foreign currency is received, say in three months from now, use it to pay off the foreign currency loan plus the interest.

For example, a US company has sold grains worth £1,000,000 to a British company. The sale is made in March for settlement due, say, in three months. The current spot rate is $/£ 1.764, the UK three-month borrowing rate is 10% per annum, while the US three-month investing rate is 8% per annum. The foreign exchange advisor of the US company forecasts that the future spot rate in three months will be $/£ 1.760, resulting in a loss of 0.004 $ per £ for the US company. In order to hedge this exchange rate risk it can take the following steps:
- Calculate the present value of £1,000,000 to be received in three months (=1/4years) from now. This will be: £1,000,000 / (1 + 0.10/4) = £975,610.
- Borrow £975,610 and convert it to $1,720,976 (= £975,610 x 1.764) at the prevailing spot rate of $/£ 1.764.
- Deposit the $1,720,976 for three months, resulting in a compound amount in three months of $1,755,396 [= $1,720,976 x (1 + (0.08/4)].

- In three months, when the foreign currency of £1,000,000 is received, repay the foreign currency loan of £975,610, plus the £24,390 [= £975,610 x (0.1/4)] owed in interest.

In this way, the US company receives now the sum of £1,000,000 it expects in three months, and converts it into home currency using the current exchange rate of $/£1.764 rather than the $/£ 1.760 rate that will prevail in three months from now. It has thus saved $4,000 (= £1,000,000 x $/£ 0.004) by locking the exchange rate at today's level.

When an outflow of foreign currency is expected and it is expected that the home currency will depreciate in the meantime, a typical series of transactions using money market hedges are the following:

- Determine the present value of the foreign currency to be paid in the future, using the foreign currency interest rate as the discount rate.
- Borrow the equivalent amount in home currency, calculated using the spot exchange rate prevailing today.
- Convert the home currency into the calculated present value equivalent of the foreign currency in the spot market now, and deposit this foreign currency at the interest rates prevailing abroad.
- On payment day, withdraw the foreign currency deposit, which by the time of payment equals the payable amount, and make the foreign currency payment.

This way, the amount to be paid in the future abroad is secured using today's exchange rate.

For example, a US company is expected to pay A\$300,000 to an Australian exporter of coal three months from now. The A\$ interest rate is 12% and the US\$ interest rate is 8%. The spot exchange rate is US\$/A\$ 0.710. However, it expects the exchange rate to change adversely, say to move to US\$/A\$ 0.750 in three months, when it will need the A\$. It can avoid paying the higher amount of US\$ by hedging its exchange rate risk as follows:

- The present value of the A\$300,000, to be paid in three months (= 1/4 years) from now, is: A\$300,000 / (1 + 0.12/4) = A\$ 291,262.14.
- Borrow US\$206,796.12 (= A\$291,262.14 x 0.710) and convert it to A\$291,262.14 at the prevailing spot rate of US\$/A\$ 0.710.
- Deposit the A\$ at the 12% interest rate, which grow to A\$300,000 in three months. Pay this A\$300,000 on the due date.
- Repay the US loan, including interest, of US\$248,155.34 [= US\$206,796.12 x (1 + 0.8/4)].

Through these moves, the US company locked its loan of A\$300,000 at today's exchange rate of US\$/A\$ 0.710. Had it done nothing it would use the US\$/A\$ 0.750 rate prevailing in three months time to convert its debt of A\$300,000, costing the US company US\$225,000 rather than US\$213,000, which it would have cost had it used today's rate of US\$/A\$ 0.71. This is a saving of US\$12,000, through this strategy of hedging.

Companies find that the use of currency derivatives contracts for hedging exchange rate risk is more profitable than the use of money market instruments. This is because in practice companies find that: (i) they borrow at interest rates which are higher than the inter-bank offshore lending rate; and (ii) they earn interest rates on deposits, which are lower than the inter-bank offshore deposit rates. Derivatives are cheaper to use, and moreover, they are more flexible in terms of reversing positions as market expectations regarding future movements of exchange rates change.

6.2.2. Currency Forwards

The currency forward market is the market for the future delivery of a currency, in terms agreed today. According to market sources, typical contract maturity is one, two, six, nine and twelve months. The forward rate is determined by market participants' expectations of the future spot value of the currency which, in turn, depends on the economic variables described in the first section of this chapter. Hence, the forward market provides information about expected future spot price movements in the currency markets. Currency forwards may be used for hedging when a company:

- **Expects inflows of foreign currency:** Forward contracts are used to sell the foreign currency at a future date, at a specified currency rate agreed today, to insulate against an expected drop in the value of that foreign currency.
- **Expects outflows of foreign currency:** Forward contracts are used to buy the foreign currency, at a future date at a specified currency rate agreed today, to insulate against an expected increase in the value of the currency.

6.2.3. Currency Futures

Currency futures are commitments to buy or sell one currency for another currency in the future. The underlying cash instrument is the actual exchange rate of the two currencies. The price of the underlying instrument is the value of this currency, which is determined by the interactions of supply and demand for each of the two currencies[72]. Currency futures are cash settled and are traded on centralised exchanges with highly standardised contract specifications in terms of size and maturity[73]. The associated clearing-house is the counterparty to every transaction, operating the typical margining system of initial margins, of mark-to-market, and of variation margins. Currency futures offer great leverage possibilities due to the fact that only the initial margin (typically 5% of the total position) is required up front to commence trading.

Table 6.2 compares the characteristics of currency futures with currency forwards. It is observed that forwards are customized to the needs of the user, in terms of contract maturity and size, location and timing to access these contracts, while futures are standardized and offered only during the trading hours of the exchanges. The credit risk which exists in forwards is eliminated in futures, through the use of the clearing house and the margining system. Settlement for futures is on a daily basis through the mark-to-market procedure, as opposed to forwards where settlement takes place on the maturity date of the contract.

---

[72] A currency that has lost value relative to another currency is said to have depreciated in value in relation to that currency. A currency that has gained value relative to another currency is said to have appreciated in value in relation to that currency.

[73] Some derivatives exchanges that offer currency futures are the following: the International Monetary Market (IMM) (a subsidiary of the CME), the Philadelphia Board of Trade (PBOT) (a subsidiary of the Philadelphia Stock Exchange), the Bolsa Mercadorias & de Futuros (BM&F) in Brazil, LIFFE in London, Singapore International Monetary Exchange (SIMEX) in Singapore, and the Tokyo International Financial Futures Exchange (TIFFE) (a subsidiary of the Tokyo Stock Exchange), amongst others.

Table 6.2. Comparison of Currency Futures with Currency Forwards

	Currency Forwards	Currency Futures
Location	Interbank	Exchange floor
Maturity	Negotiated	Standardised
Contract Size	Negotiated	Standardised
Fees	Bank's bid-ask spread	Negotiated commissions
Counterparty	Bank	Clearing-house
Collateral	Negotiated	Margin account
Settlement	At maturity	Most are settled early
Trading Hours	24 hours	During exchange hours

6.2.3.1. Applications of Futures/Forward Contracts

To hedge a foreign exchange exposure, the customer assumes a position in the futures/forwards market, which is opposite in direction to the exposure in the spot market. For example, if a company is long (short) the British pound, it will short (long) the futures/forwards market[74]. A company which is long in the futures/forwards market is expecting an increase in the value of the currency, whereas a short position is assumed when expecting a decrease in the value of the currency. The following examples illustrate the concepts of hedging and speculation (leverage) that currency futures/forwards provide.

6.2.3.1.1. Hedging with Currency Futures (Expected Cash Outflow)

It is currently July and a US shipping company has to pay a shipyard in Southampton (UK) £1,000,000 in September, for the repairs of the engines of two vessels. The shipping company expects an increase in the price of sterling. The current forex rate is US$/GB£ 1.692 and the futures price is $/£ 1.685. Futures contracts, for $/£ currency rate, may be found trading in LIFFE, for instance. The futures contract size is £62,500. In order to protect itself against the possible appreciation of the pound, the US company purchases 16 (= £1,000,000 / £62,500) futures contracts and locks the forex rate at $/£ 1.685 for the September payment of the £1,000,000.

Table 6.3 summarises the positions for the shipowner in both the spot and the paper markets, under two alternative scenarios; a market rise and a market fall in forex rates. Under the first scenario (forex rates increase to $/£ 1.695) the shipowner loses $3,000(= $1,692,000 – $1,695,000) in the spot market, while in the futures market it gains $10,000 (= $1,695,000 – $1,685,000), giving a net gain of $7,000. Under this scenario, the realised losses of the shipowner in the spot market ($3,000) are covered by the gains in the futures position ($10,000). Under the second scenario, presented in the second column of the same table, forex rates fall to $/£ 1.675. The shipowner saves $17,000 (= $1,692,000 – $1,675,000) in the spot market, while in the futures market he loses $10,000 (= $1,675,000 – $1,685,000), giving a net spot/derivatives portfolio gain of $7,000. Under this scenario, the realized gains of the shipowner in the spot market ($17,000) are lowered by the losses in the futures position ($10,000).

---

[74] A company that is, for example, long the British pound, has pound denominated assets that exceed in value their pound denominated liabilities. A company that is short the British pound, has pound denominated liabilities that exceed in value their pound denominated assets.

Table 6.3. The Two Possible Outcomes of Currency Futures Hedging (Cash Outflow)

July	
Spot Market	**Futures Market**
Forex rate: $/£ 1.692	Action: Buy futures contracts
Exposure in foreign currency: £1,000,000	Futures September price: $/£ 1.685
Cost in domestic currency: $1,692,000	Value of Futures: $1,685,000
(= £1,000,000 x $/£ 1.692)	(= £1,000,000 x $/£ 1.685)
First Scenario: Exchange Rates Increase	**Second Scenario: Exchange Rates Decrease**

September: Spot Market	
Forex rate: $/£ 1.695	Forex rate: $/£ 1.675
Amount Cost: $1,695,000	Amount Cost: $1,675,000
(= £1,000,000 x $/£ 1.695)	(= £1,000,000 x $/£ 1.675)
The shipowner loses $3,000	**The shipowner gains $17,000**

September: Futures Market	
Action: Sell futures contracts	Action: Sell futures contracts
Futures price: $/£ 1.695	Futures price: $/£ 1.675
Value of Futures: $1,695,000	Value of Futures: $1,675,000
(= £1,000,000 x $/£ 1.695)	(= £1,000,000 x $/£ 1.675)
The shipowner gains $10,000	**The shipowner loses $10,000**

Portfolio of Physical and Futures Positions	
Net gain for shipowner: $7,000, instead of $3,000 losses	**Net gain for shipowner: $7,000,** instead of $17,000 gains

6.2.3.1.2. Hedging with Currency Futures (Expected Inflow)

A US spare parts company has concluded a sale of two vessel engines to a British shipping company for £1,000,000. The sale is made in January for settlement due, say, in three months. The current spot rate is $/£ 1.7640. The US company decides to hedge this exchange rate risk, against the possible depreciation of the pound, using currency futures. The futures contract size at LIFFE is £62,500. In order to protect itself, the US company sells 16 (= £1,000,000 / £62,500) futures contracts and locks the forex rate at $/£ 1.7540 for the April cash inflow of £1,000,000.

Table 6.4 summarises the positions for the US company in both the spot and the paper markets, under two alternative scenarios; a market rise and a market fall in forex rates. Under the first scenario, forex rates increase to $/£ 1.767, the US company gains $3,000 (= $1,767,000 – $1,764,000) in the spot market, while in the futures market it loses $11,000 (= $1,765,000 – $1,754,000), resulting in a net loss of $8,000. Under this scenario, the realised gains of $3,000 of the US company in the spot market are lowered by the losses in the futures position of $11,000. Under the second scenario, presented in the second column of the same table, forex rates fall to $/£1.760. The US company loses $4,000 (= $1,760,000 – $1,764,000) in the spot market, while in the futures market it gains $6,000 (= $1,748,000 – $1,754,000), giving a net spot/derivatives portfolio gain of $2,000. Under this scenario, the realised losses of $4,000 of the US company in the spot market are covered by the profits in the futures position of $6,000.

329

Table 6.4. The Two Possible Outcomes of Currency Futures Hedging (Cash Inflow)

January	
Spot Market	**Futures Market**
Forex rate: $/£ 1.764	Action: Sell futures contracts
Sales amount in foreign currency: £1,000,000	Futures April price: $/£ 1.7540
Income in domestic currency: $1,764,000	Value of Futures: $1,754,000
(= £1,000,000 x $/£ 1.7640)	(= £1,000,000 x $/£ 1.7540)
First Scenario: Exchange Rates Increase	**Second Scenario: Exchange Rates Decrease**

April: Spot Market	
Forex rate: $/£ 1.767	Forex rate: $/£ 1.760
Income Amount: $1,767,000	Income Amount: $1,760,000
(= £1,000,000 x $/£ 1.767)	(= £1,000,000 x $/£ 1.760)
The US company gains $3,000	**The US company loses $4,000**

April: Futures Market	
Action: Buy futures contracts	Action: Buy futures contracts
Futures price: $/£ 1.765	Futures price: $/£ 1.748
Value of Futures: $1,765,000	Value of Futures: $1,748,000
(= £1,000,000 x $/£ 1.765)	(= £1,000,000 x $/£ 1.748)
The US company loses $11,000	**The US company gains $6,000**

Portfolio of Physical and Futures Positions	
Net loss for US company: $8,000, instead of $3,000 gains	**Net gain for US company: $2,000,** instead of $4,000 losses

6.2.3.1.3. Speculating with Currency Futures

It is August and it is forecasted that the GB£ will strengthen against the US$ in the next two months and a trader would like to take advantage of this opportunity. The current (August) forex rate is $/£ 1.647 and the futures price is $/£ 1.641. The trader may use the following two strategies for speculation purposes:

- **Strategy A**: Purchase £250,000 with $411,750 and deposit them in a bank account for 2 months. If the GB£ strengthens against the US$ a profit will be made, otherwise the strategy results in a loss. This strategy involves $411,750 deposit in the bank.
- **Strategy B**: Purchase October futures, through which the trader is committed to buying £250,000 at $410,250 in 2 months. If the GB£ strengthens he can sell the £ and make a gain in US$ terms, otherwise he makes a loss. This strategy involves the commitment of $41,025 (= $410,250 x 10%), in order to cover the initial margin.

Table 6.5 summarises the two strategies of the trader under two alternative scenarios; a market rise and a fall in forex rates. With strategy A, under the first scenario (forex rates increase to $/£ 1.70, the trader gains in the money market $13,250 (= $425,000 – $411,750). Under the second scenario, forex rates decrease to $/£ 1.60, and the trader loses in the money market $11,750 (= $400,000 – $411,750). Considering these amounts as percentage returns on capital committed, they represent a gain of 3.22% (= $13,250 / $411,750) and a loss of 2.85% (= $11,750 / $411,750), respectively. With strategy B, under the first scenario of a rising market, the trader gains in the futures market $14,750 (= $425,000 – $410,250) representing a Return on Equity (ROE) of 36% (= $14,750 / $41,025). Under the second scenario, of a falling market, the trader loses in the futures market $10,250 (= $400,000 – $410,250), representing a ROE of 25% (= $10,250 / $41,025). As can be seen, strategy B, due to the leverage effect prevailing in futures markets, involves higher ROE (both gains and losses) in relation to strategy A, under which the money (spot) market is used for speculation. This difference in ROE for speculation, between money and futures markets, is one of the attractions of futures markets, which make it popular with market agents.

Table 6.5. The Two Possible Outcomes of Currency Futures Speculation

Strategy A: Money Market	Strategy B: Futures Market
August	
Action: Buy £250,000	Action: Buy Futures contracts
Forex rate: $/£ 1.647	Futures October price: $/£ 1.641
Cost in US$: $411,750 (= £250,000 x $/ £1.647)	Value of Futures: $410,250
Deposit £250,000 in a bank for 2 months	(= £250,000 x$/£1.641)
	Initial Margin: $41,025 (= $410,250 x 10%)
October	
First Scenario: Exchange Rates Increase	
Forex rate: $/£ 1.70	Futures price: $/£ 1.70
Investment in US$: $425,000	Value of Futures: $425,000
(= £250,000x $/£1.70)	(= £250,000 x $/£ 1.70)
The trader gains $13,250	**The trader gains $14,750**
Second Scenario: Exchange Rates Decrease	
Forex rate: $/£ 1.60	Futures price: $/£ 1.60
Investment in US$: $400,000	Value of Futures: $400,000
(= £250,000x $/£1.60)	(= £250,000 x $/£ 1.6)
The trader loses $11,750	**The trader loses $10,250**

6.2.4. Currency Swaps

Currency swaps are derivative contracts to exchange an agreed amount of a currency for another currency at specific future dates. It constitutes an exchange of debt-service obligations, denominated in one currency, for an agreed principal amount of debt, denominated in another currency. A currency swap is often the low-cost way of obtaining a liability in a currency in which a company has difficulty borrowing from. The way this works is as follows: a pair of companies simply borrow in currencies they have relative advantage borrowing in, and then trade the obligations of their respective loans, thereby effectively borrowing in their desired currency. Commonly, a financial institution will match the interested companies, undertake all the paperwork and essentially eliminate the counterparty risk that exists when the companies arrange the swap between themselves.

The following provides a simple example of how these work. US company A would like to borrow in Swiss Francs to hedge its ongoing Swiss franc denominated cash-flows from Switzerland. A Swiss company B would like to borrow in US$ to hedge its expected US$ cash receipts from its sales to the US. Both companies are relatively unknown to the credit markets of the respective foreign countries, and thus anticipate unfavourable borrowing terms. An investment bank suggests that each company borrows in the credit market it has relative comparative advantage in. Then, the investment bank will give them sufficient cash-flows in each period to cover the obligations of these loans, in return for making the payments in the foreign currency that exactly matches the other company's obligations. The end result is that, the swap contract effectively gives each company access to the foreign debt market at reasonable terms. Both companies gain, and the investment bank charges a fee for its services, typically 0.25%-0.5% to each company.

Currency swaps only exist because there are market imperfections. If companies can access foreign and domestic debt markets at equal cost, swaps are redundant. One important reason that currency swaps are so useful is that companies engaged in a swap need not each have an absolute borrowing advantage in the currency in which they borrow vis-à-vis the counterparty. In fact, it is possible that company B, say, has better access to both the U.S. and Swiss debt markets than company A, and still gain through the swap transaction.

6.2.4.1. Swapping Liabilities with a Currency Swap

Suppose a Japanese commodity exporter sells in the US, and a US commodity exporter sells in Japan, exposing them to exchange rate risk. The Japanese company is well-known in the Japanese capital markets while the US company is well-known in the US capital markets. The Japanese company borrows from the Japanese capital market JPY105 million, at an interest rate of 1%, while the US company borrows from the US capital market US$1 million, at an interest rate of 5%. However, their businesses are in the opposite countries, such that the Japanese company's revenues are from the US and the US company's revenues are from Japan. They decide to swap their liabilities to hedge currency risk. The contract matures in one year. The current spot exchange rate is JPY/US$ 105.

Figure 6.5, summarises the above information and the cash-flows of the agreement. At the initiation of the swap, the Japanese company pays JPY105 million to the US company and the US company pays US$1 million to the Japanese company. At the maturity of the swap, the Japanese company pays US$0.05 million to the US company and the US company pays JPY6.05 million to the Japanese company. Overall, the Japanese company pays US$1.05 million to the US company. In return, the US company pays JPY106.05 million to the Japanese company. Both companies hedge forex risk associated with their liabilities.

Figure 6.5. The Transactions Involved in the Currency Rate Swap

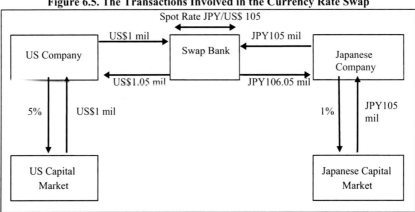

6.2.4.2. Swapping Transaction Exposures with a Currency Swap

Assume a US shipping company has a subsidiary in Italy. It sees an investment opportunity for expansion in Italy that will require €40 million, with an economic life of 5 years. The US company could raise $48 million at home through a bond issue with 8% yield, and convert these $48 million to €40 million, at the current spot rate of $/€ 1.20, to finance the investment. Since earnings in Italy are in Euros, while interest payments due in the US are in US$, there is a transaction exposure from the potential change in the financial position of the project due to currency changes over the 5 years of its lifetime. Alternatively, the US company could raise €40 million in the Eurobond market by issuing a five-year foreign bond, payable in Euros. The euro interest rate is 6% for a well-known company, but the Italian subsidiary of the US company is charged a 1% risk premium and pays 7% because it is less-known. There is an Italian company with a US subsidiary needing $48 million for an expansion project in the US with a five-year life. The Italian company could borrow Euros in Italy at 6%, and then convert them to dollars. There is transaction exposure since the dollar cash-flows would be generated in the US, while the interest payments are due in euro in Italy. The company could issue Yankee bond in the US, but would face a 9% interest rate because the Italian subsidiary is not well-known in the US.

Figure 6.6. The Transactions Involved in a Five-Year Currency Rate Swap

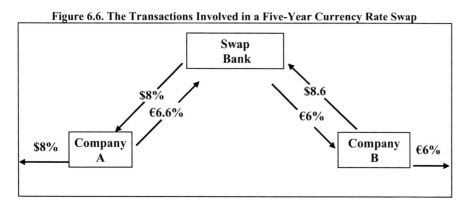

The above information and the swap deal, provided by a swap bank, are presented in Figure 6.6. The deal eliminates the long-term currency risk and reduces the interest expenses for both multinational companies. The swap provider can offer an 8% US$ rate for the US company against receiving a 6.6% Euro rate, and offer 6% Euro rate for the Italian company against receiving 8.6% US$ rate. The principal sums are also exchanged through the bank. The US company borrows in the US and transfers $48 million to the Italian subsidiary, while the Italian company borrows in Italy and transfers €40 million to the US subsidiary. Every year the US subsidiary in Italy makes a payment of €2.56 million (€40 million at 6.6%) to the swap bank, which transfers €2.4 million (€40 million at 6%) to the Italian company to pay the Euro loan. The Italian subsidiary in the US pays $4.128 million ($48 million at 8.6%) to the swap bank, and the bank transfers $3.84 million ($48 million at 8%) to the US company to pay for the dollar loan. At maturity, payments of the principal amounts are also exchanged. The swap bank gains $576,000 per year (= 0.6% x $48 million + 0.6% x €40 million x $/€ 1.20) for the next five years.

6.2.5. Currency Options
A currency call (put) option is a contract that gives the owner the right, but not the obligation, to buy (sell) a currency at a specified price at (European) or during (American) a given time. OTC currency options are most frequently written by banks, such as Chase Manhattan, Morgan Stanley, Merrill Lynch, amongst others, for US dollars and other currencies against the British Pound, Swiss Franc, Japanese Yen, Canadian Dollar and the Euro. The main advantage is that they are tailored to the purchaser, but counterparty risk exists. OTC currency options are mostly used by individuals and banks. Currency options are also traded on organised exchanges, such

as Euronext N.V., with clearing facilities provided by the clearing-houses of these exchanges. Counterparty risk is not present in this case.

6.2.5.1. Speculating with Currency Options and other Alternatives

Assume that the financial manager of a shipping company has £100,000 and is willing to speculate with this money, based on his view of how currency rates will evolve, in the spot, the forward and in the options market. The financial manager (henceforth, speculator) believes that the US dollar will appreciate in relation to the British pound in six months. The current January spot rate and six-month forward rates are £/$0.5392 and £/$ 0.5301, respectively. A call and a put option on dollars, with a strike price of £/$ 0.5394, are available and sell at a premium of £/$ 0.005 each.

Speculating in the Spot Market – see Table 6.6 panel A
The speculator uses the £100,000 to purchase $185,459.94 in January, at the spot rate of £/$ 0.5392, and holds the dollars for six months. When the target exchange rate is reached, he sells the $185,459.94 at the new spot rate of £/$ 0.5400, receiving £100,148.36 (= $185,459.94 x £/$ 0.5400). This results in a profit of £148.36(=£100,148.36 – £100,000).

Speculating in the Forward Market – see Table 6.6 panel B
The speculator uses the forward market, because he believes that the June spot rate will differ from the January forward rate of June. Therefore, during January the speculator purchases $188,643.65 using the forward six-month rate of £/$ 0.5301, with no initial cash outlay. Six months from now, in June, when the forward contract expires, he receives $188,643.65 at £/$ 0.5301, at a cost of £100,000. He simultaneously sells $188,643.65 in the spot market at the prevailing spot rate of £/$0.5400, receiving £101,867.57 (= $188,643.65 x £/$ 0.5400). This results in a profit of £1,867.57 (= £101,867.57 – £100,000), with no initial investment required.

Speculating in the Options Market (Case 1) – see Table 6.6 panel C
The speculator during January buys a call option on dollars ($185,459.94), with a strike price of £/$ 0.5394, at a premium of £/$ 0.005. As spot rates (£/$ 0.5392) are below the strike price, the speculator is not exercising this option because he can purchase dollars cheaper in the spot market. The speculator's loss currently is limited to the cost of the option, that is to the premium of £/$ 0.005. As June spot rates (£/$0.5400) become higher than the strike price (£/$ 0.5394) it becomes worth exercising the option. Thus, he buys dollars at £/$ 0.5394, which he can sell for £/$0.5400 in the spot market, making a gain of £/$ 0.0044 {= Max[(spot rate – strike price), 0] – premium = Max[(£/$ 0.5400 – £/$ 0.5394), 0] – £/$ 0.005}. This results in a profit of £816.02 (= $185,459.94 x £/$ 0.0044). The call option holder's gain is the option writer's loss and visa versa. When the spot rate is below £/$ 0.5394, the holder of the option is not exercising the option and the writer keeps the premium of £/$0.005. As June spot rates (£/$ 0.5400) are higher than the strike price of £/$0.5394, the holder of the option exercises it and the writer has to pay the holder of the option. This results in a loss for the writer of £816.02 (= $185,459.94 x £/$ 0.0044).

Speculating in the Options Market (Case 2) – see Table 6.6 panel D
The speculator during January buys a put option, to have the right to sell currency at the strike price of £/$ 0.5394, at a premium of £/$ 0.005. If the spot rate falls below £/$ 0.5394 the speculator will exercise the option for a profit {= Max[(strike price – spot rate), 0] – premium}. As June spot rates (£/$ 0.5400) are higher than the strike

price of £/$ 0.5394 the speculator does not exercise the put option, as he is better off selling the currency spot. He loses the option premium of £/$ 0.005, with a position loss of £927.30 (= $185,459.94 x £/$ 0.005). The speculator's counterparty is the seller/writer of the put option. He is obliged to purchase dollars at the strike price of £/$ 0.5394 if the holder of the put decides to exercise, and he receives a premium of £/$ 0.005. If the spot rate falls below £/$ 0.5394 the holder will exercise the option and the writer of the put option, will realise a loss, which is equal to –Max[(Strike Price – Spot Rate), 0] – Premium. As June spot rates (£/$ 0.5400) are higher than the strike price of £/$ 0.5394, the put option is not exercised by the holder, as he is better off selling the currency spot. He loses the option premium of £/$ 0.005, with a position loss of £927.30 (= $185,459.94 x £/$ 0.005). This is the put option writer's gain.

Table 6.6. Speculating with Currencies: Spot, Forwards and Options

January	June
Panel A: Spot Market	
Forex rate: £/$ 0.5392 Investment Amount: £100,000 Action: Purchase $185,459.94 (= £100,000 / £/$ 0.5392)	Forex rate: £/$ 0.540 Action: Sell $185,459.94 at £/$ 0.540 receiving £100,148.36
Outcome: Profit of £148.36 (= £100,148.36 – £100,000)	
Panel B: Forward Market	
Forward six-month rate: £/$ 0.5301 Investment Amount: £100,000 Action: Purchase $188,643.65 (= £100,000 / £/$ 0.5301)	Forex rate: £/$ 0.5400 Accept delivery of $188,643.65 Action: Sell $188,643.65 at £/$ 0.540 receiving £101,867.57 (= $188,643.65 x £/$ 0.540)
Outcome: Profit of £1,867.57 (= £101,867.57 – £100,000)	
Panel C: Options Market (Case 1)	
Options contract: June call option Call strike price: £/$ 0.5394 Options premium: £/$ 0.005 Action: Buy June call option	Spot Forex rate: £/$ 0.540 Strike price (£/$0.5394) < Spot price (£/$0.540) Action: Exercise the call option Options payoff: £/$ 0.0044 [= (£/$ 0.5400 – £/$ 0.5394) – £/$ 0.005]
Outcome: Profit (Loss) of £816.02 (= $185,459.94 x £/$ 0.0044) for the option call holder (writer)	
Panel D: Options Market (Case 2)	
Options contract: June put option Put strike price: £/$ 0.5394 Options premium: £/$ 0.005 Action: Buy June put option	Spot Forex rate: £/$ 0.540 Strike price (£/$0.5394) < Spot price (£/$0.540) Action: Put option is not exercised Options payoff: -£/$ 0.005 (options premium)
Outcome: Loss (Profit) of £927.30 (= $185,459.94 x £/$ 0.005) for the put option holder (writer)	

Table 6.7 presents the alternative strategies examined and their outcomes. From the four speculative strategies shown, the currency forward contract yields the highest profit, of £1,867.57, with no initial investment. The speculator, since he is seeking the highest profit making strategy, should go for the currency forward contract. He should also keep in mind though that if his expectations regarding the future movement of the currency market do not materialize, he can incur maximum losses, in comparison to the alternative strategies. This is not the case with options, whose downside risk is limited to the options' premium.

Table 6.7. Alternative Strategies and Speculation Outcomes

Speculating Strategy	Outcome (Payout)
Remain Unhedged	Uncertain
Spot Market	Profit of £148.36
Currency Forward Market	Profit of £1,867.57
Currency Call Option	Profit of £816,02
Currency Put Option	Loss of £927.30

6.3. Comparison of Currency Derivatives in Hedging Forex Risk

The following example illustrates the alternative financial products, which are available to market agents in the shipping industry, in order to hedge their positions in the spot markets against forex rate risk. Suppose a US marine spare parts company, has just concluded a deal for the sale of spare parts and vessel engines to a British shipowning company, for £1,000,000. The deal is made in January with the settlement being due in April, three months from now. The current spot rate is $/£ 1.764, the three-month forward rate is $/£ 1.754 and the company's cost of capital is 12%. The UK three-month borrowing rate is 10% per annum, the UK three-month investment rate is 8% per annum, the US three-months borrowing rate is 8% per annum and the US three-month investment rate is 6% per annum. An April put option of £1,000,000 is traded in the OTC market at a strike price of $/£ 1.750 and is priced at $/£ 0.0265. The US company forecasts the future spot rate in three months to be $/£ 1.760. Finally, the budget rate, representing the lowest acceptable amount, is based on an exchange rate of $/£ 1.700. The US company has the following alternatives: to remain unhedged, to hedge in the currency forward market, to hedge in the money market, to hedge in the currency futures market, or to hedge in the currency options market. Each of these alternatives is examined in turn.

Alternative 1 – Remain Unhedged
If the spot rate in three months turns out to be $/£ 1.760, then the company will receive $1,760,000 (= £1,000,000 x $/£ 1.760) in three months. However, if the spot rate in three months drops to $/£ 1.650, the company will receive only $1,650,000, which is well below the budget rate of $/£ 1.700. Therefore, under this case, the company is fully exposed to the fluctuations of the $/£ exchange rate. However, if the spot rate in three months turns out to be $/£ 1.768, then the company will receive $1,768,000 (= £1,000,000 x $/£ 1.768) in three months, which is $8,000 more than anticipated.

Alternative 2 – Currency Forward Hedge
When this deal is fixed in January for April, it is recorded at a spot rate of $/£ 1.764. Thus $1,764,000 (= £1,000,000 x $/£ 1.764) is recorded as a sale for the US company. In order to get protected against forex rate risk the company enters a short forward position in January at $/£ 1.754. Therefore, in three months, the company will receive £1,000,000 and exchange those pounds at $/£ 1.754, receiving $1,754,000. This sum is $6,000 less than the uncertain $1,760,000 expected from the unhedged position. This would be recorded in the company's books as a foreign exchange loss of $10,000(= $1,764,000 as booked – $1,754,000 as settled). However, if spot rates drop below $/£ 1.754, then the forward position will start yielding a profit for the company. On the other hand, if the spot rate in three months turns out to be $/£ 1.768, then the company will loose in both the spot and the forward markets. In the spot market, the company will loose $4,000 (= $1,764,000 – $1,768,000) while in the forward market, the company will loose $14,000 (= $1,754,000 – $1,768,000), giving a total loss of $18,000, when combined with the losses in the spot market.

Alternative 3 – Money Market Hedge

The company, using the money markets, will borrow pounds in London, convert the pounds to dollars and repay the pound loan with the proceeds from the sale. It borrows the present value of £1,000,000, which is £975,610 (= £1,000,000 / 1.025). In three months it repays this amount plus £24,390 (= £975,610 x 0.025) in interest. Then, the company exchanges the £975,610 at the spot rate of $/£ 1.764 and receives $1,720,976 today. This hedge creates a pound denominated liability that is offset with a pound denominated asset, thus creating a balance-sheet hedge.

Suppose further that the company has three choices for an investment for the next three months: (a) the loan proceeds might be invested at the US rate of 6% per annum, (b) the loan proceeds can be substituted for an equal dollar loan at a rate of 8% per annum, and (c) the loan proceeds can be invested in the company itself with a cost of capital of 12% per annum. The money market hedge is superior to the forward hedge ($1,754,000) if the proceeds are used to replace a dollar loan with a debt cost of 8% [$1,755,396 = $1,720,976 x (1 + 0.08/4)] or are invested in the company with a cost of capital of 12% [$1,772,605 = $1,720,976 x (1 + 0.12/4)]. The forward hedge would be preferable if the loan proceeds are invested at a US Treasury-Bill of 6% [$1,746,791 = $1,720,976 x (1 + 0.06/4)].

Alternative 4 – Currency Futures Hedge

The US company could also cover the £1,000,000 foreign exchange exposure by selling futures contracts at $/£ 1.754. If the spot rate in three months turns out to be $/£ 1.760, then the result of the futures position is: – Principal Amount x (Spot price – Futures price) = – £1,000,000 x ($/£ 1.760 – $/£ 1.754) = – $6,000. The loss on futures would reduce the value of the amount received to $1,754,000 (= $1,760,000 – $6,000). Just as in the currency forward hedge, if the spot rate in three months turns out to be $/£ 1.768, then the company will loose in both the spot and the forward markets, giving an overall spot-futures position loss of $18,000. The difference between the currency forward and the futures hedges is that in contrast to the latter, the former does not require any initial investment. However, the forward position is exposed to credit risk.

Alternative 5 – Currency Options Hedge

Finally, the US company could cover the £1,000,000 foreign exchange exposure by purchasing a put option. This provides the upside potential for appreciation of the pound, while limiting the downside risk to the cost of the option's premium. A three-month put option can be purchased with a strike price of $/£ 1.750 and a premium of $/£ 0.0265. The cost of this option is $26,460 (= £1,000,000 x $/£ 0.0265). In order to compare the alternative hedging strategies, the future value of the option cost in three months is calculated. Using a cost of capital of 12% per annum (i.e. 3% per quarter), the premium cost of the option as of June is: $/£ 0.0273 (= $27,254 / £1,000,000), $27,254 (= $26,460 x 1.03) overall. The company does not exercise its option position when the exchange rate is above $/£ 1.750 and would rather convert pounds to dollars in the spot market. For instance, if the spot rate is at $/£ 1.760, the company exchanges pounds in the spot market, receiving $1,760,000 (= £1,000,000 x $/£ 1.76), less the premium of the option of $27,254, resulting in a net amount of $1,732,746. If the pound falls below $/£ 1.750, the company exercises the put option. For instance, if the spot rate falls to $/£ 1.700 in June, the option is exercised and the £1,000,000 is exchanged at $/£ 1.700, receiving $1,700,000. Subtracting the option's premium of $27,254, results in a net amount of $1,672,746, rather than $1,700,000, which would have been received if the company stayed unhedged and used the money market to convert GB£ into US$.

In conclusion, the US marine spare parts company knows its exposure to exchange rate risk three months from now. It must decide on a strategy to undertake; to stay unhedged or to use one of the derivatives instruments available to hedge this exposure. The alternative outcomes must be compared for a decision to be made. Table 6.8 presents the alternative strategies analysed and their hedging outcomes.

Table 6.8. Alternative Strategies and Hedging Outcomes

Hedging Strategy	Outcome (Payoff)
Remain Unhedged	Uncertain
Currency Forward/Futures Hedge	$1,754,000
Money Market Hedge (8% per annum)	$1,755,396
Money Market Hedge (12% per annum)	$1,772,605
Currency Put Option Hedge: If Exercised	$1,722,746
If not Exercised	Limited

Two criteria can be used in order for the company to make a decision: the risk tolerance of the US company expressed in its stated policies and the viewpoint of the managers' view on the expected direction and distance of the exchange rate. Despite the fact that the money market hedge (12% per annum) gives the highest payout ($1,772,605), currency derivatives are cheaper to use, and moreover, they are more flexible in terms of closing/changing positions as market expectations, regarding future movements of exchange rates, change. Therefore, the company can use either the currency forward or the currency option. At the outset, the former is cheaper than the latter, as there is no initial investment, but the latter, at an extra cost of $26,460, can limit the downside risk.

6.4. Summary

This chapter presented examples of how foreign exchange rate derivatives can be used for speculation and hedging in the shipping industry. This is a concern in the sector when receipts are in one currency while payments are in another currency. For example, payments for newbuildings, repairs and maintenance, payment of a loan denominated in a foreign currency, management costs, indicate potential exchange rate risk exposures. The various financial instruments that can be used to hedge forex risk are money market hedges, through borrowing and lending; currency forwards, available OTC and tailor-made to the needs of the customer; currency swaps, being a combination of forward and money market instruments; currency futures, traded on exchanges; and currency options, both OTC and exchange traded, which allow companies to hedge against movements in one direction while retaining exposure in the other.

The next chapter examines the last risk exposure that was identified in Chapter 1 as a source of risk market agents in the shipping sector are exposed to; that is, interest rate risk. It introduces and analyses interest rate derivatives products as instruments, through, which this risk can be managed. After covering the possible sources of interest rate risk in shipping, the various interest rate derivatives instruments are presented, including T-Bond futures, T-Bill futures, interest rate swaps, interest rate options, etc.

CHAPTER 7. Interest Rate Derivatives and Risk Management

7.1. Introduction

The last source of risk affecting shipping companies, as identified in Chapter 1 of this book, is the risk which emanates from fluctuation in interest rates. Companies, particularly in the highly capital intensive shipping industry, borrow in order to be able to perform their investment plans. Vessels are very expensive investments and it is not uncommon for borrowing to be as high as 80%-90% of the value of the vessel. Companies borrow from their banks or directly from the public, through bond issues, in order to perform their investment plans. Either way, capital needs to be raised, and the cost of capital borrowed changes as interest rates in the world economy change. This in turn, brings about fluctuations in the cash-flow positions of the shipping company, and the greater the amount borrowed - that is, the greater the financial leverage of the company – the larger is the exposure to interest rate risk. This risk, when coupled with other sources of risk the shipping company faces, can have disastrous effects on the company if it is not managed appropriately.

The interest rate risk, referred to above, relates to the management of liabilities for the shipping company. For non-financial companies it constitutes the largest source of interest rate risk. The second most prevalent source of interest rate risk is from holding interest sensitive securities. Companies invest their assets in interest bearing securities, with fluctuating returns. Particularly, for multinational companies, differing currencies (both on the liability and on the asset sides) have differing interest rates thus, making this risk a concern. Whether it is on the left (liability) or right (asset) hand side of the balance-sheet, the reference rate of interest calculation is important[75]. As a consequence, it is important to have tools available to manage interest rate risk. Interest rate derivatives provide this set of tools, and the aim of this chapter is to show their use to that effect.

Before companies can decide on a hedging strategy, they must first form expectations or a directional and/or volatility view regarding future movements of the risk generating variables. Once the management has formed its expectations, it must then choose the appropriate derivatives tools to use in order to implement its risk management strategy. Interest rate derivatives, irrespective of whether they are exchange-traded, such as interest rate futures and options on underlying cash instruments (like T-Bonds, T-Notes, T-Bills or Eurodollars), or OTC traded (such as Forward Rate Agreements – FRAs, interest rate swaps and options), involve the exchange of cash payments based on changes in market interest rates. For example, an FRA is a forward contract that involves the exchange of cash payments based on changes in the London Interbank Offer Rate (LIBOR) (see section 7.3.1). Interest rate swaps exchange payments, based on differences between two different interest rates (see section 7.3.3). Interest rate options require one party to make payments to the other when a stipulated interest rate, most often a specified maturity of LIBOR, moves outside some predetermined range (see section 7.3.4).

---

[75] The reference rate is the rate of interest used in a standardised quotation, loan agreement, or financial derivative valuation. The most common reference rate is the LIBOR.

There has been rapid growth and pace of innovation in the market for interest rate derivatives. The first exchange-traded interest rate futures was introduced in 1975 by the Chicago Board of Trade (CBOT) and the first OTC interest rate swap agreement was introduced in 1981. These developments were due to volatile interest rates prevailing in the 1980s, large amounts of government debt, huge volumes of capital at risk and due to the increased desire by the financial community and businesses to reduce interest rate exposures. The trading in interest rate swaps was soon followed by FRAs, caps, floors, as well as other hybrid instruments, such as forward swaps, options on swaps (swaptions), and even options on options (captions).

This chapter introduces interest rate derivatives for uses in the shipping industry. Market agents in the sector may use these tools to: (i) protect the value of their financial assets; and to (ii) lock in favourable interest rates for the finance of their investments through loans and bonds. The rest of this chapter is organised as follows: Section 7.2 describes the underlying "*commodities*" of interest rate derivatives, such as T-Bonds, T-Notes, T-Bills, Eurodollar and LIBOR. Section 7.3 presents interest rate derivatives contracts, such as forwards, futures, swaps and options, providing a number of examples of their uses in the shipping environment. Finally, Section 7.4 concludes the chapter.

7.2. The Underlying Assets of Interest rate Derivatives
A bond is a security, that is issued in connection with a borrowing arrangement. For instance, a shipping company (the borrower) issues (i.e. sells) a bond to the general public (the lender) for a certain amount of cash. The arrangement obligates the company to make specific payments to the bondholders on specific dates. A typical coupon bond obligates the issuer to make semiannual (coupon) payments of interest to the bondholders for the life of the bond. When the bond matures, the issuer repays the debt by paying the bondholders the bond's par value (face value). Figure 7.1 provides a graphical representation of the cash-flows emanating from such a corporate bond issue of a company, with a par value of $1,000, yield to maturity 10% and 2 years maturity. As can be observed, an initial inflow of $1,000 takes place for the company, followed by four coupon outflows of $100 each every 6 months and $1,000 outflow at maturity representing the face value of the bond. The coupon rate of the bond serves to determine the interest payment. The coupon rate, maturity date, and par or nominal value of the bond are part of the bond indenture, the latter being the contract between the issuer and the bondholder. Bonds may be issued by companies wishing to borrow, but also by central and regional governments.

Figure 7.1. Cash-Flows from a Corporate Bond Issue of a Company

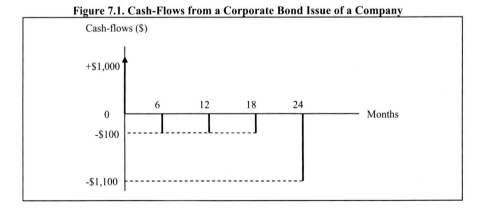

7.2.1. Treasury Bonds (T-Bonds) and Treasury Notes (T-Notes)

A US Treasury bond (T-Bond) or a US Treasury note (T-Note) is a debt obligation of the US Federal government that makes semiannual coupon payments and is issued at or near par value. T-Notes maturities range from 1 year up to 10 years, while Treasury Bonds maturities range from 10 to 30 years. Both bonds and notes are issued in denominations of $1,000 or more. Aside from their differing initial maturities, the only major distinction between T-Bonds and T-Notes is that in the past, some T-Bonds were callable for a given period, usually during the last 5 years of the bond's life. The call provision gives the Treasury the right to repurchase the bond at par value during the call period. The Treasury no longer issues callable bonds.

Although bonds are sold in denominations of $1,000 par value, the prices are quoted as a percentage of par value. The bid and asked prices are quoted in points plus fractions of 1/32 of a point. The bond point is a conventional unit of measurement for bond prices set at $1 and equivalent to 1% of the $100 face value of the bond. For instance, a price of 80 means that the bond is selling at 80% of its face or par value. Thus, a quote of 90.05 means that the indicated price for a bond with a face value of $100,000 is $90,156.25 (where $156.25 = 1/32 x 0.05 x $100,000).

The yield to maturity of a bond is a measure of the average rate of return to an investor who purchases the bond for the asked price and holds it until its maturity date. The yield curve is a graphic depiction of the relationship between the yields on bonds of the same credit quality but different maturities. Broadly speaking, the yield curves are upward sloping (**normal yield curves**) reflecting the higher yields expected from investors for parting with their money for longer periods. The yield curve may be flat, when all maturities have the same yields. A flat curve sends signals of uncertainty in the economy. This mixed signal can revert back to a normal yield curve or could later result into an **inverted yield curve**. An inverted yield curve occurs when long-term yields fall below short-term yields. Under this abnormal and contradictory situation, long-term investors will settle for lower yields now if they think the economy will slow or even decline in the future. An inverted curve may indicate a worsening economic situation in the future.

Bonds have a current (fixed) yield for life when issued. The current yield for a bond that pays $80 coupons per $1,000 nominal value to the holder each year is calculated as: Current yield = Annual Coupon Payment / Bond Value (i.e. $80/$1,000=0.08=8%). Say interest rates rise to 10%, then $80 / 0.10 = $800. If interest rates fall to 6%, then $80 / 0.06 = $1,333. That is, there is an inverse relationship between interest rates and bond prices. This inverse relationship may be understood when one looks at the marketplace as a true auction. Suppose an investor purchases a 10-year bond with a 6% coupon when yields are at 6%. Thus, the investor pays 100% of the face or par value of the security. Assume then that rates rise to 7%. The investor decides to sell the original bond with the 6% yield, but no one will pay par as bonds are now quoted at 7%. He must sell the bond at a discount to par in order to move the bond (i.e., rising rates are accompanied by declining prices). Falling rates produce the reverse situation. If rates fall to 5%, the investment yields more than market rates. The seller can offer it at a premium to par. Thus, declining rates are accompanied by rising prices.

7.2.2. Treasury Bills (T-Bills)

US Treasury Bills (T-Bills) are the most marketable of all money market instruments. The US government raises money by selling T-Bills to the public. T-Bills are issued with initial maturities of 28, 91, or 182 days. Individuals can purchase T-Bills directly, at auction, or on the secondary market from a government securities dealer. T-Bills sell in minimum denomination of $10,000. A T-Bill pays no coupons, and the investor receives the face value at maturity. T-Bills sell at a discount from the stated par value. They are examples of short-term zero-coupon instruments. A zero-coupon (discount) instrument is issued intentionally with low coupon rates that cause the instrument to sell at a discount from par value. The Treasury issues a bill for some amount less than $10,000, agreeing to repay $10,000 at the bill's maturity. The difference between the purchase price and maturity value constitutes the investor's earnings. All of the investor's return comes in the form of price appreciation over time. The income earned on T-Bills is exempt from all state and local taxes.

T-Bill price quotes are for a T-Bill with a face value of $100. A price quote is referred to as the discount rate (yield) and is calculated as: Discount Yield = (Par Value – Market Price) x (360 / Days). If for a 90-day T-Bill, the market price is 95, the quoted price would be $20.00 [= (100 – 95) x (360/90)]. The discount yield relates the income of the T-Bill to the par value rather than to the price paid and uses a 360-day year rather than a 365-day year. The discount rate is not the same as the rate of return earned on the T-Bill. The latter is calculated as the dollar return (Par Value – Market Value) divided by the cost (Market Value). In the above example, where the quoted price is $20.00, the rate of return would be 5/95, or 5.26%, per 90 days. This amounts to 5/95 x (360/90) = 0.2105 or 21.05% per annum on an actual/360 basis. Alternatively, it is 5/95 x (365/90) = 0.2137 or 21.37% per annum on an actual/365 basis. When converted to semiannual compounding, the 21.37% rate is sometimes referred to as the bond equivalent yield because it is directly comparable with the yields quoted on government bonds.

7.2.3. Eurodollar

Eurodollar refers to a certificate of deposit in US dollars in a commercial bank outside the jurisdiction of the US Federal Reserve Board (foreign banks or foreign branches of American banks). Most of the Eurodollar deposits are in London banks, but Eurodeposits may be anywhere other than the US. Similarly, a Euroyen deposit represents a certificate of deposit in yen outside Japan. Banks may prefer Eurodollar deposits to domestic deposits because: (i) they are not subject to reserve requirement restrictions by the Federal Reserve Board, and (ii) every Eurodollar received by a bank can be reinvested somewhere else before maturity.

Most Eurodollar deposits are for large sums (i.e $1 million), and most are time deposits of less than 6 months' maturity. Eurodollar certificates of deposits are considered less liquid and riskier than domestic certificates of deposits, however, and thus offer higher yields. The Eurodollar interest rate is the rate of interest earned on Eurodollars deposited by one bank with another bank. It is also known as the LIBOR. Eurodollar interest rates are generally higher than the corresponding T-Bill interest rates because a bank has to pay a higher rate of interest than the Federal government on borrowed funds.

7.2.4. London Interbank Offer Rate (LIBOR)

The LIBOR is the rate at which large banks in London are willing to lend money among themselves. One-month LIBOR is the rate offered on one-month deposits, three-month LIBOR is the rate offered on three-month deposits, and so on. LIBOR rates are determined by trading between banks and change continuously as economic conditions change. Figure 7.2 shows the LIBOR rate from January 2002 to November 2005. This rate, which is quoted on dollar-denominated loans, is the premier short-term interest rate quoted in the European money market, and it serves as a reference rate for a wide range of transactions. For example, a company can borrow at a floating rate equal to LIBOR plus 3%. LIBOR is the most commonly used floating short-term interest rate in the swap market (see section 7.3.3) and is frequently a reference rate of interest for loans in international financial markets. To see how it is used, consider a loan where the rate of interest is specified as three-month LIBOR + 0.3% per annum. The life of the loan is divided into three-monthly periods. For each period, the rate of interest is set 0.3% per annum above the three-month LIBOR rate at the beginning of the period, while interest is paid at the end of the period.

Figure 7.2. LIBOR Rate (Jan. 2002 – Nov. 2005)

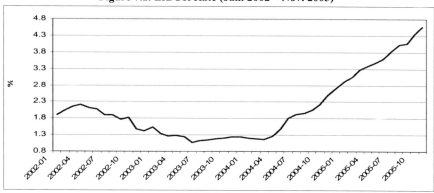

Source: Clarksons Research Studies

7.3. Interest Rate Derivatives Contracts
7.3.1. Forward Rate Agreements (FRAs)

A FRA is an interbank-traded cash-settled OTC forward contract to buy or sell interest rate payments on a notional principal amount at a given future date. FRAs are traded among major international banks active in the Eurodollar market since 1983. Most FRAs trade for maturities corresponding to standard Eurodollar time deposit maturities (one month up to six months), although non-standard maturities (from one year up to five years) are sometimes traded.

Banks use FRAs to fix interest costs on anticipated future deposits or interest revenues on variable-rate loans indexed to LIBOR. A bank that sells a FRA agrees to pay the buyer the increased interest cost on some principal amount if some specified maturity of LIBOR is above the forward rate on the maturity date of the FRA. In contrast, the buyer agrees to pay the seller any decrease in interest cost if market interest rates fall below the forward rate. On the settlement date no actual principal is exchanged. Rather, the buyer and the seller calculate the present value of the net interest owed, and one party makes a cash settlement payment.

For example, suppose a company wishes to turn a floating rate debt payment of LIBOR + 0.50% to a fixed rate. It can buy a FRA, which locks in a total interest payment of 5.5%. If LIBOR rises above 5.0%, then the company receives a cash payment from the FRA seller, reducing their LIBOR payment to 5.0%. If LIBOR falls below 5.0% then the company pays the FRA seller a cash amount, thereby increasing their LIBOR payment above 5.0%.

A 6-to-9 months FRA locks in a three-month interest rate starting six months from now. The 6-to-9 months FRA rate is such that the investor would be indifferent between buying a nine-month T-Bill versus buying a six-month T-Bill and then locking in a lending rate for the following three months through the FRA.

Example of FRAs
Two banks enter into a FRA with: (i) a forward rate of 6% on a Eurodollar deposit with three months maturity, (ii) a $1 million principal amount, and (iii) settlement in one month. Such an agreement is termed a 1-to-4 FRA because it fixes the interest rate for a deposit to be placed after one month and maturing four months after the date the contract is negotiated.

If the three-month LIBOR is 7% on the contract settlement date, the seller pays the buyer $1 million x (7% – 6%) for a period of 90 days. Since every 1 basis point change is equal to $25 [= (1% x 1/100) x 90/360 x $1,000,000], the 100 basis points increase, correspond to a change in the interest cost on a three-month Eurodollar deposit of $2,500 (= $25 x 100 basis points). But the interest on a Eurodollar deposit is paid upon maturity, whereas the settlement (maturity) date of FRAs corresponds to the date the underlying deposit is placed. Therefore, to make the cash payment on the FRA equivalent to the extra interest that would have been earned on a Eurodollar deposit paying 7%, the $2,500 difference in interest costs is discounted back three months using the actual three-month LIBOR prevailing on the settlement date. Final settlement of the amounts owed by the parties to an FRA is determined by the following formula:

$$\text{Payment} = [\text{PA} \times (\text{LIBOR} - \text{FR}) \times (T/360)] / [1 + \text{LIBOR} \times (T/360)] \qquad (7.1)$$

where, PA is the principal amount of the agreement, FR is the agreed (fixed) forward rate, LIBOR is the value of LIBOR prevailing on the maturity date, and T is the maturity date (in days) of the contract. If LIBOR is higher than the FR, the seller owes the payment to the buyer, while if LIBOR is lower than the FR the buyer owes the seller the value of the payment amount. For the above example, if the 90-day LIBOR turns out to be 7% on the contract maturity date, the amount the buyer would receive is calculated by substitution into the formula. This would be: $2,457{=[$1,000,000x(7% – 6%) x 90/360] / [1 + 0.07 x (90/360)]}.

7.3.2. Interest Rate Futures
Interest rate futures contracts typically have as an underlying asset T-Bonds, T-Notes, T-Bills and Eurodollars. Interest rate futures are exchange-traded standardised contracts, very liquid, and simple to use. The two most common exchanges trading these contracts are the CBOT and the CME.
- For example, in the CBOT market, the contract size for T-Bonds futures is $100,000 for a bond with 30 years to maturity.
- The contract size of T-Bills futures is $1million for a 90-day T-Bill.

- In the CME market, the underlying asset with a Eurodollar futures contract is a three-month, $1 million face value instrument.
- Quotes are in points and 32nds of a point. For example, 95.16 is 95 and 16/32nds. Thus, T-Bond futures prices are quoted in the same way as the T-Bond prices (see section 7.2.2. of this chapter). T-Bond prices are quoted in dollars and 32nds of a dollar. The quoted price is for a bond with a face value of $100. Thus, a quote of 90.05 means that the price for a bond with a face value of $100,000 is $90,156.25. A $1 change in the quoted futures price would lead to a $1,000 change in the value of the futures contract.
- Delivery can take place at any time during the delivery month.
- T-Bill futures prices are not quoted in the same way as the prices of T-Bills themselves. The following relationship is used: T-Bill futures price quote = 100 – Corresponding T-Bill price quote. If F is the quoted futures price and S is the cash price, this means that:

$$F = 100 - (360/90) \times (100 - S) \quad \text{or} \quad S = 100 - (90/360) \times (100 - F)$$

Since the face value of the T-Bill, underlying a T-Bill futures contract, is $1 million, the contract price is: $10,000 \times [100 - 0.25 \times (100 - F)]$. For example, the T-Bill futures quote of 82.32 corresponds to a price of $95.58 [= 100 – 0.25 $\times$ (100 – 82.32)] per $100 of 90-day T-Bills, or a contract price of $955,800 (= $10,000 \times $95.58).

A Eurodollar futures appears to be the same as the T-Bill futures contract. The formula for calculating the value of one Eurodollar contract from the quoted futures price is the same as that for T-Bill futures. However, there are some important differences between the Eurodollar and the T-Bill futures contracts. For a T-Bill futures contract, the contract price converges at maturity to the price of a 90-day T-Bill, and if a contract is held until maturity, this is the instrument delivered. A Eurodollar futures contract is settled in cash. The final mark-to-market sets the contract price equal to $10,000 \times (100 - 0.25E)$, where E is the quoted Eurodollar rate at that time. This quoted Eurodollar rate is the actual 90-day rate on Eurodollar deposits with quarterly compounding (add-on yield).

The T-Bill futures are quoted on a discount basis, while the T-Bond and T-Note futures are quoted on a fixed basis. The Eurodollar futures contract is therefore a futures contract on an interest rate, whereas the T-Bill, T-Bond, and T-Note futures contracts are futures contracts on the price of a T-Bill, T-Bond and T-Note, respectively. Moreover, Eurodollar futures cannot be transferred to another owner, while T-Bill, T-Bond and T-Note futures can.

Table 7.1 presents the specifications of T-Bond, T-Note, T-Bill and Eurodollar futures in the CBOT and in the CME.

Table 7.1. Specifications of T-Bond, T-Note, T-Bill and Eurodollar Futures in the CBOT and CME

Specifications	T-Bond Futures	T-Notes Futures	T-Bill Futures	Eurodollar Futures
Contract Size	$100,000	$200,000 (a) $100,000 (b)	$1 million	$1 million
Delivery	Yes	Yes	Yes	Yes
Settlement	Cash	Cash	Delivery	Cash
Transferable	Yes	Yes	Yes	No
Maturities	Up to 30 years	Up to 5 Years (a) Up to 10 Years (b)	Up to 1 year	Up to 10 years
Tick Size	$31.25	$15.625	$25	$25

Notes:
- (a) corresponds to a 2-year T-Note Futures.
- (b) corresponds to a 10-year T-Note Futures.

7.3.2.1. Interest Rate Futures Positions for Hedging

To see how these instruments may be used for hedging purposes, suppose first a company wants to hedge a floating rate payment due next year on a bank loan it has taken. It would sell (short) futures contracts:

- If interest rates rise, futures prices fall and the company can offset its interest payment with the proceeds from the sale of the futures contracts.
- If interest rates fall, futures prices rise and the savings from the interest payment due will offset the losses from the sale of the futures contracts.

Consider next a company, say a bank, that wishes to hedge a floating rate receipt due next year. It would buy (long) futures contracts:

- If interest rates rise, futures prices fall and the increased interest earnings due will offset the losses from the purchased futures contracts.
- If interest rates fall, futures prices rise and the company can offset its lower interest earnings with the proceeds from the purchased futures contracts.

The above two hedging strategies, using interest rate futures, are summarised in Table 7.2.

Table 7.2. Hedging Strategies Using Interest Rate Futures

Risk Exposure	Position	Scenarios	Outcomes
Paying interest on debt in the future – Exposure to interest rate increases	Sell (short) Futures	Rates increase	Higher interest payments on debt; Futures price falls; Short earns a profit
		Rates decrease	Lower interest payments on debt; Futures price rises; Short earns a loss
Earning interest on credit in the future – Exposure to interest rate declines	Buy (long) Futures	Rates increase	Higher interest earnings on credit; Futures price falls; Long earns a loss
		Rates decrease	Lower interest earnings on credit; Futures price rises; Long earns a profit

7.3.2.2. Pricing of Interest Rate Futures Contracts

Interest rate futures prices are derived from the implications of the cost-of-carry relationship, which links spot with futures prices, outlined in Chapter 2 of this book. That is, the net cost-of-carrying the commodity forward in time, is calculated as the income earned on the asset minus the carry charge, which is the interest that is paid to finance the asset:

$$F = S \times (1 + C) \qquad\qquad (7.2)$$

where, F is the futures price for delivery at time T, S is the spot price today, and C is the cost to carry the commodity forward, to time T.

If an investor can borrow money at the same rate that a T-Bill pays, the cost-of-carry is zero. Solving Equation (7.2) for C ($= F / S - 1$) yields the implied repo (repurchase agreement) rate[76]. The implied repo rate is the rate of interest on a short-term T-Bill implied by the futures price for a contract maturing at the same time as the short-term T-Bill and the price of a T-Bill maturing 90 days later than the short-term T-Bill.

If an arbitrageur can discover a disparity between the implied repo rate and the actual short-term T-Bill rate, there is an opportunity for risk-free profit (arbitrage opportunities) through the following actions:
- If the implied repo rate is greater than the borrowing rate, then the arbitrageur could borrow, buy T-Bills, and sell futures.
- If the implied repo rate is lower than the borrowing rate, the arbitrageur could borrow, buy T-Bills, and buy futures.

To see this, suppose that the 40-day T-Bill rate is 8%, the 130-day T-Bill rate is 8.5%, and the rate corresponding to the T-Bill futures prices for a contract maturing in 40 days is 8.6%. The forward interest rate for the period between 40 and 130 days implied by the T-Bill rates may be calculated using the following formula:

$$\hat{r} = \frac{r^* T^* - rT}{T^* - T} \qquad\qquad (7.3)$$

where, $\hat{r}$ is the forward interest rate, r is the spot rate of interest applying for T years, r^* is the spot rate of interest applying for T^* years, and $T^* > T$. Substituting into Equation (7.3), yields the implied forward interest rate ($\hat{r}$): 8.72% [$= 130 \times 8.5 - 40 \times 8.0) / 90$].
- For T-Bill futures contract maturing in 40 days priced at 8.6%, since the forward rate of 8.72% is greater than the 8.6% forward rate implied by the futures price, an arbitrageur should borrow for the period of time between 40 and 130 days at 8.6% and invest at 8.72%. This can be done by shorting the futures contract to ensure that a T-Bill yielding 8.6% can be sold after 40 days, borrowing 40-day money at 8.0% per annum, and investing the borrowed money for 130 days at 8.5% per annum to ensure that a rate of interest of 8.72% is earned during the time period.
- If, instead, the rate of interest corresponding to the T-Bill futures was greater than 8.72%, the arbitrageur, in order to exploit the arbitrage opportunities, would take a long position in the futures contract, borrow 130-day money at 8.5% per annum and invest the borrowed money for 40 days at 8.0% per annum.

---

[76] Repurchase agreements (or repos) are financial instruments, used in the money markets, where securities are sold now for cash by party A (the cash borrower) to party B (the cash lender), with the promise made by A to B of repurchasing those securities later, with A paying the requisite implicit interest (repo rate) to B at the time of repurchase.

7.3.2.3. Applications of Interest Rate Futures Contracts
7.3.2.3.1. Speculation with Eurodollar Futures
A shipowner wishing to speculate using a Eurodollar futures would think as follows: (i) the price of a fixed income security moves inversely with market interest rates; (ii) industry practice is to compute futures price changes by using 90 days until expiration. Assume the shipowner – speculator, during January, purchased an April Eurodollar futures contract at a price of 96.32, with a face value of $1 million. He anticipates that interest rates will decrease in the near future, which would increase futures prices in the future time at levels which will be higher than the futures price at the initiation of the contract. As a consequence, a speculative profit can be made on the futures price differential. Suppose the discount yield at the time of purchase was 2.5%. The initial price of the futures contract is calculated as follows:

$$\text{Price of Futures contract} = \text{Face Value} \times [1 - (\text{Discount Yield} \times 90/360)]$$
$$= \$1,000,000 \times [1 - (0.025 \times 90/360)]$$
$$= \$993,750$$

Assume that in the middle of April, interest rates rise to 5.0%. The price of the futures contract then would fall to $987,500 (= $1,000,000 \times [1 - (0.050 \times 90/360)]$). Thus, the shipowner has lost $6,250 (= $987,500 - $993,750$). Therefore, the shipowner's expectations of a future decrease of the Eurodollar interest rate market did not materialize, and by speculating in the Eurodollar futures market he ended up with a loss in his futures position. Had his expectations materialised he would have realised a speculative profit.

7.3.2.3.2. Hedging with Eurodollar Futures
Suppose that a shipowner has borrowed from a bank, during January, $10 million dollars, in order to pay a shipyard in three months, for the repayment of a vessel. Currently, interest rates stand at 2.5% per annum. Suppose that the bank demands to receive the first interest payment on the borrowed capital amount when the payment is made to the shipyard. The shipowner believes interest rates will increase in the near future. Therefore, he establishes a short hedge in Eurodollar futures. As each Eurodollar futures contract has a face value of $1 million, the shipowner decides to sell 10 (= $10 million / $1 million) Eurodollar futures contracts.

The initial value of the 10 futures contracts is $9,937,500 [= $1 million x [1 - (2.5% x 90 / 360)] x 10 contracts]. Table 7.3 displays the cash-flows that will result, under two possible outcomes.
- Scenario A considers the outcomes, assuming that during April interest rates rise to 5.0%. In the spot market, the shipowner has to pay $62,500[=$10million x (2.5% – 5.0%) x 90 / 360] more than what he would have paid in January. In the futures market, the value of the futures contracts falls to $9,875,000 {= $1 million x [1 – (5.0% x 90/360)] x 10 contracts}. This is $62,500 (= $9,937,500 – $9,875,000) less than the price at the time the shipowner established the short hedge, yielding a gain in the futures position. Overall, combining the outcomes of the spot and the futures positions, the shipowner has fully covered his interest rate risk, through the use of Eurodollar futures; his cash-flow is $0 (= $62,500 – $62,500), instead of making a loss of $62,500.
- Under scenario B it is assumed that interest rates decrease to 1.0% by April. In the spot market, the shipowner has to pay $37,500 [= $10 million x (2.5% –

1.0%) x 90 / 360] less than anticipated. In the derivatives market, the new value of the 10 futures contracts, after three months, is $9,975,000{=$1millionx[1 – (1.0% x 90 / 360)] x 10 contracts}. This is $37,000 (= $9,975,000 – $9,937,500) more than the January price, at the time the shipowner established the hedge, yielding a loss in the futures position. Overall, combining the outcomes of the spot and the futures positions, the shipowner gains $500 (= $37,500 – $37,000), instead of making a profit of $37,500, which he would have made had he not used Eurodollar futures. But then his expectations did not materialize. In either case, what the shipowner managed to do is to stabilize his interest costs approximately at today's (January's) level.

Table 7.3. The Possible Outcomes of a Eurodollar Futures Hedge

January 2005	
Spot (Money) Market	**Futures Market**
The shipowner needs to pay interest in three months on $10 million borrowed Interest rates: 2.5%	Action: Sell 10 Eurodollar futures of $9,937,500 {= $1 million x [1 – (2.5% x 90/360)] x 10}
April: Scenario A, Interest rates rise to 5.0%	
Action: Pays interest of $62,500 [= $10 million x (2.5% – 5.0%) x 90/360]	Action: Buy 10 Eurodollar futures of $9,875,000 {= $1 million x [1 – (5.0% x 90/360)] x 10}
Total: Loss in spot position as the shipowner pays $62,500 more interest	**Total:** Gain in futures position of $62,500 (= $9,937,500 – $9,875,000)
Spot and Futures Market Outcome: Gain/Loss 0 (= $62,500 – $62,500) Instead of loss of $62,500	
April: Scenario B, Interest rates fall to 1.0%	
Action: Saves interest of $37,500 [= $10 million x (2.5% – 1.0%) x 90/360]	Action: Buy 10 Eurodollar futures of $9,975,000 {= $1 million x [1 – (1.0% x 90/360)] x 10}
Total: Gain in spot position as the shipowner pays $37,500 less interest	**Total:** Loss in futures position of $37,000 (= $9,975,000 – $9,937,500)
Spot and Futures Market Outcome: Gain of $500 (= $37,500 – $37,000), instead of a gain of $37,000	

7.3.2.3.3. Hedging with T-Bond Futures

Suppose that on March 19th a shipping company has issued $1,200,000, in 10 bonds of value $100,000 each at 120.00 in order to raise funds for a vessel acquisition. The company is concerned about interest rate fluctuations. Interest rate is currently at 6.67%. The value of the 10 bonds during March is $1,200,000(=10bondsx$1,000x120.00), where they are traded in denominations of $1,000 par value and the prices are quoted as a percentage of par value. In order to get protected against interest rate increases, the company decides to sell 10 T-Bond futures at 120.12. The value of the 10 T-Bonds futures is $1,203,750(=10x$1,000x120.375). It has to be noted that hedging corporate bonds with T-Bond futures involves a cross-hedge and that T-Note futures or T-Bill futures could also be used instead. Because corporate bonds are structurally similar to T-Bonds – they typically pay semiannual coupons over their lives and return the face value to the bondholder at maturity – T-Bond futures are preferred as a hedging instrument.

Table 7.4. The Possible Outcomes of a T-Bond Futures Hedge

March 19th	
Spot (Money) Market	**Futures Market**
The company issued 10 bonds at 120.00 or $1,200,000 (= 10 x $1,000 x 120) Interest rates: 6.67%	Action: Sell 10 T-Bond futures at 120.12 i.e. at [120.375 = 120 + (1/32) x 12] or $1,203,750 (= 10 x $1,000 x 120.375)
May 10th: Scenario A, Interest rates rise by 1%, to 7.67%	
The value of the bonds decrease to 104.10 (= 104.3125 = 104 + 1/32 x 10) or $1,043,125 (= 10 x $1,000 x 104.3125)	Action: Buy back 10 T-Bond futures at 105.00 or $1,050,000 (= 10 x $1,000 x 105)
Total: Loss in spot position of $156,875 (= $1,200,000 – $1,043,125)	**Total:** Gain in futures position of $153,750 (= $1,203,750 – $1,050,000)
Spot and Futures Market Outcome: Loss of $3,125 (= $156,875 – $153,750) instead of a loss of $156,875	
May 10th: Scenario B, Interest rates fall by 1%, to 5.67%	
The value of the bonds increase to 136.10 (= 136.3125 = 136 + 1/32 x 10) or $1,363,125 (= 10 x $1,000 x 136.3125)	Action: Buy back 10 T-Bond futures at 135.00 or $1,350,000 (= 10 x $1,000 x 135)
Total: Gain in spot position of $163,125 (= $1,200,000 – $1,363,125)	**Total:** Loss in futures position of $146,250 (= $1,203,750 – $1,350,000)
Spot and Futures Market Outcome: Gain of $16,875 (= $163,125 – $146,250), instead of a gain of $163,125	

The outcome of the hedge under two alternative scenarios is summarized in Table 7.4.

- Scenario A, assumes that interest rates increase by 1%, to 7.67%, two months later, on May 10th. The shipping company incurs a loss of $156,875 (=$1,200,000 – $1,043,125) in the spot (money) market, as the value of the bonds decreases from $1,200,000 (= 10 x $1,000 x 120.00) to $1,043,125 (=10 x $1,000 x 104.3125). In the T-Bond futures market, the derivatives position results in a gain of $153,750 (= 1,203,750 – $1,050,000), as the value of the futures contracts it shorted decreases from $1,203,750(=10x$1,000x120.375) to $1,050,000 (= 10 x $1,000 x 105.00) when it closes the position. Thus, combining the outcomes from the spot and the derivatives positions, the overall cash-flow of the shipping company produces a gain of $3,125 (=$156,875 – $153,750), instead of a loss of $156,875, which would have resulted if the company remained unhedged.
- Under scenario B, shown in the same table, interest rates fall by 1%, to 5.67%. The shipping company incurs a loss of $146,250 (= $1,203,750 – $1,350,000) in the derivatives position, as the value of the futures contracts it shorted increases from $1,203,750 (= 10 x $1,000 x 120.375) to $1,350,000 (=10x$1,000x135.00) when it closes the position. In the spot market, the spot position results in a gain of $163,125 (= $1,200,000 – $1,363,125), as the value of the bonds increases from $1,200,000 (=10 x $1,000 x 120.00) to $1,363,125 (= 10 x $1,000 x 136.3125). Thus, combining the outcomes from the spot and the derivatives positions, the shipping company incurs a decrease of $16,875 (= $163,125 – $146,250) in the gains arising from the spot position ($163,125), due to the losses of $146,250 produced in the derivatives position.

7.3.2.3.4. Hedging with T-Bill Futures

Suppose that during March 17th interest rates are low, standing at 6.85%. A shipping company needs to borrow in two months $2 million in order to finance a new vessel purchase. The loan will be for 12 months. The company considers current interest rates low and wishes to get protected against an interest rate increase. As a consequence, it sells 2 T-Bill futures at 95.15.

Table 7.5. The Possible Outcomes of a T-Bill Futures Hedge

Match 17th	
Spot (Money) Market	**Futures Market**
The company needs to borrow $2 million in two months Interest rates: 6.85%	Action: Sell 2 T-Bill futures at 95.15
May 17th: Scenario A, Interest rates rise by 0.9%, to 7.75%	
Action: Borrow $2 million at 7.75%	Action: Buy 2 T-Bill futures at 94.15
Total: Loss in spot position as they pay $18,000 (= 0.009 x $2 million) more interest	**Total:** Gain in futures position of 1 point or $20,000 (= 0.01 x $2 million)
Spot and Futures Market Outcome: Profit of $2,000 (= $20,000 – $18,000) instead of loss of $18,000	
May 17th: Scenario B, Interest rates fall by 1.1%, to 5.75%	
Action: Borrow $2 million at 5.75%	Action: Buy 2 T-Bill futures at 96.15
Total: Gain in spot position as they pay $22,000 (= 0.011 x $2 million) less interest	**Total:** Loss in futures position of 1 point or $20,000 (= 0.01 x $2 million)
Spot and Futures Market Outcome: Gain of $2,000 (= $22,000 – $20,000), instead of a gain of $22,000	

The outcome of the hedge under two alternative scenarios is summarized in Table 7.5.

- Scenario A, summarises the possible outcome of the hedge, two months later, on May 17th, assuming that interest rates increase by 0.9%, to 7.67%. The shipping company incurs a loss in the spot (money) position as it pays $18,000 (= 0.009 x $2 million) more interest. In the T-Bill futures market, the derivatives position results in a gain of $20,000 (= 0.01 x $2 million), as the price of the futures contracts it shorted decreases from 95.15 to 94.15 when it closes the position, therefore gaining 1 point (= 95.15 – 94.15). Thus, combining the outcomes from the spot and the derivatives positions, the shipping company receives a small gain of $2,000 (= $20,000 – $18,000), instead of making a loss of $18,000, which would have resulted in the spot market if the company remained unhedged.
- Under scenario B, shown in the same table, interest rates decrease by 1.1%, to 5.75%. The shipping company incurs a loss of $20,000 (= 0.01 x $2 million) in the T-Bill futures market, as the price of the futures contracts it shorted increased from 95.15 to 96.15 by the time it closes the position, therefore loosing 1 point (= 95.15 – 96.15). The company incurs a gain in the spot position as it pays $22,000 (= 0.011 x $2 million) less interest. Thus, combining the outcomes from the spot and the derivatives positions, the shipping company makes a gain of $2,000 (= $22,000 – $20,000), instead of a gain of $22,000, which would have resulted in the spot market.

7.3.2.4. Interest Rate Futures Spreads

Some institutional investors might prefer spread products to money market (Treasury) securities, because of the higher yields these spreads offer. When the US economy seems to be thriving, and investors have confidence in the ability of issuers to meet their obligations, heavy buying pressure in the spread sectors will force prices higher and yields lower. At the same time, slack demand for money market securities will force prices of those securities lower and their yields higher. As a result, spreads will narrow. Conversely, when investors begin to have concerns about the ability of corporate issuers to meet their obligations, demand for spread products generally slacks off and demand for money market securities increases. Investors might begin selling corporate issues so they can invest their capital into money market securities. When this happens, spreads widen (CBOT, 2001). Interest rate futures contracts, with different underlying assets but the same expiration, can be combined to create interest rate spreads:

- The **NOB (Notes-Over-Bonds) spread** is the difference between the price of a US T-Note (or T-Bill) futures contract and the price of a US T-Bond futures contract. NOB spreads are used by traders who are speculating on shifts in the yield curve. If they feel that the gap between long-term rates and short-term rates will narrow (widens), they buy (sell) T-Note futures contracts and sell (buy) T-Bond futures. Suppose a speculator is forecasting a general decline in interest rates across all maturities. Since bonds with greater maturities are more price sensitive to interest rate changes than those with shorter maturities, a speculator could go long in the longer-term bond with the position partially hedged by going short in the shorter-term one. The speculator, alternatively, could form a spread by going long in a T-Bond futures contract that is partially hedged by a short position in a T-Note (or T-Bill) futures contract. On the other hand, if the speculator is forecasting an increase in interest rates across all maturities, he could go short in the T-Bond futures contract and long in the T-Note futures contract.

- The **LED (LIBOR-Eurodollar) spread** is the difference between the price of a LIBOR futures contract and the price of a Eurodollar futures contract. LED spreads are used by traders if they believe that there will be a change in the slope of the yield curve, or if there are apparent arbitrage opportunities in the existing Eurodollar rates and those implied in the forward rates.

- The **MOB (Municipals-Over-Bonds) spread** is the difference between the price of a Municipal Bond futures contract and the price of a T-Bond futures contract. It is a play on the taxable bond market (T-Bonds) versus the tax-exempt bond market (Municipal Bonds). MOB spreads are used by traders by buying the futures contract that is expected to outperform the other and selling the weaker contract. This spread periodically widens or narrows based on public sentiment, changes in tax laws, and the general economy. In an economic recession the demand for lower default risk bonds often increases relative to the demand for higher default risk bonds. If this occurs, then the spot yield spread (risk-premium) for lower grade bonds over higher grade would tend to widen. A trader forecasting an economic recession could, in turn, profit from an anticipated widening in the risk-premium by taking a long position in a T-Bond futures contract, which has no default risk and a short position in a Municipal Bond futures contract, which has some degree of default risk.

- The **TED (T-Bill-Eurodollar) spread** is the difference between the price of a U.S. T-Bill (or T-Note) futures contract and the price of a Eurodollar futures contract, where both futures contracts have the same delivery month. TED spreads are used by traders who are anticipating changes in the relative levels of risk of Eurodollar deposits; If they think that the spread will widen (narrow), they buy (sell) the spread. Similarly to the MOB spread, since Eurodollar deposits are not completely risk-less, while T-Bills are, a trader forecasting riskier times, resulting in a widening of the spread between Eurodollar rates and T-Bill rates, could go long in the T-Bill futures contract and short in the Eurodollar futures contract. Conversely, when the spread narrows, the speculator would go short in the T-Bill futures contract and long in the Eurodollar futures contract.

Example of a TED Spread

The following example, summarized in Table 7.6, illustrates how TED spreads are traded. In late May, the dollar value of a basis point for the 10-year T-Note futures is $46.10. At the same time, the dollar value of a basis point for the 10-year Eurodollar futures is $64.15.

Table 7.6. Example of a 10-Year TED Spread

	Value in Basis Points (in $)	Yield Change (in bps)	Number of Contracts	Gain/Loss (to nearest $)
	(1)	(2)	(3)	(4) = (1) x (2) x (3)
Scenario 1: Rates decrease, spread stable, no spread ratio				
Long 10-y T-Bill	$46.10	-10	100	$46,100
Short 10-y Eurodollar	$64.15	-10	100	-$64,150
				-$18,050
Scenario 2: Rates decrease, spread stable, spread ratio				
Long 10-y T-Bill	$46.10	-10	100	$46,100
Short 10-y Eurodollar	$64.15	-10	72	-$46,188
				-$88
Scenario 3: Rates decrease, spread widens, spread ratio				
Long 10-y T-Bill	$46.10	-20	100	$92,200
Short 10-y Eurodollar	$64.15	-10	72	-$46,188
				$46,012
Scenario 4: Rates increase, spread widens, spread ratio				
Long 10-y T-Bill	$46.10	10	100	-$46,100
Short 10-y Eurodollar	$64.15	20	72	$92,376
				$46,276
Scenario 5: Rates decrease, spread narrows, spread ratio				
Long 10-y T-Bill	$46.10	-10	100	$46,100
Short 10-y Eurodollar	$64.15	-20	72	-$92,376
				-$46,276

- Under scenario 1, both the T-Note yield and the Eurodollar rate decrease by 10bps. The long 100 contracts position of September 10-year T-Note futures results in a gain of $46,100, while the short 100 contracts position of September 10-year Eurodollar futures results in a loss of $64,150, yielding an overall loss of $18,050 for the TED spread.
- Under scenario 2, both the T-Note yield and the Eurodollar rate decrease by 10bps, but the investor takes a ratioed spread. To calculate the ratioed spread, the investor divides the T-Note futures dollar value of $46.10 by the Eurodollar futures dollar value of $64.15. The 0.7186 result translates into 100 T-Note futures contracts to 72 Eurodollar futures contracts. Under the ratioed spread, the long 100 contracts position of T-Note futures results in a gain of $46,100, while the short 72 contracts position of Eurodollar futures results in a loss of $46,188, yielding an overall loss of $88 for the TED spread. Thus, the ratioed spread shows no significant gain or loss given the same 10bp drop in the T-Note yield and Eurodollar rate.
- Under scenario 3, the ratioed spread is followed and both yields decrease, but the spread widens as the T-Note yield falls 10bps more than the Eurodollar

yield. Under this scenario, the long 100 contracts position of T-Note futures results in a gain of $92,200, while the short 72 contracts position of Eurodollar futures results in a loss of $46,188, yielding an overall gain of $46,012 for the TED spread.

- Under scenario 4, the ratioed spread is followed and both yields increase, but the spread widens as the Eurodollar yield increases 10bps more than the T-Note yield. Under this scenario, the long 100 contracts position of T-Note futures results in a loss of $46,100, while the short 72 contracts position of Eurodollar futures results in a gain of $92,376, yielding an overall gain of $46,276 for the TED spread.
- Under scenario 5, the ratioed spread is followed and both yields decrease, but the spread narrows as the Eurodollar yield decreases 10bps more than the T-Note yield. Under this scenario, the long 100 contracts position of T-Note futures results in a gain of $46,100, while the short 72 contracts position of Eurodollar futures results in a loss of $92,376, yielding an overall loss of $46,276 for the TED spread.

7.3.3. Interest Rate Swaps

Interest rate swaps are contractual agreements to exchange a series of fixed interest payments for a series of floating rate payments, on a nominal amount. The swap itself is not a source of capital but an alteration of the cash-flows associated with payments. Financial intermediaries, such as banks, pension funds, and insurance companies, as well as non-financial companies use interest rate swaps to effectively protect the value of outstanding debt or that of an interest-bearing asset. The first interest rate swap was a 1982 agreement, in the US, in which the Student Loan Marketing Association, named Sallie Mae, swapped the interest payments on an issue of intermediate-term, fixed-rate debt, for floating-rate payments indexed to the three-month T-Bill yield.

Early interest rate swaps were brokered transactions in which financial intermediaries, with customers interested in entering into a swap would seek counterparties for the transaction among their other customers. The intermediary collected a brokerage fee as compensation, but did not maintain a continuing role once the transaction was completed. The contract was between the two ultimate swap users, who exchanged payments directly. Today the market has evolved into more of a dealer market, dominated by large international commercial and investment banks. Dealers act as market-makers that stand ready to become counterparties to different swap transactions before a customer for the other side of the transaction is located. A swap dealer intermediates cash-flows between different customers, becoming a middleman to each transaction. Unlike brokers, dealers in the OTC market do not charge a commission. Instead, they quote two-way *"bid"* and *"offer"* prices. The quoted spread between bid and offer prices allows for payment of the intermediary's services.

If a company believes that rates would rise, it would enter into a swap agreement to pay fixed and receive floating payments, in order to protect itself from rising debt-service payments. On the other hand, if a company believes that rates would fall, it would enter into a swap agreement to pay floating and receive fixed payments, in order to take advantage of lower debt-service payments. The payments (cash-flows) are calculated based on a notional amount that is not exchanged. Only the net differential of the fixed and floating rate payments need to be exchanged. Thus, an interest rate swap can be considered as a series of forward contracts on interest rates. At each settlement date, that is, at each periodic date for the exchange of cash-flows, the fixed rate payer is obligated to exchange a fixed rate cash-flow for a floating rate cash-flow, specified in advance when the interest rate swap was entered into.

The most common interest rate swap is the fixed-for-floating swap, called generic or plain vanilla swap; a fixed-rate payer makes payments based on a long-term interest rate to a floating-rate payer, who, in turn, makes payments indexed to a short-term money market rate to the fixed-rate payer. In this initial position, the party with the floating rate obligation (say, a shipowner with a floating rate loan) is exposed to changes in interest rates. By swapping this floating rate obligation with a fixed one, it establishes a hedge against increases in interest rates and at the same time makes predictable future interest obligations. The latter helps in budgeting decisions.

The fixed interest rate typically is based on the prevailing market interest rate for Treasury securities with a maturity corresponding to the term of the swap agreement. Typically, the maturity in interest rate swaps ranges between 3 and 5 years. The floating rate is most often indexed to 6-month LIBOR, but can be indexed to almost any money market rate (three-month LIBOR, T-Bill rate, one-month Commercial Paper rate, Municipal Bond tax-exempt rate, etc.). A fixed-rate payer is the buyer (long the swap), while the floating-rate payer is the seller (short the swap). The effective date is the date interest begins to accrue, while the payment date is the date interest payments are made. However, it has to be noted that in a swap there may be counterparty risk, which refers to the risk that one party to the swap may not honour its part of the agreement.

7.3.3.1. The Comparative Advantage in a Plain Vanilla Interest Rate Swap

To see how interest rate swaps can be used to exploit differentials in the credit market, consider the following example. Company A is BBB rated and has access to 8.50% in the fixed rate market and LIBOR + 0.50% in the floating rate market. Company B is AAA rated and has access to 7.0% in the fixed rate market and LIBOR in the floating rate market. The difference between the fixed rates that the two companies can achieve is 1.50% and the difference between the floating rates is 0.50%. Company A is at disadvantage in the fixed-rate market, so it should avoid borrowing at the fixed-rate.

Figure 7.3 presents the design of an interest rate swap, under which both companies gain. Thus:
- Company A borrows four-year floating at LIBOR + 0.50%. Company B borrows fixed at 7.0%. Company A pays 7.35% to a swap bank and the swap bank pays LIBOR to company A. Company B pays LIBOR to the swap bank and the swap bank pays 7.25% to Company B.
- As can be seen at the bottom left and right of the figure, Company A has turned a floating rate into a fixed rate with a net cost of 7.85%. This is better than if the company borrowed directly from the market at the fixed rate; it would have costed the company then 8.5%, while through the swap it costs 7.85%; that is, 0.65% less.
- Similarly, Company B gains through the swap agreement; it has borrowed directly from the market at the fixed rate of 7%, which it has turned into a floating rate through the swap agreement. Moreover, its net cost is LIBOR minus 0.25%, which is 0.25% less than if the company borrowed directly floating (LIBOR).
- Finally, the swap bank has gained 0.1% for its services.

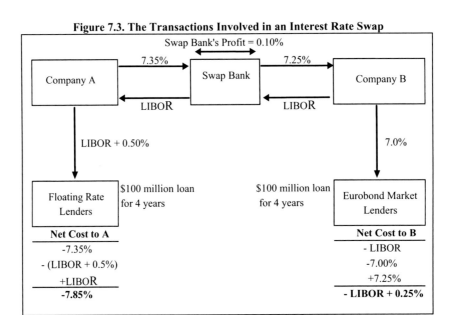

Figure 7.3. The Transactions Involved in an Interest Rate Swap

Swap Bank's Profit = 0.10%

| Company A | 7.35% → | Swap Bank | 7.25% → | Company B |

LIBOR ← (between Company A and Swap Bank)

LIBOR ← (between Swap Bank and Company B)

LIBOR + 0.50% ↓

7.0% ↓

| Floating Rate Lenders | $100 million loan for 4 years | $100 million loan for 4 years | Eurobond Market Lenders |

Net Cost to A
-7.35%
- (LIBOR + 0.5%)
+LIBOR
-7.85%

Net Cost to B
- LIBOR
-7.00%
+7.25%
- LIBOR + 0.25%

7.3.3.2. Shipowner's Schedule of Payments in a Plain Vanilla Interest Rate Swap

A plain vanilla swap was presented in the previous example, demonstrating how all parties gained from the agreement. The following example presents the schedule of payments for a shipowner, as in Table 7.7, that emanate from a swap agreement. The swap covers a five-year period and involves annual payments on a $1 million principal amount. Note that the first payment is made one period after the initiation of the swap agreement, using the interest rates of the previous period for the calculation of the payment due. Thus, the floating rate is the rate observed at the beginning of the period. The first floating rate payment is known at the initiation of the swap.

Table 7.7. The Outcomes of an Interest Rate Swap on US$ 1 million

Year	Floating Rate (LIBOR)	Fixed Rate	Floating Payment	Fixed Payment	Settlement for the shipowner
0	0.08	0.09			
1	0.09	0.09	$80,000	$90,000	-$10,000
2	0.10	0.09	$90,000	$90,000	$0
3	0.12	0.09	$100,000	$90,000	$10,000
4	0.10	0.09	$120,000	$90,000	$30,000
5			$100,000	$90,000	$10,000
Total			$490,000	$450,000	$40,000

Assume that Party A (the shipowner) agrees to pay a fixed rate of 9% to Party B (a financial institution/bank). In return, Party B agrees to pay a floating rate equal to LIBOR to Party A. The shipowner pays 9% of $1 million, or $90,000 each year, for five years, to the financial institution, as can be seen in the fifth column of the table. The financial institution's payments to the shipowners are shown on the fourth column of the table and vary according to the LIBOR rate, shown in the second column of the table. In fact, the amount changing hands is simply the differential between the fixed and the floating payments, shown in the last column of the table. It is the settlement amount, calculated as: floating (spot) rate minus the fixed (swap) rate. When the floating rate is below the fixed rate, as in the case of the first payment, the shipowner transfers money to the financial institution; in this case, $10,000. When the floating rate is above the agreed rate, as is the case in the last three years of the agreement, the shipowner receives net amounts of $10,000, $30,000 and $10,000 from the financial institution. Over the five years, the shipowner has paid $450,000 and received $490,000 from the swap bank. This yields a net profit of $40,000. It is possible that if interest rates had a different pattern the swap could have resulted in a larger profit or perhaps a loss for the shipowner.

7.3.3.3. Exotic Interest Rate Swaps

The above swap examples, named plain vanilla swaps, were an exchange of a fixed-for-floating payments. Other more exotic interest rate swaps include:

- The **basis (or floating for floating) swap**, under which the exchange of payments are based on the difference between two different floating rates. This allows a financial institution to hedge an exposure arising from assets subject to one floating rate (say, LIBOR), being financed by liabilities that are subject to a different floating rate (say, the prime rate – the interest rate at which banks lend to their best customers).
- The **forward start (or deferred) swap**, under which the cash-flows do not begin until sometime after the initiation of the swap agreement. If the swap begins now, the deferred swap is called a **spot start swap**.
- The **circus swap**, under which a plain vanilla interest rate swap and an ordinary currency swap are used to exchange a fixed interest rate in one currency for a floating interest rate in another currency. Both swaps might be with the same counterparty or with different counterparties. For example, Party 1 receives (pays) LIBOR (8% on Euros) from (to) Party 2 and Party 1 pays (receives) LIBOR (6.5% on $US) to (from) Party 3. Therefore, Party 1 is effectively paying 8% on Euros and receiving 6.5% in $US.
- The **amortizing swap**, under which the notional value declines over time according to some schedule. This might be designed to correspond to the amortization schedule on a loan or a floating rate mortgage.
- The **accreting (or step-up) swap**, under which the notional value increases through time according to some schedule. This might be designed to correspond to the drawdowns on a loan agreement.
- The **swaption**, which is an option on an interest rate swap. A **payer (or put) swaption** gives its owner the right to pay the fixed interest rate on a swap. For example, suppose a company plans to issue a fixed-rate note in 6 months, but is concerned that rates will rise in the meantime, raising the cost of the issue. Therefore, the company buys a payer's swaption, thereby locking in today's fixed price on the note issue. Should rates rise, more than the fixed price, the company would exercise its option. The increased issue rate would be offset by the higher floating rate received from the swap. A **receiver (or call) swaption** gives its owner the right to receive the fixed rate and pay the floating rate. For example, suppose a bank has agreed to lend to a company. It is worried, however, that after two years, should rates fall, it would receive an unacceptable return on its loan. Therefore, the bank buys a receiver's swaption giving the right to enter the following interest rate swap at the end of two years. Should the three-year swap rate fall in two years, the bank would exercise its option and enter into the swap, paying floating rate while receiving fixed rate at an above-market rate. The bank would pay the option premium in the form of upfront cash payment or at a swap rate below the two-year forward rate.

357

- The **puttable swap**, under which one party with floating rate payments has the option to terminate the swap early. The party with the right to terminate pays a premium in the form of a higher fixed rate. The contract may also involve a termination fee.
- The **extendable swap**, under which the fixed-for-floating party has the option to extend the life of the swap beyond the specified period. There are benefits from the ability to extend a current swap rather than negotiating a new swap at the prevailing market rates in existence when the initial swap matures. However, this feature involves a higher swap price. The contract may also involve fees if the swap is extended.
- The **constant maturity swap**, under which a LIBOR rate is exchanged for a swap rate. An example is an agreement to exchange six-month LIBOR for the ten-year swap rate every six months for the next five years.
- The **constant maturity Treasury swap**, in which a LIBOR rate is exchanged for a particular Treasury rate, say a ten-year Treasury rate.
- The **indexed principal swap**, in which the principal reduces in a way dependent on the level of interest rates. The lower the interest rate, the greater the reduction in the principal.
- The **differential (or diff) swap**, in which a floating interest rate in the domestic currency is exchanged for a floating interest rate in a foreign currency, with both interest rates being applied to the same domestic principal.

This list is just indicative and far from exhaustive as the different variations of swaps grow with each year.

7.3.4. Interest Rate Options
Options were introduced in Chapter 2 of this book, while several application of their use have been presented in subsequent chapters, outlining a number of interesting strategies for hedging and investment purposes. This section of Chapter 7 demonstrates how options may be applied to interest rate markets.

7.3.4.1. Interest Rate Caps
An interest rate cap is like a portfolio of European call options on interest rates. On each interest payment date over the life of the cap, one option in the portfolio expires. Caps are OTC instruments whose payments can be tailored to match the payment schedule of any floating-rate loan and to match virtually any interest rate maturity up to one year. Payment schedules for interest rate caps follow the conventions in the interest rate swap market. For example, interest rate reset dates (the dates with which the floating rate changes) for a cap indexed to six-month LIBOR would occur every six months, with payments due six months later. Cap buyers typically schedule interest rate reset and payment intervals to coincide with interest payments on outstanding floating-rate debt. Caps are useful to companies with floating rate liabilities. The buyer of an interest rate cap, anticipating interest rates to increase, pays the seller a premium in return for the right to receive the difference in the interest cost on some notional principal amount any time a specified interest rate market index (typically some specified maturity of LIBOR) rises above a determined (maximum) cap rate (strike price), similarly to a call option. The buyer bears no obligation or liability if interest rates fall below the cap rate.
- If the specified market index is above the cap rate, the seller pays the buyer the difference in interest cost on the next payment date, which is equivalent to the

payoff from buying a FRA[77]. The amount of the payoff of an interest rate cap is determined by the following formula:

$$(PA) \times \max(r - r_c, 0) \times (T/360) \qquad (7.4)$$

where, PA is the principal amount of the agreement, r is the index (benchmark) rate, r_c is the cap rate, and T is the number of days from the interest rate reset date to the payment date.

- If the index rate is below the cap rate, the buyer receives no payment and loses the premium paid for the cap. Thus, a cap effectively gives its buyer the right, but not the obligation, to buy a FRA with a forward rate equal to the cap rate. A one-period cap can be seen as a European call option on a FRA with a strike price equal to the cap rate (r_c).

Example 1 of an Interest Rate Cap
Consider a one-year interest rate cap that specifies a notional principal amount of $2 million and a six-month LIBOR cap rate of 6%. The agreement covers a period of one year with the interest rate to be reset on 15th of July. The cap buyer (say a shipowner) in this example will be entitled to a payment, only if the six-month LIBOR is higher than 6% on 15th of July. Suppose that the six-month LIBOR is 6.5% on 15th of July. Then, on the following 15th of January (184 days after the 15th July reset date) the seller will owe the buyer $5,111 [= $2 million x (0.065 – 0.060) x (184/360)]. If the six-month LIBOR is lower than 6%, then the buyer does not receive any payment.

Example 2 of an Interest Rate Cap
Assume that a shipping company has to pay semi-annual interest on a loan of $100 million notional value. The company believes that interest rates will increase in the near future and wishes to get protected against interest rate risk. Therefore, it purchases an interest rate cap on three-month LIBOR from a bank, with a cap rate of 7% on $100 million notional value. The price is 0.4% for a four-year cap, that is $200,000 (= $100 million x 0.4%/2). The cap buyer can schedule the cap payment intervals to coincide with the interest loan payments. At the start of each period, the actual three-month LIBOR is compared to the cap rate of 7%. If the three-month LIBOR is less than the cap rate, there is no compensation. If the three-month LIBOR is greater than the cap rate, the bank pays the shipping company the rate differential.

The first column of Table 7.8 presents the future path of interest rates. Column two, presents the loan payments at each level of interest rates, shown in column one. The cap premium of $200,000 (= $100 million x 0.4%/2), paid by the company to the bank, is shown in column three, while columns four and five present the received payments from the cap and the net cost of the loan for the company, respectively. When interest rates move above the cap rate of 7%, the interest rate cap is exercised, producing cash inflows for the company, and therefore decreasing its loan cost. For example, when interest rates are 7.50%, the cap profit is $250,000 [= $100 million x (0.0750 – 0.0700) x (180/360)] to the company. The net cost for the shipping company is calculated, in each case, by adding together the loan payment and the premium paid and subtracting the payment received from the cap. For example, when

---

[77] One difference between the payoff to a FRA and the payoff to an in-the-money cap is that a FRA pays the present value of the change in interest payable on the notional principal at settlement, while payments on caps are deferred.

interest rates are 7.50% the net cost is $3,700,000 (=$3,750,000 + $200,000 – $250,000), instead of $3,750,000 had there been no cap.

Table 7.8. The Payments from an Interest Rate Cap Hedge

Interest Rates	Loan Payment	Premium Paid	Payments Received from Cap	Net Cost
(1)	(2)	(3)	(4)	(5) = (2) + (3) – (4)
5.00%	$(2,500,000)	$(200,000)	0	$(2,700,000)
5.25%	$(2,625,000)	$(200,000)	0	$(2,825,000)
5.50%	$(2,750,000)	$(200,000)	0	$(2,950,000)
5.75%	$(2,875,000)	$(200,000)	0	$(3,075,000)
6.00%	$(3,000,000)	$(200,000)	0	$(3,200,000)
6.25%	$(3,125,000)	$(200,000)	0	$(3,325,000)
6.50%	$(3,250,000)	$(200,000)	0	$(3,450,000)
6.75%	$(3,375,000)	$(200,000)	0	$(3,575,000)
7.00%	$(3,500,000)	$(200,000)	0	$(3,700,000)
7.25%	$(3,625,000)	$(200,000)	$125,000	$(3,700,000)
7.50%	$(3,750,000)	$(200,000)	$250,000	$(3,700,000)
7.75%	$(3,875,000)	$(200,000)	$375,000	$(3,700,000)
8.00%	$(4,000,000)	$(200,000)	$500,000	$(3,700,000)
8.25%	$(4,125,000)	$(200,000)	$625,000	$(3,700,000)

7.3.4.2. Interest Rate Floors

An interest rate floor is like a portfolio of European put options on an interest rate. On each interest payment date over the life of the floor, one option in the portfolio expires. Floors are useful to companies with floating rate assets. The buyer of an interest rate floor pays the seller a premium in return for the right to receive the difference in interest payable on some notional principal amount any time a specified index of market interest rates falls below a determined (minimum) floor rate (strike price). Buyers use floors to fix a minimum interest rate on an asset paying a floating interest rate indexed to some maturity of LIBOR. Like an interest rate cap, a floor is an option-like agreement in that it represents a right rather than an obligation to the buyer. The payoff of an interest rate floor is determined by the following formula:

$$(PA) \times max(r_f - r, \ 0) \times (T/360) \tag{7.5}$$

where, PA the principal amount of the agreement, r is the index (benchmark) rate, r_f is the floor rate, and T is the number of days from the interest rate reset date to the payment date.

If the index rate is below the floor rate on the interest rate reset date the buyer receives a payment of (PA) x $(r_f - r)(T/360)$, which is equivalent to the payoff from selling a FRA at a forward rate of r_f. In contrast, if the index rate is above the floor rate the buyer receives no payment. Either way, the cost of the floor is the premium paid to the seller. Thus, a floor effectively gives the buyer the right, but not the obligation, to sell a FRA, which makes it equivalent to a European put option on a FRA.

Example of an Interest Rate Floor

An investor has a $10 million portfolio of money market securities, earning a variable rate of return. The investor is currently earning one-month LIBOR, which stands at 5% during January. Expectations are that LIBOR will decline over the next year. The investor cannot accept an index rate less than 4%. In order to hedge this risk of declining portfolio yields, the customer purchases a floor from a bank with one year duration and a strike price of 4%. The bank sells this floor to the investor for a fee of

0.10% of the notional amount, or $5,000 (= $10 million x 0.05%). Table 7.9 presents the payments from the interest rate floor for the next year. If LIBOR does not fall below 4%, as is during January to April and November to December, then the investor does not receive any payment. If LIBOR falls below the strike price of 4% the floor is exercised and the investor receives a payment from the bank. For instance, during May LIBOR falls to 3.0% and the bank will pay the investor the difference between 4% and the actual LIBOR rate. Thus, for a rate of 3% during May the investor receives $8,611 [= $10 million x (0.040 – 0.030) x (31/360)] as it is presented in the fourth column of the table. The investor will continue to receive payments until October, where the LIBOR rate is lower than 4%. The fifth column of the table presents the premium paid for the floor ($5,000). The net payment for the investor, presented in the final column of the table, is calculated, in each case, by subtracting from the floor payment the premium amount paid. For instance, during May the net payment from the floor is $3,611 (= $8,611 – $5,000) and so on for each month the floor is exercised.

Table 7.9. The Payments from an Interest Rate Floor Hedge

	LIBOR Rate	Days in Month	Payments Received from Floor	Premium Paid	Net Payments
January	5%	31	0	$5,000	-$5,000
February	4.5%	28	0	$5,000	-$5,000
March	4%	31	0	$5,000	-$5,000
April	4%	30	0	$5,000	-$5,000
May	3%	31	$8,611	$5,000	$3,611
June	3.5%	30	$4,167	$5,000	-$833
July	3%	31	$8,611	$5,000	$3,611
August	2.5%	31	$12,917	$5,000	$7,917
September	2%	30	$16,667	$5,000	$11,667
October	3%	31	$8,611	$5,000	$3,611
November	4%	30	0	$5,000	-$5,000
December	4%	31	0	$5,000	-$5,000

7.3.4.3. Interest Rate Collars

The buyer of an interest rate collar takes a long position in an interest rate cap and a short position in an interest rate floor, indexed to the same interest rate. Collars can benefit both lenders (investors) and borrowers. In the case of a lender, the collar protects against falling rates but limits the benefits of rising rates. In the case of a borrower, the collar protects against rising rates but limits the benefits of falling rates. Borrowers with variable-rate loans buy collars to limit effective borrowing rates to a range of interest rates between some maximum (determined by the cap strike price) and a minimum (determined by the floor strike price). Although buying a collar limits a borrower's ability to benefit from a significant decline in market interest rates, it has the advantage of being less expensive than buying a cap alone because the borrower earns premium income from the sale of the floor that offsets the cost of the cap. A zero-cost collar results when the premium earned by selling a floor exactly offsets the cap premium. The amount of the payment due or owed by a buyer of an interest rate collar is determined by the following formula:

$$(PA) \times [\max(r - r_c, 0) - \max(r_f - r, 0)] \times (T/360) \qquad (7.6)$$

where, PA the principal amount of the agreement, r is the index (benchmark) rate, r_c is the cap rate, r_f is the floor rate, and T is the term of the index in days.

If the index interest rate (r) is less than the floor rate (r_f), the floor is in-the-money and the collar buyer (who has sold a floor) must pay the collar counterparty an amount equal to (PA) x (r_f − r) x (T/360). When r is greater than the floor rate (r_f) but less than the cap rate (r_c), both the floor and the cap are out-of-the-money and no payments are exchanged. Finally, when r is above r_c the cap is in-the-money and the buyer receives (PA) x (r − r_c) x (T/360).

Example of an Interest Rate Collar

An investor is borrowing $10 million at one-month LIBOR from a bank. LIBOR is currently at 5.75%. He wishes to cap the LIBOR so that it does not exceed 6%. Therefore, he takes a long cap with a strike price of 6% and a premium (c) of $300. In order to neutralise the cost of the cap, he sells a floor to the bank with a strike price of 4% and a premium (p) of $300. The bank and the investor have created a *"band"* between 4% and 6%, presented in Figure 7.4, within which the investor will pay LIBOR. If interest rates move outside the band of 4%–6%, there are money transactions between the investor and the bank.

Figure 7.4. The Trading Positions in an Interest Rate Collar

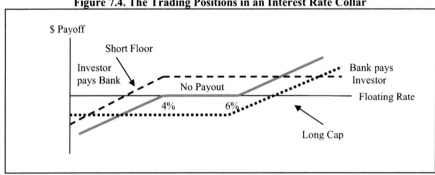

Table 7.10 presents three possible outcomes of this interest rate collar strategy for the investor, assuming three scenarios for the floating rate (LIBOR) at the expiration of the contracts, in one month. Specifically:

- Let LIBOR fall below the put's exercise price of 4%, say to 3.5%. The second column of Table 7.10 shows that in the money market the investor pays $350,000 (= $10 million x 3.5%), in the derivatives positions the put option is exercised and the investor pays to the bank $4,306 [= $10 million x (4% − 3.5%) x (31/360)]; the call option is not exercised. The investor has forgone the benefit of reduced interest rates should LIBOR ever falls below 4%. The overall derivatives position payoff, taking into account the premiums, is a loss of $4,306. Combining this with the money market position results in an overall cost to the investor of $354,306.
- When LIBOR is between the two exercise prices of 4% and 6%, neither option is exercised. The third column of the table shows the payoffs from a hypothetical LIBOR rate of 5.75%; the total cost to the investor is $575,000, as the payoff of the derivatives position is zero.
- The fourth column of the table shows the payoffs when LIBOR is above the call's exercise price of 6%, for instance, when the rate is 7%. In the money market, the investor pays $700,000. In the derivatives positions, the call option is exercised and the bank pays to the investor $8,611[= $10 million x (7% − 6%) x (31/360)]; the put option is not exercised. By exercising the call option, the investor managed to decrease his interest rate cost, by $8,611, to $691,389.

Table 7.10. Payoff Table of an Interest Rate Collar Strategy

	Case A: $S < X_1 = 4\%$ LIBOR Rate $= 3.5\%$		Case B: LIBOR Rate $= 5.75\%$		Case C: $S > X_2 = 6\%$ LIBOR Rate $= 7\%$	
Money Market Cost	-$350,000	-S	-$575,000	-S	-$700,000	-S
Less Gain/(Loss) on Options						
Put Payoff	-$4,306	$PA[-(r_f - r)](T/360)$	0	0	0	0
Put Premium	+$300	+p	+$300	+p	+$300	+p
Call Payoff	0	0	0	0	$8,611	$PA(r - r_c)(T/360)$
Call Premium	-$300	-c	-$300	-c	-$300	-c
Total Gain/(Loss) of Derivatives Position	-$4,306	$PA[-(r_f - r)](T/360)$	0	0	$8,611	$PA(r - r_c)(T/360)$
Overall Interest Rate Cost	-354,306		-$575,000		-$691,389	

Notes:
- It is assumed that p = c.
- Also, $X_1 = 4\%$, $X_2 = 6\$$.
- The time to expiration of the two options is the same, $T = 1$ month.

7.4. Summary

Exposure to interest rate risks is a main concern of shipping companies, as the industry capital is highly geared. Borrowing for vessel acquisition is often higher than 70% of the value of the vessels. Most of the liability consists of senior debt with a defined margin over the LIBOR. This chapter presented some of the interest rate derivatives available to participants in the shipping industry, to hedge against the adverse price movements of interest rates. Market agents in the industry may use interest rate derivatives to: (i) protect the value of their financial assets and to (ii) lock in favourable interest rates in shipping finance, be it in forms of loans, bonds or other interest bearing securities. Derivatives products available for hedging interest rate risks include interest rate forwards, futures, swaps and options. Several applications of their use have been presented in this chapter. These products are an extra tool in the hands of shipowners, banks and other participants in the industry to manage in a more flexible and cheaper way interest rate risks.

BIBLIOGRAPHY

Arditti, F. D. (1996): "Derivatives: A Comprehensive Resource for Options, Futures, Interest Rate Swaps, and Mortgage Securities," Harvard Business School Press, Boston, Massachusetts.

Baltic Exchange (2004a): "FFA Trading System, Manual for Principals," London, UK.

Baltic Exchange (2005): "Manual for Panellists: A Guide to Freight Reporting and Index Production," August, London, UK.

BIS (2005): "Triennial Central Bank Survey of Foreign Exchange and Derivatives Market Activity in 2004," Survey Conducted by the Bank of International Settlements, April/June.

Boland, G. (1999): "Interest Rate Futures and Options in New Zealand," *Business Development Manual*, New Zealand Futures and Options Exchange.

Calvin, D. (1994): "Summaries of Reports on Over-The-Counter Derivatives," *Unpublished Manuscript*, International Business Enterprises.

CBOT (2001): "CBOT Interest Rate Swap Complex: Trading the 10-Year Term TED Spreads," Board of Trade of the City of Chicago.

Chance, D. M. (2003): "An Introduction to Derivatives and Risk Management," 6th Edition, South-Western College Publications.

Clarkson Securities (1999): "FFAs: Forward Freight Agreements," Clarkson Securities Ltd. Publication, London.

Cockett, N. (1997): "Neil Cockett on Bunkers," Lloyds of London Press – LLP, London.

Drewry Shipping Consultants (1997): "Shipping Futures and Derivatives: From Biffex to Forward Freight Agreements (FFAs) and Beyond," Drewry Shipping Consultants Publications, London.

Energy Information Administration (2002): "Derivatives and Risk Management in the Petroleum, Natural Gas, and Electricity Industries," *Special Report*, US Department of Energy, Washington, DC, October.

Fite, D. and Pfleiderer, P. (1995): "Should Firms use Derivatives to Manage Risk," In (Eds.) Beaver, W. H. and Parker, G., *Risk Management: Problems and Solutions*, McGraw-Hill, New York, 139-169.

Gibson, R. and Zimmermann, H. (1994): "The Benefits and Risks of Derivative Instruments: An Economic Perspective," *Unpublished Manuscript*, Universite de Lausanne and Hochschule St. Gallen.

Gray, J. W. (1986): "Financial Risk Management in Shipping," Fairplay Publications.

Gray, J. W. (1987): "Futures and Options in Shipping," Lloyd's of London Press Ltd.

Gray, J W, (1990): "Shipping Futures," Lloyd's of London Press Ltd.

Hamilton J. D. (1994): "Time Series Analysis," Princeton University Press, Princeton, NJ.

Hull, J. C. (2005): "Options, Futures and Other Derivative Securities," 6th Edition, Prentice-Hall Inc., New Jersey.

IMAREX (2004): "Trading on IMAREX: A Short Introduction to Trading of Freight Futures at IMAREX, and How to Become an Exchange Member," International Maritime Exchange, Oslo, Norway.

ISDA (2003): "A Survey of Derivatives Usage by the World's 500 Largest Companies," Survey Conducted by the International Swaps and Derivatives Association, March.

ISDA (2004): "A Survey of Finance Professors' Views on Derivatives," Survey Conducted by the International Swaps and Derivatives Association, March.

Kavussanos, M.G. and S. Marcoulis (2001), 'Risk and Return in Transportation and other US and Global Industries', Kluwer Academic Publishers.

Kolb, R. W. (2002): "Futures, Options and Swaps," 4th Edition, Blackwell Publishers.

LIFFE (2000): "BIFFEX Futures and Options: Contract Information and Specification," *Commodity Products Manual*, London International Financial Futures and Options Exchange.

Natenberg, S. (1994): "Option Volatility and Pricing: Advanced Trading Strategies and Techniques," 1st Edition, McGraw-Hill.

Parker, B. (1987): "Freight Futures in Coal Shipping," *Market Report*, Published by E.D. & F. Man Futures (Inc.), November, New York.

Pillipovic, D. (1997): "Energy Risk: Valuing and Managing Energy Derivatives," McGraw Hill Publications.

Platts (2003): "Methodology and Specifications Guide: Bunker Fuels and Tankers," 30 June.

SSY Futures (1998a): "Freight Rate Risks and Hedging: An introduction," SSY Futures Ltd. Publication, London, UK.

SSY Futures (1998b): "A Guide to Oil Freight Derivatives, A New Horizon", SSY Futures Ltd. Publication, London, UK.

SSY Futures (2000): "Introduction to Tanker Freight Derivatives, SSY Futures Ltd. Publication, London, UK.

Stopford, M. (1997): "Maritime Economics," 2nd Edition, Routledge Publications London and New York.

Stulz, R. M. (2002): "Risk Management and Derivatives," 1st Edition, South-Western College Publications.

Sutcliffe, C. (1997): "Stock Index Futures: Theories and International Evidence," 2nd Edition, International Thomson Business Press, London, UK.

Veldhuizen, P. J. (1988): "Freight Futures: Targeting the 90s," *LLP Special Report*, Lloyd's of London Press Ltd.

Wakeman, L. M. (1996): "Credit Enhancement," In (Eds.) Alexander, C., *Handbook of Risk Management and Analysis*, New York, NY: Wiley and Sons.

Working, H. (1960): "Price Effects of Futures Trading," In (Eds.) Peck, A. E., reprinted in *Selected Writings of Holbrook Working*, Chicago: Chicago Board of Trade, 45-75 (1997).

REFERENCES

Abeal, P. and Adland, R. (2003): "Managing Vessel Value Risk," *Marine Money*, April, 15-19.

Adland, R., Jia, H. and Koekebakker, S. (2004): "The Pricing of Forward Ship Value Agreements and the Unbiasedness of Implied Forward Prices in the Second-Hand Market for Ships," *Maritime Economics and Logistics*, 6(2): 109-121.

Alizadeh, A. H., Kavussanos, M. G. and Menachof, D. A. (2004): "Hedging Against Bunker Price Fluctuations Using Petroleum Futures Contracts; Constant Versus Time-Varying Hedge Ratios," *Applied Economics*, 36, 1337-1353.

Allayannis, G. and Weston, J (2001): "The Use of Foreign Currency Derivatives and Firm Market Value," *Review of Financial Studies*, 14: 243-276.

Aury, P. (2003): "Forward Freight Agreements: State of the Market," Clarkson Capital Ltd., October, London, UK.

Baltic Exchange (2004b): "Baltic Exchange FFA Workshop: The Greek Perspective," *Seminar Proceedings*, 15 September 2004, Piraeus Marine Club, Greece.

Batchelor, R., Alizadeh, A. H. and Visvikis, I. D. (2003): "Forecasting Spot and Forward Prices in the International Freight Market," *Conference Proceedings*, 13th International Association of Maritime Economists (IAME) Conference, Busan, Korea, 3-5 September 2003.

Batchelor, R., Alizadeh, A. H. and Visvikis, I. D. (2005): "The Relation between Bid-Ask Spreads and Price Volatility in Forward Markets," *Derivatives Use, Trading & Regulation*, 11(2): 105-125.

Bates, D. (1996): "Jumps and Stochastic Volatility: Exchange Rate Processes Implicit in Deutsche Mark Options," *Review of Financial Studies*, 9: 69-107.

Beaulieu, J. J and Miron, J. A. (1991): "The Seasonal Cycle in US Manufacturing," *Economic Letters*, 37: 115-118.

Beenstock, M. (1985): A Theory of Ship Prices," *Maritime Policy and Management*, 12: 215-225.

Beenstock, M. and Vergottis, A. (1989): "An Econometric Model of the World Market for Dry Cargo Freight and Shipping" *Applied Economics*, 21: 339-359.

Benninga, S., Eldor, R. and Zilcha, I. (1984): "The Optimal Hedge Ratio in Unbiased Futures Markets," *Journal of Futures Markets*, 4(2): 155-159.

Bera, A. K., Garcia, P. and Roh, J. (1997): "Estimation of Time-Varying Hedge Ratios for Corn and Soybeans: BGARCH and Random Coefficients Approaches," *Working Paper*, Office for Futures and Options Research, 97-106.

Bessembinder, H. and Lemmon, M. L. (2002): "Equilibrium Pricing and Optimal Hedging in Electricity Forward Markets," *Journal of Finance*, 57. 1347-1382.

Black, F. (1976): "The Pricing of Commodity Contracts," *Journal of Financial Economics*, 3: 167-179.

Black, F. and Scholes, M. (1972): "The Valuation of Option Contracts and a Test of Market Efficiency," *Journal of Finance*, 27: 399-418.

Bollerslev, T. (1986): "Generalized Autoregressive Conditional Heteroskedasticity," *Journal of Econometrics*, 31: 307-27.

Campbell J. Y. and Shiller, R. J. (1987): "Cointegration and Test of Present Value Models," *Journal of Political Economy*, 95: 1062-1088.

Campbell J. Y. and Shiller, R. J. (1998): "Valuation Ratios and the Long-run Stock market Outlook," *The Journal of Portfolio Management*, 24(2): 11-26.

Canova, F. and Hansen, B. E. (1995): "Are Seasonal Patterns Constant Over Time? A Test of Seasonal Stability," *Journal of Business and Economic Statistics*, 13: 237-252.

Case, K. E. and Shiller, R. J. (1989): "The Efficiency of the Market for Single-Family Homes," *The American Economic Review*, 79: 125-137.

Chang, Y. and Chang, H. (1996): 'Predictability of the Dry-Bulk Shipping Market by BIFFEX," *Maritime Policy and Management*, 23: 103-114.

Cox, J. C., Ingersoll, J. E. and Ross, S. A. (1985): "A Theory of the Term Structure of Interest Rates," *Econometrica*, 53: 385-408.

Cox, J. C., Ross, S. A. and Rubinstein, M. (1979): "Options Pricing: A Simplified Approach, *Journal of Financial Economics*, 7: 229-264.

Cullinane, K. P. B. (1991): "Who's Using BIFFEX? Results from a Survey of Shipowners," *Maritime Policy and Management*, 18: 79-91.

Cullinane, K. P. B. (1992): "A Short-Term Adaptive Forecasting Model for BIFFEX Speculation: A Box-Jenkins Approach," *Maritime Policy and Management*, 19: 91-114.

Cuthbertson, K. Hayes, S. and Nitzsche, D. (1997): "The Behaviour of UK Stock Prices and Returns: Is the Market Efficient," *The Economic Journal*, 107: 986-1008.

Dinwoodie, J. and Morris, J. (2003): "Tanker Forward Freight Agreements: The Future for Freight Futures," *Maritime Policy and Management*, 30(1): 45-58.

Duffie, D. Pan, J. and Singleton, K. (2000): "Transform Analysis and Asset Pricing for Affine Jump-Diffusion," *Econometrica*, 68: 1343-1376.

Ederington, L. (1979): "The Hedging Performance of the New Futures Markets," *Journal of Finance*, 157-170.

Ederington, L. H. (1979): "The Hedging Performance of the New Futures Markets," *Journal of Finance*, 34: 157 - 170.

Engle, R. F. (1982): "Autoregressive Conditional Heteroskedasticity with Estimates of the Variance of United Kingdom Inflation," *Econometrica*, 50: 987-1007.

Eydeland, A. and Geman, (1998): "Pricing Power Derivatives," *RISK*, 11, October: 71-73.

Fairplay (2000a): "Mechanics of FFAs," *Fairplay Magazine*, 15 June, 23.

Fairplay (2000b): "Options for More Risk," *Fairplay Magazine*, 15 June, 23.

Fairplay (2001): "Baltic Proposes FFA Clearing House," *Fairplay Magazine*, 19 April, 53.

Fama, E. F. and French, K. R. (1988): "Dividend Yields and Expected Stock Returns," *Journal of Financial Economics*, 22: 3-25.

Gagnon, L. and Lypny, G. (1995): "Hedging Short-Term Interest Risk Under Time-Varying Distributions," *Journal of Futures Markets*, 15(7): 767-783.

Geman, H. and Vasicek, O. (2001): "Plugging into Electricity," *RISK*, 14, August: 93-97.

Geppert, J. (1995): "A Statistical Model for the Relationship Between Futures Contract Hedging Effectiveness and Investment Horizon Length," *Journal of Futures Markets*, 15: 507- 536.

Glen, D. R. (1997): "The Market for Second-Hand Ships: Further Results on Efficiency using Cointegration Analysis," *Maritime Policy & Management*, 24(3): 245-260.

Glosten, L. R., Jagannathan, R. and Runkle, D. (1993): "On the Relation Between the Expected Value and the Volatility of the Nominal Excess Return on Stocks," Journal of Finance, 48: 1779-1801.

Grauwe, P. D. (2005): "Exchange Rate Economics: Where Do We Stand?," CESifo Seminar Series, The MIT Press.

Haigh, M. S. (2000): "Cointegration, Unbiased Expectations and Forecasting in the BIFFEX Freight Futures Market," *Journal of Futures Markets*, 20(6): 545-571.

Hale, C. and Vanags, A. (1992): "The Market for Second Hand Ships: Some Results on Efficiency using Cointegration," *Maritime Policy and Management*, 19: 31-40.

Hamilton, J. D. (1989): "A New Approach to the Economic Analysis on Nonstationary Time Series and Business Cycle," *Econometrica*, 57: 357-384.

Haralambides, H. E. (1992a): "A New Approach to the Measurement of Risk in Shipping Finance," *Lloyd's Shipping Economist*, April.

Haralambides, H. E. (1992b): "Freight Futures Trading and Shipowners Expectations," *Conference Proceedings*, 6th World Conference on Transport Research, Lyon, France: Les Presses De L'Imprimerie Chirat, 2: 1411-1422.

Heston, S. L. (1993): "A Closed-Form Solution for Options with Stochastic Volatility with Applications to Bond and Currency Optons," *Review of Financial Studies*, 6: 327-343.

Johnson, L. (1960): "The Theory of Hedging and Speculation in Commodity Futures," *Review of Economic Studies*, 27: 139 - 151.

Kavussanos, M. G. (1996a): "Comparisons of Volatility in the Dry-Bulk Shipping Sector: Spot versus Time-charters and Small versus Large Vessels," *Journal of Transport Economics and Policy*, 30(1): 67-82.

Kavussanos, M. G. (1996b): "Price Risk Modelling of Different Size Vessels in the Tanker Industry using Autoregressive Conditional Heteroskedasticity (ARCH) Models," *Logistics and Transportation Review*, 32(2): 161-176.

Kavussanos, M. G. (1997): "The Dynamics of Time-Varying Volatilities in Different Size Second-Hand Ship Prices of the Dry-Cargo Sector," *Applied Economics*, 29: 433-443.

Kavussanos, M. G. (1998): "Freight Risks in the Tanker Sector," *Lloyds Shipping Economist*, Specially Commissioned Article, June: 6-9. Also, July 1998: 9.

Kavussanos, M. G. (2002): "Business Risk Measurement and Management in the Cargo Carrying Sector of the Shipping Industry," *The Handbook of Maritime Economics and Business'*, Lloyds of London Press, Chapter 30, 661-692.

Kavussanos, M. G. (2003): "Time-Varying Risks Among Segments of the Tanker Freight Markets," *Maritime Economics and Logistics*, 5(3): 227-250.

Kavussanos, M. G. and Alizadeh, A. H. (2001): "Seasonality Patterns in Dry-Bulk Shipping Spot and Time-Charter Freight Rates," *Transportation Research Part E, Logistics and Transportation Review*, 37(6): 443-467.

Kavussanos, M. G. and Alizadeh, A. H. (2002a): "Seasonality Patterns in Tanker Shipping Freight Markets," *Economic Modelling*, 19(5): 747–782.

Kavussanos, M. G. and Alizadeh, A. H. (2002b), 'The Expectations Hypothesis of the Term Structure and Risk-Premia in Dry-Bulk Shipping Freight Markets; An EGARCH-M Approach," *Journal of Transport Economics and Policy*, 36(2): 267-304.

Kavussanos, M. G. and Alizadeh, A. H. (2002c): "Efficient Pricing of Ships in the Dry-Bulk Sector of the Shipping Industry," *Maritime Policy and Management*, 29(3): 303-330.

Kavussanos, M. G. and Nomikos, N. K. (1999): "The Forward Pricing Function of Shipping, Freight Futures Market," *Journal of Futures Markets*, 19(3): 353-376.

Kavussanos, M. G. and Nomikos, N. K. (2000): "Futures Hedging when the Composition of the Underlying Asset Changes: The Case of the Freight Futures Contract," *Journal of Futures Markets*, 20(6): 775-801.

Kavussanos, M. G. and Phylaktis, K. (2001): "An Examination of the Relationship Between Stock Returns and Trading Activity Under Different Trading Systems," *Greek Economic Review*, 21(1): 19-36.

Kavussanos, M. G. and Visvikis, I. D. (2003a): "Financial Derivative Contracts in the Shipping Industry and the Price Discovery Function of Freight Forward Agreements (FFA)", *Lloyds Shipping Economist (LSE)*, February.

Kavussanos, M. G. and Visvikis, I. D. (2003b): "FFAs can Stabilize Revenue," *Lloyds Shipping Economist (LSE)*, July.

Kavussanos, M. G. and Visvikis, I. D. (2004): "Market Interactions in Returns and Volatilities between Spot and Forward Shipping Markets", *Journal of Banking and Finance*, 28(8): 2015-2049.

Kavussanos, M. G. and Visvikis, I. D. (2005): "The Hedging Performance of Over-The-Counter Forward Shipping Freight Markets," *Conference Proceedings*, 14th Annual Conference of the International Association of Maritime Economists (IAME), Izmir, 30 June – 2 July 2004.

Kavussanos, M. G. and Visvikis, I. D. (2006): "Shipping Freight Derivatives: A Survey of Recent Evidence," *Maritime Policy and Management*, Forthcoming 2006.

Kavussanos, M. G., Visvikis I. D. and Alexakis, P. (2004): "The Hedging Performance of Stock Index Futures: The Case of the Athens Derivatives Exchange", *Conference Proceedings*, 8th Annual European Conference of the Financial Management Association International (FMA), Zurich, Switzerland, 2-5 June 2004.

Kavussanos, M. G., Visvikis, I. D. and Batchelor, R. (2004): "Over-The-Counter Forward Contracts and Spot Price Volatility in Shipping," *Transportation Research – Part E, Logistics and Transportation Review*, 40(4): 273-296.

368

Kavussanos, M. G., Visvikis, I. D. and Goulielmou, M. A. (2005): "An Investigation of the Use of Risk Management and Shipping Derivatives: The Case of Greece," *Conference Proceedings*, 15th Annual Conference of the International Association of Maritime Economists (IAME), Limassol, Cyprus, 23-25 June 2005.

Kavussanos, M. G., Visvikis, I. D. and Menachof, D. A. (2004): "The Unbiasedness Hypothesis in the Freight Forward Market: Evidence from Cointegration Tests," *Review of Derivatives Research*, 7(3): 241-266.

Kemma, A. G. Z. and Vorst, A. C. F. (1990): "A Pricing Method for Options Based on Average Asset Values," *Journal of Banking and Finance*, 14: 113-129.

Koekebakker, S., and Adland, R. (2004): "Modelling Forward Freight Rate Dynamics – Empirical Evidence from Time Charter Rates," *Maritime Policy and Management*, 31(4): 319-336.

Koekebakker, S., Sodal, S. and Adland, R. (2005): "Modelling Freight Rate Derivatives," *Conference Proceedings*, 15th Annual Conference of the International Association of Maritime Economists (IAME), Limassol, Cyprus, 23-25 June 2005.

Kroner, K. F. and Sultan, J. (1993): Time-Varying Distributions and Dynamic Hedging with Foreign Currency Futures," *Journal of Financial and Quantitative Analysis*, 28(4): 535-551.

Levy, E. (1992): "Pricing European Average Rate Currency Options," *Journal of International Money and Finance*, 14: 474-491.

Lindahl, M. (1992): "Minimum Variance Hedge Ratios for Stock Index Futures: Duration and Expiration Effects," *Journal of Futures Markets*, 12: 33-53.

LSE (1996): "Subtle Problems of Selling Freight Derivatives," *Lloyd's Shipping Economist*, 18: 10-11.

MacKinlay, C. and Ramaswamy, K. (1988): "Index-Futures Arbitrage and the Behavior of Stock Index Futures Prices, *Review of Financial Studies*, 1: 159-172.

Mayhew, S. (2000): "The Impact of Derivatives on Cash Markets: What Have We Learned?," Working Paper, Department of Banking and Finance, Terry College of Business, University of Georgia, Athens, CA, February.

Meese, N. and Wallace, N. (1994): "Testing the Present Value Relationship for Housing Prices: Should I Leave My House in San Francisco?," *Journal of Urban Economics*, 35: 245-266.

Menachof, D. A. and Dicer, G. N. (2001): "Risk Management Methods for the Liner Shipping Industry: The Case of the Bunker Adjustment Factor," *Maritime Policy and Management*, 28(2): 141-156.

Merton, R. C. (1973): "Theory of rational Option Pricing," *Bell Journal of Economics and Management Science*, 4: 141-183.

Merton, R. C. (1990): "The Financial System and Economic Performance," *Journal of Financial Services Research*, 4: 263-300.

Montepeque, J. (2003): "The Future of Futures," *Global Energy Business*, January, Available from: www.platts.com/business/issues/0103s0103geb_futures.html.

Moosa, I. A. and Al-Loghani, N. E. (1994): "Some Time-series Properties of Japanese Oil Imports," *Journal of International Economic Studies*, 8: 109-122.

Osborne, D. R. (1990): "A Survey of Seasonality in UK Macroeconomic Variables," *International Journal of Forecasting*, 6: 327-336.

Pesaran, M. H. and Timmermann, A. (1994): "Forecasting Stock Returns: An Examination of Stock Market Trading in the Presence of Transaction Costs", *Journal of Forecasting*, 13: 335-367.

Poterba, J. M. and Summers, L. H. (1998): "Mean Reversion in Stock Prices: Evidence and Implications," *Journal of Financial Economics*, 22(1): 27-59.

Stein, J. (1961): "The Simultaneous Determination of Spot and Futures Prices," *American Economic Review*, 51: 1012 - 1025.

Stewart, P. (2001): "Hedging Marine Price Risk," *Energy Transport*, Global Energy Business Feature, Platts, September/October.

Thuong, L. T. and Vischer, S. L. (1990): "The Hedging Effectiveness of Dry-Bulk Freight Rate Futures," *Transportation Journal*, 29: 58-65.

Tilley, J. A. (1993): "Valuing American Options in a Path Simulation Model," *Transactions of the Society of Actuaries*, 45: 83-104.

Turnbull, S. M. and Wakeman, L. M. (1991): "A Quick Algorithm for Pricing European Average Options," *Journal of Financial and Quantitative Finance*, 26: 377-389.

Tvedt, J. (1998): "Valuation of a European Futures Option in the BIFFEX Market," *Journal of Futures Markets*, 18(2): 167-175.

Veenstra, A. W. (1999): "The Term Structure of Ocean Freight Rates," *Maritime Policy and Management*, 26: 279-293.

Vergottis, A. (1988): "Econometric Model of World Shipping," *Unpublished PhD Thesis*, City University Business School, London, UK.

Working, H. (1953): "Futures Trading and Hedging," *American Economic Review*, 43(3): 314-343.

GLOSSARY

Alternative Delivery Procedure: A provision of a futures contract that allows buyers and sellers to make and take delivery under terms or conditions that differ from those prescribed in the contract.

American Option: An option contract that may be exercised at any time prior to expiration. This differs from a European option, which may only be exercised on the expiration date.

Arbitrage: The simultaneous purchase of one commodity against the sale of another in order to profit from fluctuations in the usual price relationships. Variations include the simultaneous purchase and sale of different delivery months of the same commodity; of the same delivery month, but different grades of the same commodity; and of different commodities.

Asian Option: An option that is exercised against an average over a period of time.

Ask: A motion to sell. The same as offer.

At-the-Money: An option whose exercise (or strike) price is close to the spot market price.

Automatic Exercise: Following options expiration, an option which is in-the-money is exercised automatically by the clearing-house, unless the holder of the option submits specific instructions to the contrary.

Backwardation Market: When spot prices are higher than derivatives prices (the basis is positive). Also known as an inverted market. The opposite of contango.

Baltic Exchange: The Baltic exchange was formed in 1883 to bring together market participants wishing to buy and sell the freight service. The Baltic is responsible for providing the freight and vessel price indices, which are used as the underlying *"commodities"* of derivatives in the shipping industry.

Bareboat Charter: Hiring of a vessel for a period of time during which the shipowner provides only the vessel at a rate that covers any depreciation and nominal expenses and the charterer provides the crew, all stores and bunkers and pays all operating expenses.

Barge: A vessel used to carry products in navigable waterways. Inland river barges that carry oil products generally hold 25,000 barrels. Ocean-going barges range in size up to 120,000 barrels.

Barrel: A unit of volume measure used for petroleum and refined products (1 barrel = 42 U.S. gallons).

Basis Risk: The uncertainty as to whether the spot-futures spread will widen or narrow between the time a hedge position is implemented and liquidated.

Basis: The differential that exists at any time between the cash (spot) price of a given commodity and the price of the nearest futures contract for the same or a related commodity. Spot minus futures equals basis.

BCI: The Baltic Capesize Index, launched in 1999, consists of 10 Capesize routes.

BCTI: The Baltic Clean Tanker Index consists of 6 dirty tanker routes.

BDA: The Baltic Demolition Assessments consists of scrapping prices of 6 vessel types.

BDTI: The Baltic Dirty Tanker Index consists of 15 dirty tanker routes.

Bear Market: Market in which prices are in a declining trend.

Bear Spread: The simultaneous purchase and sale of two futures contracts in the same or related commodities with the intention of profiting from a decline in prices but, at the same time, limiting the potential loss if this expectation is wrong. This can usually be accomplished by selling a nearby delivery and buying a deferred delivery.

Bear: One who anticipates a decline in price or volatility. Opposite of a bull.

BFI: The Baltic Freight Index, launched in 1985, consisted of 13 dry-bulk routes and was the underlying asset of BIFFEX.

BHI: The Baltic Handysize Index, launched in 1997, consisted of 5 Handysize routes.

BHMI: The Baltic Handymax index, launched in 2000, consisted of 6 Handymax routes.

Bid: A motion to buy a futures or options contract at a specified price. Opposite of offer.

BIFFEX: The Baltic International Freight Futures Exchange contract, launched in 1985 by LIFFE, was the first freight futures contract, with settlement on values of the BFI. Ceased trading in April 2002.

BITR: The Baltic International Tanker Route Index, launched in 1998, consisted of 12 tanker routes.

Black-Scholes-Merton Model: An options pricing model initially derived by F. Black, M. Scholes and R. Merton for options, based on the theory that price volatility is random around a given trend, which was later refined for options on futures.

Box Spread: An options market arbitrage in which both a bull spread and a bear spread are established for a risk-free profit. One spread includes put options and the other includes calls.

BPI: The Baltic Panamax Index, launched in 1998, consists of 7 Panamax routes.

Broker: An individual who is paid a fee or commission for acting as an agent in making contracts, sales, or purchases.

BSI: The Baltic Supramax Index, launched in 2005, consists of 5 Supramax routes.

BSPA: The Baltic Sale and Purchase Assessments are the underlying assets of the SPFAs on six types of vessels (three tanker and three dry). All the valuations are made on five-year old vessels and based on professional assessments made by ten panellists.

Bulk Cargo: Cargo moved on a one vessel one cargo basis.

Bull Market: Market in which prices are in an upward trend.

Bull Spread: The simultaneous purchase and sale of two futures contracts in the same or related commodities with the intention of profiting from a rise in prices but at the same time limiting the potential loss if this expectation is wrong. This can be accomplished by buying the nearby delivery and selling the deferred.

Bull: One who anticipates an increase in price or volatility. Opposite of a bear.

Bundle: A stack of commodities strapped together for shipping.

Bunker Fuel Oil (or bunkering fuel): Fuel used for vessels. Generally refers to a No. 6 grade of residual fuel oil, with gravity about 10.5.

Business Day: From the initiation of the trades up to the ending of the trades for a 24-hour period.

Butterfly Spread: An options position comprised of the combination of options with three different strike prices and the same time to expiration.

Buyer: A market participant who takes a long futures position or buys an option. An options buyer is also called a taker, holder, or owner.

Buying Hedge: Also called a long hedge. Buying futures contracts to protect against possible increased costs of commodities that will be needed in the future.

Calendar (or Time or Horizontal) Spread: An options position comprised of the combination of options with the same strike price and different time to expiration.

Call Option: An option that gives the buyer (holder) the right, but not the obligation, to buy an underlying commodity for a specified price within a specified period of time in exchange for a one-time premium payment. It obligates the seller (writer) of an option to sell the underlying commodity at the designated price, should the option be exercised at that price.

Cap (or Ceiling): An upper limit. A contract between a buyer and a seller, whereby the buyer is assured that he will not have to pay more than a given maximum price.

Carrying Charge: The total cost of storing a physical commodity over a period of time. Includes storage charges, insurance, interest, and opportunity costs.

Cash (or Spot) Commodity: The actual physical commodity.

Cash (or Spot) Market: The market for a cash commodity where the actual physical product is traded.

Cash and Carry Arbitrage: In markets in contango, buy the underlying asset and simultaneously sell the derivatives instrument.

Cash Price: The price in the marketplace for actual cash or spot commodities to be delivered via customary market channels.

Cash Settlement: The settlement of an open derivatives position on expiry against a previously identified cash value which mirrors the physical market.

Charterparty: A contractual agreement between a shipowner and a cargo owner, usually arranged by a broker, whereby a vessel is chartered (hired) either for one voyage or a period of time.

Clean Cargo: Refined products such as kerosene, gasoline, home heating oil, and jet fuel carried by tankers, barges, and tank cars. All refined products except bunker fuels, residual fuel oil, asphalt, and coke.

Clearing Member: Clearing members accept responsibility for all trades cleared through them, and share secondary responsibility for the liquidity of the exchange's clearing operation. They earn commissions for clearing their customers' trades, and enjoy special margin privileges. Original margin requirements for clearing members are lower than for non-clearing members and customers. Clearing members must meet a minimum capital requirement.

Clearing: The procedures through which the clearing-house or association becomes the buyer to each seller of a futures contract, and the seller to each buyer, and assumes responsibility for protecting buyers and sellers from financial loss by assuring performance on each contract.

Clearing-house: The independent exchange-associated organisation which registers, matches and guarantees dealings between derivatives market members and carriers out financial settlement of derivatives transactions. Orders are *"cleared"* by means of the clearing-house acting as the buyer to all sellers and the seller to all buyers.

Close: The period at the end of the trading session when the closing price is determined

Closing (or Range) Price: The price of the last trade done during the close or, in the absence of trade, the average between the final bid and offer during the close.

Closing Out: Selling (or buying) the amount of derivatives to make the position zero (i.e. offsetting an existing market position).

Collar: A contract between a buyer and seller of a commodity, whereby the buyer is assured that he will not have to pay more than some maximum price, and whereby the seller is assured of receiving some minimum price (a combination of a cap and a floor). This is analogous to an option fence, also known as a range forward.

Commission: The fee charged by a broker for the execution of an order.

Contango Market: When spot prices are lower than derivatives prices (the basis is negative). Opposite of backwardation.

Contract Months: See delivery month.

Contract of Affreightment (CoA): A service contract under which a shipowner agrees to transport a specified quantity of cargo, at a specified rate per ton, between designated loading and discharge ports. This type of contract differs from a voyage charter in that no particular vessel is specified.

Contract Trading Volume: Daily trading volume.

Contract: 1) A term of reference describing a unit of trading for a commodity future or option. 2) An agreement to buy or sell a specified commodity, detailing the specifications of the product and the date on which the contract will mature and become deliverable.

Convenience Yield: In markets in backwardation, it is the marginal benefit of holding an additional unit of inventory to meet unexpected demand.

Convergence (Narrowing of the Basis): The tendency for prices of physicals and futures (or forwards) to approach one another, usually during the delivery month.

Conversion: An arbitrage transaction involving a long futures contract, a long put option, and a short call option. The put and call options have the same strike price and same expiration date.

Cost, Insurance, Freight (CIF): Term refers to a sale in which the buyer agrees to pay a unit price that includes the Free On Board (FOB) value at the port of origin plus all costs of insurance and transportation. This type of transaction differs from a *"delivered"* agreement in that it is generally ex-duty, and the buyer accepts the quantity and quality at the loading port rather than paying for quality and quantity as determined at the unloading port. Risk and title are transferred from the seller to the buyer at the loading port, although the seller is obliged to provide insurance in a transferable policy at the time of loading.

Cost-of-Carry: It relates the forward/futures price to the spot price of a commodity. It includes all costs incurred from holding the underlying commodity.

Cover: To offset a short futures/forward or options position.

Covered Option: A short call or put option position that is covered by the sale or purchase of the underlying futures contract or physical commodity. For example, in the case of options on spot positions, a covered call is a short call position combined with a long spot position. A covered put is a short put position combined with a short spot position.

Credit Risk: The risk that a counterparty to an agreement will default.

Cross-Hedge: Hedging an underlying spot position with a derivatives contract designed to hedge a different, but related, commodity. For example, hedging bunker fuels with energy futures contracts. A high correlation between the prices of the spot position and the prices of the derivatives contract is needed.

Crude Oil: A mixture of hydrocarbons that exists as a liquid in natural underground reservoirs and remains liquid at atmospheric pressure after passing through surface separating facilities.

Current Delivery Month: The derivatives contract which matures and becomes deliverable during the present month or the month closest to delivery. Also called the spot month.

Default: Failure to perform on a futures contract as required by exchange rules, such as failure to meet a margin call, or to make or take delivery.

Delivery Month: The month specified in a given derivatives contract for delivery of the actual physical spot or cash commodity.

Delivery: Delivery generally refers to the changing of ownership or control of a commodity under specific terms and procedures established by the exchange upon which the contract is traded.

Delta Neutral Portfolio: Consider a short position of one call on a non-dividend stock combined with a long position of delta units of the stock. The value of the portfolio would change as the stock price changes. The Delta of this portfolio is zero and so the portfolio is insensitive to the value of the stock.

Delta: The sensitivity of an option's value to a change in the price of the underlying commodity. Deltas are positive for calls, and negative for puts. Deltas of deep in-the-money options are approximately equal to one; deltas of at-the-money options are 0.5; and Deltas of deep out-of-the-money options approach zero.

Derivatives: Financial instruments derived from a cash market commodity. Derivatives can be traded on regulated exchange markets or over-the-counter. Derivatives involve the trading of rights or obligations based on the underlying product but do not directly transfer property.

Diagonal Spread: An options position comprised of the combination of options with different strike prices and different time to expiration.

Differentials: Price differences of the same commodity.

Dirty Cargo: Those petroleum products which leave significant amounts of residue in tanks. Generally applies to crude oil and residual fuel oil.

Discount: 1) A downward adjustment in price allowed for delivery of stocks of a commodity. 2) Sometimes used to refer to the price differences between derivatives of different delivery months.

Distillate Fuel Oil: Products of refinery distillation sometimes referred to as middle distillates; kerosene, diesel fuel, and home heating oil.

Efficient Market: A market in which new information is immediately available to all investors and potential investors. A market in which all information is instantaneously assimilated and therefore has no distortions.

European Option: An option that may be exercised only at its expiration date.

Exchange (of Futures) for Cash: A transaction in which the buyer of a cash commodity transfers to the seller a corresponding amount of long futures contracts, or receives from the seller a corresponding amount of short futures, at a price difference mutually agreed upon. In this way, the opposite hedges in futures of both parties are closed out simultaneously.

Exchange (of Futures) for Physicals: A futures contract provision involving an agreement for delivery of physical product that does not necessarily conform to contract specifications in all terms from one market participant to another and a concomitant assumption of equal and opposite futures positions by the same participants at the time of the agreement.

Exchange Rate: The price of one currency stated in terms of another currency.

Exercise Price: The price at which the underlying spot commodity will be bought or sold in the event an option is exercised. Also called the strike price.

Exercise: The procedure by which the options buyer (holder) takes up the rights from the contract and receives a long (call) or short (put) spot commodity by the options seller (writer).

Expiration Date: The date and time after which trading in options contracts terminates, and after which all contract rights or obligations become null and void.

Extrinsic Value: The amount by which the options premium exceeds its intrinsic value. Also known as time value.

Fair (or Theoretical) Value: A derivative's value generated by a mathematical model given certain prior assumptions about the term of the derivatives contract, the characteristics of the underlying spot contract, and prevailing interest rates.

FFABA: The Forward Freight Agreement Brokers Association was formed in 1997, as an independent body, by FFA brokers, members of the Baltic Exchange, under its auspices. According to the Baltic Exchange the association was formed in order to promote the trading of FFA contracts and the high standards of conduct amongst market participants.

FFAs: Forward Freight Agreements are principal-to-principal contracts between a seller and a buyer to settle a freight rate in a future period, for a specified quantity of cargo or type of vessel, for one, or a combination, of the major trade routes of the dry-bulk and liquid-bulk shipping sectors.

FIFC: The Freight Indices and Futures Committee is responsible for appointing Baltic panellists, determining index and route composition, supervising all aspects of quality control and is responsible to the Board of the Baltic Exchange.

Floor: A lower limit. A contract between a buyer and seller of a commodity, whereby the seller is assured that he will receive at least some minimum price. This type of contract is analogous to a put option.

Foreign Exchange: Foreign currency. On the foreign exchange market, foreign currency is bought and sold for immediate or future delivery.

Forward Contract: A contract between a buyer and seller, whereby the buyer is obligated to take delivery and the seller is obligated to provide delivery of a fixed amount of a commodity at a predetermined price on a specified future date. Payment in full is due at the time of, or following, delivery. This differs from a futures contract where settlement is made daily, resulting in partial payment over the life of the contract.

Free on Board (FOB): A transaction in which the seller provides a commodity at an agreed unit price, at a specified loading point within a specified period; it is the responsibility of the buyer to arrange for transportation and insurance.

Freight Market: The market into which freight rates are determined - in bulk shipping through the forces of supply and demand.

Fuel Oil: Refined petroleum products used as a fuel for home heating and industrial and utility boilers. Fuel oil is divided into two broad categories, distillate fuel oil, also known as No. 2 fuel, gas oil, or diesel fuel; and residual fuel oil, also known as No. 6 fuel, or outside the United States, just as fuel oil.

Futures Contract: A contract between a buyer and seller, whereby the buyer is obligated to take delivery and the seller is obligated to provide delivery of a fixed amount of a commodity at a predetermined price at a specified location. Futures contracts are traded exclusively on regulated exchanges and are settled daily in the marketplace.

Gamma: The sensitivity of an option's delta to changes in the price of the underlying spot commodity.

Greeks: Commonly used to indicate an options value and how this value will change as market conditions change (sensitivity).

Hedge Ratio: Ratio of the value of derivatives contracts purchased or sold to the value of the cash commodity being hedged – a computation necessary to minimize basis-risk.

Hedge: The establishment of a position in one market which is equal and opposite to that held in another market. Hedging is defined as the purchase or sale of derivatives contracts to offset adverse changes in the value of assets (or cost of liabilities) currently held or expected to be held.

Hedger: A trader who enters the market with the specific intent of protecting an existing or anticipated physical market exposure from unexpected or adverse price fluctuations.

IMAREX: The International Maritime Exchange is a web-based exchange for trading dry-bulk and tanker freight and bunker derivatives.

Initial Margin (or Initial Deposit): The deposit which users of futures markets must make to the clearing-house on buying or selling a contract (the initial collateral required to establish a futures or options position). The amount of the deposit represents only a small proportion of the full value of the contract and will be returned on closing out.

In-the-Money: An option that can be exercised and immediately closed out against the underlying market for a cash credit. The option is in-the-money if the underlying cash price is above a call option's strike price, or below a put option's strike price.

Intrinsic Value: The amount by which an option is in-the-money. An option which is not in-the-money has no intrinsic value. For calls, intrinsic value equals the difference between the underlying cash price and the option's strike price. For puts, intrinsic value equals the option's strike price minus the underlying cash price. Intrinsic value is never less than zero.

Last Trading Day: The final trading day for a particular delivery month derivatives contract. Any futures contracts left open following this session must be settled by delivery.

LIBOR (London Interbank Offer Rate): The US$ interest rate used by banks to borrow between them, in the London markets.

Lifting: Refers to tankers and barges loading cargoes of petroleum at a terminal or transhipment point.

Limit: The maximum daily allowable amount a futures price may advance or decline in any one day's trading session. Limits are also placed on the number of positions a participant holds.

Liquid Market: A market characterised by the ability to buy and sell with relative ease.

Liquidation: The closing out of derivatives positions.

Liquidity: A market is said to be *"liquid"* when it has a high level of trading activity and open interest.

Long Hedge: Purchase of futures or forwards against the future market price purchase or fixed price forward sale of a cash commodity to protect against price increases.

Long: 1) The market position of a futures or forward contract buyer whose purchase obligates him to accept delivery unless he liquidates his contract with an offsetting sale. 2) One who has bought a futures contract to establish a market position. 3) In the options market, position of the buyer of a call or put options contract. Opposite of short.

376

Lot: Any definite quantity of a futures commodity of uniform grade; the standard unit of trading.

Maintenance Margin: The sum which must be maintained on deposit at all times. If the equity in a customers' account drops to, or under, that level because of an adverse price movement, the broker must issue a margin call to restore the customers' equity. Margins are set by the Exchange based on its analysis of price risk volatility in the market at that time. See variation margin.

Margin Call: A demand for additional margin funds when futures prices move adverse to a trader's position, or if margin requirements are increased.

Margin: The amount of money or (other accepted collateral) deposited by a customer with his broker, or deposited by a broker with a clearing member, or by a clearing member with the clearing-house, for the purpose of insuring the broker or clearing-house against adverse price movement on open futures contracts.

Market-Maker: An independent trader or trading company which is prepared to buy and sell futures or options contracts in a designated market. Market-makers provide bids and asks and greater liquidity.

Marked-to-Market: Daily cash-flow system used by futures exchanges to maintain a minimum level of margin equity for a given futures or options contract position by calculating the gain or loss in each contract position resulting from changes in the price of the futures or options contracts at the end of each trading day.

Maximum Price Fluctuation: A commodity exchange's established maximum limits for fluctuations in futures prices during any one trading session.

Middle Distillate: Hydrocarbons that are in the so-called *"middle boiling range"* of refinery distillation. Examples are heating oil, diesel fuel, and kerosene.

Minimum Price Fluctuation: Minimum unit by which a futures price or an options premium can fluctuate per trade, also known as tick size.

Nearby Futures: The nearest trading months.

Net Position: The difference between an individual or company's open long contracts and open short contracts in any one commodity.

NOS: IMAREX uses the Norwegian Options and Futures Clearing-House (NOS) for the clearing of standardised listed futures and OTC derivatives.

Notional Principal (or Reference) Amount: The amount (in an interest rate swap, forward rate agreement, or other derivative instrument) or each of the amounts (in a currency swap) to which interest rates are applied (whether or not expressed as a rate or stated on a coupon basis) in order to calculate periodic payment obligations.

Offer (or Ask): A willingness to sell at a specified price. The price at which a seller is prepared to trade is known as the offer (ask) price. Opposite of bid.

Offset: A transaction which liquidates or closes out an open contract position. Risk is reduced when one side offsets the other.

Open Interest: The number of open or outstanding contracts for which an individual or entity is obligated to the Exchange because that individual or entity has not yet made an offsetting sale or purchase, an actual contract delivery, or, in the case of options, exercised the option.

Open Outcry: A method of public auction for making verbal bids and offers for contracts in the trading pits or rings of commodity exchanges.

Opening Price: The price for a given futures commodity that is generated by trading through open outcry during the opening range of trading on a commodity exchange.

Option: A contract which gives the holder the right, but not the obligation, to purchase or to sell the underlying spot commodity at a specified price within a specified period of time in exchange for a one-time premium payment.

Out-of-the-Money: An option which has no intrinsic value. For calls, an option whose exercise price is above the market price of the underlying commodity. For puts, an option whose exercise price is below the price of the spot commodity.

Over-the-Counter (OTC) transactions: Bilateral transactions between two counterparties in which (derivatives) contracts written are on a tailor-made basis.

Petroleum: A generic name for hydrocarbons, including crude oil, natural gas liquids, refined, and product derivatives.

Position Limit: For a single trader or company, the maximum number of allowable open contracts in the same underlying commodity.

Position: The net total of a trader's open contracts, either long or short, in a particular underlying spot commodity.

Premium: 1) The price or cost of an option determined competitively by buyers and sellers in open outcry trading on the exchange trading floor. 2) The excess of one futures contract over that of another.

Price Discovery: The process of determining the price level for a commodity based on supply and demand factors, which makes prices visible and readily available to the public.

Put Option: An option which gives the buyer, or holder, the right, but not the obligation, to sell a spot commodity at a specific price within a specific period of time in exchange for a one-time premium payment. It obligates the seller, or writer, of the option to buy the underlying spot commodity at the designated price, should an option be exercised at that price.

Refinery: A plant used to process crude oil. An oil refinery separates the fractions of crude oil and converts them into usable products.

Reversal: An arbitrage transaction involving a short futures contract, a short put option, and a long call option. The put and call options have the same strike price and same expiration date.

Reverse Cash and Carry Arbitrage: In markets in backwardation, short sale the underlying asset and simultaneously buy the derivatives instrument.

Rho: The sensitivity of an option's value to a change in risk-free rates of interest.

Risk Management: The use of financial analysis and instruments to control and reduce selected types of economic risks.

Seasonality: The recurrence of a pattern (peak or trough) in a series with the same periodicity within a specific time interval (e.g. increase in prices in January in relation to the average of the year, year after year)

Settlement (or Closing) Price: 1) The price established by an exchange at the close of each trading session as the official price to be used by the clearing-house in determining net gains or losses, margin requirements, and the next day's price limits. 2) The price established by the derivatives brokers in OTC markets to be used in determining net gains or losses of OTC derivatives contracts.

Settlement Period: Period(s) during the duration of the hedge when the actual prices are compared with the derivatives prices.

Shipping Route (or lane): Path through open water used for commercial vessel passage and so noted on chart (see deep water route).

Short (or Selling) Hedge: Selling futures or forward contracts to protect against possible decreased prices of commodities.

Short Selling: Sale of assets that the investor does not currently hold, with the obligation to purchase them back later.

Short: 1) The market position of a futures contract seller whose sale obligates him to deliver the commodity unless he liquidates his contract by an offsetting purchase. 2) The holder of a short position. 3) In the options market, the position of the seller of a call or a put option. The short in the options market is obliged to take a spot commodity if he is assigned for exercise.

Specifications: 1) Contract terms specified by an exchange for listed derivatives products. 2) Contract terms specified by derivatives brokers for OTC derivatives products.

Speculator: A trader who hopes to profit from the specific directional price move of a derivatives, or commodity.

SPFA: Sale and Purchase Forward Agreements are OTC forwards contracts on vessel values, which cover both the dry-bulk and the tanker markets.

Spot: Term which describes a transaction, where a commodity is purchased *"on the spot"* at current market rates.

Spread (Futures and Forwards): The simultaneous purchase and sale of futures or forward contracts for different months, different commodities, or different grades of the same commodity.

Spread (Options): The purchase and sale of options which vary in terms of type (call or put), strike prices, expiration dates, or both.

Straddle: An options position consisting of the purchase or sale of both a put and a call having the same strike price and expiration date. The buyer of a straddle benefits from increased volatility, and the seller benefits from decreased volatility.

Strangle: An options position consisting of the purchase or sale of put and call options having the same expiration but different strike prices.

Straps: An options position comprised of the simultaneous buying two calls and a put with the same time to expiration and the same strike price.

Strike (or Exercise) Price: The price at which the underlying commodity is bought or sold in the event an option is exercised.

Strips: An options position comprised of the simultaneous buying a call and two puts with the same time to expiration and the same strike price.

Swap: A custom-tailored, individually negotiated transaction designed to manage financial risk, where a buyer and a seller agree to swap underlying assets that may be more beneficial to each other (i.e. each makes a gain). Swaps can be conducted directly by two counterparties, or through a third party such as a bank or brokerage house. The writer of the swap, such as a bank or brokerage house, may elect to assume the risk itself, or manage its own market exposure on an exchange.

Swaption: Option to purchase (call swaption) or sell (put swaption) a swap at some future date.

Synthetic Futures: A position created by combining call and put options. A synthetic long futures position is created by combining a long call option and a short put option for the same expiration date and the same strike price. A synthetic short futures position is created by combining a long put and a short call with the same expiration date and the same strike price.

Theta: The sensitivity of an option's value to a change in the amount of time to expiration.

Tick: A minimum change in price, up or down.

Time Charter Contracts: The contract to hire a vessel over a period of time. Rates are commonly paid on a US$/day basis.

Time Value: Part of the options premium which reflects the excess over the intrinsic value, or the entire premium if there is no intrinsic value. At given price levels, the option's time value will decline until expiration.

Trader: (1) A merchant involved in cash commodities. (2) A professional speculator who trades for his own account.

Trading Volume: The number of contracts that change hands during a specified period of time.

Trading: Buying and selling of commodities or assets.

Tramp shipping: Vessels which move around the world, seeking mainly bulk cargos to transport, without a predetermined schedule. They operate under very competitive market conditions, with freight rates determined at the balance of demand with supply.

Trend: The general direction of price movement.

Underlying: The stock, commodity, futures contract, or cash index against which the derivatives contracts are valued.

VaR (Value at Risk): A statistical method which is used to measure the maximum loss from a trading position at a certain probability.

Variation Margin: Payment made on a daily or intraday basis by a clearing member to the clearing-house to cover losses created by adverse price movement in positions carried by the clearing member, calculated separately for customer and proprietary positions.

Vega: The sensitivity of an option's value to a change in volatility.

Volatile Markets: Commodity markets with exceptional price movements in both directions, generally driven by the economic forces of supply and demand as well as world events.

Volatility: The variation of a series around its mean value. Can be measured by the range of values of the variable, its standard deviation, the variance, etc.

Voyage Charter: A voyage whereby the shipowner places the vessel at the disposal of the charterer for one or more voyages, the shipowner being responsible for the operation of the vessel.

West Texas Intermediate (WTI): A grade of crude oil deliverable against the New York Mercantile Exchange light, sweet crude oil contract. Nominally, the benchmark crude of the U.S. oil industry.

Writer (or Issuer or Grantor): The seller (maker) of an option contract.

SUBJECT INDEX

O

AUTHORS INDEX

391

_____